THAT NEUTRAL ISLAND

THAT NEUTRAL ISLAND

A Cultural History of Ireland During the Second World War

CLAIR WILLS

The Belknap Press of
Harvard University Press
Cambridge, Massachusetts
2007

First published in 2007
by Faber and Faber Limited
3 Queen Square London WC1N 3AU
Typeset by Faber and Faber Limited
Printed in the United States of America

Library of Congress Cataloging-in-Publication Data

Wills, Clair.
That neutral island : a cultural history of Ireland during the Second
World War / Clair Wills.
p. cm.
Originally published : London : Faber and Faber, 2007.
Includes bibliographical references and index.
ISBN-13: 978-0-674-02682-7 (alk. paper)
ISBN-10: 0-674-02682-9 (alk. paper)
1. World War, 1939–1945—Ireland. 2. Neutrality—Ireland.
3. Ireland—Politics and government—1922–1949. I. Title.
D754.15W55 2007
940.53'417—dc22
2007006937

For Philly, Jimmy and Peggy

Contents

SCOTLAND

Lough Swilly *Malin Head*
Tory I.
Letterkenny • •Derry DERRY
•Lifford *Lough Foyle* ANTRIM
DONEGAL TYRONE Antrim• •Aldergrove
•Omagh **Belfast**•
Bundoran• FERMANAGH DOWN
Belmullet• Enniskillen• •Monaghan ARMAGH •Downpatrick
Inishkea Is. •Sligo •Armagh
Achill I. Ballina• SLIGO LEITRIM MONAGHAN Dundalk• *Carlingford Lough*
•Castlebar Carrick-on- Cavan• LOUTH
MAYO Shannon• CAVAN •Drogheda
▲ *Croagh Patrick* ROSCOMMON Longford• MEATH
Roscommon• LONGFORD •Navan *R. Boyne*
•Trim
Galway• GALWAY WESTMEATH •Mullingar **Dublin** IRISH
•Tullamore DUBLIN •Dun Laoghaire
Aran Is. OFFALY KILDARE
•Kildare *The Curragh*
CLARE LAOIS WICKLOW SEA
•Ennis •Portlaoise •Wicklow
Shannon Estuary •Limerick •Carlow
Ballybunion• •Foynes TIPPERARY CARLOW
LIMERICK KILKENNY
•Tralee Clonmel• •Kilkenny WEXFORD
KERRY Bowen's Court• •Wexford
•Killarney *R.* Waterford• •Rosslare
Valentia I. Mallow• •Fermoy WATERFORD
CORK Cork•
Cobh•
Berehaven• *St. George's Channel*
Bantry Bay
Cape Clear

ATLANTIC OCEAN

0   miles   50

INTRODUCTION

An Irish Theatre of War

I grew up with stories of the Second World War that stemmed from very different experiences. My mother lived the war years – her early teenage years – on a small farm in West Cork. In 1934 my grandfather, an agricultural labourer, inherited £300 from an older brother who had emigrated to Chicago some fifty years earlier, where he had done well out of a livery stable. With the money my grandfather bought the house and the thirty-acre farm, previously a tenant-holding on a once large estate, and now 'in fee' to the Land Commission. The family's new, if tenuous, prosperity matched the hopes of the new Ireland of the 1930s. The nationalist Fianna Fáil party, which came to power in 1932, was bent on gaining greater political and economic independence from Britain. Along with this went economic independence for Irish citizens, and in particular for the small farmer. The thirty-acre farm – thought large enough to maintain a family on the produce and its proceeds – was the model on which Fianna Fáil hoped to build a new, fair, if frugal, agrarian society. My grandparents' large family subsisted, in pretty typical style, as far as possible on their own crops and the small income from the sale of milk, eggs and pigs, boosted by the older children's earnings. For the boys there was rabbit snaring and seasonal agricultural work for the County Council, on jobs such as ditch clearing and drainage; for the girls, domestic service in the home of the local Minister. Except for the unaccountable fact that my grandfather had been born a Protestant (though he had long since converted), the family came close to embodying the ideal of a self-sufficient, rural, devout and independent Ireland.

Powered by a sense of duty to such people, and to the needs of a young and relatively weak state, the Fianna Fáil leader, Eamon de Valera, was determined to keep Ireland out of the war that, by the mid-1930s, was already looming. Disillusioned with the politics of collective security after the failure of the League of Nations, and convinced of the democratic right of small nations to protect themselves from becoming embroiled in the conflicts of the big powers, he was also committed to neutrality for wholly pragmatic reasons. Ireland had a small, ill-equipped army, and few defences. Still only in its second decade of independence, it was a vulnerable state, which could all too easily be swallowed up in a widespread war. The world of the small farmer and the small town, which lay at the heart of de Valera's vision of an independent Ireland, would go with it. In the late 1930s de Valera worked to regain control of Irish defences, bartering for the return, in 1938, of all naval and air facilities still in British hands. And on 3 September 1939, as Britain and France declared war on Germany, the Irish government sealed its commitment to neutrality, passing an Emergency Powers Act, which remained in force until 2 September 1946. Throughout the war years Ireland's Taoiseach resisted Churchill's – and later Roosevelt's – attempts to encourage, persuade and occasionally bully him into the war; supported by the vast majority of the Irish population, de Valera resolutely kept Ireland out of the conflict.

My mother's principal memories of the Emergency are of shortages, particularly of sugar, tea and flour; of trains on the Skibbereen–Schull Light Railway ('the tram') running so slowly on inferior fuel that you could climb on and off them as they went uphill; of visits to a pair of relatively well-off elderly Protestant neighbours who owned a working radio; and of making up stories of British successes in the Battle of Britain to tell to her father when she returned home – news of British losses was sure to put him in a bad mood. As a schoolgirl her day-to-day lessons, friendships, and fraught relationships with the nuns were no doubt more present to her than the far-off events of the world war. In addition there were domestic chores and jobs on the farm such as drawing water, collecting eggs, feeding the sow and the hens, making butter, going to the creamery. By the blueish light of the paraffin lamp, and sometimes by candlelight, she would reread the stories in the rare copies of *Ireland's Own*, books borrowed from the school 'library', and the dog-eared romance novels passed from hand to hand. She attended vocational classes in domestic economy organised by the parish priest, where – despite the shortages – she learnt fancy techniques such as how to make pastry by rubbing the butter into the flour, or how to beat egg whites so stiff you could turn the bowl upside down over your head. Yet baking at home was impossible; in common with nearly all the other homes nearby, all cooking on the farm was done over an open fire.

For her older siblings there were occasional visits to the cinema in the town, more frequent music sessions in neighbours' homes, card-playing, Sunday-night patterns, turkey-drives, fair days, dances in the town hall and a round of social activities centred on the local parish church. In many ways, the war years for my mother's family were a continuation of life in the 1930s, with its local focus, its seasonal liturgical ritual, as well as its economic privations. Frugality was the order of the day, and worries about the supply of day-to-day necessities took priority over the seemingly distant war. Even had my mother been interested in the global news she would have found it difficult to follow events. Early on in the war the family's radio became inoperable, due to the difficulty of recharging the wet and dry batteries. They lived too far from the town for daily purchase of a newspaper, and in any event transport difficulties often delayed or cancelled delivery of the *Cork Examiner* to the smaller market towns. The local weekly paper was true to its type, carrying almost exclusively local news, along with frequent government directives on emergency measures.

My future father, meanwhile, was living out the 'typical' wartime experience of an English youth on the outskirts of London – including evacuation to Wales in the early part of the war. Since his father, a hospital clerk, was too old to be conscripted, and he himself was too young (he turned sixteen in the summer of 1945), the family avoided the fears and dangers common to those in the Forces, or with relatives in the Forces (an older brother went into a reserved occupation). But in the row of terraced houses owned by the hospital, in which the family lodged, neighbours received news of the death of relatives. For months at a time the family slept each night in the Anderson shelter in the garden, later migrating to the Morrison shelter under the kitchen table. Towards the end of the war they bedded down in a huge complex of tunnels built into a hill in the grounds of the hospital. Planes from the air force base at Kenley Aerodrome flew low over his school on the South Downs each day, and everywhere there was evidence – in bomb damage, troop movements, defence emplacements – of a country wholly given over to the war effort.

Life on the British home front was undoubtedly more disrupted and perilous than life in neutral Ireland, but it was also more varied. There were weekly visits to the local British Restaurant for dried egg and chips, in order to eke out the rations, and later youth clubs and dances. As a youngster my father read the *Beano* and the *Dandy*,

s way through the adventure stories in the local library,
models of the planes droning overhead, listened to music and
on the wireless. The technology that made the war so lethal
ave him more freedom – as he cadged the occasional ride on the
of a motorbike out into the country, or took the bus every
Saturday morning (and later every Saturday night) to the Regal
cinema to watch the latest films and Pathé newsreels.

On the face of it, it would be hard to come up with two more contrasting experiences of the war. On the one hand, life in a culture
increasingly driven by technology and the beginnings of mass consumption, on the other, a rural life that was still almost pre-machine-
age: the contrast seems emblematic of the distinction between living
inside and outside the war. Many Irish people volunteered for the
British forces, out of conviction, economic necessity, or a youthful
thirst for adventure. Others, attracted by the prospect of a job with
decent wages, moved to England to work in the war industries. But for
the majority of the Irish population who stayed at home, the conflict
was distant from their own concerns.

Yet the state of economic siege, the breakdown of transport, the
sense of isolation, had more than simply material effects. As one journalist, a schoolboy during the Emergency, recalled, 'apart from the
food, fuel and petrol rationing and other inevitable discomforts or
deprivations, the atmosphere of fear, menace and foreboding was constant and almost tangible. Quite simply, one just could not shut it out,
at least for long.' As the Irish government was keen to emphasise, neutrality was not peace. While the violence of the conflict may have
seemed remote to most people, everyday life in Ireland was shaped by
the hardships, constraints, and psychological pressures of surviving in
a war-torn world. Indeed, the very fact that my parents' lives could
converge at the end of the decade speaks of a shared sensibility. Like
thousands of other Irish girls, at war's end my mother applied to train
as a nurse in the newly formed National Health Service. In seeking a
future abroad, she was typical of the thousands who left Ireland in the
years immediately after the war, and now chose as their natural destination not the United States, but Britain. The mass emigration across
the Irish Sea that occurred once wartime restrictions had been lifted
revealed the extent of the economic disaster that the war had created
in Ireland, but it also indicated a new sense of connection to Britain
(and is just one example of how the war fundamentally changed the

social order in Ireland). By the time my parents met at the end of the 1940s, the declaration of the Republic of Ireland had severed the last formal political ties with Britain, but the shared working lives of Irish and British citizens had brought them closer together.

If neutrality did not protect Ireland from all of the war's effects, this obvious truth has been overshadowed by the Allied perception that Ireland's neutrality was tantamount to opting out of the war. The weight of popular feeling in Ireland that the country's neutrality was natural and necessary, given the history of the state and its poor defences, made scarcely any dent in British public opinion at the time. British people believed that Ireland had deliberately cut itself off, and had betrayed its neighbour. Many Britons were simply unable to absorb the fact that the country was no longer a part of the United Kingdom. Ireland's neutrality was regarded by the Allies as the nadir of national protectionism, an extension of the economic isolationism of the 1930s. Ireland had cut itself off not only from the war but from the vital flow of ideas that was shaping the new world. Rather than being active, sovereign, and independent, its neutral stance was negative: defensive, distrustful and inward-looking.

Contemporary comparisons of life in neutral Ireland and that in belligerent Britain focused on the contrasts between them. Travellers' accounts of journeys to Ireland (of which there were many, partly because the 'peace' there made it a welcome destination for journalists) were keen to stress the tremendous differences, and incidentally offered a picture of life in neutral Ireland that those living in rural areas would have found it impossible to recognise. According to these narratives, to travel from Britain to Ireland in wartime was to journey from darkness into light. Passengers from England endured an uncomfortable, excruciatingly slow train ride – at night the windows were blacked out, so that it was like travelling in an endless tunnel – and a crowded, often vomit-fumed, mailboat crossing over the Irish Sea. The wartime journey was longer by about eight hours than in peacetime. But the reward for their stamina, as travellers recorded obsessively, was to be greeted by the blaze of lights in neutral Dublin – a veritable rebirth from the cave of darkness that was Britain at war. (Travellers from Ireland were just as struck by blackout-blanketed Britain.) Visitors rhapsodised over the startling sea of lights in Dublin Bay, and even noted the pale reflections in the River Liffey. And not only was there light, there were things in the shops:

Woolworths! You just can't imagine! All the little things amaze you as much as the big things – paper hankies, lead soldiers, combs, zip fasteners, bath salts.

Visitors came to buy, and to eat. Restaurants, cafés and ice-cream parlours vied with shop-window displays for their attention. (In fact Dublin's lights were supposed to be dimmed during the war, and there were restrictions on display fronts – creating what local wags liked to call 'celtic twilight – half a blackout' – but the contrast with Britain was still stark.) Steak, cream cakes, knickerbocker glories, bacon and eggs, butter, cosmetics, jewellery, leather goods, all were in plentiful supply, and at bargain prices for the British visitor. Shopping and eating could be followed up by Guinness, whiskey and pink gins in the pub, by a visit to the cinema, or the theatre, by formal dances at the Gresham Hotel for the well-heeled, at the Olympia Rooms, or at local hops. Dublin and Cork swayed to the sounds of the foxtrot, the quickstep, the waltz and the rumba. Weekends could be spent on the golf course, shooting and fishing in season, sailing in Dublin Bay, or at any one of a number of regattas around the coast. These attractions were not lost on Ireland's closest neighbours, civilians living in Northern Ireland, and above all the forces stationed there. Dublin became the favourite haunt for those on short leave, and after American troops arrived in the North in 1942, Dubliners became used to seeing trains unload their cargoes of GIs seeking twenty-four hours of indulgence. Summertime brought invasion from the North. In July 1942 bookings on the Great Northern from Belfast to Dublin exceeded all records. 'They are said to be down here chiefly to eat,' reported the novelist Elizabeth Bowen.

The evocation of luxury in accounts of life in the Irish capital generally implied disapproval (and ignored the very real economic hardship in the city, where shortages and rising unemployment were causing near destitution for increasing numbers of the poor). The stories of pleasure and plenty were tinged with a fairy-tale sense of unreality, as if Ireland were a fantasy refuge from the harsh outside world, a place where moral backsliding could be indulged. Anger at the presence of Axis legations in Dublin was a staple of Allied propaganda. And rumours of the extravagant lifestyle to be enjoyed in Dublin were accompanied, later in the war, by stories in British and American newspapers of Germans, Italians and Japanese crowding the streets, of Nazi U-boats refuelling on Ireland's coast, of swastika badges worn openly in Ireland, of Axis spies allowed freedom to roam across the country. For many in Britain and the United States the lights of Ireland were a reminder that she was, in a frequently used phrase, 'shaking hands with murder'. To the British and American public, Dublin's wide and well-lit streets screened a moral darkness: the 'small, obstinate, intransigent nation with its head still stuck in 1938' was, in reality, experiencing her blackest hour.

The Allied case against Ireland during the war was initially based on her 'betrayal' of Britain and the Empire. In 1938 Britain gave up the 'Treaty ports' at Cobh, Berehaven and Lough Swilly, which it had retained in 1921. The refusal to lease the ports back to Britain during the worst years of the Battle of the Atlantic was portrayed as the principal sign of Ireland's funk. The lack of access to the ports was blamed for many deaths during the German U-boat campaign in the early part of the war. British public opinion (fuelled by the British press) was incensed by Ireland's 'disloyalty'.

As the war was increasingly understood in Britain as a 'people's war', a struggle by ordinary civilians against the monster of Hitlerism, Ireland's neutral stance was looked upon as a betrayal of democracy itself. Neutrality involved shutting one's eyes not only to the dire consequences for lonely Britain of the lack of western defences, but to the nature of fascism: a moral as well as political failure. Ireland had cut herself adrift from the current of modern life, and from the decisive political struggle of the day.

Within Ireland, however, there was near-complete consensus on the prudence of the policy. Neutrality was above all a practical stance dictated by military and political necessities, not an ideological declaration, or the expression of a moral choice. It did not imply hostility to Britain, but expressed the Irish government's responsibility for the survival of the state and the welfare of its citizens. The wisdom of neutrality was argued first of all pragmatically – it was impossible for Ireland to choose belligerence given the country's lack of defences. But beyond this lay a fear of a return to the internal conflicts of the recent past, if the population were asked to make common cause with Britain. Irish suspicion of Britain could take many different forms, of course, from a generalised scepticism about Britain's motives in going to war, to a frank desire to see Britain beaten by Germany. Nonetheless in letters, newspaper articles, memoirs and interviews, the phrase that kept recurring to describe the policy of neutrality was that it was 'natural given our history'. That history included not only the War of Independence, concluded less than two decades previously, and the continuing problem of partition. The phrase also invoked the memory of the bloody and divisive civil war which was one of the outcomes of the Anglo-Irish Treaty. In 1939 that war, which had been fought over whether to accept the terms offered by the British, was barely sixteen years in the past.

And neutrality was also defended in terms of democratic entitlement. Ireland, as a small nation, had a right to its independence. If other countries regarded themselves as engaged in a battle for democracy, then they should accept that Ireland's neutrality was the price of democracy, a genuine expression of the popular will. The refusal to be drawn into a major war not of its making was a sign of Ireland's sovereignty, an expression of its hard-won independence.

British (and later American) anger was met in Ireland in large part by resignation – many Irish, after all, felt themselves no strangers to the British inability to understand their country's history, or respect Irish independence. But beyond the broad popular endorsement of neutrality as the country's only viable option lay concern about the costs of the policy. While the impact of economic isolation was felt right across the country, amongst the intelligentsia the worries were about imaginative and cultural isolation. The wartime generation of writers portrayed itself as 'a static generation', cut off from the real world of the war. The loss of intellectual traffic with Europe was an inevitable consequence of the difficulty of travel to and contact with Britain (and the impossibility of contact with countries on the continent), but it was intensified by the strict censorship of printed news and other media. Political censorship forbade 'unneutral' comment on the progress and conduct of the war, and opinions about the belligerents. The idea that the country could sustain its neutrality only by screening out information about the war made it all the harder to refute British accusations of culpable detachment from the struggle against Nazi Germany.

The belief that Ireland's neutrality was the extreme expression of isolationism has been an enduring one. These have been called 'lost years' for Ireland, a country that became, in the words of the novelist Frank O'Connor, 'a non-entity state entirely divorced from the rest of the world'. O'Connor made his judgement in 1942. Thirty years after the war the historian F. S. L. Lyons reached for the contrast between darkness and light in his famous metaphor for the psychological and cultural isolation of Ireland in wartime:

It was as if an entire people had been condemned to live in Plato's cave, with their backs to the fire of life and deriving their only knowledge of what went on outside from the flickering shadows thrown on the wall . . . When after six years they emerged, dazzled, from the cave into the light of day, it was to a new and vastly different world.

The idea that Britain, continental Europe, Asia and Africa had suffered the 'fire of life' while Ireland dwelt in the darkness of a self-made prison was not wholly retrospective. In an editorial published in the *Irish Times* soon after the Allied victory, the end of isolation (and the lifting of censorship) was greeted – in a striking reversal of the idea of Ireland as a well-lit paradise outside the world at war – as the dawning of a new freedom: 'We feel as anybody must feel who, having been confined in a dark cell for nearly six years, is released suddenly into the sunshine and blinded by the light.'

Isolation, incarceration, indifference – the consensus is striking. The idea that neutral Ireland was cut off from the rest of wartime Europe was shared by supporters of the Allies, but also by some Irish defenders of neutrality and even a few supporters of the Axis powers. In May 1945 the Irish novelist Kate O'Brien took the mailboat from Holyhead to Dun Laoghaire. She had been absent from the country for five and a half years, and her return was necessarily coloured by her experience of living in Britain throughout the war.

It was to sail back far, and shockingly, into the overlaid and the forgotten. I remember how the cleanliness startled me; gleaming paint and polished plate-glass of suburban houses; arrays of shining cutlery and enormous, beautifully starched white napkins in the dining room of the hotel; amazing, exquisite and long-forgotten food. As there was no petrol in Dublin hardly an engine stirred, and one heard again the old clip-clop of horse-hooves along the quiet streets. The season was in leaf, and all the gardens, public and private, were Victorianly tended and radiant with flower.

This was indeed a far, far past – and very ghostly.

There are many other descriptions like this, of Ireland as a land outside time, untouched by the devastation. Yet there are equally compelling reasons to argue that Ireland had not remained impervious to the war. And for O'Brien, returning in 1945, behind 'the amazing foreground' of unbroken windows, flowering gardens and platters of meat, 'it didn't take long to find, among the poets and middle-aged writers anyway, certain depths of shock and sorrow that kept us up to date even then, and spiritually safe enough; entrenched somehow beyond our superficial non-reality.'

O'Brien pours cold water on the idea that Ireland was 'in its conscience and heart immune in 1945 from the pain and horror which had torn the world apart'. Despite censorship, and despite a high degree of cultural isolation, the imaginations of Irish citizens were not cut off from the war raging in Europe. Despite economic stagnation and restrictions on travel, everyday life in Ireland was far from unaffected by the conflict. The country was, as many said at the time, both in and not in the war. While 'the poets and middle-aged writers' may have expressed this edgy and ambivalent consciousness, the experience went much further than that. Volunteering, migrant work, spying, smuggling, unemployment, shortages, censorship, defence: there was no home front in Ireland, but the country was nonetheless shaped by the war.

*   *   *

We now know that Ireland, as a 'friendly neutral', helped the Allies more than either side admitted at the time. There were Irish in the Allied defence forces, and in British war industries; there were well-known acts of solidarity such as de Valera sending fire engines north during the blitz on Belfast, or the repatriation of Allied airmen downed in Éire; there was sharing of information from German decodes and coastal surveillance of German planes and submarines. As the war progressed, there was increasing security cooperation between MI5 and its Irish equivalent, G2. De Valera was a realist, not only in maintaining Ireland's immunity from attack, but in his understanding that it was in Ireland's long-term interest that Britain should win. But beyond the awkward balance between political stalemate and inter-governmental entente, between diplomatic showdowns and assistance on the intelligence front, lies the story of how neutrality was experienced day to day by Irish citizens, unaware of the extent of that cooperation.

One version of Ireland's wartime story is that it is all about absence – the absence of conflict, of supplies, of social dynamism, of contact with 'the outside world'. This perspective has masked the material and psychic impoverishment that the war wrought in Ireland, and which continued long after the war ended. The effects of poverty, massive emigration, the decline of rural areas, the suppression of debate through censorship, and of political dissent through a series of repressive measures including internment, persisted like a silent damage to the culture throughout the 1950s.

The strange, ghostly existence of Ireland both in and outside the war has been replicated in the writing of this book. In focusing on the cultural repercussions of Ireland's neutrality, I have written about the country in so far as it sought to respond to chains of events outside its control. Neutrality only makes sense in the context of war elsewhere. In looking at Ireland through the optic of the war years, I have measured the country against a chronology which isn't really its own. Nonetheless, the wartime narrative is not entirely alien to Ireland's sense of itself, either. As Elizabeth Bowen wrote in a wartime short story set in Ireland, in a total war 'there is no elsewhere, no other place'.

For the most part the experience of being 'outside' or on the edge of total war has not been well documented. There has been little anatomy of the varying opinions in town and country: amongst Irish speakers in the Gaeltacht, for example, or the remnants of the Ascendancy, the middle class of the small towns, the urban intelligentsia, the young who left for war work in Britain. The testimony I turn to here comes from a wide variety of sources including interviews, letters, editorial opinion, diaries, transcripts of radio broadcasts, archives of the Department of Justice, the Department of External Affairs, and of the Irish secret service organisation G2, trade journals, magazines, and other ephemera. But I also allot a distinctive role to cultural and artistic expression in a broad sense, and in particular to poetry, fiction, and drama.

In part this is because many of Ireland's writers of the period have left us explicit and moving reflections on their own responses to neutrality (and in some cases arresting accounts of the crises of conscience that neutrality occasioned for them). But I am also convinced that the narrative turns, the verbal patterns which recur from one writer to another, offer insights into the deeper currents of feeling in Irish society as a whole. The images and figures of speech encountered in the creative work of wartime give word to the silent majority. In fact, this book began from my fascination with the glimpses into the emotional world of neutral Ireland that I encountered in imaginative literature. I wanted to understand more about the uneasy, suspended form of existence which I sensed in the writing, about the experience of being surrounded by – and yet detached from – momentous conflict.

I was also intrigued by the relationship between the creative exploration of neutrality and the demands on writers and artists to engage publicly with the war. Writers and writing play a leading role in my story because the changes in Ireland's literary and intellectual life during wartime vividly indicate the inner stresses and strains which the wider culture was under. One of the most striking aspects of Irish writing in this period is the general turn towards documentary work, something which Ireland shared with the countries at war – indeed Irish literature's new forms of public engagement were partly shaped by the wartime demands on art and writing in Britain.

Many of Ireland's wartime writers – cosmopolitan in outlook, European-minded – became during the course of the conflict vociferous critics of neutrality, or impatient with aspects of the policy. Writers such as Elizabeth Bowen, Kate O'Brien, Louis MacNeice, Francis Stuart, Denis Johnston were all separated by class and education (not to mention, barring O'Brien, religion) from the majority of Irish citizens, whether rural or urban. Much of their wartime writing has to be understood as a challenge to neutrality. In choosing to produce radio propaganda for the Allies (or in Stuart's case, the Axis powers), to secretly gather information on Irish attitudes to the war, to report on the war in Europe for the BBC, each was specifically working against the censorship if not precisely against neutrality. (Samuel Beckett's absolute rejection of neutral Ireland for Paris and later Roussillon – his stated preference for France at war to Ireland at peace – is the most vivid example of this divorce).

The idea, beloved of Yeats in his later years, of the Protestant southern minority as guardians of intellectual freedom within a nation increasingly committed to an ideal of Gaelic, Catholic Ireland, was given a form of reprieve during the war. By 1939 most of the writers Yeats had had in mind were dead: Lady Gregory in 1932, AE in 1937, Yeats himself in 1939. Others, such as the aged G.B. Shaw, seemed resolutely to have turned their backs on Ireland. Nonetheless middle class Irish writers as different as MacNeice and Kate O'Brien, living and working within a climate of British cultural opinion and indeed British propaganda on the war, but writing to and about Ireland, continued to see themselves as the – often angry – voice of the nation's conscience.

This impulse towards engagement – through polemic, commentary, reportage, propaganda work in print and broadcasting – also transformed literary culture in Ireland. Not only war but neutrality demanded public engagement from even the most 'detached' or 'aesthetic' of writers, who turned to journalism, essays, documentary film, and reportage. And it is no surprise that this public engagement on the part of the writers seeped back into their private art. In the process Irish cultural debate was changed beyond recognition.

A generation of writers born in the first decade of the century – some of whom had taken part in the fight for independence, who were educated in the university colleges in Dublin or Cork, or the new teacher training colleges – reached artistic maturity during the war. Products of a politically confident new state, they were both more self-assured and more disillusioned with that state than a previous generation had the luxury to be. The distinctively modern and critical Irish idiom in the work of a writer such as Patrick Kavanagh, or Brian O'Nolan (Flann O'Brien) for example, supportive of neutrality yet ferociously contemptuous of the new political and cultural consensus, would have been unthinkable thirty years before.

In part the wartime literary renaissance was the fruit of isolation – cut off from publishing outlets in Britain, and keyed up by the new injection of energy brought by small groups of refugees from Britain and elsewhere in Europe, writers and artists turned to an Irish audience, developing new cultural initiatives. The most well-known is the journal *The Bell*, begun by Peadar O'Donnell and Sean O'Faolain in October 1940, but the war provided the conditions too for the growth of regional drama, for Irish exhibitions of the visual arts, and even for Myles na gCopaleen (O'Brien's journalistic alter-ego) in the *Irish Times*. The boost given to writing in the Irish language was more clearly and literally tied to isolation, as the incarceration of men such as Máirtín Ó Cadhain, and boys such as Brendan Behan, in the Curragh internment camp provided them with the time to both study the language and to write it. The violent dislocations born of economic disaster in rural and working class urban districts provided the spur to new, often bitterly comic, reflections on the ideal of an Irish Ireland. Despite complaints at the time, (contemporary reviews of the Irish language theatre in particular are almost unrelievedly damning), the war proved a turning point for the movement to develop a modern literature in the Irish language, and a self-confident modern Irish writing in English. The grumbles about intellectual stagnation were, paradoxically, evidence of the energy and dynamism which was resisting that stagnation.

This book will take account of the declarations and initiatives of diplomats and statesmen, but it also seeks to open up the experience of Ireland's shadow theatre of war and the impact of being on the edge of global conflict. Ordinary Irish people, as well as politicians, and those whose vocation was reflective or creative writing, struggled to understand what neutrality meant as a condition they were living through, one whose outcome was still indeterminate. This book is a record of that experience, and of the effort of a culture to make sense of it.

This Emergent Ireland

Some months before the war began, in January 1939, three major wireless networks in the United States relayed a broadcast by de Valera from the Radio Éireann studios in Dublin. The Irish leader was announcing his country's involvement in the New York World's Fair, to be held in May. The Fair's organisers had been having a rough time; in the planning stages four years earlier, with what must have felt like zip and zing, they had hit on the theme 'The World of Tomorrow'. With a certain amount of idealism and a great deal of borrowed money they went about reclaiming the 'primeval bog' of Corona Dumps, in the outer borough of Queens, transforming it into a modernist landscape where they could display all the elements at work in the American dream of a better world.

Despite the rank commercialism at work in many of the Fair's exhibits, advances in science, technology, and social thought were all presented as exalting the freedoms and opportunities of democracy in the new world about to dawn. But by 1939 the theme 'The World of Tomorrow' was asking for trouble, given the overwhelming fear that the world might wake up at any time to another war. And in fact there were a few sticky months when the global ambitions of the Fair seemed in jeopardy, given the dire international situation. After disagreement over sharing space with countries in the Commonwealth, Ireland signalled her intention not to participate. De Valera's later volte-face was due in part to the intervention of the mayor of New York, Fiorella La Guardia, who wheedled that 'Ireland's flag would be very much missed from the family of nations'. (The mayor was nicknamed 'O'La Guardia' because of his shameless courting of the Irish vote; he was said to gain the hint of a brogue when talking to Irish immigrants.)

The benefits of attendance at the World's Fair were primarily commercial, and much of the Irish exhibit was devoted to boosting the export market, but in his January broadcast de Valera was keen to present Ireland's participation as above mere trade:

16

Our aim will not be an advertisement of goods we desire to sell; rather our aim will be to give you who have taken such practical interest in our struggle for freedom an idea of how the freedom which has been won has fructified in the developments of our national life, in our political institutions, in our national economy and in our social services.

The Fair was a chance to show the global public (and Irish-Americans in particular) what Ireland had done with her independence. It was a window on to her self-image after seventeen years of self-rule.

'I look towards a land both old and young; old in its Christianity, young in its promise of a future,' declared de Valera over the airwaves, quoting Cardinal Newman and defining what the designers hoped would be the significance of the display: Ireland's dynamic fusion of the traditional and the up-to-date. Ireland was indeed an ancient nation and it could justly celebrate not only a rich tradition of Gaelic culture in rural life, folklore, music and literature, but also a central role in the monastic life of the medieval Christian world. Yet it was also a modern state – and one still struggling to free itself from centuries of underdevelopment under British rule. Once the Fair opened in May 1939 visitors discovered a series of displays focusing on the Irish government's energetic attempts to tackle the consequences of that lag.

Prominently exhibited along one wall of the Irish Pavilion at the World's Fair, now at a good distance from the Commonwealth nations' exhibition, was an imposing Art Deco-inspired mural of the most unequivocal sign of Ireland's embrace of the modern world: the showcase Shannon hydroelectric scheme. This was a massive (German-built) project to bring electricity to the entire country, begun in the early years of the Free State. There were few more far-reaching, or more controversial, plans for the transformation of Irish rural life – electricity was to be the force behind farm mechanisation (powering grain-crushing, root-pulping, chaff-cutting, milking, milk-churning) as well as the saviour of the Irish housewife. Supply was mainly confined to cities and the larger towns, until the rural electrification scheme was put into practice immediately after the war. Nonetheless the purveyors of the new power were nothing if not ambitious – to rural dwellings that lacked even electric light and running water, advertisements and brochures trumpeted the benefits of the most complex (and expensive) labour-saving devices. But even for those who welcomed the changes to be ushered in by the new power, it proved impossible to foresee the extent of the social transformation modern technologies might bring. As one deputy put it during a debate on rural electrification in the Dáil:

I hope to see the day that when a girl gets a proposal from a farmer she will enquire not so much about the number of cows but rather concerning the electrical appliances she will require before she gives her consent, including not merely electric light but a water heater, an electric clothes boiler, a vacuum cleaner and even a refrigerator.

On top of these far-reaching practical benefits, the enormous power station at Ardnacrusha looked the part. Sean Keating's massive eighty-foot modernist mural emphasised the subjugation of nature, with the edifice set in a huge gouge hacked out of the earth, and man dwarfed by the machine. The state-run Electricity Supply Board (condemned by one newspaper as 'the first fruits of Bolshevism in this country') produced modernist prints and photographs which would have done Russian avant-gardists or Italian futurists proud. Alongside these the Irish Pavilion offered displays featuring the progress of drainage and land reclamation, the decentralisation of industry, improvement in housing and hospital facilities (funded by United States citizens gambling on the Hospital Sweepstakes), and the transformation of the transport network. Here again Shannon was seen as the hub of future developments, both as a base for seaplane flights across the Atlantic, and as the projected centre of an air-travel network linking Europe with the United States.

But in the Fair as a whole, examples of Irish corporate vigour and nettle-grasping were overshadowed by the designers' seemingly limitless ability to recycle old stereotypes. This was not entirely their fault. In recent years the country had hardly gone on a drive to diversify its exports. Predictably, the displays fell back on trying to sell Ireland as a tourist destination, for the fisherman, the hunter and the sightseer; its chief products were whiskey, stout, smoking pipes, thoroughbred horses and church ornaments (Catholic paraphernalia were an important part of the exhibit in general). Despite the fanfare over the new, locally based industries (manufacturing candles, soap, tyres, and so on) the content of the trade exhibit was firmly moored in the past; what Ireland had to offer the world in 1939 was almost indistinguishable from what it had had to offer before gaining limited independence in 1922. What had changed was the manner of its presentation.

The design of the Irish Pavilion itself, by architect Michael Scott, could justly claim to have united the traditional and the modern. The building was designed in the shape of a shamrock – though with an excess of confidence in the dawning era of mass air travel, the shamrock outline could only be fully grasped from above. Most visitors arrived by train and on foot, however, and therefore experienced the shamrock as it were by degrees. The main entrance to the trade exhibit stood at the end of the glass-walled stem, which enclosed a hall eighty feet long. The curved leaves had a certain modernist allure, but the Art Deco effect was fatally compromised by the green awnings that adorned both leaves and stem, to cut down the glare of the New York sun. Emerald-clad attendants were posted at strategic intervals to direct visitors to the different exhibits.

Scott was well aware of the problem of being both folksy and futuristic when he took on the commission. Landed with the task of finding some architectural form with which the twenty-five million Irish-Americans could connect, he pointed the problem out to his new employers:

There was no Irish architecture after the twelfth century . . . all the rest was influenced one way or another by outside sources . . . 'What do you expect me to do?' I said. 'A couple of round towers and the Rock of Cashel?'

Scott offered an ultra-contemporary solution to the problem of authentic Irishness – a building in the shape of a resonant national symbol. He later remembered, 'They thought it was marvellous, a wonderful building. They liked how I solved the problem of nationalism and made it modern at the same time.' The green-and-white shamrock plumped in the middle of the metropolis proclaimed its difference – its singular identity. It couldn't be taken for anything else. But it was also a cipher – the most traditional symbol of Irishness used as the marker for an as yet undefined future, a gesture towards a political, social, cultural identity still struggling to know itself.

Outside, the area surrounding the Pavilion was landscaped to include a miniature lake; in the centre of the lake lay a large relief map of Ireland, for which soil had been brought from the fields of each of the counties and water from the River Shannon and the Lakes of Killarney. Irish-American visitors crowded round the green-tinted mini-Ireland. They were drawn too to an enormous carved granite pillar carrying a bust of the rebel leader Patrick Pearse in the centre. The pillar's design was ingenious: integrated within the granite were stone blocks taken from buildings which had almost sacred significance in the story of Ireland's struggle for independence, because of their role in the 1916 Rising – when armed rebels proclaimed an Irish Republic, holding parts of the centre of Dublin against British forces for over a week. The pillar contained, for example, fragments from the General Post Office, the centre of the military campaign; from Kilmainham Prison, where the rebels were held; and from Arbour Hill, where they lay buried. The whole construction was illuminated by the text of the 1916 Proclamation of Independence, in Irish and English.

This, then, was the Ireland ready to take her place in the World of Tomorrow. 'The eyes of the Fair are on the future,' insisted the official literature, but apart from the shamrock itself, which was hailed as one of the most innovative structures at the Fair, the Irish exhibit seemed to have little to say directly to the world to come. The most popular exhibits were a bizarre genuine-kitsch amalgam – real soil from the land, real water from the lakes, real stones from the places where 'history' had been made, and finally even real sportsmen: to complete the aura of Irish authenticity the organisers imported the Galway and Kerry Gaelic Football teams to help open the Pavilion. Soil and water were offered up as the body and blood of Ireland – tiny scraps of an authentic world which had been forever lost to those across the

Atlantic. The shamrock itself represented a secular trinity. As though to confirm every cliché about the Holy Land of Ireland, the exhibition presented bits of Ireland itself as relics; making a visit to the Fair was to be a pilgrimage.

This clash between a Gaelic Christian past and a modern future was no accident. It echoed the conundrum of the archaic and the modern which confronted Ireland as a whole. Ancient nation and nascent state – as de Valera suggested in his broadcast, Ireland's challenge in the inter-war decades was to be both new and old at the same time.

* * *

The Free State born in 1922 was for many, twenty years and several treaties later, still waiting to grow up. 'We are today in this emergent Ireland living experimentally,' observed the writer and editor Sean O'Faolain in 1941. In this ongoing emergency Ireland's difficulty was that any recognisably Irish 'forms of life' were 'still in their childhood'. The childishness of the Irish was a common complaint, from insiders as well as outsiders. 'She is the oldest nation in Europe, though she is still in her teens,' explained Sean O'Casey in 1944, in partial apology for Ireland's wartime stance. The problem was that socially, politically, and culturally Ireland was finding it difficult to separate from Britain. The trouble lay not only in the partition of the island. The Anglo-Irish Treaty of 1921, which concluded the War of Independence (and ushered in the Civil War), had offered Dominion status within the British Commonwealth to the twenty-six counties. The country would not achieve full independence until after the war in 1949.

The inter-war years saw a number of changes to Ireland's political status, as de Valera progressively wrung concessions from Britain. Soon after he came to power in 1932 he abolished the Oath of Allegiance to the Crown, and in a series of moves limited the power of the Governor-General. During the 1936 constitutional crisis, and the abdication of Edward VIII, the Constitution Amendment Bill removed all reference to the king from the Free State Constitution. In the same year the Italian invasion of Abyssinia, and the weak response of England and France through the League of Nations (when de Valera was President of the League), confirmed his disillusion with the politics of collective security. In June 1936 he announced in the Dáil, 'We want to be neutral' (adding that he would not allow the country to be used as a base from which to attack Britain). In a referendum in 1937 the populace voted for a new Constitution, which bore de Valera's unmistakable stamp: the name Irish Free State was dropped in favour of Éire, or Ireland (a term that formally designated all thirty-two counties). The country became a Republic in all but name. And in 1938 Ireland negotiated the return of the three Atlantic seaports at Cobh, Berehaven and Lough Swilly, removing Britain's last toehold in the South, and giving Ireland control over her own defences. This move was crucial if the Irish government was to make more than a pretence at an independent foreign policy – it was to make her wartime neutrality viable. Neutrality in turn was to become a symbol of Ireland's sovereignty. De Valera announced that the 1938 agreement, granting Ireland control of her ports and harbours, 'recognises and finally establishes Irish sovereignty over the twenty-six counties and the territorial seas'. Despite the running sore of partition, by the later 1930s Ireland's politicians were able to present the country's moves towards full independence with legitimate pride. She had been steadily disentangling herself from the grip of her powerful neighbour. On the eve of the war all the conditions seemed in place for Ireland to argue her status as an equal among the modern nations of the world.

But making the break from Britain was not easy. In many respects, the dilemmas Ireland confronted were similar to those of any emergent nation, moving out from the shadow of foreign domination. The big difference was that Ireland was not located across the ocean, on the opposite side of the world, to its former ruler; it belonged to the same continent, shared the same cultural heritage, and was bound by the closest geographical proximity, with all that this implied in terms of continuing ties of trade, family, and friendship.

By 1939 Ireland had her own constitution, including her own President (the appointment of Douglas Hyde, founder of the Gaelic League and a Protestant, 'marked the first stage in political maturity', according to one commentator). She also had control of her own defences. But the country was still connected to Britain by 'External Association'. A tenuous link was maintained with the British Commonwealth, partly in order to facilitate the future reunification of Ireland. During the coming war this would lead to anomalies such as the fact that Britain kept neither an ambassador nor a High Commissioner in Dublin; the chief emissary was known simply as the

British Representative. Irish representatives to foreign governments had to be ratified by London before being able to take up position. The monarchy thus still had a role, however vestigial – indeed, the king and queen dutifully visited the World's Fair Pavilion in May 1939. (They greeted the Patrick Pearse pillar in silence.)

Quite apart from these formal connections, there were many in Ireland who still thought of themselves, at least in part, as British. Members of the former Protestant ascendancy and well-to-do businessmen – both Catholic and Protestant – maintained links to Britain through education, marriage, social ties, business and financial interests, not to mention inclination. Putting sentiment aside, the fact that nearly all Ireland's export trade was carried on with Britain, and most of her securities were in British banks (the Irish currency was linked to sterling), meant that any sudden break in relations was impossible. And for those, including many middle-class Protestants, who identified with the new Irish state, there was still the problem of what that state stood for. The severing of the last political ties to the former colonial power was poorly matched by independence in devising home-grown institutions. The apparatus of parliament, judiciary, and the agencies of law enforcement were largely modelled on British prototypes. Literature, leisure, sport, all were in danger of being governed by rules set in London or New York. What could be said to be Irish about Ireland? How would independent Irish life be different from life within the British Empire? In the years after 1922 furious battles were fought over the kind of politics, society and culture best suited to the new state – over what type of Ireland should take its place in the family of nations.

Considering the shaky foundations on which the new state had been built – with the civil war a very recent memory – the country had achieved remarkable stability by the late 1930s. Its leader, de Valera, had managed the transition from nationalist insurrection to democratic parliamentarism which many anti-colonialist fighters in the twentieth century failed to achieve. Ireland had a strong liberal parliamentary system, inherited from British rule and bolstered by a constitution; despite the continuing presence of the IRA the rule of law was accepted by a majority of the population; there was freedom of the press and, in the main, religious tolerance.

Travellers visiting Ireland in the late 1930s discovered in Dublin a once shabby provincial city slowly transforming itself into a European

capital. If the social life associated with the heyday of the rule of the British Governor-General had faded, energy flowed instead from the Dáil and from the courts. The founding of the National University in 1908 had enabled a generation of Catholic intellectuals, lawyers, politicians and businessmen to gain the qualifications they needed to take up posts in the government, the civil service and education. There was evidence of a growing social democracy as the political revolution of 1922 took effect in society: the professions were slowly being filled by the sons of comparatively poor men – farmers, shopkeepers, country doctors; increasingly the landed gentry cast in their lot with the people. Despite censorship, the universities – Protestant Trinity, the more recent, Catholic, University Colleges, the seminary at Maynooth and (in 1940) de Valera's new Institute for Advanced Studies – fostered an intensive, and Irish-identified, intellectual life, which found expression in scholastic philosophy, in empiricist history, in medical and educational reform, in journalism and in literature.

In newspapers, pamphlets and the pages of several intellectual journals such as the *Irish Monthly* and the more academic *Studies* (both Jesuit publications), the *Irish Rosary* and the *Irish Ecclesiastical Record*, debate focused on how Ireland was to develop and modernise without losing touch with its own distinctive traditions. But it wasn't all inward-looking. The national intelligentsia – academics in the new university colleges, clerics, co-operative organisers, Gaelic Leaguers – debated the future of Irish society amidst European developments. During the late 1930s there were long-running discussions about the nature of money and the kind of banking system that would be suited to Ireland, the good and bad effects of industrialisation, the nature of communism, the wording of the 1937 Constitution, the status of women within Irish society, the revival of Irish. These initiatives grew out of a sincere attempt to develop practical ways to organise Irish society on Catholic social principles, particularly as these were laid out in two Papal Encyclicals, *Rerum Novarum* and *Quadragesimo Anno*. Powerful clerics such as Father John Charles MacQuaid, who was a close friend of de Valera and who became Archbishop of Dublin in 1940, championed Catholic social teaching, including a corporatist model of representation which was intended to minimise the social injustices of capitalist democracy.

The new Catholic society which was envisaged was deeply traditionalist. At a political level the years after 1922 had ushered in a raft

of conservative legal changes designed to underline Irish Catholic morality, including legislation on divorce, contraception, censorship, education, and – in the 1937 Constitution – women's role in society. Laws such as the 1935 Criminal Law Amendment Act, which criminalised the import of contraceptives, were an attempt to regulate public morality on Catholic lines. It was not simply that sexuality was twinned with indecency in the minds of the legislators (the use of artificial birth control was associated with prostitution rather than planned parenthood). Catholic sexual morality and the ideal of the Catholic family were seen as a front line in the battle with the secular materialism of Britain and the United States. Many of these debates were thus freighted with sectarianism and xenophobia. Conservative churchmen and politicians took the lead, but there were numerous semi-clerical organisations which popularised these ideas throughout society. The Legion of Mary, An Rioghacht (the League of the Kingship of Christ), the corporatist movement, the rural co-operative movement Muintir na Tíre, were all attempts to provide a forum and practical testing ground for the intellectual, and often reactionary, ideas of Catholic Europe.

The strength of the Catholic nationalist consensus reflected the needs of a society striving to give cultural expression to its newly won independence. Barring a few notable exceptions, opposition to the conservative clerical establishment was concentrated in liberal literary circles. Liberal writers were loud in their complaints about the stifling atmosphere of nationalist, clerical Ireland. Many of them, after all, had fallen foul of the authorities themselves, in the form of the 1929 Censorship of Publications Act. The Act was designed to protect Irish readers from the immoral literature produced across the channel – everything from smutty pulp fiction to pamphlets on birth control – but the Censorship Board also banned work by nearly every one of Ireland's younger literary writers.

However, literary dissent was not simply a reaction to the fact that the writers were targets of the clerical establishment. The social role of literature had developed very differently in Ireland during the 1930s than in Britain or the United States. Partly because Irish intellectual life lacked a tradition of political theory or sociology, literature had taken on responsibility for recording Irish life, and in particular for investigating the clashing moralities and value systems of independent Irish society. At the heart of the literary work of the period lay a struggle between the modern values of self-expression and self-fulfilment, and the ethical norms championed by the religious hierarchy and its lay followers.

The liberal intellectuals associated with magazines such as *Ireland Today*, the *Dublin Magazine*, and later *The Bell*, liked to think of themselves as champions of a humanistic and universalist ethos, battling chauvinism and parochialism. There were historical reasons for this, not least the influence of James Joyce. At the beginning of the century Joyce's *Dubliners* had anatomised the social and psychological paralysis of the city, condemning both the Catholic Church and the political establishment for acceding to petty-bourgeois, conservative values. Realist prose writers such as Sean O'Faolain and Frank O'Connor – and later Mary Lavin – extended this picture of disillusion to the small towns. Many of their stories of the 1930s were portraits of failure, studies of individual creativity and idealism broken by the petty, pious concerns of provincial Ireland. The emphasis was on the damaging effect of a puritan social code designed to protect the family and its assets, rather than to nurture individuality, or even happiness. The censors objected to the representation of infidelity, illegitimacy, contraception, prostitution, abortion (and they kept banning the work), but for the writers it was the refusal to acknowledge the less palatable aspects of Irish society that lay at the heart of the country's difficulties. They saw it as a battle between romantic myths of Irish culture and grubby reality. Novels and short stories offered a way of exploring the thoughts and feelings of the creative individual, and at the same time condemning the parochialism gripping Irish society.

* * *

For the Fianna Fáil government under de Valera (who enjoyed unbroken rule as Taoiseach from 1932 to 1948), the ideal Ireland was a self-sufficient rural republic, Catholic in religion and Irish-speaking – the vision at the heart of earlier Sinn Féin rhetoric. In 1928, Seán Lemass, the future Minister for Trade and Industry, had put it bluntly: 'We believe that Ireland can be made a self-contained unit, providing all the necessities of living in adequate quantities for the people residing in Ireland and probably for a much larger number.' Rural self-sufficiency seemed possible, because by the time Fianna Fáil came to power there had already been significant land redistribution, after the Land War and subsequent Land Acts of the late nineteenth century.

Fianna Fáil rhetoric was all on the side of the small farmer. The large tracts of land on which a minority of richer farmers raised cattle for export, while the rural poor were often forced to emigrate for want of work, would be divided into small farms able to sustain the basic needs of a growing population. Excitement about the social transformation that the land redistribution was bringing about was entirely justified; the crumbling power of the Anglo-Irish Ascendancy was dealt a definitive blow by this transition from aristocratic to peasant proprietorship. 'Every thirty acres of land would represent a new family,' insisted de Valera, working on the assumption that emigration could be stemmed if the land was properly worked. The growth of wheat, animal feed, fruits, vegetables, and even tobacco was to transform the grasslands into viable tillage farms. In the pages of *Studies* and the *Irish Monthly*, experts offered opinions on how many acres were required to feed a family, and on the correct nutritional balance required for a healthy diet.

After the Wall Street Stock Exchange crash of 1929, and the subsequent collapse of the gold standard, the goal of self-sufficiency seemed all the more imperative: across the world, faith in the exchange economy based on international trade was badly shaken. Ireland's protectionist response seemed only common sense: in effect, free trade was to be abolished in the cause of national self-sufficiency. Native industries were to be encouraged by protectionist economic policies, providing work in local towns for those from the farms. Foreign firms were obliged to set up subsidiary Irish companies (so that Irish businesses could no longer be run from London). De Valera's trade and industry policies, and his decision to withhold the land annuities from the British government, provoked a bitter economic war with Britain which had a damaging effect on Irish agriculture during the later 1930s, and on the cattle trade in particular. But the widely felt sense of grievance at the economic state in which the country had been left by Britain ensured that he continued to receive support (though emphatically not from the larger farmers) for his strategy of setting Ireland free from the British market.

Farm life had changed little in fifty years and many of the farmers themselves seemed determined to resist change. They were among the most vociferous opponents of the Shannon Electrification Scheme, for example, on the grounds of the cost they would have to bear. Tractors were an unusual innovation; horses and donkeys were used for clearing the land, ploughing, and harvesting alike. The poorest farmers tilled cut-away bog; crops were worked with the spade and reaped by the sickle or scythe. Even so, much of the land was unusable because of poor drainage or rocky soil. Running water was practically unknown in many areas and it wasn't unusual for smaller farms to have no access to water either from a well or a spring; water was lifted from the nearest river or stream.

The relative poverty in many rural areas, particularly in the poorer land in the West, meant that people travelled little. Farmers congregated in the towns on market days, and women made the most of shopping trips. But few rural dwellers made the transition from local National school to secondary-level schooling in the town. A child living no more than five miles from the town might wait until he or she was seven, and taking first communion, for a first visit. Social life centred on the townland or parish. It was an affair of neighbours – from road bowling to the Stations of the Cross, from music and drinking in the local pub to parish clubs. Sunday mass, which every Catholic, young and old, attended, functioned as a focal point of the week, an important social as well as religious occasion, while the priest wielded far more than merely spiritual authority. A rhythm of life dominated jointly by the fields and by the crescendos and diminuendos of the liturgical year; an existence revolving, for the most part, around local concerns and local allegiances – de Valera's vision of a rural republic was undoubtedly idealistic, but it expressed a genuine respect for the life of the small farmer, so numerous in the Irish countryside. His dream reflected a widespread belief that the integrity of Irish existence should be defended against the commercial, industrial, cosmopolitan life of modern society.

Nonetheless that life was making itself felt. The fightback against a century of 'industrial repression' by Britain involved setting up small industries manufacturing, for example, razor blades, electric light-bulbs, beet sugar, tyres, wallpaper, silk stockings, roofing tiles, cosmetics, aluminium kitchen ware, batteries, canned food, shoes, fertilisers, cement. The success of many of these light industries led to the growth of a new petty-bourgeois class, rivalling the established big businesses such as Guinness, Jacobs biscuits, and the whiskey distilleries. A new confidence in the middle classes of the towns bred a number of entrepreneurs, with money in commerce and property, whose local influence substituted for the declining power of the Big House. Village life became increasingly attenuated, particularly in the West, as the towns became more and more the purlieu of the petty-bourgeoisie. Power now resided with the doctors, lawyers, justices, well-off farmers, local magnates and gardaí: 'a vicious and ignorant middle-class', according to the novelist Frank O'Connor, scarcely to be relied upon to embrace the Gaelic ideal. Their influence was felt, for example, in the steady advance in city and town of commercial leisure activities – such as golf, or the cinema – and the slow, and much disparaged, advent of commercial sports catering for the lower paid. While mountain hare coursing remained immensely popular, greyhound racetracks began to appear on the outskirts of towns later in the decade, a magnet for organised gambling, according to the loudly disapproving Church authorities.

The middle classes also liked to travel. For those who could afford it, there was weekend motoring, punctuated by well-watered stops at pubs and hotels. Others took advantage of the extended and mostly efficient rail system that criss-crossed the country, linking nearly all the major towns, with narrow-gauge and branch lines servicing the smaller towns and villages (a legacy of the Congested Districts Board in the late nineteenth century). 1938 saw the introduction of the new Cork–Dublin express, made – or at least assembled – in Ireland. With its steel exterior, restaurant car, toilets, heating and corridor carpets it was, said one traveller, 'a symbol, a portent of things to come'. Trains serviced the tiny factories built on the central plains, and gave the spur to novelties such as the weekend break and the annual holiday. Train-fed seaside towns grew up, such as Ballybunion in County Kerry, catering for the expanding ranks of the lower middle classes. Teachers and middle-class intellectuals, on the other hand, chose Irish-speaking holidays in the Gaeltacht. Many were Northerners, emotionally attached to the revival of Irish, and using the several Northern Railway lines that crossed the border to spend their summers in Donegal and the Rosses.

Indeed, despite outward observance, the idealisation of the simple, Catholic, Irish-speaking life of the small farmer was increasingly irrelevant to the growing middle class in town and country – and when it spelt poverty, it held little attraction for the small farmers themselves. Even if the economics were right (and often they weren't) it proved impossible to ask the population to turn their backs on the social benefits and pleasures of modern life. In 1938 Professor Michael

Tierney, one of the foremost Catholic intellectuals, and later President of University College, Dublin, complained:

In our cities suburbanity, the thin and colourless conventionalism of the puritan or post-puritan petty bourgeoisie, is if anything now more dominant than formerly; and it constitutes the ideal towards which the more well-to-do in country districts, with the help of the motor car, wireless, and the cinema, are incessantly on the march.

The difficulty lay in how to harness these attributes of modern industrial living – motor car, wireless, cinema, telephone, electricity – to the cause of Irish distinctiveness. In the absence of indigenous Irish versions of progress, becoming modern appeared dangerously close to becoming foreign; development seemed hopelessly entangled with importation from abroad.

The battle for the future shape of Irish existence was staged, in part at least, as a conflict between the measured realities of age and the irresponsible desires of youth, too easily drawn to foreign pleasures. De Valera's dream of an Ireland 'young in its promise of a future' became in effect a struggle over the meaning and direction of youth. 'That is no country for old men,' wrote William Butler Yeats in 'Sailing to Byzantium'. By the late 1920s the internationally renowned poet, now in his sixties, could write ruefully of the 'young in one another's arms', caught in the 'sensual music' of a young and vibrant nation. The potency of youth was frankly desired by this respected public figure, a senator in Ireland's second chamber, who feared the drying up of his sexual and imaginative energy. But if Yeats regretted his age and inability to take part in the erotic pleasures of the young, there were plenty of others determined to stamp out such recreation. The problem as far as the authorities were concerned was not simply that the music was sensual, but that it was not Irish.

Priests, bishops, and district justices up and down the country railed against the cosmopolitan modern imports of jazz and swing. There was too much jazz on Irish radio (the people should be satisfied with traditional music) and too little respect for native culture. During the later 1930s the Irish Folklore Commission sent its representatives out into village and countryside to try to preserve the music and oral tradition associated with the Gaelic way of life – a sure recognition that that culture was in decline. (People complained of the 'folklore ramp'. The Commission targeted schools and the suggestion was that for fear of a slap from the teacher, children were inventing tales of local pookas and sacred wells.) Parish groups and organisations such as the Gaelic Athletic Association tried to foster interest in distinctively Irish pastimes, and the GAA was hugely successful in championing games such as Gaelic football, hurling and camogie against soccer, rugby and hockey.

But they waged a losing war against foreign music, and in particular against the dance-halls. 'The fever of dancing . . . seems to have seized all classes,' wrote one conservative commentator in 1938. Irish culture was a 'vacuum', gradually being filled at one end with Hunt Balls, and with profiteering dance-halls at the other. Undoubtedly, dancing, and that other foreign import, cinema, swept all before them. County Donegal in particular became renowned as 'a sort of rock of scandal'. No fewer than seventy-eight dance-halls were licensed by the County in 1937 alone, though very few of these were the 'profiteering' commercialised variety; most were held as fundraising events for church halls and local organisations. Nonetheless, dancing was given primary responsibility for a national decline in morals, particularly among the young. Dances were regularly denounced as 'a public scandal and an occasion of ruin to many young people, especially girls'.

It was partly that the dances themselves – the foxtrot, the quickstep, the slow waltz – offered far more opportunity for physical intimacy than the strictly codified Irish dances. And there was the darkness that surrounded them (particularly in the countryside). It was taken as a matter of course that young men and women could not be trusted together after night fell. Sociability in itself was a danger when it allowed unrestricted mixing of the sexes. As District Justice Walsh of Letterkenny put it in one licence hearing in 1939: 'I don't care whether you dance every evening, so long as it is in daylight. I take it, of course, that there will be nothing but Irish dancing.' (He was horrified to learn that there would not.) In a similar vein the parish priest of Quin, County Clare, opposed a dance licence for Knoppogue Castle, Quin, on the grounds that 'It is half a mile from the public road; it is surrounded by woods, and the dance could not possibly be held under proper supervision. It is just such a place as would suit evilly disposed persons, and I ask the court to refuse the application' – which the court duly did.

The fuss about dancing was one strand of the paternalistic state's efforts to construct a stable Catholic society by regulating sexual morality. They had evidence of the need to do something. In 1930 and 1931 the Carrigan Committee, investigating the laws governing contraception and the problem of juvenile prostitution, heard statistical evidence and witness statements outlining a rising illegitimacy rate and increasing sexual crime, including sexual abuse of children. The Committee interpreted sexual crime and prostitution as part of a more general problem of sexual immorality. Contraception, the Committee suggested, was widely used in both country and town, and everywhere morals were declining. The Committee noted, for example, the 'notorious indecency prevalent today, in country districts as well as in the neighbourhood of towns and cities, in which both sexes take part and a feature of which is the misuse of motor cars'.

In these frequent moral panics, the awkward vigour of youth was the overriding issue. The idea that young people might be mature enough to be trusted with their independence was out of the question. Irish society was, of course, scarcely unusual in this. Traditions of hierarchy and deference were still dominant throughout much of pre-war Europe, though challenged by the youthful and idealistic, by political radicals and cultural bohemians of various kinds. In Ireland, however, the conflict was complicated by the dismissal of modern innovations as shallow, materialistic, above all British. In July 1939 Professor James Hogan outlined what he considered to be 'The Pre-Conditions of a Rural Revival'. These included the need to accept a lower standard of living, to reject commercialised entertainments, to get rid of luxuries (motor cars, cinemas, radios, and 'cosmopolitan dress designers'), to overhaul the banks and get rid of the parliamentary party system. Only by rejecting 'urbanised and alien standards' could the traditional culture of the countryside fight back against the 'Anglo-Saxon Mammonism' that was leading the young astray.

Utopian and frankly authoritarian politics like this did not have government backing (and they were to fade in popularity during the war). But for many people, especially the aspirational lower middle classes, religious conformity and social propriety were necessary steps on the path of self-improvement; upward mobility meant sexual and economic prudence, and the rejection of reckless behaviour and morally dubious foreign crazes. In his 1940 novel *Dutch Interior* Frank O'Connor suggested that the country was very far from de Valera's dream of youthful promise, or even Yeats's fantasy of 'the young in one another's arms'. He portrayed the young people of Cork city 'clinging to one another' less out of desire than out of desperation. The aspirations of youth had no other means of expression than the evening promenade along the main streets: 'Hundreds of boys and girls, escaping from dreary homes, put on their best clothes, their best manner. For a few hours at least they were subject to no authority, audacious, successful, invincible.'

When they were old enough, if they had the means, the young left the country altogether. Conservative fears that the dance-halls were squeezing out native culture proved to be far too sanguine. Society itself was disappearing. For despite attempts to regenerate the countryside, profits in all areas dwindled during the 1930s, partly as a result of the economic war with Britain. In 1937, for example, the proprietor of a dance-hall in Castletownbere, County Cork, applied for a licence to admit girls of seventeen, citing as his reason that all the girls over eighteen in the area had emigrated. Castletownbere was the site of one of the Treaty ports, which suggests that the English garrison had little hold over Irish girls, who were leaving such depressed areas in droves. Emigration rose inexorably in the later 1930s. Parents faced the likely prospect of their children leaving home just as had their own parents' generation – with one difference. Since the 1929 Crash and the start of the Great Depression, Irish emigrants were more likely to choose Britain than the United States as their eventual destination; indeed, for a few years at the start of the 1930s more Irish travelled back from the States than emigrated there. The fabled 'American Letter', containing yearly news but also all-important remission of funds, was increasingly rivalled by the Christmas post from England and Scotland. The dwindling of the population was, as before, more marked in rural areas. And it had serious knock-on effects as the economy staggered to keep afloat on nothing. During 1938 teachers working in rural areas had their salaries cut because of depopulation – their constituency was steadily fading away.

For all that Irish Irelanders worried about the vacuum in Irish culture, this emptying of the population created a literal void. Gaelic culture might be prized, but not enough to stop it disappearing. There were two hundred thousand Irish speakers in 1922; by 1939, the number had been cut by half. The glorification of the peasant was a tacit confession that his was no longer a viable way of life, a fact cruelly satirised in Flann O'Brien's parodic Gaeltacht autobiography, *An Béal Bocht*:

I am noting down the matters which are in this document because the next life is approaching me swiftly – far from us be the evil thing and may the bad spirits not regard me as a brother! – and also because our likes will never be there again. It is right and fitting that some testimony of the diversions and adventures of our times should be provided for those who succeed us because our types will never be there again, nor any other life in Ireland comparable to ours who exists no longer.

The trappings of modern 'suburbanity' slowly infiltrated Irish life, bringing with them increased discrepancies in wealth and new social tensions. One unlikely new menace was joyriding, which enjoyed brief popularity during the late 1930s, as car ownership rose, and before the petrol rationing of the war years put a stop to driving altogether. A sure sign of social malaise, joyriding became a mild enough outlet for underemployed and envious youth. In January 1937, for example, a Miss O'Mara, daughter of the local doctor, left her car outside the cinema in the small town of Ennis, County Clare. While she was inside enjoying the picture, four local youths promptly took the car out of the town, driving it for nearly two hours 'all around the roads and byeways'. In fact this was only one of two cases of joyriding to occur in Ennis in one night. Local papers throughout the country record numerous troubles with joyriders – in some reports joyriding appears as a barely disguised euphemism for sex, along the lines of the 'misuse of motor cars' condemned in the Carrigan report.

Ireland's roads were amongst the most dangerous in Europe. It was not that there were a great many cars, but the ones there were had an alarming number of accidents. In 1937, for example, despite very low car ownership, 209 people were killed on the Irish roads, and there were 10,583 injuries. There were similar concerns over car safety in England, where the Automobile Association successfully lobbied for an absence of any speed restrictions – insisting in effect that the law should aim to control the working classes rather than the well-to-do car-owner. In a similar vein one Irish judge decried the idea that the car-owner should have to lock his car. If people got hurt it was their own fault for getting in the way. Car magazines did their best to encourage a responsible attitude, including articles helpfully entitled 'The Use of the Clutch' and (worryingly) 'Learn to Steer'. By the late 1930s the motor car was well on the way to becoming a necessary middle-class acquisition. The Ford Factory in Cork helped to spread ownership by offering their cheapest car for £140. (This could be enjoyed for five pounds per month on top of a 'moderate down-payment'.) Joyriding, driving without lights, driving dangerously, driving unfit vehicles – motoring offences began almost to rival bicycle crime in the country at large.

Of course, increased mobility also had huge benefits. It was essential if decentralisation of industry in the rural areas was to have any effect. But mobility also brought traditional and modern Ireland face to face in new ways. One revealing case was heard in Letterkenny, Donegal, in January 1939. It concerned the theft of turf from Gaeltacht farmers. In the autumn of 1938 Moses Vance from Raphoe in the Lagan Valley in East Donegal, accompanied by his brother William and two friends, had driven a lorry-load of corn to the poorer land in the West to sell. After concluding his business, he and his companions had a few drinks and on their way back across the county stole sods of turf to the value of one pound from the turf stacks of two local farmers. The judge was incensed, all the more because Vance and his friends were, as he put it, 'well-off'. (Was there a sectarian element to his rage, hinted at in the very un-Catholic first names Moses and William?) Declaring the crime far worse than smuggling (then rife in Donegal), he determined to invert the meaning of the saying that there was one law for the rich and another for the poor. 'The farmer cannot lock up his field,' he argued, and therefore respect for the land was all the more vital. Despite the fact that on being challenged the four men had immediately paid for the turf, and had offered compensation for the damage done to the turf stacks, Vance was sentenced to three months' imprisonment with hard labour.

Those Gaeltacht farmers, their livelihoods and distinctive culture, lay at the heart of de Valera's dream of a modern rural republic. In January 1939, when their case was heard, and as the Munich settlement began to unravel, the sense of impending crisis for Europe could not have seemed greater, nor – for the farmers themselves and many of their compatriots – further away. It was not at all clear what relevance the coming war could have to these subsistence farmers on the western edge of Europe, or what responsibility they could bear towards it. It seemed reasonable that a people who did not enjoy the benefits of modern city life, the prosperity of industrial development, or the fruits of empire, should stay out of a conflict between economically advanced and highly mechanised powers.

* * *

Beyond cultural differences lay political quarrels. Before the war de Valera repeatedly stressed the political necessity for neutrality. Huge internal difficulties stood in the way of Ireland lending support to Britain. First amongst these was the continuing problem of partition, and the threat of a return to civil war. 'Any other policy,' de Valera later declared, 'would have divided our people, and for a divided nation to fling itself into war would be to commit suicide.' His minister Frank Aiken went further when he remarked that if the Irish were to join the war, they would have to fight a civil war first to decide which side they were going to be on.

Aiken may have been exaggerating for effect, but both men were pointing to the deep-seated distrust of Britain that stood in the way of support for the war. Resentment of Britain over the long history of conquest, over its retention of Northern Ireland, and over the treatment of Catholics in the province, was endemic. These feelings were compounded by memories of 'British treachery' – in particular the refusal to face down Ulster Unionism and move towards Irish autonomy, despite the sacrifice of Irish men and women in the First World War, and the notorious cruelty of the Black and Tans during the War of Independence that followed. The political impact of the First World War had given strong historical sanction to the policy of non-alignment in Ireland. Neutrality, and opposition to the threat of conscription – as the European carnage continued – had been a central plank of Sinn Féin's 1918 election campaign. The success of the separatists at the ballot box delivered the *coup de grace* to the Irish Parliamentary Party, and set the mould for Irish politics for many decades to come. With memories of the civil war kept alive by sporadic campaigns from the still active IRA violence was much more than an abstract possibility. As Elizabeth Bowen remarked in the middle of the war, 'For Ireland, between 1918 and 1939, "peace" contracted into a shorter space than people realise.'

Though there was little active support for Germany either inside the IRA or in the wider population, the Irish experience after the First World War generated sympathy for the Germans. This focused on the treatment meted out to them at Versailles. An editorial in the *Meath Chronicle* in April 1939 (a few weeks after Hitler's invasion of Czechoslovakia) captured one strand of the public mood when it blamed the coming crisis on Anglo-French greed:

The war to end war was won in 1918. Now the babies, born that year, are called upon to train as cannon fodder. Just twenty-one years ago Britain saved civilisation, drove the Huns to Berlin, made a situation which, we are told, would culminate in an era of peace and happiness for all. Lloyd George was the hero of the hour – he won the war to end war. He made the peace which has brought the babies born in the year of victory, to the shambles twenty-one years after. The boys of Britain, 20–21 years of age, are being conscripted. Today, thanks mainly to the greed of Britain and France, the world is on the brink of general war – only God's mercy can save it . . . If Hitler is the man of the moment, as he is, Britain and France made him. He is the instrument – it was England and France made the situation.

Get that fact well in mind.

There was no love of Hitler lying behind such sentiments, but a confirmed sense of having seen it all before. Even if this didn't necessarily add up to support for Britain's enemies, it certainly precluded active support for Britain – a just deserts attitude summed up in the popular sentiment, 'I hope that England will be nearly beat.' But there was also a section of the populace – focused on the sundered six counties of Northern Ireland – who hoped that England would be beaten outright. 'We resolved,' de Valera stated, 'that the aim of our policy would be to keep our people out of a war. I said in the Dáil that with our history, with our experiences of the last war, and with part of our country still unjustly severed from us, we felt that no other decision and no other policy was possible.' In this he was simply being realistic. After all, in January 1939, a number of his citizens had already declared war on Britain.

The IRA's announcement of war was the result of a series of splits within the movement during the late 1930s. The new Chief of Staff of the IRA from 1938 was the bullish Sean Russell. Under his leadership, the organisation turned its back decisively on the left-wing, anti-fascist, anti-imperialist rhetoric that had characterised some early-1930s Republicanism, and which, for Russell, was merely a distraction from the military struggle with Britain. His commitment was to physical force – he was convinced that a bombing campaign centring on Britain would compel Westminster to negotiate over partition. Accordingly, a plan of synchronised but sporadic sabotage operations in major English cities was drawn up (the 'S plan'). The idea was not to target individuals, but to disrupt transport systems and power supplies, in the hope of bringing England to its knees. Throughout the latter half of 1938 poorly trained men, with poor materials, tried to turn themselves into a credible fighting force by organising bombing classes, gathering new volunteers and resources, and raising money (through the United

States). The increased activity on both sides of the Irish border was initially ignored by complacent Irish and British police forces.

The close of 1938 saw a series of trial runs, as customs posts along the Northern Irish border were blown up – internment was reintroduced in Northern Ireland in December 1938. Then, on 12 January 1939, a formal ultimatum was delivered to the British Foreign Secretary, Lord Halifax, demanding the withdrawal of all British armed forces and civilian representatives from every part of Ireland. Three days later notices were posted throughout the country asking for the support of the population in the effort to complete a British withdrawal from Northern Ireland. During the following days and weeks there was a series of major explosions on electricity lines, underground stations and power stations – in London, Manchester, Birmingham, Alnwick, Liverpool and Coventry. Scores of Irishmen were arrested, imprisoned or deported. (When British police discovered a copy of the 'S plan' on a suspect, the first thought in Dublin was that this was part of an Orange plot to sabotage de Valera's negotiations over partition.)

That spring witnessed heavy IRA activity. In March there were explosions at Hammersmith Bridge, in Birmingham, Liverpool, Coventry and then seven more in London. Over Easter, while Russell travelled to the United States to raise money, attacks in England continued, targeting cinemas and hotels. In a token of support, gas masks were burned in nationalist areas of Birmingham, and Post Offices and letter boxes were bombed. On 24 June there were major explosions in Piccadilly Circus, followed by a series of firebomb attacks over the next few weeks. On 24 July, Sir Samuel Hoare introduced the Prevention of Violence Bill, authorising tighter control of immigration, deportation, the registration of all Irish living in Britain, and the detention of suspects without trial. There had been 127 incidents since January: one dead, fifty-five injured, sixty-six convicted of terrorist activity. More bombs were set off over the next few days, at Victoria and King's Cross stations in London, and in Liverpool. Deportations began in August, and by the 5th of the month there had already been forty-eight expulsion orders. There were also raids on the Irish side of the water. On 22 August the Offences against the State Act was brought into force, setting up special criminal courts, and giving the government additional powers to arrest, search, and detain suspects. On 25 August – as the British Parliament was ratifying the defence treaty with Poland – a bomb was detonated in the centre of Coventry, killing five people and injuring sixty.

The IRA numbered nearly five thousand at the end of the 1930s. This ready supply of volunteers not only pointed to frustration with Britain, and impatience with de Valera's negotiations for full independence and the end of partition. It also suggests that, in the eyes of republicans, wider European issues were eclipsed by Ireland's immediate grievances, a mindset which neutrality was in turn to foster. IRA membership was far from negligible, but broad republican sentiment reached well beyond those willing to join the organisation. Many shared the republican conviction that this was not a war against Hitler, nor a war to prevent the partition of Poland, but a war to protect the British Empire. This was a view accepted by many on the left in Britain as well, of course, especially during the early years of the war: the years of the Nazi–Soviet Pact. After all, Britain had notably failed to act against fascism through the League of Nations, and its record in Ireland was scarcely a model of democratic governance.

Republican agitation against the war was strongest in Northern Ireland. For those unwilling to take up active sabotage, smaller-scale interference focused on air-raid precautions. Scepticism about the hype surrounding measures against gas and chemical warfare was one issue. (The campaign in Spain was cited as good grounds for consigning the alleged dangers of gas to the realms of lurid fiction.) It was compounded, in strongly nationalist areas, by a belief that ARP was a subtle form of British domination, which should be resisted with vigour. Not only did it prove difficult in nationalist areas to recruit ARP officers, but there were incidents of burning gas masks in the street, and later of deliberately showing lights after blackout.

British 'hypocrisy', highlighted by the treatment meted out to the nationalist community in Northern Ireland, provided obvious fuel for arguments against joining in the war. In a series of articles published in Irish-American newspapers in early 1939, Eugene Coyle, a parish priest in County Fermanagh, reminded his readers that Hitler had asked Roosevelt what he intended to do about the continued aggression of England towards Ireland. 'I am living since 1929 under this Dictatorship,' Father Coyle declared, 'and I may say this, that if the Dictatorships in Italy and Germany are 1/4 as bad as that of England with Craigavon as her puppet, in the 6 Counties of Ireland, they are really bad.' By the middle of the war, M. J. MacManus, literary editor of the Fianna Fáil newspaper, the *Irish Press*, was explaining to readers of the English journal *Horizon*: 'The word democracy, in fact, has lost much of its old potency in Ireland.' The poor showing of parliamentary regimes in the face of economic and political crisis during the 1930s had bred disaffection with democratic ideals across the political spectrum in Britain too. But the centrality of the word democracy in England's wartime rhetoric was bound to make its exhortations look especially tarnished from the other side of the Irish Sea.

After the reintroduction of internment in Northern Ireland, following the bombing campaign of January 1939, condemnations of the 'fascist and undemocratic' nature of the six counties, and of the British contempt for civil liberties, were rife. An editorial in the *Donegal Democrat* of 21 January 1939 focused on the men in Crumlin Road jail being held without trial:

Surely the Empire must be bankrupt in policy, its structure crazy and rotten when it has to resort to these brutal tactics. These are the people who lecture Hitler and hold up their hands in horror at Mussolini. Well our friends on the Continent and in the USA know that the liberty of the Catholic subject is at the whim of the Orange bigot in Northern Ireland.

By the autumn of 1939 the rhetoric of the war as a clash between evil empires was well rehearsed. One republican publicist based in the small town of Ballyshannon, County Donegal, brought out a short-lived *Bulletin* on 'Ireland and the War' which was designed to counter British 'war propaganda' in Northern Ireland:

It is our settled belief that, as charity begins at home, so it is the duty of the Irish people to attend to their own affairs first, and, not to allow themselves to have their attention diverted towards acts of injustice at the ends of the earth, when a major act of injustice, the Partition of their own country and a whole host of minor outrages, are being perpetrated upon themselves.

The economic and social life of the people of 'Northern Ireland' is being profoundly disturbed by the fact that they have been dragged into a war in the wake of Imperial Britain. People are losing their chance of new houses and other improved social amenities, they are being pressed into a foreign army by Hitler methods, they are having to suffer the discomfort and dangers of a nightly blackout.

Of course, the degree of resentment at British injustice, both past and present, varied tremendously between persons, between families, between classes. For thousands of Irish people it was not sufficient to prevent them from feeling that, on balance, their choice should be to join the British armed forces, or support the war effort in other ways.

Nonetheless, it seemed clear that, without an end to partition, any attempt by de Valera to take Ireland into the war on the side of Britain would have been met by fierce resistance from the IRA. And many of de Valera's own supporters were convinced that entry on Britain's side would have meant the occupation of the ports and airfields by British troops – a renewed invasion. The Taoiseach's speech to the Dáil on 2 September 1939 clearly pointed to resentment and suspicion of Britain as one reason for the government's stance:

We, of all nations, know what force used by a stronger nation against a weaker one means. We have known what invasion and partition mean; we are not forgetful of our own history and, as long as our own country, or any part of it, is subject to force, the application of force, by a stronger nation, it is only natural that our people, whatever sympathies they might have in a conflict like the present, should look at their own country first and should, accordingly, in looking at their own country, consider what its interests should be and what its interests are.

Those interests included the basic one of survival. There were sound practical reasons for Ireland to stay out of the conflict: it made hard-headed sense for a country so little able to defend itself. It was generally acknowledged – even in Britain – that Ireland could not afford to fight; that if the country were to become caught up in the war it would last no time at all. The choice, it seemed, was either to stand aside, or be crushed by the colliding chariots of the Great Powers, trampled in the battle of titans.

Fears of aerial bombing and invasion were rife, and Ireland's vulnerable position and lack of air defences were undeniable. Dublin had few anti-aircraft guns and searchlights, for example, and until 1942 it proved very difficult to buy more from England. At the beginning of the war the Irish armed forces could boast only sixteen serviceable fighting aircraft, all of which were obsolcte. Radio equipment was also woefully inadequate. As for the ability to combat invasion on the ground, the Irish army was seriously under strength. The meagre force was neither trained nor equipped for combat. There was a grave shortage of armaments, ammunition and explosives – practically no anti-tank weapons, for example, and very few tanks. And the situation was no better at sea, for the country had no navy. The Irish Merchant Marine itself comprised fewer than fifty cargo-carrying vessels at the beginning of the war. Unable to combat seaborne invasion, U-boat incursions, or mines, Ireland also had to rely on the British navy for protection of its shipping.

Regaining the Treaty ports had been a precondition for Ireland's ability to endure isolation. But their acquisition also carried a strategic burden. As George Bernard Shaw insisted, the ports proclaimed to the world 'not only Ireland's liberty, but also her responsibility'. The government certainly intended to take that responsibility seriously, but making the dilapidated ports serviceable again was a challenge in itself. At Haulbowline, a fortified island in Cobh harbour formerly used by the British, the cobwebs had to be cleared away, and rooms made habitable, before any kind of start could be made on the task of fitting out and converting a trawler and three motor torpedo boats. The Marine Inscription service organised a fleet of small craft operating around the coast – they were supposed to assist in blocking channels in case of invasion, and also did minesweeping work. Eighty-nine coastal lookout posts were set up (with the additional benefit of bringing phone lines to Leitrim and Mayo, which had practically no telephone contact until 1940). Nonetheless the ramshackle nature of Ireland's defences made the country look like a sitting duck.

In February 1939 the government was attacked in the Dáil by opposition politicians for failing to take a lead in protecting the populace, especially in relation to the threat of attack from the air. In reply the Minister of Defence, Frank Aiken, outlined plans to increase the army from twenty thousand to a maximum strength of thirty thousand men, made up of a regular force of eight thousand, a reserve of five thousand, and a Volunteer reserve of seventeen thousand (the Volunteer force had been set up in 1934, but the training was poor). Proclaiming the government's intention to spend five million pounds on weapons and equipment, Aiken sketched a defence strategy based on a highly trained and efficient army, a network of coastal defences, motorcycle squadrons, anti-aircraft artillery and ARP, an air force, and the marine service. He also announced the government's intention to build an ammunitions factory.

The opposition countered that five million was a risible amount considering the forces the Irish army might be up against. In the months leading up to the war numerous articles in newspapers and journals pointed out the country's exposure to aerial bombing and invasion from the skies. New technology, such as aeroplane radios, had made possible long-range raids, which could easily reach Irish shores. The Italian

Count Balbo had already flown an 'Air Armada' of seaplanes to the United States via Derry. The numerous inlets of the western coast were cited as geographical invitations to seaplane (and submarine) invasion. The campaigns in Spain and Abyssinia had focused minds on the possibility of invasion by air, as well as of high-explosive and incendiary bombing raids, and there were fears too of gas attack from the air. More money should be put, Aiken's opponents insisted, into building a viable air force, rather than swelling the ground army.

The country's vulnerability prompted some to insist that neutrality was a hopeless dream. It was, in the words of one defence analyst, merely a 'pious aspiration'. For not only did Ireland appear an easy target; it was also surely a likely one. Ireland was dependent on British markets and trade for its economic survival. It was also heavily dependent on British shipping. How could the country expect to find safety in solitude, when it was becoming ever more closely linked with the rest of the world? (Roosevelt scoffed that it was like believing one can escape danger by getting into bed and pulling the clothes over one's head, and certainly – as Denmark, Holland and Belgium were swallowed up – many in Ireland worried that he was right.) Ireland's efforts to modernise had made it part of the latest networks of communication spanning the globe. New airports had been constructed at Foynes and Dublin, and the Valentia telephone cable, laid under the Atlantic, now linked Ireland and North America. Inevitably the wireless, which could bring home the reality of the war even to the remotest areas of the countryside, would facilitate attacks on Ireland from either side.

It was far from clear that Ireland had the strength to defend its independence as a neutral nation, but by the same token it had little or nothing to offer as a belligerent except the sacrifice of its citizens. If neutrality was dangerous, belligerence looked like suicide.

But on top of these practical issues of political will and military capability, to be weighed in the balance for many Irish people was a solid pride in independence. Neutrality was an assertion of autonomy; it was a marker of Irish distinctiveness, as potent as Catholicism or the Irish language. Far from being merely the counsel of a sober, even timorous realism, it was Ireland's first decisive act as a sovereign power. And it was also something in which de Valera passionately believed, as a matter of principle. In 1938, at the League of Nations, he had declared:

Despite our judicial equality here, in matters such as European peace, the small states are powerless. As I have already said, peace is dependent upon the will of the great states. All the small states can do, if the statesmen of the great states fail in their duty, is resolutely to determine that they will not become the tools of any great power and that they will resist with whatever strength they may possess every attempt to force them into a war against their will.

Conscious of the degree of feeling against Churchill's martial oratory, de Valera repeatedly asserted the 'God-given' right of small nations to decide their own fates, and suggested that if Britain truly believed in democracy it would stop trying to coerce its neighbours. Neutrality was right in principle: a moral and ethical defence of the independent rights of small nations against imperialist claims of power and jurisdiction over them.

De Valera was intending to use his speech at the opening of the New York World's Fair in May 1939 to reiterate Ireland's separation from British foreign policy, and her intention to remain neutral. In the end the worsening diplomatic situation prevented him from leaving for New York in May, and instead he sent Sean T. O'Kelly, Vice-President of the Executive Council of Éire, as his emissary. O'Kelly, a small white-haired man, lacked not only de Valera's commanding physical presence but also his capacity for measured statesmanship. On his arrival at the airport he put the case for Ireland's neutrality bluntly: 'I don't think there's a ghost of a chance of Ireland's fighting for anyone if she can get out of it, and the British know it.' O'Kelly was undoubtedly undiplomatic, but he was merely saying what everyone in Ireland already knew: that it would have been impossible for any democratic Irish politician to impose a policy of active participation in the war. Ignorance about the true nature of fascism, resentment of Britain, pride in Irish distinctiveness, recent memories of the First World War, the Anglo-Irish War and the Civil War, and above all fear of aerial bombardment – all combined to create an overwhelming consensus against becoming embroiled in yet another conflict.

Such arguments made little impression on British public opinion. Over the next five and a half years the accusation would be levelled again and again that Ireland was ducking her moral responsibilities, betraying her natural allies, hiding behind British defences, and turning a blind eye to the tyrannical, expansionist ambitions of fascism. As President Roosevelt wryly enquired, if the Nazis were to win, could Ireland hold out: would Ireland be permitted 'an amazing exception' in a world not free?

2

Talk of Escapism

On 1 September 1939 Europe woke up to the news that German forces had crossed the Polish border. Despite all the efforts to avert it, war had come a very large step closer. The situation in Europe had been steadily worsening since Hitler's invasion of Czechoslovakia in March. On 24 August, following the Nazi–Soviet Pact, the British Parliament had passed an Emergency Powers Act. The following day it copper-fastened the defensive alliance between Britain, France and Poland that had been hastily pushed through after the invasion of Czechoslovakia – though what help there could be for Poland now was questionable. Now, with the crisis suddenly on top of him, Chamberlain vacillated, unsure of the support of France and unwilling to commit to war once the guarantee to Poland had failed. There was uproar in Parliament when MPs met on 2 September to hear a lame suggestion from Chamberlain, still searching for peace at almost any price, to help open talks between Germany and Poland if Hitler would withdraw his troops.

But in Ireland de Valera seemed confident that Britain and France intended to keep their promises to the Poles. He announced a state of emergency in the Dáil on 2 September and amended the constitution to ensure that the provision for emergency legislation 'in time of war' included war in which Ireland itself was not directly engaged. Following near-mutiny by his Cabinet that same evening, Chamberlain announced over the wireless at 11.15 a.m. on Sunday 3 September that Britain was at war with Germany. The same day, the Oireachtas passed the Emergency Powers Act (1939): 'An act to make provision for securing the public safety and the preservation of the state in time of war.'

The two Irish legislative bodies, the Dáil and the Seanad, had been hurriedly summoned by telegram on 1 September. They met the following afternoon amid grumbles that TDs had been notified of the emergency session too late for those living in the country to make it up to town – some only found out about the assembly when they read about it in their morning paper. Since everyone knew that the crisis was looming, why the panic session? Couldn't the assembly have been called earlier, or meet a day or two later? De Valera and his ministers insisted that the two pieces of legislation to be pushed through – amending the constitution and passing the Emergency Powers Bill – could not wait. The two acts formed a single package. The constitutional amendment meant that the government could not be accused of acting illegally in introducing Emergency legislation even when the country was not itself at war. Despite some qualms about the erosion of democracy which the amendment might allow, the Bill was passed without opposition. The Emergency Powers Bill itself had a much rougher ride. This Bill was modelled on the British Act passed the previous week, and was designed to give the government extensive rights – all the powers necessary for protecting the state and its citizens in a volatile situation 'almost akin to war', for maintaining public order and suppressing dissent, and for regulating and controlling essential supplies such as basic foods, petrol, coal and the raw materials needed by industry.

The deliberations over the Bill went on until 5 a.m. – causing problems for some members who missed vital parts of the discussion while napping on the benches outside the chamber. Despite the lateness of the hour, the debates show a remarkably clear understanding of the difficulties Ireland was to face over the next five and a half years. There were two main areas of concern. On the economic front, the fears were of unemployment and shortages. TDs saw the difficulties of accessing shipping, protecting the export market, and ensuring equal distribution of supplies through a comprehensive rationing system (which was never properly to get off the ground).

This alarm over the state's chances of economic survival was all too perceptive. But if anything there was even more concern about the limits the Bill placed on citizens' constitutional and civil rights. The government was empowered to suspend any legislation it thought necessary, to legislate by decree, to censor public and private communications, to control citizens' movements, to search and arrest people without warrant, to intern them without trial or right of appeal. Ministers implied that they were likely to be too busy to attend regular meetings of the Dáil, leading to calls from right across the political spectrum for reassurance that parliament would meet regularly throughout the period of Emergency. TDs reluctantly agreed these 'dictatorial' and 'complete totalitarian powers'. Many felt they were colluding in the destruction of the country's painfully achieved democracy, 'stripping the people naked of any constitutional rights', unravelling its newly acquired constitution. If Ireland was to be neutral, why did the government need to copy the British Act, which was designed to cope with war? While the government offered predictable reassurances on the proper use of these powers, speaker after speaker revealed the levels of disquiet about how neutrality was going to work in practice. What were the effects of the decision going to be on the economic, industrial and civil life of the country? And did the government really think it would protect the people against invasion or aerial bombing?

What was missing from the debates as they dragged on into the small hours was any significant discussion about the rights and wrongs of the policy of neutrality as a whole. A few senators, and even fewer members of the Dáil, did raise the issue of sympathy for Britain, and the ethics of staying neutral while relying on British shipping for supplies, but even they had to acknowledge the practical difficulty in taking the country into war when the 'vast majority' of the population wanted to be neutral. There was near-unanimous backing for neutrality as the only practical option for the country, and no real sense of having to defend it politically either.

The policy seemed both logical and reasonable. Rather than turning its back on Europe in choosing neutrality, the country was, as the historian Joe Lee has put it, 'never more European'. Across the continent neutrality was the popular choice. In 1939 all the smaller states, and some large ones, signalled their intentions to keep out of the war. Ireland was able to align itself with Belgium, Holland, Luxembourg, Denmark, Norway, Sweden, Finland, Hungary, Yugoslavia, Romania, Bulgaria, Portugal, Switzerland and Italy, not to mention the United States. On the other hand the British Commonwealth dominions (a status hotly contested in Ireland) quickly joined the war on Britain's side – Australia and New Zealand stepped forward on 3 September, Canada a week later. It was the history of Ireland's long connection with Britain which made its neutrality conspicuous – distinguishing the Irish from the Belgian choice, for example. But as de Valera had been trying to hammer home for the previous two or three years, that unhappy history, and the country's more recent attempts to emerge from under the thumb of imperial Britain and go it alone as a sovereign power, also made neutrality inevitable.

All year de Valera had been stressing the fact that Ireland would be neutral. The official commitment to neutrality was blazoned across the newspapers that weekend. (On 3 September the *Irish Times* brought out its first Sunday edition since the 1916 Rising.) But the crisis mood in Britain was infectious. Official evacuation procedures had been announced on 31 August and the news over the weekend was dominated by the crowds of children who were being herded onto trains leaving London and other major cities, the new trenches that were being dug in London parks, the anti-aircraft gun emplacements on the coasts and in the cities, the sandbags, the barrage balloons. Calls for ambulance drivers, stretcher-bearers and volunteers for civilian defence were put out over the radio. The Royal Navy was fully mobilised; all army reservists were called up, and most of the Royal Air Force reserve. In Ireland, as in Britain, people hung on for news bulletins on the wireless, and there was a run on the papers. The major dailies, the *Irish Times*, *Irish Press*, *Irish Independent* and *Cork Examiner*, were full of the international crisis, and of the atmosphere of alarm in Britain – trenches, shelters, evacuation, mobilisation.

In Dublin, in Cork, and in numerous smaller towns across the country, there was real confusion over the need for air raid precautions. People had been painting their windows and buying blackout curtains for some weeks, partly under the influence of announcements on the BBC and in English papers. The Irish authorities themselves were confused, issuing a flurry of contradictory instructions about safety and supplies. On 1 September the Department of Defence sent telegrams to local authorities in east-coast towns calling for them to reduce their lighting to 25 per cent. In the game of Chinese whispers that followed, the gardaí gave instructions for a complete blackout in some areas (even 'the most remote mountainy villages'), motorists cut their lights, and public hospitals were ordered to ensure a total blackout even in isolated districts. Where house lights were left burning near Dublin on 2 September, a small plane flew low and flashed warning signals, although many shops and even the bus company failed to comply with the confused blackout orders. Meanwhile there were reports of 'hooliganism' in towns such as Sligo and Ballina, as bored young people took advantage of the darkness, leading to calls for a curfew. All this, as a TD pointed out the next day, was guaranteed to contribute to 'the nervous condition of our people'. Was neutrality going to protect the country? The Irish public sat out the first day of September 1939 'in a state of extreme nervous tension'.

The extraordinary sitting of the Oireachtas right through the following night did little to still rumours, especially since some TDs insisted on making statements contending that Britain was going to 'starve us into the war', and that the border would guarantee Ireland's involvement whether the people wanted it or not.

While the members of both houses worried about the imminent loss of Irish citizens' constitutional rights, outside the assembly people were forced to focus on more immediate difficulties. In these first days housewives dithered with their blackout curtains, and motorists experimented with sidelights to minimise the risk of accidents. And there were inevitable attempts at hoarding. After hearing the news on 1 September, people rushed out to the shops to buy in provisions. There was a run on sugar, for example, so that an ad hoc rationing system had to be hastily introduced. Protests over the sudden shortages revealed a good deal about popular standards of nutrition. One woman complained that, rather than the six or seven pounds of sugar her family used to get through in a week, they were now restricted to one. Because of panic buying, prices rose suddenly. By 2 September the price of flour had risen by two shillings a sack – a week later it was up a further two shillings and sixpence, despite the government's Prices Standstill Order aimed at fixing charges at late-August prices.

But the most obvious effect on Ireland of Britain's declaration of war was a series of sudden migrations. As the news spread, long queues formed outside post offices in Dublin and Cork, while people in rural areas pedalled to the nearest telephone to call their relatives in England. They urged them to come home – to avoid both the peril of aerial bombardment (which was expected imminently) and the more long-term danger of conscription. Many did not wait for a call. That weekend the trains from Euston to Holyhead were packed (Great Western Railways laid on extra transport), as people scrambled to the Dun Laoghaire ferry from the south of England, from Liverpool, Manchester and Birmingham. Others squeezed onto the Paddington to Fishguard train and took the boat to Rosslare. Staff at the Irish High Commissioner's office in Piccadilly worked straight through the weekend, dealing with a mass of passport and permit applications. By Monday six extra officials had been drafted in to deal with the queues now snaking through the streets, and to process more than fifteen hundred applications a day. On 2 September four thousand 'refugees' arrived in Dun Laoghaire, and a further thousand in Cork (the boats were so crammed there were several cases of men, and women, over-board). By the middle of the following week staffing at Irish Sea ports had been doubled as thousands continued to come in. The ferries from Glasgow to Belfast were also crowded to overflowing. Sir Basil Brooke, distinguished First World War veteran and Minister of Agriculture in the Stormont government, travelled back to Belfast on 1 September, from a curtailed Scottish holiday. He noted in his diary, 'Masses of Irish on the Glasgow boat. Running away . . .'

They included workers from London and other centres of Irish immigrant population, as well as seasonal labourers from Scotland and Lancashire who would soon have been returning to their rural holdings in Donegal and Mayo anyway. By 9 September, for example, *The Western People* was reporting that two hundred and fifty 'boys and girls' had returned to the small town of Kiltimagh, in County Mayo, and a further six hundred to Ballaghaderreen in County Roscommon during the previous week. Press reports liked to stress that the majority were women and children, but as the *Irish Times* reported on 3 September, there were also 'a large number of young men, who looked like labourers'.

It was not only the fear of bombing that prompted the mass evacuation, but also confusion over the rules governing conscription. In April 1939 military conscription in peacetime had been introduced in Britain for the first time in history. (The orders excluded Northern Ireland. Despite the urgings of the Northern Irish Prime Minister, Lord Craigavon, who was determined to set the seal on Ulster's loyalty to the Crown, Chamberlain had refused to extend conscription to the province, for fear of violent resistance from the nationalist community. The 1918 conscription crisis, which led to the victory of Sinn Féin in the election that year, was still fresh in political memory. The Belfast IRA may have been boasting when they claimed that they had forced Britain to back down, but the non-compulsory status of military service certainly caused difficulties for Stormont politicians, who were anxious to prove their complete and loyal backing for Britain's war effort, especially in comparison with the neutral South.) In May, cancelling his trip to the World's Fair, de Valera had tried and failed to have all Irish domiciled in England exempted from military service. The compromise was the 'two-year rule', which excused all Irish citizens who had been living in England for less than two years. This still left a large number of labourers, many in farm and building work, in an awkward position. They might have been living in England for far longer than two years, but still considered their home to be in Ireland. Certainly some felt a duty to fight for Britain, and many joined up rather than waiting to be conscripted. Others took the first opportunity to leave.

Most of the hasty travellers were Irish, but not all of them. Some of those in a hurry to get out were British citizens, many of them women with children, who had arranged to stay with friends in Ireland or in some cases booked country hotels – reservations shot up for the usually quiet winter months. And there were also men hoping to avoid conscription – border officials attempted to sift out able-bodied British men and send them back. Concerns were raised in the Dáil about the country, and Dublin in particular, becoming 'a happy hunting ground for a lot of undesirable aliens'. One TD who had been away from Dublin for his annual holidays returned at the end of August: 'I walked down town on Thursday because I had not got the car, and found quite a number of accents and faces which I could recognise as not being Irish.' He meant, of course, that they were British: they included pacifists, a scattering of Trotskyists, and a number of people against the war for their own reasons. But there were accents from further afield – including a small number of refugees from Germany and central Europe, and one or two German undercover agents.

There was also a rush of travellers in the opposite direction. Over the preceding weeks British Army reservists had been called up and asked to rejoin their units; the call-up involved an estimated twenty thousand Irish – from both sides of the border – serving in the British Armed Forces on the eve of war. They found themselves travelling with scores of volunteers intending to enlist in the British Armed Forces. Some took the boat to England – by 3 September Irish seaports were reporting that around eight thousand men, reservists or soldiers on leave, had left from Dun Laoghaire, North Wall Dublin, Cobh, Cork and Rosslare. Others travelled north. 'There were hundreds on the train from Dublin, both deserters and ordinary civilians joining up,' remembered one fugitive from the Irish army who made the trip to Belfast that weekend. One volunteer recalled that on 8 December 1939, when he joined up in Belfast, fourteen men from the south also enlisted on that day. Another remembered that out of a group of sixty who enlisted with him, forty-six were southerners. Men living in the border counties simply walked to the recruiting centres in Omagh and Armagh.

Apart from volunteers, the ferries to England and Scotland carried holidaymakers of all nationalities whose vacations were suddenly curtailed by the war, including Irish nationals normally resident in Britain who were caught out by the summer holidays and were now struggling to get back. Some of the more well-to-do English tourists, who could afford the luxury of waiting and seeing how the war would develop, inevitably chose to stay. Motorists prolonged their sojourns in country hotels; those renting hunting lodges or cottages for fishing extended their leases. Some, including the English novelist T. H. White, who was shooting in Mayo in September 1939, on the proceeds from his 1938 bestseller, *The Sword in the Stone*, were to remain in Ireland throughout the war. (In the words of his biographer Sylvia Townsend Warner, White 'remained with the women and children'.) Others left wives and children in Ireland while they returned to work in England.

But not all of those travelling to England in the first weeks of the war had the Allies' cause at heart. On 11 September members of the small German community living in Dublin and the surrounding areas gathered in Dun Laoghaire to board the mailboat for Holyhead, where they were met by British police and escorted to the German Embassy in London (from where they travelled via neutral Holland to Germany). Some Germans, including the Director of the National Museum in Dublin and Nazi Party member, Adolf Mahr, were on holiday in Germany anyway, and about three hundred German nationals (including members of the German legation) decided to remain in Ireland. There were also a very few Irish citizens, among them the novelist Francis Stuart, whose sense of wartime allegiance was to take them to Berlin.

* * *

Most of the crowds jostling to get onto the mailboat as German troops entered Poland were motivated by fear. But there were also more considered responses. Principled pacifist arguments still retained their potency. In the first days of September the Pope's appeal for peace was given extensive and serious coverage in all the papers. Cardinal MacRory, Primate of All Ireland, called for peace now, rather than a devastating war followed by peace on victors' terms, recalling, like many, the disastrous consequences of Versailles. Parish priests across the country inaugurated special 'Prayers for Peace', which took place on Sunday evenings (and therefore had the added advantage of allowing the priest to keep tabs on the young people of his parish). These initiatives were no doubt driven partly by fears for the fate of Christianity at the hands of a totalitarian regime, and even after June 1940 there were members of the British Cabinet who argued the need to sue for peace with Germany. At the other ideological pole, small left-wing groups also opposed the war, in part because of republican sympathies and because of the Hitler–Stalin pact. But most of the populace, driven neither by their stake in organised religion nor by ideological commitments, simply felt that the fight was none of their concern – this was not Ireland's struggle.

In the autumn of 1939 the correspondent for the journal of Commonwealth affairs, *The Round Table*, offered the following assessment of Irish opinion:

There are, of course, many people in Ireland who, however much they may wish loyally to accept the Government's decision, cannot be neutral in thought. The great majority of these feel that our interests economic, political and spiritual are so indissolubly bound up with those of Great Britain and France that, if those Powers were to go down before the onslaught of Hitlerism, the future of Ireland and indeed of European civilisation itself would be dark indeed. Others, while hating Hitlerism and all its works and pomps, cannot forget the cynical dismemberment of Czechoslovakia in which Poland joined, and feel that the present war is only one more move in the game of power politics from which Ireland has everything to lose and nothing to gain. They cannot see why we should participate in this war any more than Belgium, Holland, Switzerland or the Scandinavian countries, all of whom represent the best kind of democratic community.

The pro-Commonwealth angle here is unmistakable, and it is likely that the sample was weighted towards middle-class Dublin society. Even so the reporter could acknowledge the common-sense arguments for neutrality – widely shared amongst the small nations of Europe. As each of the European neutrals declared, their decisions were given prominent space in all the Irish papers; there were calls for an alliance of neutrals to sue for peace. Ireland was now sovereign and independent, and had no obligation to risk these gains by joining in someone else's war. Such views echoed de Valera's rhetoric about the rights of small nations, as well as his sceptical view of imperial Britain's democratic credentials. Looked at in this light, neutrality was the sensible, rational choice, the obvious majority decision – indeed the only democratic one.

However 'natural' and spontaneous this backing for neutrality, it was nevertheless consciously nurtured by the government. In a memo to the censor's office on 18 September, Joseph Walshe, the Secretary of External Affairs, argued that Emergency legislation should be used to press home the need for neutrality. He laid out a number of strategies for creating 'neutral-mindedness', including scaring citizens off thoughts of war:

The neutrality of the State cannot be preserved without a positive as well as a negative policy in relation to censorship. Public opinion must be built up on a neutral basis, a neutral-mindedness must be created. A list of the States which are neutral should be frequently and prominently displayed in the Press. The advantages of being neutral should be stressed. The losses and suffering of all kinds, including famine and poverty, which come upon countries at war should be stressed. For Ireland, neutrality is the only logical policy. We are not heirs, either on the positive or negative side, of the Treaty of Versailles . . . Unless we remain neutral, we cannot join with the small States of the world, and with the Vatican in particular, in attempts to bring about peace. The cost of neutrality is nothing like the cost of war. The amount of suffering we shall have to endure is part and parcel of the universal readjustment which any great war imposes.

This mixture of pragmatism and moral superiority (the virtues of the peace-loving) threaded through Fianna Fáil rhetoric throughout the war, and it proved very effective in moulding public opinion. The government liked to deny there was any such thing as positive censorship – a nice term for neutrality propaganda. And it seems possible that a mixture of fear and common sense would have been enough to steer Irish citizens off thoughts of helping Britain. But the government was taking no chances.

Walshe insisted that the greatest threat to neutrality came from 'the subtle propaganda of an ascendancy clique which will undoubtedly use this occasion to promote their dearest wish which is to bring the British back'. But at this stage in the war Ireland had not yet come in for public attack. British propaganda portrayed Ireland as a neutral like Holland or Belgium, preparing to defend herself against German aggression. On 9 September 1939 the London *Times* declared: 'From the British point of view it is more than probable that Éire's neutrality is the best possible policy that Mr de Valera's government could have adopted.' Right through the first half of 1940 the mood in the British media remained sympathetic. Newsreels presented defensive preparations, such as the mining of Dublin Bay, as Ireland making ready to repel the Nazis.

It suited British public opinion at this stage to think of Ireland as backing Britain to the best of her ability. But this was not just wishful thinking. Before the censorship regime properly kicked in, Irish papers presented a broadly pro-neutrality line which was certainly not anti-British. Far from it. Editors of all the major papers made great play out of Irish sympathy for the Poles, and for the crisis that was hitting Britain, pointing out that it was all the fault of one man – Hitler. This was also the dominant tone in both houses of the Oireachtas. And beyond the general support for Britain there was a very clear appreciation of the danger the neutral country was in.

The blackout was merely one sign of that. The Department of Defence rushed out a pamphlet called 'Protect Your Home Against Air Raids', and appeals went out for ARP volunteers. People were wanted for the Irish Red Cross, the Defence Reserves, and the coastal watch. Much space in the newspapers was given over to the importance of complying with government orders, and the need to pull together in the first days and weeks. It was not only Ireland's trade and economic links with Britain which meant danger; the border with the belligerent North was an obvious risk factor. The Dáil, the local and national newspapers, the wireless were all agreed: 'We shall have war all around us'; conditions would be 'almost the same' as the conditions in belligerent countries.

By the end of the month, however, the 'war panic' had begun to subside, as the nature of the situation 'approximating to war conditions' became clearer. No bombs had fallen (except in Poland), and people began complaining about the effects of the blackout. There had been a steep rise in car accidents, despite the lack of petrol, and irritated

STATIONERY OFFICE, DUBLIN

A.R.P. HANDBOOKS

Handbook No. 1 : Personal Protection Against
Gas .... 6d.

Handbook No. 2 : First Aid and Nursing for
Gas Casualties .... 4d.

Handbook No. 4 : Decontamination of
Materials .... 6d.

Handbook No. 7 : Emergency Lighting
Restrictions .... 2d.

Handbook No. 8 : Duties of Air Raid
Wardens .... 2d.

Handbook No. 12 : Air Raid Precautions for
Animals .... 4d.

Protection of Your Home Against Air Raids. 1d.

Air Raid Shelters : Standards of, for Persons
Working in Factories, etc. .... 6d.

Civilian War Duties : Public Information
Pamphlet No. 1 .... 1d.

Notes on Elementary Fire-Fighting .... 2d.

(Enclose 1d. stamp for postage)

FROM THE

GOVERNMENT PUBLICATIONS SALES OFFICE

3-4 COLLEGE STREET, DUBLIN

motorists pointed out that Parisian streets and cars were still lit, and France was supposed to be at war. By November the blackout restrictions had been lifted, except for public lighting in some areas on the east coast. The atmosphere in Britain too had calmed and, as local Irish newspapers reported, the 'seriously ill' and 'dying' parent telegrams sent to call children home from England were no longer having an effect on the young men and women happy to keep on their jobs in London, Birmingham or Liverpool. The navy seemed to be doing very well in the Atlantic against the U-boat menace – so that despite the losses of HMS *Courageous* and HMS *Royal Oak* it seemed to the editor of the *Irish Times* in mid-October that the chances of a successful blockade against Britain's merchant service were 'almost negligible'. As winter set in it looked as though Ireland's worries would be economic rather than defensive – focused not on attack from the air but on the difficulty of securing supplies, rapidly falling revenue, additional expenditure, and soaring unemployment.

At the beginning of September de Valera had set up two new departments: the Department of Supplies, headed by Seán Lemass, and another with the unwieldy title of Department of the Co-ordination of Defensive Measures, headed by Frank Aiken. Lemass had his work cut out to control immediate panic buying, which caused a substantial rise in prices in the provinces. Despite the Prices Standstill Order on basic goods there were serious problems with non-compliance. Throughout September a 'very large number' of complaints about overcharging were sent in to his department by 'public-spirited people' who could not bear to see the profiteering tradesmen getting away with it. In the first week of the war people had been 'stampeded', as Lemass put it, into buying sugar, and by the end of September a sugar committee was already having to meet daily to deal with the numbers of complaints over supply. By mid-October there was widespread concern over shortages. The farmers could not get hold of fertilisers, animal feed, linseed or flax seed; housewives found it increasingly difficult to buy tea, sugar, flour, soap, candles, cream of tartar; nobody could buy petrol except on a strict ration; and supplies of cement had already run out.

Shortages of fuel and raw materials such as cement and timber had serious knock-on effects on industry and employment. The building trade – the biggest single industry in Ireland since 1932 – and the motor trade were the worst hit in these first weeks. And the loss of the British export market intensified worries about unemployment (two hundred men were laid off at Haulbowline steel works at the first sign of war on 1 September). Even after some creative work with the statistics Seán MacEntee, the new Minister for Industry and Commerce, had to admit that, six weeks after the war began, over five thousand more people were out of work than at the same time the previous year. MacEntee's figures did not include the large numbers of returned workers from England – other estimates put the number of unemployed as up by twenty thousand on pre-war figures. Not all layoffs were due to the war, and amongst the war unemployed there were some unpredictable casualties. Factories closed due to the shortage of raw materials, but so too did the Hospital Sweepstakes, and those who worked in racing and betting lost their jobs following the British ban on racing.

Many of the unemployed had no safety net – they quickly faced destitution, or the humiliation of the county council relief schemes. A month after the race for the mailboat home to Ireland, despite the war and the chances of conscription, large numbers of workers began returning to Britain each week, and others left for the first time. According to a Cork TD, for example, there was an 'exodus' to England of Cork tradesmen (carpenters and plasterers) in the first weeks of October. The atmosphere of economic crisis deepened for those who stayed behind, as unemployment continued to soar and stringent price controls tightened the squeeze on small businesses. In November the opposition's fears about the repressive Emergency Powers Act seemed justified when the government rounded up and arrested groups of farmers protesting against shortages and the controlled price of milk. Coverage of the riots, and the pitched battles between police and farmers, was kept out of the papers by the censors, but in the Dáil, and for many ordinary citizens, the sense of crisis was palpable.

*   *   *

For the Irish government, and for most Irish people, the problems posed by the outbreak of war were primarily practical, and above all economic. The main questions for both individuals and the state were ones of survival. Was the government going to be able to maintain order and supply the needs of the population – including the needs of employment and essential supplies? Were the people going to be safe from aerial bombing? How were the thousands returning from England to be helped? There was broad agreement over the nature of the political and economic crisis the war posed for Ireland, if not about the solutions. Above all, there was a general understanding that if Ireland was going to be neutral it wasn't going to feel in the least like peace – this neutrality would ape many of the conditions of war.

There were even those who argued that Irish neutrality – as the only practical policy the country could have chosen in the circumstances – should be construed as part of the battle against Nazi Germany. On 26 August 1939 Elizabeth Bowen's cousin Hubert Butler wrote to John Dulanty, the Irish High Commissioner in London, from his base in Hampstead, explaining, 'I am a citizen of Éire. My home is in Kilkenny. I want to offer my services for war work and should value your advice.' He enclosed a brief curriculum vitae:

I am a member of the Irish Co-ordinating Committee and was responsible for the bringing of the first refugees from Vienna and the initiation of the work in Ireland.

I speak well German and French, with a little practice would become good in Russian, less good in Serbo-Croatian – a perfect reading knowledge of course of all. Added to that I think I can say I have a very wide experience of European countries and people.

I have written to Mr E. N. Cooper at the Home Office and to someone at the War Office but I should naturally prefer greatly to work under my own government if there was any opening for someone of my qualifications.

Polyglot, cultured, self-consciously European, Butler was a member of the Kagran Gruppe, a Quaker organisation officially concerned with helping Christian Jews leave Austria (though it did not limit its humanitarian work to Christian Jews). He had been forced to leave Vienna in the summer of 1939, and settled in Hampstead, while his wife stayed in Kilkenny and Monaghan. His letters to her in the early months of the war show him wrestling with the rights and duties of his neutral status. While in London he continued working to get refugees out. In November 1939, we find him attempting – in retrospect naively – to get to Poland as a neutral in order to help the growing number of refugees. When that proved impossible, Butler considered getting a job with the British censorship. On the face of it this seems an odd possibility for him to entertain. How could he have thought of himself as offering humanitarian assistance from his privileged position as a neutral, and as a potential agent of Allied censorship? In part, no doubt, he simply needed employment. But beyond such practicalities, as the letter to Dulanty shows, at the beginning of the war Butler was able quite comfortably to assume that Irish neutrality was part of an anti-Nazi front. Aid for the persecuted and defence against aggression – it was all 'war work' whether undertaken on behalf of Britain or Ireland, though he would 'naturally prefer greatly to work under [his] own government'.

Butler's perspective on the shared purpose of neutrality and war against Germany was unusual. Most people who supported the war looked instead for ways to square the fight against fascism with Irish policy. The Irish government had a simple solution to such dilemmas. From the outset de Valera made it clear he would place no restrictions on individuals joining the British forces, or leaving for war work in Britain (this policy would turn out to be in the best interests of Ireland's economy anyway, since it allowed the yearly emigration of the unemployed to continue). As he insisted on 2 September:

It is only natural that, as human beings, we should judge the situation and, having formed a judgment, sympathise with one side or the other. I know that in this country there are sympathies, very strong sympathies, in regard to the present issues, but I do not think that anybody, no matter what his feelings might be, would suggest that the Government policy, the official policy of the State, should be other than what the Government would suggest.

Oral history interviews with Irish ex-servicemen, and the occasional memoir, bear out this lack of friction to a large extent. Many comment on the fact that it seemed natural both for the state to be neutral and for them to fight. Judging by such responses, by the confident tone of de Valera's statements on the issue, by the absence of controversy in the Dáil, it appears that at this stage in the war feelings of sympathy with and support for Britain could be catered for relatively simply, under the broad umbrella of what was to become known as 'friendly neutrality'.

There were exceptions, of course. For dyed-in-the-wool supporters of the British Empire, the failure to fall into line behind Britain was the sign of a lack of moral courage on the part of the government. Some senators and one or two TDs suggested that although neutrality was the practical option, the 'moral effect' of the policy on the country would be bad. Senator Sir John Keane admitted that he was not voicing the opinion of the majority when he warned of 'the very thin dividing line between our national interests and our national honour'. Senator McDermot suggested that 'practical cooperation in the defence of the British Isles as a whole, and in the defence of the shipping upon which we ourselves depend just as much as England' would be a more defensible position for the country to adopt than strict neutrality. They were a small minority, made smaller by the fact that a number of the people who agreed with them had 'already left the country to perform what they believe to be their duty'. The role of self-appointed conscience to the nation fell to the wives left behind and to men of the older generation. During the autumn of 1939 there were occasional letters from such people to the *Irish Times*, such as one from 'War Widow', who proudly declared that her four sons were away in the British army, and condemned the country for its policy of 'sheltering behind England'.

It was at this point that two competing ways of understanding Irish neutrality began to emerge. One, undoubtedly the majority view, saw neutrality as practical, pragmatic, inevitable, difficult – and as time went on, both astute and successful. The other was preoccupied instead with the problems Ireland's neutrality caused for Britain, with the ethics of the situation, with divided loyalties, and with the dilemma of personal accountability in the fight against fascism. There was a vast difference, of course, between loyalty to Britain, and altruistic commitment to the struggle against fascism, a difference that supporters of neutrality were not slow to point out. But the fact that this was a war against totalitarian aggression meant that political morality and national and cultural allegiance were able to bleed into one another. The war was to increase the alienation of some Anglo-Irish, who felt forced to choose between England and Ireland. It would also widen the social and cultural distance between the small, self-consciously 'European' intellectual elite and those committed to the protection of the nascent rural Republic – not to mention the already considerable distance between the concerns of the upper middle classes and the attitudes and aspirations of Ireland's 'plain people'.

For writers such as Kate O'Brien, Louis MacNeice, Elizabeth Bowen, and Denis Johnston – and for others of their class and background – the outbreak of war was a challenge. The often fragile accommodation between an Irish identity and allegiance to cultural and political ideals associated with Britain and Europe broke apart. None of these people disagreed with the policy of neutrality – at least, not at this early stage in the war. What they describe, with varying degrees of intensity, is the way in which the war created a crisis of allegiance for them and for the people they knew. Loyalty to Ireland came into conflict with a number of other loyalties – a sense of duty to Britain, support for Churchill and the idea of the Empire, allegiance to a European identity, or commitment to the anti-fascist cause. As the war progressed, and particularly during the worst phases of the conflict for Britain, this critical, 'ethical', perspective was to become almost indistinguishable from British anti-neutrality propaganda (and after all, all these writers were to end up working for British information and propaganda services during the war). But these early wartime reflections on the rights and wrongs of neutrality also reveal the presence of genuinely torn allegiances, and real conflicts of loyalty.

* * *

On Wednesday 6 September 1939 Kate O'Brien wrote from Limerick to her London neighbours, John and Barbara Gawsworth, of her wish to get back to England as soon as possible. 'I feel terribly nostalgic at not being in my right and customary place just now.' O'Brien's background was amongst genteel Catholic business people in Limerick. Born in 1897, and schooled at a Limerick convent, O'Brien had attended University College, Dublin, and afterwards worked on the *Manchester Guardian* and as a governess in Spain. She returned to England to marry a Dutch journalist but the marriage ended within the year. For an intellectual, cosmopolitan European on the political left (she was banned from Franco's Spain for her 1938 travel book about the country), O'Brien's talk of nostalgia, to describe her longing for an adopted home, is odd and striking. Ethical and political commitment, she seems to be saying, can and perhaps should exert a stronger emotional tug than origins. But O'Brien was a chronic debtor and she also admitted to more mercenary motives: 'I am going to damn well get a well-paid (if possible!) war job. I simply must get solvent and earn a living. What jobs will there be do you think? I'll be looking for something writer-ish, if you know what I mean. I mean, I'm not going to be a Police Canteen Woman or a sergeant of the Waa[f?].' She went on:

Here we are all appalled, of course – and most of us (is the censor working yet?) think that the neutrality business has already taken a very tender and lovely curve in the right direction – but officially it is still supposed to be perpendicular as a ramrod. Feeling runs very strong, and everyone is most desperately sad for the world and for their friends. Naturally, I feel overwhelmed with sadness, thinking of all my friends. Who doesn't?

O'Brien was to be proved wrong about the strength of sentiment in support of the war, though not about the feeling of being 'sad for the world', which was to surface in various guises, from the most anguished to the most patronising, in the years to come.

By the middle of October O'Brien was back in England, where she was to remain for the next five and a half years, severed by geography and censorship from the developing sense of pride in Irish neutrality. But she had long since begun to disconnect herself from what she saw as the worst effects of Irish isolationism. Like many Irish writers of her generation, she identified with the progressive, modernist culture of 1930s Europe. Convinced of the need to fight the fascists throughout Europe, in her 1938 novel *Pray for the Wanderer* she had made no secret of her dislike of what she saw as the selfish, protectionist attitude of de Valera's Ireland, and she again painted a negative portrait of that mentality in *The Last of Summer*, a story set in the Limerick countryside in August 1939.

The novel centres on the family drama unfolding within one Catholic household at the outbreak of war. The Kernahans are a well-to-do farming family, by turns welcoming and suspicious of the half-French cousin who suddenly appears on their rural doorstep while Moscow engages in the talks that will lead to the Nazi–Soviet Pact. For the French Angèle, a little bit of Europe out of place in Ireland, the comforts and certainties of peace are appealing, if finally artificial:

Angèle had forgotten for hours that now seemed countless that there was such a thing as the nine o'clock news, with a whole world waiting on it in fear. She wondered if the others had forgotten. She looked about with sudden general love, as if she were a sister to these cousins, had sat here with them often before, and shared all their summers, all their childhood. She felt the peace of the moment as sharply as if she knew an alarm bell was about to clang against it instantly.

The ensuing love tangle between Angèle and her two Irish cousins takes place against the threatening backdrop of the coming war. ('For two pins I could make an analogy between Éire and Europe and the boys and you,' says her female cousin to Angèle.) The novel ends as the characters battle over love and war on the morning of 3 September, with Chamberlain's recorded announcement playing on the radio in the background.

It is hard not to imagine that O'Brien was recording some of the opinions she heard in Limerick that last summer before the war. For the complacent local doctor, war impinges primarily as a threat to his ability to purchase his usual sherry. For his daughter Norrie the war is simply irrelevant: 'No war for *us* anyway.' For the Kernahan matriarch the war is a threat to her comfortable family life, built upon falsehoods and a judicious courting of the local Catholic hierarchy. O'Brien doesn't question the right of Ireland to be neutral, as a matter of national policy. But at the same time she is convinced of the morally corrupting effect of neutrality on individuals. It is as though neutrality – regardless of its political logic – provides rich soil for the flourishing of the least admirable human qualities.

Against an isolationist mentality represented as petty and myopic, she sets characters who find themselves unable simply to shrug off the larger issues at stake in the war. The young Martin Kernahan, for example, 'although his Éire citizenship would probably give him a just immunity', nonetheless feels pledged to war and committed to the fight against fascism. However, he decides to join the French army, rather than fight alongside the British. His sister Jo also decides to leave Ireland, in order to join a religious order in Belgium: 'There might be something Christian one could do – for refugees or children or in air raids.' Given that the book was written after the fall of France, the fact that brother and sister face the dangers of charitable work and soldiering on the continent, rather than assisting the war effort in Britain, tells of sacrificial bravery. O'Brien leaves us in no doubt that it is these characters who make the moral choice. Like Norrie, however, most of the inhabitants of the village of Drumaninch view the war as a battle between enemies which has 'nothing whatever to do with us. A plague on both their houses.' Britain is seen as engaged in imperialist warmongering, its pretext a mere 'border dispute' between Germany and Poland. As the possessive, blinkered Hannah Kernahan (an avowed admirer of de Valera) puts it, in an attempt to deflect her son Martin from leaving: 'Danzig's a long way from Drumaninch, my son.'

How many conversations like this were really going on in Ireland in the first months of the war? Certainly it is no surprise that mothers should have tried to persuade their boys not to enlist – nor that they did enlist despite maternal protests. The archives of the Department of Foreign Affairs contain numerous letters from mothers asking for assistance in trying to get their children released from the British army. There are letters searching for minors who have volunteered under other names, letters from mothers whose sons have 'run away in a fit of temper' and joined the army, letters arguing that their boys were under age, and therefore wrongly enlisted, letters pleading for help because their son was their 'only support' and they could not do without him. As one mother from Ballina wrote in November 1939: 'I hope you will leave no stone unturned to secure his release as I do not wish a child of mine to take any part in Britain's War.'

Kate O'Brien's portrait may have been hostile, but it was also acute about the political atmosphere in Ireland in the months leading up to the war. As one British civil servant recorded, reporting back to the Foreign Office in July 1939 on Irish attitudes to the crisis:

In all quarters I found that the possibility of Danzig becoming a casus belli with Germany was regarded with horror. The Taoiseach himself during the six or seven minutes' conversation which I had with him spent his whole time deploring such a contingency . . . The numerous difficulties of the United Kingdom Government are appreciated, and there is much sympathy for them, but, nevertheless, so Mr de Valera assured me, it would be difficult, if not impossible, to convince people that a war should be allowed to take place over this issue.

But in representing the outbreak of war as a crisis of moral commitment for individual Irish people, against a background of self-satisfied neutrality for the majority, O'Brien misread the levels of fear and uncertainty over what neutrality was going to mean. Rather than the similarity between neutrality and war which the Irish government was keen to emphasise, she insisted on the immense, and increasing, difference between the two. In aid of this contrast she simplified both neutrality (pictured as almost indistinguishable from indolent, indifferent, peace) and war (synonymous with ethical commitment and altruism). In the first weeks of the war, certainly, some of those who left to volunteer their services to Britain were driven by ideological conviction – impelled by the need to fight fascism – as the historian Richard Doherty has shown. But as many were persuaded by a family history of service in the British army. Others, remnants of the Ascendancy and those with close familial ties to Britain, were driven by a broad sense of allegiance to the Crown. And for large numbers of those who took the mailboat, or the train to Belfast, the decision to enlist had as much to do with necessity, even opportunism, as with ideology.

The Last of Summer was published in 1943, and much of it was written during the summer of 1942, at the height of the dudgeon over Ireland's decision to remain neutral. The confidence of O'Brien's judgements in the novel stems, then, from the wisdom of hindsight. It is possible, in fact, that the novel was a deliberate piece of propaganda designed to prick the conscience of the Irish nation. Was this O'Brien's war work? In later years she claimed to have carried out wartime work for the British Ministry of Information, but this may have been wishful thinking. (She suggested she had given 'pep talks' on the BBC for the home front. Her biographer describes this claim as 'almost certainly not true'. She was never, at any rate, to land the 'well-paid war job' she craved.) At the beginning of the war, however, the political calculus had been far less clear. There was little consensus on the right course of action, either in England or in Ireland. Despite all the bluster about the protection of democracy, and standing up to international bullies, the war was at first essentially defensive – Britain and France effectively abandoned Poland to its fate. Principled pacifists in Britain, as well as the Communists and others on the left, were not alone in asking why this particular line had to be drawn, at the cost of plunging Europe into turmoil and bloodshed. Until the invasion of France and the Low Countries there was widespread confusion about the best response to German aggression, though this was soon masked in Britain by conscription, and the wave of propaganda aimed at concerting the war effort.

In the North, for example, where there was propaganda but no conscription, the authorities were embarrassed by the low turn out of volunteers. The Vice Chancellor of Queen's University, disturbed by how few undergraduates had enlisted by November 1939, put out a rueful plea in the university magazine in which he acknowledged his students' good fortune in avoiding compulsory military service. 'Many of us may, however, feel that the undergraduates of English, Scottish, and Welsh Universities are fortunate in not being left to judge entirely for themselves with regard to their national obligations.' He held out a series of carrots for those who changed their minds, but few were enticed at this stage in the war. One nineteen-year-old Trinity College student, from a middle-class Protestant family in Armagh, wrote in his diary entry for 3 September: 'My conscience is in an awful muddle.' Like most of his friends, he was 'dead scared of going out and prepared to stay at home until conscription'. In January 1940

Professor Montrose defended Queen's students' scepticism in responding to news of war:

The disclosures as to the last war made them suspicious of vague phrases of politicians: they held fast to their declaration that the plea of act of State is no justification for killing . . . Aggressive force they knew had to be checked, but states were not to be given the hardihood to deny all claims of justice. For them a clear and positive statement of war aims was imperative to satisfy the urge to create a world in which the realisation of their ideals was possible. They feared that unless an early statement was made of the purpose to which victory was to be put, men might lose sight in the long agony of war of the ideals which led to the taking up of arms.

In this, Northern Irish students scarcely differed from those in the rest of Britain, but the absence of conscription made their fears and uncertainties meaningful.

*　　*　　*

Kate O'Brien's experience of living in Spain, and her despair over Franco's triumph, convinced her of the need to support Britain against the fascists in Germany. But Britain's failure to come to the aid of the democratic government of the Spanish Republic produced the opposite reaction in others. Convinced anti-imperialists, and left-wing Irish Republicans, were confirmed in their suspicion of Britain. Some were also held in sway by Communist Party-led resistance to the war as a second imperialist war – a position maintained until the German invasion of the USSR and the end of the Nazi–Soviet pact.

One of the young men making the journey from Dublin to Liverpool in the autumn of 1939 was the sixteen-year-old future playwright Brendan Behan. No doubt he jostled against some of the many Irish volunteers on the mailboat, but Behan himself was not going to enlist in the British forces. He came from a staunchly left-wing republican family (though this didn't prevent one of his half-brothers serving in the British army during the war); a scion of the educated working class, he left school at thirteen to join his father's trade as a house-painter. At eight he had joined the Fianna Éireann, the Irish republican scout movement founded by Countess Markievicz. He published his first poems and prose in the youth organisation's magazine, *Fianna: the Voice of Young Ireland*, and in left-wing periodicals such as *Wolfe Tone Weekly*, *United Irishman* and *Worker's Republic*. After the family moved in 1937 to a local-authority housing estate in Crumlin, Behan transferred his membership to the IRA. Forty-eight hours after arriving in Liverpool in 1939 he was arrested at his lodgings:

Friday, in the evening, the landlady shouted up the stairs:

'Oh God, oh Jesus, oh Sacred Heart. Boy, there's two gentlemen to see you.'

I knew by the screeches of her that these gentlemen were not calling to enquire after my health, or to know if I'd had a good trip. I grabbed my suitcase, containing Pot. Chlor, Sulph Ac, gelignite, detonators, electrical [sic] and ignition, and the rest of my Sinn Féin conjuror's outfit, and carried it to the window. Then the gentlemen arrived.

A young one, with a blonde, Herrenvolk head and a BBC accent, shouted, 'I say, greb him, the bestud.'

When I was safely grabbed, the blonde one gave me several punches in the face, though not very damaging ones. An older man, in heavy Lancashire speech, told him to leave me alone, and stop making a – of himself . . . There were now two or three others in the room, and this old man was the sergeant and in charge of the raid.

He took some Pot Chlor and sugar out of the case, put it in the empty fireplace and lit it with a match. It roared into flame and filled the room with smoke. He nodded to me and I nodded back.

Since he was only sixteen at the time of his arrest, Behan was sentenced to borstal and sent initially to Feltham Prison, then to Hollesley Bay, where he spent the first two years of the war. One of the most remarkable things about his vivid recollections of his period in borstal (written in the mid-1950s) is the almost total absence of reference to the war. The first few months of Behan's detention, while he was waiting to be sentenced, coincided with the trial, appeal and execution of the men sentenced for the Coventry bombing in August. Behan was repeatedly bullied by prison guards and attacked by fellow prisoners because of his IRA activity (with reason, he admits), but according to his recollections, Ireland's neutrality in the war with Germany was never offered as a further black mark against republicanism.

When Behan was picked up, the full-scale confrontation had not yet begun. Even after the end of the 'phoney war', the closed world inhabited by prisoners and their guards may have made the war appear less urgent than it did to the majority on the outside. As the war progressed, several young soldiers, sailors and members of the RAF turned up inside. But in *Borstal Boy* the war impinges primarily through prison overcrowding, the arrival of a scattering of Polish Jewish refugees, the presence of mines off the east coast when the boys go swimming, the awkwardness 'when some bloke heard that his brother was killed or lost at sea', and – finally – in the death at sea of Behan's friend Charlie Millwall soon after he is released from Hollesley Bay to return to the navy. For Behan himself (and, he would have us believe, for the rest of the prison population) the European war is an irrelevance – certainly of no bearing on Ireland's war with Britain. Indeed Behan saw no reason to curb his own republican activity. On his release from Hollesley Bay Borstal in December 1941, he was deported to Ireland; the following year he was arrested by the Irish police for the attempted murder of two detectives during the annual Easter Sunday 1916 Commemoration in Dublin. He was sentenced by a Special Criminal Court to fourteen years' imprisonment. Sent first to Mountjoy Jail and then, in July 1943 to Arbour Hill Military Prison, he was finally interned at the Curragh Military Internment Camp in June 1944, until he was released in 1946 in the general amnesty for republican prisoners.

Behan's first statement at Lime Street police station in the autumn of 1939 included a propagandist flourish about the 'Irish Workers' and Small Farmers' Republic'. His guard remonstrated:

'Here, what's all this about small farmers? It's your statement, Paddy, and you can put what you bloody well like in it, but I never seen a small farmer, Irish or English; they're all bloody big fellows with bulls' 'eads on 'em, from eating bloody great feeds and drinking cider.'

The left-wing element in the movement would be delighted, and the others, the craw-thumpers, could not say anything against me, because I was a good Volunteer, captured carrying the struggle to the English doorstep – but they would be hopping mad at me giving everyone the impression that the IRA was Communistic.

Behan's jibe at the 'craw-thumpers' was an acknowledgement of the tremendous shift to the right which took place in the IRA during the 1930s. In 1934 the most radical IRA members split to form the left-wing Republican Congress, leaving a militant organisation which was home to a range of political views. There were IRA members on the right who supported Franco, and later Hitler, as well as those who propagandised for 'Christian Social Justice'. There were those – perhaps a majority – who saw politics as a distraction.

The war, for all these factions, posed no great crisis of faith in the cause. But for the small number of Republicans on the left, like Behan himself, the first years of the war required strenuous contortions. They had been saturated in the anti-fascist rhetoric of the 1930s, which implied that the fight against reaction and imperialism in Spain, Germany, Britain, was all part of one great struggle. (There is an echo of this in the 'Herrenvolk' head of Behan's British policeman.) As early as 1935, Charles Donnelly – an Irish republican who was later to die fighting Franco's forces in Spain – argued in *Irish Front* (a mimeographed bulletin brought out in London) for vigilance about Britain's war aims. The economic war, he insisted, was being used by Britain to subdue Ireland and 'preserve Ireland as a British war base':

Irish republican exiles in London resent and repudiate the countenance and support given by the representatives of Irish Free State Government here to the imperialist Jubilee celebrations which are being staged in an attempt to rouse the feelings of the British workers in preparation for the blood bath of another war, and by the same forces which are waging an economic war on the Irish Free State with the purpose of breaking republican resistance and so securing Ireland as a base in that war.

The subjection of Ireland, Donnelly argued, was leaving the country in danger of being sucked into an imperialist war in which it had no interest.

By 1938 the Treaty ports had been returned to Irish jurisdiction and the danger of Ireland's involvement in a further war staved off. Yet the Popular Front rhetoric espoused in some republican circles continued to warn of the danger of making alliances with any imperialist power – whether Britain, Germany or Italy. Throughout 1938, for example, the *Worker's Republic* warned against

German Nazis at work in Ireland [and] the willingness of some IRA leaders to respond to the overtures of the Nazi 'Brown Network', which has stretched its imperialist-fascist tentacles towards Ireland . . . It is a fact that both German and Italian Imperialism, like British Imperialism, deny the right of self-determination to small nations. Consider the barbarous methods adopted by Italian Imperialism against the primitive folk of Abyssinia.

However, whereas in England the Popular Front moved throughout 1939 towards support for an anti-fascist war, the vaunting of British democracy met with suspicion, if not outright derision, in Ireland.

When communist parties across Europe performed their astonishing volte-face in September 1939, after the Nazi–Soviet pact, and began to argue for a swiftly arranged peace (on Hitler's terms), left-wing Irish republicans had probably the least distance to travel in rejigging their views of the war. Shortly after the outbreak of war the Communist Party of Ireland declared that 'The British National Government is financially subsidising and guarding with British troops in the partitioned area a regime which is the nearest approach to Hitler fascism in the whole English-speaking world.' A month later, in October 1939, the Party launched a campaign for the return of the six counties. 'The declared slogans about democracy and liberty,' it proclaimed, 'are smokescreens concealing the imperialist aims of the ruling circles . . . [who] are waging war to defend their colonial plunder . . . Any fight for liberty or a better life abroad is a sham while these are denied at home. We demand therefore that the Six Counties withdraw from the conflict.'

Given the ferocity of these sentiments, it is not really surprising that, despite his left-wing leanings, Behan showed little interest in Britain's anti-fascist war. He simply wasn't persuaded by it. But his silence on the issue is striking, not least because he was no doubt surrounded by British wartime propaganda – he tells us for example that he used to read the *News of the World*, and his closest friend was a young sailor from the British navy. Did Behan find the IRA's anti-imperialist view hard to justify, in retrospect? Was he influenced by the Nazi–Soviet pact? Whatever the reasons for his reticence, it's clear that, for a bright working-class Dublin boy, the unfinished business of British rule in Ireland could overshadow Hitlerism almost entirely.

*   *   *

For many left-wingers in Britain and Ireland, not just those who shared Behan's brand of republicanism, the European politics of the 1930s and their disastrous outcome had brought demoralisation and disillusionment – the very opposite of enthusiasm for a new anti-fascist crusade. The ruins of Spain could be read as a lesson in the need to support the war against fascism, or as proof of yet another British imperialist betrayal. But for those whose aspirations had been bound up in the republican fight for Spain, their failure also confirmed the futility of ideals, the powerlessness of ordinary people in the face of national, and international, power politics.

Among those on holiday in Ireland in the summer of 1939 was the Northern Irish poet Louis MacNeice. On 1 September he was in Galway with his friend Ernst Stahl, a lecturer in German at Birmingham University, where MacNeice had taught Classics until the mid-1930s. MacNeice shared with Kate O'Brien a well-to-do middle-class background, but his family were Protestant, and he had been brought up in the North of Ireland (the son of a Rector, later Bishop of Belfast). Educated in high style at the English public schools Sherborne and Marlborough, and at Oxford, MacNeice later described his education as one that fitted him to 'never really again believe anything that anyone says'. Certainly he liked to distance himself both from what he described as the profit-driven culture of the North of Ireland and the romantic, fantasy-driven self-obsessions of the South ('Your assumption that everyone cares / Who is the king of your castle'). But he had no time either for the 'Ireland versus England match'. Friends at school with Anthony Blunt, at university with W.H. Auden and Christopher Isherwood, married while a student to a young Jewish dancer, MacNeice had the energy and brilliance to play a leading role in the left-leaning literary circle which formed around Auden, Stephen Spender, Cecil Day Lewis and John Lehmann.

But by 1939 MacNeice was living alone with his small son and his son's nanny in London, teaching Classics at Bedford College – a job he did not enjoy. His wife had left him three years earlier for an American graduate student, with whom she had emigrated to the United States. MacNeice's holiday in the summer of 1939 was a chance for him to say goodbye to his father and stepmother, and to revisit the West of Ireland before he in turn left for the United States in the autumn. There he was hoping to further his relationship with the short-story writer Eleanor Clark, whom he had met in New York the previous spring. He was also trying to write a book about the poetry of W.B.Yeats, who had died in January.

Six months before his Irish holiday MacNeice had published a long poem exploring the private and public failures of the 1930s. Written in the autumn of 1938 during the Munich Crisis, 'Autumn Journal' set the collapse of his marriage, the ups and downs of subsequent relationships, and an intensely honest description of his own aspirations, snobberies, doubts and failures of empathy, alongside the collapse of the political hopes and ideals of his generation. Like the First World War, and the war in Spain, the coming war was bound to see all principle squandered in 'panic and self-deception'. MacNeice watched as the trees on Primrose Hill were cut down for gun emplacements ('Each tree falling like a closing fan') and feared as much for the destruction of mental freedoms as for physical attack:

And we who have been brought up to think of 'Gallant Belgium'
    As so much blague
Are now preparing again to essay good through evil
    For the sake of Prague;
And we must, we suppose, become uncritical, vindictive,
    And must, in order to beat
The enemy, model ourselves on the enemy,
    A howling radio for our paraclete.

With conscription looming, and the propaganda machines getting under way in Britain in order to match the mobilisation in Germany, MacNeice grieved for subtlety, variety and complex, mixed opinion – all of which would be lost in the one-mindedness of war:

And the individual, powerless, has to exert the
    Powers of will and choice
And choose between enormous evils, either
    Of which depends on somebody else's voice.

This sense of helplessness was common among left intellectuals throughout Europe, faced with the prospect of another war. After all, the poetry of the battle between democracy and fascism had already been written, in the 1930s. The war had already been fought and lost, in Spain.

The Munich crisis was over in a month, but MacNeice's disenchantment remained. A year later the same feelings of helplessness and disillusion were played out against the backdrop of an Irish landscape. In his lyric series 'The Coming of War' MacNeice recorded the experience of hearing the news of the German advance into Poland while in Galway. The war is an abrupt intrusion:

O the crossbones of Galway,
The hollow grey houses,
The rubbish and sewage,
The grass-grown pier,
And the dredger grumbling
All night in the harbour:
The war came down on us here.

Salmon in the Corrib
Gently swaying
And the water combed out
Over the weir

And a hundred swans
Dreaming on the harbour:
The war came down on us here.

Part of MacNeice's purpose for holidaying in Ireland was to pursue the research for his planned book on Yeats. 'As soon as I heard on the wireless of the outbreak of war,' he wrote in his autobiography, 'Galway became unreal. And Yeats and his poetry became unreal also.' But so too did the literature of social conscience. As MacNeice declared in his book on Yeats, which was published in 1941, 'war spares neither the poetry of Xanadu nor the poetry of pylons' – neither the poetry of rubbish and sewage nor the poetry of dreaming swans. For MacNeice and his contemporaries the guillotine had come down on their conception of poetry, the hope that literature might be able to play a socially progressive role. But more than that it had destroyed the hope that individual thought and action might have some power for good. The sense of the wreckage of the past, and a looming future emptied of ideals, was reflected back to MacNeice by the Irish land-scape. But Ireland mirrored the mood of a whole dejected European generation.

Ireland – or at any rate Galway – seemed unreal because it was so far removed from the world of the war. In 'Autumn Journal' MacNeice had attacked the isolationist mentality in Ireland which tried to deny its connections to the political disaster of Europe. ('Ourselves alone! Let the round tower stand aloof / In a world of bursting mortar!') But for a man with so little appetite for a new war of bombs and propaganda, Ireland's lack of interest in the coming struggle must have had its attractions. In these early days MacNeice was able to appreciate the value of standing outside the new European war. Those salmon were an image of peacefulness but also of defiance – they were able to keep their places against the tide, at a moment when individuals in England, Germany, France and across Europe were being swept away by the howling on the radio, the obligation for commitment. MacNeice said of Ireland in September 1939 that it was able to 'poise the toppling hour', to give him 'time for thought' in a world where thought was being everywhere sacrificed to the demands of war. After the newsflash announcing the invasion of Poland, MacNeice and Stahl hurried back to Dublin, so that Stahl could catch the boat to England that night. MacNeice, who was on leave from his teaching job at Bedford College, extended his stay in Ireland through the autumn, unsure about what he should do and unwilling to give up on the respite from total mobilisation which Ireland offered.

That respite was to turn sour:

When Ernst had left I was alone with the catastrophe, spent Saturday drinking in a bar with the Dublin literati; they hardly mentioned the war but debated the correct versions of Dublin street songs. Sunday morning the hotel man woke me (I was sleeping late and sodden), said, 'England has declared war.' Chamberlain's speech on a record was broadcast over and over again during the day. I went to Croke Park in the afternoon to watch the All-Ireland hurling final – Cork in crimson against Kerry in orange and black. Talk of escapism, I thought . . . There was a huge crowd of Gaelic Leaguers, all wearing their fáine, one-minded partisans.

MacNeice may have been prompted to mention the team colours because, as if in divine rebuke of this escapism, the end of the game was marred by a freak thunderstorm. The rain fell so heavily that the dye ran in the players' shirts. Nonetheless, he showed how little he felt at home, and how little he understood his surroundings, by getting the teams wrong. Cork played Kilkenny that day.

The Dublin set with whom MacNeice whiled away his Saturday could well have been those habitually to be found in the Palace Bar, a well-known literary haunt during the war years. They may have included the young novelist, and soon-to-be *Irish Times* columnist, Brian O'Nolan (Flann O'Brien); the poet Patrick Kavanagh, who had returned penniless from London in the middle of August (where he too was in debt to Kate O'Brien's friend John Gawsworth); F. R. Higgins, poet and director of the Abbey Theatre; M. J. MacManus, novelist and literary editor of the *Irish Press*; the novelist Brinsley MacNamara and poets Austin Clarke, Roibeard Ó Faracháin and Donagh MacDonagh (son of poet and rebel Thomas MacDonagh, who had been executed after the 1916 Rising), painters Harry Kernoff and Patrick O'Connor, as well as the editor of the *Irish Times*, R. M. Smyllie, and writers and journalists more or less loosely associated with the paper.

Their banter, if MacNeice is to be believed, stubbornly asserted the fact that the war was none of their concern, revelling in mock pedantry about wilfully recondite and local issues – yet, in doing so, insisting defiantly on the value of Ireland's cultural patrimony. It is a picture of Dublin's drinking culture that was confirmed by many throughout the war years: 'The urgencies, brutalities and curtailments war had brought seemed very far away there.' Like the supporters at Croke Park, the drinkers in the Palace Bar are escapists, wilfully blind to the impending catastrophe. But at the same time they are waging a war – one-minded partisans – in their case a war for the primacy of Irish culture, which seems to preclude any acknowledgement of a world beyond Ireland, or even beyond Dublin.

For MacNeice, attempting to resolve his relationship to the war, the choice appeared to be between the unthinking fever of mobilisation north of the border and the limited outlook and deluded beliefs of the gombeen Republic.

I spent the rest of the year alternately in Belfast and Dublin. Belfast, gloomy at all times, was gloomier now, full of patriotic placards and soldiers; at night the tramcars moved slowly along like catafalques, glimmers of spectral blue. My family still had family prayers in the morning but the god of the house was the radio. 'And that is the end of the news.' But it never was. The favourite song both over the air and in the streets, where it was sung by truck-loads of soldiers, was 'Run, Rabbit, Run'.

Going to Dublin was changing worlds – a dance of lights in the Liffey, bacon and eggs and Guinness, laughter in the slums and salons, gossip sufficient to the day. Dublin was hardly worried by the war; her old preoccupations were still her preoccupations. The intelligentsia continued their parties, their mutual malice was as effervescent as ever. There was still a pot of flowers in front of Matt Talbot's shrine. The potboy priests and the birds of prey were still the dominant caste; the petty bureaucracy continued powerful and petty.

The starkness of MacNeice's juxtaposition – all of Dublin fiddling while Britain, overflowing with patriotic propaganda, was about to burn – was part of his attempt to process events and make up his mind about his own attitude to the war. He wrote his account of his experiences in Ireland within a few months of leaving, and his autobiography was in large part a way of discovering his own view of the conflict, and in particular trying to understand what it was in his background that led to his eventual decision to return to the war and the propaganda. It took him more than a year to decide. MacNeice had been planning to leave for the United States in the autumn of 1939, yet he allowed himself to be persuaded (by Walter Starkie, Professor of Romance Languages in Dublin and, later in the war, head of the British Council in Madrid) to apply for a teaching post at Trinity College Dublin, and remained in Ireland for some months awaiting news of his application. So it was not until January 1940, after he heard that his bid for a post had been unsuccessful, that he set sail for America. Through the American Eleanor Clark, MacNeice had an emotional tie to another neutral country. (And Clark herself was convinced that the war would be 'just a dirty war of power politics'.) His friends Auden and Isherwood had left for the United States in January 1939, and were publicly understood as turning their backs on the intellectual world of 1930s Europe and the politics of Europe in the 1940s alike. It is almost as though in his five-month sojourn in Ireland MacNeice was trying the neutral country out – would it serve him as America served Auden? He decided that it would not.

'For five months,' MacNeice wrote of that period leading up to January 1940, 'I had been tormented by the ethical problems of the war':

In Ireland most people said to me 'What is it to you?' while many of my friends in England took the line it was just power politics. Why Poland of all places? And then there was India. I had decided, however, that any choice now was a choice of evils and that it was clear which was the lesser. But it is hard to risk your life for a Lesser Evil on the off-chance of some entirely problematical betterment for most likely a mere minority in a dubious and dirty future. I felt that I was not justified in supporting the war verbally unless I were prepared to suffer from it in the way that the unprivileged must suffer. But I was not yet prepared to do this, so I made use of certain of my privileges to escape for a little to America. I had an especial reason for wanting to return to America, but apart from that I thought I could think things out there, get myself clear before I went back into the maelstrom. Clarification – it may be too much to demand of most people but a writer must demand it of himself.

There is something more than a little embarrassing about this convoluted self-justification. The capitalisation, the question marks, the repetitions – all are telltale signs of the kind of hoop-jumping that many left intellectuals, used to 'certain privileges', indulged in at the start of the war. In stating the choice as, at best, one between evils, MacNeice mirrored Day Lewis's famous declaration about defending the bad against the worse. He certainly felt uncomfortable in Ireland, ridiculed by the crowd at the Palace Bar (one apocryphal story tells of a row between MacNeice and the satirists, immortalised in Patrick Kavanagh's lines, 'Let him go back and labour / For Faber and Faber'). As he represented it, the detachment he found in Dublin was simply too detached for his liking, too redolent of escapism. Or we could look at it another way – the unconcern was too embedded in the atmosphere of Catholic Ireland. The aloofness or indifference MacNeice discerned in Dublin sprang not from the kind of disillusionment experienced by British intellectuals, which he knew and understood, but from an underdeveloped, peripheral European country's sense of distance from the struggles of the continental powers. In the end, MacNeice could only understand this remoteness as evasion.

* * *

Kate O'Brien left for Britain in October 1939. By January 1941 MacNeice was back in London, where he attempted to join the navy. Both defined themselves in the end against a neutral stance they saw as a shirking of responsibility. Their letters and fictions tell us less about the general atmosphere in Ireland than about the crisis of allegiance the war caused for those whose loyalties were divided. As the shape of the war became clearer, and more urgent, from June 1940 onwards, supporters of the Allies began to draw an increasingly sharp distinction between engagement and neutrality. The contrast between Ireland and Britain became one between irresponsible escapism, on the one hand, and conscription and the war effort on the other. This was an understandable shift in perspective. It was almost impossible not to measure life in Ireland against the fate of the rest of Europe. Ireland became a land of a fairy-tale peace, far removed from the battle front, while its inhabitants were arraigned for their detachment from reality, their isolation and myopia.

But for many people in Ireland during these first months of war it was the proximity of the conflict that bore down most heavily. No one knew exactly what protection neutrality would offer, or had any clear idea of how Ireland could survive in a world at war. At most, there was hope of escaping the worst. Several of the men putting their wives and children onto packed trains at Euston during the first week of September 1939 were interviewed by a reporter from the *Irish Times*. They suggested that they weren't convinced their families would be safer at home in Ireland, but at least they would be amongst 'their own people'. Though there was probably an element of self-deception here, it is unlikely these men were being wholly disingenuous. The mass evacuation across the Irish Sea was a race to a place of safety, but it didn't necessarily connote either escapism or indifference.

The atmosphere of menace and confusion in Ireland at the beginning of the war was not pictured in the fictions of those who turned their backs on the country, but it did feature in the writings of those who stayed. Like MacNeice in Galway, and Kate O'Brien in Limerick, the war 'came down on' the novelist Sean O'Faolain in the West of Ireland. Commissioned to write a travel book about the new Ireland, O'Faolain had set off from Dublin in the summer of 1939, visiting the towns of the midlands, south and west (along with the artist Paul Henry, who was to produce paintings to illustrate the high-class travel guide). By September he was in Mayo, where he sat at the foot of Croagh Patrick mountain 'and read in the paper that Germany had invaded Poland'. A month later he returned to Elizabeth Bowen's country house in north Cork, which he had already passed through in July. His October visit, when he found Bowen trying to haul the family mansion into the twentieth century – getting a telephone put in, having the place wired for electricity – was to mark the sputtering end of their two-year affair, another curtain lowered.

The love affair and subsequent friendship between the patrician Anglo-Irish writer Elizabeth Bowen – author by then of six acclaimed novels and several volumes of short stories – and the Catholic, middle-class O'Faolain (son of a Cork policeman) offers a unique perspective on attitudes to the war amongst the Irish intelligentsia. The affair had begun in 1937. In a letter to a former lover, Humphry House, then in India, Bowen wrote:

I have no news, except news of a very personal sort: England seems almost as far away to me as it must to you because I am, we are, someone and I are, very much in love. It doesn't feel like a love affair, it feels like a marriage . . . He is Irish, and lives in Ireland. He is the best (I think, without prejudice) of the younger Irish writers. I only read any book of his last summer, for the first time: then I thought, I must meet this person and nearly wrote him a fan letter, then didn't. Then this last April, when he was in London for a week, staying at the Thackeray Hotel and working at the B.M., he wrote *me* a fan letter, about my books. We met at the end of that week. Since then we have always met in Ireland, at B. Court or in Dublin. He was fighting with the Irish in the Anglo-Irish war, then the Republicans in the Civil War. He is not at all like anybody's idea of an ex-gunman, he is a very gentle person with fair hair – or hair, at least, about the colour of mine. We are the same age – and doing such very different things in the same years of our lives. Nothing is easy; he has a very nice wife he has been married to for ten years, and they have got one little girl of five. He would hate to upset her just as much as I should hate to upset Alan. So we are trying to pay for our happiness by being very good. We are both, by nature, extremely secretive, which helps. This, as you can imagine, makes me more homesick for Ireland than ever: I feel wedded to the country, and rooted there.

As Bowen describes it the 'marriage' between them was a secret accommodation between republican, Catholic, middle-class Ireland and the Ireland of the Protestant landed gentry. For two years the two met in London (he wrangled a meeting with Virginia Woolf through Bowen), in Ireland, and on one occasion they took a trip, along with Isaiah Berlin and a few others, to Salzburg for the opera festival.

In the summer of 1939, the affair seems to have come to an end. Though neither writer commented on the reasons for this, it's hard to ignore the kinds of strain that would be put on a marriage by the divided allegiances called into play by the war. Bowen, impatient with appeasement and an avowed admirer of Churchill, was – like Kate O'Brien – eager to get back to England in October 1939. She was to spend the majority of the war years in London, where she volunteered as an ARP warden. In the summer of 1940, as the situation worsened, she undertook clandestine information and opinion-gathering work for the Dominions Office. Although, she claimed she always thought of herself as Irish, the war called forth her obligation towards England. It was to England that she would have to answer for her choices.

O'Faolain's allegiance, on the other hand, was to neutral Ireland – but it was a tortured allegiance. Like the majority of his fellow citizens, he felt no inclination to leave his native country, and broadly supported his government's policy. But this did not mean that, like those who came and went, he found in Ireland a positive space for reflection. O'Faolain felt imprisoned – 'immobilised', he was later to say – by his distance from the world-shaping events unfolding elsewhere. But he also grasped that Ireland's experience of vulnerability connected it with Europe.

While at Bowen's Court in October, amidst the blacked-out countryside of County Cork, he wrote a piece for the *Manchester Guardian* on the atmosphere in neutral Ireland. 'Irish Blackout' described the strange and uneasy mood in the countryside where the 'boys and girls' have stopped dancing at the bridge: 'Tradition has been broken. The heart is dishevelled. Continuity has been blotted out.' Haunted by the sense of what was happening elsewhere in Europe, O'Faolain found himself longing for the sounds of the Anglo-Irish war (in which, as Bowen rather proudly tells Humphry House, he had been involved):

This silence is far more ominous. If there were even a 'plane from the aero-drome, with its red-and-green wing-tips, white tail-light, throbbing across the sky, it would be more bearable.

This silence from across Europe, this breath of mystery between the Urals and the Galtees, this vacuity, these thoughts of shuttered ships at sea, unrecorded deaths of submarines, this total darkness of the mind – it is the last ebb of the great darkness come to the rim of the world. We sit wondering what it must be like in London, Berlin, Warsaw, conjuring furnace towns, fly-ing men, and complaining beasts.

To express such sentiments at the outset of the war was unusual, to say the least. At the end of 1939 most of O'Faolain's countrymen were relieved to be out of the fight, rather than worrying about their spiri-tual and physical isolation. His use of 'we' suggests the uncommon perspective O'Faolain may have been struggling to hold onto at this point, pitched somewhere between support for Catholic Ireland's independence and allegiance to an emphatically European cultural ideal.

A year after their parting at Bowen's Court, Bowen drew a portrait of a man very like O'Faolain in her short story, 'Summer Night'. Liberal, intelligent, committed to Ireland and to Europe, Justin Cavey has got stuck in provincial Ireland in the summer of 1940, unable to take his usual continental holiday. Far from feeling relief at being spared the impact of the war, Cavey's vision of the destruction of Europe, and his powerlessness to do anything about it, send him mild-ly hysterical. 'I say, this war's an awful illumination; it's destroyed our dark; we have to see where we are. Immobilised, God help us, and each so far apart that we can't even try to signal to each other.' As Bowen declares of her protagonist (it would be wrong to call him a hero): 'The immolation of what had been his own intensely had been made, he could only feel, without any choice of his. In the heart of the neutral Irishman indirect suffering pulled like a crooked knife.'

This was a portrait of one individual who held a very particular per-spective on the war. But it was also intended as a picture of 'the neu-tral Irishman' more generally. As Bowen saw, O'Faolain's 'dishevelled heart' also expressed the public mood in Ireland. The problem of sym-pathy, and what to do with feelings of sympathy for the Poles in par-ticular, was raised in parliament, in newspapers, in churches throughout the country. 'Bhí gach duine ag breathnú léarscáile na Polainne ins na laethe úd' ('Everyone was looking at Poland's map in those days'), said the novelist Séamus Ó Néill. The dilemma of personal accountability in the fight against fascism – what MacNeice described as being 'tormented by the ethical problems of the war' – was also an issue for those committed to Ireland's independent stance, or at least for some of them. And there were real fears that the country was going to get pulled into the conflict. Alarm and uncertainty over the coming war echoed the repeated warnings by de Valera and his ministers, in the Dáil and on public platforms, that 'we shall have war all around us'. This was to be not only a war of fronts and borders, of those lines and contrasting colours on the map that most Irishmen could contemplate with a reassuring sense of distance. The country, neutral or not, would be encircled by violence. A month into the phoney war, O'Faolain was quite clear that the boys and girls who had stopped their dancing in the Irish blackout 'will meet again in wartime London'.

3

Mobilisation

Back in Ireland in the summer of 1940 Hubert Butler found himself
without war work, and indeed without 'neutrality work' either.
Neither the British nor Irish governments had come up with anything
in response to his requests to be given something to do in what he saw
as the two countries' joint battle against Nazi Germany. Jobless, and
with his father ailing, he returned to his parental home in Kilkenny,
where he was to keep a night vigil by his father's bedside for many
months, often writing through the night to his wife in County
Monaghan. In October he wrote explaining that his brother Gilbert
was considering volunteering for the British army:

I can't see why the Irish army isn't adequate . . . his line is that farming *isn't*
really now vital, nobody seems to want food, & he's feeling frightfully on the
fringe of things. I think it's just a burst of provincialism that considers
Piccadilly, or rather Sydenham & Egerton Crescent as the hub of world, –
hence lack of self-confidence in our own milieu and efforts. It seems to me
that if there is an invasion, it will be, as Churchill hinted, on both islands at
once and he's more likely to be useful and needed here than there. I dare say
he's a bit bored and wants a bit of life and doesn't think organising whist
drives for Volunteers enough.

If anything the new, threatening, situation after the fall of France had
reinforced Butler's sense that Irish neutrality was part of the war
effort. Right through the war he sought to sustain the idea of neutrality as a principled alternative to violence, as the platform for a
forthright humanitarian response to the refugee question. Rather than
a passive or negative stance – merely keeping one's head down, staying out of harm's way – he saw the possibility of 'positive' neutrality.
(He was later to argue for pacifism in the same way.) But his sense of
'equality' with Britain also sprang from the fact that both countries
were equally at risk of invasion. By the summer of 1940, as Holland,
Belgium and France were overrun in turn – neutral and belligerent
alike – it suddenly seemed all too clear that Ireland's survival was
going to depend on her ability to defend herself.

The country was totally unprepared. As far as defence went, the contrast between neutral Ireland and belligerent Britain could not have been more marked. Both countries, it was true, had become used to the calm of a war in which not very much was happening. By mid-October the battle for Poland was over: the country had been divided up between Germany and the Soviet Union, and the Polish government and many of its armed forces had escaped into exile. During that first winter the only real fighting was happening in Finland. The Soviet Union attacked all along the Russo-Finnish border at the end of November 1939 and fighting continued on and off until the ceasefire in March the following year, when Finland ceded the province of Karelia. French troops hung back from advancing across the Maginot Line into Germany, Britain dithered over sending troops to aid the Finns, and engaged in a few isolated incidents at sea, but for the most part the war at this stage was one of stand-off (and according to the Poles and the Finns, betrayal).

Nonetheless Britain was preparing for battle. In Ireland, by contrast, there reigned an almost exaggerated calm. During the winter of 1939 the nervous tension that had been whipped up on the outbreak of war had dissipated. Full mobilisation of the Irish Defence Forces had been ordered on 1 September 1939. Troops, wearing the German-style Vickers helmets that would cause so much derision in Britain, occupied railway stations and harbour positions. The soldiers of the Volunteer force appeared on the streets of small towns across the country. But gradually, as it appeared that nothing was happening, they melted back into their barracks. And some retired completely for a while. For the army was seriously underfinanced, and by December of that year de Valera was forced to order the war establishment to be cut back. Soldiers were actually demobilised in the first months of the war, so that by March 1940 the army's strength was down by one quarter on its strength at the outbreak of hostilities.

This atmosphere of relative security was dramatically shattered by Germany's sudden westward advance in the spring of 1940, and by the invasion and collapse of the European neutrals. On 9 April Germany took over Denmark and Norway (Hitler tried to claim this was a preventative manoeuvre against a planned Franco-British occupation of Scandinavia – and a means of protecting the two countries' neutrality). On 10 May France, Belgium, the Netherlands and Luxembourg were attacked. By the beginning of June Allied forces were in headlong retreat; on 14 June Paris was occupied, and by 25 June France had capitulated.

It was immediately obvious that the crisis was going to affect Irish hopes of keeping out of the war. Firstly, the threat of an invasion of Britain was guaranteed to cause panic in independent Ireland, despite the formal separation between the two states. If nothing else the government faced the serious problem of how the country would survive, given its trade, shipping, labour and economic connections with Britain.

But there was also a real fear of a simultaneous invasion of Ireland. As the troops retreated hurriedly from Dunkirk the obvious next step for Germany was to follow them. As Hubert Butler suggested, invasion was anticipated 'on both islands at once'. A German foothold in Ireland would make invasion of the North easy and inevitable, and give the Nazis passage across the Irish Sea; it would also forestall any British inclination to retreat to Ireland in order to regroup. The flattening of the European neutrals in May brought home to both government and people that there was no safety in claiming to stand outside the conflict. The country seemed, in fact, just as likely as the belligerent nations to have to defend itself against armed invasion, and the need to improve its defences became paramount. De Valera began warning of the immediate danger of invasion: 'I do not want to alarm you . . . but I want to wake you up from the apathy which seems to have settled on our people in months past . . . We really are within the war zone.'

Sound evidence suggested that invasion was being considered in Berlin. In September 1940 German defence analysts published their 'Militär-geographische Angaben über Irland'. This hefty invasion package included maps of roads, power supplies, and the main cities and towns, a booklet of photographs (many of them tourist snaps), and a seventy-seven-page survey of the country. There were descriptions of the diversity of terrain, population density, tillage, animal rearing, inland waterways, sources of energy; analyses of roads, harbours, railways and shipping; statistics concerning agriculture and industry. Other sections covered the Irish character, and areas in which the Irish language was spoken. The purpose of the booklet was obvious from the discussions of where troops should be billeted, and what diet and accommodation they could expect, the analysis of the coastline, and the street plans of the larger towns. The work had been compiled over a number of years, from geography books, ordnance surveys, tourist information and textbooks – and included pictures taken from postcards and newspapers (some more than forty years' old). The scant analysis of Ireland's defences and war-making potential suggests that these were regarded as negligible. Operation Green, as it was known, was certainly mooted, and seems to have involved plans for an amphibious landing from Brest to coastal points between Wexford and Dungarvan, before the end of September 1940. There were to be two waves of attack – the first in beach-worthy flat-bottomed transports, to be followed up by larger vessels carrying equipment and support weapons. The invaders would then advance on Dublin and Kildare. Sea manoeuvres and training for such a landing, whether feint or not, were kept up until October 1940.

Historians suggest that the Irish government's discreet assistance to Britain (above all through sharing intelligence) began in earnest during the summer of 1940, born of an edgy understanding, rarely acknowledged openly, that Ireland's continuing independence depended on Britain's ability to withstand the German assault. At the same time British defence analysts were conscious of Ireland as a weak point on their western flank. It was in May of that year, according to MI5, that security liaison between Britain and Ireland began to be taken seriously by both sides, building on the good relations between Colonel Archer of G2 and Captain Liddell of MI5. New travel regulations were put in place, and detailed plans drawn up for combined action in the event of a German attack.

A month later came a proposal from Malcolm MacDonald, then Minister of Health in the British wartime coalition government, for a Joint Defence Council to decide on matters of security and defence North and South of the border. This was followed by an offer of post-war Irish unity (subject to Northern Irish consent), in exchange for naval and air facilities and participation in the war. A declaration accepting the principle of a United Ireland was to be issued subject to various conditions:

Éire to enter the war on the side of the United Kingdom and her allies forthwith, and, for the purposes of the Defence of Éire, the Government of Éire to invite British naval vessels to have the use of ports in Éire and British troops and aeroplanes to cooperate with the Éire forces and to be stationed in such positions in Éire as may be agreed between the two Governments.

Britain's primary consideration was the need to secure Ireland against invasion, given the fate of the continental neutrals, although the use of the ports for Atlantic defence was desirable in itself. It was a sign of desperation – and de Valera knew it. The plan to secure the country with British troops was as likely to encourage German retaliation as ensure Ireland's protection, he argued. Moreover, the promise of eventual Irish unity was no more than 'a pious hope'. Not only was the consent of Northern unionists unlikely to be forthcoming (and Craigavon immediately expressed his 'shocked and disgusted' opposition to 'such treachery to loyal Ulster') but strategic as well as political factors undoubtedly made such promises seem empty. At this stage in the war, after all, most people were expecting a German victory. MacDonald reported back to Chamberlain and the British Cabinet on his fruitless discussions with the Taoiseach: 'I felt that one of the decisive influences on de Valera's mind now is his view that we are likely to lose the war.'

The increasingly polarised rhetoric on the part of both Britain and Ireland masked the genuine complexity of the defensive relationship between the two countries. On the one hand there was Anglo-Irish security cooperation, born of a general understanding that both countries together were going to have to repel German invasion. But de Valera's refusal to come into the war or lease the ports meant that Ireland remained a military risk. If the British feared an Axis invasion of the twenty-six counties as a prelude to an invasion of Britain, or in order to seize the Irish ports to bolster submarine warfare in the Atlantic, Irish authorities had double the worry, for there were persistent rumours of a British pre-emptive attack across the border. The atmosphere throughout the summer of 1940 (and for the following year until Hitler turned his attention to Russia) was one of scare and counter-scare. Rumours of a seaborne invasion by Germany on the southern coast, or of aerial assault by parachute troops dropping in the mountains, were matched by fears of a British advance across the border to secure the ports and other strategic centres before Germany got there first.

There was ample evidence of a possible British attack. There were few troops based in Northern Ireland until June 1940. The 53rd division had arrived 'in driblets', virtually untrained, between October 1939 and the following April. It was the fall of France that made clear the province's strategic importance, and the risks posed by the border.

During May 1940, the division's primary function changed from internal security to 'action against enemy forces invading Éire' and 'action to repel an enemy invasion of Northern Ireland'. The force was concentrated along the border in Fermanagh, Armagh and Down. Over the next year these troops were reinforced, until five divisions were posted throughout the province. Defence emplacements and fortifications sprang up everywhere:

The preparations along the road are fantastic . . . Barriers of concrete and railway sleepers, three and four deep, bar the exit from [the city] and entrances and exits of every village en route, usually with pill boxes as well. All the bridges even on small secondary roads are mined and a cross-roads in the heart of the country is fortified as if to hold up an advancing army.

All this activity was carefully watched in Ireland. As fear of invasion increased, so did suspicion on both sides of the border. Rumour and counter-rumour, information and disinformation, were carried back and forth by travellers and police agents. In June 1940, for example, the following Garda letter was sent to Aiken, forwarding intelligence from 'a reliable agent on the Northern Ireland Border':

On Sunday, 23 June, 1940, I was in Armagh and the sole topic of conversation was the pouring into Northern Ireland of British soldiers with tanks and mechanised equipment. As a result of my information I went to Dungannon and The Moy, Co. Tyrone. On Saturday night, 22 June, 1940, 200 light tanks and 260 Bren Gun Carriers arrived in Dungannon. 1,600 men and a full mechanised contingent arrived in The Moy three miles from Dungannon. The Monmouthshire Regiment arrived in Armagh. The Royal Ulster Rifles and London Irish Regiment, which were in the north, were sent to England and were replaced by English regiments. All bridges are being mined and Barricades with machine gun emplacements are built on all roads leading to Armagh and Newry, and all Northern Ireland towns. From the information that I could gather British troops are pouring into Northern Ireland, and the Catholic population there are in a state bordering panic. The troops themselves look on the Catholics and all persons belonging to the Free State as being pro-Germans.

Another plan adopted by the Northern Government is the sending of all unemployed Catholics to England to jobs there. No Protestants are being sent. Should Catholics refuse their unemployment allowance is stopped immediately.

Such reports did nothing to ease the jittery atmosphere in the South. Aiken drew up a series of guidelines for the ordinary citizen in case of invasion. They were printed in the national and local papers, broadcast over radio, and read out in town squares up and down the country. In July 1940 he was in Dundalk warning people to remain in their own homes at the first sign of trouble. Don't listen to rumours (the radio could be 'interfered with'), don't give the enemy information, or let them get their hands on cars or bicycles. Hand over food and transport to the Irish defence forces, obey instructions, take cover, build shelters, avoid flying glass, lie down if you get caught outside in a raid.

Military defence against a possible British attack focused on the Boyne valley. The Boyne and Blackwater rivers were to form the 'Main Line of Resistance' in Ireland's defence against invasion from the North. An infantry detachment was to be deployed along the line of the two rivers, which acted as a tank obstacle. All crossings were to be covered by blockhouses (pillboxes), and machine gun pits 'were to be placed on the north side of Drogheda, Slane, Navan and Kells'. Eastern Command received the following directive from Portobello Barracks, Dublin, on 9 July 1940:

Circumstances require the observation of the northern territory and the covering of routes from the border towards Dublin . . . Provision will be made for . . . prompt opposition to a hostile advance including delaying action by a small detachment between the border and a final line of defence. The final line of defence will be the general line of the rivers Boyne and Blackwater from the sea to Lough Ramor.

Observation groups were placed on the frontier and east coast (and also at the Treaty ports, in case the British should attempt to seize them). Behind the observers a screen of motorcyclists and cavalry squadrons, assisted by the LDF, waited in readiness to delay attackers. Motorcycle squadrons were based at Dundalk and Manorhamilton, with motor squadrons at Kingscourt, Cavan and Mohill. Three infantry battalions were deployed at outposts north of the main line of resistance. The line itself was fortified by a series of concrete blockhouses, camouflaged with sod-covered banks of earth (and constructed with an aperture which allowed firing only in one direction – towards the border). Several of these emplacements bear the scrawled initials of those who built them, along with their dates. '1942' appears on several, and one carries the late date of '1944'. It took some time, apparently, for the defence plan to be put into action, although some of the fortifications may have been erected in response to the renewed threat of invasion, after the arrival of American troops in the North in January 1942.

All these preparations cost money and manpower, both of which were in short supply. In the spring of 1940 de Valera announced that he was setting up a new, all-party, Defence Conference for discussion of security measures (thereby effectively compromising the opposition's ability to criticise his policies). At the same time the government asked for vastly increased expenditure on defence – citing a projected bill of more than three million pounds. Although the amount was voted through, it was in the face of considerable annoyance from the main opposition parties, Fine Gael and Labour – who were angry firstly that more had not been done at an earlier stage to build up the country's defences, and secondly because it was felt that the sum, though vastly more than the country could afford, was also far too little to protect against invasion by a modern army.

It was, argued members of Fine Gael, simply 'political codology', pure 'squandermania', to suggest that Ireland was going to be able to defend itself where Finland, Norway and Denmark had failed. For all that the government trumpeted the army's competence, the idea that, alone and ill-armed, it was going to be able to resist columns of tanks flew in the face of common sense. Ireland's security, argued the most allied-friendly members of the opposition, depended on the British navy and air force, and therefore, if not on British goodwill, then on the hope that Britain would find it expedient to come to Ireland's aid. There was anger too over the government's refusal to state publicly that the danger of invasion came from Germany. At the same time the vulnerability of the state gave rise to strains of fatalism. The paltry nature of Irish defences led some to argue that the goal of defence was in itself misguided: 'Is there any thinking man in this country to-day who, if he had the courage to say so, would not admit that Denmark had chosen the better part, in not spending unnecessary sums of money on defence purposes which, when the emergency arose, were found to be useless?'

Most people, however, thought that some attempt should be made to defend the country. Army reservists and first-line volunteers were called up and a major army recruitment campaign got under way. The national Call to Arms focused on the regular army, including marine defence, and on the need for volunteers to join the newly formed Local Security Force, but also encompassed other emergency services such as

ARP, the Irish Red Cross, and medical services. Legislation was pushed through allowing for enlistment in the regular army 'for the duration of the emergency' ('durationists') rather than for a period of years only, in an effort to increase the numbers of those willing to join. Older men or men who felt unable to leave their homes (such as many small farmers) could be registered for the part-time local security corps, where they would be inducted into one of two groups: either volunteering as part of an armed, local protective force under Garda control, or engaging in unarmed patrol and observation work.

The call was put out over radio, and followed up by rallies, marches and recruiting platforms across the country. Newspaper

Men of Ireland!

" Never allow it to be said of you that you are weaker than your fathers were. Let it not be said of you that you have grown soft on the freedom that your fathers have won. Show that you are worthy of them, worthy of their sacrifices. "

THUS spoke An Taoiseach to the men of Ireland a few short weeks ago. Already many thousands have answered the call; but thousands more are needed. Young men, men of mature years, and old men too, all must do their part to defend the nation in this, her hour of danger. Our freedom can be made secure — our liberties safeguarded — but only if we show that we deserve to be free, that we are worthy of liberty. Serve to defend freedom! Join one of these four national defence forces. Don't put off joining . . . . . .

Your country needs you *Now*

MAKE UP YOUR MIND—ANSWER THE CALL—JOIN ONE OF THESE FORCES TO-DAY advertisements and editorials took up the summons and for several months a large proportion of column inches in both the local and national press was given over to the recruitment drive. Initially there was dismay over the level of response, particularly in rural areas where there was, it was suggested, 'a terrible amount of apathy'. A debate in the Seanad on 7 June 1940 heard complaints that the 'lethargy in some country districts is almost incredible, due to the fact that the urgency of the matter has not been realised'. Despite the fact that de Valera had described the danger as 'immediate and imminent' and 'a matter of days not weeks', the people had not yet been stirred to 'a consciousness of the dangers that are abroad'. Part of the problem was the persistence of 'subversive propaganda' (some of it emanating from the Dáil itself) which suggested that the Irish should not attempt to defend themselves against external attack: the country was 'too small, too weak, too poor and too insignificant to fight'.

In an effort to combat defeatist rumours the government set about persuading citizens of the competence of the defence forces. They used displays of military force, bolstered by emotional appeals to patriotic duty. The trick was to balance declarations of the viability of the national defence with a picture of the country's vulnerability that was sufficiently alarming to hit home. The great triumph of what was in effect neutrality propaganda was its ability to present the fight *for* neutrality, rather than defence *against* a particular enemy, as Ireland's patriotic cause.

Rhetorically the Call to Arms might have been compromised by the lack of a specific enemy, but the cause of neutrality could be expressed as a battle for Ireland itself – in effect as an armed defence of independence. Rather than non-involvement, neutrality was reframed as the protection of the country against the war itself, or as the journal of the defence forces put it, 'Ireland versus the foreigner'. Such frankly xenophobic formulations would cause problems in Britain, and for those Irish citizens who felt most involved in the Allied cause, but the beauty of this expression was that it allowed people of all political persuasions to support the 'fight' for neutrality. Frank Aiken, Minister for the Co-ordination of Defensive Measures, argued that there was in effect no difference between neutrality and war: 'In the modern total warfare [neutrality] is not a condition of peace with both belligerents, but rather a condition of limited warfare with both . . . In cold economic and military fact it is becoming more and more difficult to distinguish between the two emergencies called war and neutrality.' Those with ties to Britain, including some Fine Gael politicians, were intensely irritated by the refusal to acknowledge publicly who the enemy might be (de Valera repeatedly insisted on the need to defend against invasion 'from whatever direction it might come'). But such studied vagueness, combined with patriotic appeals, contributed to the government's ability to galvanise public opinion in defence of the nation. The idea of Ireland versus the foreigner was, of course, the opposite of Churchill's hint that invasion would occur on both islands at once, welding the two countries anew in the face of a common enemy. But both scenarios resulted in the drive to defend Ireland – to ensure a sturdily armed neutrality.

*   *   *

The task of the Call to Arms was to establish the idea of a harmonious, if not homogeneous, democratic national community, united against the threats from abroad. The creation of political consensus was helped by the internment of members of the IRA in 1939 and 1940 – who were sealed off from the general population for the duration of the war in the Curragh camp. Public sympathy for the IRA decreased as the threat of invasion grew, but it wasn't helped either by some high-profile activity on the part of the republicans themselves.

Internment without trial for active members of the IRA was introduced soon after the war began. A series of raids in the autumn of 1939 had uncovered explosives and incriminating documents in Rathmines, an explosives class complete with blackboard instructions in Offaly, a bomb-making factory in Killiney, an arms dump in Brittas. Those caught red-handed were tried and convicted, but individuals were also rounded up for possessing illegal transmission sets, and for membership of an illegal organisation. They were arrested under the Offences Against the State Act, which had been passed in June 1939. This Act allowed for special criminal courts, extended powers of search, arrest and detention, and internment without trial for anybody suspected of involvement in a wide range of seditious activities. Several of the prisoners apprehended under the Act went on hunger strike in November, and the government, sensing lack of popular support for the policy of internment, and believing the IRA threat negligible, backed down. The strikers were released unconditionally and a number of other prisoners let out early.

Then came the Magazine Fort Raid. On 23 December 1939, fifty IRA members raided the Irish army's ammunition store in the

Magazine Fort in Phoenix Park. They got away with more than a million rounds of ammunition. This victory over the national army was a tremendous coup for the IRA, and a humiliation for the army. But it was short-lived. Most of the ammunition was recovered in a huge search operation over the following weeks. The army's success in recovering the arms was partly down to their own intelligence work, but it also had as much to do with declining popular support for the republicans. As Eunan O'Halpin has put it, the Magazine Fort raid dispelled 'any residual national complacency' about the IRA, and prompted 'a flood' of information from the public. The war had put the conflict between the state and the IRA on a different footing.

After the raid large numbers of men were caught in the search for the stolen arms and ammunition, but the government complained that there was often insufficient evidence to convict them. A series of amendments to the Emergency Powers Act and the Offences against the State Act gave the government even wider powers of arrest and detention, including the power to execute people convicted by a military tribunal, without right of appeal. The government's response to a further hunger strike in April 1940, by prisoners campaigning for political status, was evidence of the new, tougher stand. De Valera regretted the concessions he had made in November. (One of the released men, Patrick McGrath, was involved in the killing of two detectives the following August and was subsequently executed.) In April 1940 two men died on hunger strike and the IRA called off the protest without gaining any concessions.

In May, with the invasion scare at its height, the Curragh camp in Kildare was enlarged to cater for possible German and British internees, and a mass of soon-to-be-arrested republicans. The majority of the raids on houses and farms throughout the country took place during the first few days of June. Within a few weeks nearly five hundred men were interned at the No. 1 Internment Camp at the Curragh, under the revised Offences against the State Act, and another three hundred or so at Cork Jail. Sentenced republican prisoners were also held in Portlaoise prison, in Arbour Hill, as well as prisons in Northern Ireland and England. Most of the IRA internees, upwards of eight hundred of whom were held at different times during the war, were to remain in the camps until 1944, a few until the general amnesty in 1946.

From the government point of view the rationale for internment was clear. Those who intended to wage war on Britain, because British troops were occupying the six counties, were effectively waging war on the Irish state itself – jeopardising the state's policy of neutrality, and possibly dragging the country into the European conflict. IRA propaganda liked to present the force as a credible threat to Britain, and to imply the possibility of an alliance with Germany.

Come into the ranks of the IRA at once. We want you. We want to train you. We want to arm you so that when the day of battle arrives you will not be found wanting. Make no mistake about it. This war will not pass without an attempt being made to cut this country off from the British Empire. They may gaol us, they may hang us but they will never exterminate our spirit.

Rhetoric like this from the IRA's *War News* of December 1939, along with attacks on the Irish army and police force, gave the government all the excuse it needed for cracking down on IRA treason against the state. Maintaining consensus around the country's stance required the isolation of disruptive elements. By the second year of the war the IRA, with a large number of its members interned in uncomfortable conditions and with no idea of when they would be released, was suffering from a severe loss of morale. There is evidence that those who remained free lost whatever political judgement they may have had. In October 1941 G2 seized an extraordinary note, presumably to be couriered to Germany, recommending a final blitz on Belfast and requesting that the bombers avoid the Falls Road and prisons holding 'Irish Republican Soldiers'. It went along with a helpful map of the city for the Luftwaffe.

The effective suppression of the IRA as a realistic force during the war was partly down to internment, but it was also a victory for the government's ability to orchestrate and mobilise active support for neutrality. Under the slogan 'Step Together', the emergency services coordinated a series of recruitment events combining displays of men and weaponry, sporting contests and pageantry. The primary aim of these displays was to convince people (both inside and outside the country) that Ireland did have a credible army, and that joining it would be a worthwhile act – there were regular massed marches, and presentations of arms designed to impress by force of numbers. Frequently featured in Irish newsreels, the columns of uniformed, marching men also signalled a show of unity. Processions of soldiers, nurses, and Local Security Force volunteers recast isolated individuals as part of an integrated and cohesive community and emphasised the fact that the army was indeed stepping together, in the words of the 1923 Irish Volunteer marching song:

Step together – boldly tread,
Firm each foot, erect each head;
Fixed in front be ev'ry glance,
Forward at the word advance,
Serried files that foes may dread,
Like the deer on mountain heather,
    Tread light,
    Left, right, –
Steady, boys, and step together!

Aiken and other ministers spent much of the summer of 1940 rushing up and down the country to open Step Together fairs. Their rhetoric of unity, sovereignty and moral righteousness owed a good deal to the 'positive censorship' designed to nurture neutral-mindedness which was advocated at the centre of government. There were several strands to it. Ministers recalled ancient fights for liberty, and suggested that joining the Volunteers was not about taking part in war but living up to the Fianna of old. They stressed pride in national unity and patriotic duty. And they also managed to turn the defence of neutrality itself into a moral calling. As Aiken put it in June 1940:

We can see clearly the boiling European cauldron in which classes, religions and nations clash blindly with a growing violence which threatens the destruction of all. Can we add something to calm this seething mass? Can we dispel the darkness and show a way of life in which the various elements, which go to make nations and the human race, can live in peace and harmony, utilising the ever increasing power of man over nature for their mutual benefit rather than for their mutual destruction? . . . Whatever the answer, the youth of Ireland must conquer cynicism and despair and strain every nerve to prove that a full and harmonious life can be achieved in one little country.

There was nothing to prevent northerners from 'betaking themselves elsewhere to work off their belligerency', but Irish citizens wished for an early peace 'based on the principles of justice'. In Athlone, a few months later, he argued that volunteering to defend neutrality was not simply a patriotic duty. It was morally righteous in itself:

We have the strong moral basis that while we sympathise deeply with the human beings affected we seek no quarrel; that all we ask is acceptance of our right to decide our own national policy without evil intent to any. Thus morally armed we can, in my opinion, with effective organisation and with energetic training to make the best use of the equipment we have, ensure the effective defence of our country.

In addition to the more obvious forms of spectacle – military parades, precision marching to pipe bands, and parades of armoured cars and weaponry – the army also put on a number of theatrical displays and tableaux, with the enthusiastic encouragement of assistant chief of staff Major-General Hugo MacNeill, a devotee of amateur drama. Historical tableaux representing the Irish national struggle down the centuries had been a popular form of entertainment since the founding of the state – they featured, for example, in the celebrations of the Tailteann Games inaugurated in the early years of the Free State. The use of tableaux was in part an attempt to harness the popularity of traditional religious festivals, such as the annual Corpus Christi celebrations, which featured processions of floats and tableaux pulled through the streets of towns across Ireland (indeed during the war the LDF marched behind the religious in Corpus Christi processions). The Eucharistic Congress in 1932 had featured a number of tableaux vivants, including symbolic representation of the dawning of the age of Irish freedom. One of the attractions of these pageants, particularly when they featured a generalised 'Mother Ireland' figure, or representations of ancient, mythic battles, was that they were able to make their appeal across a wide political spectrum. Both pro- and anti-treaty forces could respond to representations of the eleventh-century Battle of Clontarf, for example.

In July 1940 the army mounted a three-week theatrical extravaganza designed to enhance recruitment. 'The Roll of the Drum' was performed at the Theatre Royal in Dublin three times a day and more than a hundred thousand people witnessed the combination of military display and national pageant – with actors miming battles in dumb show, and a final tableau showing the emergency services gathered to protect a female figure of Ireland, and bearing weapons reminiscent of skirmishes down the ages. Like the French revolutionary use of pageants to counteract the influence of monarchical festivals, Irish nationalist pageants were in part a response to British royalist celebrations, which many felt they had endured for long enough. 1937 had brought forth a crop of Coronation films, for example, which had given rise to protests against the cinemas by republicans and nationalists, particularly in the North of Ireland. Two further films released in 1937 and 1938, *Victoria the Great* and the sequel *Sixty Glorious Years,* were little more than hagiographical royal pageants, celebrating the pomp and power of the empire. By contrast the nameless female

figure at the centre of a tableau representing the struggle for Irish freedom stood as allegory both of national identity and of the need for its
protection.

This patriotic, emotional appeal was backed up by a celebration
of military strategy for its own sake, as actors mimed episodes of significant historic European battles. 'Representation of historic scenes
went back for generations, even to Fontenoy, and the attention given
to detail and historical facts could not be surpassed.' The eighteenth-
century battle of Fontenoy, near Tournai in Belgium, in which
French forces overpowered the British and their allies, could hardly
be said to bear directly on the situation of the Second World War,
except perhaps in terms of geography (or indeed the illustration of
Britain's vulnerability). Yet the emphasis on battle strategy rather
than ideology was part of an attempt to sidestep potentially divisive
or 'unneutral' allegiances. As an approving member of the Dáil put
it, the Theatre Royal show had managed against all the odds to
appeal to 'people of every blend of political thought'. This was
theatre as festival – the gathering together and celebration of a
community.

A new defence forces journal, *An Cosantóir*, was launched in
December 1940 with an exhortation to 'good comradeship' by the
chief of staff General McKenna: 'The present expansion of the Army
has brought into its ranks men of every political party and men of
every creed and class. This unification of the different elements of the
community is in itself one of the greatest factors in our defensive
strength today.' Ireland's cause must override 'personal motive or private jealousy'. The new Local Security Force was seen as a crucial element in the development of a positive morale:

The LSF is also of the first importance as a means of welding together in its
defence all the elements which go to make the Irish nation . . . Constant effort
is needed to make us sink our petty differences and to realise the essential
things which we have in common; to substitute the name of Irishman for
every sectional title. In the matter of Ireland versus the foreigner we are all for
Ireland . . . In modern war the strength of a nation depends in the first
instance upon the strength of the national will, upon the determination of its
people to resist aggression. The strength of an army lies more in its moral
qualities than in anything else and the moral qualities of an army – its patriotism, its discipline, its fighting spirit – will depend to a great extent upon
the spirit of the people.

After the spectacular failure of the French to protect their homeland, numerous commentators exhorted Irish citizens to learn the lesson that defence was a moral issue as much as a military one; successful resistance depended on the ability of each individual, and groups of individuals in each small area of the country, to maintain the will and determination to fight. In effect the rhetoric celebrated the transformation of passive, isolated citizen to active volunteer – as many noted at the time, Ireland's was the only *volunteer* army in Europe, with all the connotations of patriotism, unity, and commitment this implied.

The success of the Theatre Royal extravaganza, and its particular combination of aesthetics and morality, led to calls for recruitment drives across the country to include theatrical elements, along with sporting events and competitions. Local Security Force (and later Local Defence Force) fairs, often lasting for several weeks at a time, were held at regional centres across the country. Alongside marching displays by the Emergency services, and recruiting parades, they might include sporting contests, hurling and football matches (usually the army against the LDF), point-to-point, rifle-shooting competitions, army band recitals, free cinema performances for members of the services, fun fairs, military tableaux, and even amateur dramatics competitions. Each night of the fair would conclude with dancing in a marquee (sometimes with 'Kaleidoscopic Lighting Effects'). A fair at Ennis, for example, which was shown on Irish newsreels, included competitions such as Tilting Buckets, Greasy Pole, the High Jump, children's dancing, pony jumping and even duck racing. Athletics and gymnastics (and perhaps pony jumping as a modern version of early equestrian contests) were intended to recall the customs and public fairs of ancient Ireland.

The story went that the Aonach Tailteann – the two-week-long national competition of Irish sports and creative arts begun in 1922, on which the Step Together Fairs were at least partly modelled – were celebrated in Ireland more than a thousand years before Rome was founded, and that the Olympic Games were a mere shadow of Ireland's sporting contests. By 1940 there were also unfortunate echoes of the open-air exercises of the Hitler Youth, though on a far smaller scale – thirty youths in white shorts and singlets bending and stretching in a hillocky field. The fields and hedges, as well as the contributions of animals and children, were all part of the intended effect of the fairs, particularly when shown on film. Such displays made a virtue out of participation at all levels of the local community, and at the same time offered up the spectacle of vigorous, active, defence-minded local districts to cinema audiences across the country as a whole. Other events – such as marching parades – insisted rather on the separation between ordinary people and the defence forces: those out of uniform could only watch. The intended message was not only that the country was safe in the protection of these forces, but that individuals could only become truly part of the new unified community by volunteering. Joining in meant joining up.

A similar relationship between the local and national lay at the heart of the pageant competitions and the presentation of Historical and Topical Tableaux. Local amateur dramatics societies, which had increased in popularity throughout the 1930s, really began to thrive during the Emergency. This was partly because the difficulty of travel made it harder for the provincial middle class to manage the journey to Dublin or Cork for entertainment, and forced them to consider creating their own local forms of amusement, but also because of the fillip given to regional theatre and even film by the activities of the army and the LDF. At its most basic, encouragement of the dramatic arts focused on historical pageantry. A Step Together fair in County Longford, for example, concluded with a tableau of Mother Ireland (a local girl called Chrissie Mahoney) surrounded by a synchronised display of the might of the local defence forces with rifles and bayonets, massed together on a specially constructed stage. Like many of the fairs, this event was put out on newsreel. The poor-quality film shows a creaky, overcrowded stage, and the amateur display, clearly executed on a shoestring, appears slightly ridiculous – but the local, home-made, nature of the event is part of the point. This is no slick, well-lit, centrally organised and orchestrated creation but the product of the efforts of a local committee, probably comprising members of the Step Together board, along with local church dignitaries, active members of Muintir na Tíre, and the great and the good among the provincial middle class. The films celebrate the fairs as a display of the strength of local community bonds, because effective defence is local and home-made too.

At their most elaborate, Step Together fairs provided the focus, and excuse, for fully fledged local drama festivals. Local dramatic societies, and the annual round of provincial and rural drama competitions, were one reflection of the growth of a provincial middle class in small towns across the country. Amateur dramatics had a long and respectable history in the major cities – Dublin, Belfast and Cork – and some purchase in regional centres such as Galway and Limerick. The inclusion of the category of drama in the Tailteann Games after 1922 gave publicity and lent a kind of urban cachet to the activities of local drama societies, and may have been in part responsible for their increased popularity throughout the 1930s. But progress in the regions also depended on a sufficient number of educated people with enough energy and leisure time to commit to finding a play, rehearsing, making scenery, costumes and so on.

The town of Dundalk, for example, with a population of sixteen thousand, boasted several competing drama clubs. Dundalk was booming during the 1930s; with the Great Northern locomotive works, two breweries, several distilleries, three boot factories, a cigarette factory and a cement works, the town showed little evidence of its beginnings as an agricultural market. By the end of the 1930s it had its own small theatre, seating sixty, built into a room at the back of a beauty shop, under the enthusiastic direction of a chemist's assistant. The market town of Birr, with only 3,300 inhabitants (and a new boot factory), could also claim its own theatre, opened in 1934 and seating a hundred and sixty, in a room at the back of a printing house. (The Birr theatre committee was a faithful representation of the middle and aspiring middle classes of the town; it was started by the scion of a well-known local professional and business family, together with a cabinet-maker, the owner of a large shop, a lorry driver, a teacher, a plumber, a bank manager, a butcher, and so on – but no farmers.) These theatres were typical of the pre-war period, when many drama groups were located in larger, or – in the case of Birr – more prosperous towns. Louth Drama Festival, for example, which was begun in 1937, gathered entries from Sligo, Dundalk and University College, Dublin, along with a large number of competitors from north of the border – Belfast, Omagh, Newry.

The overwhelming preference of the drama societies was for realist or naturalist plays by contemporary Irish dramatists such as George Shiels (chosen by five different societies at one festival in 1940), T. C. Murray, Louis D'Alton and Lennox Robinson, but there was often a showing too for Eugene O'Neill, T. S. Eliot, Lady Gregory, and sometimes the controversial Paul Vincent Carroll (if his criticisms of small-town pieties could be got past local clerical opposition), as well as plays by local writers. Playwrights who were very rarely performed included Synge, Yeats, Martyn, Colum, O'Casey, Teresa Deevy, Shaw, Sheridan, and Goldsmith – writers with a reputation for being either too difficult, or too Anglo-Irish, or both. While Abbey Theatre writers such as Shiels and D'Alton increasingly came in for criticism in the pages of respectable literary journals for initiating the decline of the Irish national theatre into melodrama and farce, it was just these characteristics which endeared them to the local festivals. Writing a series on rural theatre in *The Bell* in 1940 and 1941, Michael Farrell – a frequent judge of regional drama festivals – attempted to suggest some suitable plays for rural amateur societies, including Synge, Ibsen, Shaw and Yeats, only to receive a slew of mail objecting to his choices and asking for more comedy, farce, melodrama, and thrillers, and more parts for women.

Country theatre was taken seriously and not just in the provinces; festivals were generally reviewed in the national papers, and in literary journals such as the *Irish Monthly*, the *Dublin Magazine* and *The Bell*. Features on regional theatre were broadcast on Radio Éireann. As the war progressed this national interest was focused on increasingly local festivals, remote from the cities and large towns. In 1941 the Sligo Feis, for example, drew competitors from Ballina and Bundoran, from smaller towns such as Ballymote and Dromore West, and from tiny villages in Sligo and Donegal such as Croagh and Glenties. Sligo was a town of twelve thousand inhabitants, with no industry to speak of, and had been hard hit by the war. As Michael Farrell put it, from a distinctly metropolitan perspective, in *The Bell*:

One can imagine what a boon this week of competition and possible triumph must be to the scattered towns of the West where nothing ever seems to break the monotone of repose except the shunting of some empty cattle-wagons within sight of a creamery's blank wall and the incongruous whistle of a new factory dredging up to the skies all the melancholy of the landscape.

For the middle class, and for women, local drama offered opportunities for involvement and socialising that others found in the GAA, in local politics, or in religious confraternities. But an element of entrepreneurship also played a role, as local communities attempted to draw tourists to their areas. For the Irish middle classes now forced to holiday at home, a trip to the theatre might prove an attraction. In 1943, a summer Drama Festival was launched in the tourist spot of

Killarney, and in 1944 in Bundoran, and even in Tubercurry in Galway. By 1946 there were thirteen amateur festivals across the country. Underlining the trend, a tourism feature in the *Cork Examiner* in May 1940 wasn't above treating the blitzkrieg as a marketing opportunity: 'It's an ill wind that blows nobody any good. In this light Ireland should stand to gain in its tourist traffic from the disturbed conditions on the continent.'

The army and LDF were not slow to capitalise on this enthusiasm, integrating drama into even the most small-scale activities. On a far more local and modest scale than the Sligo Feis, for example, the Cavan Step Together committee promoted the Cavan Drama Festival as part of the activities at their recruitment fair in 1943: a two-week run of recent Irish plays all performed by local groups ('See the cream of County Cavan's Amateur Dramatic Societies in works by leading Irish Dramatists'). Here again a large part of the point lay in celebrating the creative energy of local organisation, as well as giving those, like Hubert Butler's brother Gilbert, bored with whist drives, something to do.

The Festival's insistence that the plays should be written by Irish writers about Ireland was entirely typical, and reveals the close connection in the organisers' minds between (silent) historical and military tableaux and scripted theatrical performance. This was a connection urged by metropolitan dramatists too. Impressed by the natural theatricality of the events of Easter Week, the playwright Denis Johnston suggested in 1941 the inauguration of bank-holiday re-enactments in Dublin, arguing that O'Connell Street was the perfect space for open-air drama:

This street at the same time is the actual scene of certain events in our National history which provide a heroic theme as rich in dramatic values as anybody could wish. It is a theme which is outside the realm of controversial politics and which in fifty years' time will probably have become legendary.

This 'National Morality Play' was never staged, although the frequent military displays performed in front of the GPO throughout the war years – integrating the army, the Old IRA and the Emergency Services – could perhaps be interpreted as a form of communal theatre, emphasising the link between the rebellion of 1916 and the country's present fight for neutrality.

The celebration of a local community united against the enemy – whoever it was – lay at the heart of the Call to Arms. But it was evident that such communities were to be firmly under the control of the modern state. Indeed while local neighbourhoods were prized for their 'traditional' cooperative spirit, modern state-driven technologies, including wireless, telephone, and film, broadcast these values to the nation at large. Film of Step Together activities, including pageants, was regularly included in Movietone's Irish newsreels – which were used to substitute for sections of newsreels considered by the Irish censorship authorities to be belligerent propaganda. As the war progressed there were almost weekly items devoted to march-pasts and displays of strength, either in College Green in Dublin, or at one of the numerous provincial fairs. Long newsreel items on the army's system of field communications, on marine defence, on training, on local military exercises, and on the 1942 manoeuvres in County Cork (in which the LDF took on the army) added up to a large amount of wartime film of the Irish defence forces. Again, this was down to Major-General Hugo MacNeill, who employed a full-time cameraman, Jack Millar, to document the activities of the army:

I did filming anywhere that the General Officer commanding the division happened to visit. I was his aide-de-camp, which made it very easy for me. I carried the camera with me, did films down in the bog where the men were all cutting turf – not all of them maybe, but most of them – and visits along the Border up to Finner Camp, and places like that. Most of this was put together by Gen. MacNeill himself, who had a great talent for that sort of work – wonderful fellow – anything to do with the theatre or films or entertainment, MacNeill was an enthusiast, and wouldn't allow anything to stop it. So that facilitated the job greatly.

MacNeill's interest in entertainment extended to the production of army roadshows. A Dutch journalist who spent the war years in Dublin and wrote for the *Irish Independent* reported on one trip down to the troops billeted at the camp in Kildare. The overcrowded lorry disgorged its cargo of actors and singers, fit-up stage, costumes and scenery to reveal the makings of a 'smart city-cabaret right in the heart of the bog . . . [with] all the precision of faultlessly high-stepping, spirited chorus girls, of quick-firing comedy gags, of hilarious impersonations, the pathos of old Irish songs, and the modern bathos of Tin Pan Alley, wise-crackingly mixed by a perfect compère – professional, for his lieutenant's uniform'.

Jack Millar was chief cameraman for the 'Spearhead Film Unit', which was also responsible for the 1940 recruitment film *Step*

Together. 'Ireland Needs Her Sons' began the film's voice-over, as it featured footage of an array of guns, tanks, and weaponry, the physical training undergone by a recruit, signalling instruction, camp life, parades, as well as sporting activities ('the building of a healthy, vigorous manhood'), and music from the No. 1 Army Band. In a grand touch the recruitment message was painted on the underneath of five planes – a significant portion of the army's air fleet – which flew overhead in formation in the film's closing moments. While the film attempted to present a rosy picture of camp life – the sun shines throughout and there is no trace of mud near the neat rows of tents – the appeal was directed not just towards the prospective volunteer. The acquiring of skills such as neatness and organisation, and even basic cookery, might appeal to the mothers of the sons needed by Ireland, but not as much as the financial rewards. 'Dear mother,' says the voice-over, 'I'm sending you a little donation from my first pay. I'll be sending you more when I'm a Field Officer.' This was proof that the makers of the film knew very well which factors influenced the decision to enlist, and who would take that decision in practice – and that they were battling above all the higher rates of pay available in England.

* * *

At least some of these tactics were successful. Media saturation of the recruitment message, and all-party public platforms in aid of national defence, had remarkable success in the summer of 1940. In September 1939, the Regular Army had stood at 7,600, with nineteen thousand on full mobilisation. By May 1940 army strength had fallen to thirteen thousand. Within five weeks of the recruitment drive nearly twenty-five thousand men had volunteered for the army – almost double the number of men then under arms. By October of that year 180,000 men had also come forward to join the Local Security Force. Moreover the national call to arms echoed overseas, where the cry of 'Ireland versus the foreigner' managed to appeal to at least some of the Irish who were then living amongst foreigners. Applications to serve in the Irish defence forces arrived from Irish citizens living in Britain and the United States throughout the summer of 1940. Dulanty, the Irish High Commissioner in London, received a barrage of mail in early June from men of military age in England wanting 'to offer my services to the nation'. Much of it came from people living in and around

Liverpool who picked up Radio Éireann and who had heard the appeal for volunteers, or read it in Irish papers published in England.

Offers came too from further afield, although in at least one case it was not clear how the prospective volunteers would manage to make it to Ireland. In a decoded telegram from Washington, the Irish Ambassador Joseph Brennan announced 'Some Irish and Americans have asked if they would be allowed to join Irish Forces. Please advise.' On 3 June 1940 James Glynn of the Combined Irish Alliance wired President de Valera from Chicago: '10000 IRISH AT YOUR DISPOSAL IF ERIN IS INVADED.' On 20 June a wire addressed to 'Mr De Valera President of Ireland' was sent from Jersey:

ABOUT FOUR TO FIVE HUNDERED IRISH SEASONAL WORKERS STRANDED IN JERSEY CI ALL PREPARED TO JOIN ARMY. WHAT IS THE ACTION OF YOUR GOVERNMENT APPLY MOLONY 20 SAND ST STHELIERS.

Many of the applications received in both London and Dublin came from Irish citizens eager to get out of England, who had been informed that in order to be granted leave to travel they needed a permit to enrol in the national defence forces. The pull factor of dedication to the Irish cause was probably outweighed in a majority of cases by the push factor of fear of conscription in the British army. A great deal of this anxiety was due to ongoing confusion about the rules governing conscription of Irish citizens. Only those who had lived in Britain for two years or more were eligible for call-up, and these could claim exemption on the basis of a new arrangement which excused Irish citizens from military service if they wished to return to Ireland permanently. In such cases the British authorities would agree to an exit permit if the High Commissioner offered assurances that the applicant had a home in Ireland. The permit was valid only for the journey home, and if the individual returned to Britain he was immediately liable for military service – no further exit permit would be granted. Recruiting officers in Britain were not all equally eager to explain this exemption to Irishmen living in their areas, however, and many migrant labourers were fearful of being caught up in the war. 'Dear Sir,' began one letter to the Minister for Defence:

As an Irishman temporary living in England and on behalf of scores of our countrymen who comes over here and wait a year or two without returning to their native land in order to keep the home fires burning some of us now have been placed in a funny position as you understand if we are here over two years we must fight for England. We do not say we wont fight for England but what we do say is if our own country is in danger and the 'Irish Press' and radio is calling for the youth of the country to rally to the recruteing [sic] office why don't you Mr. Oscar Traynor call on some of the 100,000 Irishmen who are here in England to defend the shores of Éire, I myself am a native of Co Mayo and have a little farm there so why should I together with hundreds more who are in my position fight in France or Belgium while my own home and property is in danger despite the fact that we may be here over two years if we were here twenty years we are still Irish.

In July the Department of External Affairs composed a formula reply to be sent to all those who queried the procedure for those wishing to return to Ireland. Irish citizens were directed to apply to the High Commissioner in London for a travel permit to Ireland. They then had to apply for a British Exit Permit from the Passport Office: 'In this connection I am to inform you that it is understood that Irish citizens whose homes are in Ireland and who are returning thereto for permanent residence will be granted the necessary British Exit Permit.' Once in Ireland they could then apply to join the defence forces.

People continued to get caught up in the system, however. The Department of Foreign Affairs files contain many letters from young men who had only been in England a month or two, and could not, or thought they could not, get back. 'I wish to join the Volunteers and shall be grateful if you send me particulars of how to get out of this country,' wrote one young man in July 1940, who had been working in England for only nine months. His case was, theoretically, simple, but there was ample evidence that both recruiting officers and passport officials had little time for people wanting to return to neutral Ireland. After all, Allied forces had just suffered ignominious defeat in France and a German invasion of Britain looked imminent. Another young man cabled de Valera on 17 June: 'I have been refused an exit permit to leave here for not having proof that I am going home to join the home defence as I want to defend my country.' A few days earlier the Irish Citizens' League and Advisory Bureau, a Glasgow-based organisation, had written complaining that restrictions on passenger traffic were being applied indiscriminately – and arguing for the need to arrange for men to join the Irish Defence Forces through the High Commissioner in London.

There were similar requests for recruiting centres close to the border with Northern Ireland. Even though conscription had not been extended to Northern Ireland there were complaints about the difficulty for nationalists living in the North in evading the voluntary call-up. Indeed, the lack of conscription in some ways made the recruitment of Catholics in the North an even more fraught issue, for it was felt they were being unfairly press-ganged into the British army. In October 1939, the Anti-Partition Council of Ireland had urged the Department of the Taoiseach to provide better facilities, such as an enrolment bureau in Buncrana in Donegal, for the enlistment of young men from Derry in the 'Army of Ireland'. Many of the Catholic unemployed in the city were destitute, they argued (not least because poor relief was not paid to applicants under the age of forty-five), and unable to manage the fare to Dublin or Athlone:

As you are aware the Nationalist youth of the Six Counties are the victims of an economic pogrom that is daily proving more effective than the periodic anti-Catholic outbursts of previous years. Two recruiting sergeants from the British Army attend daily at the local Unemployment Bureau, and it is insidiously suggested by the Staff that the alternative to refusing to enlist may be the loss of unemployment benefit. Over 75 per cent, at a conservative estimate, of the unemployed are Catholic and Nationalist, but the proportion of Nationalists coerced in the British Army at the moment is roughly 95 per cent. In other words out of each batch of twenty marched from the Bureau to entrain at the Depot, there might be one Protestant or Unionist.

Northern nationalists regularly complained that B Specials, in particular, were not being encouraged to join the British Army. Added to this were claims that Northern Ireland's recruiting officers were in the habit of sending money to young men in the south for the fare to Belfast so that they could join up. Letters from distraught mothers asking the government to intervene mounted up: their boys had been seduced by pay and adventure to join up even though they were under age, they pleaded. Such angry rumours probably influenced the decision by the censorship to alter – in the interests of maintaining civil order – the wording of a ballad by Charles Kickham, which was broadcast during a piece on ballad poets on Radio Éireann's *Children's Hour*. The phrase 'a foreign army' was substituted in the well-known lines:

But cruel as my lot was then,
I ne'er did hardship know,
Til I joined the British Army,
Far away from Aherlow.

As an exasperated member of the Seanad put it, 'Are we to censor Kickham, who died in '82?'

By the war's end, the number of Irish citizens who had volunteered for the British armed services was estimated at 150,000. At no point during the war did the Irish government seriously consider putting a stop to the voluntary recruitment of Irish men and women in the British forces, and the majority volunteered without feeling this compromised their support of neutrality. But – particularly during the invasion crisis – there was real concern about the loss to Britain of young men needed to defend the homeland. In May 1940, the Minister for Defence, Oscar Traynor, introduced a ban on 'public recruitment for foreign armies', particularly through newspaper advertisements. Nonetheless, complaints persisted of the numbers of young men (a proportion of them deserters from the Irish army) travelling together on the train to Belfast to enlist – and there was very little the government could do to stop them. Later in the war this traffic was officially recognised by British forces in Northern Ireland, who sent potential absconders from the Irish army letters telling them to travel on the 9 a.m. train from Dublin, which would be met in Belfast by officers of the RAF and other services (copies were angrily brandished in the Dáil). Guards in plain clothes began boarding the trains in order to flush out likely deserters.

Complaints that citizens in both the north and the south of the country were being conscripted into the British army 'by hunger and want' were to increase as the war progressed. At root, however, the problem of leakage from the Irish army lay in the genuine difficulty of disentangling friend from foe when dealing with Britain. The rhetoric of the Call to Arms warned of the danger from 'the foreigner', in an attempt to persuade Irish citizens that the country was equally at risk from Germany and England, but Irish army volunteers who objected in principle to the idea that they might be asked to fight against British soldiers were apparently told, 'Don't worry, you won't have to.'

The mobilisation in the summer of 1940 was focused on the need to protect against invasion. The massed marching, the newsreels of local communities, the strictures on defence-force morale, were all aimed at securing the territory of Ireland against incursion, whether from over the border or from across the sea. But Irish neutrality was also under pressure from another quarter, for in addition to a war against invasion Britain was also fighting a war for the sea – a war in which Ireland's coast seemed strategically vital. With Germany attempting to sever the Atlantic supply lines, Ireland's neutrality began to appear to the British as an indulgence that could no longer be afforded. As Britain's attention focused more and more on the loss of the Treaty ports, the battle for Ireland's coastline began.

4

War at Sea

As dark fell on the evening of 7 August 1940, the *Mohamed Ali El Kebir*, an Egyptian liner recently redeployed as a British-registered troop transport and en route from Avonmouth to Gilbraltar, was torpedoed 250 miles west of Malin Head by U-38, under the command of Commandant Liebe. The 7,290-ton vessel did not sink immediately and nearly all the 860 men on board, including the injured, were able to make it to lifeboats and life rafts in the two hours before the ship submerged, to be picked up during the night by the escorting destroyer, HMS *Griffin*. However, as *The Times* reported on 12 August, 'because of the rough weather, some of the lifeboats filled with water, and several of the men were washed off the rafts and drowned. A number died from exposure after being picked from the water. One lifeboat, when picked up, contained only the dead body of a lascar, and was three-quarters filled with water.' When the ship sank at 10.30 that evening it did so very suddenly and some of the thirty or so men left on board had to jump clear; not all of them made it to the rafts. Approximately 740 survivors were picked up and landed at Greenock on the Clyde on 9 August.

It was several weeks before the detritus from the wreck, including the first of the bodies of those drowned, began to wash up on Ireland's western coast. Empty lifeboats were reported adrift off the Mayo coast on 27 and 30 August. On the 27th, too, the bodies of George Ironside, a forty-four-year-old Sapper with the 706 General Construction Company, Royal Engineers, and twenty-three-year-old Gunner J. A. Herdinghan were washed up in Achill Sound, and at Keel Pier in Mayo. Over the next three weeks, thirty more bodies retaining papers or tags identifying them as having been on board the *Mohamed* were brought in by the sea to the strands and coves of Mayo, Sligo and Donegal, and a further fifteen unidentifiable bodies were washed up close by. On 19 September the last identifiable casualty of the *Mohamed* came in at Rusheen, near Louisburgh, County Mayo – it was John Pratt Thomson, the forty-nine-year-old captain of the ship.

His body was found by Michael Burke of Uggoole, near Louisburgh, and was described in official reports as being in a very advanced state of decomposition. Clothed in part of a tunic and blue vest, it had been more than six weeks in the water. An inquest was held on site and the body was buried immediately at Rusheen, above the high-water mark.

Thomson had been the last to jump from the ship as it turned on end and plummeted and, in an odd coincidence, his body was the last to be recovered. Part of the reason for the length of time between drowning and recovery was the position of the ship when attacked. At 55 North, 15 West the *Mohamed* went down in the middle of the North Atlantic Drift, a slow northward-moving flow of warm water, which reaches a depth of about a thousand metres.

In the immediate aftermath of drowning, as the lungs and stomach fill with water, a body will sink quite quickly. The process of decomposition causes gas to build up inside the body's cavities, creating buoyancy and allowing the corpse to rise slowly to the surface – this can take days or several weeks depending on variables such as body density, fat, the previous state of health of the drowned person, and the temperature of the water. Once near the surface again, the casualties of the *Mohamed* would have been caught in the meandering flows of the North Atlantic Drift, in the log-jam areas of eddy currents. In time, as the flesh decomposed further, as holes appeared and the gas was expelled, the bodies would slowly sink once more, and might catch the currents moving below the surface – the more southerly, faster-flowing North Atlantic Current (a continuation of the Gulf Stream) which moves eastwards towards the Irish coast. Many of the casualties from the wreck of the *Mohamed*, and other ships bombed or torpedoed north-west of the island, were recovered considerably further south than the points where the vessels sank.

A corpse floating this long in surface water was at the mercy of fish and birds, and – as the current took it in to shore – of jagged coastal rocks. After four or six weeks in the sea much of the exposed flesh would have fallen away or been devoured, and the extremities were often missing: as a body is washed by the tide against rocks, the hands, feet and head are repeatedly knocked and tend to become detached. A body brought in by the Gulf Stream to the coast of West Cork, and described by a Bantry guard, was typical of many of the bodies washed ashore:

The body was found lying face downwards on the strand. It was in an advanced state of decomposition and appeared to have been in the water for a considerable time. The body was that of a man. It was minus the legs from the trunk. The arms and trunk were intact but the flesh was badly decayed, and the lower part of the stomach was missing, and there was no flesh on the skull.

The sinking of a troop ship was a relatively rare occurrence during the war; and in this case there were comparatively few casualties. Nonetheless the loss of the ship was a reminder of the increasingly serious situation Britain was facing in the Atlantic. More and more vessels were being successfully targeted by submarines, and British sea and air power seemed helpless against them. In 1940 over a thousand Allied ships were lost, one quarter of British tonnage. During September 1940 an average of three ships a day went down to U-boat attack. In December Fine Gael's Richard Mulcahy noted that 'a large number of sinkings are taking place close up around Malin Head. This apparently is the main stream of traffic. The next largest is in a widespread area about two hundred miles off the Mayo coast.' Not all British ships were lost off the Irish coast by any means, but the pattern of sinkings in the North Atlantic during the latter half of 1940 meant that Allied public opinion swung decisively against Irish neutrality, and in particular against the refusal to allow Britain to use naval and air facilities to aid Atlantic defence.

Following the fall of France, with nearly all of Western Europe under the control of the Axis powers, with towns and cities at the mercy of aerial bombardment, Britain was beset by fears of defeat – fears of invasion, of gas, of obliteration from the air, of gauleiters in the offing. The worst terrors were not spoken openly, and the rest were kept in check by a blanket of upbeat propaganda. But anger against those who stood by, while what appeared to be the debacle of European civilisation unfolded, could be openly indulged. There was tremendous resentment against American isolationism, and a concerted press campaign against the Irish, which now focused obsessively on the loss of the Treaty ports. As Ireland's critics saw it, the refusal of the ports was proof that neutrality had deadened ethical feeling. While sympathy might be expressed by individual Irish men and women, and citizens from both North and South volunteered in increasing numbers, the state seemed to have contracted in on itself (like a hedgehog, said Hubert Butler), refusing to acknowledge any duty to aid Britain's defences. This was the nadir of Irish–British wartime relations as critics implied that Ireland had placed its own political survival above the ethical requirement to save lives. From a less hostile perspective it might have been granted that few political issues are ever decided on a purely ethical basis in any circumstances, let alone in wartime, and that the first duty of the Irish state was to its own people. But for Allied public opinion Irish intransigence meant not merely that Ireland had failed in its duty to support Britain, but that the Irish bore some responsibility for the deaths in the Atlantic – an accusation angrily rejected across St George's Channel.

*   *   *

The southern approaches to Britain were in real need of greater protection in the first months of war. Convoy escorts operating out of Plymouth and Milford Haven were worked to breaking point, but were still unable to defend Britain's Atlantic convoys as far westward as was needed. Naval personnel looked at Berehaven on the coast of West Cork and railed at the loss of the port as a base for escorts and flying boats in their battle against the U-boats. As Rear-Admiral Tom Phillips argued in a memo prepared for the Cabinet in October 1939, the use of Berehaven would also enable battleships and cruisers to avoid 'a great deal of unnecessary steaming through submarine-infested waters'. But even inside the Admiralty only Churchill – who had after all been opposed to giving the ports back in 1938 – favoured force if negotiation failed. Throughout the crisis, strategic considerations clashed with political ones – the need for westerly operational bases was balanced against the value of a friendly Ireland, providing vital exports of civilian workers in particular. Undeniably, however, Churchill's personal attitude to Irish neutrality was also a factor. As Eunan O'Halpin has put it, Churchill 'regarded Irish neutrality almost as a personal affront'. Against those who advocated caution in squaring up to Ireland's independent stance he argued that there was no legitimacy to Ireland's neutrality – the country was, in his view, still under the crown and thus legally 'at war but skulking'. Right through the crisis in the Atlantic, and particularly after becoming Prime Minister, his comments were designed to bully and threaten Ireland into entering the war and leasing the ports to Britain.

As the situation on the continent deteriorated dramatically with the invasion of the Low Countries, Churchill blamed Atlantic losses on 'the fact that we cannot use the south and west coasts of Ireland to refuel our flotillas and aircraft'. He also gave weight to popular stories that the Irish were aiding German submarines by allowing them to refuel on the Western coasts. Recalling the IRA bombing campaign of the previous year, he reasoned that those willing to place bombs in London would be more than ready to sell fuel to U-boats. It was this accusation in particular that incensed Irish political opinion. People were convinced that the British knew such refuelling to be technically impossible (and practically impossible, too, given the shortage of fuel across the country), so that the accusation was pure scandal-mongering, designed to increase the pressure on Ireland to give up the ports. Unsurprisingly, it gave rise to a number of other fantastic stories. English newspapers reported rumours that the crews of submarines were being entertained in remote villages in the West of Ireland, that wireless transmitters up in the mountains were at the heart of a vast espionage system against Britain, that the personnel of the German, Italian and Japanese legations in Dublin had increased by hundreds.

Calls for Britain to take back the ports were periodically renewed throughout the first half of 1940, but it was in the months following Dunkirk that their loss was really felt. Because of the fears of a seaborne invasion of Britain many ships previously employed in the Atlantic were kept in home waters. At the same time a good number of armoured ships and corvettes had been lost or damaged during the operation itself. So there was less protection for the Atlantic convoys, and Germany was now in control of the coast all the way from Norway to France. Spain, Portugal and Ireland, on the Atlantic rim, were all neutral. German High Command took full advantage of these strategic gains and intensified warfare in the Atlantic. Night aerial bombing of Britain's cities – designed to destroy civilian morale – was twinned with the destruction of the British merchant fleet – designed to destroy the British economy by crippling trade and supplies. In July 1940, due to heavy losses from Luftwaffe attacks, the British suspended the use of the southern approaches, and mined the area from the south coast of Ireland to Cornwall. In August Hitler issued instructions for the escalation of the sea and air war, including a complete blockade in all shipping trade with Britain. And the pressure on Ireland to lease the ports grew.

It was during this period that Elizabeth Bowen became involved in gathering information on Irish attitudes to the war, and the leasing of the ports. She was clearly affected by the growing clamour in Britain. At the beginning of the war she had been able to acknowledge the 'sheer disaster' it would be for Ireland to become involved in the war, 'in its present growing stages and with its uncertain morale'. By the summer of 1940 she had grown impatient with what she regarded as Ireland's stubborn refusal to acknowledge the consequences of neutrality for Britain – sufficiently impatient to begin working for the British government. On 1 July she wrote to Virginia Woolf with news of her new responsibilities:

I think I told you I had asked the Ministry of Information if I could do any work, which I felt was wanted in Ireland. On Saturday morning I had a letter from them saying yes, they did want me to go. Now it has come to the point I have rather a feeling of dismay and of not wanting to leave this country. I am to see Harold Nicolson on Thursday and go to Ireland on Friday night next. I don't expect it will be for very long. I shall be at Bowen's Court first, but I expect they will also want me to move about the place. I don't know much till I've seen Harold Nicolson. I hope I shall be some good: I do feel it's important . . . It will all mean endless talk, but sorting out talk into shape might be interesting. I suppose I shall also finish my book.

While 'espionage' is too strong as well as too narrow a term for what Bowen called her 'activities' in Ireland, they did involve sending secret reports to the Ministry of Information, and meetings at the Dominions and the War Office, conveying her sense of the climate of opinion: taking the temperature amongst writers and intellectuals in Dublin, and amongst country people near her home in County Cork. Bowen's decision was no doubt influenced by the departure of Chamberlain and accession of Churchill, whom she admired enormously (as well as by the fact that the trip gave an opportunity for her to get on with her book). But it was principally a response to the catastrophic situation for Britain following the fall of France. The stakes could not have seemed higher and the sympathies and loyalties of Allied supporters in Ireland became unbearably stretched.

During the second half of 1940 an average of fifty ships a month were lost in the Atlantic. Junkers and Condors, based at airfields at Dinard and Brest in Brittany, flew up the west coast of Ireland in order to bomb the ships now using the North Atlantic routes, as well as laying mines by parachute in Belfast Lough. U-boats refuelled in Northern France took to hunting around the western and northern coasts of Ireland with increasing success. Because of the shorter distance they had to travel, smaller U-boats now became a menace. Both aircraft and submarines were hard to attack for the British bombers operating at long range, and with poor radar, out of Liverpool and Aldergrove. In November Churchill let rip against Ireland in his 'Parliamentary Review of the War', which was printed in the London *Times*, and taken up by leader writers, columnists and cartoonists in the weeks and months that followed. His description of the closure of the ports as a 'most heavy and grievous burden' was glossed by the *Belfast Newsletter* as the 'frigid and ungenerous refusal' that was assisting the German blockade. The *Belfast Telegraph* explained to its readers that the use of Lough Swilly to guard the 'trade lane' which led to the Clyde and Liverpool, and of Berehaven to secure the lane which led through the Bristol Channel, would save hundreds of lives as well as tons of supplies.

The virulence of these attacks stemmed in part from the need to deflect the attention of the British public away from the heavy shipping losses. Criticism of the Irish was, after all, popular in Britain, and the economic sanctions introduced against Ireland may at least have given the British public a feeling that something was being done. But behind the propaganda lay genuine frustration. Churchill's personal history at the Admiralty, as well as his inability to come to terms with any measure of Irish independence, fed his sense of rage, but he was also reflecting real feeling in the Forces. Nicholas Monsarrat, who spent the war years criss-crossing the Atlantic protecting convoys in a navy corvette, articulated the general fury in his 1951 novel *The Cruel Sea*:

There are degrees of neutrality, just as there are degrees of unfaithfulness: one may forgive a woman an occasional cold spell, but not her continued and smiling repose in another man's arms. Even in her grossest betrayal, however, whether of the marriage vow or the contract of humanity, there could be variations of guilt: for example, one could understand, though one could not condone, the point of view of such countries as Spain or the Argentine, which had political affinities with Germany and did not disguise their hatred of England and their hopes for her defeat. They had never been married to democracy in the first place . . . But it was difficult to withhold one's contempt from a country such as Ireland, whose battle this was and whose chances of freedom and independence in the event of a German victory were nil. The fact that Ireland was standing aside from the conflict at this moment posed, from a naval angle, special problems which affected, sometimes mortally, all sailors engaged in the Atlantic, and earned their particular loathing . . .

To compute how many men and how many ships this denial was costing, month after month, was hardly possible; but the total was substantial and tragic. From these bases escorts could have sailed further out into the Atlantic, and provided additional cover for the hard-pressed convoys: from these bases, destroyers and corvettes could have been refuelled quickly, and tugs sent out to ships in distress: from these bases, the Battle of the Atlantic might have been fought on something like equal terms. As it was, the bases were denied: escorts had to go 'the long way round' to get to the battlefield, and return to harbour at least two days earlier than would have been necessary: the cost, in men and ships, added months to the struggle, and ran up a score which Irish eyes a-smiling on the day of Allied victory were not going to cancel.

This is Ireland as fickle coquette, blind to the benefits of her liaison with British democracy, and flirting dangerously with the enemy. The rhetoric of adultery suggests marriage, that of faithlessness suggests duty – both give voice to an underlying belief that the Irish state still 'belonged' to Britain by rightful union, and should behave accordingly. However this type of imperial rhetoric did little to encourage Ireland to give up the ports, but rather had the opposite effect.

As Elizabeth Bowen argued in her November 1940 report for the Ministry of Information, the resentment engendered in Ireland by Churchill's House of Commons speech, and the ensuing propaganda war, made it impossible for de Valera to act, even if he had wanted to. She noted the impossibility of hoping for Irish cooperation when such levels of anti-Irish feeling were being stoked up in the British press, advocating 'a tactful broadcast, apparently to England, but at Éire' to cool the hostility down. The Irish censor also wanted the temperature lowered. By June 1941 anti-Irish articles and cartoons (which endlessly rang the changes on the self-centredness, naivety and stupidity of de Valera and by implication the Irish in general) had caused the censor to cut the combined circulation of English dailies and Sunday papers to a record low of twenty thousand for the whole country.

British diplomatic pressure on Ireland received support from the United States. Churchill made his House of Commons speech the day after the re-election of Roosevelt as President (indeed, he probably timed it so as not to undermine Irish-American support for the incumbent in the run-up to the poll). Roosevelt's electoral success helped to copper-fasten the United States' increasingly pro-British attitude, bringing it nearer war. De Valera complained of a vicious press campaign against Ireland from both the Great Powers. Suspicion that the

Cartoon by David Low, published in the *Evening Standard*,
8 November, 1940.

media storm was orchestrated was not unfounded. The British Special
Operations Executive (a secret organisation established in the summer
of 1940) was behind several American initiatives including the
American Irish Defense Association – a group of prominent Irish-
Americans who campaigned for Irish cooperation over access to the
ports and airfields (and who would no doubt have been surprised to
know that their strings were being pulled from London). In March
1941 the AIDA cabled de Valera to urge him to open the western ports
to Britain, because 'the life line between Britain and America has
become the life line of civilisation':

Hitler has proclaimed the downfall of all small nations. What makes Irishmen
hope that Irish liberty alone could survive a Nazi victory? If Hitler stood off
England's shores, how long would he wait to seize the Irish ports? If America,
3,000 miles away and a thousand times as strong as Ireland, feels threatened
by the Nazi revolution, how much more terrible is the threat to little Ireland,
almost defenceless and close at hand.

For her own security America is sending all the arms she can produce to

England, but it partly depends on Ireland whether these arms will ever arrive, otherwise all America's effort may be in vain. Hitler proclaims in every speech that he will torpedo our aid, and the British admit that he has four times as many submarines now as he had last summer. Already the sinkings have begun to increase with the lengthening of days and calmer seas.

But there is an answer, for the naval experts state that the use of Ireland's western ports would double the strength of the British convoys. While the American fleet stands guard for freedom in the Pacific, Britain can keep the Atlantic free with Ireland's help.

There may be risk in this course, but the risk of standing by is infinitely greater. And when have Irishmen been afraid to take a risk against the powers of evil? This is no time to haggle or hesitate. We ask Ireland to grant the use of her ports not only for the sake of England, but for Ireland, for America and for the World.

This entreaty recycled a number of familiar arguments. The plea is based first of all on self–interest – your survival depends on your willingness to help Britain. But this is closely followed not only by an attempt to enlist Irish sympathy, but by flattery of Irish courage and fearlessness. The appeal is to the bravery of the Irish, to their willingness to take risks – a gratifying version of the stereotype of the hot-blooded, impetuous, pugnacious Irish-American familiar from Hollywood films of the period.

De Valera was unmoved. To the language of risk he answered with 'prudence' and practicality:

There must be an examination of what your means are and what the consequences of your action are likely to be. Ordinary prudence is not cowardice. It is one of the powers given to us in order to enable us to conduct ourselves and live as human beings in the world. We have certain duties to perform on behalf of our people. We try to exercise the virtues of foresight and prudence in so far as it is humanly possible to do it and when people ask us why we cannot give this facility or that facility, we ask them: 'Do you realise what you are asking us to do?' It is all very well for a big nation, a nation at a distance, to give facilities and act in that particular way.

The invocation of size by both sides carried a number of coded implications. The 'small nations' rhetoric was hardly calculated to instil confidence in Ireland – which had answered the call to protect Belgium in 1914, and been rebuffed by the Great Powers in the post-war settlement. Such unfortunate echoes of the First World War were turned on their head by de Valera. Unlike big nations, he argued, and nations safely on the other side of the Atlantic, such as the United States, Ireland once in the war could not hope to influence the course of events, and would risk losing everything.

Let us consider what our position would be. After this war we might find that we would have very little to say, as little to say about the terms on which it should end as we had to say about the terms on which it began. The big nation is not in that position. The big nation will be big enough at the end to insist that the things it fought for are the things that will be accomplished in the peace. A small nation getting into the war is in no such position. Its services are availed of for the time being, but when the end comes, and when it says: 'Our people fought for such an ideal,' its views will not be considered. Certain people will sit around the table at the peace conference, the big four or five, or whatever their number may be. They will deal with the settlement, and they will be quite capable of making a settlement to suit themselves. They can give the small nations any sort of an excuse they want to.

The allusion here to the peace settlement at Versailles (gesturing not only to the causes of the current war but to the 'betrayal' of Irish hopes after the First World War) is hard to miss. But de Valera's insistence on the sovereign country's entitlement to neutrality and independence was only one plank of his argument.

Throughout the crisis over the ports de Valera emphasised Ireland's lack of armaments and air-raid defences, arguing reasonably that the attacks on Dublin, Cork, and other Irish cities which would follow leasing the ports could not be parried. Above all he maintained that the ports could not be leased without Ireland entering the war.

We are sometimes asked to give this facility or that facility, as if it were a matter of giving the loan of a grid-iron or something of that sort, quite forgetting that what we are being asked to do is to enter this war – that is what it amounts to. I was speaking to one person who happened to visit us here and he asked: 'Why do you not do this?' He observed: 'If a neighbour's house was on fire, surely you would allow the firemen to get up on your roof to put out the fire next door?' Of course we would, but that is not an analogy to what we are being asked to do. What we have been asked to do is to set our own house on fire in company with the other house. We have been asked to throw ourselves into the flames – that is what it amounts to.

What really rankled was the inability on the part of both Britain and the United States to appreciate the true costs for Ireland of leasing the ports. And given that the United States itself wanted to keep out of the war, how could it ask Ireland to put itself at risk?

The Irish Ambassador to Washington, Robert Brennan, spent his time trying 'to offset the venomous propaganda against us', which stemmed, he argued, from American special correspondents in Ireland writing dispatches 'which were loaded with charges against Ireland and which questioned the sincerity of her leaders in their policy of neutrality'. He had meetings with Sumner Welles and Cordell Hull, and tried to influence the editors of Washington and New York dailies; he wrote articles and letters to the papers and even, on one occasion, a poem.

On 21 December 1940 the *New Yorker* published a sort of global Christmas Greeting, in the form of a poem by Frank Sullivan. It concluded with the lines:

Now let's polish off a dram
To John Bull and your Uncle Sam!
Sam, be Santa! Fill John's stocking
With toys to send a Nazi rocking.
Come on Éire, be good sports!
Give J. Bull the use of your ports!
Winston, we lift this seasonal cup
And say to you and yours, Thumbs Up!

The tone of this jingle was too much for Brennan. On 26 December Brennan wrote to J. C. Walsh of the *Irish World*, enclosing a copy of his reply, and explaining that it had kept him from Midnight Mass:

Come on Éire, be good sports,
Give John B. the use of your ports.
We know 'twill put you in the fray,
And we're 3,000 miles away.
When you were fighting to be free
We gave you lots of sympathy.
We did not go to war, 'tis true,
Although a tyrant tortured you,
But we ask you to go to war,
That's what all little folks are for.

Brennan's ditty lambasted the Americans for their cavalier attitude to Irish lives, and argued for Ireland's right to remain neutral. But it also expressed another concern of the Irish government, though one less often acknowledged in the sober language of diplomacy: the belief that if the British were offered the ports, they would never give them back ('For says John, "I find those bases / Are really quite attractive places . . ."'). Where the British were inclined to think of the ports simply as military bases, divorced from the counties and communities in which they stood, Brennan, and behind him the Irish government, focused on the ports as Irish territory – as integral to the country as the Six Counties.

Allied public opinion showed no signs at all of inclining to the Irish view. Brennan was not the only public figure moved to verse by the events in the Atlantic that Christmas. On 4 January 1941 the detective-fiction writer Dorothy L. Sayers sent Churchill a poem which rolled together Irish 'treachery' over the ports, guilt and indifference – so that Ireland seems scarcely less responsible for the deaths at sea than Germany:

> O never trouble Ireland, for she may sleep sound
> While the reek of blood and burning goes up from English ground.
> She lies down lightly with a smile upon her lips,
> Her bulwarks built of English bones and the wreck of English ships.

In response to such passionate indictments of Ireland's stance came a flurry of articles, books and pamphlets aimed at defending the Irish position, or offering pro-Irish solutions to enable Ireland to lend the ports, or more. The nationalist Henry Harrison (sole survivor of Parnell's party), who had published a hefty two-volume history of English–Irish relations in the late 1930s, followed up in 1942 with *The Neutrality of Ireland*, a historical overview written out of a conviction that any other course would lead to civil war: 'Ireland's spiritual aloofness from Britain is not of her own choosing but is the result of historically traceable sources – many of them recent and even contemporary – for which she is not responsible. Neutrality follows logically, and in all the circumstances is inevitable. It is a source of grief to very many who yet insist that it is necessary and inevitable.' Harrison's suggestion that Ireland's aloofness was primarily 'spiritual' glossed over the practical consequences of neutrality for the Allies, and may well have fuelled resentment in its turn. Nonetheless his measured, academic tones contrasted with the populist Jim Phelan, self-proclaimed 'peasant novelist' from Dublin, who worked as a journalist in London for much of the war.

Phelan's real background is hard to determine. He was an obsessive self-dramatist, variously describing himself as a 'tramp' from Tipperary, an ex-convict imprisoned for murder under shaky circumstances, a former IRA operative, and a socialist 'anti-Nazi Irishman'. Phelan diversified from novel and autobiography to publish two propaganda tracts with Victor Gollancz's Victory Books and The Bodley Head in 1940 and 1941. In *Churchill Can Unite Ireland* and *Ireland: Atlantic Gateway* Phelan accepted that Ireland's neutrality was inevitable, given the history of the two islands, and the unresolved problem in the North; but he insisted that the 'peasants' and 'working men' of Ireland understood the mutual interdependence of the countries of 'the West' and would be prepared to open the ports to the Americans. In Phelan's fantastically warped understanding of the political status quo in Ireland it was the unholy Nazi-supporting alliance between the Belfast industrialists and the large farmers of the pro-treaty forces (the rump of the Blueshirts, Ireland's quasi-fascist movement of the early 1930s) which was holding the country neutral in order to further Nazi policy. The answer was not to squeeze Ireland further, but to promote Irish and American cooperation:

In the light of the American Government's present activities, and the alignment of the Democratic Party plus the American Irish, only a miracle of stupidity or atavistic 'wangling' on the British side can withhold the native Irish from cooperation and initiative on the side of their myriad relatives across the Atlantic.

Supporting a similar pan-Atlantic alliance, the journalist and travel writer Máirín Mitchell, who was serving as a stenographer at sea, argued in *Atlantic Battle*, published in 1941, that in return for the ending of partition Ireland should join in an Atlantic alliance with Britain and the United States.

For the American market, meanwhile, there were numerous publications aimed at encouraging Irish America away from isolationism, and into persuading the Irish back home to abandon their neutrality. In 1942, Tom Ireland (whose previous publications had covered less-than-pertinent subjects such as the history of the Great Lakes, child labour, and the politics of the Far East) published *Ireland Past and Present*. This thousand-page history, aimed at Irish-Americans, made no bones about its propagandist intent, including a preface by Major-General John F. O'Ryan insisting on Éire's vulnerability and its dependence on British systems of defence. Ireland argued robustly that the Irish in Britain and America were being put at risk by the Nazi advance, and that Éire must help Britain hold the Nazis at bay while the United States caught up in the development of armaments. Like many in Britain he argued that the ports at Cobh, Berehaven and Lough Swilly were held not merely for the Irish in Ireland but for the freedom of Irish everywhere. Unlike British propagandists, however, he put forward a federal Ireland, with a parliament in the North under Dublin's control, as recompense for joining the war.

*   *   *

Despite their common cause, there was a vast difference at this stage in the war between American and British arguments over the ports. This was hardly surprising, since the United States was still neutral. Where the US accused the Irish of cowardliness, and attempted to bolster 'native' Irish valour, the British insinuated treachery, with the implications of corruption which went along with it. While cowardice was associated with shame and dishonour, disloyalty implied guilt, and a failure of responsibility.

Neutrality, for the British public, became synonymous with moral numbness. The Irish were guilty of a myopic refusal to look reality in the face; they were turning their backs while catastrophe occurred on the doorstep. 'Oh yes,' says a character in Kate O'Brien's *The Last of Summer*, 'Éire will be neutral, which is only the clearest sense politically. But that's beside the point. Little patches of immunity like ours are going to be small consolation for what's coming. Being neutral will be precious little help to the imagination, I should think.' From this standpoint, neutrality deadened empathy and bred indifference. Merely by succeeding in staying out of it, Ireland was culpable. The country remained a welcome destination for those seeking the comforts of peace and respite from the war elsewhere, but the lack of anguish with which Ireland stuck to her neutrality was increasingly condemned.

The shift was palpable in British public opinion, and it markedly affected the attitude of those Irish and Anglo-Irish who felt torn in their allegiance. In one of Bowen's most bitter wartime stories, set in Ireland in the winter of 1940 and written while she was reporting for the Ministry of Information, she imagines a group of well-to-do visitors holed up in a Kerry hotel, intent on blocking out all thoughts of the war. They turn their radios off and barricade themselves in overheated sitting rooms. But the misty view over the estuary from the windows of the seafront hotel speaks in a half-heard, strangulated way of what the inhabitants refuse to face squarely: 'Now and then a soft, sucking sigh came from the water, as though someone were turning over in his sleep' – no doubt one of the many bodies taking their last sleep around that western coast. Try as the visitors might to ignore the war, somehow it pursues them. Mrs Massey, the owner of a nearby house, arrives at the hotel with her daughter Teresa, seeking a suitable stage on which to act out her grief for the recent death of a young pilot. Hysterically worked up, she refuses to acknowledge the hotel's decorum, the protections afforded by privacy – she squeezes herself into an English guest's car like an unwelcome thought into his brain. The general embarrassment reaches a climax when Mrs Massey drunkenly takes the Englishman for the dead airman ('He looks like a hero, doesn't he?') – for a hero he most certainly isn't.

Bowen's impatience with what she diagnosed as a form of moral indifference was directed in this story at the English and Anglo-Irish who used Ireland as a means of escape from their responsibilities, rather than at the local Irish themselves. By contrast Louis MacNeice lambasted the country as a whole. MacNeice's views, like Bowen's, shifted dramatically after the fall of France. He had after all considered staying in Ireland in the winter of 1939. Living in England from January 1941, he began by asking for England's indulgence:

I have no wish now to bring up the undying (though Chameleonic) Irish Question but I would ask you to remember that the feeling in Éire is now predominantly pro-British (though still opposed to participation in the War), that the pro-German minority is extremely small and de Valera's position is agonisingly difficult. Those who propose the application of the strong hand to Éire are forgetting their history.

But a year later MacNeice wrote perhaps the most heartfelt indictment of Ireland's introverted stance:

The neutral island facing the Atlantic,
The neutral island in the heart of man,
Are bitterly soft reminders of the beginnings
That ended before the end began.

Look into your heart, you will find a County Sligo,
A Knocknarea with for navel a cairn of stones,
You will find the shadow and sheen of a moleskin mountain
And a litter of chronicles and bones.

Look into your heart, you will find fermenting rivers,
Intricacies of gloom and glint,

You will find such ducats of dream and great doubloons of ceremony
As nobody today would mint.

But then look eastward from your heart, there bulks
A continent, close, dark, as archetypal sin,
While to the west off your own shores the mackerel
Are fat – on the flesh of your kin.

MacNeice's anger at the make-believe he saw at the root of Irish isolationism was palpable, as he bitterly pointed out the human cost of
Ireland's decision. Ireland's proudly vaunted self-sufficiency was, for
him, no more than a symptom of her self-absorption. What is more,
MacNeice evoked the self-entrancement in terms that recall Yeatsian
myth-mongering, not only in the swipe at Sligo, Yeats's imaginative
home, but in the bankrupt coupling of 'ceremony' and 'dream' – two
images deeply rooted in the senior poet's creative lexicon. Yeats's
mythical re-creation of Ireland has overwhelmed realism and responsibility, MacNeice suggests, in yet another reprise of the idea of Ireland
as caught in a world of childish imagining. The poem constantly hints
at circularity and self-enclosedness – in the intertwined beginnings and
endings, in the hilltop cairn, the navel-gazing, the ducats and doubloons. (Could there be an echo of de Valera's famous comment that
when he wanted to find out what the Irish people were thinking he had
only to look into his own heart?) In its narcissism, Ireland endlessly
loops around itself, obsessed with a history that might appear rich, but
has now become dead and arid. The Irish imagine themselves secure
on their cut-off island, but if they would only raise their eyes for a
moment, they would find themselves at the centre of a momentous
battle.

MacNeice opened his poem by hinting at the edenic traits of neutrality – in an ideal world, to be dispassionate might be the optimum state.
But now that the phoney war had ended, and France had fallen, the
time for standing aside was past. When 'Neutrality' was published in
Springboard in 1944 it was preceded by another poem, in which
MacNeice inveighed against the mindset of the moral purist, the man
whose capacity for commitment is paralysed by 'the permanent bottle-
neck of his highmindedness'. Deceived by self-serving declarations of
principle Ireland had, in MacNeice's account, lapsed into culpability.
The suggestions of profiteering, and – more gruesomely – of cannibal-
ism, in the final image of the feasting fish, underscores the horror of the

result. (If rumours of selling fuel to U-boats turned out to have been unfounded, they may have sprung from stories – which Robert Fisk argues are almost certainly true – of fishermen in the West selling their catches to U-boat commanders.) In a macabre parody of self-sufficiency, MacNeice indicted Ireland for feeding off the harvest of corpses produced by neutrality.

Others worried about feeding too. As both the British and the Americans were keen to point out, the ships that were being torpedoed in the Atlantic were also carrying Irish supplies. Due to the dearth of Irish ocean-going vessels, Irish trade was reliant on British shipping and on the protection of the Royal Navy – a fact repeatedly stressed in the British press. Food and fuel supplies depended on the convoys that were so badly in need of greater security – a situation which even those who most strongly supported the Irish government's line on the ports found it hard to take pride in. As Deputy Cole from Cavan argued in the Dáil, 'At the present time we are lying low. We are living, so to speak, on the lives of men who have taken risks in order to feed us.'

Cole made his comment during a long and acrimonious debate on the ports which was initiated by James Dillon in July 1941, after nearly a year of severe shipping losses. There were very few public critics of neutrality inside Ireland during the war. Dillon was the exception, a Fine Gael TD who eventually resigned over the policy of neutrality and sat as an Independent. Dillon's case for a modification of the policy of strict impartiality was a self-proclaimed 'Christian' one, based on the need to defeat Nazi tyranny in the name of persecuted Christianity. He argued trenchantly against what he termed 'indifferent neutrality' – in other words a policy which pretended indifference to the moral issues at stake in the war.

Dillon had first queried the relationship between neutrality and 'indifference' during the debate over the Emergency Powers Bill at the outbreak of war. The term was picked up by politicians and journalists sympathetic to the Allies right through the conflict. Hubert Butler, for example, used it in an article published in *The Bell* a few weeks before the July 1941 debate. Butler supported the policy of neutrality, arguing that it should be understood as a positive and principled stance against totalitarianism – the way Ireland chose to fight the war. Yet he became disillusioned by the cultural and, he implied, moral isolation he encountered on his return to Ireland in the autumn of 1940: 'Just as our island is physically protected by the sea, there is an ocean of indifference and xenophobia to guard our insularity and protect us from foreign entanglements.' Great cultures, he argued, 'have always arisen from the interaction of diverse societies', and indeed Irish culture and literature had become a significant ingredient of European intellectual life, through the influence of writers such as Shaw and Joyce. Yet perversely, Ireland was labouring under the delusion that it could go it alone: 'Today we are cut off completely from the outer world, and between north and south, between cities and provinces, barriers are rising. The war has forced on us a cultural self-sufficiency more complete than the most fervent separatist could have imposed by law.' Butler's attack on an Irish 'ocean of indifference' was born of personal experience of the refugee crisis on the continent. Like MacNeice, he suggested that Ireland's physical isolation was both symptom and cause of the 'indifference' that protected Irish citizens from the fellow feeling he found lacking. He was accusing Irish society of having allowed the political logic of neutrality to slip into an ethical stance of blank impartiality.

It is possible that Butler's piece encouraged Dillon's public attack on the government. The debate in the Dáil on 17 July 1941 was one of the very few occasions during the war when the conflict was openly discussed in terms of justice and morality – both the moral claims of the belligerents and the moral duty of the Irish state. James Dillon began the debate by arguing that the policy of neutrality was 'not in the true interests, moral or material, of the Irish people'. It was a policy of 'dishonour', because it refused to acknowledge the moral claim of the Allies: 'I say that it is not doubt as to the right and wrong of the moral issues in this struggle that deters us from making the right decision now. It is fear of the German blitz that deters us.' He was supported by another TD, Henry Dockrell who insisted that 'there are a great many people who feel that in this struggle there is a moral issue involved', and asked, 'Does anybody think that the present policy adopted by one of the belligerent Powers on the high seas is a moral policy and one that should be defended?' Dillon's rhetoric of dishonour and cowardice clearly echoed that of the American Irish Defense Association, whose March 1941 cable to de Valera called upon him to protect the Atlantic 'lifeline of civilisation'. Dillon went on to advocate the need for risk-taking in order to prevent 'the Nazi attempt to cut the lifeline between the United States and Britain'. He used the notion of an 'Atlantic lifeline' three times in his speech, suggesting that his approach was in part modelled on propaganda stemming from the United States.

The debate changed no minds, but it did enable clear and unambiguous lines to be drawn. To Dillon's argument that the moral issues at stake in the war required Ireland to respond, Irish politicians presented an all-but-united front. The bare mention of the fact that Britain required the use of Irish naval and air bases caused one deputy to explode with rage: 'I say the Deputy should be removed out of the House. I will put him out [–] quick, the corner-boy. If he does not shut his [–] mouth we will shut it for him.' Leaders of Dillon's own party quickly denounced him, arguing that the government's duty was first of all to the stability and security of the country. In one of his least inspiring moments, the Fine Gael leader W. T. Cosgrave came close to arguing for a moral equivalence between the two sides: 'If we in this country take the line that the difference between the belligerents is democracy on the one hand and autocracy on the other, the sinlessness of the one and the guilt of the other, then I want to say that neither appeals to me. Democracy may have as many sins to its credit and may be as faulty a form of government as an autocracy.'

But the primary focus of the debate was on the question of responsibility. De Valera put it bluntly: 'I do not think we have got any responsibility for the present war.' For Fine Gael, Richard Mulcahy argued that Ireland bore no responsibility 'on moral grounds' for a situation which arose from the Treaty of Versailles, and therefore should feel no obligation 'to wipe up the mess that was partially at any rate created by themselves'. To a certain extent such statements were sleight of hand. Dillon was not arguing that Ireland was responsible for the war – this much was uncontested – but that the country had a duty to help the Allies in the fight against totalitarianism, although even he drew the line at sending troops abroad. But if no one could argue that the Irish bore responsibility for the war, what remained unanswered was whether refusing the use of the bases could be held responsible for deaths in the Atlantic.

One of the most striking aspects of this debate is the relatively late date at which it took place. By the summer of 1941 there had been a huge expansion of naval and air facilities in Northern Ireland. The naval base at Derry had been built up to serve in the absence of Lough Swilly. The pre-war airfield at Aldergrove was supplemented by airfields built further west, so that bombers could reach further out into the Atlantic. Coastal

Command established squadrons of bombers at Limavady and Ballykelly near Derry; their tasks were anti-submarine patrols and air cover over the western approaches. Although it would be some time before more advanced radar systems and longer-range aircraft would succeed in closing the Atlantic gap, helped by bases in the Azores and Iceland, the Derry bases certainly substituted very well for the out-of-date defence post on Lough Swilly. At the same time it was obvious to Irish citizens that the British were no longer using the southern approaches, meaning that Berehaven and Cobh would have been little use to the Allies. The southern waters had been mined, after liaison with Irish authorities, and British mines kept washing up on the eastern coast. Convoys were no longer seen off the coasts of Cork and Kerry, and there was a sudden increase in activity off the coasts of Donegal, Mayo, and Galway.

Yet the public defence against British accusations of betrayal seldom rested on the claim that the bases were not vital for the protection of the North Atlantic shipping lanes. The question of Irish liability was discussed at length at the inter-party Defence Conference; Aiken brought charts of the North Atlantic to meetings, and ministers speculated on how access to ports and airfields in Ireland might alter the balance of air power in favour of the RAF. But although the strategic importance of the new bases in Derry, and the fact that they diluted the case for the southern Irish bases, was highlighted in private, there was very little discussion of the Northern Irish bases in newspapers, and no mention at all in the July 1941 debate in the Dáil. In part this silence may have reflected an unwillingness to acknowledge the fact of partition. But it also suggests that British and American propaganda over the need for the ports set the agenda for the debate in Ireland.

* * *

The Atlantic Battle had a profound effect on Britain's war capabilities, and also on Britain's attitude to Ireland during the war. The impact of the war at sea on Ireland itself is harder to gauge. One practical consequence of the submarine warfare was that Irish shipping itself was at risk; despite the hopeful 'ÉIRE' signs painted on the hulls of Irish-registered ships, there were regular sinkings. Fifteen Irish-registered ships were mined, bombed or torpedoed during 1940, with fifty-nine dead, and the attacks continued the following year. On 17 August 1940 (ten days after the *Mohamed Ali El Kebir* went down) Germany designated a large area of the waters surrounding the British Isles (up to 350 miles west of Ireland) as a no-go area. Any ship in this area was subject to attack without warning, because it was understood as engaging in trade with Britain and therefore considered fair game. Irish ships had no option but to cross the blockaded area, and to trade with Britain. They also had to comply with the British Navicert system, which meant that vessels sailing between Ireland and countries other than Britain had to get clearance at a British port – a procedure regarded by Germany as 'unneutral' and therefore one that opened the way for attack. This was quite apart from the many Irish marine servicemen in British service, who were as liable as any other nationality to be shipwrecked or drowned.

On land the Atlantic Battle was blamed for shortages. Not only were goods at the bottom of the sea, but Churchill's policy of a trade squeeze on Ireland meant that it wasn't easy to find other sources of supply. Dáil and Seanad debates insistently returned to the effect of the Atlantic Battle on supplies. In December 1940 Lemass stressed the need for greater tillage of wheat, given the number of sinkings. A month later the assembly debated the effect of the sinkings on the petrol supply. In March it was the tea ration. By spring the following year the crisis of supplies was openly being discussed in terms of impending starvation. But public opinion stayed firm behind the refusal of the ports, as de Valera turned the problem of getting food and fuel into a matter of English intransigence.

The state sat precariously in the middle of a blockaded area – to that extent it was 'in' the war, regardless of the lease of the ports. If the majority of the Irish population was screened by censorship from open debate about the rights and wrongs of leasing the ports, they were nonetheless aware of British anger through the filtering down of newspaper stories, news from relatives in Britain, and – for those living in towns with a strong maritime tradition, such as Arklow and Galway – the perspective of those aboard the merchant ships. And the consequences of the war at sea bore down in a very practical way on those living around the coast. In the autumn of 1940, for example, when an average of three ships a day were lost, many went down within sight of the Irish coast, or a few hours' sailing distance away.

It would be hard to overestimate the importance of the idea of the coastline in the developing sense of Irish sovereignty during the war. Coastal areas had at one time been defined primarily in economic or cultural terms – particularly in the West – as poor 'congested districts' needing economic measures to ensure survival, or as remote areas requiring protection of Irish traditions of language and culture. Now the coast was defined as territory in itself, as limit and boundary to the state. The border with the North was repeatedly described as a 'frontier' between war and neutrality, but the coast was just as much a front, or front-line, in Irish defences. (Arguably too, coastal representations of the borders of the state had the advantage of evading the issue of partition.)

Early in the war the Irish government had set up a marine-defence establishment, as a branch of the defence forces. With responsibility for port control, and for patrolling Irish territorial waters, the men of the Maritime Inscription also took on the task of mine-laying, as well as shooting drifting mines. Wartime newsreels produced for the Irish market figured the maritime service prominently, even excessively given its small size. The films repeatedly showed footage of motor torpedo boats and detonation of mines, but also of coastal batteries and fortifications. Even when newsreel items focused on land-based elements of the defence forces, such as army manoeuvres, route marches and so on, the story of Irish defence was often framed by shots of the coast, and of coast-watchers' huts.

This maritime focus was natural during 1940, given the fear of invasion from the continent. One response to this fear was the inauguration of a system of coast-watching – rather like a modern version of the Martello towers that had ringed the Irish coast as lookout posts during the Napoleonic wars. The Marine and Coast-Watching Service was a land-based branch of the maritime force, specifically detailed to monitor signs of suspicious activity around the coast, and to provide early warning of invasion from any direction. The coast-watchers' task was to monitor the borders of the Irish State – to be alert to infringements of the integrity of the state not only from the sea but also from the air.

However, despite the symbolic importance of the coast, at the beginning of the war there were repeated complaints in the Dáil about the cost and uselessness of the coast-watching service:

All round our coast, numbers of untrained country lads – picked by minor Volunteer officers because of their political leanings – are being paid at the rate of 30/- or £2 a week, and planted like palm trees on the tops of hills overlooking the sea – scanning the horizon with naked eye for, I presume, enemies of our neutrality. When they imagine they see an aeroplane or seaplane they walk five or six miles to the nearest telephone box to communicate the news to headquarters. Of course they do not know the nationality of the machine, nor does it matter a bit as nothing can be done about it or will be done about it. This whole business of having these youths wasting their time staring out to sea is farcical, and is a scandalous waste of public money.

The makeshift nature of the posts, and the poor provision of equipment, encouraged the belief that coast-watching was a do-it-yourself activity, not to be taken seriously. The coast-watchers were initially stationed in eighty-eight tents placed on strategic headlands around the coast. Advertisements for binoculars and field glasses were posted in local papers, in an attempt to provide the look-out posts with something approximating to the necessary equipment. In the first few months some posts were even without bicycles. The outfit was again ridiculed during a vote on increasing defence force funds in April 1940, after the fall of Denmark:

What is the Coast-Watching Service? What are they watching through? What are they watching from? What are they watching for? If they see anything coming what are they going to do? It is nonsense to have a man here and there along the coast who, if a fleet is arriving, will telephone or signal. To whom?

The coast-watchers' tents were eventually replaced with concrete huts. The sign 'ÉIRE', and the number of the post, was cut in letters thirty feet high on the ground, as near as possible to each station – ostensibly a warning to aircraft, the signs also served as navigational aids to Allied airmen seeking their bases in Northern Ireland. Two years into the war each post was equipped with a bicycle (or occasionally a motorcycle), binoculars, charts of Allied and Axis planes, and priority telephone access to the regional Defence Force Centres, such as the barracks at Athlone or Renmore. In July 1940, for example, the *Western People* reported that engineers were working round the clock to lay telephone connections between Belmullet and coast-watching stations at Faulmore, Annagh Head and Glenlarra in Mayo. Despite long lines of communication, particularly from the western coast, the coast-watchers could boast that most information they sent on was only fifteen minutes old by the time it reached Headquarters in Dublin. The efficiency of the service was also helped by (British) radio transmitters installed at regional reporting centres, which broadcast unencoded messages to Dublin, and from Dublin and Cobh to Air Corps aircraft on patrol (and which could be intercepted by British patrols). Economic constraints continued to have an effect on their work, however. In the summer of 1943 requests were made in the Dáil for an increase in rations of tea, sugar and kerosene for the coast-watchers, who had, after all, to keep going at night. And the shortage of bicycle tyres and inner tubes was also proving a severe handicap.

Manned by volunteers chosen from the Local Defence Force, each post was serviced by a corporal and his team of seven or eight men; there were 750 coast-watchers in all. To maintain round-the-clock surveillance, two men worked together in eight- to ten-hour shifts, one patrolling the coast, and one manning the telephone. Sightings of aircraft, in particular, were immediately phoned through, so that the flight paths of Allied or Axis planes could be tracked, and if necessary AA fighters alerted. It was a coast-watcher in Wexford, for example, who confirmed that the plane that later dropped the bombs on the North Strand in Dublin was a German machine. Coast-watchers also proved their worth by combating claims of fuelling U-boats, and through the more low-profile work of recovering wreckage. As part of their routine work the coast-watchers recorded, in a series of detailed logbooks, 'everything that moved on or above the sea', including ships and aircraft, drifting mines, floating cargo – even, on one occasion, a message in a bottle from a German captive on board an Allied ship. It was their job to alert the voluntary coastal lifesaving teams if they saw a ship going down, to haul in drifting lifeboats – occasionally bearing survivors of bombed and torpedoed ships – and to land and log any dead bodies.

In the second half of 1940 more than two hundred bodies were recovered from Irish coastal waters, though the majority were found not by those manning the look-out posts but by local fishermen. On 10 August 1940 alone, fifteen bodies were recovered on the coasts of Sligo, Donegal and Mayo; the next day a further twelve were logged. Twenty-seven bodies in two days was a high but not unparalleled number. Bodies were generally picked up out of the sea by fishermen, or discovered on rocks and beaches and dragged up to the high-water mark, to prevent them being washed out to sea again before they could be removed. In the case of John George Wallace of the *Mohamed Ali El Kebir*, for example, the body came ashore in a very inaccessible place near Glencolumbcille in Donegal. It was found by Francis Gillespie of Meenasillagh, who was a member of the LSF. Gillespie recalled that they had to take a coffin in below the cliff by boat but, once full, they were unable to get it out again. Wallace was therefore buried on site above the high-water mark but the coffined body was later washed away in a storm.

Gillespie's later account suggests that the official logs of recovered bodies fail to give a proper sense of the atmosphere on the north-western coast: 'it was a terrible time, many bodies were seen floating near the coast, but it was not possible to recover them.' A report in the *Western People* on 10 August 1940 corroborates this: 'It is believed that about 100 dead bodies are floating in the sea off Inniskea island, on the Western Mayo Coast. The sea is so rough that the bodies cannot be recovered.' In one case a body floated for a week against jagged rocks in a particularly difficult spot before a rowing boat could get close enough for men to tie a rope around the corpse and lift it above the cliff. A week later seventeen more had been pulled from the sea (many of them casualties of the *Arandora Star*, a ship that had been transporting interned Italians and Germans to Canada), but newspaper reports commented on the persistent rumours of many more yet unrecovered.

The local gardaí recorded all available information on the recovered bodies: when and where they were found, details of the state of decomposition, length of time in the water, any identifying marks, and details of any property found on them, including their clothing. They then arranged for them to be buried by the Home Assistance or Relieving Officer, who worked for the Board of Health and Public Assistance. The loss of the British trawler, *Rendlesham*, off Cape Clear Island, County Cork, on 5 November 1940 (the day of Churchill's House of Commons attack on Ireland) provides a fairly typical example. There were five survivors of the attack, who were taken to Skibbereen hospital and later returned to Britain. Six of the dead were taken by another British trawler to Milford Haven. Over the next weeks the sea slowly gave back the dead. British currency was washed up on the rocks; cigarette lighters, keys, and a further three bodies were recovered. The Skibbereen Garda Report of 5 December 1940 records the following statement by Rev. Patrick O'Donovan, CC, and Cornelius Cadogan, both of Cape Clear. The two men brought a body to the mainland on 2 December and reported to gardaí in the village of Baltimore:

The body was taken from the water by Patrick Cadogan and Kieran Cotter, Cummer, Cape Clear. The latter were out fishing at the time and noticed sea-gulls on the surface of the water. On proceeding to the spot the body was observed, floating. They took the body into the boat and had it later taken to

Baltimore. The head, legs and hands were missing. There was no clothing of any kind or nothing which would assist in identification. The body was that of a man.

The Public Health authority was informed, and the body was buried by the Relieving Officer near Baltimore.

Early on in the hostilities the system worked on the assumption that a coroner would conduct an inquest on each body recovered, but as the coroner for the Letterkenny District in Donegal argued in late October 1940, this was simply not practical. If one difficulty was the state of some of the bodies – often little more than decomposed body parts – another was the sheer number of corpses. The coroner admitted he had been flouting the regulations for some time:

The local doctor examines the body and makes a report to me and I issue a death certificate. I did this because it would be a physical impossibility for me to hold Inquests on all these bodies, by reason of the fact that a large number are often washed up on the same day at widely different parts of the coast including the islands. For example on 19th inst. 3 bodies were washed up at Cruit Island, one on the mainland at Kincasslagh, one near Derrybeg at Gweedore, one at Gola island off the Gweedore coast and a Vice Admiral at Tory Island. Tory is 9 miles off the coast and sometimes it isn't approachable for days so that you can see that even had I a seaplane at my disposal I couldn't possibly do the work.

Many of these bodies may have been casualties of the *Manchester Brigade*, torpedoed off Aran Mor on 27 September 1940. But the coroner also pointed out that thirty-five bodies had been washed up in his district in August and September. The argument was strongly put that medical reports should suffice in cases of obvious war casualties whose bodies could then be interred on the authority of the local doctor. In March 1941 the Department of Justice sent out a circular allowing coroners to dispense with inquests when individuals had died outside the state, and as the result of belligerent action. This still left the problem of airmen who crashed on Irish soil: such deaths technically occurred within the borders of the Irish state and therefore an inquest was in principle still necessary. By 1 April 1941, coroners were informed that they could dispense with an inquest in those cases too, unless it took a long time for the crash victims to die, 'as such airmen are in State custody at the time of their deaths'. In effect this was a debate on what degree of legal responsibility the Irish government had to take for these Atlantic dead.

It was not only pressure of time but also the financial strain placed on cash-strapped local authorities that encouraged the Department of Justice to do away with the need for inquests. On 24 August 1940 the *Derry People and Tirconaill News*, a Northern-based weekly, reported on the cost to the Donegal Board of Health of burying bodies washed ashore. The burial itself could amount to four pounds per body, and an inquest usually cost five pounds. Who should pay these expenses? Certainly the local inhabitants of Donegal could not be held responsible for creating the 'mess' of the war, as the Fine Gael TD Richard Mulcahy put it in the July 1946 debate, but as far as the Atlantic battle went they became, by default, responsible for cleaning it up. In late September the Mayo Board of Health put on record the need for additional funds to be given to Home Assistance Officers, pointing out that in the absence of a government grant, the burial expenditure 'would weigh heavily on the maritime counties'.

There were also numerous practical difficulties arising from the state of the bodies themselves. Dr Donnelly of Achill applied to the Mayo Board of Health for a supply of rubber gloves with which to handle them. He also recommended that a supply of ready-made coffins should be made available, since it was often many hours before a coffin could be got, and the men of the LSF were left 'standing by for several hours'. One difficulty was that larger coffins than usual were required, as the bodies were generally wearing lifebelts. (The Board agreed that while an ordinary coffin cost 19s. 11d., an additional 5s. 1d. would be allowed from public funds for the larger coffins.) Another doctor applied to the Sligo Board of Health requesting better coffins: 'They have to be carried a distance sometimes to the local cemetery, and you understand what it means to carry a decomposed corpse in a bad coffin.' The Board agreed on the need for well-made coffins without cracks, and suggested that the joins should be sealed with pitch. A further difficulty arose from the fact that several of the smaller coastal graveyards were full up, and some of the bodies therefore had to be transported a long way. In addition to the repeated requests for additional remuneration to offset the increased workload, and the need for further funds for coffins and gravediggers, numerous procedural difficulties had to be hurriedly ironed out as the bodies kept arriving – was it permissible to bury a body outside a graveyard? Should they be buried in strangers' plots and if so would more become available? What was the correct procedure for handing over the body for burial? At what point did the guard's authority cede to the coroner and then to the Home Assistance Officer? Which identification tag (red or green) should be buried with the body and which forwarded to the consular officials? Who was to record details of burials so that relatives could later be informed? Could identification be used to claim money back from the consuls? Should a special account be kept for the burials, in order that money could be later reclaimed?

Finding, identifying and burying the bodies was only the beginning. Gardaí were required to inform the local registrar of deaths, to arrange for death certificates of those identifiable, and to file a report to their superiors, which was then forwarded to the Department of External Affairs. They were responsible for sending on smaller items of property that washed ashore, such as keys, unposted letters, passports, papers and foreign currency. Some casualties who had not been long in water retained metal identification tags, and even occasionally papers, showing when and where they had enlisted. In so far as it was possible to determine the nationality of a corpse, it was the Department's task to notify the relevant national authority in Dublin. Justices liaised with the British Representative's Office, the Dutch Consul General, the German Envoy, the Belgian Envoy, on questions of identity, property, burial, and eventually the upkeep of graves.

As the war at sea progressed the system of reporting and burying bodies became more efficient, and more codified. At the beginning guards tended to write long, often moving, descriptions of the state of bodies, and the process of recovery. A year into the battle, however, they had developed a well-organised system of reporting, including a form on which they could enter the place and date on which the body was found, and by whom, the date gardaí were informed, the date the body was buried, and foreign representatives informed, and so on. However those who actually found and dealt with the bodies may have felt, the development of an official, matter-of-fact language of reportage helped to contain the horror.

But official liaison did not preclude direct correspondence. Garda stations all along the western coast, but particularly in the north-west, regularly received mail from distraught relatives searching for news of sons or husbands washed ashore, or seeking more personal information than was given in official reports from the British Navy. After the *Manchester Brigade* went down off the coast of Donegal, for example, the gardaí in Dungloe received several letters from men and women whose relatives had not been reported found, asking whether any further bodies had been recovered, and citing distinguishing marks that might help to identify them. There were requests too for precise details of the place and manner of burial – so that the Relieving Officer or local men involved in the burial might be asked to draw maps of graveyards to send on, or to describe the plot ('up a short track, through the gate and ten paces to the left').

The direct correspondence also went the other way. There were certainly cases when locals went through the property of the dead before the doctor or guard arrived. On one occasion, for example, a Scottish widow wrote to the British Representative explaining that she had been informed by letter from Donegal of the recovery of her husband's body at Fanad Head in November 1940 – much to the consternation of the local gardaí, since when they had come across the body it was naked and had nothing by which to identify it.

If this was a case of petty theft, others were not above more avert attempts to profit from the fruits of battle. At the end of April 1941 an American Air Transport auxiliary pilot, Robert Glenn Smith, was killed when the ship on which he was travelling to Europe, the SS *Nerissa*, was sunk off Galway. His body was washed ashore at Kilronan in July 1941. He was buried on Aran and a leather wallet containing two five-dollar bills, a snapshot, a driving licence, an Airman Rating record, and a medical certificate was sent by External Affairs to the American Consulate. Sometime later his widow in Indiana received a letter from Dara Connelly, a native of Killearney, on Aran.

Dear Sir or Madam,
    I and some fishermen of the North Aran Island, Galway Bay, Ireland, found the body of a Robert Glenn Smith, Commercial Air Pilot, ashore here. We secured a coffin and buried his body in the local graveyard. His description – height, six feet. Age 31 years. Blonde hair. We hope to hear from his people.

The letter included a postscript: 'Sir: I hope you will do your best for me as I got a great trouble.'

As the local Relieving Officer put it, when questioned about the affair, Connelly and the fishermen had been paid £2 10s. by the Health Board and had therefore already been 'amply rewarded' for their trouble. It is probably no accident that similar letters to British widows have not survived. It was not only that an Irishman seeking payment for burial of a corpse would have got short shrift from many in Britain because of the refusal to lease the ports. There was also a belief that American relatives were more likely to come up with generous rewards – this confidence stretched back at least as far as the torpedoing of the passenger liner *Lusitania* off Kinsale in 1915, and the stories of rewards from US families for the recovery of bodies. But valuables such as rings, watches, and currency did go astray from bodies of every nationality – scarcely surprising given the extreme poverty of many of those who found and buried the bodies.

If this was the darker side of profit from the war at sea – and the attitude attacked in MacNeice's poem – a more legitimate way of gaining revenue from submarine warfare was through gathering wreckage. The Atlantic Ocean was, month by month, becoming littered with American arms and food destined for Europe. Along with the bodies of sailors and airmen, and occasional civilians, more welcome bounty was washed up on Europe's western shores. Bales of rubber and of cotton, barrels of oil, timber – all commanded a small fee if gathered in and handed over to the Receiver of Wreck. The rate of remuneration for the fishermen who went out in small boats to try to manoeuvre this cargo came in for a good deal of criticism, however. Questions were asked in the Dáil. The Dunlop tyre factory in Cork eventually came to an agreement whereby they paid salvagers directly for rubber, substantially increasing the profit to fishermen and guaranteeing a regular if small supply for the manufacture of bicycle

A letter sent from Canada to Great Britain, 'Recovered from the Sea', and resealed in Dublin, 23 July 1940.

tyres. Other cargo might not be sold on at all, but used to alleviate local shortages. In one strange story by Margaret Barrington, the ship-wrecked men themselves become the prize, dragged out of the sea by desperate women in a remote fishing village, their own men all either dead or emigrated.

The awkward alliance of gruesome and welcome finds was discussed in local newspapers:

Every storm which has blown from the north or north-west for many moons has been a signal for alertness on the part of dwellers by our northern Mayo and Sligo coasts. There is always the chance that something of value may be washed on to our shores, and up to now almost every conceivable class of wreckage, from a ghastly dead sailor to a packet of wax, from a ship's bridge to a barrel of oil, has come ashore and been retrieved by our unofficial watchers. Not all of the finds, I understand, have been reported to the gardaí or Customs Officials, for now and then the shore-searchers have annexed a little of the flotsam as their own particular perquisite.

While on holiday in Donegal, the Belfast poet and museum curator John Hewitt overheard a local complaining that 'If the Germans don't sink a few more ships the people here will have to be buried without coffins.' It's a comment that nicely illustrates the warped economy of profit and loss, for the timber – desperately scarce in areas of Donegal and Mayo – was also used for burying bodies washed ashore. Who, then, were 'the people here' who would have to do without coffins?

A short story by Peadar O'Donnell entitled 'Why Blame the Seagulls?', published in the third issue of *The Bell* in December 1940, turns on the mixed benefits and costs in this economy of wreck. The story describes the sudden appearance of a ship battling the waves off the Donegal coast. It turns out to have been holed and abandoned, but kept afloat by its cargo of timber. If O'Donnell was writing from experience (he owned a cottage on the Donegal coast), the ship might well have been the *Elmbank*, which sailed for Belfast from Nova Scotia with cargo of timber on 19 September 1940, and was torpedoed two days later during a particularly bad few days of submarine warfare. The crew all got away to the lifeboats while the commander of U-99, Otto Kretschmer, spent several frustrating hours, and all his ammunition, attempting to get the vessel to sink in spite of the buoyancy of the timber. However, the *Derry People* of 7 September 1940 suggests another possible model for the story:

Every island off the coast of Donegal has had bodies washed ashore or some kind of wreck from torpedoed vessels, such as lifeboats, ships stores, timber etc., declared a highly placed revenue officer to me . . .

The ten-thousand ton Greek vessel, *Leonidas of Vanimas*, which was torpedoed fore and aft in the Atlantic, was kept afloat by its timber cargo, and is now on the way to the Clyde, being towed by British tugs who found the vessel abandoned some miles off the Donegal coast.

In O'Donnell's story, a jubilant party of Donegal fishermen row out to strip the vessel of its load: 'The war had sent us a prize and the islands must grab it. Timber! Timber for the world! And timber is flour, meal, tobacco, tea. Everything.' But their relief and pleasure is short-lived as they discover, under a swarm of seagulls, the floating body of a young man. (Garda reports often noted seagulls as one of the signals of the presence of a body, as well as describing the damage that gulls inflict: 'the head was damaged beyond recognition, evidently by birds or fishes'.) As O'Donnell tells it, the body of the young man ('some woman's son') brings the war 'home' to them:

. . . the war had struck us its blow. No man now stands on the cliff-top and looks out, without dread, over the wide wastes of the bay for sign of things floating. For now and then we see that cluster of seagulls. And underneath, that darkness bobbing. It is getting so that we throw stones at seagulls wherever we see them, we who looked at seagulls as part of the joy of the day. And yet, why blame the seagulls? What of the lights that had gone out before ever they picked the eyes out of that up-tilted head . . . Now you know our misery, those young faces with empty eye-sockets, up-tilted, and seagulls screaming.

Any idea of blame here falls on the war itself, rather than on the scavengers that act according to nature. The fishermen drive the seagulls away but are also twinned with them in the sense that they too depend for their survival on the sea. The activities of salvaging and scavenging share more than a number of letters.

Writers such as Bowen and MacNeice and politicians such as James Dillon suggested that Ireland was turning its back on the deaths in the Atlantic, and also on the moral cost to Ireland of maintaining a position of 'indifferent neutrality'. They portrayed the Irish as refusing to see the cost of withholding the ports, and implied that knowledge of the cost in human lives had been suppressed by a combination of self-delusion and censorship. O'Donnell's Donegal fishermen, by contrast, are blameless and powerless in equal measure. There is nothing else they can do but accept the unpleasant task of retrieving and burying the detritus of the war. As a member of the Sligo Health Board put it, in a debate about coffins, 'the sea gives up its dead and the people have to deal with it. This is a neutral country and we treat all of them the same.'

Part of the reason for the accusation of indifference may have been due to the lack of public discussion, at a political level, of the human tragedy of the Atlantic Battle. Despite the well-organised system that grew up around the recovery of bodies and property, and which involved considerable numbers of people, including coast-watchers, guards, doctors, coroners, health-board officials, and officials of the Department of Justice and External Affairs, not to mention the many ordinary civilians who found bodies or salvaged wreck, it was not until July 1942 that any official recognition of the task of recovery and burying bodies was made in the Dáil, during a debate on financing the defence forces – and by this time the incidence of bodies washed ashore had markedly decreased. (This was because submarine warfare was then taking place further out in the middle of the Atlantic – and bodies were no longer making it to Ireland.) Even then the debate focused on the problem of the upkeep of the graves rather than the recovery of the bodies.

This silence over the bodies was in marked contrast to the in-depth and protracted discussion of the problem in the local press in Donegal, Sligo and Mayo. Small items on the recovery of particular bodies were commonly included in the area news of each county, under titles such as 'Two More Bodies Washed Ashore' or 'More Gruesome Finds on Beach'. *The Mayo News* of 21 September offers a fairly typical example in terms of tone and detail: 'The body of a British naval rating was washed ashore at Stockport, Belmullet, on Sunday. The remains, which were very much decomposed, with a foot and hand missing, were buried in Termoncarra Cemetary on Sunday evening. This is the thirty-second burial of war victims in Erris during the past two months'. But as increasing numbers of bodies began to arrive, more and more column inches were given over to the issues of recovery and burial. During the period in which the victims of the *Arandora Star* were being washed up, the *Western People* gave half a broadsheet page to the problem each week.

The national press very rarely picked up such stories, however – and when they did so, it was generally when there seemed to be evidence that the body was German rather than British. For example, the *Irish Independent* of 1 August 1941 included under 'Interesting Items', 'Body Recovered From Sea. A body found at Dursey Island, Co. Cork, is believed to be that of a German airman. A notebook found contained entries in German.' Except when large numbers of survivors were landed in Ireland, such as the survivors of the SS *Athenia* who were brought to Galway in September 1939, for the most part national newspaper coverage of the Atlantic Battle was restricted to a brief record of the tally of sinkings and air strikes in the Atlantic, including rival British and German accounts, and nothing else.

The absence of the washed-up bodies in the Dáil and the national press, compared with the extensive local coverage of the issue, is a puzzle. Was the censorship less effective with regard to local papers? Or were the bodies seen as a purely local problem, not meriting national coverage? Was it simply not expedient to discuss the problem of funding the burial of foreign corpses? No doubt the silence was due to a combination of all these reasons, and there may well have been more self-censorship than official censorship of the news of the bodies. What is clear is that the level of public discussion of the bodies is no guide to the levels of public awareness of them. If local discussions, letters and recollections – not to mention the images of bodies which appear in the creative literature – are anything to go by there was intense, if short-lived, concern over all the aspects of the wreck.

The Atlantic Battle affected coastal communities directly, but indirectly news of the wreck filtered through to the rest of the country. The disproportionate amount of newsreel focused on the marine services was perhaps one sign of a more general anxiety. Another was the large number of pictorial representations of the Atlantic Battle that regularly appeared during the worst period for Ireland (before the battle moved further west), in all sorts of publications from children's annuals to *Ireland's Own*. Although photographs were often censored during the war, drawings were not. For example, each issue of *Dublin Opinion* featured, alongside the small cartoons and sketches, a full page 'serious' pen-and-ink drawing. It is remarkable how many of these drawings during the early war years were of the Battle of the Atlantic. They included pictures of dramatic rescues, such as that of the survivors of a ship who reached the Kerry coast in May 1941: the caption read, 'The survivors reached land after eleven days.' But there were also drawings of empty lifeboats, planes shot down, ships in trouble in sight of the coast, dog-fights over the sea watched from an Irish headland, young women praying for the safety of sailors in trouble. The politics of the ports may have been a closed debate, but not the tragedy occurring within sight of the shore.

5

Invisible Enemies

Probably the most celebrated treatment of the war years by an Irish writer is Elizabeth Bowen's novel, *The Heat of the Day*. Written at the end of the war and set in London, it tells the story of Stella Rodney, a woman Bowen's age, who is informed by a shady character in the opening pages that her lover – whom she met during the 'heady autumn' of 1940 – is spying for the Germans. Despite her qualms about shadowing her lover, Stella turns spy in order to discover whether or not he is a traitor, so that pretty soon all the major characters are trading in information. It is a story, in part, about the value of intelligence, about the power that accrues to those who give information, and to those who withhold it – and the difficulty of telling one from the other. The putative spy and would-be spy-catcher are both called Robert, for example, and Stella is offered the choice of becoming the second Robert's lover in exchange for the freedom of the first.

If one biographical source for this exploration of betrayal and allegiance lies in Bowen's wartime affair with Canadian diplomat Charles Ritchie, another is her intelligence-gathering work in Ireland for the Dominions Office. In her letter to Virginia Woolf in July 1940 Bowen described the work that she felt was 'wanted' in Ireland: 'I hope I shall be some good; I do feel it's important.' Talking, mostly to the 'political people', meant not only listening to their views but also trying to have some influence on them. And if she was presenting a line, so was everybody else. Bowen was only too aware that the conditions that called for intelligence-gathering were also those that encouraged the dissemination of lies and rumours. Espionage and listening in (the attempt to diagnose opinion), propaganda and disinformation (the attempt to influence opinion) – these were activities that fed off each other, and pervaded the whole of a society during war. 'You did not know what you might be tuning in to, you could not say what you might not be picking up: affected, infected you were at every turn.'

Infiltration was a concern for all countries affected by the war. But it was a particular problem for neutral states, since they were home to representatives of both sides. The Irish security services were alert to the possibility of foreign spies – either Allied or Axis – but they also had to reckon with the likelihood of 'fifth columnists' fomenting insurrection at home. As de Valera insisted in May 1940, 'danger threatens now from within as well as from without.' That summer both pro-German and pro-Allied groups stepped up their game, in an atmosphere of increasing fear and suspicion. The mounting pressure on Britain led Allied sympathisers in Ireland to try all kinds of ways of supporting Britain; intelligence work was just one of them. Tension mounted too for the much smaller number of Axis sympathisers, who also attempted to broaden their support at this critical moment. It must have looked to them as though there was a real possibility that British rule in Northern Ireland could be overthrown. A more amorphous problem was that of sympathisers with either the Axis or Allied cause attempting to drum up support, spreading rumours, or seeding propaganda. Internment was intended to deal with the worst threats, and censorship with milder breaches of neutrality. But policing non-neutral allegiance was tricky.

For a start there were the Irish citizens who were now members of the British armed services. The numbers leaving the country to join up were a problem, but so were those returning. Early on the government introduced an Emergency regulation banning wearing the uniform of a foreign army. At the beginning of the war the regulation applied in practice only to British forces personnel on leave in Ireland, though it would later also affect American forces stationed in the North, who had to change into civilian clothing when crossing for short holidays or the odd night out in a pub south of the border. One of the most haunting images of Irish neutrality is surely that of soldiers shedding their uniforms at the border. British forces quickly adapted to the Irish regulation by allowing Irishmen to keep civilian clothing with them while training or on service in Britain, or by supplying them with non-uniform kit ('Going on leave, you went to the quartermaster who issued you with a suit – I had my own'). For those returning from the battlefield, and who therefore had no civilian clothing, piles of jackets and trousers were supplied at Holyhead to enable them to merge quietly with the rest of the population. Ireland was host to a silent and invisible army. Nonetheless uniform smuggling was common – it was a particular coup to unveil British uniforms at family functions and weddings of members of the Forces on leave in Ireland.

There were also cases of uniform smuggling in reverse. Early on in the recruitment drive it was decided that Northern Irish citizens might join the permanent force in the south, but they were not eligible to become members of the local defence forces, 'as Volunteers retain their uniforms and certain equipment as personal issues'. The fear was that nationalist residents in the northern border counties might antagonise their neighbours if they were seen decked out as Local Security Force volunteers – they would, after all, be parading their neutral status within a country at war. The idea of Northern residents joining the Southern Security Force was particularly delicate because the LSF focused on intelligence gathering and surveillance. Indeed it was LSF members who tended to report on Southern residents who were members of the Northern forces. A garda report from Donegal offers one example:

Members of the Local Security Force in Castlefin area have been keeping the movements of certain persons from that Sub-District, suspected of being members of the 'B' Specials, under observation for some time past and on Monday, 15th July 1940, the following was observed.

On 15 July 1940, a member of the Local Security Force from Castlefin happened to be in the vicinity of Sion Mills, Co. Tyrone, and saw Samuel G. Hepburn and John W. Hepburn, Sessiaghallison, Castlefin, at 11 p.m. dressed in the uniform of the 'B' Specials and each carrying a rifle and the usual equipment of that Force. They were marching with other Specials on the road from the direction of Victoria Bridge towards Sion Mills. At Sion Mills RUC Barracks the party was dismissed and the two Hepburns, who are brothers, were seen entering the barracks with their rifles and equipment at about 11.30 p.m.

Our informant saw them again at about 12.30 a.m. on the 16/7/40. They were then dressed in the usual everyday clothes. Our informant then left Sion Mills and returned to this State and took cover at Clady Bridge, where he saw the Hepburns returning from Northern Ireland and cycling towards their homes . . .

The Hepburn brothers, it turned out, were twenty-one and twenty-two years old – young men bound to the defence of another country. This was not an isolated incident, as Dan Bryan of G2 admitted: 'I heard similar rumours from the Cavan–Monaghan area some time ago.' The concern was that neutrality would be compromised by such cases, and other more blatant breaches such as that of 'a person continuing to live in this country while being a member of the British

Forces in the Six County area'. De Valera's advice was to keep an eye on these characters, who might become 'a considerable nuisance and danger to us'.

At the heart of the danger lay the border – for long a political, now also a practical challenge. On the one hand the border was purely administrative – merely an 180-mile-long line drawn on the ground, one that ran athwart many more tangible phenomena, such as villages, farms, and even houses, main and branch railway lines, main and secondary roads, cart-tracks, telegraph and telephone communications. Many republicans refused to accept that it was there at all, and even Cecil Liddell of MI5 acknowledged in 1946, 'In spite of Partition, Ireland has remained to all intents and purposes, one country.' On the other hand, fears about the war spreading south encouraged reinforcement of the very frontier that the Southern state ultimately wanted to do away with.

Leakage was a problem for both the Irish and British authorities. Officially, a strict division obtained between North and South, and the contrast between the belligerence of one and the neutrality of the other made the separation increasingly rigid. Measures were stepped up to define the border more clearly. But the 'land frontier' proved impossible to close effectively from either side. After all, numerous villages and towns straddled it, and it was easy for individuals to cross. Border traffic of different kinds, both official and unofficial, proliferated. In addition to the numbers of Southern citizens who joined the forces in the North (the novelist Benedict Kiely recalled that the military barracks in Omagh was 'packed to the gates with Freestaters, as we still called them'), thousands of workers from the South commuted sometimes weekly, sometimes daily, to jobs in the dockyards of Derry and Belfast.

Although a permit system was supposed to regulate passage over the border, for much of the time it was perceived as unworkable – by April 1942 estimates were that about twenty thousand people crossed the border at recognised checkpoints each week. Anyone with work or family on the other side was allowed free access, and the British authorities found themselves with a major security headache, as Tom Harrisson reported for Mass Observation:

Enemy agents would hardly need to rely on overheard talk in Belfast, as there is a large Nationalist element working inside the Docks and with free access of a more direct sort. Many men from Éire now work in the area, especially in Haarlem and Wolff [sic] and in Short and Harland. Many of these men go regularly to and fro across the border. Many of the workers in the Dock area belong to Trades Unions in Éire, notably the Irish Transport and General Workers, a breakaway from Bevin's Transport and General Workers; these competitive unions have their respective meetings in Dublin and Belfast, delegates, shop stewards and permanent officials, in key positions for obtaining information, moving freely to and fro.

It is not suggested, of course, that these men do deliberately carry information. But there are plenty of indications that tongues almost automatically loosen in the neutral atmosphere of Éire, and that is where the agent can most safely and easily listen in and ask questions.

This problem of the *border* dominates the security set-up, naturally. Anyone with an identity card can go to and fro at will. A great many people, including serving officers and other ranks, do so. Not only those who live or have relatives in Éire, but thousands who go South for weekends or holidays away from the blackout. It is understood that the IRA and other elements have been inciting serving men to cross the border and desert.

In Derry the problems were, if anything, even worse: 'There is a constant to and fro, and at a Saturday night dance at Derry, where nearly all the men were soldiers or sailors, we estimated that nearly half the girls were from Éire.' The British authorities, disturbed by the possibility of leakage of intelligence, considered attempting to close the border on several occasions during the war, but as the MI5 report explained:

in the opinion of the Military and Civil Authorities in Northern Ireland, the Border could not be closed without large numbers of troops and the erection of the necessary obstructions would have led to serious civil disturbances. This meant that throughout the war, as far as the Security Service was concerned, the actual crossing of the Border into or out of Northern Ireland with its Naval, Military and Air establishments, dockyards and war factories, by persons resident in neutral Éire, could not be prevented or even controlled.

In fact, given the British need for manpower in the northern war industries, controls would have been counterproductive even if they had been feasible. The interchange continued (and MI5 concluded that the most effective way of dealing with it was with Irish cooperation). Workers from Éire lived a dual existence, inside and outside a country at war. And northern citizens found their statelet infiltrated by neutral outsiders. Given the unmanageable extent of this traffic,

British security services reluctantly decided the only option was to construct a 'ringed fence' round Ireland, north and south. After June 1940, new travel restrictions meant that all citizens, whether British or not, had to obtain a visa in Dublin or exit permit in Belfast before travelling to Britain. There were more restrictions on movement between Northern Ireland and the rest of Britain than within Ireland as a whole.

The constant movement of individuals between North and South reflected not simply personal choices, but the facts of economic geography. For the inhabitants of northern Donegal, for example, the obvious base for business was in Derry. Cattle dealers, auctioneers, timber merchants, ironmongers in neutral Ireland's remotest territory advertised in the newspapers and almanacs of the belligerent North. Small shops in the Northern border areas relied for trade on country dwellers in the South. Fears arose that these businesses might go under if, due to rationing, their usual customers were unable to buy provisions from them. In response, at the start of the war, the authorities handed out Northern Irish ration cards to 'Éireann citizens' living close to the frontier, who were used to doing their shopping in the North. The government had huge difficulties when it decided to collect them again in the summer of 1940. The round-up was ostensibly because of the need to conserve rations. But no doubt there was also a feeling, intensified after the blitzkrieg, that the treacherous neutrals should not benefit from their proximity to the war. Nonetheless, for shoppers (and smugglers) the border remained porous at countless points.

Trafficking was rife all along the divide, and numerous cases of petty smuggling were brought up before the district courts. The District Judge in Letterkenny, for example, became accustomed to dealing with cases such as a peddlar arrested for carrying second-hand clothes over the border, or a girl apprehended with a bag of sugar. In fact, it proved impossible to regulate this form of transaction – especially where, in places such as Belleek, the border actually bisected the town. Defendants could always claim that they were giving to a relative on the other side, rather than selling. And because smuggling into the North was not illegal in the South, some bizarre cases were heard. On several occasions people who felt they had been unfairly cheated out of their share of the profits from smuggling goods into the North brought their business partners up before the courts. One man from Dundalk, who had been cycling around the North selling blackberries illegally, and not getting paid for it, persuaded several witnesses from the North to cross the border and speak in court in aid of his claim against his employer. As his lawyer pointed out, they did so at some risk to themselves, since they were admitting involvement in an activity which was illegal in the North.

Batteries, candles, tins of cocoa, tea flowed steadily from the six to the twenty-six counties. Cattle were herded surreptitiously along unapproved roads. Butter, bacon, eggs and other produce were conveyed in the opposite direction. Boats rowed across Carlingford Lough after dark, laden with meat and eggs going north, bringing tea and sugar on the return voyage south. One County Down resident remembers her father cycling regularly to Dundalk for supplies – there was a general feeling that the guards didn't bother individual smugglers. But the volume of contraband could get out of hand. One Dundalk guard reported to the Dublin office of Garda Síochána:

I beg to report that for some short time past large numbers of Belfast people travel on special excursion trains to Border towns in Éire and buy sugar, cigarettes, tobacco, butter and eggs. Yesterday 2.10.40, three special trains arrived here about 4 p.m. carrying approximately 2,000 people, mostly middle-aged women, all armed with capacious shopping bags. They all left carrying a considerable quantity of the above goods. One grocer whom I know took in over £50 in about two hours and some shopkeepers had to close their shops while they supplied all the people they could serve at a time and then opened to have the shop immediately refilled. This traffic will develop from being a joke into being a huge drain on the food reserves of this town and except some stop is put to it I cannot visualise the bounds to which it might rise. I realise that we have power under the Emergency Powers Orders to deal with the illegal export of all commodities except under licence but on the other hand the quantity taken by each individual is small though the aggregate is large and this practice has operated and is operating all along the Border.

Shopping bags had become the weapons in a new economic war, and the Irish government was forced to fight back with a change in the regulations. Private effects not being exported for trade had been exempt from customs controls, but now most foodstuffs were regulated. Butter, bacon and eggs continued to count as private effects, however – for fear that southern farmers might be forced out of business.

The shopkeepers were delighted with the trade. As the *Dundalk Examiner* reported, between them the Great Northern Railway Works and the business of smuggling had revived the economic fortunes of the town. Smuggling became 'an integral part of the life of the town; in the old days smuggling was always in imports; today it is in exports, whether from Northern Ireland or from Éire. White bread and flour and tea from Northern Ireland; sugar from Éire have taken the place of cattle.' By the middle of the war there were no vacant shops in the town and business was thriving – with some unforeseen consequences. By the summer of 1942 the railway was receiving complaints about the 'dirty appearance and bad conduct of the Belfast–Dundalk "smuggler" passengers'. Part of the problem was that the women wanted to enjoy themselves with the money they were making. As an internal memo put it, 'Many of these objectionable passengers appear to have money to spend and desire to use the dining cars – it is not always possible to keep them out of them.' Even worse was the behaviour of the women when they had got their contraband through: 'The conduct of some of these women passengers after they have cleared Goraghwood [customs] is not good.' The railway decided to run a special train to Dundalk for this class of passenger, leaving the more genteel Belfast to Dublin passengers free to use the dining cars in relative comfort.

Northern Ireland citizens did not make the crossing south only in order to search for provisions in short supply at home. Éire became a retreat for those in the North seeking respite from wartime privations and restrictions, particularly the blackout. Donegal seaside holidays became an increasingly regular fixture for well-to-do Northern residents, while trips to the Gaeltacht attracted middle-class nationalists. Some of the better-off residents of Derry decamped wholesale to hotels on the Donegal coast; with four buses each way every day, they could easily commute from peace to war. In the summer of 1940, while both British and Irish governments attempted to monitor and curtail border movements, the Great Northern Railway began promoting its excursions, to the growing resort at Bundoran, and to Greenore, County Louth. But the most popular outing was a shopping trip to Dublin – GNR laid on five trains a day between Belfast and the Irish capital. Special guards were employed to watch the coal while the trains stood at the platform at Amiens Street.

*   *   *

Shoppers and smugglers could be a nuisance, and occasionally a boon, but rarely a threat. Government concern centred on more menacing incursions. Throughout the latter half of 1940 and the beginning of

A page of advertisements in *The Bell*, July 1941.

1941, for example, British Troops Northern Ireland began sending plain-clothes officers across the border to obtain military information about roads, bridges, and other points of strategic significance. These were deliberate and covert moves in a plan to secure the country for Britain in the event of a German invasion. However much, or little, Irish authorities, let alone the Irish population in general, may have known about Germany's preparations for 'Operation Green' during the summer of 1940, there seemed to be plenty of evidence in Ireland itself that the danger of incursion was real. The idea that Ireland might be used as a 'back door' into Britain was given credence by several advance parties who arrived in Ireland throughout the year.

In February 1940 a German operative, Ernst Weber-Drohl, a wrestler who had worked in Ireland and had two children there, was landed by U-boat at Killala Bay with a radio transmitter, which was lost when his boat overturned. He delivered cash to the IRA, along with instructions for communication and collaboration with the Abwehr. He was picked up in April, and his story splashed all over the newspapers. Weber-Drohl managed to convince his interrogators that he was merely trying to make contact with his children, and was released for the time being. But along with news of the fall of France came stories of enemy spies landing in Ireland by U-boat and by parachute. On 5 May 1940 the most successful of the espionage agents sent to Ireland from Germany, Hermann Görtz, was dropped over Meath with a radio transmitter, and subsequently made his way to the home of Iseult Gonne – daughter of Maud Gonne and wife of the novelist Francis Stuart, who was by then in Berlin. Görtz escaped capture for nearly sixteen months, but on 23 May G2 picked up his accomplice Stephen Held, along with a wireless set, enciphered messages, twenty thousand dollars and a copy of the blueprint for Plan Kathleen: a plot for combined German/IRA operations in Northern Ireland, including arms drops. Dublin was 'simply reverberating with rumours and talk'.

According to MI5 this discovery of a German–IRA plot, combined with the news from the continent, sent the government into a spin, and on 24 May government departments began burning 'secret papers on a large scale'. The fear was that enemy aliens were about to arrive in large numbers through the skies. In June 1940 rumours were circulating that Germans were buying up land in the West of Ireland, and preparing the ground for an invasion. On 8 June Richard Mulcahy, who was assembling a dossier on German activities in Éire, wrote to

Gerald Boland, the Minister for Justice in de Valera's government: 'note purchases (recent) of houses and land by Germans on South and South West Coasts – notably around Cork (Midleton etc) some of the purchasers are levelling the hedges and ditches (also at Scull? [*sic*]). Germans are known to be taking soundings at Cobh harbour and in the Kerry bays.' In July two South Africans and an Indian – all German agents – were landed on the west coast of Cork. An Irishman captured in the Channel Islands was parachuted into Ireland by the Germans later in the year. The fact that these intruders were nearly all picked up promptly did little to calm public anxieties – in some ways, it added to them. For if a handful had been caught, how many more might there be? There were stories of unmanned wirelesses being dropped in the mountains, to be later picked up by IRA operatives and used for sending signals to Germany. (In fact the transmitters were nearly all too weak for anything but local transmission.) As an Irish coast-watcher in the 1946 film *I See a Dark Stranger* drolly acknowledged, German spies

An Irish Army roadblock, County Cork, August 1940.

were everywhere: 'I read in the English papers they're swarming all over Ireland. It's almost our biggest national industry.'

Ireland's neutral status (in particular the presence of Axis legations) and her proximity to Britain made her appear to the British an ideal base for spying. De Valera had promised to prevent Ireland from being used as a base for sabotage against Britain – yet despite a panoply of repressive emergency measures, such as the Offences against the State Act, and the Emergency Powers Act, there was no law in Ireland prohibiting spying against Britain or any other foreign state. Inevitably, on the British side, there were fears that Southerners working in the North might carry back information or intelligence about war preparations. Nicholas Monsarrat, for example, on duty in the Atlantic, was convinced that Ireland, like Portugal, was 'an espionage centre' throughout the war. And IRA operatives did cross the border with makeshift plans of military camps and installations, lists of ground defences and gun positions. Ireland seemed dangerously porous, a sieve through which information could readily leak in and out.

I See a Dark Stranger was the best but not the only popular film to pick up, immediately after the war, on the fears of Irish espionage then being played up in British newspapers. Another 1946 release, *Night Boat to Dublin*, centres on the kidnap of a Swedish scientist working on the atomic bomb, and the use of Ireland as a base through which to pass documents on to German agents (handovers take place in the restaurant room of the mailboat and in a Dublin hotel). Popular treatments of the spy theme were generally indulgent to the Irish case at the end of the war, when the scale of Ireland's contribution to the war effort in terms of both service personnel and manpower had become more evident. They tended to suggest that Ireland was the stage for espionage but that the Irish themselves – either through incompetence or natural good-heartedness – were not up to the game; the major enemy agents in both *Night Boat to Dublin* and *I See a Dark Stranger* are British. By the same token, however, the friendly but dim Irish characters are powerless to stop the espionage.

Suspicion of Irish movement between the two countries was considerable. One Irish volunteer who worked in Signals recalled an immigration officer at Holyhead going through the lining of his jacket and every page of his prayer book looking for secret codes. The novelist Rayner Heppenstall, who was stationed with the British Troops

Northern Ireland, suggested that the security was just as strict for those travelling to the North: 'At Stranraer . . . they were searching everybody, even making them peel their socks off and looking at the soles of their feet.'

Suspicion of trading in secret information was an urgent matter for Britain, but the Irish authorities too were concerned that such activity would endanger the security of the state. The lack of any visible enemy only served to fuel these stories of secret agents and clandestine wireless communications, with the greatest anxiety focused on covert activity by republicans in support of the Axis powers. As the external situation worsened during the spring and summer of 1940 the government and judiciary became increasingly alarmed about the activities and recruitment of the IRA. This anxiety was not without cause. In addition to a number of attacks on Guards, the murder of state witnesses and witness intimidation, there were a series of violent incidents including armed robberies of shops and banks, and arson attacks on those cinemas in the North that persisted in playing British newsreels. The discoveries of Görtz and Held in May of that year were convincing evidence that these activities were all aimed at providing a basis for German incursions into the country. A G2 report written immediately after the end of the war reveals a clear conviction within the Security Services that the IRA were 'prepared to sacrifice the independence of the country' in return for German aid in freeing the North. It also implies that, at least some of the time, G2 equated the security of the Irish state with the need to protect Allied troops against the IRA threat:

The treasonable contacts with a foreign power, which had been established before the war, were renewed and the Government learned that German parachutists had been dropped at various points throughout the State and were being supplied with military information, including the disposition and movement of troops and plans of ports, aerodromes, and military installations of all kinds.

Throughout the whole course of the war, these treasonable communications continued and all the activities of the organisation were directed to involving the country at war. In June 1940, the most active members to the number of about three hundred were interned, but many whom it was felt to be in the public interest to intern succeeded in evading arrest for a time. The security of the State was thus endangered, particularly in view of the presence of large numbers of British and later American troops across the border, with regard to whose military establishments and armaments there was evidence that information was being sought by the organisation. It required the greatest vigilance on the part of the authorities to prevent such information from being conveyed to German agents and the existence of this possibility was a continuous source of anxiety.

The discovery of Plan Kathleen was not the only thing the security services had to go on. Throughout the war, members of the IRA who were still at liberty brought out a number of mimeographed bulletins and news sheets, including *War News*, which was produced by the 'Republican Publicity Bureau', variously operating out of Belfast and Dublin. An issue of December 1940, for example, included a rallying call for the coming battle:

Were it not for the friendly attitude of the German Reich towards the Irish Republican Army, we and our women and children would even now be suffering the logical consequence of the situation. De Valera's statement is clear enough – the two Imperial armies, the 'Free State' Army in the South, the British Army in the North, will together make this island difficult for the Germans to enter. In other words, native slave and FOREIGN INVADER combine to hold Ireland against – whom? . . . who is the common enemy of both Irish traitor and foreign invader? The Axis Powers, in the first place, because the enemy of the Imperial master is naturally the enemy of the native slave . . . and whatever lie the 'Free State' soldier has swallowed, he holds Cork and Dublin for the Empire.

But the enemy is fast weakening – THE SHOW-DOWN IS AT HAND!

A later issue struck at the heart of de Valera's policy when it asked, 'So you're neutral, are you?':

Has it ever struck you that your bogus neutrality is of far more value to Britain than if you had openly joined up with her and declared war on Italy and Germany three years ago? Has it ever occurred to you that your alleged neutrality is the cleverest plan ever thought of in connection with the old war between Ireland and England? Have you ever suspected that it was arranged in London by de Valera and the British Cabinet that you should declare yourself neutral for the greater safety and benefit of the good old Empire?

It would be risky to divine republican sentiment more generally on the basis of these publications; most active members of the IRA were interned after June 1940, and of those who remained at liberty the men (and possibly women) who produced *War News* may not have been representative of the movement as a whole. But the surviving publications do provide some indication both of IRA methods of underground circulation, and of the public's response.

Files in the National Archives contain copies of the bulletins obtained in a number of ways. Some were forwarded to the police after having been sent to GAA members in Kerry through the post: a number were received in Abbeydorney, for example. Others, forwarded by County Tipperary Guards, had been pushed under doors in Tipperary town, in Nenagh and in Cappawhite. Moya Woodside recorded the appearance of IRA leaflets on the counters of shops and travel agents in Belfast. Others were left in public places where they might be found; *War News* invariably included an exhortation to its readers to pass their copy on to as many people as possible. It also advertised the illegal republican radio station, which broadcast every Friday night at 9 p.m. from Belfast during the early months of the war. The capture of the radio and arrest of its operators caused an inevitable lull in transmission, but a year later it was back on air with three broadcasts a week, on Sundays at 1.30 p.m. and Wednesdays and Fridays at 9 in the evening. The station issued calls to young men to join the IRA, in order to replace those 'held prisoners because they would dare to assert the right of this Nation to independence'. It broadcast news of arrests in Britain, and IRA activities in the North, as well as the occasional escapes and release of prisoners.

A favoured method of circulating *War News* was to send parcels by train or bus to non-existent addressees, care of rural post offices or stations. Theoretically guards who became aware of these parcels only had to wait for someone to turn up to collect them in order to apprehend IRA sympathisers. But as one guard ruefully wrote, his request of the postmaster to inform him who came to collect the parcel was 'unlikely' to bear fruit. The postmaster's reluctance may have had little to do with his own political sympathies. In part the Irish authorities were up against the 'traditional' suspicion of the police in rural Ireland, and the deep-rooted hatred of informers that was one legacy of British rule. It was simpler to turn a blind eye to whatever clandestine activities might be going on. How many copies of *War News* were never handed in, despite the government's calls for vigilance?

Given the apparent levels of subversive activity, the government was determined to get the population to report their suspicions. On 8 May 1940, following the Görtz/Held discoveries, and as the Low Countries fell, de Valera spoke at a meeting in Cork requesting volunteers for a network of informants – who were to form the Local Security Force – to report on any secret manoeuvres. He addressed his countrymen as citizens of a fledgling national democracy, closing ranks against violent outsiders, and in particular against a return to the chaos of civil war:

I am speaking to you tonight for a few minutes to remind you of a duty which each of you owes to himself, to the community as a whole, and to Ireland. This moment, when small nations throughout Europe are devoting all their efforts to strengthening national unity, in order the better to defend their independence, is the moment that a group in this country has chosen to destroy our organised life.

In the last few years, as you know, every obstacle has been removed which could in any way be used to justify a recourse to violence. Today every Party within this State is free to seek to achieve its political aims by peaceful means. The use of violence is, therefore, not only unjustifiable, it is a wanton attack upon the whole community engaged in with a cynical disregard of the vital need to keep our people strong and united in the face of universal danger . . .

The Government will do its part in ridding the people of the armed menace. But the people also have a duty. If they value what has been won for them they will now, as in the days of the Black and Tans, be the eyes and the ears of the national defence. What has happened in the last few weeks – the exploding of a time-bomb in the police quarters at Dublin Castle with utter disregard for human life, the attempt yesterday to shoot down without mercy two Garda officers – these things must have opened the eyes of everyone to the seriousness of the position. Were these deeds allowed to continue, civil war would be the inevitable consequence, and such a weakening of our strength as would make our country easy prey to any invader.

In addition to being on guard against incursions ('to keep an eye out for parachutists or submarines in coastal areas and on suspicious looking strangers'), the Local Security Force were encouraged to report both on the activities of IRA sympathisers, some of whom were found inside Special Branch itself, and on those with obvious pro-British sympathies.

The Local Security Force was a 'visible' one; it did not operate under cover, though arguably whether in or out of uniform its members were never off duty. But the new Force was only one of a number of measures designed to control security and information, most of them under the control of the security services, G2. This organisation was responsible for control of communications, including censorship and covert interception, investigation of resident aliens, advising on travel permits, spying on foreign diplomats, and monitoring the activity of a range of possible enemies of the state, from members of the IRA, to anti-semitic groups, to pro-Allied circles.

The censorship of communications was a major aspect of G2's security policy, and one that caused a great deal of resentment. Restrictions placed on the public media (press, radio, cinema) were aimed at controlling covert propaganda, disinformation, and stories planted by the belligerent powers. Control over private communications (telephone, cable, and letter) was intended to control the dissemination of seditious plans and rumours. Telephone calls were openly monitored by operators, press reports were sent for vetting to the censor's office, but the largest section was the postal censorship. In the Post Office in Dublin nearly three hundred people were employed to open and read private letters. Both outward and incoming mail was inspected. There was, however, no censorship of mail to and from Northern Ireland. Although both governments would have liked to regulate the traffic of mail across the border, it proved impossible to reconcile the inhabitants of either jurisdiction to interference with their mail. At the beginning of the war Britain had tried to impose censorship on the post to Ireland; it was forbidden to send a newspaper, or picture postcard or photograph, though a shop or agency with a permit could send such items on your behalf. But eventually the government had to admit defeat. The censorship ceased to monitor mail from Northern Ireland to Éire – as Cecil Liddell of MI5 put it, 'the open border allowed any person to defeat such censorship by walking over a field with a letter in his pocket' – though the censoring of mail to England continued.

Ostensibly, the Postal Censors were looking for sedition or treason. But as Aiken admitted, a 'secondary object' was 'to collect as much information as possible', for example by monitoring those applying by post to join the British forces. By its nature, the postal censorship affected more citizens in more intimate ways, and caused more indignation than other forms of interference.

One unintended – though no doubt welcome – consequence may have been to put a stop to mail orders of birth control devices. The sale and importation of contraceptives had been illegal in Ireland since the Criminal Law Amendment Act of 1935, but wealthier couples had continued to send off for them to British companies, which sent them into Ireland in plain parcels, addressed by hand, in order to avoid customs. It was just this type of parcel which was opened by the wartime censors. There may be a case for suggesting that contraceptive smuggling across the border grew during the war, and not only because when the American troops arrived in the North they brought with them ready supplies. Since it was possible to send mail-order contraceptives to the North without fear of the censorship, it may have seemed easier to bring them over the border than risk the Emergency postal censorship in the South.

The policy of censorship aroused much indignation: there were complaints of letters received in ribbons, protests at the intrusion into family correspondence, and arguments in the Dáil that citizens were entitled to express private opinions. The avowedly pro-Allied Senator Keane insisted that the individual should be allowed the 'right to his conscience', and that the censorship was 'undermining morality and sapping moral judgement by preventing its exercise'. Why should the government's neutral policy mean that Irish citizens had to speak and even think neutrally? But the government did not think state neutrality could co-exist with citizens' strong commitment to either side. As soon as any *parti pris* was disclosed to others, even in the form of a confidential letter to a relative or friend, it was seen as a threat to the government's stance. Maintaining neutrality meant far more than preventing partisan action within the borders of the state. The attempt to enforce a 'neutral' public opinion became, for the government's critics, as destructive of democracy as the civil conflict it was supposed to help prevent.

Beyond the workings of the Postal Censor, which were known and often resented, there were also other more clandestine networks of information gathering. Early in the war G2 set up an intelligence-gathering operation, which included a radio-detection service (the use of the German legation wireless was monitored, for example) and a telephone listening-in service. Other undercover activities included the Supplementary Intelligence Service (SIS), a secret unit of the LDF, made up of one-time 'hardened republicans' who would not wear a Free State uniform, but carried out secret surveillance, primarily in the Munster area. The SIS, drawing on long-established War of Independence networks, managed to induce some old republicans to serve the state in secret. Systems of informing and reporting ramified throughout civil society, and intelligence files were held on large numbers of people. Interception and monitoring activities targeted individuals and groups with a range of political sympathies, from pro-Allied politicians such as James Dillon and Senator McDermot (as well as Jewish TD Bob Briscoe), to communist and left-wing organisations, to members of the 'Irish Friends of Germany' and other anti-semitic or pro-German

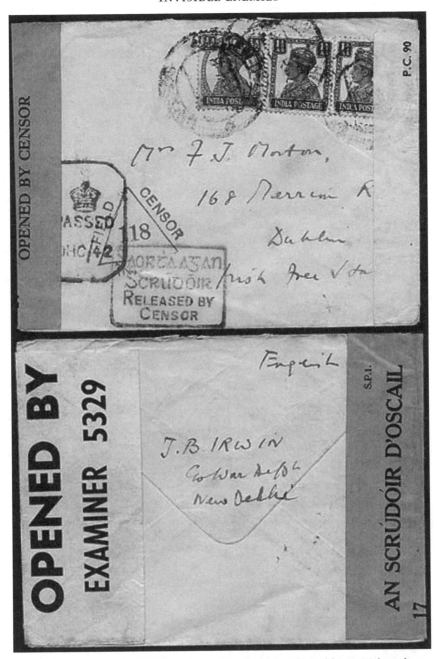

A letter sent from India to Ireland in 1940, and read by British and
Irish censors.

groups. The regular police played their role in the process, opening letters at post offices, for example. Such covert interception, however, differed from censorship: the recipient in these cases received no warning in the form of the familiar stamp, 'Passed by Censor'.

Local-government inspectors also proved useful in forwarding information. The historian Margaret MacCurtain recalls how as a schoolgirl in Kerry she was passed information in the school playground on planned republican movements, which she was to convey to her father, the local Schools Inspector. Civil servants of all kinds became unofficial conduits for intelligence, and here the distinction between observation and knowledge came into its own. De Valera's call for citizens to act as the 'eyes and ears' of the security services implied looking out for unusual activity and reporting it. But suspicous-looking strangers were probably the least of Ireland's worries (the Indian national landed by the Germans, for example, was picked up in double-quick time). Since much of the danger was home-grown, citizens were being asked to report not what they saw, but what they knew. They were being recruited not as spies, but as informers.

These grassroots networks were just one of the measures employed by the Irish government to maintain security. Overt censorship was aimed at keeping the lid on potentially dangerous political passions, while surveillance and interception helped to build up a picture of popular allegiances. Internment contributed by physically excluding potential subversives. The population acquiesced in these measures, by and large, because they were seen as necessary to preserve cultural and social cohesion, and hence to protect neutrality. Not many people went as far in embracing the new surveillance culture as the editor of the art magazine *Commentary*, however. Sean Dorman even titled one of his articles 'Irishmen Should Be Informers', and argued that:

[The Emergency] has afforded us the opportunity of showing that, as well as possessing our traditional courage, we can also display restraint and citizenship . . . It has, by three-parts isolating us from a dangerous world, vividly brought home to us the need for unity and sober strength. The welfare and safety of Ireland, ruled by Irishmen, through Irishmen, for Irishmen, has depended upon the discipline which each individual one of us has placed upon his tongue and act, upon our cooperation with authority, and our unyielding firmness at the moments of crisis when the national sovereignty was, or seemed about to be, challenged.

The informer, he argued, was not a traitor but a man with a properly mature sense of civic responsibility; it was the black marketeers who were the real traitors.

The idea that informing had become socially acceptable was wishful thinking on Dorman's part. But the drive to form a national consensus around neutrality was having an effect. The Step Together fairs and pageants were part of an effort to build local morale, and reinforce the government's message through sport and recreation. But professional theatre did its bit too in maintaining the post-civil war political consensus, particularly the plays produced at the Abbey in Dublin. If the early Abbey had been tinged with an Anglo-Irish ethos, under Yeats, Gregory and Synge, by the 1940s Ireland's national theatre had a reputation for asserting political and religious orthodoxy more and more loudly. One of the directors of the Abbey was also a film censor during the war, and explicitly charged with guarding the nation's neutral conscience.

One of the most popular productions at the Abbey during the war played for more than twelve weeks during the summer and early autumn of 1940. George Shiels's *The Rugged Path* tells the story of two families – the Tanseys and the Cassidys – divided by lingering civil-war animosity. Their rural community is at the mercy of a violent outlaw clan (the Dollises) who, as the play opens, have murdered an old man for the sake of two pounds. Despite fears of reprisals, which prove to be well founded, one of the Tanseys decides to inform the police, and finally to stand witness at the trial of the murderer. The drama turns on the need for a new consciousness of citizenship and community – for a new alliance between those for and against the Treaty – in order to combat the destructive presence of violence and intimidation. In effect, it provides justification, in the name of community relations, for the ongoing internment of militant republicans in the Curragh.

Many plays of the 1930s and 1940s touched on the importance of national unity and consensus, and the need to turn away from violence, in the cause of a stable, peaceable, constitutional and democratic society. But what was striking about Shiels's play, and perhaps a key to its popularity, was that this message was explicitly set in the context of the world war. This topicality assured it a keen reception on the amateur circuit – *The Rugged Path* had a long run in Wexford's semi-professional theatre in 1942, for example. As the play begins, a farming family tries – in vain – to resurrect the battery and tune the wireless to hear news of the air war over Britain. Three acts later, as the play closes, the wireless has been mended and threatening news of fighter planes and bombings is broadcast into the stage sitting-room – and into the theatre. Technological innovations in the Irish countryside, such as the wireless and electric light, suggest the benefits of a forward-looking, stable community. The resurgence of an archaic violence from within the community, and the menace of foreign belligerence from without, blend into one – both are portrayed as threats to the new, democratic nation-state.

The play's message – that the demonisation of informers was fit only for pre-independence Ireland, that justice (and peace) required speaking out against violence – fitted in neatly with the government's call for volunteers to put the civil war behind them and turn in active members of the IRA as enemies of neutrality. Encouraged by the success of his play, Shiels wrote a sequel. *The Summit*, performed in the Abbey in February 1941, made the analogy between civil-war reconciliation and current security even clearer. In the second play the audience witnesses the healing of the civil-war breach as the Tanseys and the Cassidys make common cause against lawlessness – and eject the Dollis clan, who represent violent republicanism. The play ran for only four weeks, however, despite the fact that Denis Johnston hailed it as 'so much better a play than the original', suggesting that the sudden accommodation between the two sides stretched the credulity of the audience, who seemed happier with the earlier, tragic version of the story. No doubt too the waning of the invasion threat, after the panic of the summer of 1940, also reduced its appeal.

* * *

The Irish security services proved both efficient and energetic in their surveillance of potential Axis sympathisers. By contrast, the size of the Allied-friendly population, and the fact that so many informal networks of family, trade, and cultural exchange already linked Britain and Ireland, ensured that pro-Allied activity remained much more difficult to track. The government was sensitive about British attempts to influence Irish opinion and alter the bent of neutrality through news and other media, particularly during the invasion scare. But it was also on the alert for cases of organised spying and rumour-mongering, not to mention attempts at amateur espionage, on behalf of the Allies.

Here postal and telephone censorship, covert interception, and the LSF information network played their part.

In an environment where rumours, planted or spontaneous, could swing neutral opinion, intelligence was a potent weapon, and MI5 was far from being the only British undercover operation in Ireland during the war. The British SIS had a number of operatives working in Ireland. Some worked semi-openly, such as the officer attached to the British Passport Control Office in Dublin, who was able to make inquiries and provide information about those wishing to travel to Britain. Others operated undercover, such as two wireless operators using the disguise of domestic servants of the British Air Attaché. (G2 were on to them as early as 1940.) On top of this, after 1941 the American Office of Strategic Services began operating clandestinely in Ireland. Undoubtedly, also, a number of individual British and American nationals in Ireland were engaged in undercover activities of one kind or another. These included both those coming to Ireland for apparently bona fide purposes – journalists, for example, or envoys of the movie industry such as Martin Quigley, who worked undercover for the American Security Services for nearly a year – and others who were already living in Ireland at the beginning of the war.

There was a sense, which the government did little to discourage, that anyone from outside the country was suspect, and citizens were urged to report any suspicions. The British novelist T. H. White spent the first years of the war finishing his *Arthur* trilogy in Mayo. His evidence in a letter to David Garnett suggests that some people responded with enthusiasm to de Valera's request for them to act as 'the eyes and ears' of the defence forces:

Things are slightly troublesome personally, because I am always being reported to the police as a spy, but they can't make out whether I am a German or an English one, which confuses the issue . . . The boring part about it is that it hampers my movements. I can't, for instance, go out to my beloved Inishkea, because it would be thought I was refuelling a submarine, etc., while even my hawks are interfered with. When I wave the lure round my head, a hundred zealous watchers are sure that it is semaphore.

White may have been somewhat more than disingenuous. During the summer of 1940 he travelled and camped around Achill and neighbouring islands in the West. Given that on the outbreak of war he had volunteered his services to the Ministry of Information, it is quite likely that his several sojourns on the uninhabited island of Inishkea, ostensibly to follow up folklore tales of a primitive deity, did have an undercover aspect, involving observation of U-boat movements and possible local trading of fish and fuel.

Activities of external spies were, of course, far easier to track than those of internal sympathisers. The long period from summer 1940 to June 1941, when Hitler invaded Russia, proved very hard for Allied supporters in Ireland. The dire situation for Britain, rumours of Britain's desperate need for pilots, the daily tally of losses in the Atlantic – all seemed to call out directly for their loyalty and support, but public expression of sympathy for Britain was not allowed. It was driven undercover, and for fear of destabilising the neutral balance in the country the Irish security services were determined to root it out. Letters to the office of the UK Representative were intercepted; there was the occasional discovery of a radio transceiver in the home of a pro-British citizen on the southern or western coast – and above all, there was the postal censorship. People were convinced that this was vindictive rather than necessary. Professor Alton argued in the Seanad: 'You have letters between father and son, between mother and daughter or between brother and brother in which the news that is being censored is, as far as I can see, of no military importance.' But Aiken defended the policy: 'we have been able to stop a number of stories going out of a scare-mongering type which would indeed have done great damage to the people of the country,' namely by casting aspersions on 'our state of preparedness'.

It is understandable that people felt aggrieved at not being allowed to write to relatives in England, explaining their feelings about the war, or simply mentioning the dearth of guns and ammunition for the LSF. But what G2 was intent on controlling was communication that fell in the grey area between personal feeling and 'national intelligence'. In *The Heat of the Day*, Bowen offered a portrait of an elderly Anglo-Irish man carrying on his own war in Ireland:

His real object in making the journey to England had been to offer that country his services in the war – his own country's abstention had been a severe blow, but he had never sat down under a blow yet. Bound to Mount Morris both by passion and duty, he had waited two and a half years for Éire to reverse her decision: hopes of German invasion had for part of that time sustained him – he had dug tanktraps in the Mount Morris avenues – but as those hopes petered out he resolved to act.

Once the threat of a physical enemy recedes, Cousin Morris offers his services to the British government in passing on intelligence. Throughout the war republican propagandists liked to insist that the real 'fifth column' in Ireland was to be found amongst the Anglo-Irish, and others friendly to Britain. Within government too, men such as J. J. Walshe, Secretary for External Affairs, equated anti-Irish activity with 'collaborationist elements in the Ascendancy class'. The problem was not just information leaks. Almost more dangerous were stories making vague claims about pro-Axis sympathy in government or among the people, since these stoked anti-Irish feeling in Britain. Evidence that Allied-friendly citizens continued to warn of pro-German sentiment (Nazi spies, fuelling of U-boats, and so on) is contained in the British Representative's reports to his superiors in London. Asked to comment on claims of rampant pro-Axis sympathy, Maffey repeatedly complained of the mischief-making reports that were making their way into Britain, either by post or in person, and he did his best to scotch the wildest rumours.

Throughout 1940, the Department of External Affairs attempted to control the activities of British sympathisers drumming up support for the Allies. The rumours that circulated ranged from suggestions that the British Legion was acting as an unofficial recruiting agency to reports of fundraising activities to collect donations for the British Forces. In January 1940, for example, Cobh Council lodged an objection to a fundraising dance, arguing that an event intended to provide cigarettes for British soldiers in France might give rise to protests, or even rival dances for the IRA: 'From the ordinary national point of view of the neutrally-minded population, there can be no justification at all for permitting the raising of money and the export of "comforts" to a foreign army when our own military forces enjoy no such support from the Irish public.' The suggestion that any 'rival' events would be those held in support of armed republicanism is telling. It implies that the neutrality of the Irish armed forces placed them not so much equidistant from Britain and Germany, as in between the British and the IRA. And it supports the view that neutrality was less about balancing between foreign powers, and more about containing potential civil strife between pro-British and republican elements within the country.

The following month residents in Monaghan wrote to the Chief Superintendent of Monaghan Barracks asking him to put a stop to a whist drive in aid of the British Minesweepers and Sailors. The event was 'a provocative display' and 'a direct infringement of our neutrality and is in absolute conflict with the wishes of the people'. There were whist drives, bridge parties, raffles, private parties – all in order to raise funds for the British and Allies Comforts and Victims of War Fund. Early in 1940 the Department of External Affairs listed eighteen functions in the space of a month, not counting less clearly definable 'seditious' acts, such as the collections taken in Protestant churches for the purchase of wool, or the Enniscorthy ladies' knitting circle making garments to forward to Lady Maffey for the Forces. Frank Aiken, as Minister for the Co-ordination of Defensive Measures, was keen to introduce legislation to ban fundraising events, but others were wary of amending the Emergency Powers to deal with the problem. To officials at the Department of Foreign Affairs it seemed better simply to keep it quiet:

I don't think it would do our international relations any good if we were to have superintendents and sergeants of the Garda standing up in District Courts and opposing the grant of dance licences on the grounds that the proceeds of the function were destined for a belligerent purpose and the holding of the dance would therefore be contrary to our neutrality.

There was a danger that the nuisance would be driven into private houses 'and give those who indulge in it a stronger sense of solidarity'. The main thrust of security policy was towards a less heavy-handed monitoring and containing of sympathies, for fear of making the situation worse.

Just as the IRA *War News* circulated throughout the country, along with newsletters from German and Italian sources, pro-Allied leaflets did the rounds. Many of these encouraged fundraising, for example through the 'Spitfire Funds'. In September 1940 the Postal Censor wrote that it was impossible to stop Fund leaflets coming over because they were sent in open 'printed paper' packets, and time and manpower meant that only closed letters could be examined. Instead, gardaí took to targeting the fundraisers. In September 1940 three young men were arrested in Monaghan, for example, for making a collection for the *Belfast Telegraph* Spitfire Fund. In the same month a woman from Cavan was observed by a member of the gardaí making collections; a woman employee in a garage in Milford, County Donegal, was reported by a bus driver for soliciting donations for Spitfires, and taken in to the local garda station to make a statement. A report from Letterkenny in November 1940 listed eight collectors for the *Belfast Telegraph* Spitfire Fund in the local area, and gave names and addresses of subscribers. Meanwhile there were rumours circulating that a Dublin Spitfire Fund had been set up in the Guinness brewery. G2 was sent leaflets produced by the Dublin Spitfire Club hailing the bravery of 'heroic airmen' struggling against overwhelming odds 'in endeavouring to prevent the insensate and barbaric annihilation of innocent civilians particularly Women and Children'. In October the *Daily Express* duly carried a note from the British Ministry of Aircraft Production thanking the Dublin Spitfire Club for a donation of four hundred pounds. The principal agents of the Club, according to garda investigations, appeared to be in the coast-watching service and the LSF.

On 11 October 1940 a concerned citizen wrote directly to the Department of the Taoiseach listing a number of fundraising events in his area: 'The Taoiseach may be interested to have this information as it indicates that a certain "rot" has begun in relation to our neutrality which he will wish to put an end to at once on account of the dangers, internal and external, which are sure to follow if the "rot" is unchecked.' There was an example of more rot in a letter, dated 8 October 1940, from John Downes, an employee of Baxendale & Co., to Herr Hempel at the German legation (clearly an intercepted letter, with a copy forwarded to External Affairs):

I am a member of the staff of this firm but on no account would I contribute towards this Club. A number of my fellow workers would not contribute and abhor the whole idea, firstly because it is Anti-German and secondly because it is a direct contravention of our neutrality. Our number is not great however and therefore we could not complain to the management (which incidentally is pro-British and sponsors this collection here) as we would in all probabilities be dismissed.

Downes suggested that Hempel should lodge a protest with the relevant government department.

In November 1940, a new British fund was set up: the 'Civilian Air Raid Victims Aid Society'. G2 launched an investigation, and eventually a new Emergency Powers Order was introduced to proscribe collecting. November 1940 also saw the 'ladies of the Killarney/Killorglin area' being taken in for questioning by the gardaí for supplying wool for scarves and socks 'for the Forces regardless of whether they were British or Irish'. Mrs MacGuillycuddy, wife of the local grandee, had asked the ladies during tea if they would knit some garment for the soldiers (the distant organiser of the effort was Lady Maffey). The image of genteel Anglo-Irish ladies being cautioned and forced to make statements about their pro-British activities goes some way to explaining the atmosphere of impotence, combined with incipient panic, that typified these months. For all their ties to Ireland, the Anglo-Irish could not help but feel cut off from their natural environment, and somehow in the wrong place at the wrong time. Many of their men were away in the Forces, or working in ministries in England. For them, neutrality meant not a benign state of suspension, but the political suppression of their spontaneous sympathies. Above all it must have seemed both cruel and nonsensical to these women that young Irish men and women were free to join the British forces and perhaps to die fighting for the Allies, while they were not allowed to knit them socks. From the security point of view, of course, the government did not mind what Irish people did outside the country. Their task was to control the various enemies of neutrality within.

A masterful short story by Elizabeth Bowen presented the mood during the summer of 1940 as one of barely suppressed hysteria, and particularly so for the embattled 'collaborationists' of the Ascendancy class. The events of 'Summer Night' take place against the backdrop of the Battle of Britain – insecurity and invasion fears are rife in both countries. In this setting, Bowen tells a tale of adultery and betrayal, exploring again her abiding preoccupation with allegiance. In the process she paints a negative picture of the 'corrupting' atmosphere in Ireland. 'Summer Night' revolves around an assignation between Emma, the young wife of a retired Anglo-Irish major and a middle-class factory owner, Robinson, who lives in a small town in County Cork. (The latter was a portrait of one of Bowen's friends, Jim Gates, the manager of the creamery in Kildorrery, County Cork.) As Emma hurtles through the evening in her car, she leaves behind, in the large country house that is her home, her husband (an 'unmilitary-looking man' who nonetheless fought in the previous war), her two children and her husband's aunt, whose primary relationship is with the wireless.

Aunt Fran, 'so frightened something will happen', can hardly bear the atmosphere in which she is forced to exist, and cannot settle until the house has been closed up at night (turned into 'a fortress') to protect those inside from the forces of destruction she senses around her. In part, these are the powers unleashed by the war. Aware of a strangeness in Emma's behaviour as she prepares to leave for her tryst with Robinson, Aunt Fran imagines an invading stranger (a 'black tide') pressing into the house from outside, just as the news on the wireless presses in. 'Something has got in,' she cries when the children pick up on Emma's mood and she hears dancing in the rooms upstairs. Aunt Fran has become engulfed by the heightened atmosphere of rumour and mistrust which followed the fall of France. 'No one speaks the truth to me but the man on the wireless,' she cries. 'Always things being said on the telephone, always things being moved about, always Emma off at the end of the house singing, always the children hiding away.' The threatening night is full of violence as an air battle takes place elsewhere (men are 'destroying each other' in the Battle of Britain), but the house is also part of the 'infected zone', a place where men and women destroy each other without weapons. The only recourse is to pray for protection from this indeterminate foe:

There is not even the past; our memories share with us the infected zone; not a memory does not lead up to this. Each moment is everywhere, it holds the war in its crystal; there is no elsewhere, no other place. Not a benediction falls on this apart house of the Major: the enemy is within it, creeping about. Each heart here falls to the enemy.

Emma's unspoken betrayal betokens the precarious, inside/outside position of the Anglo-Irish in this moment of historic crisis.

It is worth pausing a moment to reflect on this picture of Anglo-Irish life during the war. At the time she was writing 'Summer Night' Bowen was also reporting back to London that 'the worst defeatism, on behalf of Britain' was to be found among the Protestant Anglo-Irish. Bowen's unashamed preference for Churchillian values made her deplore the Anglo-Irish 'cagey and negative attitude' in support of neutrality. Like the Mass Observation diarist, the Trinity College student from Armagh, who was 'prepared to stay at home until conscription', young Anglo-Irish men, she discovered, were surprisingly indifferent to the war. Encountering a number of Trinity College students in November 1940, she found them 'unexpectedly detached about European affairs. They denied having any point of view, and professed no interest in politics.' Bowen was of course unlikely to meet in Ireland those Anglo-Irish, or Irish-Irish, who had decided to volunteer in Britain. Nonetheless, in her view, the war was intensifying the disconnection of the Anglo-Irish from both England and Ireland.

In *Bowen's Court*, the family history that she had begun in 1939 (presumably while still feeling 'wedded' to the country through her 'marriage' to Sean O'Faolain), and which she completed during her intelligence-gathering trips in 1940 and 1941, Bowen recorded the 'centripetal and cut-off life' of the Protestant Ascendancy in Ireland. She lamented the isolation of the Anglo-Irish from contact with the world outside the Big House demesne (echoed in the 'apart house' of 'Summer Night'). Their aloofness began from the moment of their arrival in Ireland, she argued, but increased with the Act of Union in 1800. From this moment Anglo-Irish culture was, by necessity, directed politically and economically towards England, though a social life centred in Ireland continued. As Hubert Butler suggested, the sense of withdrawal increased again with the Anglo-Irish war: 'For our parents of the ascendancy it was easy and obvious to live in Ireland, but we of the "descendancy" were surrounded in the 'twenties by the burnt out houses of our friends and relations. England beckoned us and only an obstinate young person would wish to stay at home.'

For those who did remain in Ireland after the founding of the Free State in 1922, political and social allegiances had to be revised, for political power had passed to the dominant culture, lying beyond the walls of the estate. And there was a further increase in isolation on the outbreak of war, when many Anglo-Irish men (as well as many others) left to fight or work for Britain. The Big Houses became house-islands: 'singular, independent, and secretive', as Bowen put it. Inside them the last representatives of a dying culture struggled to continue in isolation, seeking connection with England through the wireless, through 'belligerent' acts such as knitting for the Allied Forces or collecting for Spitfire Funds.

Bowen's English friend Henry Green painted a vivid picture of these islanded Anglo-Irish in his wartime novel, *Loving*. Green set his story in an Irish fairy-tale castle, suggesting the persistence of the old colonial fantasy: Ireland as the only country in Europe where the world of make-believe and enchantment was still possible. As in 'Summer Night', the drama takes place in the summer of 1940, at the height of invasion scares in both Britain and Ireland. It focuses on the attitudes of the English servants marooned in the castle while their masters pursue their amatory and business affairs elsewhere. The servants – despite their isolation from Britain – manifest all the stereotypical prejudices and fears aroused by Ireland's 'betrayal' after the fall of France. All agree 'we're practically in enemy country here'. They take care not to talk to 'the natives', not to believe anything printed in 'these Irish rags', and fuel their fear on tales of the IRA and on Irish indifference: '"The war's on now all right," Kate said, "and do these rotten Irish care? They make me sick."' Their fears of attack, Green implies, are exaggerated by an unacknowledged guilt over living in a peaceful haven, while England suffers aerial bombing. They even feel driven to imagine that, despite appearances, they are somehow contributing to the war effort. Mrs Tennant is responsible for the house, while her son is away at the front: 'In a way I regard this as my war work, maintaining the place I mean. Because we're practically in enemy country here you know and I do consider it so important from the morale point of view to keep up appearances.' Absurdly, she stresses the need to protect her French furnishings, implying that especial vigilance is called for following the blitzkrieg: 'There'll be so little left, when this war's finished.'

Green's knowledge of Ireland was less than comprehensive. It was drawn from a fishing holiday he had taken in Connemara during the Munich Crisis. As the situation worsened he and his wife attempted to listen to news bulletins on the radio, but – he maintained – were repeatedly thwarted by the indifference of the soon-to-be neutral Irish. The upshot was a deeply unsympathetic and condescending portrait of a country complacent rather than tortured about its detachment from world affairs. 'The British papers were two or more days old and the Irish press, in an attitude accepted as far as we could tell by all the natives, maintained that nothing could ever happen to the great Little Republic.' A crowd of priests in the midlands talk loudly over the wireless, and in a hotel in Cork the locals are more interested in hearing a relay of a boxing match than the possible declaration of war – and stupid with it.

Shown to a combined sitting room and office already laced with cigar smoke, a tumbler of neat whiskey in my hand, I found five or six powerful citizens of Éire tight round a huge wireless. They had the thing full on, but in their cups had mismanaged the knobs. It was bellowing out wild deadly cheering and applause which followed as it always did the end of what had obviously been a big speech to some National Socialist rally at the Sports Palace in Berlin.

Now we had no German, my wife and I, yet these screaming, shouted, harshly expectorated speeches had drawn us at home to listen in an ever-increasing anguish of terror night after night; in spite of which when we would read the translation in newspapers next morning it was with complete disbelief. It did not seem possible such things could be said. I was therefore familiar with the uproar the Irish were now listening to, therefore it came as no surprise when the German audience broke into its usual chants of '*Sieg Heil – Sieg Heil*' each louder than the last, a kind of rising invocation each step higher than the next like a grand staircase to slaughter.

But my drunken hosts were taken in. 'Ach, the fight's ended in a foul,' they said.

I tried to explain they were on the wrong wavelength but they were too far gone. Then, as the fight might still be on, I felt it a shame they should miss their programme, so I tried to get at the machine to tune us to London. They pulled me away. 'Let's hear how they robbed the boy,' they said. On which *Deutschland Über Alles* bellowed into the manager's office. This they did recognise and all broke down in laughter.

In *Loving* this highly dubious picture – surely coloured by wartime and post-war anti-Irish prejudice, for even a drunken Irishman can tell the difference between a Nazi chant and a boxing match – is transposed onto the English, and Anglo-Irish, in Ireland. Like Aunt Fran, the servants' fear of leaving the house is matched only by their fear of the house being invaded. As incursion threatens, they struggle to work out what should be their patriotic duty in this neutral war zone – should they stay and risk the arrival of the panzer grenadiers, or take the opportunity to cross quickly to 'the other side'? The sole Irish servant, the lampman, insists that the IRA would be able to hold back the Germans, but also that Ireland is not a sufficient prize for the Germans to bother with. That, for the English servants, is hardly the point:

'Because the country's too poor to tempt an army he reckons, all bogs and stones he says' . . .

'But let 'im satisfy me in this respect,' Raunce cried, 'what the condition of Ireland has to do with it? For one thing if it wasn't rotten land fit only for spuds we'd've been 'ere to this day, our government I mean. No we gave Ireland back because we didn't want it, or this part anyway. Nor Jerry doesn't want it. Then what is 'e after? I'll tell you. What 'e requires is a stepping stone to invade the old country with. Like crossing a stream to keep your feet dry.'

In the atmosphere of fear and confusion, the servants' fear of the Irish outside the castle grounds merges with their fear of Nazi conquest. The invading enemy becomes indistinguishable from the enemy within. After all, the IRA are fifth columnists, fighting against England. And who can tell whether an Irishman belongs to the IRA or not? (In one hilarious scene, an official from the Irish Regina Assurance Company, who calls to investigate the loss of a sapphire ring, is taken for a paramilitary.) Even though the walls of the castle are there to divide the bad Irish from the loyal English, the servants feel increasingly guilty at remaining in a neutral enclave. In the end neutrality seems as invasive as war; at the very least it is just as unsettling. Two of the servants opt to elope for safety to bombed-out England, and the youngest member of the household decides to join the RAF as an air gunner – perhaps the most dangerous of all combatant roles.

Green's novel was not really about Ireland, or even the Anglo-Irish, and no one comes out of it very well except those who leave for England. But it does capture the standoff between Britain and Ireland at this point in the war. This persisted in spite of tremendous efforts on the part of the British propaganda services at the Ministry of Information to get the Irish on side.

6

War in the Air

For more than twelve months after the collapse of the European neutrals, Ireland suffered under a war of nerves. For de Valera, at any rate, the success of neutrality depended on keeping his nerve in the face of threats, and occasionally promises, from the two belligerents. The drive to bolster the national consensus in favour of neutrality, to build up a viable defence force, to sideline republican radicals, to suppress the activities of Ascendancy 'collaborationists', and to control the war of rumours and intelligence were all directed towards keeping the country stable and quiet. But the problem for the government was that however well they succeeded in monitoring and containing internal dissent, they could do little or nothing to stop material coming in from abroad, particularly over the wireless. Radios are ideal means of infiltration across borders, speaking public messages within the private space of the home. The pre-war pastime of 'listening in' suggested both active participation in a wider community outside the home and an almost clandestine eavesdropping. But if the Irish government could – and did – utilise the radio to plant neutrally minded ideas (Grow More Wheat, Join the LDF), the wireless could also be used to send Allied or Axis propaganda into neutral Irish homes. (By contrast, in the late 1930s wireless sets were on sale in Germany which made it impossible to tune in to other national stations, and enemy broadcasts were jammed.)

This was not simply a question of propaganda. From the summer of 1940 much of Britain's war was getting live radio coverage. In July 1940, in preparation for the seaborne invasion of Britain (Operation Sealion), the Luftwaffe attempted to knock out the RAF; the most intense phase of the Battle of Britain stretched on until October of that year. By that time the blitz on London had begun. The aerial bombing of Britain's cities was not to end until May 1941. While people living on the north-west coast of Ireland had visible evidence of some of the effects of the Atlantic Battle, many more could tune in to live radio reports of the bombing raids and the dog-fights over southern

England. Later they could follow the war in North Africa, and in the East. Elizabeth Bowen noted the oddness of this contrast between tranquillity and war:

Bowen's Court, in that December of 1941 in which this book was finished, still stood in its particular island of quietness, in the south of an island country not at war. Only the wireless in the library conducted the world's urgency to the place. Wave after wave of war news broke upon the quiet air of the room and, in the daytime when the windows were open, passed out on to the sunny or overcast lawns. Here was a negative calm – or at least, the absence of any immediate threat. Yet, at the body of this house threats did strike – and in a sense they were never gone from the air. The air here had absorbed, in its very stillness, apprehensions general to mankind.

Like a rather less hysterical version of her character, Aunt Fran, Bowen imagined the war over Ireland as a war of airwaves. She described her house in Cork as 'struck' by threats from the wireless (this from a woman working as an ARP warden through the London blitz); she depicted individuals as ill-tuned receivers ('You did not know what you might be tuning in to'), picking up all sorts of signals from unknown sources.

Both Britain and Germany used the radio as an instrument of war. But the kinds of propaganda the two governments came up with were very different. German broadcasts to Ireland were 'external' and involved putting across carefully targeted propaganda, principally the need to maintain Ireland's neutral resolve and to combat any tendency towards sympathy and support for Britain. (They probably had most in common with British broadcasts on the European service to the Occupied countries.) The BBC, under the direction of the Ministry of Information, did introduce programmes consisting of directly targeted propaganda to Ireland. But the bulk of Irish listening in to the BBC, whether on the Home Services or the Forces Programme, was to entertainment, information and propaganda designed for a British wartime audience. Irish listeners were addressed as part of the British war effort – a situation viewed by the Irish censorship as uniquely destabilising, and one which gave rise to some rather unpredictable effects.

The BBC played a crucial role in mobilising the civilian war effort in Britain, in maintaining national unity and morale in a war in which, increasingly, the whole population were viewed as combatants but few were fighting. Home Front propaganda was complex, and became more subtle as the war progressed. The need to inform the population about a vast number of new regulations, and exhort them to greater efforts in industry and agriculture, was combined with more covert attempts to influence opinion. As Angus Calder has shown, the myth of British morale under the Blitz, of pulling together in adversity, encouraged stoicism during the air raids, as people strove to live up to their heroic reputation. The BBC's role in helping to create a communal spirit on the Home Front has itself achieved mythic status, for its ability to balance security with the public's demand for information, to encourage without condescension.

The ability of the BBC to inspire confidence was far from obvious in the first months of the war, however, and least of all in Ireland. During the period of the phoney war listener research in Britain reported considerable impatience with patriotic broadcasts of the 'There'll Always Be An England' type, patronising messages from the Ministry of Information, and censorious statements from politicians about digging for victory and careless talk. BBC wireless propaganda proved singularly ineffective in raising civilian morale and capturing the interest of citizens. And in persuading them that it was telling the truth. Those in Ireland inclined to interpret all information from British sources as misinformation had their prejudices confirmed by the repeated stories of thuggish Germans and Nazi atrocities, which seemed merely to repeat the excesses of First World War anti-German propaganda. But even for those most sympathetic to the Allied cause, the tone of the early wartime radio was alienating, consisting largely of 'calming' music interspersed with government announcements about new wartime regulations and embargoed 'news'. To the dismay of both the Ministry and the BBC, British listeners began turning to overseas radio stations for entertainment.

In his comfortable family house in Cushenden, County Antrim, in the first weeks of the war, MacNeice recorded the disturbing clash between catastrophe and propriety:

> Only in the dark green room beside the fire
> With the curtains drawn against the wind and waves
> There is a little box with a well-bred voice:
> What a place to talk of War.

The incongruity stemmed not only from the distance between peaceful (unconscripted) Northern Ireland and the battles in Poland, but also from the gap between the cultured voice and its barbaric subject, a gap that seemed harder to close in Ireland.

A large number of Irish wartime stories, articles and plays feature the wireless prominently. Listening to the BBC, and occasionally to Radio Éireann (never to German broadcasts), was almost always used as a device to frame a discussion of domestic issues, as though to emphasise the condition of being both in and outside the war. Patrick Kavanagh, for example, in one of his first articles for the *Irish Press*, in October 1939, began with the war on the radio:

Midnight in Dublin. A wild but not cold October wind is driving rain against my window. The last buses are swishing by on glassy-bright streets. The radio in the flat above me has stopped forwarding to this address the mixture of blather and jazz, which is called propaganda, and which is supposed to influence the masses.

Such of it as has filtered through the ceiling has had another effect on me.

Being an Irishman I would be abnormal if I didn't dream, think and write of far-past peace and quiet in pastoral fields when everyone else is thinking in terms of war.

For Kavanagh, Dublin – neutral or not – had been invaded by the conflict. The city was porous, helplessly vulnerable to the pressures from outside. With no barriers against infiltration from beyond Ireland's borders, and with the flimsiest of partitions between inhabitants crowded together in the city, infection was spreading. Kavanagh represented war and urban life as equally disruptive, but suggested he had some sort of immunity to the invasion of war news because of his nationality. 'Being an Irishman' he had the natural scepticism towards British propaganda born of the experience of Irish history. This type of scepticism might have been just what the Irish censors hoped for, a form of insurance against being affected by British propaganda, since there was nothing the censors could do to control the frequencies to which people chose to tune in.

There is plenty of evidence that the propaganda from the early wartime BBC was an unwelcome irritant in Ireland in the first phase of the war – a reminder of issues that were uncomfortable, of dubious relevance, or simply boring. One Mass Observation diarist, who followed the war while at home in Armagh, going regularly to watch the newsreels and listening to the radio every day, found it was a different matter south of the border: 'the war didn't affect me while I was away. I just lost interest in it.' While in Dublin (at Trinity College) he stayed with his well-to-do uncle and aunt who were Protestant business people in the city: 'We had the news of course on the wireless, but we only listened to it if it happened to follow some other programme which happened to be switched on. For days on end I didn't have a single thought about the war.' Admittedly he was talking about the early part of the hostilities in the winter of 1939 and spring of 1940, when many in England too were finding it hard to credit the reality of the war. To some extent the gap between war and not-war closed 'naturally' in England as the Battle of Britain, the industrial war effort and above all the blitz brought the conflict inside the home, and as all aspects of British life became regulated by war's requirements – although the BBC also learnt that it needed to be more interesting. By contrast, outside the war zone in Ireland it was down to the British Ministry of Information to attempt to narrow the distance between peace and war by spreading information and covert propaganda.

*   *   *

The Ministry was in some ways a congenial environment for Irish activities. From 1941 the Minister of Information was Brendan Bracken, an Irishman and son of a republican, who had arrived in London from Australia and built up a successful newspaper business. Bracken became a Conservative Member of Parliament who was so close to Churchill that it was rumoured he was his illegitimate son. He was heard to describe the Irish as 'those lousy neutrals' and insisted that 'people of Irish stock overseas are heartily ashamed of Éire's attitude.' But under him worked another Irishman, Nicholas Mansergh – head of the Empire Division at the Ministry, a historian who was to become Master of St John's College, Cambridge. A liberal nationalist, Mansergh was keen to promote friendly relations between Britain and Ireland: he published a measured account of the history of relations between the two countries in 1942. After the fall of France he was joined by the future English poet laureate John Betjeman, who worked for two and a half years in Dublin as Press Attaché at the Office of the United Kingdom Representative Sir John Maffey. Betjeman's post, like that of most press attachés in Europe, was a front for his work for the British Ministry of Information, which he had joined at the beginning of the war, having been judged mentally unfit for military service. Along with Mansergh, Betjeman attempted to highlight the difficulties of the Irish position in the British press, and soften the most blatant attacks on Ireland's neutrality, while encouraging in the Irish the most benevolent interpretation of neutrality for which England could hope. He endeavoured to rein in some of the more vicious or patronising versions of the British view, and he managed to put a stop to the Ministry's plan to disseminate propaganda leaflets in packets of tea, soap and toilet paper.

Betjeman got the Dublin posting on the strength of a report he had written for the Ministry following a trip to Ireland in June 1940, in which he argued for the need to soft-pedal propaganda directed to Ireland. Irish censorship was acutely concerned about British attempts to influence opinion, particularly during the invasion crisis. Betjeman counselled, first of all, against trying to whip up fears of a German invasion, or criticising Irish politicians. He also pointed out that the BBC's habit early in the war of presenting German war communiqués alongside British ones had the effect of pro-enemy propaganda in Ireland.

Betjeman's line was that overt propaganda was 'a waste of time' since it could so easily offend Irish sensibilities. In effect he spent his time in Dublin working at public relations; he cultivated a friendly, witty, tolerant persona, interested above all in cultural exchange. He fostered friendships with journalists, civil servants, artists and writers, including Sean O'Faolain and Frank O'Connor. He arranged St Patrick's Day Specials for them and got their stories broadcast on the BBC, he stood Patrick Kavanagh drinks and lent him cash, he arranged for the poet Ewart Milne to take up land work in Britain in 1941. Cyril Connolly's *Horizon* special issue on Ireland (which included part of Kavanagh's 'The Great Hunger', as well as articles by O'Faolain and O'Connor) was down to Betjeman's efforts, as were numerous other smaller-scale features in British newspapers and magazines, including several issues of *Picture Post* devoted to Ireland. His days were spent organising cultural functions, liaising between the Ministry and Irish censorship, introducing literary, academic and intellectual visitors, making contacts in the press, the government and the church, disseminating English Catholic publications, helping those who wanted to join the Forces, and sifting through advice and information sent to him by many (often anonymous) pro-British correspondents around the country.

Through all this his task was to emphasise that the Allies were going to win the war, and the inescapable fact of Ireland's military and economic dependence on Britain. There are also some suggestions that he was liaising with naval intelligence in forwarding information on the presence of U-boats around the west coast of Ireland, and he may have been engaged in other clandestine intelligence-gathering activities. But he refused to get involved in planting rumours, presumably because that might have compromised his credible, neutrality-friendly persona.

He was, by all accounts, very good at his job. Six months after he arrived in Dublin he was a well-known and popular figure, frequently encountered in the pub, and at house parties and literary functions. But to friends in England he revealed a rather different side:

Just over two months ago I got the job of Press Attaché here. I did not want it, as I was just beginning to enjoy myself at the M of I and had made many friends and was actually making films . . . I move now in diplomatic circles and have moved Propellor [his wife Penelope] and the child over here, where I find myself very pro-British and absolutely longing for the darn old blitzes. It is most surprising. I would give ten pounds to see a nice over-restored church in England and would embrace the first piece of polychromatic brick-work I could clap eyes on. I have to see pro-Germans, pro-Italians, pro-British and, most of all, anti-British people. The German legation here is pretty dim and repulsive. I have to see journalists, writers, artists, poets. I have to go about saying 'Britain will win in the end' and I have to be charming to everyone and I am getting eaten-up with hate of my fellow beings as a result. The strain is far greater than was living in London under the blitz.

Taking a break from the stress of all this cultivating and socialising, Betjeman divided his targets into the following categories 'in descending order of magnitude':

1 pro-British with relations fighting, but above everything pro-Irish
2 pro-Irish and not caring who wins, so long as Ireland survives as a united nation
3 pro-Irish and anti-British, but also anti-German
4 pro-Irish and pro-German

But it doesn't really matter what they think. One friend gained for England is one enemy for Germany and that is my job.

Although Betjeman's job description read 'Press Attaché' – and he spent a good deal of his time liaising with newspaper editors and journalists in both England and Ireland – he was acutely aware of the new power of the radio. In the run-up to war defence analysts had expressed concern that wireless technology would fatally harm Ireland's attempts to remain isolated. Immunity from attack seemed an impossible dream with wireless communications vastly extending the possible scope of air war. But in the event, it was in the area of propaganda that the wireless was to have its greatest impact on the country. British, German and Vatican radio stations took broadcasting to Ireland extremely seriously, and poured their incompatible versions of events across the airwaves.

It was ironic that it should be the wireless which so often breached the dyke of Ireland's wartime isolation. The inauguration of a national radio station (to counter 'British music-hall dope and British propaganda') had been announced with fanfare in the period immediately following the founding of the Free State. It was imperative that British influence should be held at bay, allowing a fragile Irish identity to put down firmer roots. Regarded as a nation-building institution, as important in its own way as the school system, the radio was employed as a means of fostering Irish identity along the 'right' lines. Through radio those living on isolated farms, or in remoter districts of the country, could be drawn into the life of the nation, without the need to migrate to the towns and cities.

Radio could also reach out to the 'greater Ireland': the communities of emigrants beyond the country's shores. De Valera himself was alert to the potential of the medium, using his St Patrick's Day broadcasts to outline his vision of the national culture. In his broadcasts to the US he sought to maintain the sympathy of the diaspora, as well as putting the Irish point of view to the American public at large. But if broadcasts could be transmitted outwards (in fact, despite attempts to relay Irish news bulletins and traditional music to the United States throughout 1940 and 1941, programmes had to be recorded and replayed, as the Irish transmitter was not strong enough to reach the States), they could also come streaming in from abroad.

Long before the war, in fact, wireless had revealed its ambiguous potential. As early as 1924 there had been a foretaste in the Dáil and in the Irish papers of debates that would erupt during the war. One deputy warned

We cannot set up a Chinese wall around the country, or establish an exclusive civilisation. If we wish to do that let there be no wireless broadcasting, let there be no telegraphic cables, no foreign postal service. If we are to pursue that policy, let us pursue it to its logical conclusion. We are not a little island in the middle of the Atlantic between America and Europe. For good or evil, we are a part of Europe. In the past – the distant past – we influenced Europe profoundly – and I hope it will be our lot to do so again. We shall not do it by pursuing a policy of isolation and by shutting out the education that comes from European civilisation.

This debate returned with urgency in the first two years of the war. Above all, argued P. J. Little, Minister for Posts and Telegraphs (who had responsibility for radio), the Irish station must preserve and deepen its 'distinctively national' character. To this end he put his energies into developing the 'purely Irish' aspects of programmes – distinctive features such as the Irish news bulletins, nightly Irish music programmes (mostly devoted to céilidh music), plays by Irish authors or in the Irish language, talks on Irish subjects, concerts of music by Irish composers. If this was Ireland's equivalent of British home-front propaganda, it was also powered by the idea that the station should be engaged in 'external' propaganda on behalf of the country, to combat the criticisms of neutrality being presented in the British and United States media. Arguments were put forward for broadcasts in French and German, and for targeted broadcasts to Britain and the United States. Given the poor reception on the Athlone frequency, however (which made it difficult to listen even in Wexford after about seven in the evening), the station's major focus was on the home audience. The difficulty was in reaching the right balance between what people wanted to hear – in order to encourage more listening – and what it was felt they should hear, within the financial and technological constraints of the service.

Despite the dream of cultural independence fostered through the radio, by the 1940s Radio Éireann was an under-financed subsection of the Department of Posts and Telegraphs. Barring a series of pioneering and hugely popular live broadcasts of major football and hurling matches, Irish radio had the reputation for being at worst unutterably dull and at best a poor copy of the BBC. The extent of its poor reputation was not entirely warranted given the financial restrictions under which it operated. Programming – at an average of six hours a day – consisted mainly of music, religious and sporting commentaries, and programmes for schools. Schools programming was discontinued in 1941 because of the lack of batteries and the fact that there was insufficient petrol for teachers to take their sets to school. A fair proportion of the musical programming (which took up more than half the total airtime during the war) was given over to gramophone recordings of chamber and symphony music, and traditional Irish tunes. There was an hour-long light-music programme at lunchtimes, and occasional modern dance music in the evenings. In 1941 relays of fortnightly Mansion House symphony concerts were introduced, and by 1943 (after some tinkering with phone lines) there were regular relays of provincial concerts, often put on by amateur groups. Waterford, Limerick, Sligo and Wexford all contributed music and theatre, in a move which emphasised the importance of amateur societies in the regions. Drama was expensive but considered popular and by the middle of the war there were relays from the Dublin theatres, particularly productions by the Abbey Players and Longford Productions, and the Galway-based Irish-language theatre, Taidhbhearc na Gaillimhe. Towards the end of the war there were also studio productions of sixty-minute plays, dramatisations such as a long-running version of Kickham's *Knocknagow*, as well as frequent short plays in Irish (often aimed at children). Nearly sixty plays in Irish were produced in 1942 – more than one every week.

Air-time was given to talks on Emergency regulations, the tillage campaign, rules governing the prevention of foot-and-mouth disease, and advice for those city-dwellers newly planting their gardens with vegetables. There were frequent exhortatory descriptions of the activities of the Volunteers and the LDF, which aimed to keep them in the public consciousness and at the same time give them a sense of importance. There were discussions of sport and religious affairs in Irish and English, poetry readings and readings of short stories, as well as attempted innovations such as the *New Verse Competition* begun by Austin Clarke in June 1939 (ridiculed as far too highbrow in the Dáil), and the popular *Information Please*, in July 1941, in which a panel of experts responded to letters from listeners. One of the most popular programmes was the Sunday-night *Gaelic Sports News*, and the sporting commentaries on GAA football and hurling matches, horse-racing, boxing and (from 1944) rugby matches.

Nonetheless there were regular complaints in the press about the poor quality of the service: reception was patchy in places, announcers had indistinct voices (particularly Irish-language announcers), and the 'niggardly' fees paid to writers and performers led to penny-pinched presentations. Drama suffered from doubling and tripling up of parts so that characters often became mixed up and plots impossible to follow. Low fees were a particular problem when it came to providing Variety on the Irish station; high-class performers simply took themselves elsewhere. For example, when Jimmy O'Dea and Harry Donovan asked for forty guineas to relay their pantomime *Hansel and Grettel*, they were offered ten. They took it to the BBC. Radio Éireann did showcase one extremely popular programme: the Sunday-night audience-based *Question Time*, a live, roving, participatory programme, which was mainly confined to Dublin during the war years because of petrol shortages and travel restrictions. *Question Time*'s popularity had a great deal to do with the wit of its compère Joe Linnane, and its unscripted, impromptu contributions. On one occasion when the show was aired from Belfast the host asked a competitor for the name of 'the world's best-known teller of fairy-tales': the expected answer of Hans Christian Andersen was skipped over in favour of 'Winston Churchill', to the delight of nationalists in the audience, and the fury of unionist politicians (questions were asked at Westminster). *Question Time* grabbed its listeners, but there were persistent worries that 'foreign stations' were generally more entertaining than Radio Éireann, and that most citizens listened 'for nine-tenths of the time to a British station'.

The News department struggled with few resources and a tiny budget. The News staff was increased to three in 1940, broadcasting three bulletins a day, at 1.40, 6.45 and 10.30, and eventually two at weekends. With such meagre staffing resources it was obviously impossible for the station to gather news in the manner of the large newspapers, which might have four or five reporters on duty at any one time. For national news Radio Éireann relied on government bulletins, the digest of the Dáil debates and second-hand newspaper reports. Opposition politicians complained that as far as national news went the station might as well be called 'Radio Fianna Fáil', given its tendency to mouth government views, and above all to broadcast de Valera's speeches. Meanwhile war news had to be filleted from foreign newspapers, and from British, German, US and Vatican Radio broadcasts.

The News department's task was to present the incoming war news in as neutral a way as possible. In effect this meant taking the 'emotion' out of reports, and relaying simple facts as far as they could be ascertained. Very often it meant giving the facts as both sides construed them. It was inevitably hard to inject much passion into the repeated 'lists of planes shot down, ships sunk, or tanks shot up'. A great many of the complaints about the service voiced in the Dáil focused on the airtime given to these digests of the war. One deputy insisted in 1941, 'There is certainly too much war news and it is really annoying to hear it on the radio. I think the less we hear about the war the better . . . The people of this country have not that terrible interest in war news which the manner of its presentation might tend to represent.' A year later similar opinions were being aired: 'since the war started we have really got no news at all about our own country. I hope some more time will be devoted to news of Irish interest, instead of having each news bulletin devoted almost entirely to war news.' Another deputy argued, 'There is too much in connection with war in the news coming from Radio Éireann. Goodness knows, we hear enough lies from the two sets of belligerents, and I think we should hear more of our own news.' The station had its priorities wrong: 'I think it was a week last Monday that Cardinal MacRory made a statement about his pastoral being held up and that it was almost the last item in the news. All the English war news was given before it. Surely the Minister does not suggest that for Irish listeners the war news was more important than Cardinal MacRory's statement?'

All these TDs agreed that the war news was irrelevant to Ireland, or less relevant than domestic news, and that it was dull. By contrast, P. J. Little insisted that the Irish war news was valuable precisely because of its measured and even downbeat quality:

There is good ground for thinking that, by reason especially of the impartial manner in which news items are presented, particularly those relating to the international hostilities, the news bulletins of Radio Éireann are now followed with considerable interest not only within the country but even in places outside.

One of the most striking aspects of these debates is the assumption on nearly all sides that everybody was listening to the BBC. Deputy Corish, for example, who regularly complained about the amount of war news on Radio Éireann, insisted that it was unnecessary given the fact that everyone had heard the news already – and that nobody believed it:

We get all the war news from the English stations at 1 o'clock every day, and then we get a rehash of it from Athlone at 1.40. Nobody wants to listen twice to the same news. But there are certain announcements and certain items of Irish news which one wants to hear at 1.40. Surely it is not too much to ask that the Irish news items should be given preference and put first. Government announcements and matters like that should be given preference to English war news. Everybody is sick and tired of war news. People do not believe a word of the war news they hear on the radio.

Despite the best efforts of Little and the staff at Radio Éireann, the Irish station maintained its reputation for lifeless broadcasting. When wartime difficulties caused the programmers to cut back on hours of transmission (due to the need to conserve electricity) and variety of programmes (due to the inability to attract advertising sponsorship from Irish-based manufacturers who were themselves going out of business), there were plenty of other stations to take its place. As R. M. Smyllie, the editor of the *Irish Times*, suggested in an editorial of May 1940, 'No matter how bad the Irish programmes may become, 170,000 will continue to take out licences every year in order that they may listen to the BBC.'

*   *   *

Smyllie's pro-Allied bias may have made him rather sanguine about the listening habits of the Irish in general. Others pointed out that the numbers of 'Irreconcilables', dreaming of a British defeat, chose to 'feed their animosity on German broadcasts'. To service this audience there were firstly the immensely popular broadcasts aimed at English listeners by Lord Haw Haw (William Joyce, himself of Irish extraction). While Haw Haw achieved popular notoriety in England, he was also enjoyed by a wide variety of Irish listeners, many of whom switched regularly from the BBC news to the Berlin wavelength to listen in to 'Germany Calling' – in order, as they said, to hear 'the other side of the story'. According to a Czech diplomat, writing in May 1940, not only more extreme elements, but also the large numbers of Irish who remained suspicious of Britain, were drawn to the German broadcasts:

The Irish, in accordance with their traditions have considered this war only from the standpoint of their relations with Great Britain, from the standpoint of old wrongs and from the standpoint of Irish political aims. For the ordinary Irish person who does not know Germany it is sufficient that Germany is striking the English. Of anything further he does not meditate. Even the educated man finds it difficult to free himself from the logic of the ideas which arise from an anti-British complex consciously maintained by the Irish after a decade . . . The Irish were and are in these circumstances very easily accessible to the arguments which flow on the ether from Hamburg and Bremen in an intonation familiar to them. The Irish voice of Lord Haw Haw gains thus many and willing hearers.

The German propaganda services also set up a dedicated Irish radio station called Irland-Redaktion. This service, which broadcast only in Irish for the first two years of the war, was initially manned by several German scholars of Irish language and folklore, who had spent time in the Gaeltacht during the 1930s. It was broadcast immediately following Lord Haw Haw's popular Sunday-night transmissions, in order to maximise the number of listeners. And it was put out in Irish because, the programmers reasoned, Irish-speakers were the most nationalist, most anti-British, of de Valera's citizens. A section of Séamus Ó Néill's wartime novel *Tonn Tuile* suggests that they may have been right. In September 1940 the narrator, an Irish-language enthusiast, travels to the Donegal Gaeltacht to speak the language and immerse himself in folklore. He visits the house of a famous storyteller but is disgusted with the evidence of the decline of folklore and scholarship within everyday Gaelic culture. Instead of the tales of the seanchaí the neighbours crowd into the house to hear Haw Haw on the radio; the Gaeltacht 'crows' are full of praise for the Germans and look forward to the invasion of England as divine justice. They reject the visitor's arguments that Germany hardly has Ireland's interests at heart by insisting that Dubliners have been infected by British propaganda: '"What do you know of Germany," said one, "except what you get from the English papers?"'

The first broadcast on Irland-Redaktion, by Irish scholar Ludwig Mühlhausen, was heard on 10 December 1939; Mühlhausen spent his airtime combating Allied 'lies' about the situation in Czechoslovakia and Poland and reminding his listeners of atrocities committed in Ireland by British forces during the War of Independence: 'Is cuimhin libh fiche bliain ó shin na Black and Tans.' Such flashbacks into the history of English cruelty in Ireland became a regular feature of the broadcasts, and were carried over into the later English-language programmes. From September 1941 Irland-Redaktion expanded to include nightly bilingual transmission, under the aegis of the former director of the National Museum in Dublin, the archaeologist Adolf Mahr, who worked for Ribbentrop's propaganda division throughout the war.

In the spring of 1941 Mahr tabled a report on radio propaganda to Ireland at a meeting of the Cultural Section of the Foreign Office. In it he argued for a huge expansion of the service, consisting entirely of English-language programmes, and for the introduction of new wavelengths targeting 'Irish' listeners in Australia and America, alongside secret stations purporting to be broadcast by the American Irish, with a target audience in Ireland. Given the increasingly bellicose noises being made in the United States following the fall of France, Mahr was particularly alive to the need for 'active support' for Irish-Americans in their arguments for neutrality. Throughout 1941 the American Friends of Irish Neutrality, and other groups supporting Ireland's stance, came under increasing pressure from the heightened patriotism in the United States and growing support for Britain. The broadcasts directed to Irish listeners, encouraging them to stick with their neutrality, were part of a much larger propaganda offensive designed to stem the growing disillusion in the States with 'America First' isolationism. Mahr wrote:

The programmes are supposed to appeal to the independent national identity of the Irish around the world, to strengthen the neutral position of the country spiritually and to encourage reform into a *non-belligerent stance*, while the line can be maintained that upkeep of this neutrality is not only in their interest but also in the interest of world reconstruction after the war. Elimination of the Ulster injustice is a basic demand of all Irishmen; it serves the economic future of the country, as well as the satisfaction against England and support for a new, better, world order.

For all the effort put into German broadcasts to Ireland, however, the Irish censorship was far more concerned about the BBC. Despite the inclination of a section of the populace to look on Germany as the enemy of the enemy, the Axis powers remained throughout the war both remote and foreign. The BBC could appeal to a strong base of sympathy with Britain. And as programming improved the mixture of entertainment, exhortation and encouragement characteristic of British Home Front propaganda was liable to appeal to a large number of 'neutral' Irish citizens too. The earlier diet – Gracie Fields singing 'There'll Always Be An England', and patriotic images of the British nation as an English rural village – had not been guaranteed to appeal to Welsh, Scottish or even Northern British citizens, let alone the Irish, and such fare was soon suppressed as the Ministry of Information made strides in evolving a propaganda system suitable to the majority of the population. Regional broadcasting, including broadcasts in Welsh and Gaelic, made a difference, as did the sheer quality of much of the feature programming on British history, political traditions and character. But it was the tremendous and universal popularity of stars such as Vera Lynn and shows such as *ITMA* and *The Brains Trust* that really worried the Irish censors, since they encouraged tuning in to the BBC.

The ability of British radio to appeal to Irish listeners was underscored by the number of Irish nationals on air. Early in the war the Dublin-born playwright Denis Johnston was recruited for the Ministry of Information's propaganda offensive. Johnston came from a liberal Protestant background. His father had supported Home Rule, and despite – or perhaps because of – his education at Merchiston and Cambridge he was well disposed to the independence of the Free State (indeed, of a united Ireland) and supportive of Ireland's neutral position. Early in the war Johnston shared with Bowen, Butler and MacNeice a sense that Ireland simply did not have the option of fighting. This created some difficulties for him on the outbreak of war, when he was employed at the BBC's fledgling television station in London. Television was closed down at the beginning of September 1939, and Johnston was moved to radio, where he feared he might be asked to produce anti-Irish propaganda, or attacks on her neutrality. In the event the BBC sent him back to Ireland in 1940, where, as Johnston's biographer puts it, for two years

he was to be enlisted in the drive to win Éire's support for the war or, if that was not possible, at least making its neutrality as pro-British as possible. His task was to investigate whether radio talks and other material could be provided from Dublin, for transmission on the BBC's Overseas service, which could reach the tens of thousands of Irish citizens who were already serving with the British forces abroad. The thinking was that supporting Irish soldiers in the field with news and reminders of home would be a first step towards winning hearts and minds in Éire.

In addition he was to supply programme ideas for use by the BBC in Northern Ireland, aimed at encouraging Éire to enter the war, in order to fulfil the British Ministry of Information's policy objectives. From the very beginning, then, Johnston found himself having to compromise his belief in Ireland's right to be neutral. In 1940 he joined the

Local Security Force in Dublin, where his brief was the protection of the country from both sides in the war. At the same time he was making programmes designed to undermine Ireland's non-partisan status.

Alongside Betjeman he corralled Southern writers such as Sean O'Faolain and Frank O'Connor to give St Patrick's Day talks and personal accounts of the atmosphere in Ireland, as well as broadcasting their short stories. From the North he recruited Denis Ireland to give a series of talks on the cultural renaissance in Ulster. And he contributed his own regular Irish commentary to the overseas service, in which he tried to modify visions of Ireland's tactless wartime partying by explaining the severity of shortages and rationing south of the border, the plight of the poor in Dublin, the efforts made in coast-watching and minesweeping, the consequences of air-raids. Of the effects of the bombing in Dublin in 1941 he suggested, 'It was painfully like what we have seen elsewhere.'

The aim of his talks was to underline connections between North and South – an objective that annoyed both unionists and nationalists. J. J. Walshe complained in December 1941 that Johnston's broadcasts from Ireland were creating a 'wrong impression' in America. Instead of descriptions of day-to-day life, he wanted Johnston to stress

the unity of the country behind the Government in its policy of neutrality and their constructive policy aimed at reconstructing the nation after centuries of wars and invasion . . . That would lead to the conclusion in the American mind that there could be no question of a country like ours, which has lost almost all the elements of national life, risking its final destruction in a great war.

But Johnston was an unlikely conduit for Walshe's 'positive' brand of neutral-minded censorship, and he continued to broadcast on community kitchens, theatre, fuel shortages and the everyday experience of living in Dublin.

Johnston's job was difficult because all the time he was aiming at different audiences – some programmes targeted Northern resentment against the South, others attempted to court moderate nationalist opinion south of the border. Still others were broadcast to the rest of the British Isles, and aimed at persuading English listeners of the strength of Northern Ireland's war effort, which – in the absence of conscription – was causing a good deal of resentment. A typical attempt to convince listeners of the seriousness of Northern Ireland's contribution was *The Six Counties at War*, broadcast in August 1940. From the perspective of today's spin doctors, the programme used very crude persuasive techniques, including scripted interviews with locals professing their cheerful acceptance of wartime impositions, such as longer hours, and the hardships of unfamiliar work:

I've been about 35 years cutting turf and I can say that the war has made a big difference to us all in these parts. About a third more people have started to cut turf – and mind you it's skilled work, just try it yourself and you'll find out. The rest of us have been cutting more and more to meet the demand . . .

Such contributions were interspersed with stirring editorial commentary:

In Derry you can still hear the bugles echoing across the River Foyle. But apart from its ancient history that stretches back through wars and sieges to St Columba and the first golden dawn of the Christian era, Derry today can provide other sounds besides the explosion of shells or the tramp of marching armies. For over a century Derry has held a foremost place in the world manufacture of shirts, and now in wartime her well-equipped factories have switched over to the production of SHIRTS FOR THE ARMY.

These scripts sound crude, but technical conditions meant that there was very little use of 'authentic' voices in documentary features until after the war. The technology of taped recordings came in later, though Johnston was among the first BBC correspondents to use the 'midget recorder' in Egypt, and later in Italy and Germany. The midget enabled front-line actuality reporting to be recorded on discs, which were then flown home for incorporation in the centralised 'War Report'; this technological advance transformed radio reporting of the war and made a vital contribution to civilian and Forces morale in the final stages of the conflict.

Johnston also had to perform a complex propaganda job in Northern Ireland itself, with listeners divided in their allegiance as nowhere else in Britain. He produced features aimed at reconciling a fractious populace to the need for postal censorship, for example, or at drumming up support for the Dig for Victory campaign. In 1940 and 1941 he made several programmes in two series designed to bolster Herbert Morrison's rearmament campaign: *Go To It* and *Keep At It*. The aim was to speed up the industrial war effort and combat the deterioration of industrial morale. The MOI liaised with both the local and national press to publicise stories and pictures of 'happy factory life' alongside the programmes. Perhaps inevitably the programmes were criticised by the workers themselves for 'artificiality and smugness'.

In January 1941 Johnston was joined at the BBC by Louis MacNeice, who had sufficiently resolved his feelings of being 'guilty of the war' to return from the United States to Britain. He had planned to return six months earlier but was hospitalised with a near fatal attack of peritonitis and spent the autumn convalescing in Connecticut, New York and New Jersey. On his arrival in England in December he applied to join the British navy – this was the height of the Atlantic Battle – but was turned down because of his recent illness and his short-sightedness. Instead he offered his services to the Features Department of the BBC. He had previously ruled out this activity, writing to his friend Eric Dodds from Dublin on 24 September 1939, 'There must be plenty of people to propagand, so I have no feeling of guilt in refusing to mortify my mind.' The transformation of the geopolitical balance by the fall of France and isolation of Britain caused a sea change in his opinions, but it was probably also significant that he had spent the past year listening to this transformation over the radio. MacNeice was impressed by Ed Murrow's accounts of the atmosphere in London, after Dunkirk and later during the London blitz. Murrow had developed a technique of pure news reporting: listeners to the Columbia Broadcasting Network in the United States could hear his blow-by-blow accounts from the roof of a building or ARP station in the middle of an air raid.

MacNeice's brief at the BBC, like Johnston's, read 'Features', but meant 'Propaganda' – though MacNeice's output was almost entirely aimed at the English market. Most of MacNeice's wartime output – over seventy programmes – were news features, exploring the background to current events, often at quite a distance. *Dr Chekhov* and *Alexander Nevsky* were two of his responses to Hitler's invasion of Russia, and his first radio play, the acclaimed *Christopher Columbus*, was a celebration of Britain's new ally, the United States. In his boss Laurence Gilliam he had a sympathetic and imaginative superior, who worked with Dylan Thomas and other well-known writers and composers, including Elisabeth Lutyens and Benjamin Britten (who returned to Britain in 1942). Nonetheless, MOI directives had to be followed. These might include instructions to highlight stories from Nazi-occupied Europe and accounts of German barbarity, for example; or to represent voices from around the British Isles, to feature Irishmen serving with the British Forces, to praise British democracy, the freedom of the press, religious freedom, or the relationship with the Dominions.

The titles of some of MacNeice's broadcasts give a sense of the kind of fare he was required to produce: *Salute to the United Nations*, *Salute to the US Army*, *This Breed of Men*, *The Debate Continues* (subtitled 'In honour of the House of Commons on the first anniversary of the destruction of the debating chamber'); a series entitled *The Four Freedoms* (which explored the concept of freedom as illustrated in history); another titled *Black Gallery* (Number 10 was a portrait of Adolf Hitler). Despite the brief, MacNeice produced some innovative forays into radio documentary, then a newly developing form. Traditionally the airwaves had carried spoken essays, monologues, or lectures, but not the collision of viewpoints, or the portrayal of character. By bringing the techniques of drama to his documentary work, MacNeice sought to grip his audience's imagination in new ways. Short series such as *The Stones Cry Out . . . But the People Stand Firm* (aimed at the United States and featuring accounts of the bombing of Britain, including one on 'A Home in Belfast') and *The Four Freedoms* were far from simply propagandist, and vied with some of his most interesting radio plays, such as *He Had A Date* or *The Dark Tower*. One of MacNeice's favourite techniques was to include fictional 'listeners' to the programme as characters in the drama. These would interrupt, comment on or express scepticism about the propagandist intent of the features, allowing some of the weariness with morale-boosting war talk to be addressed openly. They were intended to go some small way in combating the sense that people were being talked at by their radios, and fed only half-truths.

These features by MacNeice and Johnston could be picked up by radios in Ireland, particularly in the Dublin area, but the difficulty for the programmers was that material broadcast on the British Home Service was either listened to with scepticism (if not rejected outright as propaganda), or regarded as preaching to the converted. This was particularly true of straightforward features. In addition to regular news broadcasts and occasional features, therefore, towards the end of 1941 the BBC inaugurated a series of programmes entitled *Irish Half Hour*. Ostensibly designed for Irish people serving in the forces, the real target was the Irish audience at home.

The popular Dublin comic Jimmy O'Dea was signed up for a string of appearances as Biddy Mulligan, the Pride of the Coombe, and as the shopkeeper in a series of skits on small-town life during the Emergency. These sketches, set in the town of 'Ballygobackwards', were a very obvious attempt to produce an Irish *ITMA*, with its more or less direct lampoon of wartime conditions. These alternated on a weekly basis with songs from Count John McCormack and a group of musicians and storytellers. Betjeman argued that the programmes were popular – O'Dea more so than McCormack – but not sufficient. He was convinced that the Germans still had the upper hand in the propaganda war:

Half-an-hour's variety is not enough. The Germans at the moment broadcast two programmes a day to Éire, one on a medium wave and a Gaelic programme on Sunday evenings. The BBC programme would be most effective if broadcast simultaneously with one of the German broadcasts, or Haw Haw – preferably the latter – and could thus diminish the Germans' audience.

There is a widespread impression in the country here that of the two BBC programmes, Home Service and 'Forces', the 'Forces' is the one to listen to as it is not BBC and, therefore, is not propaganda. If mention of men of Irish birth or descent who have been given awards could be made on the Forces programme, perhaps before the Sunday half-hour, that would be a grand thing. There is little possibility of getting these awards printed in Irish papers, owing to the Irish censorship; few British papers have a wide circulation here though such information should always be put in those papers which print Irish editions – mentioning the birthplace of the awardee or his parents' birthplace in Éire!

There were further difficulties with *Irish Half Hour*. From the very beginning the arrangements for a regular cross-border Irish magazine programme involved delicate dealings with officials in the North, for whom any negotiation with Ireland amounted to appeasement. As the Northern Ireland Prime Minister, J. M. Andrews, put it:

This, in my view, would be an insidious form of propaganda which would entirely misrepresent the position of Northern Ireland in the United Kingdom and would slur over the neutral and most unhelpful attitude which Éire has taken up during the war.

What bothered both the government and the BBC in Northern Ireland was the idea that they should be linked in any way with the South, because by default Northern Ireland therefore seemed to be detached from the United Kingdom. There were remonstrations over the title of the programme (which should surely be called *Éire Half Hour*, not *Irish Half Hour*, they reasoned) and fury over the introductory tag that led into the programme: 'It's All Yours Ireland!' In the end the Dominions Office wrote to Betjeman in August 1941: 'We have had so many remonstrances from the Northern Ireland government on the lines of "shaking hands with murder" that we have decided to exclude Ulster from the programme for "Eirishmen" in the Forces.'

Meanwhile the Ministry of Information was convinced that *Irish Half Hour* was an important contribution to the propaganda war. The comedy of the programme was its great strength, giving it the upper hand over any number of more 'directed' propaganda messages. The watered-down stereotypes of well-meaning, hopelessly disorganised Paddies, with a fondness for drink and a penchant for roguish rackets, interspersed with popular Irish tunes, might serve on the one hand to defuse English hostility towards the Irish, and on the other to take the edge off the anger against Irish intransigence. But the primary target audience were the Irish who were presented as 'in it' with the English, cheerfully struggling through the funnier side of wartime restrictions. It was as though the English and the Irish were belligerent and friendly sides of the same coin.

Despite O'Dea's popularity it is difficult to gauge what people really thought of the programmes. There is nothing subtle about the characterisations, nor the intention, and it is hard to tell how well this went down with the Irish in the British forces, let alone those in Ireland. In the spring of 1944, for example, Con Leventhal, writing the Dramatic Commentary in the *Dublin Magazine*, records that he was 'still depressed by memories of the BBC *Irish Half Hour* . . . [which] rivalled in vulgarity any stage Irishman performance of other years'. Certainly the comedy series did not suit all tastes, especially in the Gaeltacht, which had never had the same degree of cultural contact with Britain. Nicholas Mansergh was keen to introduce more programmes in Irish: 'a most valuable form of indirect publicity. The Germans pay a good deal of attention to Celtic and Gaelic broadcasts.' He was also bothered about the clash between *Irish Half Hour* and *American Commentary*:

There is an almost morbid desire on the part of confirmed 'neutrals' to hear what the USA is thinking and saying about Éire's attitude to the war in general and the ports in particular – (and a corresponding disappointment when no mention is made of it) and this makes some people choose the Home Service.

On the other hand the lure of Jimmy O'Dea deters some who would be none the worse off hearing American opinion, from doing so. Both programmes have definite propaganda value and it seems a pity that they should clash.

* * *

With the BBC transmitting from London and Belfast, and Irland-Redaktion broadcasting from Bremen, Berlin, and Luxembourg, not to mention CBC, NBC and Vatican Radio, the airwaves over Ireland were an ideological battleground. Certainly Radio Éireann and the BBC led the field, but it is impossible to estimate with any accuracy how many people were listening in, and to what. For despite the keenness of the audience, the main difficulty, as the war progressed, was maintaining the technical means to listen to anything at all.

There were nearly 170,000 licensed radio sets in Ireland on the outbreak of war, together with at least 25,000 unlicensed sets (probably many more). Nearly half the licensed radios were concentrated in the Dublin area. The numbers of licensed sets rose to over 180,000 during the first years of the war, but then fell steadily because of a shortage of batteries. Many houses, particularly in rural areas, were without electricity, so that by 1942, when supplies of batteries had nearly run out, the radios outside the cities were largely silent. Wireless technology required the use of two batteries, one 'wet' and one 'dry'. A failing radio first needed diagnosis – was it the wet or the dry battery that had gone dead? The wet battery – about the size of a large hardback novel – had to be taken to a local garage or bicycle shop for recharging. Regular listeners ideally needed two wet batteries, therefore, and the presence of mind to charge one up a few days before the other went. Soon enough, with shortages of power, the garage could not help, and the supplies of dry batteries also began to run out. 'More Zinc for Éire!' urged John Betjeman in increasingly frenzied letters to the BBC, as he explained that the propaganda value of programmes such as *Irish Half Hour* was being seriously undermined by the diminishing number of people able to hear them. P. J. Little, Minister for Posts and Telegraphs, advised storage of sets with wireless dealers or traders while the battery difficulty continued, so that people would not be liable to pay the licence fee (which increased from 10 shillings a year to 12s. 6d. on 1 July 1940) while their sets were out of action. David O'Donoghue has estimated that in 1941 approximately one in nine people in Dublin had a radio, and one in sixteen in Cork, but that figures were much smaller for Donegal, Galway and Kerry, where it was nearer to one in thirty.

It is impossible to say, however, how many people might have been listening to each of these radios. One young man from Connemara recalled the early Irish-language broadcasts from Germany:

It was difficult to hear the Irish talks on German radio because there were practically no radios. People in the Gaeltacht were desperately poor and could not afford to buy radio sets. You would have to be a parish priest or a teacher to afford one. People would gather outside the window of the local post-office trying to listen to one of the few radios in the locality. I heard Mühlhausen. I knew the thing was going on.

Three years into the war the airwaves in the Irish countryside were all but silent. Elizabeth Bowen, reporting back to the Dominions Office in July 1942, was in no doubt about the keenness of Irish people in the countryside to keep up with the news, nor about the difficulty they faced in doing so:

In this rural part of Éire (Co. Cork, approximately 135 miles from Dublin), which is, I suppose, typical, I notice a very much greater degree of cut-offness, since last year, with regard to up-to-date war news. This for two reasons – 1) The scarcity, and late arrival of newspapers; even the local paper, *The Cork Examiner*, does not reach the village until the late afternoon of each day.

2) The difficulty, nearing impossibility, of obtaining new high tension batteries for wireless sets. Wireless sets, other than those run on electricity (ESB or the plants of the big houses), are gradually going out of commission. Almost all the cottage wireless sets are now silent, and likely to remain so.

The break in the habit of listening in is energetically regretted by the country people. Cottages that had wireless were much frequented by neighbours after working hours. Young men and boys who did not possess a wireless had the habit of walking miles in the evening to listen in at a friend's house – always to the war news.

The virtual suspension of wireless, and the greater difficulty in obtaining newspapers, only bring into prominence the keen interest felt by rural South Irish people in the progress of the war. I have gathered opinions on this from many people – employers of labour. All are struck by the intelligence, the grip and the up-to-dateness shown, on the subject of war news, by country working men. The interest would appear to be keener than in many parts of rural England.

In this, I notice a contrast between the Irish country and Dublin. Dublin was more apathetic. In the country the men (though not, I think, the women) are keen readers of newspapers – even when they are, owing to present conditions, a day or two out of date. The increasing uselessness of country wireless sets is felt as a deprivation and injury. At those informal gatherings of country working men that go on in the evenings, at the crossroads and bridges, I am told (and can gather from what I have overheard) that 'they talk of nothing else but the war'.

Bowen's diagnosis of a 'greater degree of cut-offness' was supported by numerous stories of travel difficulties, as well as John Betjeman's desperate pleas for zinc to replenish fading wireless batteries. To make matters worse, as the war progressed, printed news also became more exiguous, with paper shortages forcing newspapers to grow thinner and thinner – a two-page spread was all that many could manage.

War news was experienced both as too much, then, and too little. Complaints about the amount of war news on the Irish wireless station were coupled with insistence that everyone listened to the BBC. Annoyance that war news preceded Irish domestic issues on the radio was mirrored by arguments in the press that citizens were more interested in international than national or local reports. In July 1942 the *Cork Examiner*, which regularly featured maps of far-away theatres of war, somewhat paradoxically complained that its readers knew more about what was happening in Russia than in the upcoming local elections. In the same way, said Bowen, 'The pros and cons of the second front question are eagerly debated':

" All right ! All right ! It's the price we have to pay for Peace—now, don't say it again."

I would say there was passionate interest in the war as a topic; and at the same time, there is a dispassionate tone to discussions, as few people are willing to declare themselves parti pris on either side.

I have met, and heard of, almost no explicit pro-German feeling in this part of Éire. But there continues to be an almost superstitious admiration for the German fighting technique.

One psychological explanation of this interest in the war is that it is a form of escapism. With regard to Éire domestic affairs the country people are at once bored and depressed. A sense of immediate dullness, fretted by deprivations, seems to cloud life here. 'The war' stands for drama, events in a big way, excitement. All this appeals to the Irish temperament.

205

Leaving aside the patronising flourish, there seems little reason to query Bowen's view of the detached interest with which people followed the war. No doubt part of the attraction lay, as Bowen suggests, in the war's inherent dramatic interest; stories of advances and reverses on the battlefield, the tactics of generals, or the daily tally of planes downed over the Channel, provided matter for debate and discussion even for those who felt personally unaffected by the news. The pub talk of the Monaghan farmers in Kavanagh's 'The Great Hunger' suggests that the rural populace were well up on strategy, for example:

After that they went on to the war, and the generals
On both sides were shown to be stupid as hell.
If he'd taken *that* road, they remarked of a Marshal,
He'd have . . . O they knew their geography well.

Beyond an interest in campaign technicalities, however, there was clearly also an intense concern for the progress of the war, and this was perhaps particularly true in the more remote rural areas. The high rates of emigration from the West created a situation in which some of the most isolated and inaccessible areas of Ireland had the closest connections to Britain, through the large numbers of men and women now working in the war industries, or serving as members of the armed forces. The rapid economic decline in Ireland during the 1940s gave rise to a curious situation in which some of those most 'cut off' were at the same time most drawn into the war.

Outsiders often commented on the growing sympathy for Britain. As Axis aims and Axis methods became clearer throughout 1940 and 1941, through news and private correspondence, tacit support for Britain grew – but it did not shake the popular commitment to neutrality. In this respect the Irish censorship appeared to have achieved its aims remarkably well. A battle was being fought over the airwaves, in which the sympathy for one side or the other was determinedly wooed; in the middle Radio Éireann maintained its resolutely neutral stance, and, argued Little, gained trust and respect for doing so:

I have heard it said from other countries, as well as from Ireland, that the news, as we present it, is very objective, that we give both sides and give people an opportunity of forming their own opinions. Naturally the belligerents producing the news give it from their own angle, and it is very difficult to find exactly what the truth is, but part of the interest in reading the newspapers or listening to radio stations at present is the attempt one makes to see where the truth lies between them, in order to get oneself correctly informed on what is going on.

Listening to the BBC provided information which came, as it were, with a health warning attached – you could be in no doubt that you were listening to propaganda. (Deputy Hickey complained, 'Of what use is it when you cannot know whether it is true or not?') In effect tuning in to either of the belligerents, for the true neutral, meant knowingly listening to distortions and lies, and relying on an ability to sift out the likely and the plausible. Listening to 'balanced' or 'objective' reporting on Radio Éireann, on the other hand, was supposed to enable citizens, firstly, to be accurately informed about world affairs without any such effort, and secondly, to shape their own opinions, independent of propaganda.

Yet the problem was that the impartiality of the Irish State's reporting did not give listeners confidence. In effect, the practice of simply purveying two rival versions of events – according to Allied sources this, according to German sources that – left the reader or listener with no way of telling what was true and what wasn't. Despite P. J. Little's fanfare for the objectivity of Irish radio news, for many people the coverage was simply too neutral – it ceased to mean much at all.

Jaded and sceptical reaction to the news was not a prerogative of the Irish, of course. In Britain the constant stimulation of patriotic responses led to weariness with (and cynicism about) anti-German and anti-fascist reporting – after a while it became hard to believe that the war really was being fought for democracy and civilisation. The main character in *The Signpost*, a popular 1943 novel by the English novelist E. Arnot Robertson, for example, is an Anglo-Irishman from Cork who has become a fighter pilot during the Battle of Britain. Invalided out of the air force for a time he becomes desperate to get away from the highly charged propaganda in London, where strangers treat him with exaggerated concern and respect:

In Ireland, he knew – grateful at last for her fantastical quality – he would feel further away from the war than he could have done by travelling halfway across the world in his three weeks' reprieve . . . Thank heaven in that other place . . . almost everyone would consider him a plain fool for getting mixed up in the wrong fight; if not, indeed, a bit of a traitor.

He finds himself in a small village in Donegal where only the feuding priest and local gombeen man have radios, tuned to opposite sides in the war.

Such was the level of propaganda emanating from Britain that British media reports had a reputation for falsehood not only in nationalist circles, but also amongst those supportive of the war. In October 1940, for example, Moya Woodside reported from Belfast on the newsreels being shown in the city, which focused on military and ARP activities, rather than informing the audience about the attacks on London: 'The whole effect was of complete unreality, when everyone in the audience knew that air raids are of daily occurrence and creating havoc in the normal routine of life, yet they were not so much as mentioned.' When combined with reports of raids being cut out of letters from England and Scotland, she argued, 'the immediate effect is to make one doubt the adequacy and inclusiveness of *all* press reports and wireless bulletins.'

Disbelief in official statements over air-raid damage and casualties increased throughout the Blitz, because of Ministry of Information embargoes on some forms of information. Indeed, not just doubt, but active suspicion of official versions of events, became widespread. In Ireland, however, distrust of British statements was combined with a lack of clear directives from Irish sources. The upshot was a situation in which rumours could run wild. This was vividly illustrated by the response to several incidents of bombing on the east coast in the first days of 1941.

On 1 January three bombs were dropped between Drogheda and Julianstown. The following day, a bomb fell at Borris, County Carlow, killing three people. That same night, three bombs fell in Wexford, four in Dublin, and three more at the Curragh racecourse. More than twenty people were injured, and forty were made homeless. The bombings, which took place at a time when invasion fears were at their height, created a crisis in the diplomacy of neutrality. Since Germany appeared to be in the ascendant at that stage, the Irish government felt obliged to tread cautiously. In public, members of the government initially refused to confirm that the bombs were German, while in private they puzzled over what the motive could have been. De Valera had recently refused a German request to fly in a considerable number of extra personnel for the Dublin legation. Was the bombing a rebuke for this lack of compliance, the result of a temper tantrum in an office somewhere in Berlin? Or was it part of a more systematic attempt to scare Ireland away from any thoughts it might be entertaining of improving cooperation with Great Britain?

On 4 January newspapers briefly announced that fragments of the bomb which fell at Drogheda had been examined and found to be of German origin, and that the government had made 'strong protests' to Germany. Most editorials resolutely ignored the bombings, however. The *Irish Press* editorials, which read rather like government communiqués, focused on the language question and the need to conserve bread supplies. The *Kilkenny People* of 4 January risked an editorial on the bombings, for which the paper was promptly censored. This was partly because of the tone of the editorial, which argued for the need for the 'ham-strung' parliament to meet during the crisis and criticised Fianna Fáil's 'dictatorial' style of government. The fact that this was censored lent support to the argument that the real target of the censorship was not inflammatory comments about the belligerents but any sign of internal political dissent.

The combination of allowing the facts of the bombing to be published but suppressing debate and discussion had a strange effect. The English diarist J. L. Hodson visited Dublin in January 1941, in the days immediately following the bombing of the city. His assignment was to put the moral case for war, and to sound out opinion on attitudes to Britain and to the leasing of the ports. He found a populace 'more aware of the war than we are . . . Everybody listens to the British wireless, even to the midnight news so that most pieces of news become well known.' (He clearly stuck with well-to-do Dubliners, still well supplied with batteries and electricity.) Nonetheless, even he found himself affected by the neutral atmosphere into which bulletins fell: 'How swiftly one drops into the atmosphere of lights and good food and the feeling that not all Germans are bad!'

If Hodson's report was accurate, it suggests that the Irish government's policy was a resounding success, producing a well-informed but non-partisan population. But the extreme caution of the Irish reporting could also encourage rampant, ill-founded speculation. In the newsreel of the bombing shown in Ireland, the caption spoke of bombs dropping from an unidentified plane, in accordance with a government statement. However, the statement had gone on to report that fragments of the bombs had been recovered, clearly identifying the ordnance as of German origin – but this fact was suppressed in the newsreel and on the radio, though it was published in the papers. At the end of January 1941 the pro-Allied Senator MacDermot, in a wide-ranging attack on the censorship, asked for public confirmation that the bombs were German. Despite the fact that fragments of German bombs had been recovered, there were persistent rumours that they were British – circulating, according to Hodson, even amongst recently arrived refugees from Europe. Edward Murrow, of the Columbia Broadcasting Company, who visited Dublin in January 1941 to sort out some technical details for broadcasting in the event of an invasion, claimed to have met several people who insisted it was all British propaganda: 'Oh, yes, they were German bombs, but who knows the British didn't drop them?' T. H. White had complained of similar rumours the previous year, after a bomb fell in Campile, County Wexford, killing three women:

I only hope you are right about the Germans cracking up in a year. Here the feeling is definitely more pro-British than it was twelve months ago, but still apathetic. The attitude is (1) 'If only they would settle', (2) 'Ireland cannot help by joining in any more than she can by staying out: indeed, she can probably help more by staying out.' We are quite powerless. The 'if only they would settle' attitude is weakening, as people realise that settlement with such a party is impossible. Hitler has helped the English a little by bombing a few ships and an Irish creamery: but there are still a few dyed-in-the-wool nationalists who hint that this was done by the English in disguise. Fortunately a bomber crashed, and was found to be full of Germans. I have rubbed it in what marvellously cunning people the English are, not only to steal German bombers and bombs for their outrages on Ireland, but also to train crews for them from childhood, so they can only speak German.

The government reacted angrily to suggestions that people thought the bombs were British. This, they argued, was simply anti-neutrality propaganda. One way of getting at Ireland for not coming on side with the Allies was to suggest that the people were all wandering around in a miasma of misinformation. But White may not have been exaggerating the waves of rumour and counter-rumour, and indeed seems to have got carried away by them himself, since there is no evidence that a German bomber crashed on this occasion. In February 1941, after the New Year bombings, the IRA's organ *War News* revealed:

Another secret, only now beginning to leak out is that one of the bombs that fell at Dun Laoghaire has been identified as British. The bomb crew made a mistake there. It was their job, naturally, to drop German bombs in order to make the Irish people think that the Germans are their enemies, and this they did successfully in other places. If the Germans had any reason to drop bombs here, it would be natural for them to drop British bombs, of which they must have a huge supply, though it would be nothing to what the British have of theirs.

The government's announcement that the bombs were German was put down to the fact that it was 'so pro-British', and wanted to influence the populace against Germany.

The Irish censorship was aimed, in part, at protecting the populace from foreign propaganda. But it did nothing to counter the jittery atmosphere in which rumour and counter-rumour could flourish. Even many who supported the censorship admitted that the rigours of the system accounted in some degree for the 'nervenkrieg' in Ireland, what Professor Alton referred to in the Seanad as 'this unhealthy atmosphere of rumour and half-truths'. When even reports of the British weather were cut out of private letters, or film newsreels, it seemed nothing could be believed. The 'mental blackout' caused by the strict impartiality in reporting of the war, even when it visited Irish territory, was blamed for engendering a crisis of confidence in Irish attitudes (implicitly contrasted with an increasingly confident Home Front mentality across the Irish Sea), and an ideal environment for rumour-planting and whispering campaigns. German agents were believed to be increasing bomb-nervousness by 'plugged talk'; later on they were thought to be spreading the belief that America's entry into the war would increase the threat of invasion.

This is certainly the mood in Séamus Ó Néill's *Tonn Tuile*. The novel is intriguing for the way it presents the search for a truly 'Irish', truly 'neutral-minded', attitude to the war. The action of the novel takes place during the first two years of the war, as the narrator shifts between Donegal, Dublin, Belfast and rural Northern Ireland. In the Gaeltacht he encounters simplistic pro-German views; in the North he finds resentment over the treatment of Catholics and a wish to see England beaten; among Protestants and middle-class Catholics in Dublin ('especially civil servants') he finds uncritical support for Britain. '"Tá muid neodrach in éadan na Gearmáine," adeireadh siad.' ('"We are neutral against Germany," they used to say.') He keeps running into rumour, debate and partisan opinion about the war and Ireland's role in it – none of which adds up to anything coherent. Ó Néill lamented the lack of a united Irish perspective on the war, growing out of a shared cultural understanding. The novel is a plea for a return to a traditional Irish-language culture uninvaded by either

Britain or Germany – it is full of criticisms of the growing commercialism in Irish life. His remedy was securely traditionalist, but his diagnosis of the variety of opinions on the war chimed with comments from across the political spectrum. The basic difficulty was that neutrality in itself was empty of cause, as it had to be. It was built upon maintaining distance from both sides, and suppressing partisan comment about them. Paradoxically it left both sides plenty of leeway to battle it out in public opinion.

'There is no public opinion,' complained Frank O'Connor in 1942. And a senator in the Oireachtas admitted to Hodson in January 1941: 'There is really no public opinion which you can seize hold of, so mixed is it.' The senator was implicitly equating public opinion with mass opinion, a more or less uniform view taking its cue from official pronouncements, if not moulded by propaganda. Clearly the range of Irish political views was far less orchestrated than the outlook of the British on the war, let alone the more forcefully homogenised state of German opinion. But if Ireland lacked the mass-mobilised atmosphere engendered by the war effort and by the experience of the Blitz, the Irish public were nonetheless united in their solid backing for neutrality. This was partly down to censorship and the government's 'neutrality propaganda'. But it was also common sense. The war was a threat to the country whichever way it came – safety lay in neutrality.

* * *

Dublin was bombed one more time. The most serious air attack was the bombing of the North Strand area on 30 May 1941. Thirty-four people were killed, several hundred injured, and three hundred houses were destroyed. On this occasion, however, there were no conflicting rumours about who was responsible. This was partly because of the number of casualties – speculation seemed both inappropriate and undignified. And it was partly because the government quickly established a strong line on the attack. De Valera protested to the German government, who apologised for the accident, which may have been caused by British interference with Luftwaffe radio beams. But it was also because by then Belfast had been blitzed, with huge casualties. Rumours about British involvement in this latest attack on Dublin would have been tasteless, to say the least.

Faith in neutrality was both confirmed and unsettled by the bombing of Belfast in the spring of 1941, which occurred towards the end of the Luftwaffe's attack on British cities. From September until mid-November 1940 an average of two hundred bombers had blitzed London every night. In late November the German campaign broadened to target a wide range of strategically important and industrial cities: Coventry, Southampton, Birmingham, Liverpool, Bristol, Plymouth, Cardiff, Manchester, Sheffield, Portsmouth, Avonmouth. In February 1941 the German policy changed. Attacks were now focused on British ports, with the aim of supporting the Kriegsmarine in the Battle of the Atlantic: Plymouth, Portsmouth, Bristol, Swansea, Merseyside, Clydeside, Hull, Sunderland, Newcastle were attacked – and on the night of 15/16 April, Belfast.

The bombing of the North – an area over which the Irish government claimed jurisdiction – brought home with a shock the cost of belligerence north of the border and the relative immunity lent by neutrality. But at the same time it reinforced the sense of vulnerability in the South. The Belfast blitz confirmed that Ireland was in the war, and at the same time strengthened the South's neutral resolve. Nobody wanted to bring the bombs down on themselves.

The Belfast raid killed nearly nine hundred people, more in one night than almost any attack on the United Kingdom throughout the war. This was not because there were more bombers, but because there was less protection for the city – almost everyone had thought Northern Ireland too far from the continent for the bombers to reach. During the first weeks of war, when no one quite knew what kind of aerial attack might be in store, gas masks had been publicly burnt, and streets and houses left illuminated in Nationalist areas of Belfast, in defiance of the blackout (in retaliation Catholic workmen were turned out of the Belfast shipyards). The British papers duly condemned such 'betrayal', but in fact the nationalist refusal to play ball was only a more extreme version of a general apathy. At an ARP meeting in Omagh in April 1939, for example, only eleven recruits turned up. Benedict Kiely's 1945 novel *Land Without Stars* is set in Omagh and gives some sense of the pre-blitz atmosphere, as the nationalist Davey Quinn rails against the blackout: 'under God what self-respecting German would bomb this place? He wouldn't have much to crow about back in his beer-garden.' Brian Moore's 1965 novel, *The Emperor of Ice Cream*, paints a similar picture. The story centres on the character of Gavin Burke (a barely disguised version of Moore himself), a Catholic boy from Belfast who risks the censure and ridicule of his nationalist family to join the fire service. Not only is the teenager working for the imperialist powers, but the very idea that ARP might be necessary is dismissed as laughable. Gavin's older brother treats him to a lecture on geopolitics:

'Go on. Hitler never heard of this place. Look, he's got France to beat first. And after that there's the whole of England, Scotland, and Wales. It'll be years before he gets around to this benighted outpost. I'll tell you something. The war's been on how long, two months? Know how many fellows in my year at Queen's have joined up? Four. Which just proves there's no difference between Loyal Prods and bomb-throwing papists when it comes to laying down our lives for Stuttering George. And anyway, why should the Germans worry about a place where half the population will take to the hills at the first rumour of a conscription bill?'

In August 1940 Moya Woodside recorded seeing barricaded police stations and graffiti on the walls of 'RC Districts' in Belfast: 'ARP stands for Arrest, Robbery, Police', 'No Conscription Here', 'Join the IRA'. Even discounting the political scepticism of a large minority, the war, for many people in Northern Ireland, seemed very far away. She described the North as 'probably the pleasantest place in Europe. We are unbombed, we have no conscription, there is still plenty to eat and life is reasonably normal.' Even after the blitz on British cities began, the feeling lingered that ARP was redundant, partly stemming from a belief that the neutrality of the South would somehow cast a protective shield over Northern Ireland. Late in 1940 Woodside reported rumours that the North's freedom from attack could be put down to the fact 'that de Valera has indicated to the German Embassy that Ireland is to be regarded *as a whole*. As long as the English keep out of Éire, this [conception?] of affairs will be respected.'

Others saw more practical reasons why Northern Ireland seemed exempt. Lindsay Keir, the Vice Chancellor of Queen's University in Belfast, wondered 'if there isn't some force in the suggestion that the immunity of Northern Ireland from aerial attack may be connected with the absence of important munitions plants here. It is at least possible, and the corollary might well be that immunity would cease were ordnance factories to be set up . . .' The authorities, however, seemed to doubt the risk. In June 1940 there were no searchlights or mobile anti-aircraft batteries in Northern Ireland. Even after the shipyards, docks and aircraft factories were in full war production, Belfast had only seven fixed guns to protect it, and no other town in the province had any defences at all. By March 1941 the city still had only half the anti-aircraft cover it was thought to need, and the Auxiliary Fire Service was not trained to use the newly acquired fire pumps and hoses.

The first raid, a relatively light one, occurred on the night of 7/8 April, targeting the docks and shipyards. On Easter Tuesday, 15 April, the bombers returned in force and dropped incendiaries, high explosives, and parachute mines in the north of the poorly defended city, setting factories and warehouses alight, and flattening whole rows of the shabby working-class houses where people lived densely packed together. Telephone communication was knocked out, severely damaging the ability to coordinate defence and rescue, and cutting the line to the RAF in England so that Hurricane fighters were not sent to attack the bombers. By 2 a.m. fires had begun to blaze across the city, and, with water mains ruptured, the firemen could not get them under control. At 4.30 John MacDermott, the Minister of Public Security at Stormont, telegraphed a request to Dublin asking for assistance, and de Valera agreed.

Irish newspapers made a good deal of the fact that thirteen brigades of fire engines and ambulances were sent from Dublin and border towns on 16 April. They reported on the 'gratitude' of Northerners for this 'Good Neighbour' policy. And they gave a lot of space to the flight of the refugees out of Belfast. There was something incongruous about the official neutral presentation of the rival British and German communiqués on the raid – placed in many papers in separate printed boxes side by side on the main page – along with quite detailed and disturbing coverage of the effects of the raid on the people of the city. There were eye-witness accounts from Air Raid personnel and nurses trying to cope with the wounded, estimates of the mounting death toll, descriptions of the bodies and body parts laid out in the public baths because the morgue was over-full, and individual stories of tragedy and escape.

In the days that followed there were pictures of the devastation, stories from reporters visiting the bombed-out areas, first-hand accounts by refugees from the city, and tales of the 'ditchers' – some ten thousand Belfast residents too scared to stay in the city after dark, and who slept each night instead on Cave Hill or Divis Mountain. (Their fears were confirmed by a further, smaller raid on the night of 4/5 May, though this time the bombers targeted the shipyards and aircraft factories and casualties were relatively low.) The flight of Belfast's poorest inhabitants into the ditches of the surrounding countryside night after night was officially censured as a crude and chaotic precaution, but it highlighted the lack of faith in the government's ability to protect the people. What looked like funk, a failure of collective resilience, had as much to do with a feeling of being let down by the neglectful authorities. In a secret memorandum to the Cabinet, John MacDermott complained of 'a general feeling that we are neither one thing nor the other, and I think this has contributed to the unsettling effects of the raids'.

For those living south of the border much of the drama of the raids in the first days was gleaned from the refugees who streamed out of the city on 16 April. There were forty thousand homeless, but many more who were unwilling to risk another raid. Many went to relatives in rural parts of Northern Ireland but others crammed themselves into trains going south, or cadged lifts to the border. On 18 April newspapers were reporting the arrival by train of three thousand refugees into Dublin (and another three thousand into Dundalk). There were whole pages of pictures of desperate families being received by the Red Cross or the Local Security Force, and of the military and the gardaí meeting the incoming trains. (The *Belfast Telegraph*'s pictorial record of the blitz, published towards the end of 1941, included photographs of families arriving in Dublin, but the captions described them simply as 'evacuated children', suppressing the fact that they had gone south.) Feeding centres were set up, and requests for donations of food and money to the Red Cross were put out over the wireless.

Both border movements – the fire engines going north and the refugees coming south – were offered as proof that the country was one nation all along. An *Irish Independent* editorial on 18 April was typical: 'If anything further were needed to demonstrate the utter unreality of the artificial border that divides our country, the welcome that has been given to the refugees from Belfast provides it.' And two days later, in a speech at Castlebar, de Valera made the point clearly: 'In the past, and probably in the present too, a number of them did not see eye to eye with us politically, but they are all our people – we are one and the same people – and their sorrows in the present instance are our sorrows.' As the young writer Maurice Craig put it, it looked for a time

as if it were a stage nearer being a united Ireland. The still blazing streets were full of firemen from Dublin, Drogheda and Dundalk, and Dublin was full of refugees from Belfast. The calculations of those who predicted that the populations of Irish cities would never stay still under the bombs as they tend to do in Britain, were proved correct.

Much of this was clearly wishful thinking. The raids were just as much proof that the people were not one people, or at least that they were going to have to suffer differently. Pretty soon Northern unionist rhetoric was using the raids to prove the North's integral part in Britain's battle and underline once again the political distance from the South. But de Valera's rhetoric of humanitarianism and popular national unity did resonate widely in the population. People seemed glad to have been given the opportunity to show compassion and charity to the victims of the war. This was brought home by the popular response to a play performed in Dublin the following year.

In June 1942 Shelagh Richards, the estranged wife of Denis Johnston, and her business partner, Michael Walsh, created a new theatre company to stage Paul Vincent Carroll's play about the Glasgow blitz, *The Strings Are False*. Subtitled 'A Drama of the Clydeside Air Raids' and offered 'In Memory of the Common People of Clydeside who died during those fearful nights March 13th and 14th, 1941', Carroll's drama was set in the presbytery and crypt of a parish church, in an area of Glasgow that had been badly hit by the raids. The analogy between Clydeside, with its sectarian divide, and Belfast was clear to the audience, and so too was the allegory of the choice between pacifist non-involvement versus humanitarian aid which the play hammered home.

Carroll held the Irish response to the challenge of wartime cruelty and suffering up to question. The play's central action focuses on Jerry Hoare, an Irishman and a pacifist, who refuses to join the firefighters, because he is embittered against the British system that caused the death of his father. His choice not to volunteer help is shaped by the injustices of history. At one point he tries to sign on to a boat going to Ireland, but is refused. Against him Carroll sets the parish priest, who is also Irish. While his housekeeper pleads with him to 'go back home to Arrandell and the quiet places in Mourne', he insists 'there is no such thing as my people or your people. People in trouble and with broken lives anywhere in the world are our people.' The priest pleads with Jerry to see the ethical principle that lies beyond countries and beyond history: 'This is not war that comes to us out of the skies – this is the expression of the demon in man, the cult of evil and ugliness vomited over the earth out of a vile conception.' After another night of brutal violence, complete with the sound of bombs and the roar of AA guns, in which scores of people are killed, a child is blinded, and – pointedly, given what had happened in Belfast – the telephone exchange is destroyed, Jerry joins the firefighters. The battle becomes his.

Carroll could hardly have drawn a more explicit connection between the cross-border firefighting in April 1941 and a humanitarian response to the war – and Dubliners responded to it. Richards had touted a version of the play around various theatres (including the Abbey) in late 1941, but no one would touch it for 'political reasons'. The implied critique of neutrality was presumably too dangerous, so it was a much toned-down version that ran at the Olympia in the summer of 1942. Booking the Olympia for the production – a venue known only for music hall and variety – was a risk. But the play, as it turned out, was a runaway success. Dublin audiences flocked to the production. Sixty thousand people came to see it at the Olympia theatre alone, and the record run in Dublin was followed by a long season at the Opera House in Cork. Such was the play's popularity that it was revived again the following year. Shelagh Richards put the success down to 'topical and humanitarian appeal mixed with plenty of blood and thunder. We . . . decided to run it for three weeks, though we knew it might be taken off in two days because it dealt with a war which we're not supposed to know is going on.' In the event it ran for twelve weeks. It was the first time a play put on in Dublin (apart from Jimmy O'Dea's pantomimes) had been allowed to run itself out. The play became a topic of debate in the newspapers, in *Dublin Opinion*, on *Question Time* on Radio Éireann, in the Commonwealth quarterly *Round Table*, and on the BBC.

There is no doubt that the play touched a nerve – but what exactly was it that the audience responded to? In part, they may have been seeking a way of 'experiencing' war without danger. Much of the action takes place inside the crypt, which is being used as an air-raid shelter, bringing to the Dublin stage the noises and sights of the blitz. Shelagh Richards recalled:

One of our difficulties was to get something to make a 'blitz' with. All firearms are controlled, and special permits are needed to get them. Using a lot of influence, we obtained a 'blitz' record from the BBC, but it got broken in transit. Fortunately, feeling it might not come through in time, we had already looked for alternatives, and we found a few noises from the last war. Also the electric maroons, a large drum, and a record with a musical title, Feet Marching over Duckboards, and these had to do us in place of our 1942 'blitz' record.

But the audience also had to deal with the message of the play. One way to understand it was as a blatant indictment of neutral Ireland – the pacifist Irishman is so blinded by resentment against his oppressor that he refuses to help alleviate suffering until he sees that it is affecting the people close to him. The priest's echo of de Valera's words, 'they are all our people', might suggest that the neutral government's response to the victims of the blitz fitted with the Christian humanitarian message of the play. But the priest wasn't talking about a particular nation, but about the human race. How, the play asked, can you put a limit on 'our people'? 'People in trouble and with broken lives anywhere in the world are our people.' Carroll borrowed the rhetoric of the war as a 'people's war' that had developed during the blitz of Britain's cities, and which was just then getting a great deal of attention in the 1942 patriotic box-office hit *Mrs Miniver* – another drama that makes its point through an air raid, civilian casualties, and a clergyman. And Carroll implied that the commitment to suffering humanity had to overcome national bitterness.

But the audience didn't seem to see it like that. Looked at in another light, the play confirmed the morality of neutral Ireland's stance, and the response to the attacks on Britain. It said that a Christian response to the war lay not in belligerence but in aid. It confirmed the individual Irishman's capacity for courage and moral responsiveness, overriding the fact that it was not 'his' war. And it underlined the fact that charity and compassion could be more than just attitudes – they could result in action. A humanitarian response to the war was also a practical response, one that avoided politics and one that every neutral could take part in – indeed, was forced to take part in. As the priest says of the blinded child, 'For even this one crime alone, Man, all over the world, stands indicted. No one can escape. No one can go like Pilate and wash his hands. To your awful challenge we must all answer – the dead and the living, the future and the past.'

7

Immobilisation

In June 1941 the course of the war changed dramatically, as Germany invaded the Soviet Union. On 4 July Charles Ritchie, a Canadian diplomat in London (and later Elizabeth Bowen's lover), wrote in his diary:

This war between Germany and Russia has made things seem different all over again. We have entered into yet another phase of the war. This war is like a complicated piece of music – a great symphony in which motifs are started then disappear and reappear in many combinations. Now in a way it is like not being in the war any longer and yet it is not in the least like being at peace. We are back again in the 'phoney war' feeling of that first year before Dunkirk. Of course the situation is completely different but the feeling of it is rather the same. The German pressure has momentarily been removed. We are not in physical danger . . . the attack on England is off for the time being.

The most welcome sign of this release of pressure was the end of the aerial bombing of Britain's cities, which was all but over by late May. It took some time for people living in the worst-hit areas to credit the fact that the bombers were not coming back (for a while anyway) – but everyday life slowly returned to something near normal. And the pressure was off Ireland too, at least in terms of the threat from Germany. But if the effect on England of Operation Barbarossa was an almost tangible loosening of belts (as well as the hasty cultivation of Soviet friendships), its effect on neutral Ireland proved both more inchoate and more complex.

The danger of a German back-door attack on England receded, but a whole new threat to the stability of the country opened up. Large numbers of IRA activists were safely shut away in the Curragh internment camp in County Kildare and other prisons. But there were new fears that disaffected Catholic anti-communists might attempt an alliance with the Soviet Union's new enemy. In the summer and autumn of 1941, for example, the German spy Hermann Görtz, on the run since his parachute drop into Ireland in May 1940, was sheltered by a considerable number of German sympathisers. He later claimed that, after having given up on the IRA as a likely source of German aid, 'I met, at a cautious estimate, far more than 500 persons, with whom I had more or less exhaustive discussions.' There are suggestions that he met with several officials high up in both the government and the military, including Major-General Hugo MacNeill (the Forces' film and drama enthusiast), who apparently attempted to explore possible cooperation between the Irish army and the Wehrmacht.

On the other hand the new alliance between Britain and the Soviet Union encouraged the small numbers of Irish communists to change tack. Some signed themselves out of the Curragh, renouncing the IRA campaign against Britain in favour of international labour's struggle against fascism. (The British armed services were understandably wary of signing them up and most took up land work in England.) The new situation threw up some unedifying attempts at self-justification – and possibly self-delusion. Sean O'Casey, for example, spent the war in Devon, where for two years he had been vocal about the corrupt nature of Britain's imperialist power struggle. In January 1940 he published an article in *Irish Freedom* in which he argued that Ireland should cease being neutral and come out definitely against the war. The nature of English rule over its subject peoples did not 'fit it to fight for liberty and justice'. A month later he argued, 'There is no use mentioning "Nazi tyranny" to an Irishman. English Government in Ireland, setting aside the Black and Tans, has often been soft-brained, but never soft-handed.' The ports, he argued, should belong to everyone under socialism and until that day there was no point asking Irish people to die by giving them up. On 9 July 1941 he wrote to a friend that Hitler's attack on the USSR 'has somewhat bewildered me too. I thought Hitler would go Left.'

His bewilderment resulted in a flurry of propagandist tracts championing individual Irishmen's role in the war, though he still maintained support for the neutrality of the state as the only practical option for the country. Fellow communist Leslie Daiken put together a collection of articles, featuring a long piece by O'Casey, which all stressed the vital contribution Ireland was making in terms of volunteers and manpower. As Daiken put it in his preface:

The instincts of many people have been peculiarly sound. They have rushed to the aid, under arms, of fascism's victims. *They* do not sit on the fence and await the outcome. Casualty lists and obituaries proclaim this exodus before the world. THEY GO, THE IRISH. How many do not come back?

There was nothing wrong with pointing out the sacrifice of individual Irish men and women, of course, and the almost unrelieved anti-Irish propaganda in the British popular press must have made it seem vital to put the opposite case. But O'Casey tried to rewrite history. The main character in his dreadful play *Oak Leaves and Lavender* is an Irish communist living in Devon (no surprises). He defends Stalin, ridicules stories of persecution in the Soviet Union and champions the glory of the Red Army; meanwhile he trains as a fighter pilot during the Battle of Britain. ('In this fight . . . righteousness and war have kissed each other.') The action of the play suggests that the Red Army has been fighting the fascists since the beginning of the war, in fact that the Nazi–Soviet Pact never happened. O'Casey tried to bury his own tacit support for fascism during the first two years of war.

In Ireland itself nothing quite so dramatic was happening. Newspaper headlines confirmed both the vastness of the new theatres of war, and their foreignness. On the radio and in the papers people followed news from the Russian front, and later stories of the terrible weather and the Soviet advance. They read long, and often contradictory, items on the battles for Singapore, Burma, and Tobruk. Small items giving rival versions of the numbers of ships, U-boats and planes downed in the Atlantic were squeezed off the front page. In any case, despite British protestations, by this stage in the Atlantic Battle the Irish bases were less vital. Although the tally of dead in the Atlantic Battle remained high until late 1943 (when between them the homing torpedo and British codebreakers cracked the submarine system), the British base at Lough Foyle in Northern Ireland began to make up for the loss of the Irish ports. The presence of large contingents of the British army (including many Irish people) north of the border only emphasised the quiet down South. The feeling of isolation intensified once more after the arrival of US troops in January 1942. The South now found itself right next door to a hive of military activity, with a consequent increase in tension, even fears of being overrun. But the friction between the six and the twenty-six counties also brought home the contrast between a society that was ferociously reaping the economic benefits of its new war industries and a stagnant one. Ireland's status as neutral became increasingly irrelevant to the progress of the war – but at the same time the war's effects began to bite hard.

For the bulk of the population the Emergency had settled into the fixed realities of restrictive legislation, censorship, shortages, and

rationing. For the worst hit it meant poverty, unemployment, and emigration. Neutrality had been embraced as a positive symbol of Irish
sovereignty and independence from Britain, but as the logic of war
unfolded, it seemed that the country's vigour was being eroded, rather
than enhanced, by its stance. The energy and dynamism of the country were being sapped, its manpower was leaching away, town and
country were sinking into inertia.

The government's struggle to maintain army recruitment after the
invasion crisis passed was one sign of this inertia (though it was also a
measure of increased security). The Call to Arms in the summer of
1940 had touched a patriotic nerve, galvanising twenty-five thousand
men to volunteer for the army in the space of a few weeks. These were
impressive numbers, and rather more than the Forces could hope to
absorb and train quickly, especially just as they were preparing to
defend the country against imminent invasion. There were difficulties
with accommodating the troops: empty barracks at Naas, Longford,
Mullingar, Boyle, Castlebar, Waterford, and Wexford were opened up,
and additional accommodation huts were built, but many men
remained under canvas for months. It was also a challenge to find
competent officers, and to provide sufficient weapons and equipment.
Weaponry was a particular problem for the LDF, who initially had to
train with wooden rifles, and other weapons. 'We had cubes of wood
from the local sawmills marked clearly with a "G" for our hand
grenades' – the phoney war lived on.

Men were employed on routine tasks such as patrol of the coast and
the 'land frontier', and operating the few AA guns, but the average
infantryman's job was to keep watch. They guarded IRA activists and
others interned in the Curragh and Mountjoy Jail, watched over barracks and police stations, and stood protecting strategic buildings such
as the Bank of Ireland, the Pigeon House Generating Station, the
Naval Service Depot at Alexandra Basin, and Government Buildings.
Away from the city the infantry undertook low-cost route marches of
up to thirty miles at least once a week. They were trained in guerrilla
tactics, particularly hedgerow fighting (they were said to excel at tun-
nelling through and under hedges). Much of the focus of training was
in dealing with the 'subversive activity' of the IRA.

As the fear of invasion receded, the poor rates of pay, lack of
weaponry and dullness of routine work proved less and less of a draw
to the volunteers. In the summer of 1942 the army took on the LDF in

large-scale manoeuvres in the Blackwater valley in County Cork. This injected purpose for a time, and generated vast piles of reels of film by Jack Millar and his team. But difficulties with equipment and provisions continued. By 1944 the shortage of petrol, tyres, and vehicle parts meant that large-scale and even small-scale training movements were stopped. Defence personnel had to get around on bicycles. The most serious problem for morale was that the army never fought – instead, from 1941 large sections of the force were employed on turf-cutting. Soldiers spent the summer months under canvas on the bogs.

Step Together Fairs were brought back with a vengeance in 1942 and 1943, to combat declining morale and to increase recruitment. Despite the fears of civil-war rivalries, even during the initial invasion scare it was 'veterans of past wars' and in particular members of the old IRA who joined the volunteers in the greatest numbers. Younger men tended to stay away either through 'lethargy', or because they joined the British armed services instead. Publicity for the 1943 Cavan Step Together week attempted to tackle this problem head on. While the call to volunteer in defence of the nation had proved effective amongst older recruits – so 'fathers' and members of the older genera-tion 'who may have been estranged through political differences, have already decided to act as one in the face of the common danger' – the army faced real difficulty in persuading younger men to come for-ward. Like other border counties, Cavan faced a particular problem with maintaining its force: the highest incidence of desertion was amongst the border units where it was easy for men to leave for work or recruitment in the North. Cavan's recruitment drive called on 'the boys who were too young for enrolment when their elder brothers ral-lied to the nation's call, while some of the more mature, who have so far forgotten their duty, are expected to do their part instead of occu-pying the position of spectators'.

The problem of morale also dogged the Local Defence Force. Publications such as Charles J. F. MacCarthy's *Regional Defence* offered advice on laying minefields, siting and holding roadblocks, reinforcing fences and houses, and defending a town. But it also laid out detailed instructions on maintaining local morale, along with warnings about what the lack of a confident, collaborative fighting spirit had led to in countries such as France. With no clearly identified enemy, and insufficient petrol for extended manoeuvres, training

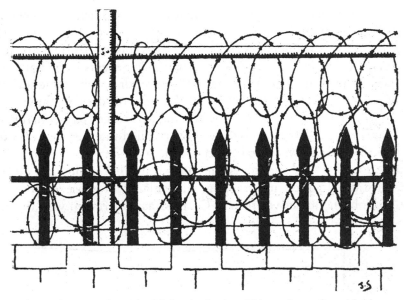

Garden railing reinforced with barbed wire. This makes a formidable
obstacle to an infantry assault upon a position. The obstacle should be
covered by fire.

naturally centred on repelling attacks and holding positions. Some of
the directions seem farcical in retrospect. With advice about how to
turn your front room into a defensive outpost, including sightlines
from behind the sofa to the bay window, or how to fortify your garden fence by wrapping barbed wire around the posts, such booklets
gave little sense of the reality of the enemy. They confirmed the static,
even stay-at-home, nature of resistance. It was an immobilised form of
warfare which held little attraction for many of the young men asked
to undertake it.

At the end of the war the Irish intelligence service, G2, estimated
that approximately five thousand non-commissioned officers and men
of the Defence Forces were absent without leave, and many had been
gone since early in the war. The assumption was that most had either
volunteered for the British forces, or were working in England. Those
who deserted the Irish army for the British were in effect swapping
inert, defensive warfare for the challenges of mobilisation. As General
McKenna admitted later in the war, 'those who have a natural taste
for military life are more inclined to join the British Services, where a

more exciting career is expected'. And for young women there were no opportunities at all in the Irish forces. One Dubliner who volunteered for the ATS in 1941 explained: 'Even if Éire is staying neutral I am not. I don't want to be left out of war [*sic*] shaking events – the Battle of Britain decided me on that.' A natural desire for mobility and adventure, a fear of 'being stuck here' and the need to 'do something', led many young Irish people to enlist. The higher rates of pay available in England were one factor – one deserter recalled that he received 13s. 6d. in the Irish army, compared to a basic pay of £3 10s. in the RAF. But so too was the desire to use the skills learnt in training in a meaningful way. Much of that training, particularly for those involved in skilled jobs in gunnery or the Air Corps, was undertaken with the aid

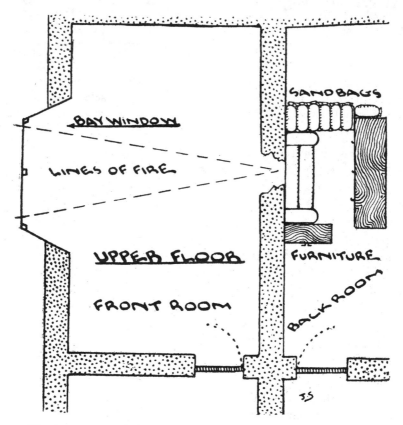

Fire Position inside house constructed with furniture and other available material.

of the British Services anyway. Two RAF liaison officers were stationed at Baldonnel Aerodrome, and the RAF also supplied instructors and flight-training manuals, so that a move from one service to the other can hardly have felt like straightforward desertion. As one volunteer recalled, 'I was in the Irish Army Air Corps up to 1942–43 and there was a mass exodus into the RAF. By 1943 there was no risk of invasion of Ireland and our time in the army seemed a waste of time in many ways.' The date of 1942–43 is significant, for by then there had been a new invasion scare – only this time the fears were focused on the Americans.

*   *   *

The attack on Pearl Harbor had a profound effect in Ireland. It was the polar opposite of the relief in Britain that America was now in the war. Although American government statements had been critical of Ireland's neutrality for some time, throughout 1941 the Irish government, and Irish public opinion, could comfort itself that America was still technically neutral, and could count on American isolationists for support. With America in, fears of becoming embroiled in the war increased, along with an obscure feeling that Ireland had been 'deserted' by the United States.

A diplomatic crisis loomed, threatening Ireland's historic ties with the United States. These were not simply a matter of the large Irish-American community across the Atlantic. The US was a powerful friend, which had intervened at crucial moments for Ireland in the past. In 1921, for example, it had helped put pressure on the British to come to terms with the Irish demand for statehood. Furthermore, as one official in the American Office of Strategic Services put it, 'The neutrality of the United States set the pattern for Irish neutrality.' What were the consequences of America's entry into the war going to be? What would happen now that Ireland's counterweight against Britain was allied with Britain in war?

A week after Pearl Harbor, de Valera gave a speech in Cork in which he sought to reassert the bonds of transatlantic friendship, without giving way on matters of principle:

There is scarcely a family here which has not a member or near relative in that country. In addition to the ties of blood there has been between our two nations a long association of friendship and regard, continuing uninterruptedly from America's own struggle for independence down to our own.

The part that American friendship played in helping us to win the freedom that we enjoy in this part of Ireland has been gratefully recognised and acknowledged by our people.

It would be unnatural then if we did not sympathise in a special manner with the people of the United States and if we did not feel with them in all the anxieties and trials which this war must bring upon them.

For this reason strangers who do not understand our conditions have begun to ask how America's entry into the war will affect our State policy here. We answered that question in advance. The policy of the State remains unchanged. We can only be a friendly neutral.

From the moment this war began there was for this State only one policy possible – Neutrality. Our circumstances, our history, the incompleteness of our national freedom, through the partition of our country, made any other policy impracticable. Any other policy would have divided our people, and for a divided nation to fling itself into this war would be to commit suicide.

The implied threat from 'strangers who do not understand our conditions' became more acute as the 'America First' Movement, and organisations such as the American Friends of Irish Neutrality lost momentum and support across the Atlantic. In joining in the patriotic surge during the war, US citizens of Irish descent were in effect severing their residual emigrant ties with the homeland, and copper-fastening their new 'Irish-American' identity. Irish nationalist newspapers in the States found themselves in an awkward corner. They got around the difficulty of defending Irish neutrality, while also supporting the US war effort, by highlighting the patriotic fight against Japan, and downplaying the struggle in the European theatre. After Pearl Harbor, the *Gaelic American* repeatedly complained about the lack of British cooperation in the Pacific. In January 1942, the paper suggested that the Anglo-American alliance was deploying its forces poorly. There was no need to send US troops to Northern Ireland, it argued, comparing the 'grim tough Americans' who were 'hurl[ing] back ten times their number of veteran Japanese troops in the Philippines' with the 'fully trained British force of close to half a million troops' stationed in the North.

Faced with this increasing political isolation, Ireland more than ever felt the need to maintain American sympathy. It was not only the waning influence in America which caused anxiety, but also the prospect of how the United States would treat the country after the war. This new worry, however, was a sign that an Axis victory now no longer seemed likely, or indeed possible, with the United States in the war and the Soviets pushing back the German attack. Earlier precautions aimed at placating the Germans, half-thoughts that some good might even come of a German triumph, no longer applied. Calculations that a victorious Axis would deal sympathetically with neutral Ireland had lost their relevance. Now the fear was that American impatience with Irish neutrality would undermine the American public's sympathy for an end to partition. The need to behave as a friendly neutral was stronger than ever, and demonstrative gestures such as the surveillance of Axis legations and the clampdown on the IRA were duly intensified.

The bullying tone that the United States government suddenly began to adopt towards Ireland – exemplified for the average Irish person by the attitude of the American press – did not help to calm the situation. In response to hostility in the United States press, the Irish government stressed the obstacles to joining the war, especially partition. 1942 was, after all, the twentieth anniversary of the foundation of the State, and de Valera lost no opportunity to remind American journalists of this example of aggression against a small nation.

At the same time he attempted to wake the populace from the new wave of lethargy that had descended on them in the latter half of 1941. Government ministers chanted on about the dangers of apathy – local and national newspapers decried it in regular editorials. Yes, the nights were cold and the training was boring, but Ireland still needed her sons, the message went. At a speech in Navan on 16 January, de Valera warned, 'You are not in the war, but you are threatened – your position threatens you – and it is a constant threat.' Attempting to scotch the wild rumours of an alliance with the United States (and in some versions a treaty with Germany), he insisted that no bargains had been struck with any side since Pearl Harbor. No, he had not, as the whispers suggested, taken a secret trip across the Atlantic to parley with Roosevelt: 'I was in my office every day for the past month or so.' There were no deals, and the need for people to rally against imminent 'hostile action' was paramount:

This country has been the subject of violent articles in newspapers in foreign countries. Everything that could be said to inflame other people against us was being urged. You don't see these things in the newspapers because we have adopted the policy of not letting into the newspapers anything that was going to stir up bitterness and ill-feeling.

He could easily, he said, read out some of these articles in order to 'stir up feeling so as to get rid of the apathy', but declined to do so. As opposition members in the Dáil complained, the effect of refusing to specify which foreigners and which papers were threatening Ireland was once again to fuel conflicting rumours and rising panic.

The crunch came with the posting of belligerent American troops on Irish soil. The first US contingents arrived in Northern Ireland on 26 January 1942, stoking fears of an invasion across the land border and the end of any hope of preserving a neutral stance. By stationing its soldiers in the North, the US had issued a rebuff to Ireland's most cherished political aspiration, had given de facto recognition to partition. The next day de Valera addressed the nation:

The people of Ireland have no feeling of hostility and no desire to be brought in any way into conflict with the United States. For reasons which I referred to a few weeks ago, the contrary is the truth, but it is our duty to make it clearly understood that no matter what troops occupy the Six Counties the Irish people's claim for the union of the whole of the National territory and for supreme jurisdiction over it will remain unabated.

The new situation set rumours buzzing. Elizabeth Bowen reported that the arrival of American troops was causing a wave of war panic south of the border:

There is also a heightening of the fear that Éire is on the verge of 'being dragged into the war'. I believe that with many people there is a nebulous fear that war is infectious: the more belligerents accumulate in the Six Counties, the more likely it is that the 'germ' will spread. War, in fact, is not entered but 'caught' – or picked up – just as, passively and unwillingly, one catches or picks up measles.

The panic may have been partly induced by German radio propaganda which (through the mouth of Irish novelist Francis Stuart, among others) was warning of the loss of immunity which the presence of the American soldiers in the North might bring. Rumours had it that the Americans had come to take possession of the ports, that the troops were meant to intimidate de Valera into agreeing to lend the ports, or worse, that this was a new occupying force and that a southward offensive could be launched at any moment. (At a meeting of the right-wing Irish-language organisation Craobh na h-Aiséirí in February 1942, Denis Ireland denounced the American and British troops who were 'garrisoning Ulster' against the south, to keen applause from his audience.) In Washington the Irish Minister Robert Brennan warned Under-Secretary of State Sumner Welles of the 'increasing belief [which] existed on the part of his Government and people that these American troops were going to be used to attack the Irish forces'.

These fears were not entirely groundless. The troops in the North were indeed making ready to invade in the event of a German attack on Ireland (they reckoned they could occupy Dublin in seventy minutes). With such plans being drawn up, it was a simple matter for armchair strategists to draw the logical conclusion, and advocate a pre-emptive strike. July 1942, for example, saw the appearance of a US pamphlet titled 'Is Ireland Next?' Describing Éire as a 'No Man's Land', the brochure insisted it was only a matter of time before the country was invaded. 'American troops in North Ireland await "over the top" order, wondering whether it will be across the North Sea or south into neutral Éire. Will the AEF beat the Nazis to Ireland's strategic bases?' 'It is inevitable,' another article went on, 'that Ireland – all of it – must be drawn into history's greatest war sooner or later. That is the opinion of virtually everyone except the people of Éire and a section of the many Irish scattered abroad.' According to the US consul in Belfast, it was 'common talk in Northern Ireland, not only in the American Army itself, but among the general population, that the purpose of the American Army in Northern Ireland is to take over the whole of Ireland'. The border, fragile and porous at any time, began to feel especially vulnerable. For all the laments about being cut off, Ireland's problem now was that the war was too close.

On the face of it the two government campaigns of early 1942 – to get rid of apathy and to calm the panic – were contradictory. What did it mean to be anxious and indifferent about the war at the same time? In June 1940, after all, when invasion threatened, thousands had joined up. The fall-off in recruitment and rise in desertions from the Irish army and LDF suggest that although there was real fear that Ireland would become swept into the war in America's wake, people didn't believe anything could be done about it. Could anyone imagine the Irish forces taking up positions against an enemy from the United States? The thing was impossible, both practically and psychologically. The arrival of the AEF in Northern Ireland underlined once and for all the fact that Ireland's ability to maintain its neutrality did not depend on its physical defences, but on politics and diplomacy. The government's verbal sallies and diplomatic moves stressed Ireland's

"IT'S NO GOOD ELMER — HE SAYS WE CAN'T GO LOOKING FOR IT UNTIL AFTER THE WAR"

Cartoon by Neb [Ronald Niebour] published in the *Daily Mail*,
28 January 1942.

opposition to the situation in the North. But at the same time there was a complicated sense for many Irish people that the Americans were 'their' forces (far more so than the British), and so the country felt more in the war than ever.

For committed republicans, however, the American presence in the North was an insult and a provocation. The IRA had already declared war on Britain for its occupation, and it regarded the US military as legitimate targets. Sporadic attacks on GIs occurred across the province, though Londonderry was a particular hotspot. Had the US government sent its soldiers to a place less remote from conflict than it might have imagined? In contrast to the rest of Britain, which was relatively safe after the summer of 1941 until V-bombs fell on British cities in June 1944, the North was vulnerable, the border creating all kinds of security headaches. The Office of Strategic Services reported to the US government in early 1943:

The situation in Northern Ireland is not quite so good, for two reasons: a) the presence of large bodies of American and British armed forces with their equipment, and b) the fact that the somewhat repressive attitude of the Government of Northern Ireland towards its large nationalist Roman Catholic minority, seems to have strengthened the hand of all the more radical elements there, and probably has accounted for an increase both in numbers and activity of the IRA within the last three years.

This observer offered a reasonably measured account of the causes of republican resentment, especially compared to the openly anti-Irish material given out to the troops themselves. Magazines and leaflets issued to the American Forces painted a picture of the cowardly and perfidious Irish without qualification, and offered some insight into what was being said across the Atlantic. The IRA campaign of January 1939 was put down to Goebbels's strategic planning (so that the war had in fact started nine months earlier than most people realised). Barely veiled threats were implicit in depictions of the German legation as the centre of a spy network, co-opting large numbers of treacherous Irish:

Adolf Hitler found a ready-made Trojan Horse in Ireland when the war began.

There were, first of all, thousands of disgruntled Irish Republican Army members and their families in both Éire and Ulster, who were only too willing to help Germany lick the British.

There was a considerable group of followers of Gen. Owen O'Duffy, organiser of Éire's outlawed Blue Shirts, some of whom were sympathetic to the Axis and had fascist ambitions of their own.

These magazines were straightforwardly propagandist in intent, but even official publications played the undercover Nazi card. The *Pocket Guide to Northern Ireland*, issued to GIs in 1942, insisted that danger was everywhere:

Éire's neutrality is a real danger to the Allied cause. There, just across the Irish Channel from embattled England, and not too far from your own billets in Ulster, the Axis nations maintain large legations and staffs. These Axis agents send out weather reports, find out by espionage what is going on in Ulster. The Ulster border is 600 miles long and hard to patrol. Axis spies sift back and forth across the border constantly.

United States publications took British anti-neutrality propaganda to new levels – accusations of betrayal and moral failure were now compounded by allegations of a general, underlying sympathy with fascism. 'Embattled England' was at the mercy of her corrupt neighbour. In effect, the men of the AEF were being warned that the girls they met at dances, the Irish lads they befriended on their bases, were likely IRA informants and spies for Germany.

The hysterical American view that neutrality really meant collaboration with the Nazis drove de Valera mad, but it wasn't entirely the fault of the US. Irish government sources also kept up their insistence on the IRA threat. An American soldier who picked up an Irish newspaper on his arrival in the North in January 1942 would have had all his suspicions confirmed. 'Plot to Embroil Country in War', read the headline of the *Irish Press* on 30 January 1942. The report, replicated in nearly all the papers, outlined the threat posed by the IRA conspiracy to take the country into war against Britain and to cause civil war at home. Yes, civil liberties were being curtailed under sections of the Emergency Powers Orders (such as the policy of accepting witness statements from people who did not have to appear in court) but this was the price of safety – the only way to control the violent pro-German plots of the IRA.

To judge by the stories of the GIs' popularity and success with women they didn't take too much notice of 'undercover IRA' warnings. In a matter of months both English and Irish communities adjusted to the American presence. Louis MacNeice – fresh from his spell in the United States – was drafted in to write a leaflet explaining the habits of the new arrivals to the British populace. Along with instructions for what to do 'when you meet a doughboy', *Meet the US Army* included helpful explanations of the American GI's love of dance-halls and baseball, plus a handy glossary of American terms. As long as United States troops stayed firmly garrisoned north of the border, alarms about invasion lost some of their urgency, and Irish opinion came reluctantly to terms with the situation. GIs, less conspicuous in their civvies, took to flouting orders and crossing into the South for diversion and entertainment. Donegal was a popular destination (especially on Sundays when the pubs were closed in the North), while Dublin was favoured for longer breaks. In this atmosphere of détente, the presence of the Americans on Irish soil had the effect of increasing Irish sympathy with the Allies, and contributed to the rising number of desertions from the Irish army. Several short stories published in 1942 and 1943, such as 'Mild and Bitter' by Jim Phelan, set in a pub frequented by Irish-American soldiers on the southern side of the border, capture this uncertain relationship with the new American enemy/ally.

The most unsympathetic diagnoses of Irish opinion put this down to self-interest – they could see now that the Allies were likely to win, and began to store their eggs in the Allied basket. But there was also simply greater understanding with the Americans. A year after the first troops arrived in Northern Ireland an OSS report suggested that, since the United States' entry into the war, Irish newsreels had begun to incline more towards the Allied side, and neutral-mindedness had become less rigid:

Despite the existence of a very rigorous news, movie and radio censorship, which prevents the population of Éire from having any real understanding of the true nature of Nazi-ism and Fascism, it can be said quite truthfully that the sympathies of the vast majority of the people are on the side of the Allies. This is especially true since America's entry into the war, and the turning of the tide of battle in favour of the Allies. The newsreels previously confined themselves exclusively to recording such innocuous activities as race meetings and cattle shows, whereas by January, 1943, various newsreels concerned themselves with aspects of Allied war preparations and activities. A similar trend is noticeable in the press and on the radio. Much more space is devoted to Allied communiqués in the press and on the radio. Allied news is now read first and in more detail, in contrast with the previous attitude, when Axis dispatches took first place in news broadcasts, and were of equal length to those from Allied sources.

The Irish authorities did their best to persuade America that the country was not in fact a quasi-fascist peace paradise. There was intense diplomatic activity in Washington, backed up by de Valera's broadcasts, and numerous interviews with US journalists. And there were other, slightly less official approaches. Books such as M. J. MacManus's 1942 biography of de Valera were intended to explain the background to neutrality to a trans-Atlantic audience as well as consolidate the neutral consensus at home; foreign journalists were treated to tours of defence emplacements, Red Cross meetings, and the sites of the Dublin bombings. Cameramen shooting sequences for the *March of Time* documentary newsreels were directed to feature coastal patrols and army manoeuvres as well as romantic tourist images of rural Ireland. Both, in different ways, were calculated to appeal to American viewers. Irish control over the newsreel scripts was obvious in statements such as: 'neutrality has become the very symbol of their ability to stand on their feet as a nation', neutrality was 'a strategic asset to the United Nations', and 'although collectively Éire is neutral, individually the Southern Irish have contributed their labour when labour was vital'. The 1944 *March of Time* documentary on Ireland explained that a hundred thousand workers had left for Britain, 'even at the risk of the immobilisation of Éire's army', as though this was all part of Ireland's pro-Allied plan.

Soon after the arrival of the American troops Sean O'Faolain made a direct attempt to set the record straight in a script for the BBC's American service:

I have a feeling that you may think that if you want to know what war does to people you must think only of France or Great Britain or Germany. And you may think that Ireland is a little bit off the map. It isn't of course, in any sense. The bombers have visited us north and south. We have our own problems of food-shortage and fuel-shortage. Especially fuel-shortage. Our defence forces have been increased enormously. There is hardly an able-bodied man in the country who is not in one or other of the defence-forces. Our national expenditure has rocketed. So that although we are officially a neutral country we are, in effect, just as much IN the war as many parts of Great Britain herself. As a matter of fact Ireland shews (sic) that in Europe to-day the word Neutrality is a very relative term.

The script was never broadcast. This is hardly surprising; it is not easy to imagine British or American listeners responding favourably to the news that things were just as bad for the Irish. It reads like a rather pathetic attempt to persuade himself that Ireland really is on the global map, 'IN the war' – and the fact that he refers to an Ireland which includes 'north and south' would have incensed official Northern Irish opinion. But O'Faolain did paint a genuine picture of the condition of neutrality for many people – it was a war effort without a war.

In early 1942 the economic difficulties which the war created in Ireland reached crisis proportions. While England's war industries created jobs and money, Ireland's Emergency spelled disaster for the livelihoods of many of its citizens. As commentators were keen to point out, the bright lights of the big city belied a dire economic situation throughout the rest of the country (and indeed for many in Dublin itself). While hostile outsiders were suggesting that the country was both a peaceful haven and a hiding place for Nazi sympathisers, many ordinary citizens were facing poverty, destitution, even starvation.

This decline into penury came to many as an unwelcome surprise. Irish farmers had looked back to the First World War for a sign of their prospects in 1939, and rubbed their hands in anticipation. A 1937 article in *Ireland Today* described the attitude of the nation's farmers in anticipation of another war as one of 'quiet optimism'. The Great War had proved a boon to them. Their supplies were in heavy demand across the Irish Sea, and fetching record prices, ironically making 'the last seven years of the Union with Great Britain the most prosperous years that had been experienced in modern Irish history', as James Meenan argued. The same was not to be true of the Second World War. Whereas in the First World War the absence of price controls had enabled Irish farmers to rake in very large profits, in the Second, British rationing and a strict price-control mechanism kept prices steady – even below pre-war prices, for some goods. Farmers selling livestock to England made very little profit. In a stroke of spectacularly bad luck, foot-and-mouth disease hit Ireland in 1941, not only restricting movement in the countryside, but ensuring a complete ban on meat exports. Tillage farming increased during the war, but the crops were needed to feed the Irish population, since grain imports all but disappeared with the pressure on shipping.

At the same time the flow of raw materials into the country was almost completely cut off, causing a 25 per cent fall in industrial production and employment. The drive for self-sufficiency had established small industries in Ireland, but they were reliant on imported raw materials, making the country in some ways more rather than less dependent on Britain. The attack on Pearl Harbor had its effect here too, as the United States moved to full war production and trade arrangements painstakingly worked out during 1940 and 1941 were abruptly forgotten. It proved impossible to continue making soap, for example, or candles, tyres, machinery of all kinds, rope, clothing, and many other goods. It was bad enough that none of these products could be obtained any longer; worse that the closure of factories led to further loss of jobs and increasing emigration.

The hardships caused by Ireland's drive for self-sufficiency were talked down in the press: censorship forbade the publication of any but official announcements on supplies, for fear of causing panic and unrest. But they were talked up incessantly in pubs, kitchens and parlours across the country. As O'Faolain suggested, shortage of fuel was a major problem. If lack of petrol proved a major irritant for the middle-class car owner, and lack of coal crippled the railways (which were never to recover), there were at least pre-motorised alternatives in the donkey, the horse and the bicycle for local journeys. A far greater concern was that lack of fuel was causing the destruction of Ireland's fledgling industries. Before the war Ireland burned about two and a half million tons of coal and three and a half million tons of turf in a year. The supply of coal from Britain fell sharply and in 1941 de Valera announced that if hardship were to be avoided the country must cut three million extra tons of turf that summer. Some of that was to be achieved by the turf companies, some by private individuals and families – schools were closed for several weeks so children could help out. In addition the County Councils set up schemes employing sixteen thousand men and boys on the bogs, but many were unused to the work and the yield was low. Then there were the difficulties of housing the turf-cutters in the summer months (all tents were in use by the army), and of transporting the turf to the towns and cities once it had been cut, for petrol was at a premium.

Coal was fundamental to the country's electricity supply, particularly in the east of the country. The effects of the war began to be seriously felt in the electricity industry in late 1940. The increase in the price of coal in 1941 drove up electricity charges by 10 per cent and consumers were urged to economise. By May 1942 the sale of cooking and heating appliances was discontinued, in order to conserve resources. A year later rationing was introduced as supplies of coal became even more scarce, and the Pigeon House coal-burning plant received only pit-head rejections from Britain. By 1944 new deliveries of coal were confined to a virtually unusable slurry. It was not unusual to find grass growing on consignments of coal which had been scraped from the top of slag heaps. While laboratory tests were designed to analyse its combustible properties, the workers in the electricity plants devised a simpler method of telling whether the stuff would burn. They threw a handful of coal at the wall – if it stuck it was too wet to use.

The economic life of the country was seizing up, and there was paralysis too in the micro-economy of the Irish household. Rationing of coal for domestic use was a major hardship, especially in the cities, where turf was hard to come by. Eventually the Long Straight in Dublin's Phoenix Park was used for storing huge mountains of turf, and was renamed the New Bog Road. But unprocessed turf was hard to burn (a poor quality sod could be nine-tenths water) and it gave off little heat. Lack of oil and paraffin, in a country where most households still had no electricity supply, was also a great burden. But it was nothing to the disappearance of tea.

Ireland had the second highest consumption rate of tea in the world, with an annual intake of just over seven pounds per head of the population. With few ships of her own, the country was dependent on Britain for bringing imports of tea from India, but British ships were now needed elsewhere and could supply only 25 per cent of normal requirements. For a while Irish firms had managed to import a small amount separately from Calcutta through America, but the war in the East effectively closed down that route. Tea was not regarded as a luxury but a necessity, particularly for Irish women, and they became frantic about losing it. The tiny weekly ration was reused repeatedly, and a thriving black market grew up around women keen to avoid undrinkable commercial alternatives such as the infamous chicory-based 'Coffee Éire' (a repackaged version of Camp Coffee) and 'Draw-Well'. Some people in rural areas took to drinking dandelion or nettle tea. And in the cities others turned to coffee – ground coffee became a new item in grocers' stocks. One British servicewoman stationed in Northern Ireland wrote to her mother of her Dublin shopping trip: 'Tea is the only thing that people are really desperate about, and you can exchange it for practically anything, so we had taken as much as we could get hold of. The tea ration in Éire has been reduced to 1/2 oz a week for each person, so you can understand their desperation. Most of the restaurants will only serve tea at certain times.' Clothing rations came in later, but these proved something of a boon to Irish women, many of whom – especially the older generation – bought few new clothes at the best of times. A lively trade in clothing coupons sprang up on the platforms of Dublin's Amiens Street station. Visitors from the North came bearing tea, bicycle inner tubes (rubber was unobtainable), soap, candles and other desirables, and went home with silk stockings – men could wear multiple pairs wound round their legs under their trousers – and the latest in utility fashion.

If restaurants served little tea, they hadn't much to offer in the way of bread either. Even when supplies of wheat could be purchased abroad, there was the problem of getting the ships to transport the grain. By the end of 1941 the country was importing a thousand tons

" Would you ask Mr. Lemass if he'd mind tastin' this?

of grain a week, but consumption was a thousand tons a day. Despite increased tillage, bread became blacker and blacker as the months went on. In October 1940 wheat extraction was fixed at seventy-five per cent, a figure that steadily rose to ninety, then ninety-five per cent, until by February 1942 it was compulsory to mill the whole grain. Housewives would attempt to sieve the flour themselves. The Minister of Supplies' announcement at the end of February 1942 that bread supplies would have to be cut by one-fifth caused panic and a run on bakers' shops in the cities and towns. In March the government found it necessary to censor reporting of the Dáil debate on bread queues and flour shortage in order to forestall panic. Statements such as 'the poor are like hunted rats looking for bread' (Richard Mulcahy, quoting a letter from a resident of Cashel), stories of women in bread queues collapsing with fatigue and having to be taken away in ambulances, criticisms of the 'unequal' system of distribution – these were not guaranteed to increase confidence, so the government thought.

As imports of flour dwindled, the government passed a series of Compulsory Tillage Orders, which included the threat that those who did not put their fields to wheat would have their land confiscated. In the spring of 1942 the government launched the Grow More Food Campaign; ministers fanned out across the country, speaking on town-square platforms and urging the farmers to greater efforts. Newspaper headlines announced that 'Only the farmers are between us and famine.' Part of the problem was lack of fertiliser. The amount available fell from nearly a hundred thousand tons in 1939 to fewer than ten thousand tons in 1941 (and a mere thousand tons in 1942). Radio broadcasts were given over to the need for wheat sowing, for using animal, and even human, manure, for gathering kelp to use as fertiliser. In March de Valera was urging the need for another hundred thousand acres of wheat and fifty thousand of potatoes. One quarter of all arable land should be under tillage, he argued, suggesting that the fines were too small: there should be a minimum penalty of twenty pounds, though in fact, fines of twenty-five pounds for failure to comply were common. Laggardly farmers protested their innocence. Much of the land, particularly in the West of the country, was unsuitable for wheat growing; lime, which might have helped the acidity of the soil, was not available. Farmers got round the order by sowing oats among the wheat, or by claiming ownership of fewer acres than they really had. In one case the District Judge suggested the defendant's obstinacy was the result of dubious political sympathies, causing him to use unusually large steps in pacing out his land: 'They weren't by any chance goose-steps?'

As the situation worsened, the Department of Supplies urged economy in order to avoid strict rationing. Menus were printed with the legend, 'It is illegal to serve wheaten foods with more than one course.' Daily papers gave more and more space to articles on managing nutrition, and finding and cooking alternative foodstuffs. The Catholic Truth Society of Ireland published a pamphlet on food supplies in 1941, noting the 'increase in the numbers of those who are shrinking below subsistence levels' and the real danger of malnutrition. They argued that cereals (such as barley) ordinarily fed to livestock should be transferred to human use and that production of onions, peas, tomatoes, swedes, carrots and potatoes should be increased. There were severe penalties for farmers caught feeding animals with grains suitable for humans; the government even mooted a plan to cull farm animals in order to conserve food for human use.

All this required not merely changes to farming practice, but a re-education of those who cooked and ate the food. There was no 'Irish Ministry of Food', but there were concerted efforts to confront the problem of nutrition – efforts directed, as in Britain, at wives and mothers. The popular novelist Maura Laverty published a pamphlet entitled *Flour Economy* in 1941. In it she responded to the 'national necessity' by explaining how to cook bread, pastry, doughnuts, scones, puddings and all sorts of cakes from potatoes and oatmeal. Saving wheat through flour economy was a woman's duty, a rehearsal of good citizenship – the ethos was not so far from the military language employed by the British Ministry of Food in propaganda for the 'Kitchen Front'.

The problem of nutrition was addressed 'officially', in the Department of Local Government and Health's 1942 pamphlet, *A Simple Guide to Wholesome Diet* and Cathal Brugha Street's 1943 *All In The Cooking*. Radio too played its part: in 1940, Radio Éireann had introduced a new thirty-five-minute weekly feature, *Scrapbook for Women*, which featured advice on cookery, needlework, gardening, baby-care and 'beauty-culture'. There were also weekly dramatisations of the lives of patriotic Irish women in the series *Women in History*. A year later, however, radio fare for women had become focused almost exclusively on their duties of housewifely frugality during the Emergency. A number of series were introduced, all giving advice on wartime shortages: *Between Ourselves* and *Food and Health* in 1941; *For the Housekeeper* (later *Housewives' Half Hour*) and *Meeting the Wheat Shortage in the Home* in 1942; *Making and Mending in the Home* and *Habits for Health* in 1943.

And there were numerous less official versions of food and household economy propaganda, including books published for the urban middle classes, who cooked with gas and electricity (Ann Hathaway's 1944 *Homecraft Book*, Laverty's 1946 *Kind Cooking*), and rural classes in cookery often organised by local parish priests. Much of the emphasis, particularly in the classes in Domestic Economy, was in teaching Irish women and girls to use a greater variety of foodstuffs in order to eke out increasingly meagre supplies. Laverty's 1942 popular novel, *Never No More*, went so far as to include a passage of thinly veiled propaganda on behalf of Indian meal (cornmeal or polenta), which had a very bad reputation since it had been blamed for deaths during the famine of those unable to cook it properly.

One side-effect of this focus on women in the drive towards frugality was a growth and confidence in women's organisations. The Irish Countrywomen's Association had been going for decades but the war years saw a big rise in their activities, focused on rural craft, cooking, and traditional farming and vegetable-growing techniques; women members also took an active part in rural cooperative organisations such as Muintir na Tíre. Wartime shortages and the increasing poverty of Dublin's underclass was the direct impetus for the formation of another women's organisation, the Irish Housewives' Association, which was founded in 1942. Its membership was primarily middle class and Protestant (with a good number of Quakers). In May 1941 a group of these women had drawn up a 'Housewives' Petition' which called for a fairer system of production and distribution of food, compulsory tillage of 40 per cent of arable land, and more help for farmers. They argued for national registration of essential foodstuffs and immediate rationing of those in short supply. Lemass kept protesting that the expense of a national registration scheme was prohibitive – too heavy a burden for the taxpayer to bear. And the difficulty with bringing in a proper system of rationing was that even when the householders had coupons, if the traders were without supplies there was nothing to be done. Unlike in Britain, where wartime rationing had the effect of raising nutrition levels for the poorest in society, the half-hearted system of rationing in Ireland hit the urban poor worst of all. Queues lengthened outside bakers' shops in the city, the price of bread, flour, tea, sugar, kerosene, and coal rose dramatically, and the poor became worse off than ever. Among other disastrous effects, the flour shortage was responsible for what may be Patrick Kavanagh's very worst poem, published in his column in the *Irish Press*:

> White bread, you give us hope; you break
> The grey monotony of the story.
> It is not how you look or taste,
> But the imagination that blossoms in the waste
> When we look on the loaf that is not hoary.
> White bread, you are a mirroring back
> Reflecting mid-night lighted streets
> Cigarettes, tea, sugar, gas always on,
> Busses coming home at a quarter to one –
> All that's evoked by the name of peace.

*   *   *

For those with money there was still plenty of everything except petrol. Travellers choosing to protect themselves from wartime austerities in Britain, and the bombing of British cities, found no better haven than the cushioned existence of the Irish country hotel. Moya Woodside painted a picture of a well-to-do rural sanctuary, indifferent to the war, in her description of her Donegal hotel: 'The tables groan under food, papers don't arrive till 2 p.m. and nobody minds, the wireless is relegated (thank God) to an obscure sitting room, and *no uniforms* are to be seen.' Woodside made her comment in the summer of 1940, but visitors continued to marvel at the luxury they found. American journalists and members of the Forces, British servicemen and women on holiday, residents of the North – all commented on the pleasures to be enjoyed in this 'outpost of peace'. In January 1941 the British diarist J. L. Hodson was appalled to be offered a seven-course dinner at his Dublin hotel; he ate it with difficulty, remembering the austere conditions he had left in England. A month later the American journalist Ben Robertson described getting to Dublin as 'like reaching heaven . . . Dublin at the present time is bright and gay. There is sugar in the bowl and butter on the plate, there are pitcherfuls of milk, and you can even have cream.' The following year Beverley Nichols described the light, glamour and riches of the city: 'We enter a restaurant in which the menu is so long that you feel it will take you a day to read it. (Yes, you *can* have eggs *and* fish *and* steak *and* cream pie.)'

The idea that Ireland was a land of plenty was promoted by gatherings which met the mailboats from England, providing tea and provisions for hard-pressed English refugees. Irish travellers to Britain brought bacon and butter, or sent it through the post to relatives in need of extra luxury. Holidaymakers from the North commented on the sight of bakeries displaying sugary confections piled high with cream, and on the delight of finding packed restaurants offering knickerbocker glories and buttery cakes. Dublin also saw the opening of several new restaurants during the early part of the war – including an Austrian and an Indian – catering for the well-to-do and the visitor. One reviewer for *The Bell* described the menus available in the capital:

At the Unicorn the Hors d'Oeuvres are said by some to be among the best in Dublin, the furnishings most tasteful, the servants the prettiest and politest. The little Austrian cakes owe much to the generous use of pure cream; modest prices mark half-bottles of reliable Burgundies. For sweeter tastes, there is a good Vouvray.

Dublin was a city of contrasts. The tempting availability of luxuries was combined with the real difficulty of getting hold of the staples of everyday life. Cartoons appeared in *Dublin Opinion* and *Passing Variety* showing shops displaying signs which read 'No Supplies' adjacent to those reading 'Send a Parcel to your Friends Abroad'. Following a visit to the capital in late 1941 the English writer and journalist Cyril Connolly strove to explain to readers of his new journal *Horizon* the striking disparities of the metropolis:

The shops are full of good things to eat, the streets of people who cannot afford to buy them. Light and heat are desperately short, for there is very little coal, and turf is scarce through lack of transport. The coal ration is three-eighths of a ton per two months, unless one is in a district where turf is compulsory, and that costs 64s a ton and burns badly. Doctors and Government inspectors have less petrol than the average English motorist, the great country houses have their bath night once a week, bread is rationed, tea and coffee are very scarce, trains run slowly on inferior fuel, the Archbishop of Dublin has inaugurated free soup kitchens, an army is training without modern equipment, and even the Gaelic is slipping . . . And emigration – the silent indictment of a civilisation which no censor can suppress – continues to threaten its human resources. This is a black picture, but it is important for the English reader to stop thinking of Ireland as an uncharitable earthly paradise.

The English reader wasn't mollified, however. The hostile vision of Dublin fiddling while Europe burned was firmly fixed in the British mind. It was not unusual to hear that it would be good enough for the Irish to be invaded, either by the British, or – perhaps a more fitting punishment – by the Germans. Even those who had some sympathy with Ireland's decision to stay neutral often failed to understand conditions there. In the middle of the war the central character in Elizabeth Bowen's novel *The Heat of the Day* travels to a Big House in County Cork on family business. While kindly disposed towards the servants of the house, she is careless of their difficulties. She keeps two oil lamps alight unnecessarily, and blithely burns the last of the candles. 'Up here in her bedroom, down there in the library, she was burning up light supplies for months ahead. Well on into the winter after Stella's departure the Donovan family went to bed in the dark.'

As the Emergency dragged on, more and more goods became scarce. It became increasingly hard to get hold of leather, for example, so that, as the boot factories closed and more people were put out of work, people turned to clogs and timber-soled shoes; children went barefoot in the summertime. Bicycle inner tubes were impossible to procure but they could be temporarily mended with wet grass. One Irish volunteer stationed in the North regularly smuggled inner tubes down to Dublin under her clothes. Wild sage and beet pulp became common substitutes for tobacco in the country. Flann O'Brien joked that visiting the cinema in Dublin had become a health hazard, as eyes streamed with the fumes from incinerated ragwort. Articles appeared in the popular monthly magazine *Ireland's Own* explaining how to make paper from peat moss, cigarettes from potato leaves, syrups and sugar from potato starch. The magazine's letters pages fail to report whether any tried the handy hints for turning potato starch into combs, knife handles, piano keys, pipes, buttons, even billiard balls. It was suggestions such as these that no doubt prompted Flann O'Brien, in his *Irish Times* column, to recommend contraptions for saving the bubbles from boiling potatoes to employ as shaving water, the manufacture of fishing rods from pressed slack, the retailing of second-hand smoke (exhaled into bags and stored for future use), and the pulping of 'limited quantities of the Abbey theatre audience' for use in making recycled paper. Shopping became what one housewife described as an

" How often do I have to be refused to become a regular customer ? "

'exciting adventure' as customers tried to wait to be served last in the shop, then to 'use all [their] wiles to secure another half pound of butter or tin of cocoa'. Even when shoppers had the coupons it often proved hard to make the shops take them, either because the supplies hadn't come through, or because retailers could make a handsome profit by selling instead on the black market. Black marketeering caused immense hard feeling. Local newspapers were full of reports of neighbours bringing each other up before the courts on charges of overcharging or selling over the ration – the latter the more serious charge. Farmers and local co-operatives got round the regulations by direct selling and barter.

The almost weekly addition of items to the list of rationed goods, and the sudden proliferation of government officials, went along with a farcical lack of communication about how and when to introduce the new rules. Ration books, and guidelines on rationing in the local papers, were written in a peculiarly impenetrable bureaucratic prose which was regularly ridiculed. It seemed that everything was under the hammer. Jimmy O'Dea, the Dublin comic, joked that kisses were the latest commodity to be rationed: 'That's right. You can't carry on without a capoon (sic). Look. Here's the book. You can't go coortin' your girrl now without you have this book on you.' In 1941 allowances of gas and electricity were restricted. Motorists who had adapted their cars to run on town gas (with the addition of a rubberised tank on the top) responded bitterly to the news that it was now illegal to use gas for transport. People with gas cookers were only permitted to use them at certain times, and each week the ration periods grew shorter and shorter. Gas supplies were cut off in between times, but in practice sufficient fuel stayed in the mains to give a weak flame – a glimmer of gas, enough to boil an egg or make tea. This led to the introduction of a further government inspector to swell the already mighty ranks of punitive officialdom – the glimmer man. These domestic policemen were sent to patrol the city streets and swoop on houses in random checks for those using gas outside permitted hours. One Dubliner who had volunteered for the British Services commented ironically on the seriousness of Ireland's wartime struggle, which he witnessed while at home on leave from a very different battleground:

The movements of the 'glimmer man' were watched and passed on with the same devotion and skill as that of the underground guerrillas in Europe. Even if one turned off the gas before the 'glimmer man' pounced, he could tell from the heat of the burners whether or not it had been in recent use. If it had, the scene was at one with that where people hide a fleeing fugitive in their house, only to see in horror when the pursuers enter an overlooked garment or personal possession has been left in the open to betray.

The idea that life and death might hang in the balance with a visit from the glimmer man had its own cruel bathos, of course, since it was obvious that Irish citizens were protecting nobody but themselves. Nonetheless stories of outwitting the glimmer man, of tea-withdrawal symptoms, of transport trauma, were eagerly recounted, suggesting as they did a population united in their 'hour of need' and facing their difficulties with good humour. In January 1941 Hodson found a number of people 'almost glad that the petrol supply has been cut – they now feel they are doing something to help win the war'. Bowen too reported that 'many of the public seem to derive a mild self-importance from being "like England" – in fact, in the movement.'

" Glory be ! The Glimmer Man ! "

These were safe stories, in contrast to tales of the increasing homelessness and destitution that were one result of wartime seclusion. In one sense, rationing increased the atmosphere of isolation from the war (as Ireland became more insular, and returned to almost nineteenth-century living conditions). But it also helped Irish citizens to manufacture a sense of struggle. As many noted at the time, Ireland was asked to embrace austerity without the 'wartime spirit' and sense of pulling together which was the accepted line on the British response to war both then and now. 'At present Éire suffers, in all senses,' said Bowen, 'and while her deprivations are far less than Britain's, they have to be met without the heroic stimulus that comes from participation in the war.' Britain itself was cut off from the main theatres of war, of course – indeed, part of the problem was that there were so many theatres to be isolated from. It may be that the stories of British stoicism under the Blitz were so powerful precisely because they could fill the void in people's imaginations, when faced with trying to understand the war elsewhere. But while communal loyalties reshaped the individual's private world in Britain, transforming it through a myth of public-spiritedness, the problem in Ireland seemed to be that there was too much privacy. If the idea of hearth and home was in disarray in bombed-out Britain, in Ireland home was impossible to escape.

A very British view of this atmosphere was captured by the comic team of Jimmy O'Dea and Harry O'Donovan, in their facetious look at Irish life in the BBC's *Irish Half Hour*. A series of skits on small-town life under Emergency Powers ran throughout 1942 – and here again the emphasis was on the population's good-humoured response to shortages, as though Ireland might vie with Britain for wartime indomitability. Events in the small town of 'Ballygobackwards' are shaped by anxiety over ration books and 'capoons' (inevitably coupons are issued only for unwanted items – 'Yeh have to take what the government orders. There's a war on'); by the always imminent arrival of government inspectors; by the impossibility of carrying out government directives; and above all by the difficulties of making contact with the outside world. Post office, telephone exchange and railway station rolled into one, the proprietors of the central stores in Ballygobackwards repeatedly attempt to connect with 'abroad' only to be foiled by the aberrations of the train timetable, or the antediluvian nature of Ireland's communications system. Outsiders arrive, such as an American GI rerouted from the North, or a Scottish visitor over for the fishing, and of course the inevitable Government Inspectors. But – in a massive suppression of the continuing emigration – no one ever leaves.

Above all, Ballygobackwards is without fuel. Trains fail to run on waterlogged turf – 'Ah, there's no fuel like a national fuel. Am I right, Dublin?' Government officials pop up to ask, 'Is your journey really necessary?' Cars adapted to town gas are of little use: 'There's a taxi outside with no petrol. It's got a balloon on top, but that doesn't go up either.' The vagaries of Ireland's transport system were a glorious and reliable source of woe, and stories of train hell became more and more fantastic. Until the new turf-processing plant at Inchichore came on stream in 1943, producing dryer and more efficient fuel, the journey from Dublin to Cork, which should have taken at the most five or six hours, often took over twelve, or on a couple of occasions over twenty. Flann O'Brien's 'Research Bureau' came up with an ingenious plan for bypassing the processing plant altogether:

I have been looking further into the problem of maintaining efficient railway services in these days of inferior fuel. My latest solution is expensive, but highly ingenious. My plan is that all the lines should be re-laid to traverse bogland only, and that locomotives should be fitted with a patent scoop apparatus which would dig into the bog underneath the moving train and supply an endless stream of turf to the furnace. Naturally, it would be dried in the furnace before being burned. This principle is at present recognised in taking up water when the train is at speed, and must, therefore, be quite feasible.

The Research Bureau was not entirely a product of O'Brien's imagination. The government set up an Emergency Scientific Research Bureau in February 1941, to look into the feasibility of producing raw materials and commodities which were disappearing as imports dried up. Plans to produce substitute materials for petrol – including burning turf charcoal to fuel producer gas plants for motor transport – got nowhere, as did schemes for the manufacture of artificial fertiliser from sewage sludge, or pulp for paper manufacture. The scientists had better luck with formalin, carbon dioxide (used in refrigeration at creameries), and other chemicals such as glycerine and home-grown digitalis. In the end, however, they were reduced to suggesting that farmers use more seaweed and kelp to fertilise the land, and to hoping for improvements in the imports of coal and petrol.

By mid-1942 transport had broken down altogether. Travel jokes became de rigueur, like the one told by the BBC's Dublin reporter, Denis Johnston, about a train that went slower and slower until eventually it stopped altogether on a bridge:

Presently the guard came along the carriage shouting, 'Who owns the bike in the van?' 'I do,' said one of the passengers. 'Well, get on it,' said the guard, 'and ride to the next station and ask for another engine or we'll be here till the war's over.'

It was probably best to give up on modern forms of transport altogether. In some areas stagecoaches were resurrected, such as the service between Limerick and Rathkeale which began operating in May 1942. But even here there were problems. There were stories of horses going without shoes because of insufficient blacksmith's coal to heat the iron to make them. In a little rhyme published in the *Irish Independent* on Christmas Eve 1940 Kavanagh saw through the veil of modernisation:

O, is it nineteen forty
Or a thousand years ago?
We are not going home by train
We're riding through the snow.

*   *   *

Shortages of food and fuel were felt across the country but were particularly bad amongst the working class in Dublin, and in the more remote rural areas. It was true that compared to the poor in the cities, people living in the country generally had a better deal in terms of access to food and fuel. Farmers were able to sell directly to local customers, and in the co-operative creameries a simple barter system developed, which enabled people to avoid the worst shortages. It also helped that farmers in rural areas had become used to living a straitened existence during the Economic War in the 1930s. Petrol rationing was irrelevant to them as they used either a bicycle or pony and trap for transport; gas and electricity rationing did not affect them; they had access to their own turf for the fire so the shortage of coal passed them by.

In one respect rural dwellers were slightly better off during the war years. A lucrative market in rabbits grew up across the country, which was a godsend to young countrymen. Between October and March young men could go west, to the Beara peninsula, for example, where rabbits were more than plentiful, and where they could subsist on a mixture of rabbit-snaring and odd jobs. The rabbits were collected each week from outlying areas by middle-men, who hung hundreds of carcasses on their bicycles. The rabbit catchers were not told why the rabbits were wanted, or why they fetched such a high price, but the rumour was that they were for use in the British war effort. They were taken to Cork and Dublin and exported to Britain, where the fur was probably used as lining for airmen's uniforms. And since rabbit meat wasn't rationed in Britain, butchers and their customers were ready to pay good prices for it. At a shilling a rabbit a man handy with a snare could net himself a handsome profit.

To an outsider, at least, the countryside must have looked unchanged. So Moya Woodside, on holiday from Belfast in south-west Donegal in September 1940, considered: 'This must be the last corner of Europe where war has made no difference to people's [illegible] way of living.' She was wrong. Underneath the tourist idyll of sparsely populated farms and villages there was growing economic destitution. Donegal was an area with very high rates of poverty and unemployment. At the end of the war 48 per cent of homes, and 91 per cent of rural homes in the county, were without running water. In some areas there was no well on the land and farmers had to collect rain or river water. Much of the land was poor, totally unsuitable for wheat. What flour there was didn't get to the remoter areas as the bread agents preferred to conserve their rations of petrol (and sell to the black market) rather than distribute it evenly. Supplies destined for shops in the South were smuggled across the border where they could command higher prices, and then sometimes smuggled back again to fetch exorbitant black-market prices. There were several cases in which wheat supplied to a mill in Donegal was used illegally in the manufacture of white flour – this was then sold on the black market as smuggled flour at £120 a ton. By the spring of 1942 there were repeated claims (admittedly from the Opposition) that people in remoter areas of Donegal were actually starving: they had been without either bread or oatmeal for two weeks and supplies of Indian meal had also run out.

The death of rural Ireland, which became the accepted wisdom of the next decade, was well under way by the middle of the war. As the economy ground to a halt, and transport links faltered, maintaining connections within the country itself became more difficult. City and countryside found themselves more estranged, and the centres of population in the east were cut off almost as much from the rural west as they were from life in England. It was possible in April 1942 for one elderly farmer, 'a regular Rip Van Winkle', to successfully defend himself against a charge of breaching the tillage order on the grounds that he had not heard that there was a war on, let alone that the government had issued orders for growing wheat. In 1946 Muriel Gahan, of the Irish Countrywomen's Association, reported of a trip to County Westmeath: 'They were like a people cut off from the rest of the country, shut in on themselves.'

The most famous portrait of rural Ireland during the war years is also the most bitter. Patrick Kavanagh's poem 'The Great Hunger' was published by the Yeats sisters' Cuala Press in 1942 as an expensive edition, and so was read at the time by only a handful of people, but a well-established critical consensus now views it as one of the great achievements of twentieth-century Irish literature. The poem excoriates the spiritual, sexual and emotional poverty of rural Ireland in the 1930s and 1940s. Kavanagh charts the life of Patrick Maguire, a subsistence farmer who is barely able to scrape a living from the land, scarcely managing to distinguish himself from the soil which he works. 'Half a vegetable', he clings to – and is clung to by – the clay which his body will fertilise in death. The narrow conventions and straitened circumstances of small-farm life mean that sheer economic survival is the overriding concern, crushing any aspiration to human fulfilment. Maguire passes a monotonous, twilit existence, dominated by the tyrannical ageing mother with whom he lives, starved of sexual contact, deprived of fellow-feeling. The farmer's inarticulate loneliness carries a great deal of the force of the poem. The ageing bachelor, too late for love, marriage or children, embodies a dying rural culture. The defeat of men like Maguire is the triumph of impotence – and stifling maternal power.

Kavanagh began the poem in the autumn of 1941, while the Russian front was the main focus of the war, and there is a sense in which he understood the struggle of the Irish peasant as analogous to that of the Russian. Maguire is described as a soldier fighting a long war for survival. 'A wind from Siberia' blows across Monaghan and connects the farmer's battle with that of the Soviet conscripts. But Maguire's existence, and his potency, has contracted to the futility of a 'no-target gun fired'. This is a neutral war – a war without a target – and a war of the powerless.

The title of Kavanagh's poem linked the desolation of the Irish countryside in the war years with memories of the famine a hundred years before. Land-hungry farmers, haunted by the historical memory of starvation when the potato crop failed, were either unwilling or unable further to divide their farms, leaving large numbers of young men and women with no prospects whatsoever. But the hunger Kavanagh described was not simply a longing for meaning and fulfilment. The poem also evoked actual starvation and the depopulation of the Irish rural landscape. The famine repeated the famine of the previous century, except that this time instead of there being no potatoes, now there were only potatoes to eat. Throughout the autumn of 1941 and 1942 the alarm was repeatedly raised in the Dáil over impending starvation. To add to the shortage of bread, the war years saw a rapid decline in pig-rearing and poultry-raising, because there were insufficient cereals for livestock. Opposition members from the Labour Party and Fine Gael (and later a new farmer's party, Clann na Talmhan) lambasted the government for the shortages of bacon and butter: there were rumours it was still being exported. The spectre of the famine years was even raised in stories of evictions of destitute tenants for non-payment of rents.

James Dillon (who was a deputy for Kavanagh's home county of Monaghan) painted a vivid picture of his destitute constituents, forced to live on potatoes for three meals a day. Schoolchildren were taking a cold potato for lunch to school because there was neither grain for bread nor oatmeal for stirabout. As he pointed out in the Dáil, 'even in famine years people could be kept alive on stirabout':

Who would have believed that we would live to see the day when the people of Ireland would go hungry for bacon, when the people of Ireland would not have butter to put on their bread and when the people of Ireland would not have a pot of stirabout to take off the fire? . . . If you create a situation in which there is a famine of bacon in the West of Ireland, accompanied by a shortage of bread and oatmeal, I warn you that the atmosphere will be analogous to that which obtained in the West of Ireland in the year 1847.

In Kavanagh's poem the Monaghan farmers are one step away from the famine dead – all are kin, living the same half-life:

Their voices through the darkness sound like voices from a cave,
A dull thudding far away, futile, feeble, far away,
First cousins to the ghosts of the townland.

Kavanagh picks up the image of the cave, later used to describe Ireland's wartime self-enclosure, and suggests that a spectral half-life

The Importance of POTATOES !

The drastic reduction in the importation of human and animal foodstuffs renders essential a greatly increased production of home-grown food. An increased acreage of Potatoes is particularly important because POTATOES

- ARE AN IDEAL AND INDISPENSABLE HUMAN FOOD
- PROVIDE EXCELLENT FEEDING FOR ALL TYPES of FARM STOCK including POULTRY
- YIELD FAR MORE FOOD PER ACRE THAN ANY OTHER CROP
- CAN BE SUCCESSFULLY GROWN IN ALL PARTS OF THE COUNTRY

ORDER YOUR SPRAYING MATERIALS EARLY !

PLANT MORE POTATOES

Issued by the Department of Agriculture

K.A.A.

has been the condition of the impoverished all along. The only consolation is that this living death is good preparation for existence in the grave. The poem ends with a famous image of the farmer buried alive – a living corpse:

> Maguire is not afraid of death, the Church will light him a candle
> To see his way through the vaults and he'll understand the
> Quality of the clay that dribbles over his coffin.
> He'll know the names of the roots that climb down to tickle his feet.
> And he will feel no different than when he walked through Donaghmoyne.
> If he stretches out a hand – a wet clod,
> If he opens his nostrils – a dungy smell;
> If he opens his eyes once in a million years –
> Through a crack in the crust of the earth he may see a face nodding in
> Or a woman's legs. Shut them again for that sight is sin.

Kavanagh's acrimony was one response to the featureless and futureless life of the small farmer. The poem brilliantly used simple language, rhyme, and repetition to suggest the narrowed horizons and meagre resources of the farming community. Kavanagh showed this barrenness to be the result of a long historical process (not least through the title), but he indicted the contemporary rhetoric of self-sufficiency too. The farmer has been literally stripped bare of reserves – he becomes nothing but a mound of wet clay. Kavanagh's interweaving of powerlessness, emasculation, and neutrality was not lost on his readers. A Northern Irish reviewer commented at the time:

The peasant's hunger is for personal freedom and sexual satisfaction, two fairly reasonable ambitions for a human being: he achieves neither – hence the poem in its full flow of power. Now this monstrous frustration-complex is typical and true of Southern Ireland at the present time: the country is neutral not because of a positive and pacifist attitude, but because of one that is negative and neuter. The best youth of the country has been so persistently drained for the British Army and War Industries that now there is a huge population of elderly, ineligible bachelors and spinsters. If such conditions prevail unchecked, of which grandmotherly Censorship is symptomatic, Éire is leaving herself open to the loss of her few remaining forts of vitality and individuality.

This attack by the young poet Robert Greacen, who was to decamp to Dublin in 1943, has its risible side. Supporters of the Allies liked to interpret the psychological consequence of Ireland's decision to steer clear of the war as a morally culpable detachment. But Greacen went further, suggesting that the decline of rural Ireland should be read as a 'frustration-complex', a reflection of the country's lack of potency and vigour, essentially of its refusal to stand up and fight. For neutrality read neuterality – a state peopled by the old and poor, a country with no future – the polar opposite of the sovereign, independent state which had been intended. It might be best, Greacen concluded, for this 'emasculated' culture to suffer invasion. Given the fact that his review was published as United States forces gathered in the North, this may not have been read as an entirely idle threat.

*   *   *

'Malnutrition is just a 12-letter word for starvation,' argued one deputy in June 1942. A good deal of the famine furore could be put down to the Opposition's attempts to make capital out of the problems of supply and unemployment. But the government also used the fear of famine to promote their campaigns for conservation of resources and greater tillage: 'Only The Farmers Are Between Us and Famine.' The centenary of the famine of 1847 was coming up, and arguably thoughts of famine were in the air. Certainly the historical memory of the famine was being cultivated. In 1943 Professor Delargy of the Folklore Commission approached de Valera for funds to begin a countrywide historical investigation of famine memories. By 1945 famine questionnaires had been sent out. Uncovering memories of the famine definitely paid dividends during the dreadful autumn of 1946, when the government managed to recruit thousands of young people from the cities to help gather in the harvest before it was ruined by the wet weather.

But the ghosts of the famine of the 1840s were also raised by the sudden return of diseases associated with poverty and malnutrition. It seemed incredible, but typhus, which had vanished from the rest of Western Europe (though it would resurface in the Nazi concentration camps), not only still existed in Ireland but threatened to become epidemic in 1942. Lice-borne typhus was known during the famine as Irish fever – it was responsible for hundreds of thousands of deaths in cottages, workhouses, fever hospitals and the coffin ships taking people to America. Typhus infection enters the body through bites or scratches on the skin, causing high fever, delirium, body aches and a rash over most of the body. In the worst cases it can cause death within fourteen days. The fact that by 1942 there was no soap to speak of, and little fuel to heat the hot water needed for washing, let alone people's homes, meant that lice were resurfacing in large numbers. Problems of dirt and overcrowding were compounded by the almost complete lack of petrol, so that doctors and nurses were confined to the towns and disease went unnoticed both in remote rural areas and the overcrowded tenements of the city. Typhus, said one deputy, had the capacity to cause 'more casualties in one month than total war', and the collapse of the public health system under the twin pressures of poor finance and lack of resources meant it seemed likely to do just that.

Typhus was only one of several preventable infectious diseases that grew alarmingly during the war years. The simultaneous dramatic rise in infant mortality, due to gastro-enteritis, pointed to an overall crisis in the country's public health. By 1941 the numbers of infants dying from epidemic enteritis in Dublin alone had shot up from five hundred to a thousand each year (and twelve hundred by 1943): a 'holocaust', as Ireland's new Chief Medical Officer James Deeny called it, equal over five years to the destruction of an average Irish town. (A Northern doctor, Deeny was appointed in 1944 and did a good deal to improve the crumbling health system, which was still based on the Poor Law. He also brought the formula for DDT from his wartime responsibilities in Lurgan, which meant that the lice problem could eventually be eradicated.) The situation was equally bad in Cork. There were fears of scurvy and rickets due to malnutrition. Citrus fruits were unobtainable and in the cities milk, eggs, butter and fish were prohibitively expensive for the poor. Cases of typhoid rose dramatically between 1942 and 1944, especially in small towns where the water supply was inadequate. Worst of all tuberculosis, that disease of the poor, which was fast disappearing in much of Europe, rose sharply in Ireland during the war. During 1942 nearly four and a half thousand people died of TB in Ireland, and many more suffered chronic disease. Like the deaths from typhoid, most of the casualties were young men and women in their teens and twenties.

These infectious diseases hit the urban poor worst of all. In the cities, absolute poverty and destitution were increasing as a result of shortages and unemployment. In 1939, small industries gave employment to a sixth of the working population; lack of essential raw materials, replacement parts, new equipment, and fuel meant that by 1944 industrial output had fallen to three-quarters of the pre-war level. Unemployment and 'more or less continuous short time' was the result. As early as July 1941, Sean T. O'Kelly was warning in the Dáil:

The taxable capacity of the nation is declining as the economic machine runs slowly down. Diminished supplies of industrial raw materials and semi-manufactured goods, of petrol and coal for transport and of other essential commodities are leading everywhere to unemployment and short time.

Unemployment schemes and outdoor relief were intended to help the most needy, but the economics often did not add up. With industrial production and average incomes down between 1939 and 1943, the costs of living soared but wages and social payments remained strictly controlled. In May 1941, the government introduced a deeply unpopular Wages Standstill Order. However, it was even worse for the unemployed, many of whom didn't qualify for welfare payments or food vouchers. These were often useless anyway, because the food wasn't in the shops.

The war did not create Dublin's underclass, nor did the levels of poverty and malnutrition compare with the situation for many peoples on the continent – the displaced, those living in battle zones, those who had had no chance to plant any crops at all. (The Irish government did make attempts to send food to Greece, Spain and India during the war.) But the war made the problems of the urban poor, and the government's failures, more visible. In 1939 Dublin Corporation set up a Housing Inquiry which revealed that the city's tenement problem was worse than in 1914. There were more than 110,000 people living in crowded one-room tenements. Alarmed by these statistics and under pressure from the churches, labour organisations, and the medical profession, the government instituted its own inquiry into working-class housing which reported in 1944. It found that there had been a rise in the city's population, a greater shortage of housing, and lower wages. As Mary Daly has shown, the average general labourer in 1938 earned between fifty-nine and sixty-four shillings a week. By the middle of the war a quarter were on twenty to forty shillings a week, and a further fifth on between five and twenty shillings. The average weekly income from benefit was twenty-five shillings. In 1939–40 there were 23,250 registered unemployed in Dublin, and 13,598 on benefit. Many others received nothing at all except charity.

A further inquiry into poverty and housing conditions was undertaken by the Rockefeller Foundation in 1942, on the invitation of the

Irish Red Cross. Dr D. P. O'Brien reported to the Foundation that there were still 'over 20, 000 families of four to six persons per family who live in one room dwellings'. Thousands of people were living in insanitary conditions, with no fresh water supply, little or no electrification, little access to medical care, bound to the pawn shop for their bare necessities. In the spring of 1943 the unfortunate poor were hit by a pawn strike, which caused real consternation in the slum districts of the city. Rather than pawn the Sunday suit, families were driven to sell their bedclothes and then their furniture. Others may have been driven to make money through the stolen bicycle racket, which seems to have been highly organised. The numbers of bicycles stolen in Dublin in any one week ran to three figures, suggesting that Flann O'Brien's famous stolen-bicycle sketch in his novel *The Third Policeman* owed as much to fact as imagination. The bicycles were dismantled and reconstituted with different parts – worth it when they might fetch five or eight pounds each.

Public attention was focused on the growing crisis by an unusual collaboration between medicine and the arts. Robert Collis was a young Dublin paediatrician, and a member of the Citizen's Housing Council, which campaigned for better living conditions for the urban poor. He published several articles on Dublin health in the *Irish Journal of Medical Science* during the war. Encouraged by Frank O'Connor, then a director of the Abbey Theatre, over Easter weekend in 1939 Collis wrote a play about tenement poverty which he entitled *Marrowbone Lane* – named after one of the sites of resistance during the 1916 rising. Collis implicitly attacked the failure of the republican dream in his portrait of current conditions: his play was poor drama but good social-realist propaganda. It tells the story of Mary (played by Shelagh Richards), a young girl from Mayo who moves to the city to marry. There she lives with her unemployed husband in one room in a condemned tenement which houses fifty other people. Her child becomes ill and then, since all the hospital wards are full, and she has no money for a private doctor, dies of pneumonia. Much of the force of the play comes from witnessing the good faith and aspiration of youth turn, through hopeless struggle with a cruel and unfair system, to bitterness and grief.

Marrowbone Lane was performed at the Gate in summer 1939, and proved an immediate success. The two-week run was extended to four, with a further two weeks booked out later in the year. It was revived at the Gaiety in 1941, and then brought out in book form by the small Runa Press in 1943. Collis made the most of the controversy it caused, calling a public meeting in the Metropolitan Hall a week after the play opened to hammer home the message about the conditions of the tenements and the paucity of hospital beds. The meeting launched the Marrowbone Lane Fund, to help children when they came out of hospital, to provide food and to improve housing conditions. It was the catalyst for the formation of the Irish Housewives' Association and was later to revolutionise the treatment of and attitude to cerebral palsy in Ireland.

By the time the play was revived in 1941, conditions in the city had worsened further. The Catholic paper *The Standard* gave a weekly report on the rising numbers of homeless attending the St Vincent de Paul centres. Christian Benevolent societies and the Dublin Corporation provided food and fuel where they could, and soup kitchens served thousands of dinners every day to the destitute. Because of lack of fuel, even when the poor had food they could not cook it. Communal feeding centres were set up to provide simple meals at low cost – Judge Wylie's 'Goodwill Restaurants' in Dublin and numerous smaller-scale communal kitchens in provincial towns. It was these conditions, argued two wide-ranging reports into TB commissioned by the Dublin Corporation in 1943 and 1945, that were causing the rising number of deaths. Deaths from pulmonary tuberculosis owed a good deal to people's reluctance to admit they had the disease, which meant not only that they didn't get the treatment they needed, but also that they stayed at home infecting their families. But the sanatoria were also woefully overstretched, so that even those wanting treatment might wait a year or more before admission, and by then it was too late. The reports pointed to the need for isolation wards, X-ray machines, and operating theatres, for tuberculin-tested milk in order to eradicate bovine TB, and above all for more beds in sanatoria. But both reports stressed that the overwhelming cause of the crisis was urbanisation and poverty. Poor diet, lack of heating, and overcrowded conditions made it difficult to avoid breathing in the disease, and once having caught it to contain it. Previously healthy young men and women, unable to find work in their home towns and villages, were being forced into the unhealthy atmosphere of the city tenements, only to die there.

The TB reports, along with another wide-ranging analysis of ways to reform the Health Service, which was published in 1944, show that the government was certainly not blasé about the crisis in social health. They introduced children's allowances in 1944, and free milk for pregnant women, both of which alleviated conditions for poor families to a degree. But TB became the symbol of the government's failure to tackle social deprivation and inequality. It was the spur to the formation of the new political party, Clann na Poblachta, which developed out of campaigns such as the 1942 Anti-Tuberculosis League. The Clann was to gain ten seats in the 1948 general election, forming part of a coalition government that finally broke de Valera's long run of power. Although this popular move away from Fianna Fáil had a good deal to do with the fact that poverty and unemployment actually worsened in the immediate post-war years, the seeds were sown during the war. As Deputy O'Leary put it in 1942:

The Minister will have fought this war, or maintained our neutrality position during this war, by disease to some degree, by the onset of crime, by the dissipation of small men's small resources and by the deprivation that some people have had to put upon their children in the matter of education and other social conditions.

8

The Static Generation

The war in Europe gave new impetus to Ireland's internal battles over culture. What had once been seen as a struggle between the Gaelic and Anglo-Irish strains in the national tradition was recast as a battle between self-sufficiency and a 'Europeanly-minded' version of Irish society. It became for some an urgent battle over Ireland's European identity.

Ireland's culture wars had long been fought on a native versus foreign axis. Attacks by the Gaelic League and the Gaelic Athletics Association on foreign games, foreign dances and especially foreign languages (by which they meant English) were intended to foster a truly national life. Advocates of an Irish Ireland had argued since the turn of the century that the 'de-Anglicisation' of the country was vital if it was to have any hope of fully emerging from centuries of colonial rule, and fostering its own native forms of creativity and political organisation. They called for a language and a literature which would champion the Gael against 'the dope of foreignism'. Unfortunately these arguments could feed all too easily into an ultra-conservative, sectarian attitude, a rejection of all that was 'non-native', of everything that did not display the signs of Gaelic 'race consciousness'. In practical terms they led to the denunciation of external influences such as radio, cinema, the foreign press, English publishers. Liberal writers liked to see themselves as the champions of modernity and enlightenment, in opposition to such benighted hyper-traditionalism, and to self-absorption in a narrow racial definition of Irishness. They argued against cultural self-sufficiency, and for the need for intellectual intercourse with the world 'outside' – especially, given the historic links between Britain and Ireland, with Anglo-Saxon culture. It was a viewpoint that often got them denounced as agents of the Ascendancy or remnants of unionism in Ireland.

For liberal Irish intellectuals Ireland's intensified wartime isolation could hardly have been more traumatic. They found themselves not only cut off from travel to England, but victims of a strict literary – and intensified political – censorship. 'You will find, I believe, that the year 1940 is the crucial year for any study of modern Irish literature,' wrote Frank O'Connor in retrospect. 'By that time Mr de Valera's government had complete control inside the country and nothing whatever to fear from liberal opinion abroad.' Echoing the image of the Irish entombed in Plato's cave, watching flickering shadows rather than sunlit reality, he declared that 'the intellectual darkness of the country was almost palpable'. It is hard to imagine a more extreme contrast with MacNeice's sense of Ireland in the opening months of the war as a possible haven, a space for reflection in a world sliding towards Armageddon. The poet's notion that Ireland might be a place to find clarity had gradually lost all plausibility – at least for certain sections of the educated middle classes. Instead they had become culturally marooned.

Amongst this section of society – numerically a small minority, of course – there were repeated complaints that the war had caused intellectual introversion and stagnation. 'Today we are cut off completely from the outer world,' wrote Hubert Butler in *The Bell* in 1941. He pointed to xenophobia and indifference to the fate of the outer world as the marks of this isolation. Margot Moffett, an Englishwoman married to Irish architect Noel Moffett and resident in Dublin throughout the war, recalled in 1945: 'During the first two or three years of the war it was possible to sense hysteria. The nation was thrown in on itself. There was no escape from this intensification of insularity: water on one side, blood on the other.' The actress Betty Chancellor concurred: 'This city is dying. The frightful censorship and narrowness is sapping the life out of everything,' she wrote to Denis Johnston, then serving as a BBC war correspondent in Egypt. Stasis and immobilisation became a standard complaint as the war progressed, and these notions have shaped the accepted image of Ireland's war years ever since, with educated Dubliners in particular described as a 'paralysed' generation, existing in 'limbo', on the margin of world events. Critics have argued that English writers living in London during the war felt awkwardly envious of French intellectuals, caught at the heart of the maelstrom; they had to make do, for example, with the vicarious thrill of publishing Louis Aragon's poems, smuggled out by the underground. By the same token, Irish literary culture worried that it was merely on the periphery of the periphery. As Flann O'Brien put it in *The Third Policeman*, it was 'negative nullity neutralised'.

O'Brien's novel was completed in January 1940. It would be wrong to interpret it as a portrait of the stagnation caused by the war. Nonetheless the novel's surreal take on rural Ireland – a hell in which the protagonist, guilty of murder and theft, is condemned to repeat for ever his encounters with a series of inscrutable policemen – drives home the feeling of confinement. The afterlife of the central character (who is unnamed) has odd similarities with the 'real' world of Ireland in mid-century. The rural community, populated only by policemen and ageing bachelors, and cut off from commerce with the world outside, runs according to its own arcane laws. Bicycle crime, of course, is rife, but the community also boasts its own band of violent clansmen joined together in secret brotherhood – the 'hoppy' one-legged men a comic version of the outlawed IRA. As one of the policemen notes, it all adds up to 'a beautiful commentary on home rule', a portrait of a culture neither one thing nor the other, neither sovereign and independent nor imperial dominion.

For all its wackiness, *The Third Policeman*'s surreal exploration of the decline of post-revolutionary fervour into greed and self-interest offered a critique of Irish society not so very different from that of the realist short-story writers, O'Faolain, O'Connor and Lavin. One of the reasons the idea of stagnation and paralysis in Irish wartime culture could take hold so easily was that it had been a staple of Irish literature for several decades – particularly of the short story. For the liberal writers the war was simply worsening the problems of surviving in that narrow community.

At the top of the list of complaints was the censorship of books and periodicals on the grounds of indecency and immorality. The Board of Censors, under the chairmanship of a one-time Professor of Literature at the National University, had long been the target of angry protests by more liberal writers. Established in 1929 with the aim of protecting impressionable Irish readers from the steady stream of low-brow periodicals, mildly scandalous popular fiction and pamphlets on birth control flowing from England, the Censorship Board also banned literary work it considered obscene, including books by nearly all of Ireland's younger writers.

The *Irish Times* mounted regular campaigns against the philistinism of the censors. Frenzy over the suppression of literary works reached fever pitch in the middle of the war, fuelled by anxieties over the country's seclusion. In 1942 Kate O'Brien's *The Land of Spices* was banned

(the second of her novels to fall foul of the censors), along with *The Tailor and Ansty* by Eric Cross (with a foreword by Frank O'Connor), and a book advocating the 'safe period' approach to birth control, *Laws of Life* by Halliday Sutherland. This triple whammy triggered protests in the papers and led to a four-day debate in the Dáil. Senator John Keane's motion of no confidence in the Censorship Board (which he described as a 'literary Gestapo') was overwhelmingly defeated. It went some way in proving the *Irish Times* right on philistinism, however, flushing out some particularly noxious xenophobic and sectarian attitudes. The information on the safe period, it was argued, would do 'untold harm' in the country: not only married but even engaged couples might be tempted to read *Laws of Life*. The book was yet another product of the campaign in England ('financed by American money') to undermine Christianity by advocating homosexuality, 'concubinage', and promiscuity.

There were intriguing literary opinions too. Kate O'Brien's novel about an Irish Mother Superior was described as a book 'whose central interest is sodomy'. At one point the chairman of the Board turned the Irish genius for short-story writing on its head. Ireland's writers, he argued, were in fact only able to write short fictions. Their forays into the alien genre of the novel were simply stories 'padded out with sex and smut', to make them attractive to English publishers. Another senator on the Board insisted that the young literati had only themselves to blame, for seeking higher sales 'by pandering to the lowest instincts of human nature'.

The workings of the Censorship Board provided ample evidence of intellectual darkness. What bothered Frank O'Connor (founder and President of the wartime 'Irish Society for Intellectual Freedom' – butt of many Myles na gCopaleen sketches) was that the cultural gloom seemed to be aggravated by the war. O'Connor, probably more than any other writer who remained in Ireland during the war, regretted the policy of neutrality and in particular the strict censorship which went with it. Though entrapment and disillusion had been a feature of the 1930s short stories, a new, more bitter, note entered into his wartime writing. The title of his 1944 collection, *Crab Apple Jelly*, evoked the sour autumn fruit of the Irish countryside, boiled down to a clear, sweet preserve – recommended by herbalists for cleansing the body of poison. There is plenty of venom in the collection. In 'The Star That Bids the Shepherds Fold', a puritanical priest and his henchmen try to frighten two girls caught in liaison with visiting French sailors. Whatever small cracks have appeared in the morality of the town clearly spring from the priest's refusal to acknowledge the real needs of his flock. The story focuses not on the priest, or on the girls, but on the curate whose ability to resist the priest's empty piety has been worn down through slow years of isolation. Several of the stories touch on gestures of defiance made long ago. In one of the most successful, 'The Grand Vizier's Daughters', the narrator listens to the town clerk telling a tale to his two grown-up daughters, of a Turkish Grand Vizier who long ago defied the power of the 'muftis' in the small town where he lived. ('As well as that he was after travelling a good deal: Paris, Vienna, Rome; the whole blooming shoot! Oh, he was none of your stick-in-the-muds at all, none of your country yobs, but a jing-bang, up to the minute Europeanised Young Turk.') As the story unfolds, the daughters realise they are listening to their father tell a 'censored' story about himself, and the decades spent enduring the slights of the town for standing up to the corrupt power of the Church. In a society that rarely offers escape, characters must live up to, or live down, choices made long ago.

O'Connor identified with the Europeanised Young Turk. After the Seanad debate on censorship he wrote to a friend, 'I have now discovered why I always wanted a house on Sandymount strand. It's the nearest I can get to England.' By 1944 he was spending long stretches of time in England working for the BBC. His Allied-friendly perspective needs to be understood as just that. Yet a significant portion of the liberal literary and intellectual elite agreed with him – if not about neutrality then about the obscurity into which it had plunged Irish culture. Unlike debate over neutrality itself – which all but disappeared except for a few speeches by James Dillon and Senator MacDermot after the first few months of the war – criticism of the censorship gathered strength and support as time went on. Writers, politicians and pressmen repeatedly complained of the censor's suppression of 'non-neutral' opinion aired in the Irish press, books, film and theatre.

Arguably, the 'average' citizen did not feel particularly disdvantaged by this censorship and may not even have been strongly aware of it. Some were keenly in favour. But for those who had been used to finding their cultural stimulation in Britain, or further afield in continental Europe, this was the final blow in intellectual freedom's losing battle against conformity and stagnation. Knowing that the censor was at work gave Irish Europhiles and Allied sympathisers a feeling of being trapped in an information vacuum. They didn't know what was really going on, and they could not write what they thought. The over-zealous authorities, said their critics, were interfering with 'the right of every man to think, speak and act freely within the law, and have free access to the thoughts of others'. When combined with the censorship of personal correspondence, and difficulties of travel, Irish cultural and intellectual life seemed entirely turned in on itself. Political censorship not only compounded the existing moral and religious censorship – it made it appear patriotic, and so all the harder to criticise.

*   *   *

Not all the defences of wartime censorship came from the ultra-conservative 'Irish Ireland' contingent or sprang from downright xenophobic attitudes. There were plenty of people (writers among them) who argued that the censorship was a good thing, providing protection from propaganda rather than insulation from knowledge of events. Even Sean O'Casey, who was vociferous in his attacks on the literary censorship, argued that the political censorship was not only mild but far less menacing than the control exercised by the British Ministry of Information: 'The Irish censorship is largely a farce: it is comic; but here, as I can prove, the censorship is silent, sinister and severe.'

Politically there was a clear case to be made for the censorship in Ireland, and the government went on trying to make it. In January 1944, during a debate on Emergency censorship, proposed (yet again) by Sir John Keane, Frank Aiken gave one of his most trenchant defences of the system. The censorship protected citizens from losing their sense of perspective on the war and so helped to maintain neutrality: 'if we are to have a very hot controversy here . . . we may split the unity of our people, and the net result will be that the people will lose their balance in the whole affair, and it is not neutral a lot of them will be.' Aiken's apology gave him the chance to launch a thinly veiled attack on the *Irish Times* campaign against the censorship. Shorn of its posturing, this was simply a cover for support for the Allies; it was anti-neutrality, and so de facto anti-national:

There is no other country in the world at the present time, I maintain, where the people have had a better and a clearer opportunity of getting all the news of this war in an unbiased manner. There has not been a single bit of news from the beginning of the war that was worth talking about that has been banned in our papers . . .

There has not been a single word uttered by any of the leaders of any country, whether they were Prime Ministers or sovereign heads, that has been banned by the Irish censor – not a single one. I should like to know in what other country have the people an opportunity of reading every word that has been said by these people without the censorship operating. What we have objected to, and what we have stood firmly against, is our people being oppressed by a barrage of propaganda from one side into taking a completely unbalanced view of what is going on in the world. That is what is objected to, not the censorship.

. . . We have allowed all the news to go through but we stopped the propaganda and we have enabled the Irish people to keep their balance during this disastrous war.

The government fear that popular feeling might at any moment be unbalanced by 'biased' coverage of the war was focused in particular on the cinema. The immense popularity and reach of the medium had no rivals in the world of entertainment during the 1940s, far outstripping that of radio in Ireland. Cinema was a vital form of recreation for the average man and woman in the towns and cities. There were upwards of 150 picture houses across the country, with a combined seating of more than a hundred thousand. Most were filled several times a day, most days of the week. In Dublin alone there was seating for thirty-two thousand people at each sitting. Mass popularity made film a well-recognised and valuable form of propaganda for both sides in the war, though given the fact that Ireland was part of the UK distribution network, Irish citizens were most 'at risk' from British and American versions of events. The British Ministry of Information laid out its tactics in its 'Programme for Film Propaganda':

[F]ilm propaganda will be most effective when it is least recognizable . . . The influence brought to bear by the Ministry on producers of feature films and encouragement given to foreign distributors, must be kept secret. This is particularly true of any films which it is hoped to distribute in America and other neutral countries.

The Irish film censor Richard Hayes commented on the resulting headaches in an interview in the journal The Bell: 'a full 90 per cent of films we get from England and America these days have more than their fair share of propaganda, even the non-war films. And it's the devil's own job cutting it out.' Hayes persevered in his work, nonetheless, in a grim, even desperate pursuit of impartiality. Large numbers of feature films were cut, and *Dublin Opinion* entertained its readers by parodying the impossible-to-follow plots that resulted. One minute the audience might be flying in an aeroplane, the next they would find themselves in a hotel bedroom, only to be catapulted suddenly onto a London bus. Other films were banned altogether, as posing a threat to law and order. Hayes said, for example, of Charlie Chaplin's *The Great Dictator*, 'If that film had been shown in this country it would have meant riots and bloodshed.'

The requirement for neutral entertainment precluded all films dealing with war preparations (troop movements, air-raid shelters), war news, propagandist or partisan comments about any of the countries involved in war, films which glorified the British empire or colonial rule, references to 'our troops' or 'we' (meaning the British people), and pictures of rulers, statesmen, warriors or flags of any of the belligerents. In practice this ruled out most newsreels. Frank Aiken (who was, according to the US ambassador, 'about as friendly as a disappointed rattlesnake') believed that 'if a newsreel is shown in which one belligerent or another is prominent, somebody may start to "booh" and somebody may start to cheer, and we do not want that sort of competition to start.'

There were good grounds for this fear. There had been a history of IRA attacks on Irish cinemas through the 1930s. Their target was the diffusion of 'continued depictions of British imperialist functions and British War Office propaganda', as *An Phoblacht* put it. In December 1934, for example, the Savoy in Dublin had been invaded by republican demonstrators, while screening newsreel footage of the marriage of the Duke of Kent and Princess Marina. Some newsreels shown early in the war caused disruption in cinemas both south and north of the border, if not quite on this scale. One diarist for Mass Observation recorded the booing and cheering which greeted newsreels shown in Armagh in September 1939 – on one occasion the Pope was cheered, the King received mingled boos and claps, but both Chamberlain and Hitler were greeted in silence.

It was not unusual for newsreels to elicit applause in British cinemas. In the first months of the war audiences clapped spontaneously at scenes of ordinary soldiers, and when this became too familiar, they still applauded during films of individuals represented as 'doing their bit'. Later on, newsreel producers tried to elicit clapping and cheering by inserting 'applause points' in voice-overs, such as 'Well done the RAF' from the commentator. Not everyone was happy with the blatant character of the propaganda. British Mass Observation diarists commented that (barring occasional more probing newsreels from Paramount) most cinema coverage was entirely uncritical of the conduct of the war, often verging on the most simplistic propaganda. The jingoism got worse as Britain's plight became more extreme. A report for Mass Observation on newsreels from August 1940 pointed out that what used to be presented as simple news footage was increasingly being cut and shaped into items that were 'very similar, though shorter, to the Ministry of Information's propaganda films'.

It is easy to see why the Irish government was intent on restricting films of this sort, but the censors' zealousness quickly led to a kind of manic rigour. When Hayes was on holiday his deputy took his duties so seriously that he began cutting the word 'war' itself. Faced with such draconian restrictions British newsreel companies produced special editions for the Irish market, though even these could be subsequently cut by the Irish censor. Bizarrely inoffensive items were excised, such as film of children visiting London Zoo (it showed them carrying gas masks). In fact zoo and animal scenes made up such a large proportion of the special Irish newsreels that when they were stopped in 1943 because of insufficient raw film stock, Irish cinema owners expressed few regrets.

It's a sign of the importance of cinema to wartime life in Ireland that the US could sneak a spy into Ireland posing as an emissary of the American Motion Picture Industry. His official task was to investigate the best way for American film-makers to respond to the censorship without losing revenue – in reality, he was there to report as fully as possible on Irish attitudes to the war. Martin Quigley Jr represented the acceptable face of Hollywood. His father, Martin Quigley, was a devout Catholic and powerful Irish-American publisher of film magazines and journals. He had been an important power broker in the parleying between the Catholic Church and the movie industry on the issue of moral censorship, and was the author of a 1937 bishop-pleasing treatise, *Decency in Motion Pictures*. In 1943 Quigley Jr spent some weeks in Dublin watching the work of the censor and trying to build up pressure for American pictures amongst the cinema owners. Inevitably he got on the wrong side of Aiken, who suggested to the cinema lobby that they should tell Mr Quigley where he got off. That there were some gentlemen who threatened if we did not do as they desired they would not give us pictures and that they would not give us wheat and they wouldn't give us a lot of other things: and that if we didn't stand united against them with a stiff back-bone they would kick us around and make us do everything they desired.

On top of his regular reports back to his masters in Washington, Quigley wrote up some recommendations for John Betjeman. He advised the poet, then back in London at the British Ministry of Information, on the most effective way to slip newsreels round the censorship, and get a British perspective on the war across to Irish viewers. As Quigley stressed, it was more often the commentary than the pictures that caused the trouble:

So far as a newsreel is concerned, I believe that many of the current war pictures will pass the censor, provided care is taken to exclude those which the Irish may classify as propaganda: for example, I doubt that the Irish film censor would pass scenes of Allied troops being received with pleasure by the natives of Italy. Also it would be necessary to cut out 'horror' scenes, such as of Axis dead and the like. Plain, objective battle scenes should pass the censor. It must be remembered that Irish film censorship is primarily concerned with excluding material which might cause disturbance in an Irish cinema.

With regard to the newsreel commentary: for Éire it should be spoken in an entirely objective and unemotional way. The Irish object to having English forces called 'our boys', Axis forces called 'the enemy' and so on. At first it might be necessary to avoid stressing which side is which. (The public will know anyway.)

The knowing public were nonetheless kept as much in the dark as possible. The newsreels managed to recreate on film the strangely abstract quality of government addresses, with their refusal to be specific even about which of the belligerents was being discussed. It was like hearing a film without seeing it, or watching with the sound turned off. While cinema audiences in the rest of Europe watched coverage of battles, shattered towns and cities, refugees, prisoners, the shell-shocked and wounded (albeit from very different perspectives), the war was glossed over for Irish filmgoers, who were informed instead about horse racing, annual festivals, the work of the Irish army and the LDF, and the activities of the Pope.

There were other sources of information, of course, including English newspapers, English, Italian and German radio, and bulletins such as *Letter from America* which was distributed in Ireland and set out to 'tell the Irish people what their Censorship did not want them to know' – not to mention private correspondence from relatives in England. But for many outside Dublin foreign newspapers were unobtainable. Meanwhile, as with wireless broadcasting, tight press censorship obliged Irish newspapers to maintain a balance between Allied and Axis perspectives in their coverage of the war. In practice this was pretty hard to achieve because Ireland had no press bureau and no war correspondents of its own; papers relied heavily on news from British and American sources, along with official communiqués from belligerent countries. The censors' response was to disallow any report that could be construed as biased to one side or the other – even book reviews were expurgated. As a character in Henry Green's *Loving* puts it: 'Well, there's one thing . . . they're neutral enough, they print what both sides say against one another.' All the same, there were persistent complaints from the Germans and Italians, and occasionally the Japanese, that war reporting was biased towards the Allies.

War news in the papers could be baldly reported, but with little leeway for opinion or comment. As far as possible events were covered in a detached manner, without any emotional charge or affective colouring; as with the radio, a balance had to be struck between contending views. This led to the practice of printing rival communiqués side by side. Editorials were very often confined to national issues, or vague generalisations about the conflict. In large measure the censorship achieved its aim of taking the heat out of discussions of the war. Compared to foreign news media, Irish newspapers produced a strangely blank description of the conflict. Rather like contemporary TV images of 'precision bombing' and 'smart missiles', the dead and dying were curiously absent. There were few pictures of wartime devastation, and none of the bodies of those killed or injured.

But in practice it proved impossible simply to stick to even-handed reporting, avoiding any slant towards either side. The material itself had its own story to tell. Reports from Stalingrad were extensively cut, for example, for fear of eliciting non-neutral sympathy among Irish citizens, as was coverage of the invasion of Belgium and Holland, and the fall of France. In fact all stories of atrocities committed by either side were stopped, for fear of their propaganda value. Irish readers learnt nothing of the Katyn massacre, for example; they remained ignorant of outrages committed in the war in the Far East. As Quigley put it, despite the publication of maps and rival accounts of battles such as the battle for Singapore, 'from the Irishman's point of view . . . the war in the East seems as remote as if it were being fought on Mars.' And the Irish knew nothing from their own sources of the persecution and cruelty in German-occupied Europe. Critics continued to argue that a play-safe approach had led to the sanitising and distortion of the real course of the war.

Many newspapers did struggle to present a fuller picture of Britain's war in Europe, such as the avowedly pro-Allied *Irish Times*, and other dailies such as the *Cork Examiner* and the *Irish Press*. Others seemed to do their best to show neutrality in a pro-Axis light. The right-wing weekly *The Standard*, the main Catholic paper, with a circulation of fifty thousand, focused overwhelmingly on news from the Vatican, on reports of reconstruction in Spain, and propagandist coverage of social reforms in Portugal – both Spain and Portugal were neutral countries and therefore fell outside the censorship. This was not so much the result of any out-and-out pro-fascism on the part of the editor, but rather an expression of the paper's support for a broadly Catholic corporatist view. *The Standard*'s coverage of the fall of France, however, was extraordinary: it excluded any mention of the dead or wounded. The paper occasionally printed a photograph of bomb damage, and reports from priests serving on the continent which touched on the refugee problem. But *The Standard*'s war was almost entirely bloodless. Most astonishing perhaps, in contrast to British papers, was that for readers of *The Standard* there was no British Expeditionary Force and no Dunkirk. Instead, they learned of the masterful diplomacy of Marshal Pétain.

Of all the attempts to control public information, press censorship aroused the most objections. Newspaper editors were Irish citizens, after all, not representatives of foreign film corporations or the British Ministry of Information, and they objected to having to trim the news to suit the government. Newspapers were not in any case simply channels of information; they also offered a public forum in their letters and opinion columns. For the relentless James Dillon, by April 1941 censorship was 'being used at present unduly to restrict legitimate free speech and prevent the natural expression of public opinion in this country'. Discussion of both international and domestic issues, so the protests went, was being muted and suppressed. There were complaints that Vatican statements on the Nazi persecution of the Catholic

Church went unreported, as did bishops' pastorals on the same problem, but German pronouncements were given space, for fear of
offending members of foreign legations; complaints that letters pages
allowed the expression of pro-German and pro-Italian sympathies,
but not pro-British ones. And on top of this – a particular bugbear –
there were cuts in the obituaries of those who died in battle.

The censors were also accused of suppressing 'legitimate discussion
about domestic affairs', such as calls for parliament to meet. They
seemed happy to clamp down on any dissent, whether or not it had
anything to do with the belligerents. Letters to the papers criticising
the handling of supplies and shortages were restricted; the experiences
of Irish people living abroad were refused publication. Far from keeping the country calm, this heavy-handed censorship was credited with
worsening the atmosphere of anxiety and rumour. The weekly rhymes
in *Dublin Opinion* obsessively harped on the censorship:

> No news evades the narrow grilles
> Of stodgy censorship
> Except the few well-coated pills
> They're willing to let slip.

For the Allies the Irish censorship was a deliberate attempt to suppress debate, and thus in effect an agent of misinformation. In 1942
the *Picture Post* ran a photo-story on Ireland, with text by Cyril
Connolly. The feature's central image was, unusually, not of Irish isolation. Headlined 'De Valera Hears What is Happening in the Outside
World', the picture showed the Taoiseach receiving 'voluminous
detailed reports' of events not only in Ireland 'but in Britain, Europe,
America, the world at large', every day. Rather than suggesting connection and contact, however, the story implied that ordinary citizens
were being deliberately kept in the dark about the news from 'the outside world'. Neutrality was being maintained by suppression of those
detailed reports. The censorship was a government ploy to keep the
populace in a neutral haze of misinformation. The ultimate expression
of Ireland's insularity, it was warping the country's responses and perceptions. 'Returning from Ireland,' wrote Connolly, 'gives a great fillip
to morale for it is clear that Ireland is experiencing every privation of
the war without the moral satisfaction of fighting for anybody.'

According to the protesters, with films and publications gagged, the
whole society felt muffled and subdued. Starved of information,

citizens found it hard to credit the reality of the war. 'The result is a queer feeling of unrealism,' complained Sean O'Faolain. 'This perpetual silence, this guarded reticence' he likened to the atmosphere of a genteel tea party, where the topic ends up being the weather – though in fact even the weather was censored, as possibly helpful to invasion plans. Elizabeth Bowen went even further, evoking not just the constriction of thought and discussion, but what she called 'a ban on feeling'. In her view, it was as though the whole country had been anaesthetised. Of course, the governments of belligerent nations, too, strove to desensitise citizens in their own way, through an incessant diet of propaganda. But combatant propaganda sought to drown out private anxieties and wayward sympathies by arousing powerful collective emotions, whereas Irish censorship aimed in effect at nullifying any strong feelings about the war. Anodyne, emotionless reports of advances and reversals on the battlefield were intended to foster a sense of detachment. While Irish people might follow the bare narrative of the war – might indeed become well versed in questions of military strategy, the ebb and flow of victories and defeats – they were not supposed to feel involved. Facts were denied context, resulting in what one commentator called a 'life lived in half-tones', and, one might add, half-speech. For those hostile to Ireland's stance, this state of suspension represented the triumph of euphemism – the very term 'Emergency' was a refusal to name the war explicitly.

*   *   *

Restrictions on travel abroad strengthened the sense of isolation induced by the censorship. Dublin's middle and upper-middle classes had been used to frequent travel and contact with England and the continent, especially France. But by mid-1940 travel to England was hedged around with difficulty, unless you were going on a labour contract, and it was impossible to go further afield. While for holidaymakers and occasional travellers this meant mostly inconvenience, for writers and artists, used to dealing with English agents, publishers, and galleries, and to placing material in English newspapers and magazines, cultural dialogue with England was abruptly severed. And as O'Connor suggested in his lament for the lost perspective of 'liberal opinion abroad', the difficulty of getting out of Ireland was compounded by the difficulty of others getting in. During the 1930s English and French touring theatre, art exhibitions, lectures by visiting continental and American academics and writers – all had confirmed the sense that Dublin was part of the modern European intellectual environment. All now seemed decisively shut down.

The negative effects were not simply on the life of the mind. Travel difficulties also meant a significant drop in income for artists and writers, so that literary circles found themselves sharing a good deal with Irish businessmen, crushed by the trade embargo. The issue was not so much long-term commitments – Jonathan Cape, Longmans, Macmillan, and Michael Joseph (all based in London) continued to publish novels, short stories and travelogues by Irish writers. But this brought infrequent and unreliable remuneration, dependent on sales. Meanwhile smaller amounts of regular income from journalism (for example with the *Manchester Guardian*) dried up almost completely. The BBC had been a reliable source of income for short-story writers during the 1930s, but such work became harder and harder to come by – the archives at Caversham contain a number of begging letters from both O'Connor and O'Faolain (Sean O'Casey quipped that he could 'rarely distinguish between the two') asking for more work, and more invitations to England. Above all they wanted money, but they also missed the cultural ambience of metropolitan London. The affair between Bowen and O'Faolain had, after all, begun after a meeting at the British Library, not in Ireland.

It is not surprising that writers such as Kavanagh, O'Faolain and O'Connor, committed to writing about Ireland, and with Ireland in mind, should have railed against the sudden divorce from an English reading public and English publishing outlets. There were few Irish publishing ventures then open to their more literary work. The Yeats sisters' Cuala Press produced several expensive works by O'Connor and Kavanagh during the war years, and there were other small ventures which actually started up during the war, such as Robert Greacen's New Frontiers Press, the Parkside Press, and English émigré psycho-analyst Rupert Strong's Runa Press. One of Runa's first titles was *Marrowbone Lane*, which Strong published alongside several anthologies of poems and short stories by both English and Irish writers, including the writers associated with the New Apocalypse movement. Runa Press publicity explicitly stated that since travel was so difficult nowadays the books were intended to cater for local reading groups in country areas. There were also new, independent initiatives for work in the Irish language, such as the publisher Sáirséal agus Dill, the journal *Comhar*, and the newspaper *Inniu*. But difficulties with supplies of paper and other raw materials caused other small concerns to go under. In March 1942, for example, the employees of Three Candles Press, which specialised in high-class printing and artwork, and in Irish-language books, were all given a fortnight's notice. The Talbot Press in Dublin was the exception. By the 1940s it could boast a large and respectable list of five hundred titles, which ranged from middle-brow fiction, religious books and lives of the saints, to Abbey Theatre plays, and work by Synge, Pearse and MacDonagh. Contemporary writers published by Talbot included Daniel Corkery, D. L. Kelleher, Francis Macmanus, Brinsley MacNamara and the popular romance novelist Annie M. P. Smithson. All the same, the fees to be had in England were much higher. And some authors no doubt looked down their noses at the national slant of the list, regarding themselves as fit for more cosmopolitan company, and aspiring to a larger readership.

The worst thing about the war from an Irish perspective, insisted Sean O'Faolain, was 'immobilisation'. In his 1942 script for the BBC's American programme he asked his imaginary listeners to picture what it was like

to have to stick in one place for several years on end, to have a very limited contact with your neighbours, to be thrown on your own local resources almost absolutely. This immobilisation is true of England, and Ireland, and every part of Europe. But for us it is particularly emphatic because we are an island, and because we are neutral, and cannot therefore even cross over to England – except under all sorts of wartime restrictions. So we have the curious effect of being IN the war, IN Europe, and yet as cut off from it as if we were two or three hundred miles out in the Atlantic.

O'Faolain suggested that what made Ireland least like being in the war (being cut off from it) also made it most like it; the restrictions of neutrality mirrored and even outdid those of belligerence. The physical immobilisation caused by travel restrictions was responsible for a cultural and psychological state of siege.

Elizabeth Bowen suggested that the 'abnormal isolation' caused by the suspension of travel between Ireland and Britain was muffling intellectual debate. In an essay on Ireland in the *New Statesman* in 1941 she lamented, 'And Éire is as hard to leave just now, as she is to enter: claustrophobia is the threat to the civilised mind.' There is more than a hint of colonial condescension here, as if Ireland depended on England for grown-up intellect – just the kind of attitude that was bound to irritate a nationalist politician such as Frank Aiken beyond measure. In a report Bowen wrote for the Dominions Office in November 1940, and on which the *New Statesman* piece was based, she enlarged on this feeling of stifling confinement:

Dublin, as a society – or rather as a complex of societies – seemed to be suffering from claustrophobia and restlessness. The suspension of travel to and from England is being very much felt. Socially and culturally speaking, the virtual closing of the Irish Channel is equivalent, for the more intelligent and Europeanly-minded people in Dublin and throughout Ireland, to a closing of the Burma Road. An increasing threat of parochialism in Dublin talk, interests, artistic outlook and social amenities is being recognised, and deplored. As 'someone from the outside' I was kindly met and frequently and hospitably entertained.

As a portrait of Dublin in general this description hardly held water, but as an insight into the world of the Allied-friendly Dublin intelligentsia it was right on target. If it closely reflected O'Faolain's views, this was scarcely surprising, given that he and Bowen were friends, and had been lovers. Bowen's information-gathering trips to Dublin from July 1940 onwards undoubtedly included meetings with O'Faolain and his circle, and their views will have been among those she reported back to London.

The idea that intelligence went along with being 'Europeanly-minded', and had been devastated by the difficulty of getting across the Irish Sea, was scarcely guaranteed to please the more 'nationally-minded'. The would-be Europeans were suffering from a loss of dignity, and from their lack of confidence in Dublin as a cultural capital in its own right. The sense of being cut off from the European mainstream went to the heart of the cultural predicament of neutrality. Out-and-out nationalists could focus their efforts on the cultivation of indigenous traditions. But for those whose self-definition relied on the context of a cosmopolitan, enlightenment culture, the loss of an international dimension was a blow to their identity. Isolated from the movement of ideas in Europe, abruptly divorced from Britain, they fell prey to anxiety and lack of direction. Who, now, was Irish culture in dialogue with? What was it for?

It is hardly surprising they were dismissed in some circles as pampered anglophiles, afflicted by a species of national inferiority complex. ('Wot? Benned in Ahland? Bet wy?' goaded Myles na gCopaleen.) To the unsympathetic eye, they were simply stuck in what would now be called a 'post-colonial' mindset, desperately mimicking the metropolitan centre – borrowing second-hand standards of taste and value. In a Gaelic League pamphlet of 1941 Daniel Corkery argued that Irish literature written in English was 'far more colonial today' than twenty years ago, fit only for the 'English and denationalised Irish' to read. Viewed from this angle, attacks on the wartime censorship were a cover for attacks on neutrality itself – products of a 'denationalised' mentality.

*   *   *

Given the vociferous complaints about isolation, it's easy to overlook the fact that Dublin's bid for the status of European cultural capital was in some ways given a boost by the war. A number of writers and artists left the country, either to work or to fight for the Allies. Travel restrictions cut down on the number of short-term cultural visitors. But to compensate, the outbreak of war also produced an influx of 'refugees' to Ireland, who had a decisive, if ultimately short-lived, influence on aspects of Irish cultural life. Some stayed only a few months, waiting to see how the war would develop. Many stayed for the duration. A good proportion of these migrants were returning émigrés, or would-be émigrés – artists and poets such as Norah McGuiness, Patrick Kavanagh and Geoffrey Taylor left England in the summer and autumn of 1939. Belfast-born painter Gerard Dillon returned from London to Dublin (or rather, like Louis MacNeice, stayed in Dublin, where he happened to be at the outbreak of the war); several architects, graduates of the modernist-influenced course at Liverpool, either returned or came to Ireland in the autumn of 1939. Irish painters based in France such as Ralph Cusack, Patrick Hennessy, and Louis and his mother Sybil le Brocquy fled to Dublin in 1939 and 1940. And there were also a number of refugees from the North – young novelists and poets such as Benedict Kiely, Robert Greacen and Roy McFadden all set themselves up in the Southern capital. Writers, artists and musicians who might once have gravitated towards London now chose Dublin as their cultural metropolis.

Then there were those who chose Ireland, who had never lived there before. Probably the most famous was the German theoretical physicist Erwin Schrödinger, who found a niche at de Valera's new Institute for Advanced Study. There were writers such as T. H. White, looking for a place to carry on their artistic work uninterrupted by the war. Ireland also proved a magnet for pacifists, and a small number of left-wingers, trade unionists and writers such as Yeats's old friend Ethel Mannin, who set up home in Connemara in the autumn of 1939, until she got caught out by travel restrictions after a trip to London and couldn't get back to the West. The English painters Elizabeth Rivers, Phyllis Hayward and Nick Nicholls all deserted London for Dublin. Stephen Gilbert, an English artist associated with the Cobra Group in Paris, and his Canadian wife decamped from France. A group of artists, psychologists and poets known as the White Stag Group and led by pacifists Basil Rakoczi and Kenneth Hall initially set up studio in Mayo, but moved to Dublin when the hardships and isolation of country living proved too much.

An international atmosphere was fostered by genuine refugees, conscientious objectors, artists and musicians. The numbers of these more permanent newcomers were boosted by an elite tourist trade, made up of wealthy Britons no longer able to get to Cannes or Monte Carlo, plus US military personnel, journalists and officials based in Northern Ireland or Britain – some brought family from the States and kept them in Ireland for the duration. There was more rather than less high-class travel to Ireland, principally by those for whom Dublin would have been off the map before the war. Now they were attracted by good food, entertainment, and the absence of blitz. The sophisticated aura lent by the foreign ('enemy') legations may have acted as a further draw. German, Italian, British, French and American diplomats created a 'consular coterie' who 'brought a sparkle and gaiety to first nights'. Almost overnight, Dublin had become 'a city with a rakish international life'. The cosmopolitan style was given a raffish gloss in the US press: 'Today Dublin vies with Lisbon as the most continental city in Europe. Americans, Britons, Italians, Germans and even Japanese mingle in the crowded streets and dance-halls.'

This influx of talent and energy, and of those on the look out for leisure, could not fail to have some effect. Margot Moffett, another new arrival, insisted that 'locking up' local Irish artists and mixing in a leavening of refugees, including those from the North, had had a dynamic effect on the Dublin cultural scene: 'We have raged and fought, with paint, poems and perspectives, against the mental paralysis which threatens the New Ireland.'

Those perspectives had a self-consciously European – particularly French – flavour. There was an unmistakably Gallic tone to the struggle for intellectual and artistic freedom during the war years –

inevitably, perhaps, given the Occupation. There was, for example, a noticeable crop of French translations in the theatre – some making explicit reference to the question of European freedom. November 1940 saw the staging of Lennox Robinson's *Roly Poly*, a version of Maupassant's story of the Franco-Prussian war, *Boule de Suif*, set in a contemporary and embattled France. The play focused on a group of refugees fleeing invading German forces – it was taken off after three nights after complaints from both the German and French legations. The story of the humble prostitute is also a leitmotif in O'Faolain's 1940 novel *Come Back to Erin*, where reading French literature and dreaming of getting to France is one release – along with visiting brothels – for the ageing, disappointed brother of the protagonist. In O'Connor's *Crab Apple Jelly* provincial puritanism can be briefly held at bay by speaking French or owning a few French books. Characters cling desperately to an idea of abroad. A more direct influence of the artists returned from France was evident in a production of Jean Giraudoux's comedy *Amphitryon 38*. This was a joint venture by the Longfords and Shelagh Richards, translated from the French by Sybil le Brocquy, with set designs by Louis le Brocquy. There were political messages to be decoded here also. Giraudoux, a French diplomat, had served as Minister of Information in Edouard Daladier's government at the start of the war, but was lying low under Vichy rule – Daladier himself had been imprisoned by the Germans.

Probably the most adventurous and active of the new wartime ventures was the White Stag Group. In addition to several group shows and one-man shows in small galleries in Lower Mount Street and Upper Baggot Street, Rakoczi and Hall organised regular lectures on art, architecture and psychotherapy, given by Noel Moffett and Mainie Jellett among others. The group specialised in post-surrealist work – what they called 'subjective art' – a mixture of styles and influences from Picasso, Klee, Miró, Masson, Henry Moore, plus elements of surrealism. Francophilia was marked here too. Henry Silvy of the French legation gave a well-publicised lecture to the group on the 'Legacy of Cubism'. There were gramophone-recording recitals and meetings in the gallery of the Society for Creative Psychology, which – in the form of psychologist Herbrand Ingouville-Williams – had relocated from London to Dublin.

The group's major project, the 1944 Exhibition of Subjective Art, showcased modern, non-representational work by the new arrivals and a small number of Irish artists, including Patrick Scott. The doyen of the modern English art scene, Herbert Read, was due to open the exhibition amid a good deal of fanfare. In the event he was denied a travel permit and John Hewitt stepped in (Read's opening lecture on 'Subjective Art' was later printed in *Horizon*). Read's catalogue introduction was nothing short of ecstatic about Dublin's new art scene: 'Here in Ireland one rejoices to find that not only has art found a secure shelter, but even fresh vigour.' Insisting (handily) that art flourished best 'where the spirit of man is free but his horizon circumscribed', he found Dublin the perfect seed bed for experimentation:

Here in Dublin I would not expect, nor do I find, a provincial art. These paintings and carvings seem to me to belong to the mainstream of European culture. And that, I venture to say, is something new in the modern history of this country. Thirty years ago your painters and your poets fled to London or to Paris because only in such artificial communities was there any semblance of that integral and organic faith and brotherhood in which alone art arises.

Now London and Paris were fleeing to Dublin, transforming it from a provincial city into a European one, a beacon of creative freedom.

Read's diagnosis was understandably celebratory, given his brief. Yet there were signs that the pressure-cooker atmosphere in cut-off Ireland was genuinely having a beneficial effect on cultural life. The battle between the moderns and the old guard had already reached a kind of climax in the Irish Exhibition of Living Art, a display of Irish avant-garde painting first held in 1943. The show grew out of the rejection in 1942, by the selection committee of the Royal Hibernian Academy, of work by a number of younger artists, including some such as le Brocquy who had newly returned to the country. The publicity for the rival exhibition cautioned against a narrow isolationism in Irish art, which was leading the Academy to value only dead imitations of dead styles. For the young experimentalists isolation, far from nurturing a 'national' art, was merely encouraging fossilised imitations of academic convention. Responses to the 1943 show split along predictable nativist-versus-cosmopolitan lines. 'European influence was the dominant note,' said Con Leventhal, 'nothing that smacked either of insularity or narrow regionalism.' By contrast Máirín Allen, writing for the *Father Mathew Record*, found only alien styles:

If any exile visited the Irish Exhibition of Living Art recently held in Dublin he must have emerged bewildered . . . by the utter foreign-ness of so much presented to him as Irish art . . . the mass of the painting shown is affected, imitative, and empty . . . rightly or wrongly one gets the notion that this strange foreign-ness . . . is the result of an absence of contact between these artists and the normal, native, cultural background.

'Insularity' versus 'imitation' – the familiar buzzwords of Irish aesthetic debate had come round again. At their best the new arrivals brought an injection of fresh energy, disrupting the tired Gaelic versus Anglo-Saxon ping-pong. What was Irish art? Paintings of Irish peasants and Irish plays at the Abbey? Was it possible to be both Irish and avant-garde? Yet it didn't take much for the wrangling to slip back into the routine opposition of local and European, native and foreign. In August 1944 the Friends of the National Gallery mounted a Loan Exhibition of Modern Continental Paintings, comprising works in Irish public and private collections, including cubist, impressionist, post-impressionist, and some German Expressionist works. The official *Irish Times* line was flag-waving: 'To a country which is pursuing cultural isolation, without seeing that it will mean cultural suicide, any breath from outside is of value.' In his column Myles na gCopaleen responded with predictable ferocity: 'A certain tasteless catholicism', he remarked, had 'impelled the selection committee to whip in a lot of very sorry imitative trash, probably just because the smell was foreign.'

At its worst, the behaviour of the European blow-ins simply ratified suspicions of the 'alien' nature of self-conscious continentals. Some of the irritation they aroused seems to have been well founded; being cultured was all too often synonymous with being Europeanly sophisticated, more at home in Montmartre than Killiney or Sandymount. A note in the January 1942 number of the new magazine, *Commentary*, announced the redesign of the White Stag gallery in central Dublin in Francophile style. Rakoczi and Hall had chosen white walls and 'gay curtains of striped blue', in order 'to create a Parisian atmosphere reminiscent of the art galleries of the Rue de la Boétie'. It was just this kind of slavish imitation which was guaranteed to raise hackles, especially when accompanied by complaints about the censorship. *Commentary* catered for a small 'elite' – an affluent, self-consciously modern, European-oriented readership, who liked to hear about the refitting of Jammets (Dublin's high-class French restaurant) and the latest fashions in food and clothing. The gossip about society weddings ('A wedding is generally an occasion for a display of fashion. That of Dr and

A page of advertisements in *The Bell*, June 1941.

Mrs Devane at Foxrock last month was fashionable and interesting'); the style features ('Winter to my mind always means a fur coat'); reports on the society at the Leopardstown Races; the recommended menus for 'at homes' and dinner parties ('Grapefruit, fried filleted black sole, and tartar sauce, with roast duckling to follow, served with apple sauce, and I believe the meal was rounded off with Meringues Chantilly. The wine was a fine Burgundy') – all this revealed a readership as much concerned with status as genuine aesthetic values.

This crowd was ripe for ridicule by Flann O'Brien, in his relentlessly satirical portraits of the 'immigrant flyboys' dressed in corduroy and stinking of oil-paint, liable at any moment to bore you with stories of Braque or the 'Rue des Grues-Nues', if not discourses on Kafka and existentialism. (O'Brien's language betrays a not very subtle attack on the small gay subculture that grew up around the White Stag Group, and Edwards and MacLiammóir at the Gate Theatre.) Far worse were those Irish swayed by such posturing – people tempted to join the Society for Intellectual Freedom and kick up a fuss about the censorship. The censorship ramp was a racket enabling second-rate pens to flounce around feeling persecuted, moaning about having to go and live in exile in Paris: 'They and Anatole France become brothers under the skin.'

A 'blushing self-conscious foreignism' was rampant not only in artistic circles. The National Planning Exhibition, in spring 1944, gave a group of architects and planners the chance to publish a series of Reconstruction Pamphlets. Imbued with a visionary gleam, these brochures advocated new towns linked by motorways, modernist architecture, pre-fabricated holiday villages, and so on. Several of these pamphlets, though decidedly ambitious, do reflect a sincere attempt to improve living conditions for the poor and apply modern social principles to the Irish situation. O'Brien attacked again:

It is my considered view that Paud keeping step with world hysteria in the belief that he is being 'modern' is a woeful spectacle, is nowise funny . . . He has got himself a lot of graphs and diagrams and he is beginning to babble about 'built-in furniture' . . . Could Paddy leave off from copying just for five minutes?

O'Brien reserved his most scathing attacks for the two major attempts at post-war planning in Ireland: the Report of the Commission on Vocational Organisation and Bishop Dignam's outline of an Irish

Social Security scheme (hailed as 'Éire's Beveridge Plan'), both of which were also published in 1944. As Private Secretary for the Department of Local Government and Public Health (and Acting Principal Officer of the Department from 1943), O'Brien was nominally responsible for implementing any changes in health provision. As Myles na gCopaleen he concluded that Bishop Dignam's recommendations for reorganising the service – welfare centres and clinics were to replace outdated medical dispensaries – were simply a slavish and ill-conceived copy of British models: 'foreignism in its filthiest guise stalks the land.'

From this perspective Irish culture was not inward-looking at all, but the opposite – guilty of 'a disgusting aping' of foreign culture. It's hard to have much sympathy with O'Brien's attacks on plans for a fairer medical system. After all, he didn't have any alternative schemes to suggest. His pillorying of the Europhile literati had more substance. The most self-consciously 'cultured' persisted in thinking that everything good and intellectually stimulating came from Europe – for which read Paris and London rather than Berlin or Madrid. Occasionally the source might be the US. By 1944, for example, the jive ('a young people's dance, of the swing persuasion, and American in origin') was being taught at a dancing academy in Lower Baggot Street, so that young socialites might feel confident when they went to a ball: 'It is no longer a matter with them of just standing up and getting through the Waltz, or the Fox-Trot, as best they can. Instead, people now take private lessons from here before they go dancing in public.' Clearly it wouldn't do to stumble through a dance with an American officer on furlough – Ireland's cultural isolation was not quite what it seemed.

O'Brien offered his own farcical version of this slavish relationship to foreign culture – finding Europe not in the cultural sphere, or in leisure, but in warfare and belligerence. In one piece he describes his acquaintanceship with Tom O'Shenko, brother to the celebrated Irishman Tim O'Shenko – presumably the hero who reached the position of Marshal in the Red Army, and successfully defended Moscow against the Wehrmacht. O'Brien recalls a conversation with Tom back in 1934:

'I've had a letter from Tim,' he said, 'and he takes a very poor view of what is happening in Germany. He says there will be a world war in seven years, if not sooner. He has joined the Red Army as a private.'

'Well, well, well,' I said. I was genuinely surprised at this rather idealistic move on the part of Tim, whom I had always heard of as a hard-headed business type. I knew that he had made plenty of money operating some suet cartel east of the Urals.

'I think I will be going away soon myself,' Tom said. 'After all, when one's brother is out there . . .'

That, I thought, was big-hearted Tom all over. He is out there now and in the thick of things. One does not take sides in these neutral latitudes, but I hope most of my readers will join me in expressing the hope that we will yet see both Tom and Tim O'Shenko back in Ireland safe and sound . . .

The Irish are taking a leading role in the war; indeed, what is most obviously Irish about them – their names – is also what is most international. But the joke also boomerangs – hinting at the impossibility of imagining anything beyond Ireland which isn't Irish, such is the insularity of the nation. It's an introversion that O'Brien both mocks and backhandedly defends. All news becomes Irish – and the Irish become the news.

The Soviet theme recurred in an item entitled 'Steppe Together', which neatly conflated the Russian landscape with the rallying cry of Ireland's volunteer army. O'Brien's strategy was a persistent blurring of the contrast between nationalism and internationalism. Ireland is not just part of Europe – it is Europe itself, particularly its main warring parties. Such is the wisdom of the people:

THE PLAIN PEOPLE OF IRELAND: Isn't the German very like the Irish? Very guttural and so on.

MYSELF: Yes.

THE PLAIN PEOPLE OF IRELAND: People do say that the German language and the Irish language is very guttural tongues.

MYSELF: Yes.

THE PLAIN PEOPLE OF IRELAND: The sounds is all guttural do you understand.

MYSELF: Yes.

THE PLAIN PEOPLE OF IRELAND: Very guttural languages the pair of them the Gaelic and the German.

Slow, thick, vainglorious, blind to any of the underlying issues, O'Brien's 'plain people' are nonetheless haunted by a sense of Ireland's ancient affinities. They sense at least that the European heritage means more than the bohemian quarters of London and Paris.

O'Brien's decision to write in Irish, in the first years of his column in the *Irish Times* and in his 1941 novel *An Béal Bocht*, meant that he risked – even invited – being caricatured as a Gaelic League nationalist. But he was equally vociferous in his attacks on the ideology of the Irish language as it was used to prop up a saccharine version of traditional Irish culture. In many ways O'Brien's natural allies were those liberal writers who attacked the 'Celtophilism manufactured by Civil Servants in . . . the Department of Education, with their fairy-tale textbooks on history and their quite unrealistic school-readers', as O'Faolain put it. In fact he wrote articles for O'Faolain's journal *The Bell* when it first started – on pubs and on dog-racing – but he soon came to detest its tone of liberal angst. In his surreal novels and satirical columns – part storytelling, part pun, part comic drama – he showed an appetite for experimenting with language and form which went far beyond the 'modern' realism of his fellow writers. But he was determined to experiment through Irish forms (parodying Irish legend in *At Swim Two Birds*, the Gaeltacht autobiography in *An Béal Bocht*) and for an Irish audience. The work he produced during the war amounted to an argument for an experimental and modernist cultural nationalism. If he was against Celtophilism he was also against Europhilism; indeed, he saw them as two sides of the same coin. The war exacerbated the divide between Ireland and 'abroad' and in doing so widened the gap between the plain people and the self-consciously liberal elite devoted to 'the European idea'. O'Brien (the bureaucrat in the middle) became increasingly suspicious of the internationalists. He saw the liberals not as more broad-minded but as more British-minded, jumping at the chance to turn their backs on Irish culture – unable in fact to notice Irish culture as it really was.

* * *

For artists and intellectuals used to commerce with Britain and the continent, the flip side of being cut adrift was the difficulty of adjusting to an indigenous Irish market. Dismayed by their new situation, forced into a dialogue with the plain people themselves, liberal intellectuals condemned the Irish cultural scene as benighted by censorship, hamstrung by narrow definitions of religion and nationality, stifled by reverence for the Irish language and folk tradition. In their eyes, cultural nationalists were reluctant to embrace the modern, let alone the experimental. It all amounted to a rejection of the enlightened or, as Bowen put it, 'the civilised mind'. To go by their published comments, many writers and artists did little else but complain. But the war also provided Dublin with the opportunity for an experiment in self-sufficiency.

The Bell was one example. A joint venture by Peadar O'Donnell (who raised the money) and Sean O'Faolain (who edited the magazine for the first five years), *The Bell* was intended, at least in part, as a remedy for isolation. It was an attempt to answer the question: what was the purpose of Irish culture? Modelled on John Lehmann's *New Writing* and on Cyril Connolly's *Horizon*, which were credited with enlivening intelligent cultural debate in England, the first issue was published in October 1940, a significant moment in terms of the worsening dialogue between Britain and Ireland. As O'Faolain's editorials liked to insist, 'emergent' Ireland was at the beginning of a new period in its history, for which it needed a new literature, new cultural forms, and – crucially – a new audience. If Ireland were to be cut off from intercourse with the 'outside world', then standards of writing, and of taste – for so long imported from the literary salons of London, and perhaps Paris – would need to be developed from within.

The great achievement of *The Bell* was that it flourished at the very moment when Irish culture was felt to be at its most insular and lifeless. O'Faolain had been a regular contributor to *The Criterion* and *The London Mercury*, and was to contribute to *Horizon*. He was impressed by the documentary impulse behind the new British magazines, of which there had been an explosion in the 1930s, with their attempt to reach out to new audiences, and their engagement with major social and political issues of the day: Communism and the rise of the USSR, the Spanish Civil War, the decline of religion – *The Bell* developed these themes, but hibernised them. Rather than being concerned with impending war, industrial labour, social transformations in 1930s Britain, or the relationship between art and commitment, the overwhelming focus of *The Bell* was on what O'Faolain called 'the realities of Irish life'. This impulse fitted nicely with the rejection, amongst the younger realist writers, of Yeatsian romanticism.

Throughout the 1930s they had waved the flag of realism in the face of what they saw as Yeats's fantasy-laden myths, focused on the West of Ireland. Here again there were links with the English journalistic and documentary movement of the 1930s. At some level O'Faolain probably saw his project as similar to that of a writer such as MacNeice. Both were impatient with romantic images of Ireland and dedicated to a literature of contemporary life – what the Scottish documentary film-maker John Grierson called 'the creative treatment of actuality'. The difference was that O'Faolain was committed to Irish neutrality, and to creating an identifiably Irish modern culture.

The Bell's backers were impatient with the mythology of de Valera's state. O'Faolain relentlessly took on the censors and the romancers, including the Gaelic League:

The Revival of Gaelic and the Revival of industry are not happy bed-mates. The Gaelic Leaguer watches uncomfortably even our development of tourism. We tried to establish a network of decentralised factories, and for that we had an ideal picture of little industries in the small towns and villages. The census returns replied in the name of Realism with the flow from the fields to the cities, the decay of the small villages, and even some of the smaller towns. A natural urge to keep out the alien supported the censorship. World Radio replies night after night. On the other hand a world-war has assaulted our isolation, and we have replied by armed neutrality.

The aim was to record the real life of country and city, rather than the idealised life of peasant Ireland. The Bell carried striking documentary articles, often written in the first person, about life in the provincial towns of Ireland, North and South; it ran items on being a music teacher or bank manager in a small town, and on the booming amateur theatre in the country. Beside these more personal contributions stood discussions of social and political issues, such as sex and censorship, penal reform, the hospital system and history teaching in schools, as well as new fiction and poetry, and theatre reviews. In his editorial in the third issue O'Faolain inveighed against the Irish penchant for endless, ill-informed controversy:

The Bell believes that the first thing we must do in Ireland is to see clearly – voir clair – to have the facts and understand the picture. This has never been attempted before. When Ireland reveals herself truthfully, and fearlessly, she will be in possession of a solid basis on which to build a structure of thought; but not until then.

The Bell prized the signs of a confident Irish modernity wherever it found them – it was hostile to insularity, against the utilitarian use of the Irish language, against censorship, and against the pieties of the provincial middle class. But in attempting to shape the literature of a progressive, open-minded, enlightened country it was also compelled to reach out to the provincial petty-bourgeoisie. O'Faolain's first editorial recognised the need for the bell to ring out across the country if it were to be heard at all:

People will hear these chance notes to the north and to the south, and when they say in field or pub, in big house or villa house, 'There is the bell', they will echo the replication of its notes, and the air will carry the echo wider and wider.

The trouble was getting the message out to those who might respond. Outlets for literary material were sparse: there were few circulating libraries, few small bookshops, and on top of this there was the problem of censorship. By the 1940s, the censors were backed up by an army of vigilantes across the country, who saw it as their task to root out unsuitable material. Even ordering reading matter through the newsagent was fraught with difficulty. One librarian in Ennis, County Clare, recalled a scene in his local shop:

I observed a curious bit of mime between the assistant and a secondary teacher standing behind some people at the counter. 'You got it?' His whisper was barely audible, but her finger shot up, and down she went to root underneath the counter, and came up with *The Bell*, cover downwards. 'I had a mind to send it, but . . .' She got an approving nod. He was at the back door when her voice followed him. 'And next month?' Another nod from him, and his pointed finger to the hole-in-the-ground, for which he got a smile of instant understanding.

The isolation of such readers was a spur to the magazine, the very thing it was seeking to overcome. To survive, *The Bell* had to pull in the middle classes of the country towns. Practically speaking, a new platform was needed for Irish writing, because of the blocking of British and American outlets. But almost inevitably, *The Bell*'s national and provincial focus acted as a drag on O'Faolain's European ambitions. From 1943 onwards, the journal ran a series of leaders entitled 'One World' – 'our modest contribution against Isolationism and Little Irelandism'. One such leader proclaimed that 'The truest Irish patriot of today is the man who can look at Ireland as a modern man, and as a Citizen of the World, who happens to be resident in this corner of it.' Nonetheless, in Frank O'Connor's view, *The Bell* showed scandalously little interest in, indeed 'refused to recognise', the war – a criticism echoed, predictably, by British commentators. There *was* the problem of the censorship, of course: for example, an article by Con Leventhal on Judaism and anti-semitism was so severely cut that O'Faolain pulled it. But *The Bell*'s idea of Europe was curiously flimsy – it was the pre-war Europe of literature, theatre, and art-house cinema, not the continent that was going up in flames. The 'International Number' of March 1943 contained articles on Tolstoy and the USSR, on P. G. Wodehouse, and on the Italian novelist Antonio Fogazzaro by O'Faolain himself. If this roster was meant to affirm the ideal unity of European culture, in the face of a continent at war, its effect was to suggest a state of denial. Unacknowledged impotence lent a hysterical edge to many of O'Faolain's self-justifications:

There is a merit in detachment; in being *au dessus du combat*; in imperturbability; in not being fussed and bothered all the time. But there cannot be any merit in this if one takes it too far and gets cut off from the rough common-sense and strength of first-hand experience.

It is not surprising that O'Faolain's declamations so often suggest paralysis, an underlying impasse. He was a champion of the concerns of modern Catholic Ireland – but in desperate need of English approval. (This was where he parted company with Flann O'Brien.) He argued for greater connection with the North, and with Anglo-Ireland – but at the very moment when the war was cementing the border, and when the Anglo-Irish he most wanted to link up with were leaving. He needed to create a writership and a readership right across the country – but despised the provincial mentality that had led to the earlier banning of his own fiction. He hated insularity but supported neutrality; he was 'Europeanly-minded', but conscious of the need to protect the 'emergent' nation.

One of the most curious things about the documentary realist movement in Irish writing was the way in which it became bound up with a form of provincial nostalgia. Tourism was of course one of the 'realities of Irish life' and the writers clustered around *The Bell* certainly weren't going to ignore it. But a good deal of their writing during the war years played directly into the hands of the tourist romancers.

There was nothing new about green-tinted representations of the Irish countryside, of course – the New York World's Fair had shown what could be done in the way of turning Ireland into a souvenir for emigrants. In 1943 the Dublin publisher Browne and Nolan brought out a new edition of *Ireland of the Welcomes*, a guide for the foreign

traveller seeking 'the old standards of courtesy and hospitality', the traditional 'Céad Míle Fáilte'. Advertising typical attractions such as the
scenery of the western coast, the horses, the fishing, the literature and
the stories of romantic and heroic history to be found in every small
town and village, the author, D. L. Kelleher, did acknowledge in the
final pages the hammering Belfast had taken in the blitz. If the idea of
bringing out a tourist guide in the middle of a world war seems optimistic (if not insensitive), the publishers were clearly aiming their text
at the new types of American visitor – GIs stationed in the North and
journalists and army personnel based in England, several of whom
deposited their families in Ireland for the duration. The potential of
foreign tourism as a serious source of cash flow was just becoming
apparent. But what was unusual about most wartime images of country life was that they were aimed at people living in Irish towns and
cities, for whom rural Ireland was only a generation away, at most.

This process had begun before the start of the war, and had initially
been spurred by the growth of Ireland's fledgling tourist industry. As
excursion trains became more and more fashionable in the late 1930s,
and motor-car ownership rose, the market grew for material aimed
not solely at the foreign visitor, but at the Irish city dweller, who was
encouraged to discover his own country. Sean O'Faolain's *An Irish
Journey*, which he had been researching on the outbreak of war, envisaged a new sort of readership, in addition to the English and American
tourists targeted in the past: he wrote too for the burgeoning Irish
middle class. His travelogue reflected – much as *The Bell* was to do –
provincial not primitive Ireland, the life of the towns rather than the
rugged coast, English-speaking Ireland rather than a romanticised
Gaelic culture. By the time O'Faolain's book was published, however,
its value as a travel guide was in question. Travel in Ireland had
become so restricted that the book turned into what O'Faolain had
probably wanted it to be all along – a work of literary tourism, a guide
to an Ireland that could be visited in an armchair.

O'Faolain was not alone in combining the roles of social critic and
provincial romantic. Patrick Kavanagh gave Ireland 'The Great
Hunger' (encouraged by O'Faolain) and enjoyed the beginnings of a
career in documentary journalism in articles he wrote for the national
press, including one on country farmers' reluctance to marry, and a
series on religious pilgrimages. But he was also forced by economic
necessity to jump on the nostalgia bandwagon when he arrived in

Dublin (by way of London) in 1939. An 'authentic' countryman turned *littérateur*, he lived partly by churning out articles for the newspapers 'on the pleasures of country life which, fifty miles away, calls me to return'. He wrote for the *Irish Times* on corn threshing, on Christmas in the country, on country marriage, on the Dundalk market train; for the *Standard* on cutting turf, on harvesting, on the November Fair, on Sunday in the country; for the *Irish Independent* on bogs, and on ploughing. Fantasies of rural Ireland, like nostalgia for an unspoilt England, were solace for those bruised by the effects of the war. They represented the known, the familiar, that which we like to imagine continues elsewhere despite all the chaos and disruption of our lives, and they made Kavanagh money, though not vast amounts of it. Newspaper editors could bank on readers' interest in benign and evocative portraits of rural life.

The public's appetite for rural reminiscence was high, and could be satisfied by novels, memoirs, even recipe collections. In books, magazines and newspapers the vogue for misty retrospection was fed by readers' appetite for reminders of what was being lost in Ireland's struggle to become modern. This went along with more practical attempts to preserve rural culture. The Irish Countrywomen's Association and the Homespun Society, although founded earlier, were both very active during the war, holding summer schools, shows, fairs and co-operative country markets, and giving lectures on crafts. Despite travel difficulties, in March 1943 the Homespun Society began a four-year survey of traditional crafts throughout the state, and lobbied for greater emphasis on crafts in rural vocational education. At the same time, however, there was an acceptance that crafts such as home-spinning and weaving were dying, and from 1941 Society members began sending artefacts for preservation in the National Museum – the collection that would later become the Folklife Collection. This uneasy relationship between 'active' and 'passive' preservation of rural customs was replicated in the work of the Irish Folklore Commission. The Commission's massive *Handbook of Irish Folklore* was published in 1942, a 'comprehensive guide' for folklore collectors intended to facilitate the garnering of endangered traditions:

Here as elsewhere the shoddy imported culture of the towns pushes back the frontiers of the indigenous homespun culture of the countryside, and the ancient courtesies and traditional ways of thought and behaviour tend to disappear before the destroying breath of 'the spirit of the age'.

Meanwhile there were numerous popular novels and short stories about village and small-town life, often set at the turn of the century. More highbrow writers such as Michael McLaverty and Mary Lavin produced literary versions of this homesickness for the recent past. Though there was often rather more sting in the tail of their depictions of rural life, they contributed nonetheless to the phenomenon of rural – or at any rate, village – Ireland being recycled for consumption in the cities and towns.

It was no accident, then, that the most popular novel in Ireland for much of the war was *Never No More*, Maura Laverty's idyllic story of growing up in a village on the edge of the Bog of Allen. First serialised in *The Bell*, the novel was published to huge popular acclaim in 1942. Its attractiveness undoubtedly had to do with its unbridled nostalgia for an unspoilt Ireland, the simplicity of childhood and youthful innocence, and a land of burgeoning plenty. Laverty was also a cookery writer and her novel dwells on traditional recipes, which must have been mouth-watering for those unable to get hold of ingredients during the war. The elements of rural custom, neighbourly cooperation, petty jealousies, first dances, and above all lack of want, compared especially to the unhappy life of the towns, were replicated in a score of less accomplished fictions. *Never No More* was above all a novel of escapism, which may explain its huge attraction for the republican prisoners interned for the duration of the war. Brendan Behan, during his incarceration in Arbour Hill Military Prison, wrote to the author about the desperate measures taken by the prisoners to get hold of the book after they had read the serialisation in *The Bell*:

Mrs Laverty, ma'am, I give you my solemn word there was nearly bloodshed over it. Each of them started taking a peep here and a peep there, and having once pept . . . they wanted to go on reading irrespective of the fact that there was a fellow waiting his turn to have it. And in the heel of the reel, we got a bit of order into the reading of it. And, God help me, altho' I was last, I had it longest.

The breathless tone of Behan's fan mail may have been copied from the adolescent palpitations of Laverty's main protagonist, though in fairness he was little more than an adolescent himself when he read the book. Laverty's novel ends as the central character Delia Scully leaves childhood and rural Ireland behind – like Laverty herself, and Kate O'Brien, she travels to Spain to work as a governess. The association of childhood with the Irish countryside was bound to resonate for a large majority of Laverty's readers in the 1940s, since so many had been forced to leave the economically stagnant rural areas to seek work in Cork and Dublin, if not Manchester, Liverpool or London.

Laverty's novel was sentimental, but – as O'Faolain saw when he serialised it – there was no necessary contradiction with its realism. The novel was certainly read for its depiction of contemporary country life. In 1942 it was referred to in the Dáil in a debate on tuberculosis: Laverty's description of a young man dying in the Bog of Allen, having waited too long for a place at Newcastle sanatorium, was used to highlight the problems of underfunding and lack of equipment in the treatment of TB.

The Bell's attempt to create an Irish literary culture which spread beyond the confines of a small Dublin elite to the towns of provincial Ireland was one result of the closure of the English cultural market. It was also a way of looking westward, to the countryside beyond the Wicklow hills, without having to deal with the Gaeltacht, and with the version of traditional culture in vogue at the Department of Education. And it provided a way of looking northward without having to worry unduly about politics. O'Faolain produced two 'Ulster' numbers of the journal during the war, and in both of them he argued for the need for more cross-border cultural exchange. This would leaven the insular nationalism of the South, he suggested, but it would also provide roots for the over-international culture of the North, where there was 'no sieve at all'.

Unlike British documentary realism of the 1930s, much of which was underpinned by socialist utopianism, Irish realism was about discovering and documenting modern Ireland. It was in the service of creating a modern Irish identity. In the end the provincial focus of the writers associated with *The Bell* fitted in well with the government's drive towards an independent Irish consensus, fostered through Step Together, frugality campaigns, and even country theatre. As Conor Cruise O'Brien put it, in his 1946 critique of *The Bell*:

In its caution, its realism, its profound but ambivalent nationalism, its seizures of stodginess and its bad paper, it reflects the class who write it and read it – teachers, librarians, junior civil servants, the lettered section of the Irish petty bourgeoisie.

The drive to nurture 'national life' rather than allow it to become swamped by cheap cultural imports underpinned the wartime developments in Irish film production. There had been a number of campaigns championing the power of film to promote Irish culture during the late 1930s, and these gathered strength during the war.

A very few Irish fiction films were made during the 1930s, but they were expensive to produce and required a good deal of equipment. Interest soon focused on the documentary. The members of the Irish Cine Club, for example, were keen to use film in the manner suggested in the 1936 Papal Encyclical, *Vigilanti Cura*, which warned against the moral harm films could do – not only because they told immoral stories, but because they did so in a seductive way, with pretty pictures and music, and even in the dark. But the Pope also argued that, in the right hands, moving pictures were a useful tool for instruction and education. The Irish Cine Club was in effect a film branch of Catholic Action; it made 16 mm film shorts of religious pilgrimages, and accounts of saints' lives, Catholic social work in Dublin, and the St Vincent de Paul holiday camps for poor children. It got a lot of coverage in *The Standard*: the paper's editor took the Catholic nationalist film project seriously and published long debates about the need for Irish-made films – which meant an Irish production company, studios, technical training, and above all investment. Much of this material was written by the film enthusiast Fr Richard Devane SJ, who in 1938 managed to persuade de Valera to set up an inquiry into the viability of a National Film Institute, which would encourage, educate and help fund large-scale productions on standard film.

Meanwhile short documentaries on sub-standard 16 mm film were in vogue. The rural corporatist movement Muintir na Tíre set up a mobile film unit early in the war to make educational films – records of Muintir na Tíre agricultural summer schools, the work of the folklore institute, films about milk production, pigs, cattle and dairy farming. There was no shortage of black-and-white sub-standard film, which accounts for the almost obsessive documentation of every aspect of army life and army training during the war. Some of this went into the Irish newsreels; some was for educational use inside the army itself, and some went into government propaganda such as the 1940 *Step Together* film. Michael Scott, architect of the World's Fair shamrock, was pulled in to help make other government shorts, including the 1943 tillage campaign film, *Our Daily Bread*. Even short tourist publicity films were conceived in documentary style, not least because of the tremendous success of Robert O'Flaherty's 1934 *Man of Aran*. O'Flaherty's film had carefully shaped island life to depict it as a struggle between nature and community. It was a romanticisation of folk life which also claimed to be 'real' – a potent mixture which tourist publicity shorts did their best to emulate.

It seemed that everyone with a camera – including a significant number of priests and Protestant ministers – was making films about 'real' Irish life. In 1943 Father Devane produced the *Irish Cinema Handbook*, covering every aspect of films from production, censorship and distribution to the design of the cinema interior. (The booklet was clearly intended to come out at the same time as the government report into the viability of a state-aided Irish Film Institute, but Lemass refused to make the findings public.) The Handbook included a survey on 'What Kind of Films Should We Make?' There were calls for the production of Irish plays and novels, including Kickham's *Knocknagow* – then a long-running and popular radio serial. But nearly everyone consulted voted for documentary: realist pictures would be 'in the national and cultural

---

"TO-MORROW'S BREAD"

Well made — Home made

THE FILM OF THE GROW MORE WHEAT CAMPAIGN

Ready for release early in December

PRODUCED BY

The Irish National Film Unit for

THE DEPARTMENT OF AGRICULTURE

interests of the people'. For the Gaelic League, documentary film offered the opportunity for the 'Gaelicisation of the screen'. Screen drama-documentaries were the natural way to develop the already 'distinctively Irish' brand of theatre of the Abbey and the Gate.

Foreign films had 'nothing of value to contribute to us'. 'We cannot be sons of the Gael and citizens of Hollywood at the same time.' Much of this rhetoric recycled the arguments for 'Ireland versus the foreigner', except that this time the foreigner most at fault was American. The moral crusade against modern romance focused on Hollywood, with Elstree running a poor second. In fact Irish film campaigners could take comfort from the documentary movements in countries such as Denmark and Britain. When Father Devane called for realistic publicity films to be made by the Electricity Supply Board, the Cement Company, the Transport Company and the Gas Company he was clearly thinking of the influential films made by John Grierson with the British GPO film unit. *Night Mail* and *The Face of Britain* had escaped the tyranny of the box office by gaining government and corporation sponsorship. This, it was argued, was the model needed in Ireland. The real enemy was not foreign film but commercial cinema.

It was partly by chance that wartime censorship and travel restrictions coincided with propaganda on behalf of home-grown film. The movement for an Irish alternative to Hollywood's eternal triangle had been gathering momentum throughout the later 1930s. But restrictions on imports of foreign films and the censor's zeal did offer an opportunity for Irish film to make headway. There were practical reasons for this. The need for newsreels suitable for an Irish audience forced the pace of film technology. Small teams of young men moved about the country with the army, gaining a fast apprenticeship in camerawork and the techniques of production. (Several men who worked with the army film unit later joined Liam O'Laoghaire's film school, which championed Grierson's socially conscious documentary work.) The war also brought an unexpected boon in the shape of a German reconnaissance cameraman-turned-prisoner-of-war. Lieutenant George Fleischmann was downed in Ireland in April 1941 complete with high-class camera, reserve lenses, and cassettes of unexposed film. In 1944 Fleischmann was granted long-term parole from the Curragh to go to university in Dublin. His camera and his experience were vital assets in Irish film-making towards the end of the war.

And the war had an impact in another way – through providing aspiring Irish realist film-makers with a greater range of models for their own work. There was no necessary clash between the realist movement in art and corporatist publicity or even state propaganda. That much was clear from collaborations such as W. H. Auden's script for the GPO's *Night Mail*, as much as Eisenstein's work. And the link between film and state information and propaganda only deepened during the war. In Britain the GPO film unit became the Crown Film Unit, for example. It was taken over by the Ministry of Information, and set to making films about public health, hygiene, ARP. Even though many of the British wartime documentaries were censored, some work filtered through to Ireland. Campaigners also pointed to the *March of Time* series, and to films commissioned by the US navy and large American industrial firms. Irish enthusiasts could take comfort from the fact that, because of shortage of standard film, 16 mm film was increasingly being used to make documentaries and newsreels shown in small US cinemas.

In all the general excitement about the propaganda power of film, celebration of the Russian model was the most unexpected. Russian film-makers such as Eisenstein, Pudovkin and Dovshenko could hardly be ignored in the search for film about the ordinary life of the people. But it does seem surprising that strongly Catholic, and normally virulently anti-communist, organisations should have pointed so readily to the Russian example. The manager of the Muintir na Tíre film unit – dedicated to a Catholic corporatist renewal of rural areas – argued in 1943:

We want to see a proper portrayal of simple Catholic life and its ideals, a story of Irish country life with non-professionals as actors and produced on the lines the Russians have followed so well. For once let us see the spiritual, rather than the material, values presented on our screen.

This suggests again that the problem was with commercial, romantic (and therefore unrealistic) cinema rather than with foreign films, whatever the ideology behind them. But it was also a sign of wartime softening towards the Soviets following the German attack on Russia. The Soviet-friendly rhetoric in Britain filtered through to Ireland, and so too did an awareness of the awful costs of the war for Russia. The image of the Russian conscript appeared not only in literary works such as 'The Great Hunger', or in bizarre form in Myles na gCopaleen's column *An Cruiskeen Lawn*. There were frequent descriptions of Soviet battle strategy in the defence forces journal *An Cosantóir*.

This was a marked shift (and it wasn't to outlast the end of the war). The first Russian film to be imported into Ireland – Eisenstein's *Battleship Potemkin* – had caused a furore in Dublin. The *Irish Catholic* denounced the Irish Film Society, which imported the film under special private licence, as a communist cell. The Society was founded in 1935 by a group of enthusiasts keen to watch foreign art films – animated work by Lotte Reiniger and Len Lye, films of Swedish rural life, Fedor Ozep's *Tarakanova*. As Liam O'Laoghaire recalled, 'the reason we wanted a film society was not that we had any specific objection to British or American films – or English-speaking films, but the whole world of the continent was cut off.'

Cumann na Scannan

THE IRISH FILM SOCIETY

announces for its

EIGHTH SEASON

a series of Matinees at

THE OLYMPIA THEATRE

of Films by

PUDOVKIN, PABST DUVIVIER, FEYDER STERNBERG, LANG, Etc.

Complete programme of Film Shows, Film School and Children's Film Committee available from The Hon. Sec.

IRISH FILM SOCIETY
5 NORTH EARL STREET, DUBLIN

The society was given a boost in 1939 by a legal change allowing cultural bodies to import films free of duty. This meant they could bring in 35 mm films. By 1940 the Film Society had a membership of six hundred and had moved up from a hired room in the Mansion House to the Classic Cinema in Terenure. (The first showing at the Classic raised comments in the papers about the 'exotic continental-style crowd' flocking to the cinema.) The following year O'Laoghaire ran a series of lectures on film production which kickstarted the Irish Film School. A small group met twice a week for theoretical and practical classes in film-making, with a particular focus on documentary. There was a syllabus of lectures and even examinations. O'Laoghaire drew up a rather unusual list of required reading for admission to the school – which took twelve student members. In addition to four Irish texts – by Liam O'Flaherty, James Joyce, Eibhlín Dubh Ní Chonaill and James Connolly – applicants were required to study François Mauriac's *God and Mammon* (for education in 'Art and Ethics'), *Citizen Kane*, T. S. Eliot's 'Journey of the Magi', *Of Mice and Men*, Eric Gill on art and part of Walt Whitman's *Leaves of Grass*.

By 1943 members began showing their films – nearly all of them documentary records of contemporary Irish life, such as Kevin O'Kelly's *Campa* (about the boys' Construction Corps), or O'Laoghaire's study of the right-wing language movement Aiséirí. These films were dedicated to an artistic treatment of their subjects, but the subjects themselves were very similar to those chosen by the government educational film unit, or Catholic Action (which made shorts about the Catholic boy scouts and the St Vincent de Paul holiday camps). Everyone seemed to be looking at the same 'realities of Irish life'. And there was general agreement that it was all in the service of building a national consensus. As O'Laoghaire argued in 1943:

One of the uses of the modern documentary is to put the life of the nation on the screen in such a way that it will be easier for cooperation to be secured from the public as a whole in the interests of national well-being.

The Film Society's goal of 'a native Film Industry truly expressive of National Ideals' was almost indistinguishable from the rhetoric of the government or the Catholic hierarchy. It was not until after the war that members of the Irish Film Society were to produce a hard-hitting social documentary, which took a distinctly oppositional stance. *Our Country* – a look at poverty, emigration, ongoing shortages, public health – was political propaganda on behalf of the new party Clann na Poblachta, even though the Clann's name was not mentioned. It was filmed in November 1947 by O'Laoghaire and Brendan Stafford of the Film Society and written by Maura Laverty.

For the moment, though, the nascent film industry clearly perceived its duty as being to support the official line. As in wartime Britain it would have been difficult to put the spotlight on contemporary social issues while political and national survival seemed to be at stake – while the country was being threatened. But the lack of sustained cultural criticism, apart from persistent anger over the censorship, suggests the strength of the consensus on behalf of neutrality, and the success of de Valera's message about the need for national cooperation.

The documentary film-makers' impulse to chronicle the 'real' Ireland of the 1940s mirrored the ambitions of *The Bell*. There was a certain irony in the fact that all these groups – Catholic Action, the liberal Film Society, Muintir na Tíre, *The Bell*, the Gaelic League, even the Abbey Theatre – were battling over the ground of realism, while being lambasted from abroad for living in a fantasy world.

By mid-1944 new restrictions on electricity use were harming the commercial cinemas. But long before that, film censorship and restrictions on imports had begun to damage Hollywood's authority. 16 mm films and newsreels were one response. Another was the boom in new theatre productions and theatre attendance. As Shelagh Richards recalled, of her decision to set up a new theatre company to stage *The Strings Are False*: 'I felt that during the war there was bound to be a boom in the theatre, firstly, because the cinema was on the down grade with its necessary repetition of pictures' and secondly, 'because there were a lot more actors in Dublin'.

The theatres flourished, and more plays were presented annually in Dublin than ever before. In October 1942 Lord Longford saluted 'a Dublin teeming with new theatrical ventures'. Within the space of a few weeks punters could take in plays by Pirandello, Sheridan, Shaw, Molière, Christine Longford and Sheridan le Fanu. 'At the moment competition is keener than ever,' remarked one observer. 'In spite of the fact that there are barely enough professional actors with any experience to go round the established concerns, fresh groups are springing up on every side, often getting hold of quite interesting plays to produce.' The main established companies were the Abbey Theatre Company, the Longford Players, the Company of Edwards–MacLiammóir, each catering for slightly different clientele. Louis D'Alton formed a company to produce his own plays at Olympia, while another troupe was established by Maurice O'Brien. The ferment was encouraged by Radio Éireann, which broadcast a series of discussions, in early 1942, on Dublin and provincial theatres. As Hilton Edwards put it in July 1942:

Considering the present upheaval, there seems to be little to complain about in the position of the theatre in Ireland. There has been a mushroom growth of new companies, frequent productions, apparently a very healthy attendance and the creation of a virile theatre organisation.

Writers, artists, actors and musicians displayed their new confidence by getting together in a new organisation called WAAMA to campaign for better pay and conditions (once again providing column feet and inches for Myles na gCopaleen). The comparable surge of interest in modern art was covered in *Commentary*, which also pioneered another venture: the Picture Hire Club. At the Picture Hire Gallery in

Molesworth Street would-be collectors could either buy art outright, or on instalments. This was just one outgrowth of the increased public interest in painting during the war. Overall, the number of exhibitions and sales of art works began to rise. Private concerns such as the Waddington Gallery and Dawson Gallery in central Dublin did well. Elsewhere in the country, smaller galleries were opening, including in Limerick, where an Art Club was founded in 1944. Even R. M. Smyllie found a silver lining:

Up to the present war, the Press in Ireland suffered severely from English competition and it was getting worse every year, but luckily the war has changed all that. Transport difficulties have made it impossible for Dubliners to have English newspapers on their breakfast tables.

Smyllie was less willing to acknowledge the beneficial effects of censorship on these wartime artistic ventures. Before the war, the agenda had been dictated by the powerful distribution networks – the BBC, the Motion Picture Association, the leading British and American publishers. Irish writers had been almost completely dependent on them. One of the consequences (if not intentions) of the censorship was to counteract this cultural domination, at least for the duration of the Emergency, allowing Irish voices to be heard without being drowned out by foreign ones. The vivid colours and dramatic movements of Dunkirk, the Battle of Britain and other heroic high points, as well as British social and cultural debates (such as those prompted by the work of the WEA), provided very stiff competition for Ireland's concerns. Not only did the Anglo-Saxon circuits already have a stranglehold, but their material was, on the face of it, infinitely more gripping than anything Ireland had to offer. Censorship, by definition a negative activity, ended up having a certain positive effect. By the end of the war Irish culture and politics had achieved a measure of separate identity they had not enjoyed five years earlier, and which they could not have gained within that space of time, had the Anglo-Saxon monopoly remained fully in force.

Dublin was home to a boom in professional theatre during the war years, and hosted more art exhibitions. Paintings were bought and sold at a brisker rate, documentary film-making got under way, several new presses sprang up. Initiatives such as the founding of the Irish Psycho-analytic Association, the Society for Creative Psychology, and the Capuchin Annual group, which imported the philosopher

Jacques Maritain to Dublin for a series of lectures in 1942, enriched
the intellectual life of the capital. Irish-language writing also enjoyed
a new boost, through associations such as Cumann na Scríbhneoirí,
and plays and pantomimes in Irish staged at the Abbey; there was
a comparable upsurge in radio drama. Outside the cities, on top
of a thriving amateur dramatic scene, home reading groups mush-
roomed. The main provincial centres put on more concerts, more
ballet, and more opera, and there were major achievements in
creative writing – 'The Great Hunger', *An Béal Bocht*, Myles na
gCopaleen's column, *The Bell*. By the end of the war, some of the
literati were starting to congratulate themselves on everything that
had been achieved. In September 1945 Stephen Rynne, writing in the
Leader, praised the war years for clinching the popularity of Irish
modernism.

We have not been so dumb here at home after all and Neutrality has suited
our art as much as it has suited our consciences . . . It is . . . solace and encouragement to know that we here in Ireland have now safely and soundly established our own Living Art . . . proof of the liveliness of our artists.

Yet all this points to a contradiction at the heart of the cultural life of
neutral Ireland. If there was more of everything, why were Dublin's
intellectuals so convinced there was less? Why the complaints about
stasis and stagnation?

Part of the problem was the fear of parochialism. When did a concern with national culture become navel-gazing? The attempt to create
a new, modern, and national film, theatre, and literary culture, to put
the centre of cultural gravity in Ireland rather than England, meant
turning away from an international audience. The sense of being 'cut
off' in Ireland spoke of a fear that no one outside Ireland was listening, or no one who mattered.

But the loss of connection was only one aspect of the problem.
Isolation forced the question of what it meant to be 'Europeanly-
minded'. Could Ireland really begin to make its distinctive contribution to the culture of the continent, while having no purchase on the
actual fate of Europe? The trouble lay less in being 'cut off' than in
being neutral. What could neutrality really offer Europe? The basic
difficulty was powerlessness. 'A European consciousness can hardly be
said to exist in Ireland,' wrote the philosopher and critic Arland
Ussher. But it wasn't quite true. The consciousness was there, but

without the power to make it mean something. In the absence of any political choice apart from belligerence, of any practical channel for humanitarian concern, the only option was an ineffectual hand-wringing. Concern for Europe could find verbal (or privately prayer-ful) expression – but could this ever be enough?

9

The Vanished Generation

In the clay body of the farmer Maguire, Patrick Kavanagh indicted the poverty of the small farm. When a section of 'The Great Hunger' appeared in *Horizon* early in 1942 the issue was banned in Ireland. The guards who came knocking at Kavanagh's door to question him about the poem were probably more concerned with obscenity than social radicalism. But the poem's political message was far more dangerous. It asked what was the difference between life above or below ground for the rural poor. Their only future lay in emigration, and depopulation was destroying the rural communities further. By the middle of the war the problem of emigration had become acute.

In the spring of 1943 a new play by a twenty-five-year-old farmer from Miltown, County Galway, was staged at the Abbey Theatre in Dublin. Michael J. Molloy's *The Old Road*, a three-act comedy about rural depopulation in the West of Ireland, made no bones about the impact of world war on Irish life. The play, which later became a staple of amateur dramatic societies around the country, is set in the kitchen of a poor farmhouse in Galway in the spring and summer of 1939. The principal characters, farm labourers and servant girls of Molloy's age, spend their time card-playing, going to dances, rabbiting for extra cash, trying to do the miserly farmer out of a few shillings, and dreaming of better futures. Their circumstances are badly straitened, strung out somewhere on a line between slavery to the older generation and death from TB. For the girl without a fortune, rural Ireland offers only service, or marriage to an ageing bachelor; for the boy without a farm, only day-labouring or the mailboat.

While the local land-grabber thinks solely of the economic benefits of the coming war ('Wance this war starts the price of land'll rise up till 'tis striking the sky'), for the young the war is a further addition to their impossible futures. With no living to be made in Ireland they cannot think of marriage. But the wages to be had in England must be balanced against the dangers:

Wance we'd marry in England we'd have to stop in it for life; then, when my two year'd be up, the lorry'd come for me for the war, and she'd be left there, maybe for many a year, maybe for good if I was killed on her.

In the end the young people decide to risk conscription and aerial bombing. They leave for England, war and marriage.

Molloy knew what he was talking about. As an evocation of rural Ireland in the summer of 1939, the action of *The Old Road* may be skewed. But it offers a very accurate picture of the depopulation of the western counties, two or three years into the war. During the Emergency around a sixth of Ireland's working population left for England. Girls went into service in Grimsby, Chester, and Swansea, joined the land army in Scotland, Lincolnshire, Warwickshire and Yorkshire, or found nursing or factory work in Liverpool, Huddersfield and London through advertisements in Irish newspapers. Men went harvesting in Scotland, working in arms factories in the Midlands, to the Ford factory in Dagenham, to the construction works in East Anglia and Hampshire, and so on. In the words of the popular song:

> The year was 1939
> The sky was full of lead
> Hitler was headed for Poland,
> And Paddy for Holyhead.

The cost of neutrality in terms of the destruction of rural life – precisely what was held to be most distinctive about Irish culture, and so most in need of protection – was overwhelming. It was Ballygobackwards for real, as the social and economic consequences of Ireland's stance bit hard. Lack of imports and the loss of an export market were to be expected, given the inadequacy and dangers of shipping, though anticipation didn't make the failure of businesses any easier to stomach. Far more disturbing was the effect of the Emergency on the traditional life of the small farmer.

The high levels of emigration from the West punctured the dream of rural self-reliance. It was no longer 'a question here of who is to inherit the holding, but who is to be stuck with it, and with it the task of seeing to the old folk'. The strained economy of the small farm – many with as little as five or ten acres of poor land – collapsed utterly. Registers of Population for 1941 and 1943 show that net emigration in this two-year period reached eighty-five thousand. The province of Connacht suffered the highest rate of emigration (and the lowest marriage rate), with the counties Leitrim, Cavan, Kerry and Longford at the top of the list – counties where most people lived on small, impoverished farms, or in very small villages, with correspondingly low town populations.

The political irony of all this was uncomfortable, to say the least. Ten years previously Fianna Fáil had gained power on its promises to protect the world of the small farmer, and to continue the struggle of those who had died in 1916 fighting for an Ireland united, Gaelic-speaking, and free. In April 1941, on the twenty-fifth anniversary of the Easter Rising, de Valera had cloaked himself in the mantle of the Republic as he stood in front of the General Post Office in Dublin before the massed ranks of the Old IRA, the Defence Forces and the Emergency services. The celebrations went ahead despite requests from opposition members in the Dáil to tone them down in acknowledgement of the disastrous situation facing many of the poor and unemployed. Men such as Pearse and Connolly 'would turn in their graves' if they could see what had become of the republican dream. The unemployed were worse off in 1941 than in the hour of Ireland's 'august destiny', as the Proclamation put it. Starvation and despair were now caused not by the 'aggressor' or 'foreigner', as a labour deputy put it, but by twenty years of self-government which had led to 'destitution, hundreds of thousands of unemployed, and people doing everything in their power to get out of the country, to try to go to the foreigner and one-time enemy to beg a living'.

The government had done no better on the revival of Irish or the ending of partition. The shrinking Gaeltacht areas were suffering the worst depopulation. And to cap it all the men who were continuing the fight for a united Ireland had spent months – which would turn into years – detained without trial in internment camps. The erosion of the republican vision through the steady haemorrhage of emigration, the decline of the Irish language, the internment of republicans fighting for a thirty-two-county Republic (and in the case of four men, execution by hanging or firing squad) – all suggested a government paying merely lip-service to the ideals of 1916. A rural Ireland, a Gaelic Ireland, a united Ireland: the dreams of a generation earlier had been abandoned.

Much of this was opposition rhetoric, but there was no doubting the dire situation in the poorer rural areas. Subsistence farmers and agricultural labourers were ill equipped to withstand the economic hardships of the Emergency. Life for the small farmer in the north-west, for example, worsened because seasonal migration of labourers to Scotland ('tatie-hoking') became increasingly difficult; prospective labourers were held up for weeks, mired in the permit system. Farmers were used to supplementing their annual income with a clear fifty pounds from this seasonal work. During the summer of 1941 labourers were bused from Donegal to the central plains to dig peat on the Bog of Allen as part of the County Council turf scheme, but the wages could not compare with those in Scotland and the coastal farms were increasingly abandoned as labourers left for good, attracted by the higher wages of factory work in England. Peadar O'Donnell insisted in *The Bell*:

There should be only one attitude towards the migrant – to smooth his going and coming, and make his journey cheap. Of late his journey has been full of difficulties. I know men to have lost the best part of this season through mistakes in the documents on which they sought visas. And for lack of guidance Donegal men, who should have gone from here direct to Glasgow, via Belfast or Larne, travelled first of all to Dublin to have their permits and visas fixed up, spent a day or two there, and then back to Belfast or Larne. For a brief period, too, there was even a partial Government ban on the issue of permits. If the costs pile up then migrants will have to spend more time abroad, and may even narrow down their time at home to short holiday periods. This is but a step towards permanent residence in Britain for the whole family.

Abandoned houses littered the countryside, their inhabitants seeking employment or charity in Dublin (other cities such as Cork grew barely at all during the war), or war work in Britain and Northern Ireland. Their alternative – according to O'Donnell – was to become 'penned in among the rocks'. For the old, there was, as Kavanagh bluntly put it in 'The Great Hunger', 'No escape, no escape'.

The young, denied the chance of inheritance, work or marriage, had no option but to leave, and the promise of well-paid work in Britain was a decisive pull. Far from achieving self-sufficiency, rural Ireland's failure to thrive questioned the very economic survival of the state. In large measure Ireland had remained a backward part of the economy of the British Isles, and this dependency seemed only to be getting worse. The departure of young men and women, with no prospects of a livelihood from the family farm or in local industries, led to a further contraction of rural life for those who stayed. Depopulation produced its own vicious circle. As the numbers dwindled, there was less and less work for those who stayed behind. With farms abandoned, small businesses closed down, school teachers in outlying areas laid off, there were fewer and fewer opportunities for socialising, and so diminishing prospects of marriage and a family. The choice was either to board the emigrant boat or be buried alive at home, in a world with no future.

O'Donnell's beefs about the permit system were not without cause. In the first months of the war there were few restrictions on travel between Britain and Ireland, so that Irish workers were able to return home swiftly when war was declared. But on 11 June 1940, as invasion threatened, Britain announced that visas and permits were to be given only for 'business of national importance'. The United Kingdom Permit Office was set up in Dublin to handle applications – with covert surveillance a further aspect to the job description. Almost immediately the British authorities faced the problem of the 1940 harvest, particularly the potato crop in Scotland, which was lying in the fields with no one to pick it. Private contractors, used to recruiting Irish labour, gathered a thousand agricultural workers, furnished them with through tickets, and presented them to the permit office – which eventually agreed to grant permission to sail on three-month visas. By insisting that labourers were restricted to agricultural work, the British authorities hoped they could be kept away from industrial centres, with all the opportunities for espionage these offered. But within a matter of months it became clear that far greater numbers of workers were needed, in factories and munitions plants, and particularly on civil-engineering contracts. In June 1941 the demands of wartime production triggered a decision to allow Irish workers to work in Britain for six-month stretches (or three months in the case of agricultural workers), though many were working in England from earlier in the war. Six- and three-month stays were aimed at cutting down on the dangers of leakage of information by returning labourers, though in fact they had the right to return home permanently at any time – except during the two months before D-Day, when security was particularly tight. In the North, large numbers of Southerners were employed in the dockyards in Derry and Belfast, returning home every weekend, or even daily.

Ireland was officially regarded as an invaluable reservoir of labour for the British war effort. According to the official MI5 report on

Ireland, completed in 1946, 'So great was the need for this Irish labour before and during the Battle of Britain in 1940 that without it the aerodromes, so desperately needed, could not have been built, and great as the need for Irish labour was then, it increased throughout the war as the calls on our own manpower became greater.' MI5 estimated that there were up to 120,000 workers from Éire in Britain and Northern Ireland during the war, including women. The Northern Irish government calculated in turn that about sixty-five thousand workers had transferred to England during the war, nine thousand of them women. Despite his republican background, between 1942 and 1944 Peadar O'Donnell spent some time in England investigating conditions for Irish workers as the Fianna Fáil government's Advisor on Migratory Labour. He estimated in 1945 that there were a quarter of a million Irish workers on war contracts, in addition to seasonal migrants.

The exodus was young and mostly male. Almost half the men who received travel documents during the war were under twenty-five, and two-thirds of them were under thirty – the majority unskilled labourers, used to building or farm work. Three-quarters of the women were under twenty-five, and more than half described themselves as domestic workers. Male Irish labour was overwhelmingly used in construction – Irish men built underground air-raid shelters, armaments factories, housing, military camps, airfields, and storage depots. Four hundred and fifty airfields alone were completed during the war. There was also high demand for skilled mechanics in heavy armaments factories and, given the collapse of the motor trade in Ireland, there were considerable numbers of men willing to migrate for this work. Initially the labour was organised by private agents representing individual British employers. These agents liaised with the unions, posted information at the employment exchanges, or placed advertisements in newspapers, such as the following, which appeared in the 'Situations Vacant' column of the *Irish Independent* in October 1940:

Tool Makers, Centre Lathe and Milling Machine Operators and Capstan Setters Required Urgently.

Must have First Class experience. Fares paid to suitable Applicants.

Apply: Newman Engineering, Ltd. Palace of Industry, Wembley, England.

Arrangements were made for visas to be swiftly granted to the recruits; travel permits were only offered to those whose employment had been approved by the British Labour Exchange. The men who were taken on traded a nomadic lifestyle, often moving between camps and factories every few months, for a decent wage and financial provision for their families.

Early on it was not clear whether the censorship would object to advertisements for war work as contravening neutrality. But with an eye to the levels of unemployment in Ireland, the Department of Industry and Commerce admitted 'the present scheme is of some positive advantage to us'. As the taxable revenue of the country declined, unemployment insurance claims rocketed, and it proved impossible for the government to square the circle. (The monthly average for unemployment assistance rose from £21,230 in 1939 to £23,320 in 1940. The following year social security was paying out £24,260 per month, from vastly reduced resources, and the amount continued to rise.) There was, however, embarrassment about using official employment exchanges to organise migrant labour in the first years of the war. Initially, local employment exchanges were not allowed to recruit openly for jobs in Britain, but could put applicants in touch with agents. As unemployment reached higher and higher levels these qualms faded, and official sanction of the international labour market became the norm.

The number of hopefuls was staggering. Precise figures are hard to glean but one historian states that over two weeks in February 1941 1,500 people applied to the Dublin employment exchange alone for work in Britain. This was at the height of the Blitz. Another has estimated that by early spring 1942 6,500 prospective migrants were applying for exit visas each month, although hold-ups in the permit office, as papers and political allegiances were checked out, meant that slightly fewer than 4,000 actually took the boat. Other accounts put the figure nearer 2,500 a month. British ministries began openly contacting their Irish counterparts in order to speed up and maintain the flow of labour power. In February 1941, for example, the Scottish Department of Agriculture wrote directly to the Department of Agriculture for Éire asking them to interview girls who had applied to join the Women's Land Army, in order to assess their suitability. Throughout 1941 young women wanting land work across the Irish Sea travelled for interview to the department's offices in Dublin – reports on each applicant were forwarded to the Scottish and Northern Irish departments. If the girls lived a long way from Dublin (such as several who applied from Castlefin in Donegal), the agricultural inspector conducted the interviews when he was in the district. A year later, in another attempt to smooth the application process, and speed up the supply of labour, the British Federation of Civil Engineering Contractors centralised recruitment in the whole of the building industry. By the following month 60 per cent of Irish workers, or nearly two thousand a month, were going to Federation jobs – building factories, digging shelters, preparing airfields, and so on. By the summer of 1942 the ministries of Labour and Agriculture were feeling the lack of manpower; later still the needs would be in Aircraft Production and War Transport.

Such was the extent of the traffic that Elizabeth Bowen recommended that propaganda should be directed at Irish workers in Britain:

The amount of these people, and their possible effect, while on holiday, on an Éire otherwise cut off from news from England, impressed me . . . On the whole I should say their effect on Éire was bad. They are great carriers of defeatist rumours, and tend to exaggerate to their Irish listeners, any stories of disaffection in British factories.

Bowen confessed that she wished for a 'better class' of Irish travellers.

Whereas emigrants in earlier decades would be gone for years, if not for a lifetime, Irish people employed in wartime Britain could return at more or less regular intervals, bringing stories of a very different world. One librarian who stayed in County Clare recalled the discrepancy between rural inertia and wartime urban life experienced by people working in war factories: 'One listened goggle-eyed to real and imaginary exploits in shattered cities, to abuse of conventions, attitudes and beliefs of which a year or two before they were themselves wholemeal examples in our streets.' Though this friction between emigrant and stay-at-home was a long-standing feature of Irish life, it was exacerbated both by the abnormal conditions of life in England, and by the fact that these were not so much emigrants as commuters earning a livelihood in England in short stretches. The contrast between the drama and catastrophe in England and Scotland and the narrow concerns of rural Ireland became more pressing: 'I can still see one lad just arrived from burnt-out Coventry bringing to a dead stop a particularly hot argument on our press censorship of war news, by quietly drawing our attention to a two-column headline in the local paper:

"Mare Would Not Mow – Claim for Warranty."' Even the horses were at a standstill.

The traffic was increased by Irish citizens already resident in Britain, who could return home if they were eligible to receive permits for holidays in Éire, for example to visit parents or relatives. An army of workers and combatants shuttled – both physically and emotionally – between two worlds; indeed, despite her strong pro-British sentiments, Bowen's 'activities' were her own way of satisfying the need to be able to pass to and fro. The claim, heard so often at the time, that Éire was 'cut off' obviously needs qualification. People *could* travel, under restrictions, both across the Irish Sea, and across the border.

Yet the fact that so many people were moving back and forth between Ireland and the United Kingdom did little to relieve the sense of entrapment. The poor of the Gaeltacht and the western seaboard decamped to the war zone because they were better off there. The young had been 'conscripted by hunger and want' into the war in England. (University graduates, over-qualified for their miserable clerking jobs in Skibbereen or Thurles, were unlikely to throw them in for a six-month stretch in a British armament factory.) By the middle of the war the West, home of an idealised authentic Irish identity, was increasingly empty – gone to England, and certainly financed from England. One of the strangest results of this population movement was a closer bridge to the European war in the far west of the country than in the east.

*   *   *

Some economic historians argue that wartime emigration didn't greatly increase over the already high rate of departure to England during the late 1930s. The figures are difficult to interpret because before the war there were no restrictions on the free movement of labour between Ireland and Britain, and therefore no reliable statistics. Then there were the thousands who were living in Britain in 1939 who returned home in September, only to apply for permits to leave again a few months later. There is also considerable disparity between the Irish and British figures for the numbers of Irish war workers in Britain. But contemporary commentators were convinced that the numbers were rising fast. This was partly because the gender balance of the emigrants changed during the war. Far more men now went on labour contracts than previously (the huge surge in post-war emigration was partly to do with women catching up). The sight of large groups of young men leaving the country may account for the increased anxiety about the loss of labour power through emigration – male agricultural and industrial labour was more valued than female domestic or nursing work. But the principal reason for the crisis over emigration was that the system was more organised during the war and therefore more visible. The permit system, identity cards, group contracts, queues, health checks, hostels, camps, dormitories – all brought attention to a process that had been going on for some time. The fact that the emigrants were leaving for a war zone made the crisis seem even greater.

Two years into the war, the vast majority of Ireland's economic migrants were now hired on group contracts. Stories of walking to Dublin from as far away as Kilkenny or Carlow, of selling a bicycle, or a shotgun, in order to afford the fare, of borrowing money for the journey on the promise of a return from first wages – all slowly faded as the traffic in Irish labour became centrally funded and managed. Young men could be interviewed for a Federation job in their local employment exchange. Once a job was secured and a travel permit arranged by the agent through the Permit Office (a process that took about six weeks), the fare to Dublin was forwarded to the prospective migrant. Men and women travelled by bus or train to Dublin to receive their papers, if necessary to lodge overnight in the city (paid for by the Ministry), and eventually to embark at Dun Laoghaire. The process was streamlined to ensure a minimum of inconvenience with travel and immigration.

At best this made for a trouble-free passage; at worst it could be dehumanising. In 1944 H. L. Morrow – who had left London in the summer of 1940 – took a return trip on the mailboat:

Steerage passengers still cattle-herded in tin-roofed quayside shed. Lumpy luggage in brown-paper parcels, cracked fibre suitcases. Shiny-faced pippin-cheeked girls and youths. One or two whey-faced middle-aged men. All – or nearly all – hatless. All with coat-collars upturned – like umbrellas blown out by the wind. Wretched-looking. The song knocked out of them. As they stumbled on board noticed why: Each wore a label – like stock cattle. 'British Factories,' it said, simply. As if on their way to be spam-canned.

The feeling of being treated as livestock, bid for at market, intensified as workers were hired without knowing their future jobs or destinations. They were reduced to labour power, to their status as able bodies. The application process made a distinction between skilled and unskilled labour, but agreements struck in Ireland were often ignored once 'on the other side'. As one TD protested, 'people find overseers going through the ranks of our people as they are landed at Holyhead and cutting them out in different classes according to their physical build. Men who appear to be strong and able to do difficult work have been packed off to do underground work in aerodromes and air-factories and things like that,' despite the fact that they might have been hired for skilled work.

The labourer's physical health was also a medical issue. Given the degree of poverty and malnutrition, and the slum conditions endured by some of the workers, there were fears in Britain over the spread of infectious diseases. Alarmed by outbreaks of typhus and typhoid in Ireland in 1942, the British Ministry of Labour instituted medical examinations at Holyhead. Travellers who were found to be carrying infection were returned on the next boat to Dun Laoghaire. (In retaliation the Irish authorities suggested there was a need to quarantine returning workers for fear of VD.)

The last thing Irish workers needed – on top of their reputation for drunkenness, for taking other people's jobs, for non-payment of rent, and for terrorist activity – was a reputation for being dirty and verminous. Stories of lice-ridden workers merely compounded the difficulty of billeting the Irish in private homes, and the British Ministry of Labour reluctantly faced the fact that if they were going to import large numbers of Irish workers they needed to build hostels in which to house – and in effect segregate – them. Lice-ridden workers did not make good publicity for Ireland either. The poor press, not to mention the cost of wasted journeys, forced the Irish government to act. In mid-1943 the Department of Local Government and Public Health, where Flann O'Brien worked as the Minister's private secretary, took over issuing the Health Embarkation Certificate in Dublin. On arrival in the capital, prospective workers, as well as those travelling to join the Forces, reported to one of two centres – the Globe Hotel in Talbot Street for men, and the Fitzwilliam Hotel in Fitzwilliam Square for women – where they would be examined, and if necessary treated for scabies or lice. If found unfit to travel they were given their fare back home. James Deeney, who took over as Chief Medical Officer in 1944, recalled a visit to the Iveagh Baths, where the men at the Globe Hotel were processed:

The baths had been emptied. On the floor of a pool were large sherry half-casks. Men with rubber aprons and Wellington boots were hosing people down and bathing them with disinfectant in the casks. All around were naked men, seemingly in hundreds. The place was full of steam and the smell of disinfectants.

Now naked men *en masse* are not a pretty sight and the atmosphere of shame, fear and outrage was easy to feel.

Once through this procedure, safely arrived in Holyhead, and assigned work, labourers were transported to their camps or factories. Migrants often complained of confusion and melee at the port, and long delays in processing and customs. The Ministry of Labour posted a reception officer at Holyhead, specifically to deal with Irish labour, and a further two welfare officers were stationed at Crewe to cut down on the numbers of lost and overwhelmed travellers. For a good proportion, who would work in the south of England, the journey meant the train to Euston and a likely overnight stay in the Camden Town transit hotel, which could accommodate about a hundred people, before they were sent on to their billets the following day.

During 1943 many of the men were allocated work on the preparations for D-Day – building aerodromes, military camps and depots in East Anglia and across the southern counties. They were housed in camps of Nissen huts – concrete structures roofed with arched corrugated iron. Consisting of dormitories, a canteen and a recreation area, the camps had a reputation for cleanliness but little comfort. Often several miles from villages or towns, there was little to do after work beyond card-playing. In 1943 the National Conference of the socialist Connolly Association, which took place in London, estimated that there were approximately three hundred thousand Irish working in factories, building camps, and serving in the armed forces in England – if true this was nearly 10 per cent of the population of the South, and a vastly higher proportion of the active working population of about 1.3 million. Officials from the Association were attempting to organise these Irish 'transferred workers' into a union – to campaign for better conditions, for example in relation to bonus pay, and the purchase of sailing tickets for twice-yearly visits home. Their report uncovered persistent minor, and not-so-minor, rankles: migrant workers resented the regulations which bound them to report regularly to the police, and other indignities associated with their alien status. There were complaints of landladies overcharging or refusing the Irish billets, and a real sense of grievance stemming from the belief that they were deliberately kept in heavy, dirty and unattractive jobs, on low pay, for which it was difficult to get British labour.

But most of the workers who were questioned seemed happy enough with their lot. Industrial canteens provided double the civilian ration of meat, butter, sugar and jam, 'and as much vegetables as they can eat'. Factory workers lodged in hostels were exempt from the ration card. Whenever they were moved to a new factory their fares were paid, and they received extra 'settling in' money. Above all wages were good. According to a 1944 report, labourers earned 1s. 6 1/4 d. an hour, and craftsmen, 1s. 11d. an hour for a sixty-hour week, with a guaranteed minimum of forty-four hours. The average weekly wage of Irish labourers in summer was £4 5s., and in winter £3 11s. Skilled workers could earn more than a pound a week on top. Even after the expenses in camp had been paid, there was generally enough to send £2 or £3 a week home to dependants.

The Catholic Church in Ireland was far less sanguine about the group contract system. Emigration as a whole triggered fears for the faith of the Irish living in England. Priests and curates were sent to the new towns where the Irish were now living, and to the camps servicing factories and building sites. Pastoral work focused on issues such as homesickness, drink and, inevitably, sex. In 1942 Archbishop John Charles MacQuaid set up The Catholic Social Welfare Bureau (a branch of the Legion of Mary) to look after the welfare of emigrants, 'principally women and girls'. The task was to try to combat the decline in morals to which the loss of home life must surely lead. There were fears for young girls spending their first months away from home in lodgings. Technically life in the camps should have been easier to monitor, but alarms were raised when camps were sited too near towns or Forces' bases. Many of the clergy were driven by a genuine feeling of responsibility for the safety and well-being of their flock, but the basic fear of the Church authorities was loss of control over the war workers.

We get some sense of the catastrophic effects which work in a British munitions factory might have upon Irish girls from Frank Carney's 1946 religious melodrama *The Righteous Are Bold*. The play, which ran for a record-breaking fourteen weeks at the Abbey and thus ranks as *the* most popular 1940s play for Irish audiences, is set in the kitchen of a small farmhouse in County Mayo in 1945. Nora, who has been working in a factory in Lancashire, is sent home to her family by the local priest, afflicted by a mysterious malaise. It turns out she has become satanically possessed by a modern, secular outlook which causes her to have fits and throw the kitchenware about the place whenever she sees a crucifix or a picture of the Sacred Heart. Several reviewers warned audiences to go to the play well protected against flying crockery but no doubt its main attraction lay in the thrill of the exorcism scenes, in which the young woman – dress torn and blaspheming – is restrained by the priests and men of the neighbourhood. England, and its pleasures, are literally beaten out of her.

If Carney's play was an extreme version of the clergy's panicky attitude to English irreligion, it chimed with paternalistic attitudes to Irish women away from home nonetheless. Even Peadar O'Donnell, when on a visit to Burghfield Residential Camp for women near Reading in February 1944, noted that 'unfortunately a considerable strength of American forces are camped nearby', with all the opportunities for congress in pubs and at dances that this afforded.

Sexual licence was also a problem far closer to home, in Northern Ireland. Throughout the war, and particularly after the arrival of the American troops, Catholic (and Protestant) clergy warned in sermons and Lenten pastorals of the dangers of the new looser morality. Much of this concern focused on Catholics living in the North. As in Britain, large numbers of confident GIs transformed the social and sexual landscape, at least for a time. And there was real concern about licentiousness spreading over the border, not only through the GIs on furlough in the South, but via southerners working in the North. The Bishop of Derry, speaking at a confirmation service in Donegal in 1944, attempted to wake the congregation up to what was going on just across the border: 'I wish I could take some of the people to see the conduct of their girls in Derry – girls from Donegal and Inishowen. It would be better for them to live on potatoes and salt.'

Were the Churches right to worry about a decline in sexual morality, associated with the war? The evidence for Northern Ireland suggests that, as in Britain, the combination of large numbers of soldiers, more women in work and living away from home, and the heightened wartime atmosphere, did impact on sexual behaviour. The numbers of illegitimate births rose between 1942 and 1945, and we can assume that a good number of other women solved the problem of their pregnancy by marrying their GI or British soldier lovers. The later war years saw increased attendance at the Marie Stopes clinic in Belfast, probably in part a knock-on effect of the fact that US troops had ready access to contraceptives, and there was a big push by the military authorities to get them to use them. Sex for single people, and extra-marital sex, did become more common, if not more acceptable, during the war years. There was also a marked increase in prostitution in Northern Ireland. Prosecutions went up from ten in 1941, to 171 in 1942 and 185 in 1943. This huge rise was probably in part down to increased surveillance, but it also reflects a rise in the number of women trading sex for money. Much of this trade was 'informal'. The poet and art critic John Hewitt, writing to Patrick Maybin at the Front, retailed an encounter told to him by Joseph Tomelty, then an aspiring novelist. Tomelty 'was in the corridor of the Ulster Hall and [overheard?] a US soldier and a chit of a girl. The yank said "Yea – honey – I'll give ya four dollars." The girl toucht (sic) the fingers of her hand with her thumb slowly then said briskly: – "Come on." Tell it to yourself with actions – it's largely visual.'

Irish war workers, both men and women, were as affected as any-one else by the new sociability in wartime Britain. But it is far harder to gauge the impact of the war on sexual behaviour in neutral Ireland. War workers travelled back across the border, and across the Channel; GIs drank and holidayed in the South. Both brought with them differ-ent attitudes to personal relationships, as well as, no doubt, at least some supplies of contraceptives. It is easy to see why wartime migra-tion made the battle to nurture a stable, Catholic morality seem all the more urgent for the religious and state authorities. And there was some evidence that the spill-over from the North and from Britain was having a negative effect. For a start prostitution in Dublin began to develop along new lines. In December 1946 Deputy Commissioner Garret Brennan reported to the Inter-Departmental Ad-Hoc Committee on the Suppression of Prostitution:

During the emergency years there developed a big increase in the number of loose women to be seen in the principal streets at night, attracted by visiting soldiers on leave and visitors from Northern Ireland and the provinces . . . a number of these women are not previously convicted, but are of the loose type of married women living apart from their husbands, and young girls of the domestic servant type.

Other reports suggested that in the area of Lower O'Connell Street and Eden Quay (and to a lesser extent Upper O'Connell Street,

Marlborough Street, and Talbot Street), 'There seems to be an increase in the number of women working as prostitutes and this is not just the "unfortunate women" who are well known to the gardaí but young women of apparent respectability who practise immorality in a surreptitious manner. A very large majority of these are young girls who have never been arrested.' Single women, it was alleged, were operating out of private houses even in the country towns. To confirm the picture of immorality, rates of venereal disease increased. According to one survey, in 1938 1,940 people were treated for VD by private doctors. By 1943 the number had increased to 2,938. As the Department of Health report admitted: 'It is very probable that these numbers do not accurately represent the position as a large number of medical practitioners failed to furnish the information.' There was a larger increase in the numbers who went to hospital to be treated, and this pattern was as true for rural as for urban areas. An article by J. C. Cherry of the venereal disease clinic at Dr Steevens' Hospital, Dublin, published in the *Irish Journal of Medical Science* in June 1943, reported a steady rise in the numbers of VD patients since 1940. Cherry warned that by 1943 venereal disease constituted a greater public health problem 'than in any previously recorded period'. The following year a Department of Health memo, headed 'Urgent Problems Relating to Public Health Which Must Be Dealt With', argued along similar lines:

There is substantial evidence of an alarming increase in this disease among married as well as single persons, and much more radical measures must be adopted on a very much wider scale to cope with it and to mitigate to the greatest extent possible its disastrous consequences for the future of the race.

Whether or not the rise in cases of VD was real, or had anything to do with the war, there was a strange kind of relief in being able to point to British and American soldiers as the cause of the rise in 'indecency'. Before the 1921 Treaty both lay and religious groups had focused on the British garrison in Ireland as the source of moral and physical contagion. The moral purity campaigns during the 1920s and 1930s had reluctantly had to face the fact that with the British soldiers gone there was still just as much, if not more, improper behaviour going on. Blame for the continuing blights of contraception, prostitution, illegitimacy, and sexual crime was placed squarely on imported 'evil literature', Hollywood cinema, dances, motor cars, and very often women themselves. With the foreign soldiers back the portrait of Ireland's moral climate returned to something more like a reassuring black and white. The war was to blame for drawing impressionable young people into sinful behaviour in Britain and Northern Ireland, and for landing foreign soldiers on Irish territory yet again.

What the Church authorities were reluctant to acknowledge was that sexual 'immorality' in Ireland often had less to do with exposure to English or American urban secular mores (as Frank Carney's play implied), than with indigenous failures. As far as illegitimacy went, the problem often lay with the poverty and poor education of both rural and urban girls. Several women witnesses to the Carrigan committee in 1930 and 1931 had argued that illegitimacy rates were far higher than official accounts suggested. They lamented the innocence of rural Irish girls compared to canny young women who had been in England, and asked for more sex education, arguing that many girls fell pregnant simply through ignorance of basic sexual facts. A 1944 short story by Mary Lavin suggested that not much had changed. 'Sunday Brings Sunday,' chants an old woman outside the parish church each week, like the chorus in a Greek tragedy. And the fate of the biddable sixteen-year-old girl at the centre of the story is just as inevitable. The parish priest enjoins her to prayer and devotion; farmers, neighbours and the doctor's wife with whom she goes into service praise her obedience. They warn against sin but never explain about sex:

Company-keeping was no harm. The priest meant something else. Why couldn't he speak out more particular? Why couldn't he say out straight what was wrong and what was not? Why couldn't he? If he only gave an idea; only an idea. They should give people some idea.

In Ireland, as in the North, numbers of illegitimate births rose slightly during the war. 1944 saw the highest rate of illegitimacy between 1922 and 1976, slightly over four per cent of all births – though it is possible that this rise reflected the introduction of the children's allowance, which may have encouraged more women to register their babies, rather than a greater number of births. As well as this statistical increase, however, some historians argue that back-street abortions and infanticide also increased. In both these cases, though, it is likely that the problem arose not because there was more contact with wartime Britain but because for vulnerable women and girls there was less. Throughout the 1930s women faced with an unwanted pregnancy had often dealt with the problem by travelling to Britain to have their baby in secret. English rescue homes in Liverpool and London were familiar with the young women who arrived from Ireland in order to give birth and, often, to leave the baby for adoption. During the late 1930s Catholic agencies in Ireland and Britain worked together to try to 'repatriate' pregnant Irish women, because they were putting a strain on Catholic resources in Britain. Women who chose to keep their babies often preferred to live in Britain rather than suffer censure back home. And there is some anecdotal evidence that before the war wealthier women went to England for clinic rather than back-street abortions, which were easier to obtain there.

From 1942 onwards travel restrictions meant that it was hard for poorer and younger girls to get to England except on a group contract, though it was not impossible. Once factory or land work was arranged it could take months for work and travel permits to come through. It was not only that permits came too late for some women, but travel to Britain on a group contract, with its rigid processing, hardly provided the privacy that women carrying unwanted babies needed.

There were other, messier effects of the migrant workers' system. Some of the cases of infanticide give an insight into how the war impacted on women carrying an unwanted pregnancy. In one case a thirty-year-old woman from rural Limerick, who had been working in England, returned home in the summer of 1943. Fifteen months later, towards the end of 1944, she had a child, who was initially boarded out. In the spring of 1945 she seems to have killed the child by strangling, because she wanted to return to England, and she could find no one to look after it. She also feared that her travel permit would not be renewed because the local police knew she had a child. Two cases heard in 1944 and 1945 involved married women whose husbands were working in England during the war years – in one case a thirty-four-year-old woman with seven children, whose husband intermittently returned to the family, killed her baby at birth. A case in County Westmeath in December 1943 involved a woman whose husband had been away for three years in England. She and her lover drowned the baby at birth, fearing the husband would hear of the child and stop sending his wife money. Any of these tragedies might have occurred before the war, though the impact of war work is marked in all of them. None of them fits the dangerous picture the hierarchy liked to paint, in which foreign and urban sexual immorality caused the ruin of Irish purity.

＊　　＊　　＊

Irish men and women slotted themselves easily into the traffic in migrant labour, partly because seasonal migration had long formed a traditional part of rural Ireland's economy. Labourers regularly travelled not only to Scotland, or Lancashire, but also to other counties in Ireland. This practice of internal migration was given a new lease of life during the Emergency. The term 'Culchie', shorthand for someone from a 'backward' rural background, derives from the Second World War period: it is a corruption, via 'Culchie Mac' or 'Culshemok', of the name given to labourers from the area around Kiltimagh in County Mayo, who migrated for work to the more fertile areas of Munster – cutting turf, binding corn, saving hay and hoeing sugar beet. A good deal of this migration was a matter of individual initiative; young women from Connemara found work as domestics in East Galway, young men from Cork spent months rabbiting in Castletownbere, Mayo labourers trod a path to East Cork. But the government was also keen to encourage internal migration for work as a way of meeting emergency demands, and of hanging on to the young.

There were numerous small-scale and local county-council relief schemes. Local councils did their best to compel men receiving unemployment assistance in their areas to undertake low-waged seasonal work such as land drainage, road building and maintenance, and above all winning the turf. The government goal of three million extra tons of turf a year was a huge amount, especially since nearly all of it had to be cut by hand. The Department of Industry's optimistic target was a ton of dry turf a day for every man on the bog, but the slanesmen themselves estimated that a team of three men and one boy could cut and spread about fifteen tons in a six-day week. In areas such as Clare, and West and North Cork, where local authorities were able to requisition bogs for emergency fuel supplies, the men were set to turf-cutting. In all about sixteen thousand men and boys were employed during the summer of 1941 on the County Council schemes, cutting and drawing the turf, laying makeshift roads into the mountain bogs, knocking up barrows, transporting the turf to the towns.

The principal government scheme was the large-scale turf-cutting on the Bog of Allen in County Kildare, which could employ more than a

thousand men at a time – if it could get them. In the summers of 1940 and 1941 young men on the dole, particularly from the congested districts of Galway, Donegal and Mayo, were transported to the townlands bordering the bog and billeted in farms and tents for the summer months – owing to the lack of materials, the promised hostels had not been built. Complaining of poor accommodation, insufficient food and dreadful wages, many drifted away. By the summer of 1942 proper camps of wooden huts had been erected – almost identical to those at the internment camp at the Curragh – but the government found it could not fill them. Not only were conditions on the bog miserable, particularly in wet weather, but the weekly wage of 32s. for a forty-eight-hour week (minus 5s. to the camp) could in no way compete with wages in England. Unemployment assistance was terminated for the men from Connacht who refused work in Kildare, but this only increased the numbers on the mailboat. The government had to call in the army to cut the turf.

This paradox of rising unemployment combined with a shortage of labour recurred in other areas of the labour market. In March 1941, for example, the managers of the Arigna Coal Mines in County Roscommon attempted to step up production in the wake of British restrictions on coal imports. The problem, as they saw it, lay with a workforce committed to their own farms and to dancing and drinking, rather than to the wages which could be earned in the mine. The management applied for leave to build a hostel housing up to fifty men which would allow them to recruit labour from outside the district:

We have always suffered from certain handicaps which are inherent in the character of the labour available to us. Our employees are nearly all small farmers or farmers' sons. They always leave off work at the mine in the spring and harvest so as to attend to their farms. This explains the recent drop in our output. Many of the young men stay at home on the day following a dance or the day following pay day. We are satisfied that no inducement we can offer will be sufficient to overcome these difficulties. Recently after repeated warnings we dismissed a number of men for absenting themselves from work without a satisfactory explanation but the improvement which followed this action was only temporary. Most of the men concerned are drawers who are paid on a tonnage basis, the rate 1/5 a ton to men who worked full time in any pay period of two weeks, and 1/- per ton to those who did not work full time. Even this has not produced the desired result. We still have a number of men who do not qualify for the 1/5 rate. There seems to us to be no prospect of securing any more labour locally and we fear our difficulties will be much increased this year as a result of the campaign for increased tillage.

It would be hard to overestimate the level of concern in government, and in the Church, over the loss to Ireland of these farmers' sons. Anger grew at the lack of effective action on emigration, and against the ills of poverty that were fuelling it. Beyond the worries about the economic consequences of migration – less and less taxable income, leading to fewer funds for projects and services – and the social consequences of depopulation for rural communities, lay a practical concern with maintaining sufficient labour reserves, and even sufficient defences. The government was lambasted for allowing a situation in which young men were leaving the LDF and heading for England. Economic necessity was forcing them to cross over to 'the other side', risking death from aerial bombardment for the sake of a living wage. It wasn't just the Opposition who were making a fuss. Officials at the Department of Industry and Commerce worried that emigration was eating into the labour supply, so that there wouldn't be enough men to produce the food and fuel to meet the country's needs.

Dissatisfaction over the worsening economic situation played a key role in the general election of June 1943. After a particularly acrimonious campaign, and despite overwhelming popular support for the policy of neutrality, Fianna Fáil lost ten seats and over a hundred thousand votes. De Valera was returned to power but as the leader of a minority government. Electoral gains were shared between the Labour party and the new farmers' party, Clann na Talmhan, which saw itself as the voice of the rural population and could call on an especially strong following in Galway and Mayo. When the Dáil reconvened with its new members in July 1943, the debates focused above all on the problems of essential supplies and the need to tackle rural poverty and emigration. Deputy Davin, for example, speaking for the Labour party, decried 'the exodus of able-bodied young Irishmen from the rural parts of this country':

I see young fellows, coming off trains at Westland Row, from the West, emigrating every day with permits supplied by the Department of Industry and Commerce, to work on war work in England instead of doing the work which will be urgently necessary in the parts of the country from which they are now going away. Where are we to get the agricultural labourers that will be required to gather in the harvest?

From an administrative point of view, it should have been possible to stem the tide. The advantage of the centralised recruiting system for

Britain was a fast and efficient supply of labour, targeted at the point of need; the advantage for Ireland was a measure of protection of the interests of Irish citizens, and nominal control over those who were leaving. With little fuel or equipment to provide schemes of work the Irish government felt powerless to prevent the outflow entirely, but they did attempt to place limitations on it. When large companies such as ICI and Ford started using unofficial agents to procure Irish labour in the spring of 1941 the government introduced a ban on direct recruiting through agents. In December 1942 they banned newspaper advertising for work abroad. There were restrictions on men and women under twenty-two, for example, and on those in work or with the prospect of work – such as in the mines. Attempts were also made to stop those in turf production or agriculture from receiving permits, leading to complaints that young men who admitted helping out on the family farm were being denied exit permits. Yet the regulations were fairly elastic. With determination, pretty much anyone could obtain a permit. It was very common for female migrants – young girls eager to escape domestic service – to sidle through under the minimum age.

A revealing 1941 memo unearthed by historian Enda Delaney outlines some of the reasons why the Department of Finance was glad enough to see the back of the rural unemployed. By ridding the country of thousands of dissatisfied youths, emigration acted as a 'safety-valve against revolution'. Nobody wanted resentful young men hanging around ready to join the republican struggle. It also had distinct economic advantages:

Involuntary idleness tends to sap the ability to work and the courage of workers and the minister feels that it is better that they should be employed at good wages in Great Britain than that they should remain without work at home, dependant [sic] for existence on unemployment assistance or other forms of assistance. Moreover the worker employed at good wages in Great Britain is in a position to send substantial contributions to his dependants at home, and thereby break for them the monotony of continuous poverty.

Better money and work from England than nothing at all, went the thinking. Better that those who might become revolutionary malcontents should be removed. And better that the depleted Irish coffers should save their resources for others.

There was some logic to this. Just as the availability of well-paid work had an enduring impact on the status and social experience of

British women, so involvement in the war economy transformed the lives and perceptions of many Irish people, both male and female. Those small farmers' sons in Roscommon, able to earn 50s. a week drawing coal from the mine in good times (not to mention the thousands who never earned more than a few shillings at a time on odd jobs), suddenly found themselves with four or five pounds a week in their pockets. In *The Death of an Irish Town*, journalist John Healy recalls the return of such migrants to Mayo at Christmas time, 'new suits and flashy ties, spiv-knotted and the jackets wide-boy padded', still unfamiliar with the handling of money. Many would not return to Ireland at the war's end. In this sense the high rates of emigration brought social and economic catastrophe to rural areas, but also a kind of dynamism.

As the war dragged on, however, the wisdom of allowing English wages to filter back into Ireland came into question. Certainly the money coming into the country – weekly savings combined with overtime, double-time, bonus money – could not be denied. In mid-1942 the Post Office traced three hundred thousand pounds a month (over three and a half million a year) entering the country in the form of wired money orders. By the end of the year, including postal orders for smaller amounts which had been enclosed with letters home, the figure stood at £4,576,594. Although a significant proportion of this sum remained in the Post Office as savings, there was no law against spending. As small towns and villages suddenly became awash with new money, there were complaints in the Dáil that the high wages available in England were worsening the situation for those who remained at home. Because of the Wages Standstill Order (introduced in 1941) and the fact that there was no proper coupon system to control the pricing of goods, the money sent home by workers in England had the effect of raising prices in Ireland. This in turn created a cycle of less disposable income, less demand for goods, and less employment. The purchasing power of Irish wages in both agriculture and industry decreased, just as the cost of living rose by 70 per cent. The search for work abroad, which was meant to provide a lifeline for those left behind, was worsening the decline and depopulation of the rural areas.

The high wages available in the North were a particular problem, since they were so easy to come by. With only the sorry prospect of 10s. a week unemployment assistance, or 32s. a week on the turf, it proved all too easy to lure Donegal labourers to the far higher standard of living on offer twenty or thirty miles (or even two or three miles) away. At one hiring fair at Donegal in 1942, Northern farmers arrived en masse offering wages of £70 a half year. For the significant numbers who remained living in the South, while working across the border, commuting meant not only shuttling between peace and war, but between poverty and relative wealth. It made little sense for these migrant workers to think of themselves as insulated from the war. But even for those living far from the border the frequency of letters, containing postal orders, or giving notice of the wired funds available at the Post Office, made life in the war zone real, something with which they were connected.

*   *   *

On St Patrick's Day 1943, de Valera broadcast a speech to the nation that was to become one of his most renowned – a speech that seemed to lay out a programme for the future, but in fact evoked an impossible past. Cloaking himself this time in the mantle of Thomas Davis and the Young Irelanders, de Valera outlined his dream of a frugal, hard-working, pious and Irish-speaking nation, 'a land whose countryside would be bright with cosy homesteads, whose fields and villages would be joyous with the sounds of industry, with the romping of sturdy children, the contests of athletic youths, and the laughter of comely maidens'. If Thomas Davis, or any of Ireland's lost leaders, had been listening, they might well have wondered what was going through his mind.

Certainly the viability of an independent, sovereign Ireland had taken root during the war, as de Valera's independent foreign policy built on the political freedoms established in the 1937 constitution. But by 1943 most other pieces of the Republican dream looked to be in tatters, with the collapse of rural Ireland one of its greatest failures. The small-farmer class was either buried alive by rural poverty or gone to England. And along with the vanishing Irish went the vanishing Irish language. De Valera reminded his listeners that 1943 was the fiftieth anniversary of the founding of the Gaelic League. It was up to every individual in the country to further the 'noble task' of restoring the language as the everyday speech of the nation, by learning it and using it in their daily lives. A cynic might have responded that it was indeed imperative for more people to begin learning the language, as the native speakers in the Gaeltacht areas were vanishing at a faster rate than ever. As one of the corpses puts it in Máirtín Ó Cadhain's novel, *Cré na Cille* (written in 1944–45), the only youths in the Connemara Gaeltacht who don't emigrate are those who have already died from TB: 'Eitinn. Sin í an cailín. Tá an roillig seo reamhar aici . . .' ('Tuberculosis. That's the girl.* She has swelled this graveyard . . .'). Poverty and disease, not the war, were the real killers.

The title of Ó Cadhain's extraordinary novel translates as 'Churchyard Clay'. Set underneath the ground in Cois Fharraige in Connemara, the novel is peopled entirely by the dead of the village, interred in their coffins. It is hard to imagine a clearer way of suggesting the mortuary atmosphere of the Gaeltacht areas by the last year of the war. The grave is a figure for the moribund state of the Irish language and the community that speaks it, trapped in a vicious cycle of poverty, disease, and emigration.

Ó Cadhain was a native of Cois Fharraige, where he had been a schoolteacher in the 1930s. He spent the war years, however, in No. 1 Internment Camp at the Curragh. In 1937 he was dismissed from his post for membership of the IRA. Having moved to Dublin, he continued his IRA involvement as a recruiting officer. 'I know what it was that brought me into the IRA,' he later said. 'It was the need to solve the plight of my people, the country's poor.' Yet unlike other socially aware republicans active in the 1930s, such as Peadar O'Donnell, Ó Cadhain was fully in support of the IRA's declaration of war in January 1939, and of the Russell faction. He was a member of the IRA Council from 1938, and secretary to the Council in the run-up to the English campaign. Accordingly, in 1939 he was interned by the state for his republican affiliations. Imprisoned initially at Arbour Hill, Ó Cadhain was released in December 1939 under the Court of Appeal ruling that detention without trial was illegal. He remained free for four months, returning to his activities with the IRA. He was rearrested in April 1940 under the revised Offences against the State Act, and sent to the Curragh, where he remained until July 1944.

Internees were arrested and detained without being charged with specific offences, and with no sense of when their internment was going to come to an end. News coverage of events in the camp (hunger strikes, riots, the death of one internee shot by a guard during a

---

* an cailín (the girl) was a well-known euphemism for TB.

food protest) was kept to a minimum or censored completely, in the interests of preserving the neutral consensus. At the same time news from outside was strictly controlled. Each hut received one newspaper, which was read out loud to the internees. In this respect, as one inmate recalled, the men in the Curragh were better off than those in prison:

There was no radio in Arbour Hill nor in the Curragh, although one newspaper was delivered to each hut there. However no radio, no newspapers and no outside news whatever – except family news – was permitted into Arbour Hill. There was however a PA there who occasionally held his paper high enough for the headlines to be read.

News which might filter in through personal correspondence was heavily censored: 'At that time there were allowed two letters out per month and two in; some of those inward were so vigorously censored with a razor blade that the pages were ribboned with cuts.'

Imprisonment in the Curragh, combined with the difficulty of communication, produced an overwhelming feeling amongst those locked away of having being forgotten. On their release, many internees commented bitterly on the fact that former IRA comrades, rather than carrying the flag while they were shut away during the war, had opted to join the Defence Forces instead. Ó Cadhain described the wartime internees as the *glúin imithe* or 'vanished generation' (literally the 'gone' generation); they were doubly cut off, forcibly severed from the life of an isolated nation. Their fight was no longer Ireland's fight.

By the early 1950s the idea of the vanishing Irish was firmly associated with the exodus to England. Ó Cadhain's insistence that the internees too were the disappeared suggested strong parallels between republican activists and migrant workers, the poorest of the rural unemployed. Both were the focus of the government's fears of social revolution, and both were excluded as far as possible from the neutral community. There were also more incidental connections – such as the fact that they were all living in camps. Migrant turf workers transported from the Gaeltacht areas in Galway, Mayo and Donegal to the boglands of Kildare were housed in huts almost identical to the newly built sixty-man huts at the Curragh internment camp a few miles away. Still more of their compatriots – the soldiers at the Curragh military camp – were housed in similar huts across the way. Fittingly, perhaps, in 1944 and 1945 a large proportion of the released prisoners were employed on the turf in Phoenix Park, excluded from their former jobs because of their record and political affiliations. 'In O'Connell Street in those days in 1945 the total bloody internment camp were walking up and down the street every day,' remembered one prisoner. 'You could meet everyone in it, all as broke as yourself.' The poverty and unemployment, the fate of the language, the incarceration and even the endless turf were all brought together in Flann O'Brien's parody of a Gaeltacht autobiography, *An Béal Bocht* – another futureless narrative. The central character, Bónapart, is one of those inhabitants of the western seaboard 'whose like will never be seen again', not least because prison walls don't offer great prospects. At the beginning of the novel Bónapart's father is in jail. Father and son meet for the first time eighteen years later when the father is released, to be replaced in prison by Bónapart himself.

If the unemployed youth of the country were in the war in England, republican activists were in it in another way – as soldiers in the Curragh concentration camp. Even if the government could cavil at the appellation 'soldiers' (though it did grant the internees political status) there was no doubt that the IRA men were there because of Ireland's position in the conflict. Among their activities featured many of the typical pastimes of prisoners-of-war, including escape attempts. Inmates tunnelled towards the perimeter fences from under the floors of the huts, hiding the soil in side tunnels or carrying it away in their trouser legs to the latrines. A rota system was organised, whereby a tunneller could go underground after breakfast and not re-emerge until the evening.

The comparison only goes so far. Contract-labour migrants had a choice about their situation, after all, even though it may not always have felt like that. And they earned good money. But the connection between poverty, emigration and incarceration was made by observers at the time. In the first days of July 1943, when the new Fianna Fáil minority government was sworn in following the election, debates in the Dáil focused not only on the disastrous situation in rural Ireland with regard to supplies and emigration – on the starvation in the congested districts – but on the republican prisoners in the Curragh, and the voluntary starvation occurring there. A few days before the election had been called back in April, eight men campaigning for release had begun a hunger strike. This was the third such strike that had been staged during the war: in April 1940 two men had died on hunger strike for political status in Mountjoy Jail. By July 1943, three of the new strikers were still refusing food, but the facts of the protest action had largely been withheld from the public. Labour TDs complained that because of censorship, rumour was rife, and relatives outside did not know if members of their own families were striking.

Conditions at the Curragh ('the Siberia of Ireland' as Ó Cadhain put it) were notoriously bad. On top of the physical cold, hunger, dysentery, and material shortages, came the mental hardships of isolation, tedium and extreme boredom. It all helped to fuel a series of rancorous splits and conflicts which convulsed the camp from the end of 1940 onwards. Political divisions between communists, socialists, pro-German sympathisers, defenders of the Church's social teaching, were overlaid by regional affiliations and loyalties. The huts were organised primarily along geographical lines: there was a Limerick hut, for example, a Leitrim hut and a Cork hut – this last was ostracised for drawing coal after an embargo ordered by a CO inside the camp. There were several Irish-speaking huts, where prisoners who wished to learn to speak the language more fluently mixed with native speakers such as Ó Cadhain: Brendan Behan was a pupil. In the mid-1930s some Irish-language enthusiasts had put forward arguments for 'campaí dluithe' ('concentration camps') to promote Irish, along the lines of Mussolini's Italian camps in the Tyrol. As Éamon Ó Ciosáin has suggested, the Irish classes in the Curragh camp were one warped version of the proposal – a forerunner of the more recent H-block 'gaoltacht' of the Provisional IRA.

Apart from a valuable series of interviews with former internees collected by Uinseann Mac Eoin there is little testimony to the experience of life inside the camp. Against this backdrop, Ó Cadhain's published letters and the novel he partly based on life in the Curragh take on a particular importance. Ó Cadhain's letters from prison reveal a man immersed in literature, and otherwise concerned primarily with daily necessities, with the intermittent arrival of cigarettes, socks, books and drink. The question of physical and mental survival predominated, pushing into a poor second place the world war raging beyond Ireland's borders. Numbed by isolation, and lacking any personal stake in its outcome, Ó Cadhain experienced the war as a reader might experience a literary drama – the only material, bar second-hand newspapers, he had to go on:

I have done nothing . . . but read constantly and it going in one ear and out the other – the poetry of Donnchadh Bán mac an tSaoir, books by Gorky, Tolstoy's *War and Peace*, Racine and Corneille and passages of the Bible now and again. *War and Peace* is a powerful book, and it doesn't seem likely that there is anything being said about Hitler now that was not said long ago about Napoleon as far as it can be understood . . . It is strange how the war is going these days. The English did something finally no matter how long it took them. But there's one thing, there's no sign of it being over, no sign at all. It could last three or four years. The Germans, I'd say, are worn out in Russia. No matter how long or short it lasts, neither side is likely to defeat the other decisively.

It is certainly possible that Ó Cadhain was sent a copy of Kavanagh's 'The Great Hunger' in the Cuala Press imprint of 1942, and picked up the idea of a half-alive buried clay community from there. If not, then the idea of rural life as half-death, endless imprisonment within a 'mud-walled cabin', was in the air. Ó Cadhain described the kind of graveyard he had in mind for his story:

There are some graveyards in Cois Fharraige in which it could have happened. When I was released from the prison camp, I was at home that winter. A neighbour of mine died in the short dark days of Christmas [1944]. There was a flood of rain mixed with sleet, so that it was not possible to dig the grave until the day she was being buried. Five or six of us went to speed it up. We opened two graves but didn't find the right coffins in them. They sent for a map of the graves but the map was like a small boy doing sums with the tongs in the ashes of the hearth.

Ó Cadhain's vignette emphasised the role of chance and confusion in the life of the community. But like Kavanagh in 'The Great Hunger', he was also interested in how such a community survives. The witty, caustic and exuberant language of those who are buried alive is a lesson in what you can do with meagre resources, how you can create in the most impoverished circumstances.

Like the prisoners in the Curragh the villagers of Ó Cadhain's novel are caught in a state of limbo, suspended between life and death. (It's hard not to hear, in English, a play on the near-identity of 'interment' and 'internment'.) The time of the novel is, as Ó Cadhain says, 'eternity' – a reflection on the endlessness of imprisonment with no prospect of release. Above ground, however, the war is clearly raging. The most salient fact about the war is its remoteness. Even more than the life of the village above ground, the war represents all that is elsewhere and in another time. As in prison, as in neutral Ireland more generally, the

CRÉ NA CILLE
MÁIRTÍN Ó CADHAIN

The cover of Ó Cadhain's novel, published in 1949, illustrated by Irish
artist Charles Lamb.

half-life lived under the clay is without progress. There can, of course, be no sense of purpose for the dead in their graves because there is nowhere for them to go (the chapters of Ó Cadhain's book are not stages in a story but 'interludes'). Nothing can happen except more talk, and the talk itself goes round and round. The villagers, each in his or her little plot, pass the unending hours in gossip and story-telling. But communication is desultory and faltering; sentences trail off, the text is full of gaps. Even gossip requires something to feed it, but these characters are trapped, frozen at the moment of their deaths, imprisoned not only in their grave plots but in the curtailed narratives of their lives. Rather than weaving a dialogue, the villagers' speeches are a series of competing comic monologues, with each character voicing his or her obsessions, regardless of whether anyone else is listening, let alone concerned.

In the graveyard, as in a prison or in a remote rural community, all news is old news. Information can only make its way underground when another person is buried, just as a new inmate might be eagerly ransacked for fresh news:

It's the same life here, Caitríona, as it was in the 'ould country', but for the fact that all we see is the grave we're in, and that we're not able to leave the coffin. You won't hear the living either, nor will you know what happens to them, except according as the newly buried tell you.

When the newly buried arrive they are asked for news of goings on in the village, tittle-tattle about those still alive. As with Ó Cadhain's worries over cigarettes and socks, most of the characters are bothered about small personal details rather than the progress of the war. Are still-living relatives behaving themselves? What news of births, or marriages? Who is making money and who is failing? The world war is a source of gossip and rumour – but in no sense a struggle in which one might take sides. One character, buried for the last thirty years, mistakes the current conflict for the Great War, and stubbornly refuses to be enlightened. There's a point to his obduracy, however, for he keeps referring to 'The War of the Two Foreigners': a phrase that highlights the irrelevance – as Ó Cadhain perceived it – of both wars to those on the rim of Europe. Another grave dweller quotes a newspaper he read while alive years ago as the basis for his views.

As one of its many resonances, Ó Cadhain's graveyard suggests an Irish-speaking hut at the Curragh – in which the war features primarily as diversion from the misery and tedium of camp life. After Pearl Harbor, Ó Cadhain wrote:

It is sometimes worth reading the papers now. The Yanks were bragging a lot but the Japanese soon put a stop to that. There would be great fun if the boat on which Churchill returns from America were sunk, as happened with the 'Prince of Wales', the pick of the fleet. But they will be too vigilant. It seems as if there is neither beginning nor end to this war, or that it is only beginning still.

Ó Cadhain's nonchalance was born of the feeling that for ordinary Irish citizens, walled in by poverty and the hardships of rural life, there could be little meaning in the grand notions for which the war was supposedly fought. But it was also the fact that while there was no end to the war there was no end to internment.

In so far as the war does matter to some in the novel, it does so because of concerns about its impact on the economy, given rural Ireland's dependence on the English market: 'If England is hit, the country will be in bad shape. We've already lost the market.' Connections with England are constantly emphasised – not out of any political sympathy, but because it represents prosperity and livelihood. And if England offers a market for goods, it also offers work for those willing and able to travel: 'Upon my word, indeed, England isn't to be blamed. There is great work there. Without England what would the young people of Baile Dhoncha do, or the people of Gort Ribhigh, or Clochar Shaibhe?' One of the newly buried is a teenager who explains that just before he died he was about to emigrate, along with all the other youth, from the village of Baile Dhoncha.

In the middle of the novel, the war comes to the buried community. It is brought underground by a French airman, whose plane has crashed into the sea off the Galway coast. This is a realistic touch, given the numbers of Allied servicemen buried on the Western seaboard, but it may also be Ó Cadhain's portrait of the English and Germans interned in the Curragh. (The analogy between interment and internment may seem overstretched, but at least one Garda report, on the burial of a drowned seaman in Donegal, in 1940 referred to the 'internment' of the body.) The pilot's French can't be understood by his grave-mates (the schoolmaster claims his language is 'sluggish' after being so long in the sea), but he learns to speak a mixture of Irish and French, and argues for the eventual victory of the

Gaullists allied with Churchill and Roosevelt. The impassioned inter-nationalism of the airman contrasts sharply with the petty vanities and jealousies of the other dead, obsessed with details such as how many mourners there were at their own funerals. Those who worry about Ireland's economic future, should England be invaded, seem grossly small-minded compared to the airman, with his indignation at the human rights abuses in the 'prison camps':

– . . . Mon ami, the United Nations, England, les États unis, la Russe, et les Français Libres are defending human rights against . . . quel est le mot? . . . against the barbarity of des Boches Nazifiés. I already told you about the prison camps. Belsen . . .

– . . . Neil Pháidín is on Churchill's side. Huntsmen and fishermen from England, of course . . .

– She was treacherous before, the little vixen! *Up Hitler! Up Hitler! Up Hitler!* Do you think that if Hitler comes over he won't knock the new house to the ground again on her?

– The Post Mistress is on Hitler's side. She says that the post mistress is a very important official in Germany, and if she suspects anyone, that part of her duty is to read the letters of that person . . .

It is difficult, with the wisdom – or perhaps the false knowingness – of hindsight, not to feel shocked by this. The juxtaposition of Belsen and the petty ambitions of the village postmistress is a provocation. At one point a character makes a direct comparison between the graveyard/internment camp and the concentration camps: 'Is measa an chill seo anois, ná na háiteachaí sin a raibh an Francach ag trácht orthu an lá faoi dheireadh: Belsen, Buchenwald agus Dachau . . .' ('This graveyard is worse now than those places the Frenchman was talking about the other day: Belsen, Buchenwald and Dachau . . .').

Cré na Cille records a world with a past, but no sense of a future. The calls of the pro-Allied intelligentsia, of anti-fascists, to join a war in the name of democracy and freedom, fall quite literally on barren ground. The non-communication between the villagers and the Frenchman reveals a gulf between worlds. Both literally, and in terms of its sentiments – the struggle for the future, for liberation and humanity – the pilot's language is incomprehensible to them, an alien European tongue. His arguments make no impression on his fellow dead. They continue to talk past one another, their voices intersecting like the babble of crossed wires in an old-fashioned telephone exchange, as they repeat their petty concerns, political prejudices, and confusions. Even the foremost champion of the Germans calls out 'High for Hitler, High for Hitler', in a mistranslation, via English, of the Nazi salute.

It is hard to resist interpreting Ó Cadhain's characters not just as Connemara villagers, but as stereotypes of the various groups in the Curragh – his fellow prisoners included Trotskyists, German-supporting IRA, pro-English, a small group of Communists who signed out of the camp following Germany's invasion of the Soviet Union, as well as large numbers of people interested only in their personal concerns. Like the villagers, Ó Cadhain's fellow inmates, cooped up in their huts with scant information to rely on, no doubt banged on endlessly about their views, until they stopped really listening to each other. And many spent long stretches of time underground, patiently scraping tunnels through the clay. But – as we are reminded by the central character's repeated calls for a headstone made of 'the island greenstone' – this is also an island community, and an image of Ireland as a whole. The villagers are frozen in their limbo-like existence, confined by their poverty, by the lack of opportunities except those promised by emigration. Though the attitude of Ó Cadhain's characters to the war may seem like wilful ignorance or culpable moral disregard, it is surely far more a reflection of their powerlessness. They are simply playing the cards that life – and death – have dealt them.

10

Sacred Egoism

Ireland's neutrality was born in large measure of its powerlessness. It promised survival for a nation with poor prospects of defending itself. But leaving aside this limited military capability – the small army, no navy, little air power, DIY defences – neutrality was not presented to the world as the result of weakness. Government declarations dwelt on sovereignty and self-determination, and the democratic rights of small nations. One of the things that stuck in the throat of Allied public opinion was the rhetoric of intellectual and moral superiority that often gilded Irish policy throughout the war.

There was a political dimension to this rhetoric, of course. Partition and discrimination against Catholics in the North had tarnished the idea of British democracy in many people's eyes. And Irish hands were clean of the diplomatic failures of the inter-war years. Frank Aiken's speeches as Minister for the Co-ordination of Defensive Measures repeatedly turned on the 'moral basis' of Ireland's right to decide its own national policy, 'without evil intent to anybody'. But the tendency to describe Irish neutrality as superior to British warmongering also sprang from a belief in the finer virtue of Catholic spirituality, untainted by a world at war. Catholic social theory provided much of the inspiration for this attitude. Arguments for corporatism, and for Catholic, Gaelic Ireland's distinctive contribution to the culture of Europe, were given a boost during the war. But despite Allied suggestions that the Irish government as a whole was a front for theocratic dictatorship, as the war progressed Catholic corporatist ideas were pushed further into the background of practical politics. Right-wing intellectuals loudly debated Catholic social theory, but it ceased to have any real influence on policy.

Claims for Catholic Ireland's special vocation ranged from the frankly sectarian and xenophobic, to sincere attempts to formulate the basis for a just Christian society. These complexities were usually lost on hostile commentators, who had no incentive to make distinctions. The assumption of Catholic superiority encountered prejudice in its turn:

344

The Irish Roman Catholic Church looks upon the United States by and large as an immoral, irreligious, materialistic Protestant country chosen by God to be led along the paths of salvation by the Irish and Irish-American Roman Catholic clergy.

The immorality of our movies, the luxury of our daily lives, the vulgarity of our music and the lack of all forms of discipline in the conduct of our human relationships: these are all adduced by the Irish as proofs of our wickedness, and now that thousands of those 'wicked' Americans are occupying Northern Ireland the suspicion and hostility of the Irish Roman Catholic Church have reached an all-time high. The Irish Roman Catholic Church is much more preoccupied with fear of the moral infection from the American armed forces in Northern Ireland than it is with the possibility that these Americans may physically invade the rest of the Island of Ireland.

Though this report, by an officer of the American Office of Strategic Services (the forerunner of the CIA), may have reflected one strand of militant Catholic opinion, its caricature of the Irish Church's moral views set the stage for even more damaging political accusations. Hostile to the ethos of modern democracy, so the argument went, the Church's natural affinities were with the continent's dictatorial regimes:

Itself a body organised and controlled on authoritarian lines, the Irish Roman Catholic Church, by its affiliations with Franco Spain and Mussolini Italy, its open adulation of the Salazar regime in Portugal and of the Pétain Land–Labor–Family cry, is in large part responsible for the complete conceal-ment of the real nature of continental Fascism from the mass of Irish people, who have very little grasp of the state of affairs in Europe. The attitude of the Church arises directly and logically from its immemorial and still very active detestation of all forms of liberalism, all manifestations of the rights of indi-vidual conscience. One of the policies which enjoys most Church support in Éire is the Family Vote advocated by Pétain, which would mean the disenfran-chisement of everyone except the heads of families.

This report suggested there was no real difference between author-itarian Catholic thought and totalitarianism: the Church was delud-ing its flock about the 'real nature of continental fascism'. This was misguided. Irish Catholic culture did throw up its fair share of fascist ideologues and eager potential quislings, who liked to cloak them-selves in the rhetoric of the true faith. But many Irish Catholic intel-lectuals and lay people expressed concern at what they saw as the corrosive individualism and materialism of modern society, without at all approving of the police states on the continent. They were looking for solutions to economic inequality, for social cohesion and social rights, and for the redistribution of wealth. They believed that to confront these problems Ireland should draw on its own social patterns and religious traditions, rather than borrowing 'alien' systems. But the OSS reporter was right about the increased level of interest in these ideas. The stimulus of the Emergency brought a spate of publications – and practical programmes – by Catholic thinkers seeking to re-evaluate the country's religious heritage, and to affirm its significance for a world at war.

'It is not rash by any means to say that the whole scheme of social and economic life is now such as to put in the way of vast numbers of mankind most serious obstacles which prevent them from caring for the one thing necessary; namely, their eternal salvation' – Pope Pius XI's 1931 encyclical *Quadragesimo Anno* (On the Restoration of the Social Order), which built on Leo XIII's *Rerum Novarum* (On the Condition of Workers) of forty years before, inspired – explicitly or tacitly – much of the Catholic social thought of the period. These papal documents were intended as blueprints for taming the harshness of the capitalist system, and so forestalling the threat of socialism and communism. They called for a widening of social participation, based on broader and more generous notions of equality. Representation in terms of vocational groupings was to minimise state control, and encourage harmonious relations between classes. National life would be organised on a spiritual rather than material code. These ideas were interpreted in some quarters as a rebuff to the liberal political tradition, and the parliamentary system as a whole.

Irish Catholic social thought harmonised here with ideas in vogue in Italy, Spain, and Portugal, as well as amongst sections of French intellectual opinion, such as that represented by Action Française. In its most militant versions it became simply sectarian and authoritarian – an excuse for denouncing the current form of government as British, pagan, and the ally of Mammon. But there was a real sense in which the parliamentary system seemed unsuited to a largely agricultural and patriarchal society. For Catholic corporatists representation should be on the basis of social role – opinion should be transmitted through vocational groupings, guilds, and corporations, rather than political parties. There were even occasional suggestions (latched onto by unfriendly observers, such as the OSS informant) that adult suffrage in the Free State should be qualified by granting votes only to the head of each family, according to the number of family members.

The sense of the failure of democracy was not, of course, unique to Ireland. After the Great War, parliamentary government was in retreat all over Europe. Capitalism and the norms of a liberal, individualistic society appeared manifestly to have failed to give a fair deal to all. Against this background, Ireland seemed to have at once a stronger and a weaker tradition of democratic institutions than many other European nations. It could claim a long-standing liberal parliamentary tradition, but not one it felt fully at ease with. The legacy had been skewed by its association with British rule – the democracy of the oppressor had never truly given a voice to the people. And partition meant its continuing failure to do so. At the same time the generation who lived through the violence of the 1920s in Ireland were not about to take the value of the new representative institutions for granted. There were frequent criticisms that political debate in Ireland was overshadowed by civil-war divisions. Allegedly obsessed with replaying the past rather than looking to the future, party politics was a brake on progress.

Even outside Catholic, nationalist circles, corporatism seemed to have a lot to say to Ireland as a rural society where communal identities were still strong. Walter Starkie, who was Professor of Romance Languages at Trinity College, Dublin, and associated with Yeats through the Abbey Theatre from the early 1920s onwards, stood out amongst those who gravitated towards such ideas. He was a complex character. Best known for his ethnographic work amongst the European Romany population, Starkie married an Italian in the early 1920s, and from then on divided his time between Ireland and Italy. He met Mussolini and – like many foreign guests – was greatly impressed, becoming a kind of unofficial Italian spokesperson in Ireland. Inspired by special audiences with *il Duce*, his work of the 1930s is often barely disguised propaganda, focusing on the parallels between the economic and social situations of Ireland, Italy and Spain. In 1935 Starkie was sent on a two-month trip to Abyssinia as a guest of Mussolini's forces, and he wrote up six articles for the *Irish Independent* the following year, arguing against de Valera's position on sanctions. A later book, published in 1938 as *The Waveless Plain* (and paid for by a grant from the Italian government), recounts his growing interest in Mussolini's transformation of social life in Italy, extolling the virtues of his revamping of politics and education. This mattered, because Starkie had been a key adviser to the Cumann na nGaedheal government on educational policy.

Ten years before the publication of *The Waveless Plain*, Starkie contributed an article to the International Fascist Organisation's *Survey of Fascism Year Book*, entitled 'Whither is Ireland Heading – Is It Fascism? Thoughts on the Irish Free State'. After approving comments on the Shannon Hydro-electric Scheme and Irish educational reforms (mostly designed by Starkie himself), he located the Irish fascist movement in a perhaps unlikely place:

The civilisation we build must destroy all servility and allow the individual to be free within the solidarity of the Nation. In the last five years there are not wanting signs that there is a spiritual awakening among a people that had endured years of anguish, and it is quite possible that Ireland may come to assimilate a great deal of fascist doctrine, properly understood.

Starkie went on to call on the ideas of Hungarian fascist sympathiser Odon Por, to the effect that fascism was in fact a blend of the ideas of Machiavelli and none other than Yeats's friend and sparring partner, the poet and social reformer AE (George Russell). Amongst his range of achievements Russell could count his leading role in founding the local co-operative movement in rural Ireland. Sure enough, Por's weighty volume *Fascism*, published in 1923, includes a long chapter entitled 'Motives and Tendencies of the Dictatorship', in which AE's corporatist thought features, rather surprisingly, as the very foundation of fascist ideology. Por also contributed several articles to AE's short-lived journal, *The Irish Economist*, in 1922 and 1923.

It's odd to think of the Celtic Twilight poet on a par with Machiavelli as political thinker, or of the local dairy co-op, still a familiar feature of the Irish countryside, as the forerunner of the fascist guild. But the idea that the corporatist vision somehow had an Irish genesis was calculated to boost its local appeal. Corporatist ideas briefly featured as part of opposition policy in the early 1930s.

It was during this period that Irish politics most closely echoed the turmoil on the Continent, as parliamentary parties forged links to Ireland's fascist group, the Blueshirts. The movement had grown quickly. The birth of the Army Comrades Association (later to be known as the National Corporate Party) in 1932 was largely the result of old civil-war animosities, and suspicions arising from de Valera's election success. There were fears that under the new dispensation the IRA would be given free rein to attack former members of the Free State Army, or those who had acted against gunmen during the Cosgrave administration. After all, de Valera, who less than ten years previously had been in arms against the parliamentary state, was hardly a convincing champion of constitutional norms. By the following year the Blueshirts had attracted over a hundred thousand members, under its new leader, General Eoin O'Duffy, who had been sacked by de Valera as Commissioner of the Civic Guard. In September 1933 O'Duffy's movement (then called the National Guard) merged with the two main opposition parties in the Dáil, Cumann na nGaedheal and the National Centre Party, to form a new political movement, United Ireland – or as it was to be known, Fine Gael. The Catholic hierarchy gave its blessing to ideas that, after all, echoed papal teaching. Professor James Hogan, a historian at University College, Cork – accused by Peadar O' Donnell of being the 'theoretician of Fascism in Ireland' – and Professor Michael Tierney, a classicist at University College, Dublin and a senator, cranked out articles and pamphlets extolling the ideal of a corporate society. Clerical intellectuals also joined the campaign. For a while, this current seemed to bring new ideas and new energy to Irish political life.

Under O'Duffy, the Blueshirts explicitly linked themselves to right-wing movements on the Continent, adopting the requisite flummery of flags and emblems. In salute, the right hand was to be swung up with flat palm outstretched. Blue shirts appeared on the streets of market towns across the country, especially in Munster, and some were even sported in the Dáil. Ireland, like the European mainland, was gearing up for the battle between Christ and godlessness. 'One thing, at all events, is certain,' asserted Hogan. 'It was the growing menace of the Communist IRA that called forth the Blueshirts as inevitably as Communist anarchy called forth the Blackshirts in Italy.' Despite the glaring absence of any plausible left-wing menace (though the IRA did launch a short-lived radical initiative, Saor Éire, in 1931), Hogan published a series of articles, and later a celebrated pamphlet, *Could Ireland Become Communist?*, in which he expatiated on his fears of the 'communistic' IRA. It was a tract that travelled far and wide. As a fourteen-year-old radical writing in a pre-war issue of *Worker's Republic*, Brendan Behan recalled that the pamphlet was used by the Christian Brothers at his Dublin school to instruct him in his catechism.

But O'Duffy lacked the gravitas necessary to lead this movement; in fact, he was a liability. He couldn't be trusted to stick to his script, coming out with ever more extreme and inconsistent policies. An Irish fascist leader not a million miles from O'Duffy was guyed by Louis MacNeice – then teaching Classics at Birmingham University – in a farce he wrote for the University Dramatic Society in 1935. Set in the buffet of a Dublin railway station, *Station Bell* follows the fortunes of Julia Brown, Ireland's would-be dictator, who has made a fortune for the country on the proceeds of an edible seaweed, Carrageen Moss, which she sells to the colonies. ('Everyone's Nationalists now. No more Orange Billy or Fianna Fáil or the devil of the rest of it. No more parties in this state.') The cast comes complete with drunken cleric, communist plotting to assassinate Julia, and Nationalist propaganda corps 'betokening the spontaneity of our movement, a body of men and women of typically national appearance symbolising the new Ireland which is superseding the old, but is yet the consummation of what was good in the old. I should like people who can do a turn or two – we must have one or two who can talk Gaelic.' Julia, whose company has been secretly making armaments, and taking control of the state's banking and financial interests, is mildly worried about the shortage of Jews in Ireland on whom to blame cock-ups, but uses the Communists instead. The dictatorship finally collapses under the weight of intrigue, plot and counterplot. In the final scene O'Halloran, a defeated de Valera figure, belatedly grasps his mistake in unleashing fascist forces, and tries unsuccessfully to call on help from the United States; stranded alone in the station buffet, he resolves instead to 'complain to the League of Nations'.

Like Julia's Nationalists, by 1935 the Blueshirts had faded as a mass movement – an indication of the strength of Ireland's fledgling democracy. (They did not entirely disappear: German superiority early in the war led to a flurry of activity among Irish fascists keen to lay the groundwork for the reception of the victorious Axis powers. O'Duffy, an object of ridicule after the debacle of the Irish Brigade in Spain, enjoyed a brief return to prominence among the far right through a number of small groups, such as the Celtic Confederation of Occupational Guilds and the Irish Friends of Germany, before they were broken up by the Security Services.) But corporatist ideas continued to circulate, in more or less viable forms. They inspired many of the small activist groups devoted to mobilisation in the countryside.

Muintir na Tíre or 'People of the Land', led by an energetic canon from Tipperary, advocated parish guilds based on vocation. Farmers, labourers, the unemployed, rural professionals – all were to have separate representation on a council that could work out a fair system of local business exchange, in which economics would be subordinated to community and not the other way round. On the theoretical front, the Jesuit journals *Studies* and *Irish Monthly* often ran articles on the potential of corporate organisation. These appealed to the affinities between traditional Irish society (Catholic and Irish-speaking) and corporatist ideals. With the backing of organisations with a strong nationalist agenda, such as the Gaelic Athletics Association and the Gaelic League, corporatist social theory was conservative and respectable.

All the same, advocates of corporatism had to take increasing care to keep their distance from communist and fascist regimes. Their aim, they insisted, was to achieve a uniquely Irish form of government. In a 1937 article in *Ireland Today* Michael Tierney declared that Irish Catholicism and Irish nationalism could together give birth to Irish democracy. A year later James Hogan was arguing for 'a conception of society radically different from that of communism or fascism whose doctrine is unitary and statist through and through'. He denounced the 'sordid and stagnant state of party politics in Ireland', suggesting that progress would only come through separating the economic and political functions of government. These were to be allotted to the guilds and to parliament respectively.

Interest in corporatism did not wane as war approached, or even during the war itself. But as the totalitarian features of Mussolini's regime became more evident, theorists grew keener to demonstrate that they were not in favour of a corporate state, but of the corporative organisation of society. Corporatism was not fascism, but rather a kind of 'social democracy'. The pole of comparison was less and less Italy, or war-torn Spain under Franco, but Salazar's Portugal. The dictator's apparently successful moulding of his country into a Catholic rural republic was not lost on Irish intellectuals. Major Catholic journals such as *Studies* and *Irish Monthly* regularly published articles explaining Salazar's experiment, and pointing out the lessons to be learned for Ireland. At a more popular level there were leading articles in the national newspapers, such as the *Independent*, but more particularly the Catholic *Standard*, which ran a story on Salazar nearly every week for years. In the local papers, too, Portugal was a frequent topic.

The attraction of Salazar's regime lay in its rhetoric of order and social harmony, rather than violent upheaval and militaristic expansion. Admirers could reassure themselves by drawing a contrast with the aggressively totalitarian, anti-religious ideology of Nazism. By 1940 memories of the Spanish Civil War were fading and giving way to paeans of praise for Franco's social reconstruction. The new regimes on the Iberian peninsula seemed to promise order rather than revolution; these were anti-democratic, authoritarian systems, but they were not to be confused with violent fascism or communism.

Enthusiasm for the Salazarist experiment did have a basis in reality, in the social, economic and religious affinities between the two countries – though it neatly overlooked Portugal's exploitation of its overseas empire. The appeal of comparisons with southern Europe sprang from the vision of a small-scale economy, based on peasant agriculture. The watchword was self-sufficiency. Local organisations, like the parish guilds advocated by Muintir na Tíre (though in fact this organisation drew support from the big farmers), were to be the building blocks of society. The rights of small tillage farmers had to be championed against the big cattle ranchers, the homestead defended against the Big House. And small nations must ensure they could supply their own needs, standing up against the imperialist bullies.

*   *   *

With the intensive drive towards self-sufficiency in food and fuel, Irish rural organisations came into their own. In June 1940, as invasion threatened, de Valera stressed the value of Muintir na Tíre and the importance of parish councils and guilds in time of war. By October 1940, the newspapers were reporting that the war had given further impetus to rural associations. Townlands began to recover their status as a focus of community, through cooperation and Emergency parish committees. At least until economic decline and emigration began to bite, it looked as though the isolation of the countryside was going to prove a boon to Irish distinctiveness.

The government backing for Muintir na Tíre was in part about building strong rural communities on the home front. Members of Muintir na Tíre tended to be active in Step Together committees, recruitment drives and local entertainments, as well as useful advocates for wheat drives, the use of home-made fertilisers, and other campaigns. But de Valera may also have valued corporatist groups as a grassroots bulwark against the IRA. The internal and external threats of the Emergency drew Catholic social organisations into a working relationship with de Valera's administration, in a movement for national survival.

Corporatist ideas also enjoyed continued currency at an intellectual level. Writers such as Aodh de Blácam (one of those keen on the family vote) and Roibeard Ó Faracháin, who were associated with the *Irish Monthly*, acted as popular advocates. De Blácam had a regular column in the *Irish Press* (under the pseudonym Roddy the Rover); Ó Faracháin was talks organiser for Radio Éireann, a job he was given in preference to Kavanagh. Both de Blácam and Ó Faracháin declared their commitment to writing that would represent, as the *Irish Monthly* put it, the 'Real Ireland of Today' – the Catholic, pious, rural, and parish-based one. Where, Catholic intellectuals complained, were the Irish counterparts of Hilaire Belloc or G. K. Chesterton?

More left-leaning strands of Catholic opinion were also committed to a search for alternatives to the social dislocation and injustice of the capitalist path to modernity. In 1942 Father Senan, editor of *The Capuchin Annual*, formed a discussion circle in Dublin to explore the philosophical background to such issues. The group, which met in the Ritz café in Upper Abbey Street, attracted writers and intellectuals such as the Northern novelist Benedict Kiely (then living in Dublin), the poet and art critic Thomas MacGreevy, who returned to Dublin from a job at the National Gallery in London at the end of 1941, and Irish-language writers Eoghan Ó Tuairisc and Donal Ó Murchú. They studied works of neo-Thomist thought. They argued over such issues as social rights in a Catholic context, mechanisms for the redistribution of wealth, and the idea of the priest as social worker. They worried about the damage wrought by economic injustice, and the materialism of modern urban life. In 1942 the group invited Jacques Maritain, the leading neo-Thomist philosopher of the age – professor at Princeton and Columbia, and one-time member of Action Française – to lecture to them in Dublin. Maritain's philosophy showed the influence of papal-sponsored corporatist thinking, but by the 1940s he was also committed to the defence of liberal and democratic norms. His attempt to define a *via media* between individualism and socialism, and his inclusive conception of human rights (he was later to contribute to the writing of the UN Declaration of 1948), added a further strand to the Catholic debate over economic and social policy. This more benign version of Irish Catholicism's links with Europe offered an intellectually cogent alternative to the liberal Europe championed by *The Bell*.

The rise in public discussion of corporatist and vocationalist ideas during the war was partly due to contingencies. In 1938 de Valera agreed to set up a Commission on Vocational Organisation, to look into the feasibility of including some vocational element in elections to the Seanad. The 1937 Constitution had sketched the possibility that the new Seanad could act as a vocational chamber, representing branches of 'the social and economic life of the nation'. But in practice it was mainly a party-political chamber. The Vocational Commission met for four years. It consulted widely, and its discussions were recounted in the newspapers, naturally fuelling interest in the idea. It sought to define a role for vocationalism within parliamentary democracy. 'There is no more reason for thinking that vocational organisation is equivalent to "fascism",' the final report asserted, 'than there is for thinking that it is equivalent to syndicalism, socialism, or communism.' The aim was a corporate society, not a corporate state: a vocational sphere of social and economic activity that could go with any form of political regime. Local vocational structures would actually provide a 'bulwark of freedom' against totalitarianism, as Bishop Browne put it, keeping the central state bureaucracy in check. At their summit would be a National Vocational Council (the Commission's alternative to a vocational Seanad), offering impartial technical advice on social and economic questions, and resolving social disputes.

None of this mild, earnest discussion of vocationalism could account for the degree of hysteria about Catholic 'fascism' in the Allied – particularly US – press. But the war also gave impetus to attacks on liberal democracy guaranteed to cause suspicion and disquiet – if not downright fury – among the Allies. For some adherents of Catholic social theory the war proved the superiority of Christian society. And they were not shy about saying so. In January 1940 Salazar's Faber book *Doctrine and Action* was reviewed in the *Standard*, with the accolade of 'Book of the Week'. The reviewer took the opportunity to point out the many ills which had sprung from liberal democracy. 'Making the world safe for democracy' would not appeal much to Dr Salazar:

There is scarcely a paragraph in this book which does not find a practical application in this country . . . At the present time when intensive efforts are being concentrated on an attempt to persuade people that 'democracy' is the only system which will preserve civilisation, it is refreshing to find an intelligent critic of Dr Salazar's calibre giving his views on the subject.

In July 1940 the paper was hailing the 'Dawn of a New Europe'. Corporatism's enthusiasts had watched with excitement the rebirth of Italy, Portugal and Spain. France was now the crucible of the new social order. At least some good had come of the blitzkrieg: 'There are now more Catholics in the French government than in the dangerous days of pre-war complacency.' The paper's editor Peadar O'Curry saw his role as aiding the emergent Catholic world order. One *Standard* response to the Blitz on London in October 1940 was the headline: 'Divorce is Destroying more Homes than Bombs.'

It is hard to know how far these ideas percolated in Irish society. In July 1940 the Secretary for External Affairs, Joseph Walshe, wrote a tart memo to the Irish envoy to Vichy who had been sending back some critical appraisals of the Vichy regime: 'The sympathy of the whole country is with Pétain . . . It is felt here that our destiny henceforth will be cast with that of the Continental Catholic countries.' Even if Walshe was right about the sympathy of the country, which is doubtful, ideas of Ireland's Catholic continental destiny were soon revised. Undoubtedly the high point of Vichy sympathy was immediately after the fall of France, when it seemed clear that Germany was going to win the war, and an alliance with the neutral Catholic bloc would suit Ireland in the new world order. But this view quickly faded in political circles as it became clear that not all of France was given over to defeatism, and as Germany's triumphal progress began to falter.

Nonetheless the war was grist to the mill of those, like O'Curry, who were keen to argue that the failure of materialist social systems was down to the dominance of economic values, and the rejection of 'the spiritual factor' in human existence. It was here that the tone of intellectual and moral superiority grated most. Europe, so the argument went, had been on the wrong track since the Reformation. Catholic Ireland had acted for centuries as the haven for pre-Reformation spirituality, which was lacking almost everywhere else in Europe. This version of corporatism hadn't got beyond the model of the medieval guild. So Father James Devane could argue in *Irish*

Rosary in 1941 that Ireland must be 'a force in the rejuvenation and re-Christianisation of a post-war Europe'. Irish society was 'a resuscitation of a medieval polity', only better because more Catholic than any country the world had yet seen.

This was one way of introducing a European perspective into Irish cultural debate. Catholic commentators welcomed the increase in discussion of the outward thrust of Irish Catholicism as a turn against insularity. Catholics should be wary of equating Catholicism and Irishness, they argued. In fact, Catholicism was European, but only Ireland remembered it. Here was a turnaround in right-wing thought. The need to 'restore Ireland to Europe' now had less to do with what it could learn from the continent than with what it could teach it. Ireland had preserved the values of civilisation that Europe had forgotten. The editorials of militantly Catholic and nationalist local papers such as the *Donegal Democrat* exuded self-satisfaction:

True to Catholic traditions, Ireland, Spain and Portugal may yet be the salvation of the world . . . There can be no peace of any description without Christianity, and Europe has been going pagan for a long period undoubtedly. It will ruefully wish for a return to simpler things and find that solace is only to be had in the discipline of devotion.

The idea of an alliance of Catholic nations to act as a bulwark against pagan Europe had strong backing in Ireland throughout the 1930s. It gained ground as pagan Europe seemed increasingly bent on destroying itself. As Conor Cruise O'Brien argued in 1945, to this extent the Catholic press was less a reflection of popular religious opinion in Ireland than a weapon in a worldwide ideological battle. The more militant thinkers and members of the Catholic hierarchy saw themselves as still fighting the battles of the Counter-Reformation. Archbishop McQuaid, for example, tried to put a stop to interdenominational discussion and Catholic–Jewish dialogue. Any suggestion that Catholicism was one faith among others could only weaken the Church's position. Ireland was to be a bastion in the worldwide combat with the forces of liberal individualism and irreligion. There was much talk of a bloc of neutral Catholic nations – a goal that became more pressing after the fight with Russia began.

It was handy for the continent that Ireland was so geographically isolated, protected from the corrupting effects of modern European cultural movements. Ireland, the land of the saints who had Christianised Europe, had retained its pristine spirituality. One need only look to the number of domestic sites of pilgrimage. All corporatist movements looked back to the medieval past. But only Ireland could claim an unbroken descent from the Christianity of the middle ages. Movements such as Pétainism could not equal this purity of pedigree. The sense of Ireland's distinctive history was not all bunkum, of course. The question was: how far did it really imply a distinctive Irish destiny? This was a live question for many more than those inhabiting the further reaches of Catholic utopian thought.

Denis Devlin, then first secretary to the Irish legation in Washington, a former lecturer at Trinity College and associate of Samuel Beckett, was not one to buy into corporatist ideas – which would have seen him, along with most of the civil service, out of a job. But he was clearly interested in the notion that Catholic Ireland had 'escaped' the forces which were bringing Europe down. In 1942 he wrote a poem about the medieval pilgrimage to St Patrick's Purgatory, the island on Lough Derg in County Donegal, which was still a site of devotion and penitence. The penitiential protocol required three days without food except bread and water, walking barefoot and moving on one's knees round the cold, bare, stony island. It offered a powerful image of a small, poor, intensely religious, not to mention hungry island. Devlin's flawed, intellectually ambitious poem 'Lough Derg', hovering between bathos and grandeur, charts the arc of a civilisation whose slow development and flourishing has largely passed Ireland by. The rude devotions of the Lough Derg pilgrims are remnants of a backward Christianity, untouched by the refinements of European thought and culture. But now 'Kent is for Jutes again, and Glasgow town / Burns high enough to screen the stars and moon.' Could this primitive, marginal Christianity retain some special healing value in the face of the continental catastrophe?

> With mullioned Europe shattered, this Northwest
> Rude-sainted isle would pray it whole again.

It was a moot question, of course, whether such a neat distinction could be drawn between the rough integrity of a Celtic Christianity and the religion that inspired the vaulting cathedrals of Chartres and Milan. As a diplomat in the pay of the neutral Irish government Devlin had a professional stake in the notion that his country's response to the world crisis had its own unique contribution to make. But he was too urbane and cosmopolitan a man not to be beset by doubts about the idea of a national mission, especially one cast in such pious terms.

> We pray to ourself. The metal moon, unspent
> Virgin eternity sleeping in the mind,
> Excites the form of prayer without content;

If the depressing circularity of praying to oneself weren't enough, the oddness of the word 'ourself' forces us to think of what should be there: ourselves. Ireland has taken the route of separateness, summed up in the phrase 'ourselves alone', but this may be less in response to a calling, than out of a desire to close in on itself. Prayer ends up both complacent and vacuous.

In the same year Patrick Kavanagh also wrote a poem about Lough Derg – a far earthier, even satirical production. Kavanagh's prime motive in going to Lough Derg was to earn some much needed cash; he was to write an article on the pilgrimage for the *Standard*. Despite a few examples of genuine spirituality, his narrative is crammed with those he calls 'petty mean people' praying for help with their everyday lives. What Kavanagh saw at Lough Derg were the priests and people of a family-centred culture, caught up for good or ill in the needs of those around them:

> That my husband may get his health
>   We beseech thee hear us
> That my son Joseph may pass the Intermediate
>   We beseech thee hear us
> That my daughter Eileen may do well at her music
>   We beseech thee hear us.

Rather than a culture with its thoughts on Europe, his miniature theocratic fiefdom was a dismal portrait of 'all Ireland that froze for want of Europe'. This was Kavanagh's 'Europeanly-minded' social conscience talking. But he was uneasy about this kind of judgement. Kavanagh never published his poem; he clearly felt uncomfortable about the fact that, with the war going on in Europe, it seemed impossible not to judge these pilgrims as inadequate and self-centred. How could even sincere prayer measure up to the war?

The idea that neutral Ireland might pray Europe out of its mess had no purchase whatsoever in far more secular Britain, let alone the United States. But given the quasi-confessional character of the state, the question of religious pacifism was almost bound to get mixed up with the issue of Ireland's wartime neutrality. People usually overlooked that the state's neutrality was armed, the country on standby for a military response to invasion. In the public mind, as well as in the reflections of religious commentators, neutrality and pacifism tended to become aspects of a single Irish identity and perspective on the world. Individuals prayed fervently, priests organised parish retreats and pilgrimages for the whole congregation. (Pilgrimages increased in popularity in all the Catholic European countries during the war.) In some places parishioners, only recently returned from mass, and with barely time to down their Sunday dinners, were expected back in church in the afternoon for 'Prayers for Peace'. There is no reason to doubt the sincerity of the sentiments expressed by Agnes Farrelly in *The Leader*, in spring 1941:

Here in our little island we may be saved – indeed, I firmly believe we shall be saved the woe that is the lot of so many of our fellow men. But if we are immune from the struggle that does not save us from responsibility. We are not as a planet apart. We are part and parcel of the European system and our future is largely bound up with its future . . . We owe it to humanity and to the God who spares us to do what little we can in the cause of peace. In these days of brute force a nation as small as ours can only make itself felt on the moral plane. Let us think peace, for thoughts fly hither and thither to find nesting places in the soul of man. Let us speak peace – not the ill-considered peace of unreasoned and unreasoning pacificism but the just peace of the Christian – the only peace likely to lead to stability and happiness. Let us preach peace on the highways and by-ways of Irish life for without peace there is no going forward – all life is either retrograde or at a stand-still.

The inescapable problem, though, was that prayer, however sincere, did not seem to help much. Certainly, it could not bring very obvious or fast solutions. If praying was indeed a heartfelt reaction to the war, its effectiveness could scarcely be assessed in the same way as practical responses such as volunteering, or engaging in relief work.

The clash between self-congratulation and a genuine openness and vulnerability, so tangible in Farrelly's homily, was pinpointed by Elizabeth Bowen. She was commenting on Irish Catholicism for the Dominions Office in 1943:

I find a great readiness, in talkers of all classes, to stress the 'spirituality' of Éire's attitude towards world affairs. At the root, this is not bogus: that this country *is* religious in temperament and disposition as well as in practice is, I take it, an accepted fact. Unhappily, religion is used to cover or bolster up a number of bad practices. I mentioned in *Notes* last summer, and still see, a threat of Catholic-Fascism. And officially the Irish RC Church is opposed to progress, as not good for the people.

The most disagreeable aspect of this official 'spirituality' is its smugness, even phariseeism. I have heard it said (and have heard of it constantly being said) that 'the bombing is a punishment on England for her materialism'. The better side, or aspect, is – that it can breed a very genuine charity, that it makes the people capable of imaginative pity and distress. There is no doubt that 'the bad state of the world' is more than conventional, a genuine source of sorrow to many people, especially to the simpler people, here . . .

I do, however, continue to hear, among enlightened Catholics, considerable criticism of the RC Church for its failure to take up a more positive attitude in this world crisis. This ranges from criticism of parish priests for their lack of outlook, their ambiguous and teetering attitude – ('They tell us to pray for peace, but how are we to work for it?') to criticisms of the Vatican's political feebleness.

Even with the best of intentions, any non-activist response to the war was bound to look to the unsympathetic like complacency. But the sense of superiority could also take far worse forms than Farrelly's naivety: war was a judgement on sinful Europe. While others were engaged in a materialistic and physical combat, Ireland was commit-ted to a battle for the true faith. A sincere commitment to prayer on the part of many of the laity was liable to be exploited by the zealots of the Counter-Reformation. Inevitably, it was religious arrogance and indifference that caught the attention of hostile commentators. For sceptical outsiders there was plenty of evidence that prayerfulness could slide into a culpable smugness; that a belief in Ireland's special vocation for peace led to a condescending attitude towards 'continen-tal quarrels'. In the eyes of such critics the stance of the Catholic hier-archy was typified by aloofness, myopic complacency, and offensive claims to moral superiority. T. H. White, for example, joined a Peace Pilgrimage to Knock in July 1940, and had this to report to David Garnett:

The sermon consisted of raking over old animosities against the English, of implications that war is a punishment for slighting the vested interests of the clergy (synonym: 'turning away from the Catholic Faith'), of dramatic or histrionic clap-trap about the Blessed Virgin and finally of the assumption that the only purpose of the Peace Pilgrimage was to pray for peace in Ireland. This man, this wicked man in priestly garments, did not mention one word of sorrow or commiseration or pity or supplication for all the millions in tormented Europe. Now I think I shall never be a Catholic.

* * *

By the middle of the war Allied descriptions of Ireland as home to a 'benevolent' Fascism were common. US attacks tended to be vitriolic – not least because the US Ambassador David Gray was personally prejudiced against 'illiberal' Catholicism. In Britain even as friendly a critic as Cyril Connolly described Ireland as 'closest by inclination to the other Western theocratic dictator-republic Dr Salazar's Portugal. Ireland has, however, no empire, very few industries, and no ships.' In the 1942 issue of *Horizon* devoted to Ireland, L. T. Murray suggested that Irish parliamentary democracy might be in serious danger:

Should conditions deteriorate, it would not be very surprising if eventually Éire had a Government on the Salazar model. Labour has never had any important following. The number of Labour members in the Dáil of recent years has been so small that the Party representatives were referred to once as 'the seven deadly sins'. Poverty, shortage of supplies and unemployment demand a remedy, and the Irish public would arrive quite happily at a benevolent form of Fascism introduced to carry out the principles of the encyclicals on economic matters published by the late Pope.

But in reality they were hearing the swansong of the Catholic corporatist movement. Despite the widespread debate, the war scotched hopes of the Irish polity ever putting corporatist ideas into practice. Though strong at a grassroots level, particularly in fertile farming areas, during the war corporatist economic organisations lost ground against the increasingly centralised state control over industry and supplies.

In fact de Valera and Lemass used organisations such as Muintir na Tíre to roll out state policy – over defence, rationing, food and fuel drives – into the countryside. And at the same time the government decisively rejected recommendations for a vocational element to political representation. When the Commission on Vocational Organisation presented its vast report in 1943, recommending an assembly that would sit alongside the Dáil to deal with social and economic issues, the government buried it. There was very little discussion of the recommendations in the Dáil and silence in the major intellectual journals when the report was published in 1944. The idea was simply pushed aside. There were several reasons for this. By 1944 the whole idea of vocationalism had become faintly embarrassing. The war was being fought on behalf of the freedoms guaranteed by liberal democracy, and it was not the right time to argue for alternative systems, particularly not those that could be tarred with a quasi-fascist brush. In 1944 the economist James Meenan published a mordant exposé of the Italian corporatist system, which did Irish apologists no favours. Even James Hogan, in *Election and Representation* (1945), was driven to qualify his earlier enthusiasm (though he still held out for extra votes for the family unit). Modern guilds, he pointed out, would have very little in common with the medieval versions which had been 'true communities in miniature'. Like it or not Ireland was part of the modern industrial world and any associations based on employment would have more in common with trade unions than with self-sufficient guilds. By the end of the war campaigns on behalf of corporatism and vocationalism had shrunk back to the clerical organisations. Bishop Browne published his argument on behalf of vocationalism, *Bulwark of Freedom*, as a Catholic Truth Society pamphlet in 1945. It was not the type of freedom the government was interested in handing over.

De Valera had won a massive election victory in 1944 and he could afford to ignore clerical pressure. But the war had also consolidated the power of the state by shrinking the role of the democratic opposition. Throughout the war de Valera rejected calls for him to form a national government which would include members from the other main political parties. This was partly because Fianna Fáil had begun to resemble a national government in itself. Through repressive measures such as censorship and internment, and arguably through emigration, as well as through more positive morale-boosting measures, de Valera's government had managed to fatten up the middle ground of support for the state. Five years after the war began in Europe, Ireland's civil-war divisions were far less of an issue than they had been in 1939. With clever use of grassroots organisations and clerical support, de Valera's wartime government had managed to create a form of national consensus within the liberal parliamentary system so that arguments for vocationalism began to seem redundant.

The public had also grown wary of some rather disturbing variants on 'benevolent' fascism that flowered during the war. One of the attractions of Catholic social theory was its international aspect – Ireland was one of a group of European nations that were really seeking an alternative to both British democracy, with all its pitfalls, and the totalitarian regimes on the continent. The more militant versions of corporatism focused instead on national recovery. They were basically fascist and totalitarian in outlook. And they were mostly the work of cranks.

In 1942, for example, a pamphlet entitled *National Action* was published by the GAA under the pseudonym Josephus Anelius. The writer was Joseph Hanly, author of popular textbooks on farming during the 1920s. His plans for National Government recycled many of the Catholic corporatist arguments of the 1930s. He was against the imitation of English systems, including the political party system. He was full of praise for Salazar. He advocated a national government combined with a 'well organised system of parish Guilds and Councils' such as that run by Muintir na Tíre. Election to the National Government would be by constituency; voters could choose between a selection of young 'strong, selfless, enthusiastic and persevering' people who would carry out an agreed national plan. Hanly strongly recommended frugality. Like James Hogan earlier, he argued that many of Ireland's ills could be put down to greed for too high a standard of living. He would get rid of foreign dances, foreign sport and foreign fashion. There would be penal servitude and the lash for traffickers in birth control – partly in order to solve the population problem. Education was to focus on physical health rather than maths and literature. Hanly argued:

Nations today are vying, under the banner of Mammon, for ultra-modern superiority. We can show to the world that ultra-modern development can be achieved, and achieved successfully, under the banner of Christ.

Gaelic Ireland saved Europe for Civilisation and Christianity before the Middle Ages. Our duty now, and our only hope for a national future, lies in making Ireland once again not only free but Gaelic, not only Gaelic but a missionary power and example of practical Christianity in the only way that twentieth century scepticism will heed it – a successful example of an exemplary Christian State.

He then made a typical anti-semitic move. In response to the 'national decay' – depopulation, the decline of the language, the failure of social and economic systems – Hanly warned against the infiltration of aliens, 'backed by powerful international financial organisations'. There was a glaring contradiction in this world view. If Ireland had maintained its unique and exemplary status as Christian crucible through all the centuries of invasion and colonisation by others, why the overwhelming need to protect it against outside influences? (Critics made the same point about the censorship – if the Irish were so naturally pure and moral, why the need to protect them from 'immoral' literature?) The idea of infiltrating aliens was also ludicrous. Very tight immigration restrictions during the war, which were targeted particularly at any group thought likely to upset the national consensus, including Jews, ensured that Hanly and his like did not need to worry. But the slippage from national protectionism, and pride in Ireland's distinctive Catholic destiny, to xenophobia and from there to anti-semitism was not unique to Hanly.

There is no evidence that Hanly's ideas gathered much active support, though the fact that his pamphlets were published by the GAA suggests a degree of respectability. The most popular far-right-wing movement during the war was Ailtirí na h-Aiséirí ('Architects of the Resurrection'), led by a former member of O'Duffy's organisation, the Irish Friends of Germany. The movement grew out of a branch of the Gaelic League founded in September 1940 by Gearóid Ó Cuinneagáin, who had earlier left his civil-service job in Dublin to perfect his Irish in the Donegal Gaeltacht. The group (Craobh na h-Aiséirí – 'Branch of the Resurrection') began as a militant wing of the League. Fed up with the moribund nature of most branches of the Gaelic League, the group's members wanted to speed up gaelicisation. These members included the film-maker Liam Ó Laoghaire, the novelist Séamus Ó Néill, and Flann O'Brien's brother Ciarán Ó Nualláin, who edited the newsletter *Aiséirí*. Most of the members were civil servants, teachers, young university students and graduates, and they certainly brought energy to the League. They held street marches and meetings; organised musical evenings and Sunday walks in the countryside; under Ó Laoghaire's influence they showed films in the street, projected against a wall or onto a sheet. The war was an opportunity for the Irish to pay more attention to their own affairs, the Craobh group argued, and the most important of these were the revival of Irish and an end to partition. The propaganda paid off. Within a year there were 1,200 new members of the branch and fifty-seven new Irish classes had been set up.

It was at this point that Ó Cuinneagáin grew dissatisfied with the scope of his organisation. In the summer of 1942 he disaffiliated from the League and set up a new, clearly fascist, organisation working for a 'Free, truly Christian, Gaelic Ireland'. Aiséirí's manifesto insisted

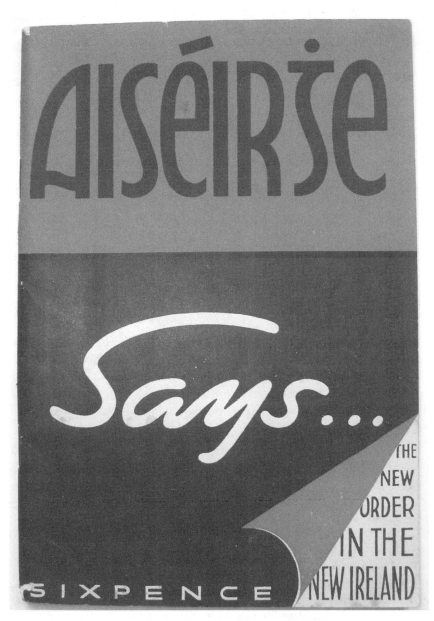

Ailtirí na h-Aiséirí propaganda booklet, published in 1943

that now was the time to get rid of the outmoded system of party politics based on civil-war divisions. The country should have one leader (himself) and one political organisation. Aiséirí urged that neither communism nor fascism, but 'actualised Christianity' was the answer to Ireland's problems. Irish was to be restored as the national language – 'This result will be achieved speedily by the adoption of twentieth century propaganda methods' – and the 'godless liberalistic corrupt government system' inherited from England was to be replaced by corporatism, 'the modernisation of the mediaeval guild system, being so successfully reintroduced into Portuguese life by Salazar today'. There was to be a single National Party, drawn from all walks of life; economic production was to be planned; and all male workers would receive a family wage and two weeks' paid holiday. 'In addition, a number of old medieval church holidays will be revived.' Partition would of course be abolished, by force if necessary. Northern Protestants would be allowed a little longer to learn Irish. Eager to proselytise, Aiséirí sent Irish-language books and pamphlets to the prisoners in the Curragh. Its manifesto no doubt raised some eyebrows amongst the republicans there, but nonetheless well-produced Aiséirí posters bedecked the camp's dining hall.

More moderate revolutionaries, including Ciarán Ó Nualláin, left the organisation at this point. But Ó Cuinneagáin gathered new followers, amongst them Ernest Blythe, Chairman of the Abbey Theatre and one-time Cumann na nGaedheal Minister for Finance. Blythe made several corrections to Aiséirí propaganda leaflets, adding attacks on the 'foreign and British Parliamentary system'. The 1943 pamphlet declared that the war was helping to ready Ireland for the coming political change:

Observe how already destiny prepares the way, how the youth of Ireland is being trained to accept leadership in the new emergency forces which have arisen in the south. Soon these will have little or no patience with the cumbersome indirect methods of our imposed corrupt, unchristian, Godless, inefficient brand of parliamentary democracy. They will appreciate the value of national discipline. As a result of the war we are, all of us, becoming very much accustomed to government by state decree, the legislative method which will be practised hereafter. What is lacking at present in the state decrees and the military and semi-military forces of the emergency and government administration generally is national force and character, a courageous national outlook, true national idealism. The fundamentally essential force and motive power and faith which are absent will be made available by the Aiséirghe movement. The young men of the new national resurgence will be impregnated with the Aiséirghe spirit and faith and the public eventually will appreciate that and act accordingly.

Aiséirí went on to win twelve seats in local elections in 1944, but this was the high point of Ó Cuinneagáin's career. A 1943 film of Ó Cuinneagáin energising his troops with street oratory and on a march across the border to Belfast shows him as a rather ridiculous figure. The Aiséirí emblem looked a good deal like a Celtic swastika and Ó Cuinneagáin certainly liked to present himself as the new charismatic leader Ireland needed. But the small group of followers in the film suggests instead a very amateur set-up. The march across the border – with cardboard signs denouncing partition and a ticket inspector stopping the group as they get out of the train in Dundalk – comes across as the very opposite of a powerful take-over. Predictably, Ó Cuinneagáin was arrested when he got to Belfast. The film was made in 1943 by Liam Ó Laoghaire and the tone of it suggests that by this time Ó Laoghaire himself had left the movement and wanted to send it up. Nonetheless outsiders, including members of MI5, continued to think Aiséirí might pose a real political threat. In October 1943, the poet John Hewitt, on a visit from Belfast to Dublin, observed the would-be caudillo in full spate:

In O'Connell St. I heard a meeting of a new party spelt Ahsearte or something like that, pronounced Asharce. Amplifiers and well printed literature, headed by one Cunningham – a pocket Hitler – with bulging veins and raucous voice – anti-masonic, anti-democratic, anti-alien, anti-jobbery – His programme is the usual skilful mixture of real abuse and fascist abuse. Some following I hear among university students and civil service. It'll just be ripe for the Éire slump after the war when 300,000 return, workless, to starve at home, conditioned to good English wage levels.

Rabidly Catholic and xenophobic Aiséirí may have been, but anti-semitism was not the central plank of its programme. Far more virulently anti-semitic and openly fascist doctrine was preached by extreme groups such as O'Duffy's Irish Friends of Germany, and its offshoot, the People's National Party (Penapa). Penapa's leader, the former Blueshirt George Griffin, made attacks on Jews a prominent feature of his oratory. At the party's founding meeting, according to the G2 reports, he laid into the Jewish presence in the Dáil Éireann with no holds barred:

A mobile poster encouraging citizens to take direct action against Partition.

An Taoiseach's father was a *Portuguese Jew*. Erskine Childers's grandmother was a Jewess. Mr Ruttledge has Jewish connections by marriage – and 'Jew' was written all over the face of Mr Seán Lemass! Practically all the Fianna Fáil TDs are in the clutches of the Jews!

The PNP's newspaper, *Penapa*, ran to only two issues, both of which were filled with anti-semitic imagery and diatribe. In January 1941 detectives seized nearly two thousand copies, following the issue of a direction by the censor. The second number was confiscated wholesale by the authorities, and Griffin ended up in court being sued for the printing costs of both issues, his political ambitions broken. Though the membership of these far-right organisations was extremely small, a G2 report acknowledged that 'the Germans have had some success in spreading the virus of anti-Semitism in Ireland with the help of such elements as General O'Duffy's Irish Fascist Party which has adopted a Nazi-inspired "Jewish peril" line.'

The activities of groups like this may have been partly responsible for the loss of political respectability which corporatism suffered during the war. There were stories that whenever Ó Cuinneagáin himself visited branches of his movement outside Dublin they quickly shut down, disturbed by his rhetoric and totalitarian ambitions.

* * *

There were a few Irish revolutionaries who made direct links with Germany, including IRA activists from both the right and the left. Early in the war the IRA Chief of Staff, Sean Russell, and Spanish Civil War veteran and ex-prisoner of Franco, Frank Ryan, turned up by separate routes in Berlin. They became involved in a plan to travel back to Ireland to foment insurrection, in a more hopeful rerun of Roger Casement's journey to Ireland of Easter 1916. They fared no better than Casement. Russell died of a perforated ulcer while at sea and Ryan returned to Berlin, where he lived the last years of the war in isolation and ill health, an unlikely fascist collaborator. Amateur revolutionaries, such as a man from County Clare who was working in the Channel Islands when Germany invaded, got involved in plans for spying and parachute drops – often motivated as much by a desire to get home to Ireland as by political conviction. And in January 1940 the novelist Francis Stuart also made his way to Berlin, where he immersed himself in fantasies of a revolution that would be as much artistic and spiritual as economic or political.

Francis Stuart appears as a kind of parodic mirror image of Denis Johnston. Both came from middle-class Protestant backgrounds, both were moderately successful writers in the 1920s and 1930s, both left Ireland during the war (both, to some extent, because of disastrous marriages), and both engaged in radio propaganda – but for opposite sides. Stuart was completely out of sympathy with the liberal view of politics and human relations that propelled Johnston through the war. He liked to think of himself as a social rebel. He was born in Australia in 1901; his father committed suicide when he was a year old and Stuart returned with his mother to County Antrim, where he spent his youth rejecting the norms of his Protestant upper-middle-class background. At seventeen he eloped to London with, and then married, Iseult Gonne, the daughter of W. B. Yeats's recalcitrant muse Maud Gonne MacBride, and so became involved in republican activities centring around the Gonne MacBride household. By the early 1930s he had written several novels and one book of poems, which had earned him plaudits from Yeats. Imprisoned for a short while during the civil war, he dramatised himself as a perennial outsider – converting to

Catholicism despite the perceived betrayal of his family, disillusioned even with the republican organisation (though this did not prevent him from carrying a message to the Abwehr from the IRA). Stuart put his faith in what he liked to call the anarchy of the imagination, a form of extreme, antisocial, mystical romanticism. He also seemed to want to outdo Yeats, not only in netting Iseult Gonne (who had refused Yeats), but in his collaboration with fascism. In his fictionalised autobiography, *Blacklist, Section H*, he described his brief involvement with the Anti-Treaty side during the civil war, through his mother-in-law Maud Gonne, and his imprisonment by the Free State government in the early 1920s. Yet he presented his political commitment negatively, suggesting it had to do with revolutionary ambitions of a different sort:

He was embarked on a private war which he hoped might cause a few cracks in the walls erected by generations of pious and patriotic Irishmen around the national consciousness. Then perhaps the dawn of the imaginative and undogmatic mood, that he saw as the prerequisite of true revolution, might set in.

Blacklist, Section H was written during the 1960s, with all the benefits of hindsight. Many of the opinions and actions of the Stuart figure in the book are sanitised or at the very least misremembered accounts of Stuart's actual activities during the war. Yet his vision of himself as romantic outcast was not wholly retrospective. It was his impatience with 'moral righteousness' (as well as a need to earn money) which, he suggested, impelled him to leave Ireland in January 1940 and return to Berlin, where he had taught English the previous spring, and where a post at the University of Berlin was waiting for him. He was to remain in Germany for the duration of the war. It was a move, so he afterwards claimed, that put him on the side of the condemned, where the life of the imagination was sustained by the very intensity of defeat and humiliation – although in 1940, of course, it was far from clear that Germany would lose the war.

In reality Stuart's move seems to have had more to do with the ideological hotchpotch of his politics. Apart from the need for a job, Stuart stated in his broadcasts that his reason for going to Germany was that

like I daresay a good many others of us, I was heartily sick and disgusted with the old order under which we've been existing and which had come to us from the great financial powers in whose shadow we lived. If there had to be a war then I wanted to be among those people who had also had enough of the old system and who moreover claimed that they had a new and better one.

In addition he acted as courier between the IRA and the German Abwehr, delivering a message from Jim O'Donovan, an IRA operative who was attempting to strengthen ties between the IRA and German Intelligence.

Like many in Europe in the 1930s, Stuart's dismay at the spiritual dilapidation of the modern world led to disillusionment with the norms of democratic politics. English parliamentarianism had delivered precious little to Ireland, and the Free State that followed on from British rule was now hopelessly corrupt. Only the far right aspired to the requisite kind of total social renaissance. In an early memoir, *Things To Live For*, written while he was in his early thirties, at the height of the fascist rumblings in Ireland, Stuart presented himself as disillusioned with all available structures in Ireland, including marriage; in his self-dramatisation he lives the life of the gambler, and political, social, and imaginative outcast. Stuart's alter ego despises the 'spirit of liberal democracy':

Democracy is the ideal of those whose lives as individuals are failures and who, feeling their own futility, take refuge in the mass and become arrogant in the herd. The productive worker, who takes pride in his work and exults in it, is never democratic because he feels no need for this refuge. He stands alone. He does not believe in the rule of the majority because he does not feel himself to be one of the majority.

Stuart's memoir merges familiar anti-democratic impulses with his own brand of fervid Catholic mysticism. At one point the book relates an unusual meeting which took place, so Stuart claims, in a large country house in County Meath in the autumn of 1933:

The small man in the centre was an ex-officer. He was in the midst of formulating a plan for establishing an independent Irish Catholic Monarchy. He was a complete reactionary. As such he attracted me. He believed in the complete isolation of Ireland from Europe and from all the so-called world tendencies and trends. The cause that he had at heart was of course a completely hopeless one. We were waiting, with his 'aide-de-camp' and pilot, for he always flew everywhere, the arrival from Dublin of the youth who had been chosen for the projected throne.

Towards evening the car arrived. I went out on to the stone steps. A priest stepped out first followed by the pretender, a young peasant of magnificent physique.

The priest, who I knew slightly, shook hands with me while the youth stood shyly beside the car. The priest called him and introduced him to me. He had vividly blue eyes in a lean brown face and close clipped hair of a deep gold. I brought them into the large room where the other three were already on their feet.

The leader of this extraordinary movement took the young peasant into a corner by the window and began to talk to him with his back turned to us. A maid came in with a lamp and started to lay a table for tea. I offered the priest a drink.

'No. Many thanks. I don't drink,' he said smiling. He was quite young too with grey eyes set wide apart and very long lashes. It was he who had suggested my own presence on this 'council' because of a novel I had written called *Pigeon Irish*. That book had raised considerable controversy. One writer to an English daily had called it, 'A piece of unpardonable impertinence to suggest that Ireland could become the saviour of Europe' and so on.

'Indeed,' the priest now said to me, 'that book of yours was in a sense instrumental in originating this idea of ours.'

'It must be the first time,' I said, 'that a novel has ever had a part in king-making.'

Keen, as always, to showcase his own reckless, maverick nature, Stuart juxtaposes the conversation in the castle with a perilous, irresponsible night flight in the ex-officer's plane. Unable to see where to land, he brings the plane down safely, thanks simply to luck. Stuart loved to cultivate his image as an inveterate risk-taker, obsessed with betting on horses, ready for any kind of chance. He pictured gambling as a way of cocking a snook at the established financial system. And these are all elements that feature in the bizarre novel which attracted the attention of the ultra-Catholic nationalist fringe.

Pigeon Irish must rank as one of the strangest books to be written about Ireland during the last century. Published in 1932, it is set in an imaginary future in the wake of a successful war for the Irish Republic. Masters of a wholly free and self-governing nation, Ireland's rulers nonetheless mistake the trappings of 'outward independence' for the 'continuance of the deep supremacy of the Irish spirit'. They fail to nurture the true soul of Irishness and attempt instead to jockey for power among the materialist nations of the world. The country becomes embroiled in a massive, mechanised European war, fighting on the side of the Allies, who are losing the battle against a rationalised enemy. Ireland thus faces the imminent possibility of occupation by a hostile power. The action of the novel takes place over three days, as the central characters (one a mystical figure based on St

Catherine of Siena) consider how to respond to the threat of occupation, how to protect 'this island the last stronghold of Western Culture against the expansion of over-civilisation'. Their aim is to set up communes in the countryside which will act as a second ark, where 'Ireland's destiny as the saviour of humanity' can be upheld:

Malone was smiling. 'Irish conservations in the modern world. You'd have a street of turf commission agents, public houses, and convents. And outside the model town you could wall off a bit of mountain and bog with a few mud cottages, a round tower and a race course.'

'You're about right, Malone,' I said. 'You've got the externals pretty right. But what you haven't got clear is the unique mentality that only thrives on these contrasts.'

As if this weren't odd enough (and oddly ironic, given Stuart's subsequent choices when war against a 'rationalised' society did come), the novel's subplot tells of the adventures of three pigeons (who converse with each other in Pigeon Irish, a soundless, intuitive speech), used to carry messages to and from the battlefields in Europe. These pigeons, with their instinctive connection to the past, and the dove sent out from the ark, embody all that would be lost in an Ireland given up to the floodtide of the new Europe.

On 13 January 1943, any Irish listeners to the German propaganda station would have heard Stuart refer to the book he had published more than ten years previously:

Let us in Ireland be true to the great tradition behind us. I mean the tradition above all of taking some hold on truth in the midst of untruth and chaos. We did it in the Dark Ages and we must do it again. Over ten years ago I wrote a book called *Pigeon Irish* in which I foresaw the coming war and the part we would have to play in it, and although a few of the outward facts are different I still see our part very much as I saw it then. It is to keep to true and lasting values in the face of the war hysteria and diversion of truth and hypocrisy all around us. I believe that is exactly what you are doing. May you go on doing so until the end.

With its mystical resonances and visionary disclosures, its critique of the rampant materialism overtaking European society, it's easy to see why the plot of *Pigeon Irish* might appeal to certain sections of Irish Catholicism. Ireland's duty was to keep out of the fray, preserving something uniquely precious for civilisation – to be the ark of European spirituality. Given the pagan, nordic, anti-Christian tenor of Nazi ideology, it might seem strange that Stuart, from this starting point, was able

373

to make the leap to Hitlerian notions of Europe's destiny. But in fact his pre-war views and social connections already displayed the affinities that would enable him to make Berlin his home. His mother-in-law was friendly with the German minister Hempel, who visited Laragh castle, home of Stuart and her daughter, while Francis was in Germany in April 1939. According to Garda surveillance reports, Hempel became a regular visitor to her home in Dublin during the war. One woman, Róisín Ní Mheara, who worked with and shared a flat with Stuart in Berlin, argues in her (often inaccurate) autobiography that he was sent by the German ambassador, to work officially as an English lecturer in the University, but actually as a colleague of Görtz, as the resident IRA man in Berlin. Since Stuart had very little German it was her job to assist him. The task was to set up a reliable radio link between Dublin and Berlin, so that Görtz could realise his objective: to impress upon the IRA the need to resolve the internal feud and to persuade them to pull together with de Valera himself in a united effort to free the North.

The extent of Stuart's collaboration with the Nazi regime has long been a source of controversy. Publication of transcripts of the broadcasts he made to Ireland for Irland-Redaktion between 1942 and 1944 fuelled the dispute. Stuart himself insisted that his move to Germany indicated not a pro-Nazi stance, but a neutral one. He wrote articles and books on the Irish struggle for freedom for a German audience, including a piece on de Valera for a collection of essays on *Irische Freiheitskämpfer*, and a book on Casement which concludes with praise of the new Germany. He argued that his broadcasts home were an attempt to combat the overwhelming stream of British propaganda on Irish airwaves – in effect, he was battling against fellow Irish writers such as Johnston and MacNeice. Soon after his arrival in Berlin he was asked to write some talks for transmission by Lord Haw Haw. His diary records that he contributed three scripts: 'The theme of my contributions, which I know is not exactly what either the Germans or Joyce wants, is a recollection of some historic acts of aggression on the part of the United Kingdom, similar to those which British propaganda is denouncing the Nazis for.' Stuart may have been right about what Haw Haw wanted, for he was soon dropped as his scriptwriter, but the historic aggression theme was perfect for the revamped Irland-Redaktion, then headed by another Irish folklore scholar, Hans Hartmann.

Whether openly or covertly, by bullying or persuasion, the British devoted a great deal of effort to bringing Ireland into the war. The

Germans, by contrast, perceived Irish neutrality as already serving their interests. Their broadcasts focused on encouraging Ireland to maintain its status, especially as the United States became more and more entwined in the war. The new English service from Irland-Redaktion broadcast for fifteen minutes a day, and half an hour at weekends. The programming included items on German cookery and housewifely hints from Stuart's flatmate Róisín Ní Mheara, a series on Celtic studies from Hans Hartmann, half-hour drama adaptations of Irish works, and Stuart's talks. Mahr's suggested lines of propaganda for the service were firstly historical, including 'horror propaganda of historical content', the cruelty of the English ('a nearly inexhaustible topic'), the disinheritance of the Irish, the persecution of Catholics, the struggle for Irish freedom, the contribution of the Irish to the spiritual and literary heritage of the world, Ireland's importance to America, its importance to Christianity, the courage of the Irish, and so on. He also advocated highlighting contemporary injustice in Northern Ireland, the effects of Britain's blockade on Éire, the rightness of neutrality given Ireland's experience in the past ('the Home Rule Swindle'), and the inevitable danger of bombing or invasion should neutrality be given up. These, then, were the topics Francis Stuart was asked to pursue when he began to make his broadcasts to Ireland on St Patrick's Day 1942.

Stuart's broadcasts fitted nicely into Adolf Mahr's propaganda template, touching on 'the spirit of Easter Week', Belfast as 'the Irish Danzig', 'the sacred soil of Ulster', Parnell the Uncrowned King of Ireland, and the perfidy over Home Rule. Occasionally he was handed a propaganda gift, such as when the British government planned to execute six members of the IRA for the murder of RUC Constable Patrick Murphy (five of the six were reprieved), or when IRA prisoners broke out of Crumlin Road jail in Belfast. To attacks on the 'hypocrisy' of Roosevelt, and the evils of the 'propaganda machines' of the democracies, he added frankly pro-German material, including references to the heroism of the German Sixth Army at Stalingrad, and even 'the amazing exploits of the submarines at Scapa Flow'.

The first broadcast that we can definitely say was by Stuart was heard on 17 March 1942, a St Patrick's Day special which rivalled Sean O'Faolain's on the BBC. He declared that he was 'not trying to make propaganda'. It was an assertion he returned to repeatedly, arguing that his broadcasts were not political except in that they supported Irish neutrality. But since neutrality forbade the use of the

Treaty ports to Britain, it was perceived by the Germans to be in their best interests. Indeed Stuart admits as much in *Blacklist, Section H*, where he reasons that the German authorities requested him to undertake weekly broadcasts to Ireland because they were 'afraid that America's entry into the conflict would influence Ireland to abandon her neutrality, though this seemed a very slight threat in the light of the powerful forces that the Germans had managed to line up against them'. Astutely, Stuart homed in on Irish dismay at the recent stationing of US troops in Ulster – a move against which de Valera protested – and went on to portray a small but unintimidated nation, uniquely untainted by the debasement of modern commerce. 'What a blessing it is,' he went on in his first broadcast

that we are celebrating this day at peace, not having escaped war by dishonourable and cowardly means but by refusing – as far as lay within our power – to waver from our strict and fearless neutrality. As an Ulsterman it is galling to me that a large number of foreign troops are today occupying that corner of the country. But though we have escaped the war, and I hope may be able to do so until the end without sacrificing our national integrity, we cannot nor do we desire to escape taking our share in the building of a new Europe . . . To put it plainly we have had too little contact with countries that have something to give us. We have on the other hand been surrounded by communities whose life is [based] on money and the power of money. Whether we turn to England or the United States we see the god of money . . . Ireland belongs to Europe and England does not belong to it. I believe that after this war our future should be linked with the future of Europe and no other.

Stuart started as he meant to go on. Many of the early broadcasts were taken up with propaganda on behalf of the new Europe (which, in 1942, still seemed to be on the cards), and attacks on the decadence of democracy. He portrayed the war as a conflict between the 'liberal materialism' of Anglo-American civilisation and the culture of Europe. Ireland, he frequently asserted, needed to connect culturally with Europe, rather than with Britain, and to be wary of liberal democracy as a trickery of finance capital: 'we must break from an alien social, cultural and financial system, which came to us from the great democracies and has been responsible for endless unhappiness'; 'this war is the defence of the system by which life is dominated by money'; 'for us Irish there is only one reality, our own life on our own soil free from the tyranny of money.' Sometimes he touched on his reasons for being in Germany:

I began to find out something about Hitler and the new Germany and then of course I was completely fired by enthusiasm, for here was someone who was freeing life from the money standards that dominated it almost everywhere that I had ever been, not excluding my own country; here was someone who had the vision and courage to deny financiers, politicians and bankers the right to rule. Nor did the word dictator frighten me – I saw that as it was. Our lives were dominated by a group of financial dictators and it seemed to me at least preferable to be ruled by one man whose sincerity for the welfare of his people could not be doubted than by a gang whose only concern was the market price of various commodities in the world markets. I was under no illusion as to our position in Ireland; we might have a certain political freedom but very very little social freedom, and life in Ireland was largely based on money standards just as in England and America.

The crudeness of Stuart's language suggests – though he would have hated to admit it – that, for all his pride in his own idiosyncrasy, he was swayed by propaganda he was hearing in Germany. The denunciation of international finance was staple fare of Nazi propaganda, usually seasoned with anti-semitism of the 'Jewish banks' variety. On the other hand, similar attacks on finance capital can be found in Stuart's early work, indicating a more complicated lineage. Denunciations of the injustices of high finance were common in Ireland throughout the 1930s. The control of banking and credit was seen as the cornerstone of Empire by groups as various as left-wing elements of the IRA, theorists of Social Credit and Distributism, and proto-fascist cells. The fact that Pope Pius XI had condemned some of the more objectionable aspects of capitalism was fuel to the fire of those arguing for a new form of social justice based on Christian principles: the Pope's endorsement made it possible to express anti-capitalist sentiments without being tarred with the brush of communism. In practical terms, this meant arguing that self-sufficiency in Ireland should also entail separation from the English (imperial) banking system. It was the link with sterling that was causing underdevelopment; Ireland's economic well-being hung on the fluctuations of the London Stock Exchange, and the profits made for their companies by Irish workers were going out of the country, with unemployment in rural areas the inevitable consequence. An influential academic at University College, Cork, Alfred O'Rahilly, a resident intellectual on the *Standard*, popularised these ideas. He proposed, on the basis of Catholic social teaching, that the money system should be dropped in favour of social credit. Amongst the Catholic hierarchy and for many poorer farmers these theories held a real attraction. The second edition of O'Rahilly's huge volume *Money* appeared in 1942; throughout the war years, social credit arguments were debated in pamphlets, journal articles and newspapers – including the weekly local papers.

There is no inevitable link between theories of social credit and fascism, of course, as present-day Credit Unions make clear. One of Stuart's radio rivals, Denis Ireland, a renegade Ulster Protestant who founded the Ulster Union Club in order to lobby for Irish unification, made the failures of the money system a major part of his argument. Ireland produced numerous pamphlets denouncing the country's status as a 'prisoner of Anglo-American financial imperialism' right the way through the war. In 1941 he brought out a booklet, *Eamon de Valera Doesn't See It Through*, made up of articles he had published during the previous two years in *The New Northman*, the *Standard* and the *New English Weekly*. His argument centred on the iniquity of 'dictation by taxation', and on the need for real economic independence as a foundation for self-sufficiency; Irishmen, he argued, were 'beginning to waken from a dream wherein green pillar-boxes, green postage-stamps, and income tax forms copied from the English but containing a few Gaelic words, appeared as the symbols of nationality, whereas they were in reality merely a convenient cover for the operation of Western Finance-Capital in its most international and dangerous form'. The provenance of Ireland's argument is not hard to discern: he is fond of quoting Ezra Pound, for example, but also Major Douglas, who had tried the social credit scheme in Alberta during the 1930s. Ireland spoke on Craobh na hAiséirí platforms, but he was also at pains to differentiate his financial theories from totalitarian doctrine. He argued that Nazism had 'inverted a sensible theory', and he looked to democracy to apply it properly.

Others of Stuart's listeners may have been less choosy. Social-credit arguments, and attacks on finance capital, were not made from a democratic standpoint by the rump of the Blueshirts, nor by other members of the Catholic extreme right, such as Joseph Hanly. Nor indeed by a section of the IRA. The war encouraged the growth of anti-semitic and openly fascist sentiment within this organisation, or at any rate within the group of republicans who remained free. Some of them, eager to make use of any link with Germany, began courting right-wing would-be despots such as O'Duffy. They seemed happy to turn a very blind eye on his Blueshirt war against republicanism ten years previously.

In Sean O'Faolain's 1940 novel, *Come Back to Erin*, the disappointed revolutionary Frankie Hannafey grandstands a version of the social-credit argument to Irish-Americans in New York, hoping to shake them from their complacent belief that Ireland's fight has been won:

The whole country is being run on the old lines. We are under the thumbs of the big bankers who are under the thumbs of London. Half our business firms are owned by Jews. Do you realise that the Irish government is still paying rent for Irish land to English landowners? Our money system is buckled tight to English gold. The whole commercial community is falling in the shadow of Manchester, Birmingham and Liverpool. The whole idea of the new bourgeois class is to make a quick turnover and squeeze what they can out of the workers and the farmers. It's not Irish. The whole blasted thing isn't Irish. It's no more free than you fellows are free of Wall Street.

'He's Red,' conclude some of the listeners, turning away, but others are not so sure.

The difficulty of disentangling right from left on this issue was part of O'Faolain's point. During the mid-1930s the IRA had moved to the right, following a schism. A group who had communist affiliations and argued they were fighting for the workers' and small farmers' republic broke away, and formed the Republican Congress. (They were championed, rhetorically at least, by Brendan Behan.) The rightward move was in part a response to Church denunciations of the red menace. Republicans wanted to distance themselves from the Irish Communist Party, however tiny it was.

But the IRA was still committed to attacks on capitalism, and arguing for a major reorganisation of society. This was to be based on the control of banking and credit, which Moss Twomey, Chief of Staff of the IRA in this period, argued was 'the cornerstone of the Imperial system'. Articles in *An Phoblacht* argued for the overthrow of capitalism, and its replacement with a system based on true Christianity; again, the influence of Pope Pius's social teaching was evident. *An Phoblacht* carried regular articles advocating theories of Social Credit and Distributism. Stuart's mother-in-law, Maud Gonne MacBride, contributed a series of articles to the paper on 'usury'. In the final issue of *Ireland Today* in 1938, in an article entitled 'Fascism, Communism and Ireland', she argued the need for Ireland to learn some social and financial lessons from the totalitarian regimes – such as a planned economy, a rigorous control of finance, population control, and self-sufficiency – in order to prise itself free from the vulture of the British Empire:

After 'the Reformation' freed England from the restraints of the Church, her alliance with the Jewish money powers and her proficiency in the unholy science of Usury enabled her to make London the centre of the Banking system, which is based on usury . . . This control of Finance has been England's great weapon in fomenting war. She lends money to the nations she wants to see fighting, to buy the arms she manufactures and to repair war devastations, reaping double profit from usury and trade and enabling her diplomacy to dominate the after-war peace treaties; prospective borrowers are in no position to dictate terms.

During the war itself this type of rhetoric became more and more prevalent in IRA propaganda. The principal publication, *War News*, liked to inveigh against the Jewish 'parasites' now running Ireland in terms which were almost indistinguishable from the language used by the Irish Friends of Germany or the People's National Party. Against this background, Stuart's convictions emerge as a warped and anti-semitic version of the right-wing Catholic conception of Ireland's distinctive destiny, of the opposition between Irish culture and the brutal commercialism of the Anglo-American world.

Stuart may have been able to count on a sympathetic hearing from some of his Irish audience, at least at first. But were they listening? Some of those who might have been most receptive to his ideas were interned and unable to hear anything, let alone a poor relay from Germany. And in fact most recollections of the Curragh camp suggest that there was very little active support for Germany amongst the internees. In later years Stuart claimed to have found very few people who had heard his broadcasts, and it is likely that even those who did tune in found his message less and less congenial. His increasingly sharp attacks on the closed-off, complacent aspects of isolationism scarcely fitted the way the populace had been encouraged to view neutrality. They mirrored instead Allied propaganda on Irish indifference. Culpable 'immunity' and indifference were staples of the Anglo-American line on neutrality by this point in the war, but Stuart took up these ideas to deplore his homeland's imperviousness to the turmoil in Europe. His broadcasts explicitly attempted to break through the indifference of his fellow countrymen, fantasising that the horror of war might somehow be the prelude to spiritual renewal. Stuart's autocratic impatience with Irish provinciality, his lambasting of his audience in ever more uninhibited terms, may well reflect something of his Anglo-Irish background. Catholic social theory proved dangerous in combination with an elitist impatience with the dull complacency of the general population. What is surprising is that such attacks should have come from someone sympathetic to the German position, for the continuing neutrality of Ireland was one of the war aims of the Third Reich.

In his broadcast of 13 February 1943, Francis Stuart commented on some of the 'good effects' that war had had:

As far as Ireland is concerned, there are several of these. To begin with . . . we are being forced to become self-supporting. I believe that this, quite apart from the war, is a very good thing. It is right and natural for a people like us, with our rich soil, to live on it; it binds us closer to it, makes us realise the preciousness of it and also does something towards giving back to country life and farming the value and importance it was losing to the modern mania of the towns and cities.

This reads like straightforward Irish Ireland rhetoric, an amalgam of de Valera's drive for self-sufficiency and championing of self-governance, with a romantic disdain for commerce and modern industry, with which the de Valera administration was also scarcely enamoured. In his more fanciful moments de Valera could sound a little like Stuart, as he did in his 1943 St Patrick's Day speech – barely a month after Stuart's broadcast – in which he extolled the virtues of a simple rural life.

But while de Valera sincerely looked forward to the realisation of his vision, the problem for Stuart was that the comfortable cocoon of country living (the Taoiseach's ideal of 'cosy homesteads') was a barrier to his message of revolution and transformation. The government's control of information was meant to prevent any upset to that rural sense of community. Each day Stuart broadcast from Germany he was engaging in a struggle with Irish censorship in order to get his message through, and to persuade his listeners to think about the war from his point of view. The battle between Stuart's incendiary creed and Irish isolation became all too easily a battle between Stuart's war and Irish indifference:

I believe that neither you nor I have the right to cut ourselves off from the storm that is raging round us no matter how much we may feel inclined to do so. Being neutral does not mean to remain unaffected by or insensitive to events that are going to determine the sort of civilisation that is going to develop in Europe.

As the radio talks continued, and the situation in Germany worsened – particularly during the bombing of Berlin, where Stuart was living – the defence of Irish neutrality became synonymous with a defence of Irish parochialism, and even the traditional goals of Irish republicanism became tinged with negative connotations of myopia and self-interest:

There is no good of saying, we want our lost provinces back, we want freedom and security and then we want to be left alone . . . No if we hope to find national fulfilment after this war, in the new world, as I believe we shall, then we must not be merely intent on taking, we must give too.

The vague image of a new, spiritual European order which Stuart, in 1942 or even 1943, could still delude himself would arise from the conflagration, reflected, of course, a perverse kind of internationalism. But it was one that still sat uneasily with the isolationist complacency he increasingly imagined in Ireland.

Stuart began by extolling Ireland's special destiny as a Catholic nation, as the ark of Europe's spirituality, and ended up attacking God and the moral order in the sub-Nietzschean tones he shared with so many other twentieth-century sympathisers of the far right. In one sense, Stuart's itinerary, however aberrant and idiosyncratic, disclosed the inconsistencies that, right from the start, had been built into notions of Ireland's special destiny. The option for neutrality in the face of the European conflict seemed, to some, to offer the very platform that was needed in order for Ireland to exercise its spiritual vocation. Stuart certainly managed to persuade himself, at first, that neutrality could be equated with a kind of imaginative openness, a vulnerability to the strivings and sufferings of the world, which the ideologically regimented parties to the conflict could not feel.

Like some religious commentators and political ideologists who remained in Ireland, Stuart freighted neutrality with more significance than it could bear. In the first instance neutrality was a pragmatic, well-nigh enforced response to the political situation, both internal and external, in which the country found itself at the end of the 1930s. Attempts to interpret it as the sign of some privileged capacity for empathy, or as the mark of the nation's superior spiritual calling, were bound to founder as the war progressed. Stuart's post-war flight into a fervid ethic of the imagination, of extreme suffering and redemption, represented, all too obviously, an effort to deny the moral dimension of the conflict and to assuage his own sense of guilt. But deep down, it also reflected the disappointment of the revolutionary fantasist that, despite its neutrality, Ireland was part of the humdrum modern world, a country more or less like any other.

11

Paying for Neutrality

In the summer of 1940 the London publishers Faber and Faber brought out a cautionary tale about 'moral surrender' – the steady, remorseless erosion of Britain's will to resist the Nazi invader. *Loss of Eden* proved a great success, and was republished the following year under the more arresting title, *If Hitler Comes*. According to the authors Douglas Brown and Christopher Serpell, the Führer did not need to come in violence. The novel imagines a gradual scaling down of British resistance, in the face of the Nazi conquest of the continent, with initial peace moves being followed by a form of union in which Britain accepts the minor role. Finally comes the German conquest – and the setting up of a protectorate along the lines of Norway or Vichy France. Britain would eventually succumb, the authors conjectured, because of war-weariness on the part of her people, combined with the 'hypocrisy and greed' of would-be quislings and profiteers eager to make money out of defeat. But further encouragement for Nazi expansion across the Channel is offered by the Irish-born leader of Britain's own fascist organisation, the Greyshirts:

His motives in founding and organising the League of Britons are equally obscure. Those who regarded Rosse as endowed with a Satanic hatred of England and an equally Satanic ingenuity in accomplishing her ruin believe that the League of Britons was founded with the deliberate intention of building a bridge to the German domination of England, and that it was an IRA conception no less murderous and devastating than a bomb.

Violent, anti-semitic, rebellious, Rosse crystallised English prejudices about the Irish. Realising too late his mistake in welcoming the Nazis, he retreats to the hills in Ireland to foment rebellion against the New Order in Britain. Though his cooperation with the invader turns out in some respects to have purer motives than that of many Britons, either out for personal gain or simply too fearful to resist occupation, it is collaboration nonetheless. It was this charge of collaboration, in more and less explicit forms, which was to be levelled repeatedly against the Irish as the war drew to its end.

With the approach of D-Day the tension between Ireland and the Allies was ratcheted up once more. To stem potentially disastrous security leaks, procedures had to be tightened right across the board, and the British authorities were forced to pay attention to the threat posed by Irish workers in British and Northern Ireland factories. Travel between Britain and Ireland was suspended on 15 March 1944, for fear that information might be carried along with less dangerous contraband, though a rueful MI5 report pointed out that the Services Department continued to allow Irish nationals to go on leave back home. Civilians, too, could still be granted compassionate leave. The previous day Churchill had put a sting in the tail of his announcement of the travel ban, in a statement to the House of Commons, describing it as

the first step in a policy designed to isolate Great Britain from Southern Ireland and also to isolate Southern Ireland from the outer world during the critical period which is now approaching. I need scarcely say how painful it is to us to take such measures in view of the large numbers of Irishmen who are fighting so bravely in our armed forces and the many deeds of personal heroism by which they have kept alive the martial honour of the Irish race.

Churchill's rhetoric evoked the confrontation between Ireland and the Allies in the early war years, with an embattled Britain being forced to take measures against its irresponsible and treacherous neighbour. In fact the security cooperation between the two states was by this point well established. After a meeting between Irish and British officials in London in April 1944 a series of measures required by military security were agreed. These included clamping down on sea and air routes, so that Aer Lingus flights were suspended, as were sailings by Irish ships to Portugal and Spain: the ships were chartered by the British, who collected and delivered Iberian cargoes to Dublin. All public telephone services between Britain and Ireland were to be suspended, and an effort was made to tighten up diplomatic channels to prevent leaks. Once more, however, the idea of closing the border between the six and the twenty-six counties was abandoned as hopeless.

Ostensibly, the travel ban was to stop information getting through – by accident or design – to Axis spy networks. There were separate fears about the German (and according to the United States, the Japanese) legations in Dublin. By the middle of 1943 the possibility of landing on the continent was being widely canvassed, and the Axis diplomats in the Irish capital were a potential security threat. The German legation had possessed a wireless transmission set since the beginning of the war, but it hadn't been used (or at least detected) since February 1942, under threat of its immediate confiscation. At that point the Irish authorities had stepped up their efforts to ensure that neutrality could not be used to harm Britain, following angry British suggestions that weather information transmitted by the German radio had helped the battleships *Scharnhorst* and *Gneisenau* to break through St George's Channel. The Irish decided on the compromise formulation of allowing the legation to hang on to the radio while warning them not to try to use it. Eighteen months later, in view of the preparations for Operation Overlord, British and Irish security services agreed that the Irish government should ask Hempel to hand the set over. In the event, the sudden parachute landing from German aircraft of two Irish nationals (John Francis O'Reilly and John Kenny) in County Clare, in December 1943, gave the Irish authorities the excuse they needed to demand the surrender of the legation's transmitter. O'Reilly and Kenny were arrested within a day of landing, but the wireless they were carrying with them heightened fears of German espionage. The legation transmitter was deposited in a Munster and Leinster Bank safe on 21 December 1943.

But the United States was not satisfied. In February 1944 David Gray, the US ambassador, drafted a request for the expulsion of Axis missions, which became known as the 'American Note'. Considering 'the opportunity for highly organised espionage which the geographical position of Ireland affords the Axis and denies the United States', the country was neutral only in name, he argued. State policy favoured the Axis powers.

We should be lacking candour if we did not state our hope that this action will take the form of severance of all diplomatic relations between Ireland and these two countries. You will, of course, readily understand the compelling reasons why we ask, as an absolute minimum, the removal of these Axis representatives, whose presence in Ireland must inevitably be regarded as constituting a danger to the lives of American soldiers and to the success of Allied military operations.

Gray privately called the legations 'Axis spy missions' and argued that, considering how easy it was to get information in Dublin about troop movements north of the border, the American forces 'might just as well be in Vichy France'. Irish security services were confident that there was very little opportunity for passing on sensitive information. But even if he had felt the force of the security argument, it would have been impossible for de Valera to comply with Gray's request without tearing up five years of work. To break off diplomatic relations with either side, especially under duress from the other, would have sounded the death knell of neutrality. It appeared that the Americans were simply trying to discredit de Valera by asking from him what they knew he could not give if he wished to maintain his independent neutral policy.

There had been several approaches to de Valera during the war, urging him to side with the Allies. The most urgent was probably Churchill's 1940 offer of Irish unity (an offer de Valera did not believe would be delivered); the most dramatic – and cryptic – his famous telegram to the Irish leader the day after Pearl Harbor. The Prime Minister's communication read: 'Now is your chance. Now or never. "A Nation Once Again." Am very ready to meet you at any time.' If this was a way of luring the Taoiseach with the prospect of his country's unification, de Valera evidently felt the risks too great, and popular support for neutrality too overwhelming, to take the offer seriously. This further, fruitless US approach, made with British backing, was followed up in the closing months of the war by a US request for de Valera not to give asylum to fleeing Axis war criminals. De Valera refused to give any assurances on this, and in doing so became the only neutral to do so – even Portugal at least conceded verbally. His stand won praise from an unlikely quarter. George Bernard Shaw, who had earlier lambasted Éire over the ports, argued that every neutral should have taken de Valera's stand. Every country should reserve the right to give asylum, when 'justice, charity, or the honour or interest of the nation' required it.

Since many of the US troops who were to land in France were stationed in Northern Ireland, paramount importance was attached to the prevention of leaks across the United Kingdom's only land border. Nonetheless, given the existing level of security cooperation, it was hard to avoid the impression that Gray engineered the crisis, with the aim of damaging relations between the two countries, and deepening the disaffection of Irish-Americans with the country back home. The ambassador had sent the note, as an MI5 report bluntly put it, 'so that it could be put on record by the Americans that the Irish Government had refused a request which might have removed a danger to the lives of American soldiers'. A year earlier, Gray had advised similar tactics in quite explicit terms:

I am sure that Mr de Valera intends to appear at the post war Peace Conference and basing his claim on the Atlantic Charter will seek the repeal of partition. We may therefore expect an intensified campaign immediately at the end of the war to mobilise British liberal sentiment and Irish and Irish-American sentiment in the US. To counteract this I should advise that great emphasis be given in the American press to Irish and Irish-American names in American casualty lists and that an intensive campaign be carried on in the American Press to point out the difficulties which Éire's neutrality creates for the Allies, especially in the maintenance of the Atlantic Patrol. The object of this should be the complete disillusionment of certain Irish and Irish-American elements with Ireland's domestic troubles, so that the American delegation to the Peace Conference could quite truthfully reply to Mr de Valera that Ireland's problems, because of Éire's neutrality, had ceased to interest anyone in America.

In effect, the United States was trying to tar the Irish with the accusation of collaboration. When the business of the note was made public in March the US press went into a frenzy. Several newspapers, including the *New York Times* and the *New York Herald Tribune*, claimed that Japan, Germany, and Italy all had extensive spy networks operating from their embassies; Irish security officials were portrayed as either incompetent, or complicit. The *Detroit News* declared the Irish to be living under a 'fascist-like' regime, one that was 'blind' and 'insulated' from the outside world, and hammered home the need 'to drive the Axis snakes from Irish shores'. Such views were replicated in Australian papers. A columnist for the *West Australian*, for example, commented on the way 'Nazis and Japs strut around the country', and claimed to have seen some of the six hundred Nazis who sported huge swastika armbands in the streets. In this new scenario, neutrality was no longer to be condemned as short-sighted, self-interested and inward-looking, but as a source of peril spreading outwards towards others. The fear that precious information would seep out now mirrored the Irish anxiety that the war would somehow work its way in.

Gray's note was greeted in Ireland with a mixture of outrage and defensiveness. Fears resurfaced of invasion by the Americans, or the imposition of economic sanctions by Britain – hadn't Churchill promised to 'isolate' Southern Ireland from the outer world? There were rumours of battleships off the coast, the army was put on high alert, and de Valera spoke out again about the need for maintaining local and national defence.

Three months later, following a defeat in the Dáil, he called an election. The result was a landslide in his favour. Fianna Fáil was comfortably returned with a majority of fourteen seats and de Valera was no longer obliged to form a minority government. This could only be taken as the expression of widespread popular support for his defence of Irish neutrality, in face of what was resented as American and British bullying. A piece in the *Irish Press* on 21 March 1944 captured the national mood:

In replying to questions asked him by American Press representatives some days ago, Mr Robert Brennan . . . mentioned that he had recently been called to the State Department to explain a report from Ireland that 3000 Japanese had landed there and were living in disguise. He replied: 'Is there no limit to the credulity of Americans?'

On hearing the story, the first questions an Irishman would have asked are: Where did those Japanese come from? – how was the influx concealed in a country whose total Japanese population numbers 47 – and if it comes to that how *do* you disguise a Japanese as an Irishman? But nobody on the American side seems to have been grown-up enough to ask those questions. These are not the only fantastic tales that have been spread about us on the 'other side'. We can recall quite a few. In the early days of the war we were supplying German submarines with petrol, night, noon and morning – until it was suddenly discovered by the authors of the fiction that submarines did not burn petrol at all. The fable mongers were in no way embarrassed. For the next story was that our fishermen brought fresh vegetables and fruit far out to sea to supply the submarines, which, of course, came to the surface and risked destruction for those succulent Irish cabbages. When this story proved too thin to deceive anybody, it was followed by a circumstantial account of how German U-boat officers (gold braid and all) and their crews were being entertained royally at our seaside hotels – no doubt having hitched their submarines in the meantime to the nearest lighthouse! This story went quite well for a time until suddenly someone thought of asking the British if they thought it was true – then it vanished.

The author, clearly getting into his stride, went on to enumerate stories of the lights of Dublin guiding German bombers to British cities, of Axis legation staffs numbering hundreds, and of military secrets being sent out in diplomatic bags or transmitted over secret wirelesses. These wilful attempts to misrepresent the situation in Ireland were infuriating not only to those in the inner circles of government, who knew that United States officials were well aware of the Irish cooperation over security and intelligence. Even for those not in the know about the high-level assistance, these unjust slights on Irish neutrality simply increased defensiveness about the policy.

* * *

The crisis provoked by the 'American Note', and the intensification of security fears until after the Normandy landings in June 1944, reflected genuine concern that Ireland's stance should do nothing to hinder or damage the Allied military campaign. The target had moved on from the need for the ports in the Atlantic Battle, but the complaints about espionage and the threat to 'isolate' Ireland continued the line that Irish neutrality was endangering the lives of the Allies. The implication yet again was that the policy of neutrality was an immoral one.

As the war in Europe ended, several events occurred in quick succession which seemed to confirm this view. Adolf Hitler was reported dead on 1 May; the following day de Valera, ignoring advice from several of his colleagues, visited the home of the German Envoy to Ireland to offer his condolences. Allied attempts to discredit de Valera paled in comparison with this. No other action by the neutral government during the war did more to harm de Valera's reputation or to bring his policy into disrepute. It is still the best-known event in Ireland's wartime history, and the most infamous. Hempel himself was apparently bewildered by the visit, many of de Valera's supporters were very unhappy, and the Allies were predictably outraged. In a letter to Robert Brennan in Washington, de Valera explained the visit as merely correct diplomatic procedure:

I could have had a diplomatic illness but, as you know, I would scorn that sort of thing . . . So long as we retained our diplomatic relations with Germany, to have failed to call upon the German representative would have been an act of unpardonable discourtesy to the German nation and to Dr Hempel himself. During the whole of the war, Dr Hempel's conduct was irreproachable. He was always friendly and invariably correct – in marked contrast to Gray. I certainly was not going to add to his humiliation in the hour of defeat . . . It is important that it should never be inferred that these formal acts imply the passing of any judgements good or bad.

Despite the barrage of criticism de Valera did not admit to regretting his action. Later in the Dáil, in response to jeers from Dillon, he again insisted that his action was 'in accordance with procedure', and that he had not expressed sympathy with the dead leader. It was a normal and necessary action for any neutral – and those who made a meal out of it were simply intent on maligning and misrepresenting the country.

While foreign commentators described the visit as evidence of 'neutrality gone mad', de Valera clearly felt it important not to be seen as climbing on the Allied bandwagon in their final victorious weeks. His use of the language of defeat and humiliation suggests that he was still thinking of the war as a war of equal adversaries. Or rather, he believed that he must maintain his public position in relation to the belligerents on the basis that this was a war of political equals, whatever he may have privately thought about the stakes in that war.

A week later celebrations of VE day were marred in Dublin when a commotion occurred outside Trinity College (traditionally supportive of Britain). Some of the students climbed onto the roof of the College and ran up the British, Soviet, Free French, and Irish flags on the flag-pole. Censored reports explained that bystanders (who included the future Taoiseach Charles Haughey) 'took exception to the position of the Éire flag', which was on the bottom. A riot ensued as the students appeared to burn the flag, though the burning was suppressed in reports, one of which added in tantalising code: 'There were cheers and catcalls from various elements as youths made attempts to snatch emblems from the coat lapels of some passers by.' After the censorship was lifted, the *Cork Examiner* described these emblems as swastika badges, but they may have been Aiséirí symbols. On the evening of 7 May, Aiséirí militants were heard yelling 'Give us the West Britons' and threatening 'those brats in Trinity College'.

Meanwhile, stones were thrown through the windows of the American legation, the seat of the British Representative in Dublin, and the French restaurant Jammet's; a Union Jack was burned in Cork, and a swastika flag flown in Galway, though none of these events was properly reported until the censorship was lifted on 11 May. On 9 May, Trinity College students attempted to hold a debate on the motion 'This House is Ashamed of the History of Ireland'. De Valera's refusal to reach agreement on denying asylum to war criminals, his condolences on the Führer's death, the stone-throwing and disturbances, were brought together in a question posed in the House of Commons a few days later: 'Is de Valera harbouring Hitler?' A year after the crisis over the removal of Axis diplomats, Ireland found itself accused of acting as a haven for the worst of war criminals.

It would be too much to follow this irate British MP in assuming the disturbances disclosed an underlying Irish support for Germany and fascism. But the rioting and displays of partisanship do suggest that the end of the war took the lid off feelings that had been suppressed under neutrality, and masked by the censorship. Indeed one way of interpreting these events was as a justification of the strict enforcement of censorship. If these were the currents bubbling under the surface of Irish society, the government had been right to suppress partisan reporting, in the interests of civil order. Or so one argument went.

Predictably, British public opinion allowed itself free rein in the first weeks after VE day, fulminating against an Irish neutrality which was portrayed as tantamount to support for Germany. Churchill himself seemed to give sanction to these attacks by his criticism of de Valera's stance, broadcast on British radio on 13 May. He pulled few punches, as he portrayed his neighbour's 'shame', and vented his anger over the refusal of access to Ireland's ports and airfields:

This was indeed a deadly moment in our life, and if it had not been for the loyalty and friendship of Northern Ireland, we should have been forced to come to close quarters with Mr de Valera, or perish for ever from the earth.

However, with a restraint and poise to which, I venture to say, history will find few parallels, His Majesty's Government never laid a violent hand on them, though at times it would have been quite easy and natural, and we left the de Valera Government to frolic with the German and later with the Japanese representatives to their heart's content.

The Irish response to accusations of treachery was strident and confused in about equal parts. De Valera's reply defended the right of small nations to go their own way, and pointed out that violation of Irish neutrality because of need for the ports 'would mean that Britain's necessity would become a moral code and that when this necessity became sufficiently great, other people's rights were not to count'. He continued:

Mr Churchill is proud of Britain's stand alone, after France had fallen and before America entered the war.

Could he not find in his heart, the generosity to acknowledge that there is a small nation that stood alone, not for one year or two, but for several hundred years against aggression; that endured spoliations, famines, massacres in endless succession; that was clubbed many times into insensibility, but that each time on returning consciousness, took up the fight anew; a small nation that could never be got to accept defeat and has never surrendered her soul?

The Taoiseach's rejoinder was generally hailed as a brilliant and restrained piece of oratory. It sold on the streets of Dublin in broadsheet form. Even the *Irish Times* proposed that Churchill had gone 'too far' in suggesting that the Irish had 'frolicked' with the Germans. As so often during the war, Churchill had sought to make neutrality a moral issue, implying a culpable frivolity on the part of the Irish in the face of depotism. De Valera refused to take the bait, turning back instead on his opposite number the political language of sovereignty, national pride and self-defence.

'Listen and Learn'
Cartoon on the front cover of *Dublin Opinion*, June 1945.

IRELAND : " Thank you, Dev."

Dublin Opinion, June 1945.

Nonetheless, it was far from easy to hold the moral questions at bay, especially as more and more news came from Europe about the nature of the Nazi regime and its treatment of prisoners. De Valera's visit to the German Envoy took place two weeks after news broke of the liberation of Buchenwald, on 11 April, and Bergen-Belsen, on 15 April. There was a great deal of press and radio news coverage of the camps in Britain and throughout Europe, including a famous report by Ed Murrow from Buchenwald on 15 April. Ten days later, parties of British and American politicians and international observers visited the camps, generating more pictures and more commentary. People faced the sudden realisation that their worst fears about Germany's persecution of the Jews lagged far behind the reality. And for those unsympathetic to Ireland's policy, neutrality became synonymous with turning a blind eye to persecution and mass murder. Neutrality meant sympathy with Nazism, and Nazism in its worst aspect. Hostile British and American public opinion had its prejudices confirmed by de Valera's visit. Even for de Valera's supporters, it was hard to understand why he thought the demands of diplomatic protocol outweighed the wish to protest against gross inhumanity. There were letters to the papers describing the visit as a 'moral horror' – though there were others complaining that the country which had supported Chamberlain's appeasement had no right to lecture Ireland on 'standards of international morality'. Sir John Maffey wrote on 21 May:

In the public mind, Mr de Valera's condolences gradually took on a smear of turpitude, and for the first time, and at a critical time, a sense of disgust slowly manifested itself and a growing feeling that Mr de Valera had blundered into a clash with the ideals of decency and right and was leading away from realities.

The response in Ireland grew more uneasy, and more polarised, when ten days after the visit wartime censorship was lifted. This allowed a far more in-depth analysis of the general situation in Europe, including reports of the destruction of cities, the numbers of displaced persons, and problems of starvation across the continent. And it also finally allowed news of Germany's persecution of the Jews and the horror of the concentration camps to be reported through the Irish media.

De Valera and his government had been aware of at least some aspects of the persecution of the Jews since the middle of the war. In December 1942 the Allies had issued a strongly worded resolution confirming the Nazi persecution of the Jews. The statement included details of the deportations from the Warsaw Ghetto, and estimated the death of a million Jews in Poland. It also made public the transfer of Jews from occupied countries to Poland. Anthony Eden read the resolution out in Westminster and it received very wide publicity in the press and on air. In April 1943 British and American officials met at the Bermuda Conference to try to work out ways of rescuing Jewish refugees – this again provided publicity for the crisis although the Conference itself came up with almost nothing in the way of immediate relief.

British media focus on the Jews faded, but the Irish government also received direct requests for help. As a neutral the Irish government did not have the option of bombing the camps, aiding the Warsaw Uprising, or putting the rescue of the Jews above the war aim of unconditional surrender. Its efforts were limited to offering asylum, possibly sending food aid and – arguably – publicising the persecution. From the end of 1942 onwards, Rabbi Herzog, the former Chief Rabbi of Dublin, whom de Valera knew well, had been sending the Taoiseach frantic telegrams from Palestine, pleading for help. Herzog repeatedly begged de Valera to intercede with the German authorities, or with the Pope, in the case of Italy's threatened Jews. Much diplomatic energy was devoted to the case of some two hundred Polish refugee families, who were trapped in Vittel, in Vichy France. The Chief Rabbi urged de Valera to grant them entry visas and temporary residence permits for Éire, but diplomatic representations to both the Vichy and the Berlin governments proved fruitless, and the families were eventually shipped east to their deaths. In another move towards the end of the war, de Valera agreed, at the request of David Gray, to admit five hundred orphaned Jewish children as refugees, with the possibility of another five hundred after the war. But there was no question, at that late stage, of the German authorities allowing any such thing to happen. All in all, possibly as few as sixty Jewish refugees came to Ireland as a result of the war.

Memos on immigration from Military Intelligence, as well as the Department of Foreign Affairs and the Department of Justice, written from the mid-1930s onwards – when Germany passed the Nuremberg laws and the refugee question became more urgent – make depressing reading. The Irish constitution and the policies of the Irish government offered no institutional foothold for anti-semitism, and certainly nothing to vie with the officially endorsed racism and xenophobia to be found in some continental countries. Yet the Irish governmental response displayed an exaggerated fear that admission of aliens would cause political difficulties, giving rise to prejudice and tension, as if Jews themselves were responsible for their persecution. Suspicions were also voiced concerning the dual allegiance of Jews – to international Jewry and to Ireland. The working assumption was that Jews would not become assimilated, and that disruption, discontent, disturbance of the peace would ensue if Ireland admitted large numbers of aliens. These typical immigration fears were reproduced in Britain, and many other countries. Given the background of the economic depression of the 1930s, concerns about unemployment were also added to the mix. Jewish refugees were usually only allowed in when they were seen as bringing obvious economic benefits: Jewish entrepreneurs opened hat factories in Mayo and Galway, for example, and a Jewish ribbon factory was established in County Longford. Essentially the policy towards refugees, based on national self-interest, was illiberal and ungenerous – it took scant regard of humanitarian considerations. Jews were treated as potentially troublesome aliens rather than as people suffering from persecution. Policy towards them was determined more by fear of civil unrest – and anti-semitism and xenophobia did increase during the war – than by charitable concern.

There was explicit anti-semitism among some ultra-nationalists and a few political renegades (including one or two members of the Dáil), occasionally expressed as the feeling that all the fuss about the Jews was distracting attention from the persecution of the Irish. But in general Irish policy towards Jewish refugees shared far too much with the British attitude. Granted that few rescue missions could realistically be mounted by the middle of the war, especially from Ireland, more often than not de Valera's attempts to provide humanitarian assistance during the war took their cue from Allied priorities. For example in 1943 he attempted to send a boatload of food to ease the situation in Greece, in line with Allied actions. The government tried to send food aid to India, and to help refugees in Spain, but there was no direct Red Cross help to the Jews.

Over and above this assortment of prejudices and inhibitions, however, the crucial factor which lamed the humanitarian response was the inability to contemplate, let alone comprehend, the true meaning and scale of the Jewish persecution until it was far too late. It is tempting to put this down, at least in part, to the censorship. Though the authorities may have regarded the censorship as simply excluding propagandist, truth-distorting views, the reality was that a reporting of the war denuded of all commentary, stripped of all specific reference to atrocity, produced its own kind of falsehood. Nowhere was this more evident than in the gap between what was known through diplomatic channels, and ordinary citizens' lack of information about the Jewish catastrophe. Despite de Valera's full knowledge, and the efforts of the Irish diplomatic service to save Jews in occupied Europe, nothing was said in public by the Irish press or Irish authorities until after the defeat of Germany. Nothing was heard except the rumours of mass extermination camps aired on BBC radio and in American bulletins. Irish citizens were able to pick up foreign reports on radio, but they heard nothing from their own neutral authorities, and even after the liberation of Auschwitz in early 1945, and of Belsen and Buchenwald in April and May, no official recognition of the genocide came from Irish sources. Censorship instructions meant that only general allegations contained in official statements could qualify for publication – no details of specific atrocities were allowed. From early 1943 the censorship was blocking numerous stories of Nazi criminality in Eastern Europe.

As the Minister responsible for squashing these stories, Aiken may have believed that they were exaggerated for the sake of propaganda, though that doesn't completely square with de Valera's efforts to help certain groups of Jews escape from Italy and France. He may also have sincerely believed that reporting atrocity stories was bound to disrupt the carefully balanced neutral consensus, although if even some of the reports were true this objective conflicted with a responsibility to disclose information about the abuse of human rights. Arguably the condemnation of Nazi persecution by a neutral could have carried more weight than criticisms of Germany coming from Allied propaganda, and Irish policy is vulnerable to the charge that officials remained silent in order to keep Germany sweet.

But not all blame can be put at the foot of the censorship. Lack of active and proportionate concern about the fate of the Jews was not just about ignorance. Some channels of information remained open. In addition to English newspapers, and the reports on the BBC, Irish nationals had news from relatives in Britain, as well as from Irish volunteers in the army, some of whom saw direct evidence of the camps in Europe. As Bernard Wasserstein has argued of the response to the genocide in Britain, it was not ignorance but disbelief which overshadowed the rescue efforts of the Allies. People were sceptical because they had been taken in once before, by the anti-German atrocity propaganda from the First World War. There was a tendency to assume that reports that came from Jewish sources couldn't be trusted – they were bound to exaggerate. After the Russian advance into Poland in July 1944, further evidence of the systematic plan to annihilate European Jewry became available in the West, but much of the evidence was still dismissed as Russian propaganda. The scepticism in

Ireland was scarcely surprising given the disbelief with which many in Britain and the rest of Europe greeted the reports. Even those who witnessed atrocities were often unable to process what they had seen, and downplayed their significance. Inevitably, the relentless manipulation of news in wartime Britain created a culture of suspicion. The intelligentsia thought themselves too smart to be taken in by the details of outrages. As an exasperated George Orwell declared in 1943, 'unfortunately the truth about atrocities is far worse than that they are lied about and made into propaganda. The truth is that they happen.' Wasserstein argues of Britain that 'It was only with the liberation of the concentration camps in western Germany by British and American troops in the final weeks of the war that there was a dawning realisation in Britain of the magnitude of the catastrophe which had befallen European Jewry.'

But Ireland's six years of neutral policy, with its official equidistance from the warring parties, made it all the harder for Irish people to accept the facts of Nazi persecution and extermination, even when the eye-witness reports and newsreels started to appear at the end of the war. Even after 11 May, when censorship was lifted, there was remarkably little coverage of the camps in Irish papers – and much of what did appear was sceptical. (There was far more discussion on the letters pages than in the news or editorials.) But reports from the camps were broadcast on radio, and within a month uncensored newsreels were being shown at cinemas around the country. Censorship (and the lifting of censorship as news of the camps broke) helped to focus the question of Irish attitudes to the Nazi regime, particularly for hostile observers; it was not the ultimate cause of those attitudes.

The response to reports of the camps was at first overwhelmingly dubious. Distrust of any stories coming out of Communist Russia coloured this reception, as well as a belief that the horrors of reports from the camps must be the exaggerations of British propaganda. Britain was the traditional enemy, and even the evidence of unheard-of barbarity had to contend with the sceptical effects of this mindset. On 14 May, a letter appeared in the *Irish Times* expressing dismay at the general scepticism towards the articles and photographs then being published in all the leading British papers, detailing atrocities which had occurred in the concentration camps of Europe. The letter writer urged that an Irish commission should be appointed to tour the camps, to verify the stories from a 'neutral' standpoint. On 16 May came the following reply from another correspondent:

The reason for this suggestion is obscure, but if we are to celebrate the removal of the censorship by washing other countries' dirty linen in our public press, why not send the party of ghouls to India, China, Palestine or Russia? In case their findings make us feel self-righteous, our own history could be so presented as to balance the picture. And what a picture! We should see, with all the gruesome details, to what depths of savagery any nation can descend.

Now that the war is over, there is a real task before us – that of building the peace. We now need to strengthen our confidence in human nature, not undermine the last tottering ruins of it. It would be more encouraging at this point to be shown the great things of which mankind is still capable; there is already too much evidence of its failings.

Outside of Ireland too there was concern about the use of the camps as propaganda. The corpses of victims at Buchenwald were left to rot for a further ten days after the liberation, rather than being buried before the international observers arrived; there were complaints that food and medical aid for the survivors should have been given greater priority. The familiar point in the *Irish Times* letter that it would be invidious to single out one form of inhumanity also had an obvious cogency. But it was overshadowed by regret at the consequences of lifting the censorship. This wish to hold back stories of the horrors of war was echoed by numerous journalists and commentators in the final weeks of the conflict. It was like a last attempt to maintain the protective 'immunity' from the war which had been one result of the censorship. It was the kind of attitude that seemed to confirm the complaints of people as far apart politically as Elizabeth Bowen and Francis Stuart: that neutrality had bred insensitivity and complacency.

The dismissive attitude towards coverage of the camps stemmed in part from the long-running battle with Allied propaganda over neutrality. It was not simply that it was difficult suddenly to admit publicly that the Allied war had been just, but that it was hard to acknowledge that Allied propaganda was 'true' – because Ireland had also been a target of that propaganda. An *Irish Press* editorial on 17 May 1945 blamed Churchill's attack on neutrality on Anglophiles associated with the rival *Irish Times*:

Now in 1945 that little Ascendancy group which is still unreconciled to the loss of its powers and privileges has begun to fawn around the knees of the

victors, or perhaps 'grovel' might be a better term, in view of its atrocity stories and atrocity photographs. And it appears as if Mr Churchill, with his fab-
ulously false conception of Irish affairs, thought that it was to the voices of
this handful he should listen.

This statement is remarkable for several reasons, not least its tone.
Could anyone really believe at this point that British anger over Irish
neutrality was all the fault of the Anglo-Irish who had been poisoning
Churchill against the state and its policy? The accusation of a grovel-
ling reproduction of atrocity stories is also hard to understand. By the
middle of May no newspaper – not even the *Irish Times* – had yet covered the story of the camps in a proper article. The *Irish Press*, like the
Standard, the *Cork Examiner*, and numerous smaller and more local
newspapers, had made no mention at all of atrocities until this point,
bar the occasional sentence buried in the testimony of a released Allied
prisoner of war. The *Irish Press* editor felt able to comment, in a context where rumours abounded, and information was pouring in via
the radio and English papers. Nonetheless, there must surely have
been some readers who simply did not know for certain what the
atrocities were. Readers may have been equally confused by a comment the following day (18 May) in the *Standard*, which referred to
the *Irish Times* letter suggesting representatives from the Dáil should
visit the camps to verify the rumours:

We would warmly support such a search for truth – on condition that our
representatives could also visit the concentration camps and slave labour disposal centres in Poland, the Baltic and Balkan states, not to speak of Russia
itself. This one-sided condemnation of brutality does not appeal to us who are
not trained to parrotry.

A political brawl was breaking out in the press over the Nazi death
camps and their implications, yet most of the Irish public, particularly
outside Dublin, had still not had access to the evidence that the argument was all about.

This was partly due to a kind of censorship time-lag – many of the
stories from the camps had broken before the censorship was lifted.
The fact that the papers could confidently expect their readers to
know what they were talking about suggests not only that there was
general acceptance that people were listening to the BBC, if not reading the English papers. It also indicates that the negative response of
many Irish papers was because the camps had become the latest

episode in a propaganda war with external news reporting. Now, rather than simply ignoring British reports, Irish editors were able to fight back.

The lack of straightforward coverage was also due to a form of censorship conditioning. Barely a week after the censorship was lifted, no newspaper was ready to print something which six years had accustomed them to not believing. This was compounded by the disbelief common to many in Europe. Even people in a position to know, such as the pro-Allied editor of the *Irish Times*, seemed unsure of the appropriate response. Smyllie had had stories about the persecution landing on his desk for years, not to mention hearing about it on the BBC. Yet contrary to the *Irish Press* attack, the *Irish Times* had not been slavishly retailing atrocity stories. On 17 May the first article to be run on the camps was headed by a title in which the word 'Horror' was put in inverted commas. On 26 May the editor, Smyllie, writing as 'Nichevo' in 'An Irishman's Diary', explained that he needed to hear it from Denis Johnston – recently returned from covering the American advance through Germany for the BBC – before he could believe the information about the camps: 'During the last war I had been in one or two of the worst POW camps, and found when I got back that conditions had been grossly exaggerated.' Johnston, as a 'neutral' reporter, Smyllie asserted, 'has no prejudice against the Germans'.

The defensiveness stemmed, in part, from the difficulty of forming a view of the evidence concerning the camps, without constant regard to its political implications for Ireland's relationship with Britain. It was a job that was not made any easier by continuing attacks coming from Britain, and from British sympathisers, on the immorality of Ireland's wartime stance. There was a feeling that the 'West Britons' were now exploiting the end of war to get a crack at the other side. The hoisting of Union Jacks, defended by some as a celebration of the triumph over fascism, was seen by others as a deliberate provocation. The Trinity College kerfuffle provided fuel for outraged nationalists for weeks. Galway students threatened to leave the Irish students' union, Leitrim County Council passed a vote of censure, and local newspapers throughout the country engaged in heated discussion of the problem of 'elements hostile to Irish independence'. Even Hubert Butler, who had been critical of the 'xenophobia' and 'indifference' he found in neutral Ireland, wrote supporting the angry reaction against the TCD students.

There was no necessary link between irritation with the triumphalist anglophiles, who were interpreted as attacking neutrality, and lack of support for the Allies. In fact many of the local papers that complained most vociferously about the insult to the flag, Churchill's affront to neutrality, and the propaganda of the concentration camps, at the same time compiled lists of Irishmen who had shown bravery in the war. Some even ran a weekly section on the wartime experiences of local volunteers. Defensiveness over the choice of neutrality combined relatively easily with pride in the gallant Irish who had fought in the war. An editorial in the *Cork Examiner* on 15 May welcomed the fact that, with censorship lifted, 'the public will learn more about the surprisingly large number of Irishmen of all classes who were involved in the war.' Under the heading 'Irish Heroes of War', the *Irish Press* printed the Irish names that appeared in the American honours list. To some extent this was a way of getting back at people who were attacking Ireland for being lily-livered and sitting on the fence. And much of the coverage was aimed at comparing the 'bravery' of Éire's citizens favourably with that of those of the North, rather than showing support for the Allies. Nationalist border papers printed lists of local volunteers partly as a way of getting at the North for its triumphalist loyalism. But there was also genuine pride in those who had fought, and in a state policy that had both protected the country and allowed them to fight.

Throughout May the political temperature continued to rise. Legal steps were taken, and questions were raised in the Dáil, over the flying of 'foreign flags' – the occasion was a small Union Jack which had appeared in the window of a house in the town of Raphoe, though there were doubtless others around the country. On 23 May a letter from J. Riversdale-Colthurst, published in the *Irish Times*, criticised people's reluctance to acknowledge that Irish immunity from attack had been due to the bravery of British and US forces. Why shouldn't people fly flags in gratitude? 'This is not surprising', the letter continued, 'from those who seem still to plume themselves on maintaining a moral, or rather immoral neutrality as regards the major issues of the war.' Ireland's inability to acknowledge the cost of the war for the Allies was part and parcel of its failure to recognise what was at stake in the conflict.

Riversdale-Colthurst was a mathematician at the Institute for Advanced Study, but his name unfortunately echoed that of Captain

Bowen-Colthurst, who had executed four men during the 1916 Rising. Comments such as his simply confirmed the Anglo versus Irish battle. On 30 May, a letter appeared in the *Irish Times* arguing that the Irish should not have gone to fight. The war had not been about the prevention of atrocities, or the defence of democracy, but about the political balance of power:

I hope that such individual sacrifice will be prevented in the future. It is sad they should have gone forth to fight and fall, perhaps, for a cause of which they really knew so little. Their comrades at home stood ready to fight against hopeless odds for their country's right to a mind and conscience of its own; for the right to be a nation among nations. Had the occasion arisen – they would have given as good an account of themselves. It may well be . . . that their quiet readiness to resist saved the country from occupation and the lot of Denmark.

The debate revealed the deep divisions in Irish society which the censorship had attempted to smother. Even after six years of public suppression, the opinions expressed split along sadly predictable lines: national independence versus support for Britain. Those who suspected that the clamour about the morality of the Allies' fight was a cover for an arrogant identification with imperial Britain countered with an insistence on the principle of respect for independent nations. In its worst manifestations, this was simply a cover for smugness and self-satisfaction.

*   *   *

These political differences were reinforced by opposing views on the ethics of neutrality. While Allied complaints implied that neutrality was a form of collaboration by omission – refusing to help the Allies was tantamount to hindering them, and by extension the cause of democracy – the Irish response stressed the objectivity of neutrality, the fact that it lay outside the corruptions of propaganda. Louis MacNeice had traced the slippage from one argument to another. At the beginning of the war he had prized the neutral perspective possible in Ireland as a bulwark against wartime indoctrination, but later he argued that it led to culpable detachment, and indifference to the deaths in the Atlantic Battle. At the end of the war, MacNeice's BBC colleague Denis Johnston made the same accusation in relation to the deaths in the concentration camps.

By 1942 the Irish playwright had wearied of his job with the BBC in Ireland, and wearied also of his failing marriage and the time it was taking for the divorce to come through. He applied to work as a front-line reporter, and covered campaigns in North Africa, Italy and Germany in the last three years of the war. Johnston insisted that he acted as a neutral in reporting the war, indeed that only a neutral could be sufficiently detached to report 'objectively'. But faced with mounting evidence of Nazi brutality, his faith in the morality of detachment came under severe strain.

In April 1942 Johnston was sent by the BBC to join the Middle East News Division as a correspondent. His biographer Bernard Adams notes a diary entry Johnston made at the time:

Before he said his goodbyes in Dublin he carefully explained to himself why he had chosen to go: 'it is my belief in Ireland's neutrality that has so largely sent me forth. Only those who are prepared to go into this horrible thing themselves have the right to say that Ireland must stay out.'

He maintained this position on the dilemmas of partisanship and neutrality, involvement and detachment, throughout the volumes of War Field Books which he wrote during the next three years in three separate theatres of war, and which formed the basis of *Nine Rivers from Jordan*, his fictionalised autobiography. Johnston began reporting from Egypt with the 8th Army, and later covered their advance through Italy. Later still he followed the advance of the Americans through Holland and Germany. *Nine Rivers from Jordan*, published in 1953, is a highly worked-over version of his diaries, filtered through several literary genres, as well as parodies of the Catholic liturgy, Celtic myth, *Ulysses* and *Finnegans Wake*, and many other works besides. Two sections of the book appeared in *The Bell* in 1950 and 1951. But Johnston also deposited a three-volume typescript of the work in the British Library in 1946 or 1947. This typescript, entitled *Dionysia*, is anonymous (and undated). It is an extraordinary document – a mass of typescript pages, sometimes double, sometimes single-spaced, with numerous handwritten corrections, and with Johnston's own photographs pasted in, as well as staff directives, 8th Army directives, and German and British propaganda leaflets. A comparison of the typescript with both the War Field Books and *Nine Rivers from Jordan* shows that it corresponds far more closely with the 1953 text. This suggests that Johnston worked on the diaries very soon after his return from Europe in May 1945. Johnston seems to want the reader to take his text as the immediate presentation of his wartime experiences. His use of tenses, and some odd jarring moments, suggest that this is writing 'as it happens'; but it is clear that a great deal of artifice has gone into the book's construction. Johnston uses composite characters, for example, and rather bizarrely, imposes the narrative structure of a novitiate in the Catholic Church, with bits of the mass and the catechism thrown in.

The artifice has to be borne in mind, for the naivety of the 'detached observer' persona Johnston adopts at the beginning of both *Dionysia* and *Nine Rivers from Jordan* stretches credulity:

Knowing what was wanted under our system of free and objective reporting, I was not going to concern myself with propaganda. I was going to describe soberly and sensibly exactly what I saw, and give the people at home the Truth, the whole Truth, and nothing but the Truth, whether unhappy or unfavourable.

He soon realises it isn't that simple. The diary records his frustration at being unable to act as an impartial voice. As a spokesperson for the BBC, Johnston wants to be a neutral and objective recorder, but he is caught in the snares of propaganda, and the journals are his response – the place he will be 'truly neutral'. Here, he says, he will tell the stories of 'good German soldiers' and of fraternisation which are supposed to be bad for morale, and to endanger the war effort. He begins his work – he would have us believe – full of idealism: 'I am not in this war as a belligerent, and so long as I remain firmly fixed in my own role and refuse to carry arms, the war can do no harm to me.'

The narrative is peppered with anecdotes belittling the earnestness of the propaganda merchants on both sides, who come off badly in comparison to the soldiers themselves. It begins from an idea of war itself as heroic and decent, and the encounters between Montgomery and Rommel in the Western desert, as Johnston reports them, seem to confirm this view. But it's an idea that becomes increasingly strained when the author returns to Europe. In Italy Johnston loses the naivety of youth, as he bemoans, 'Too many liberated adolescents thinking of war in terms of the desert and excitement and pursuit and loot. But war isn't really like that.' Yet he continues to express disgust with the way that peace is being imposed, insisting that the active fight against evil cannot help being infected by what it confronts:

I had just been given a lecture . . . on the evils of Irish neutrality – the text being that people who benefit from the blessings of justice and democracy ought to help in their preservation. Fair enough, if we really know that this is what we are fighting for. But do we know it? According to these papers, we are fighting for as vindictive and as horrible a peace as Hitler's would ever have been. What that priest on the Sangro said was true. Evil is like a Vampire. When you take arms against it and destroy it, you find in the end that you are evil too – that it is living on your own actions.

In parallel with these reflections there runs a quest narrative of sorts. It begins in the first part of the book, after Johnston finds a packet of letters from a German woman to a soldier who has been killed in the retreat from the battle of Alamein. He becomes obsessed with the woman and in April 1945, finding himself in the region of Germany from which she wrote the letters, he decides to go in search of her. He is met with stony stares, and realises that for the ordinary villagers he is not a neutral, but wearing the uniform of an invading army. The distinction between looking British and being neutral, which Johnston has struggled to maintain throughout the last three years – primarily through being unarmed – begins to break down at this point, just as he is given other reasons to feel himself a belligerent. He is advised by an American soldier to visit the local camp, which turns out to be Buchenwald. Johnston was in fact one of the first reporters to enter Buchenwald: his diary records his visit on 13 April, two days after the camp's liberation. In the novel the Johnston figure has already seen a concentration camp in Alsace – but in keeping with his status as a confirmed neutral, he has rejected the worst interpretation of the conditions there as propaganda. Buchenwald shatters his protective 'non-belligerent status':

– Here's the Block you want to see, said Quick. Don't come in if you don't want to.
   I went in. At one end lay a heap of smoking clothes amongst which a few ghouls picked and searched – for what, God only knows. As we entered the long hut the stench hit us in the face, and a queer wailing sound came to our ears. Along both sides of the shed was tier upon tier of what can only be described as shelves. And lying on these, packed tightly side by side, like knives and forks in a chest, were living creatures – some of them stirring, some of them stiff and silent, but all of them skeletons, with the skin drawn tight over their bones, with heads bulging and misshapen from emaciation, with burning eyes and sagging jaws. And as we came in, those with strength to do so turned their heads and gazed at us; and from their lips came that thin unearthly sound.

Then I realised what it was. It was meant to be cheering. They were cheering the uniform that I wore. They were cheering for the hope that it brought them.

We walked the length of the shed – and then through another one. From the shelves feeble arms rose and waved, like twigs in a breeze.

Admittedly the mechanism is rather forced: Johnston thinks he is looking for the woman, but the reality he needs to 'find' is Buchenwald. Having found it, he picks up a gun; he is no longer a non-belligerent. Some weeks later, Johnston ends his journal – in fact, ends it twice. In one version he comes across a high-ranking Nazi official who has been trying to escape into neutral Switzerland, but has reached the border too late. He offers to shoot the Nazi, partly in atonement for his own neutrality – but then hands the gun to the German, who turns it on Johnston and kills him. In another version he passes a car with a dead German in it: clearly the Nazi official who has killed himself after failing to cross the border. The awkwardness of the contrivance again reveals the depths of Johnston's dilemma. Unable to resolve the conundrum of neutrality, atrocity, guilt and moral engagement, he leaves us with a fragmented tale, with a nightmare vision of the split self.

As Johnston presents it, his support for neutrality was not shaken by the issue of the ports, or any other military consideration. Not only was neutrality the only possible option for Ireland, but he suggested it provided a valuable counterweight to the propaganda of war. The novel certainly simplifies his growing disillusionment with the politics of neutrality, but there is no reason to doubt the shattering effect of his arrival at Buchenwald. Yet however painfully personal Johnston's fiction may be, it was also intended as a sustained and ironic reflection on Ireland's neutral stance. Johnston's actual diaries and wartime notebooks reveal a slowly increasing irritation with the Irish Catholic Church's stance on the war, and with the regime of censorship. They chart a growing alienation from de Valera's version of Ireland. But very little of this finds its way into *Nine Rivers from Jordan*. Instead the Johnston character displays patterns of behaviour that echo and parody de Valera's public persona. The narrator mimics, for example, the obsessive observation of 'protocol' with regard to the Germans, and the refusal to be swayed by anything that might be regarded as propaganda. On several occasions, including the visit to the concentration camp in Alsace, this amounts to a form of censorship. More specifically, de Valera's visit to Hempel to offer condolences on the death of Hitler, and his refusal to deny asylum to war criminals, are echoed in Johnston's fictional conversation with the SS officer over war guilt, in the final pages of the journal. The discovery of Buchenwald overshadows both meetings, and Johnston's fictional 'death' at the hands of the high-ranking Nazi official suggests a profound criticism not only of his own former championing of neutrality, but of de Valera's stance. *Nine Rivers* not only questions the possibility of an objective stance on the war. It also warns that a belief in the superior virtue of impartiality can blind people to the real issues at stake. As an Irish RAF chaplain wrote sharply to the *Irish Times* in May 1945, 'folks in Ireland . . . don't understand the horror of this war because it has not been brought home to them. They have spun their own little cocoon, and have been indifferent, to a great extent, to the sufferings of humanity.'

Through the experience of the war years, neutrality had become ingrained as a central element in the Irish world-view. As Johnston learnt the hard way, though neutrality was not in itself a moral position, the lure to endow it with moral status was almost irresistible. There were hints of this in de Valera's reply to Churchill, in his portrayal of the small nation that had never surrendered her soul. Indeed, many of de Valera's actions, and much of his rhetoric, at the end of the war, can be understood as being born of his determination to preserve Ireland's independence, not to be intimidated by the prestige of Allied success. In de Valera's mind, maintaining the right to sovereign action had nothing to do with asserting a moral equivalence between the two sides. Theoretically, at least, it should have been possible to forge an independent path, while responding in appropriate terms to the appalling lessons in inhumanity the war had bequeathed. But psychologically this twin-track approach was hard to maintain. The assertion that Ireland should and would retain the right to choose its own line had somehow fused with the claim that it was not possible to choose between the two sides.

* * *

It is also possible that Johnston's criticisms were directed not just at de Valera, but at some of the attitudes he encountered when he returned to Ireland. The view that those who expatiated on the horrors of the camps were tamely repeating Allied propaganda, that condemnation of Germany's treatment of the Jews was a sign of West Britonism, persisted even when films of the camps were shown. On 11 June the *Irish*

Press carried an article by Liam MacGabhann entitled 'Buchenwald becomes Box-Office':

When pitifully emaciated bodies, skeletoned before they died, are flashed before your eyes by a carefully selective camera, the bodies being placed, unclothed, or ragged, in the positions which are most likely to arouse the emotion of revolt, two feelings begin to result – horror, and then distrust.

The horror of death by starvation is there in the film. Bodies of those who died thus are seen being removed from incinerators. Close-ups of faces of survivors show marks of starvation.

The sequences are brief, except that the camera plays long on the heaps of bodies, which, according to Mrs Tate [voiceover] have been preserved, as shown, for the MPs to see.

To one rather used to watching films for possible flaws, doubt comes creeping, not with regard to what the camera shows, but as to what was behind what the camera shows. People have taken sides on this already. But all admit that there was incredibly horrible and slow death by starvation and disease in the two places, Belsen and Buchenwald. What part the collapse played, and what part deliberate cruelty, the film cannot show.

A week later the same film critic was bemoaning the fact that the censor, having lost his emergency powers, could no longer stop pro-Allied films, especially propagandistic feature films, from being put on release:

It has not been a characteristic of the Irish race, whatever else may be said of us, to delight in kicking men when they are down. It is because of that we do not like aiding and abetting mentally the idea of the war film when it is lavished with crude and often silly propaganda. Being fair-minded and criticising the new pollution of the science of cinematography seems to leave one open to the charge of being biassed on the opposite side to that taken by Hollywood and Elstree.

In the same week the young Northern Irish novelist Benedict Kiely – who had been living in Dublin since 1941, where he had joined several groups exploring Catholic social democracy, including Father Senan's Capuchin Annual group – reviewed newsreels of the camps for the *Standard*. Like the *Irish Press* reviewer, he took the line that the camera cannot lie, but can nevertheless fail to disclose the whole truth:

A photograph of charred bodies in ovens can be very horrifying; but for men with a sceptical bias there would also be necessary a photograph of what exactly happened when the bodies went into the ovens . . .

Kiely went on to profess amazement that people should be amazed that 'horrible things can happen in times of war':

Such depravity could be found anywhere, at any time, in any nation; made more possible by the appalling philosophical unbalance of our time . . . The men who did these things were no more outside the boundaries of our common humanity than the men who suffered these things, no more than the Germans who bombed London, or the British, and Irish and Americans who bombed Berlin.

All over Europe and in the United States people were not able to take in the meaning of what they saw on the films – arguably the scenes made no sense at all if they were not understood as part of warfare. But Kiely tried to mute the horror of the images of the death camps by arguing that they were simply one more example of the atrocity in which all sides had been engaged. One implication, of course, was that non-combatant Ireland had at least escaped the moral degradation. But for Kiely this was not enough. He succumbed to the standing temptation to transform neutrality into a superior moral condition:

These films will come to your local cinema. They will inundate your local cinema. You will see fictitious films of men and women in bondage, and real pictures of men and women in prison camps; and the entertainment value of the one will be as low as the entertainment value of the other. Take them always, not with the proverbial pinch of salt, but with a detached comprehensive charity. Remember that we are still neutral, that the man who genuinely feels for the weary burden of humanity will always be neutral to horrors and stories of horror, for neutrality does not mean cowardly shrinking from the truth, but a genuine compassion for all suffering. And for heaven's sake, keep the children at home.

Irish commentators were not entirely mistaken in perceiving a propagandistic element in the reporting of atrocity, an attempt to utilise the suffering of others which might almost be regarded as a second violation of the victims. It was also true that the cognitive bullying of Allied propaganda was unlikely, in itself, to have generated simple compassion. The films themselves presented the death camps not only as witness to suffering but also as justification. On the most generous interpretation this was what critics such as MacGabhann and Kiely were trying to say, however ineptly. The values of dispassionate judgement, balance and detachment were central to a truly just response to

410

the horror. The idea that detachment from the war *should* have enabled an undiscriminating compassion for all the war's victims was voiced not just by the Catholic Church, but also by essentially secular thinkers such as Hubert Butler.

The main problem with Benedict Kiely's reasoning was not that compassion should not be extended to all the victims of war, but that he put the capacity for true empathy down to neutrality. He attempted to justify neutrality by transforming it into an ethically privileged state. He equated detachment with compassion, and argued that it was a good in itself. The refusal to be swayed hither and thither by the evidence of atrocity was evidence of a steadfast objectivity, which in turn should lead to an all-embracing sympathy. Kiely's contortions revealed the difficulty of standing by the politics of neutrality, when faced with the evidence of a cruelty so profound that it seemed no price could have been too high to prevent it. But it also showed just how strong the attachment to neutrality had become. For many Catholic thinkers the distinction between neutrality and pacifism was by now completely blurred.

One sign of this was a wry little note sent by Thomas MacGreevy to the *Irish Times* and printed on 18 May 1945. It suggested that Bach's 'Though Reviling Tongues Assail Us' should be played regularly, if not continuously, on Radio Éireann, in order to raise morale. Art in the service of national pride. It was a joke, but there was a serious edge to it. MacGreevy, who had fought in the British army during the First World War, certainly could not be dismissed as an insular scholar of the Irish Ireland persuasion. A modernist poet and art critic, he had lived in Paris, where he moved in avant-garde literary circles – he introduced his close friend Samuel Beckett to James Joyce and Eugene Jolas, editor of the modernist magazine *transition*. Later he moved to London where he made a living from his art criticism and from giving lectures at the National Gallery, until the Blitz ended this work and he returned to Dublin in 1941. There he became a leading member of the Capuchin Annual Group, and editor of the journal from 1943. Serious Catholic thinkers such as MacGreevy and Kiely, and sections of the Catholic clergy, were partly responding to negative Allied propaganda, but they also truly believed in the value of a 'neutral' perspective on the war.

This comes across clearly in MacGreevy's study of the painter Jack B. Yeats, which was published in 1945. Most of the book, which analyses Yeats's work from a self-consciously Irish perspective, had been written by 1938, when MacGreevy was living in London. But he added a postscript in April 1945, where he attempted to account for the development of Yeats's work over the last seven years. He recalled being startled by the work shown at an exhibition shortly after he arrived back in Dublin in 1941, and in particular by a new painting entitled *Tinkers' Encampment: The Blood of Abel*:

The pictorial quality of this astonishing work could be appreciated without difficulty. It was self-evidently a great masterpiece of colour and design – probably the greatest that Jack Yeats had produced to date. But what was the literary, the intellectual, content of it? What did it mean? 'Tinkers' Encampment' explained itself. The artist had always treated strollers, tinkers, gypsies and tramps of every kind, seriously, with respect. They were symbolical of the whole human odyssey. The world, after all, is no more than a temporary camping place, to which men come, and from which they go, like travelling tinkers. But *The Blood of Abel*! Obviously there was a reference to strife between brothers. But phrased like that what was the connotation? Unexpectedly I found it. I happened to open a Missal at the Gospel for Saint Stephen's Day and read:

> all the just blood that hath been shed upon the earth from the blood of Abel the just, even unto the blood of Zacharias, the son of Barachias, whom you killed between the temple and the altar. Amen, I say to you, all these things shall come upon this generation.

Upon this generation! Surely the wonderful picture was a statement about the most terrible war that had ever come upon any generation, the war that had been brought about through a succession of the most revoltingly cynical treasons against the unoffending just that history has recorded. Studying the picture more closely it seemed to lend itself fully to the suggested interpretation. All the scattered figures in the foreground are in shadow. One of them has switched on an electric torch and by the light of it one sees that the ground is red with the red of blood. A world that is dark, a world in which individual human beings are isolated from each other, a world in disorder, above all a world in which blood has been spilt. What in 1941 should that mean but the world of war that was all about us? And then, beyond the middle distance in the picture, looking past the dark foreground, there is a river. Perhaps it is the river of Time. For beyond it again there is a land of more romantic aspect, a hilly, rather Irish-looking land, indistinctly defined but brighter of atmosphere. And from between the hills, dim figures, which by the rules of perspective seem to be larger than those in the foreground, are advancing. Do they represent the men of a happier world that should replace this immediate world of darkness and spilt blood?

MacGreevy's argument here echoes Kiely – that the Irish may have a privileged position in the new world, born of having avoided the brutalising effects of war. It is easy to ridicule his description of the 'men of a happier world' advancing from the 'hilly, rather Irish-looking land', and argue that either his nationalism or his Catholicism has warped his perspective on the world. But many neutrally minded Irish were trying to articulate the country's responsibility to the 'world outside', which stemmed from having been spared. In the months that followed the end of the war in Europe, discussion in the media and in the Dáil revealed a strong sense of Ireland's humanitarian responsibility. Neutrality was not something to be boastful about, but to be thankful for. Having been spared the horrors of war, Ireland had a duty to help those less fortunate, including civilians in Germany. The Dáil voted through donations for food to help alleviate starvation in the war zones; local communities in some areas recommended meatless, tealess and milkless days in order to raise money to buy food for Europe; the Irish Red Cross set up a hospital in one of the most devastated areas of occupied France, which had been flattened during the Normandy landings.

One member of the hospital staff at Saint-Lô was the writer Samuel Beckett, who had lived in Paris for the first three years of the war. After the fall of France he had felt the effects of invasion at first hand, and witnessed the persecution of his Jewish friends: 'You simply couldn't stand by with your arms folded.' He joined a French Resistance cell, codenamed 'Gloria', and became involved in passing information to Britain. When the cell was betrayed by a Catholic priest who was working for German intelligence, Beckett escaped with his partner Suzanne to a village in the Vaucluse, where he lived for the rest of the war, earning money through farm labour and writing *Watt* 'to keep [his] hand in'. In the summer of 1945 Beckett returned to Ireland but he was uncomfortable with the atmosphere. (As he wrote in a letter, 'My friends eat saw-dust and turnips while all of Ireland safely gorges'.) He applied for the job as Red Cross hospital storekeeper partly as a way of getting back to France: because of food shortages, restrictions had been placed on resident aliens. In June 1946, long after he had left the hospital, Beckett gave a talk on Radio Éireann on the work of the Red Cross, in which he took up the issue of an Irish humanitarian perspective. While he praised both the Irish and the French who had come together through the work of reconstruction, he was also reacting to complaints in the Irish press that the French were not grateful enough for the help: 'Those who were in Saint-Lô will come home realising that they got at least as good as they gave.' Towards the end of his talk he went further, suggesting that the hospital staff in Saint-Lô 'got indeed what they could hardly give, a vision and sense of a time-honoured concept of humanity in ruins, and perhaps even an inkling of the terms in which our condition is to be thought again'.

Beckett's line here, that involvement with extremes of suffering may bring deeper understanding of the human condition, was not so very different from Paul Vincent Carroll's critique of the Irish pacifist or 'detached' stance in *The Strings Are False*, though Carroll's view of humanity itself was far less pessimistic. Beckett's argument was the opposite of the idea that the capacity for compassion and empathy could be preserved by maintaining distance from the war. It is not surprising to learn that Beckett and MacGreevy's friendship never recovered after the war. As with the relationship between Bowen and O'Faolain, which cooled on the outbreak of hostilities, it is hard to ignore the strain imposed by such divergent views on the value of 'pacifist' neutrality. In a review of MacGreevy's study of Jack Yeats, published in the *Irish Times* in August 1945 as he prepared to leave for Saint-Lô, Beckett explicitly rejected the reading of *The Blood of Abel*, arguing that Yeats's art could not be understood 'nationally'. The relevance of Yeats's work was not 'local'; it was important rather because it brought light 'to the issueless predicament of existence'. It was this predicament that Beckett was to place at the centre of his post-war writing. Much of the work on which his reputation rests, including the *Trilogy* and *En attendant Godot*, was completed in a 'frenzy of writing' in Paris between 1947 and 1950. The figures of confusion, persecution, authority, and punishment haunt this work, so that even though he rarely referred explicitly to his experience of the war, it nonetheless casts its shadow. 'I'm working with impotence, ignorance,' he later said – neither of which played well with the 'men of a happier world'.

Beckett's perspective on the lessons humanitarians could and perhaps should learn was unusual. By the end of the war the idea that neutrality meant 'being fair-minded' was almost unquestioned, except by those who identified with the Allies. This in itself was a triumph for the neutral consensus that the government had built up over the years through positive defence campaigns and the negative propaganda of media censorship, as well as more repressive measures such as internment. Fianna Fáil had in effect done a tremendous job in transforming a relatively divided post-civil-war society into one that would fairly meekly accept wartime austerities for the sake of maintaining Ireland's independent neutral stance. But one result was a society with a tendency to believe that while the rest of the world was being bullied by propaganda and misinformation, Ireland had managed to remain in privileged contact with truth.

This attitude was confirmed in more right-wing Catholic circles by a long-standing suspicion of the Soviet Union, and its role in the Alliance. No truly 'neutral' response to the picture of victors and vanquished at the end of the war could overlook the fact that the war crimes of the Soviet totalitarian regime were being ignored – thus went the conservative Catholic argument. Here neutrality seemed to have a definite edge over wartime Allied propaganda. Ever since June 1941, as part of the balance between Allied and Axis commentary on the war, the Irish press (particularly the Catholic papers) had been publishing German statements about the communist threat. As the war ended this grew more pressing. On 2 May 1945 the *Cork Examiner* quoted the comments of Germany's new leader Admiral Doenitz that the fight against Bolshevism was being hindered by the British and the Americans. This was not merely a matter of what the Soviet Union had done in the past, but of what – with British and American collusion – it was at that very moment doing to Poland. Indeed, since the fate of Poland had been the *casus belli* in the first place, her abandonment to Russian domination offered prima facie evidence that the war, rather than being a moral crusade, had been about power-mongering all along. On 15 June an editorial in the *Standard* complained:

Today the air is loud with lamentations over the black things that the coming of Peace has revealed in tortured, war-torn Europe. To an observer not likely to be moved by sudden bursts of sentiment, horror or hate or pity, there is something quaint and pathetic, something also at times slightly malevolent, in this sudden outcry.

In the *Standard*'s view, the blackest thing of all was the Soviets' takeover of Poland, which, far from raising an uproar, was being passed over in silence. 'The more the so-called "peace" progresses,' declared the *Standard*, 'the deeper will be our conviction that we were justified in holding aloof from any share of responsibility for what is even now happening.'

This scepticism of the victors' motives did not go unchallenged: 'Granted that the films on "Belsen and Buchenwald", on Italy or on Stalingrad are propaganda, they are so overwhelming that if our minds are not hermetically sealed the effect is completely horrifying and conclusive.' So Lucy Glazebrook (an American actress married since 1940 to Irish academic Vivian Mercier) noted in her review of war films for *The Bell*, in August 1945. Nonetheless, the flood of material that poured into the country from May 1945 onwards left even the most earnest and discriminating viewer confused as to what to think. The lifting of censorship allowed a sudden spate of war movies into the country, as the 'now-it-can-be-told' angle was played up by the film distributors. As Glazebrook remarked, 'VE Day, which brought Peace to the rest of Europe, was the signal for celluloid War to descend on Dublin.' Kavanagh joked along similar lines in the *Standard*: 'We have paid and are paying for our neutrality with the cinematic equivalent of blood and tears and toil and sweat.' Imaginations that had been shielded for years from the impact of moving images of violence and destruction suddenly had to process a six-year backlog all at once. As Glazebrook argued:

Dublin has seen these films in unique circumstances. For instance, many of the films are several years old, they appeared from time to time during the War, and as the films increased in intensity so did the experiences of the audiences for which they were made, so that the temperature of the films just about reflected the temperatures of the audiences. But there has been no such experience in Dublin, and audiences here, suffering from the subnormal temperature of pretty complete isolation, have been landed with no preparation into the climax of the fever. The result has been either shattering or bewildering, or both.

Glazebrook encountered one viewer who found the fictional portrayal of brutalities on the part of the Norwegian resistance, in *Commandos Strike at Dawn*, 'immoral'. In response she framed a new, post-war version of *The Bell*'s staple argument. Ireland had cut itself from the mainstream of human events – only by squarely confronting the horrors it had been spared could it ever hope to make up for lost time. The claim was by now a familiar one: political neutrality, especially when bolstered by a censorship which allowed only the skeletal reporting of world events, was bound to produce an impoverishment of the moral imagination, a crippling of spontaneous human impulses and affections. Ireland was suffering from an

THE
BELL

Edited by Sean O'Faolain

M. J. MacMANUS writes
IN DEFENCE OF
EAMON de VALERA

THOMAS DAVIS
T. W. T. DILLON

WHAT IT MEANS
TO BE A JEW
A. J. LEVENTHAL

One Shilling and Sixpence

JUNE   Vol. X. No. 3   1945

The first issue of *The Bell* after Emergency censorship was lifted, with A. J. Leventhal's uncensored article on the Jewish community in Ireland.

emotional and cultural lag from which it would not be easy to recover. O'Faolain put the case himself in July 1945:

Isolationism was the great rule of thought during those five and a half years. The censorship, for example, was obsessed in this regard. We saw no war-films; we had no correspondents abroad; unlike other neutrals, more accustomed to the uncomfortable position of small nations, our press and public men were not allowed to comment on anything that occurred . . . We took in no refugees from Europe. We virtually disowned those of our own people who went abroad to fight Nazism. Gradually we became so mathematically punctilious that, in the (obviously) last weeks of the war our External Affairs department committed the appalling correctitude of uttering public sympathy on the death of Adolf Hitler. Our Prime Minister did well, then, to reply soberly to the British Prime Minister. We had got away . . . by the skin of our teeth, and we have fully realised it. But we have paid for that escape. We have suffered by the prolonged suppression of our natural sympathies with tortured humanity, our admiration for endurance and courage; our moral judgement has been in abeyance; our intellectual interest in all the ideas and problems which the rest of the world is still straining to solve has been starved. We emerge, a little dulled, bewildered, deflated. There is a great leeway to make up, many lessons to be learnt, problems to be solved which, in those six years of silence we did not even allow ourselves to state.

*   *   *

Just as Ireland sought to assimilate and make sense of the welter of documentary, reporting, and wartime drama that the lifting of censorship had allowed in, another event jolted the balance. On 6 August 1945, the United States dropped an atomic bomb on Hiroshima, and within a few days another on Nagasaki. In the days and weeks that followed, the Irish media, and Irish citizens, attempted to process the meaning of this new weapon – for warfare, for international relations, and for the future. In the midst of day-to-day reports from Pétain's trial, the newspapers record the slow dawning of the implications of the bomb. This was an armament that could not be directed at specific targets, which allowed no calculus of civilian suffering and military gain. By the end of August reports of new deaths from radiation sickness began to filter in.

The news of the destruction of the Japanese cities was treated very differently to the reports from the death camps. It was not only that, with the lifting of censorship, the event could be reported in its full horror. It was also the fact that it had been perpetrated by one of the Allies, by a country which – despite neutrality – the Irish regarded as their natural friend. The atomic bomb seemed to have torn up all the known rules of war. For the Irish-language novelist and poet Eoghan Ó Tuairisc, who had also been involved in the Capuchin Annual group, this was the decisive event of his life as a writer. As the news broke, he was travelling back from honeymoon with his wife Una. He later recalled:

When I read the paper – I was coming home on the train – I understood – Hiroshima – bomb – . . . 70,000 people blown up . . . Something within me broke. A bad minute. I do not know if I understood or if I understand. From that bad minute sprang *The Weekend of Dermot and Grace*, and an understanding of the devilry in man.

In 'Aifreann na Marbh fuair bás ag Hiroshima, 6th Lúnasa 1945' ('Requiem Mass for those who died in Hiroshima, 6 August 1945'), a poem not published until the 1960s, Ó Tuairisc described Ireland too as guilty of the bombing. Suggesting that for all the trumpeting of neutrality, Ireland was in reality in hock to the Anglo-American alliance, he intercut scenes in Dublin and Hiroshima on the morning of the bomb. Christianity, Anglicisation, modernisation had all led to the 'indifference' to non-western lives that made the horror possible.

When the Bomb fell, even the relentlessly ironic Flann O'Brien lost his poise. After a swipe at the 'peace criminals' at Potsdam for carving up Poland, and Europe, without reference to the leaders of the countries concerned, O'Brien (writing as Myles na gCopaleen) unleashed his fury at the news of the attack:

Why should this outsize barbarity be visited on the Japanese? It cannot be because Japan was at war with America, since human rights remain intact even in war and the admirable Red Cross Society exists to see that these rights are meticulously respected. No, it must be because the Japanese are considered unpleasant folk; few of them are Knights of Columbanus, Elks or Rotarians, they are not afraid of death, they respect authority and live frugally.

A few weeks later, O'Brien was 'talking still of the abombic tomb – I *meant* atomic bomb but leave it, I am a neutron in such matters . . .' The destruction of Nagasaki and Hiroshima, O'Brien implied, can be understood by neutrals for what it truly is – as an abominable tomb, rather than a justified act of war. His macabre punning reflects once more the notion that the Irish have at least escaped the numbing effects of propaganda and political indoctrination. Furthermore, O'Brien seems to want to imply, they have escaped the poison of anti-Japanese racism, all the blather about the 'yellow peril' which helped

419

to make the mass attacks on civilians acceptable to US public opinion. Irish nationalists in the United States had jumped without compunction on the anti-Japanese bandwagon, as a way of deflecting attention from Ireland's neutrality in the fight with Germany. But in Ireland O'Brien was not the only writer to acknowledge the racist dimension of the attack. As Ó Tuairisc later recalled, 'There was no need for the bombing of Hiroshima. It was American business men who looked at the Japanese as *little yellow men . . .*'

Why was the Irish response to Hiroshima and Nagasaki so much more forthright than the reaction to the death camps? Partly, perhaps, because the atomic bomb was more recognisable: it had more continuity with what people understood about war. Fears of aerial bombardment had been rife throughout Europe since the Spanish Civil War, and the destruction of the Japanese cities realised this common dread in the most nightmarish form. For citizens who had spent the last ten years hearing ever more, learning ever more, about the destruction of cities, whether Spanish, English, German, French, or Russian, the attacks on Japan raised the terror of aerial bombing to the power of *n*. The corollary of this was an apparent difficulty in comprehending the kind of intimate, face-to-face cruelty and killing that the Germans had perpetrated on such a vast scale. It was the combination of ruthless mechanisation and personalised brutality that made events so difficult to comprehend, just as it was almost impossible to confront those faces that stared at the audience out of the newsreels. As the reviews of death-camp documentaries testified, a tacit wish kept surfacing to believe that the exterminations had not been fully deliberate, but somehow a consequence of the inhuman wartime conditions in which both inmates and their guards had found themselves. That the German state could have consciously put in motion the extermination of millions simply failed to make sense. The dropping of the atomic bomb, by contrast, could not be seen as anything other than an act of state: a monstrous, premeditated civilian massacre.

It would be foolish to deny that Hiroshima may have been experienced as helping to relieve the pressure on neutrality at the end of the war. Ireland had been tragically vindicated in its refusal to see the conflict in terms of black and white – and several letters to the papers in the aftermath of the atomic bombs attempted to draw up a balance-sheet of horror. The frequently voiced concerns that a new and ruthless world order was emerging, one in which the big powers would rule on the basis of their capacity for endless destruction, confirmed the feeling that Ireland had been right to avoid belligerence, to play no part in the machinations that had brought humanity to this frightening pass. In the mid-1950s, with Cold War antagonisms at their sharpest, Sean Keating (painter of the power station at the New York World's Fair) argued that the bombing of Japan had irreversibly confirmed the validity of pacifism:

When the Americans atom-bombed Hiroshima, destroying the just with the unjust and sterilising the survivors, they made a more brutally effective statement of the mechanistic theory of existence than any materialist has ever proposed. But it blew away for ever the clouds of sentimental humbug and hypocritical 'patriotism' from the face of war. Now sincere Christians and convinced materialists can, and must, agree to declare against war. Not to do so is to become an accessory to mass murder.

It is in such a perspective that we should set de Valera's complaints, in the autumn of 1946, that the death sentences imposed on Nazi leaders at Nuremberg were contrary to international law. For the first time in history, the victors had put the vanquished on trial, formally proclaiming not just a martial, but a moral triumph over their enemies. Despite the appalling crimes against humanity of which the political chiefs of the Third Reich were guilty, the inclusion on the charge sheet of indictments for 'launching aggressive war' could only serve to lend credence, in German eyes at least, to the idea that this was victors' justice. It was felt that hostilities were being perpetuated by other means – those of ritual public humiliation and political theatre. Stalinist participation in the judicial process, given the recent memory of the Moscow show trials, left the Allies open to accusations of employing double standards. The glossing over of the Katyn massacre, for example, was not easy to swallow, given the self-righteous demeanour of the Allies in their presentation of the war as a crusade against evil. While the United States was concerned that the trials should be seen as lawful – and there was certainly something unprecedented about the vanquished being given the chance to put their case in court – for de Valera, and for others too, they were also undeniably political.

In questioning the justice meted out to the defendants arraigned in the dock at Nuremberg, many of them undoubtedly moral monsters, de Valera demonstrated consistency, if nothing else. In his eyes, it was important to show that neutrality was not simply a pragmatic response to the problem of wartime survival. Neutrality was not to be apologised for; it was a legitimate status, recognised by custom and international law. As throughout the conflict, de Valera's aim was to preserve his country's capacity for autonomous action. Ireland must retain, as far as possible, its independence from the Great Powers, at the dawning of the new post-war world. But in his determination to pursue this goal, de Valera failed to understand the way the war had changed that world.

The elevation of Ireland's neutrality from the domain of practical politics into the realms of moral virtue was one of the striking outcomes of the Emergency. In 1945 the Irish Assurance Company ran advertisements for life insurance in local papers across the country:

The past few years have taught us that if we hope to exist as a nation, we must be self-reliant and rely on our own resources. Our farmers have worthily performed their part and saved the nation from hunger, if not actual starvation . . . In the future we must all become more self-reliant in our own lives too, and not be content to benefit from the labour of others.

The equation of neutrality with independence, and independence with uprightness, had become the widely accepted wisdom. No wonder national pride was injured when Ireland learned that, because of a Soviet veto, it would not be admitted to the new United Nations along with once-neutral countries such as Holland and Belgium, but on the same terms as the former enemies of the Allies.

Afterword

By war's end views of Irish neutrality were all but set in stone. The Trinity College riots were proof, if proof were needed, that the fear and uncertainty of the first months of war were long gone. Divided opinions had polarised still further under the cover of censorship. Despite all the attempts to think across national lines – to identify with the suffering in Europe, to support neutrality and back the Allies at the same time – arguments for and against neutrality kept falling back on national loyalties. And this rhetorical battle has cast a long shadow: attitudes towards wartime Ireland are still primarily determined by national allegiance. In Britain the story is still the refusal to hand over the ports, and de Valera's condolences on Hitler's death. In Ireland it is a story of national survival.

Either way, it was a battle of darkness against light. In Britain the Irish were portrayed as dwelling in a cave, lost in the dark, fumbling around in a state of ignorance induced by the harshness of the censorship, but also by their own lack of interest in a world from which they had deliberately withdrawn. In Ireland the right to an independent foreign policy, and to protect the Irish state, was also argued in moral terms. Political and religious imperatives seemed to overlap as neutrality was associated with pacifism, and with an ability to feel compassion for all suffering, regardless of which side the victims were on. According to this account, neutrality was a source of enlightenment. Irish society might be called on to 'dispel the darkness' of the 'seething European cauldron', as Aiken put it – to calm the warmongering on both sides. An editorial in the *Irish Times* in May 1945 set these rival moral claims against one another, arguing that de Valera's policy clearly lost out in the comparison:

He elevated the idea of neutrality into a principle . . . he contrived to convince the people of this country that Irish neutrality had a high spiritual basis, whereas, of course, when great moral issues are involved, the consistent saying of 'no', however holy it may be, cannot be otherwise than a policy of national emasculation. Moral issues of the highest kind were involved in the war which has just come to an end. No man with a conscience could be really neutral; and we are convinced that no citizen of this country, not even Mr de Valera, ever was neutral in the normal sense of the term.

Neither the story of national emasculation ('neuterality') nor the story of national power and sovereignty did justice to Ireland's oblique experience of the war, though there was something to be said for both versions. In particular it was true that by the end of the war the power of the Irish state over its own citizens had expanded dramatically. In part this was due to events outside Irish control. The fear of invasion during the crisis period of May 1940 to June 1941 did more than anything else to secure the power of government. The old politics based on civil-war rivalries were swept aside in favour of a new compact: the cause of Ireland versus the foreigner.

The government slowly built up a consensus around the need to cooperate, and to exclude violence from Irish society, whether home-grown, British or German. In the process, despite verbal flag-waving over partition, the focus shifted from the goal of national reunification, to the survival of the partitioned Irish state. Although neutrality put Ireland back into conflict with Britain once more, the war allowed for a period of political consolidation, in which the phase of revolutionary insurgence was left decisively behind.

Emergency social and economic regulation played an important part in consolidating the power of government. The rhetoric of survival turned on patriotism, but also on the need for self-sufficiency – the turf drive, the wheat drive, the frugality campaign. With the exception of the poorest in the country, who suffered real hardship, the experience of shortages rarely meant intolerable suffering. Instead the apparatus of rationing lent neutrality a much-needed epic tone. It is for this reason that the Irish wartime experience was so often lampooned in both the British and the Irish media. But the shortages also brought economic regulation into new areas of Irish society, as more and more aspects of everyday life and work came under the control of government edicts and local-authority inspectors. Even if people ignored the dictates, as they frequently did, a shared language of 'cooperation' helped to knit rural and working-class urban communities into a civic 'neutrally minded' whole, at least for the duration of the Emergency. Despite the high level of concern about poverty, disease, emigration, and economic crisis right across the political spectrum, the government managed to keep a lid on the disaffection until after the war was over.

The sense of civic responsibility that grew up around neutrality brought its own post-war reaction. In 1947, impatient with the prolonged economic crisis, the electorate ejected Fianna Fáil from power and voted in a new coalition, which included the radical new party Clann na Poblachta, with its social agenda centred on poverty and unemployment and outspoken criticism of the government's treatment of republican prisoners. The 1945 Labour landslide in Britain was the result of a vastly increased workforce looking for a social pay-off for their commitment to the war effort, in the context of a booming economy. The situation was very different in Ireland, where employment had shrunk and wage levels dropped (and where a large proportion of the workforce was abroad in Britain). But what the two populations shared was an unwillingness to put up with austerity any longer, and a strong belief in the government's responsibility to its citizens.

Reaction to the wartime consensus quickly set in amongst the intelligentsia too. The growth of a confident, independent Irish cultural sphere which went beyond the GAA and official Irish-language concerns such as the publishing house An Gúm was one of the most striking outcomes of the Emergency. *The Bell* became well known, partly because of Sean O'Faolain's liberal take on Irish affairs. But it was not a lone star. Small publishing houses, magazines, amateur theatre, Irish-language presses, art exhibitions, film-making, all testified to a new vitality in Irish culture. Wartime censorship had kept rival material out; writers and artists needed new markets because London and Paris were closed to them. But the atmosphere of neutrality also had its effect. In particular it encouraged a focus on Irish circumstances, which chimed with a literary, and cinematic, fashion for realism and documentary. Like the political consensus, which had collapsed by 1947, this cultural activity was to fade in the post-war years. Many writers chose to live outside Ireland, and to produce or publish their work first in London or the United States. By the early 1950s *The Bell* had died, and other magazines such as *Kavanagh's Weekly*, *Irish Writing* and *Envoy* quickly went the same way. The editors liked to put this down to the philistinism of the population, but it had far more to do with the dissipation of the wartime atmosphere, and the closed world of the literary elite. Dublin's brief spell as a European cultural capital was over.

The battle over the rights and wrongs of Irish neutrality continued, though Allied attacks grew more muted as the scale of the contribution to the war made by individual Irish men and women became better known. For most Irish people the question of whether neutrality had been right or wrong, moral or not, had always been the wrong one. The political quarrel over neutrality, and the story of the triumph of democracy that followed the war, left no room for their edgy experience. Their concerns had been about *how* to be neutral, how to keep themselves apart from the war without denying that, inevitably, the war was also a part of them.

Bibliographical Essay

KEY TO ARCHIVES:

NA National Archives of Ireland, Dublin
  DFA Department of Foreign Affairs
  DT Department of the Taoiseach
  DJ Department of Justice
PRO Public Records Office, London
PRONI Public Records Office Northern Ireland, Belfast
TCD Trinity College Archive, Dublin
UCD University College Archive, Dublin
BBCW BBC Written Archives Centre
MO Mass Observation Archive, University of Sussex
VP Volunteers Project, University College, Cork
IFC Irish Film Archive, Irish Film Centre, Dublin
IWM Imperial War Museum, London

For Dáil and Seanad Debates see *www.historical-debates.oireachtas.ie*

My research into Irish culture during the Second World War is indebted to several ground-breaking studies. The political and military events of the period are deftly handled by Robert Fisk, *In Time of War: Ireland, Ulster and the Price of Neutrality 1939–1945* (Dublin, 1983). Despite lack of access to Irish diplomatic sources, many of which only became available in the 1990s, Fisk's study is particularly helpful on Irish–British relations and on the early period of the war. Chapters 5 and 6 of Eunan O'Halpin, *Defending Ireland: The Irish State and its Enemies since 1922* (Oxford, 1999), provide an incisive and beautifully written account of Irish defence planning and threats to Irish security, both foreign and home-grown. O'Halpin has also edited and introduced *MI5 and Ireland, 1939–1945: The Official History* (Dublin, 2003). This report, completed in January 1946, offers important insights into British–Irish security and economic co-operation, counter-intelligence and German espionage in Ireland. The series of essays published as *Ireland in the War Years and After, 1939–1951*, ed. Kevin B. Nowlan and T. Desmond Williams (Dublin, 1969), still presents an excellent introduction to Irish politics, economics and culture during and immediately after the war. Despite limited access to archives Joseph T.

Carroll provides a clear historical account focusing on politics and diploma-cy in *Ireland in the War Years* (Newton Abbot and New York, 1975). John P. Duggan, *Neutral Ireland and the Third Reich* (Dublin, 1989) is also still the standard work. Duggan's *Herr Hempel at the German Legation in Dublin, 1937–1945* (Dublin, 2003) makes use of a great deal of original research in Irish and German archives to offer a reassessment not only of Hempel but of German–Irish wartime relations. Both Helen Litton, *The World War II Years: The Irish Emergency, An Illustrated History* (Dublin, 2001) and Ian S. Wood, *Ireland During the Second World War* (London, 2002) contain excellent visual material. I have kept returning to chapter 3 of J. J. Lee, *Ireland: 1912–1985, Politics and Society* (Cambridge, 1989) for analysis which places the politics and diplomacy of the war in the context of the development of Irish society as a whole. In particular Lee's balanced account of the reasons for and effects of censorship and domestic security, and the development of an aura of 'moral superiority' around the policy of neutrality, was a spur to the writing of this book.

The National Archives of Ireland (NA) were established in Dublin in 1988, enabling a great deal of new research on international relations and diplo-macy. Several recent edited collections bring together scholarly work based on recently released documents; see in particular Michael Kennedy and Joseph M. Skelly, eds., *Irish Foreign Policy, 1919–1996: From Independence to Internationalism* (Dublin, 2000); Mike Cronin and John M. Regan, eds., *Ireland: The Politics of Independence, 1922–49* (Basingstoke, 2000); Dermot Keogh and Mervyn O'Driscoll, eds., *Ireland in World War Two: Neutrality and Survival* (Cork, 2004). For political analysis of the concept of neutrality and the development of the Irish policy see: Thomas E. Hachey, 'The Rhetoric and Reality of Irish Neutrality', *New Hibernia Review* 6.2 (2002), 26–43; Garret FitzGerald, 'The Origins, Development and Present Status of Irish Neutrality', *Irish Studies in International Affairs* 9 (1998), 11–19; Patrick Keatinge, *A Singular Stance: Irish Neutrality in the 1980s* (Dublin, 1984); Ronan Fanning, *Independent Ireland* (Dublin, 1983); Raymond James Raymond, 'Irish Neutrality: Ideology or Pragmatism', *International Affairs* 60.1 (Winter 1983), 31–40; Trevor Salmon, *Unneutral Ireland* (Oxford, 1989); Michael Kennedy, *Ireland and the League of Nations, 1919–1946: International Relations, Diplomacy and Politics* (Dublin, 1996).

In recent years scholarship on wartime Ireland has begun to focus on the ways in which Ireland, and Irish individuals, were involved in the war. The history of Irish members of the British armed services is explored by Richard Doherty in *Irish Men and Women in the Second World War* (Dublin, 1999) and *Irish Volunteers in the Second World War* (Dublin, 2002). Brian Girvin and Geoffrey Roberts, eds., *Ireland and the Second World War: Politics, Society, Remembrance* (Dublin, 2000) offers new perspectives on the relationship between Britain and Ireland, focusing in particular on the history of Irish volunteers for the British services and Irish workers in Britain. Some of this work grew from the Volunteers Project, a research programme on the oral history of Irish volunteers based at University College, Cork. The interviews are not yet open to researchers but I am grateful to Geoffrey Roberts for allowing me access to the written summaries of the interviews.

Research on Irish literary and popular culture during the war has been less well served. The best analysis of Irish literary culture in the war years is still Terence Brown's chapter on the Emergency in *Ireland: A Social and Cultural History 1922–1985* (London, 1981). Much of this present book is an attempt to expand and interrogate Brown's concise and illuminating analysis of the development of Irish cultural life in the 1930s and 1940s. Brian Fallon's two studies of the period, *An Age of Innocence, Irish Culture 1930–1960* (Dublin, 1999), and *Irish Art 1880–1950* (Dublin, 1994), offer a welcome corrective to the standard picture of wartime Ireland as one of unrelieved gloom and stagnation. Donal Ó Drisceoil, *Censorship in Ireland, 1939–1945: Neutrality, Politics and Society* (Cork, 1996) is indispensable on wartime censorship (of the press in particular); see also Kevin Rockett, 'Film Censorship and Irish Politics', *Irish Film Censorship: A Cultural Journey from Silent Cinema to Internet Pornography* (Dublin, 2004). Bernard Share, *The Emergency: Neutral Ireland, 1939–1945* (Dublin, 1978) and Tony Gray, *The Lost Years: The Emergency in Ireland 1939–1945* (Dublin, 1997) both offer lively pictures of everyday life during the war years. Given the cultural and literary connections between Ireland and Britain in the period, I have also drawn on studies of literary and popular culture in wartime Britain, such as Angus Calder, *The Myth of the Blitz* (London, 1991) and *The People's War* (London, 1971); Samuel Hynes, *The Auden Generation: Literature and Politics in England in the 1930s* (London, 1976); Robert Hewison, *Under Siege: Literary London 1939–1945* (London, 1977); Adam Piette, *Imagination at War: British Fiction and Poetry, 1939–1945* (London, 1995). In addition I have drawn on biographical and critical studies of writers which I have noted as sources for individual chapters.

The best guide to debates in Irish intellectual culture is to read (with an eye to the censorship) through wartime runs of journals and magazines such as *Ireland Today* (1936–1938), *The Bell, Irish Ecclesiastical Record, The Capuchin Annual, The Catholic Bulletin, Studies, Irish Rosary*. See also Frank Shovlin, *The Irish Literary Periodical 1923–1958* (Oxford, 2003); Gerry Smyth, *Decolonisation and Criticism: The Construction of Irish Literature* (London, 1998); Susannah Riordan, 'The Unpopular Front: Catholic Revival and Irish Cultural Identity 1932–1948', in Cronin and Regan, eds., op. cit.; Liam O'Dowd, 'Intellectuals in 20th Century Ireland, and the Case of George Russell (AE)', *Crane Bag* 9.1 (1985) 6–25.

For public attitudes and discussion of both neutrality and war I found the local and national newspapers extremely useful, particularly the editorials and letters pages (though again bearing in mind the censorship). I read daily papers (*Irish Times, Irish Press, Irish Independent, Cork Examiner*) and some weeklies such as the *Standard* for the weeks and months surrounding specific events, such as the outbreak of war, the fall of France, the bombing of Dublin and Belfast, the German invasion of the Soviet Union, and so on. I chose to read yearly runs of some local papers (such as the *Clare Champion* for 1937 and 1940; the *Donegal Democrat* for 1940 and 1942; the *Meath Chronicle* for 1945, etc.). In researching the effects of the Atlantic Battle in Ireland I read papers such as the *Southern Star*, the *Western People* and the *Mayo News* for eight months from June 1940. *Ireland's Own* and trade magazines such as the *Irish Grocer* offer interesting ways to think about frugality and household rationing during the war. The complete run of the *Irish Messenger* from 1939 to 1945 was a revelation: individuals' prayers, intentions and letters about favours received add up to a moving (and occasionally disturbing) picture of everyday Catholic life during the war. I also looked to the Dáil and Seanad debates for a sense of changing public opinion during the war. Both government and opposition members may overstate their case during parliamentary debates, but I found evidence such as letters from constituents, TDs' personal experiences and prejudices, and descriptions of the situation in their areas extremely valuable in building up a picture of the country as a whole.

The following description of sources for individual chapters is intended both as a guide and as an acknowledgement of my debt to individual writers and scholars. When the source of a quotation is clear from the context I have not reproduced the reference here.

INTRODUCTION: AN IRISH THEATRE OF WAR

The quotation from the journalist on page 4 is from Brian Fallon's *The Age of Innocence*, op. cit., 214. Numerous foreign travellers' accounts of journeys to Ireland during the war were reprinted from English and American newspapers in the monthly *Irish Digest*. Several were also subsequently brought out in book form such as Ben Robertson, *I Saw England* (London, 1941), and James Lansdale Hodson, *Towards the Morning* (London, 1941). *Picture Post* produced several special issues on Ireland during the war, managing to blend tourist images with a measure of political analysis. One such is 'The Story of Ireland' in the 27 July 1940 issue, written by Tania Long, an American journalist based in London, who had left her mother and young son in Ireland. The happy Woolworths shopper was S. M. Batstone, whose letters to her mother from her posting in Northern Ireland are held at the IWM (86/61/1). Bowen's statement about GIs is taken from her 'Notes on Eire' report for the Dominions Office of July 1942, available at the PRO DO 130/28. The reports have also been published (with numerous typographical errors and an extremely partial attack on Bowen) by the Aubane Historical Society as *Elizabeth Bowen, 'Notes on Eire', Espionage Reports to Winston Churchill, 1940–2; With a review of Irish Neutrality in World War 2* by Jack Lane and Brendan Clifford (Aubane, County Cork, 1999).

The description of Ireland as still stuck in 1938 is from Cyril Connolly, 'Comment', *Horizon* 5.25 (January 1942), 3–11. Frank O'Connor's judgement on the 'non-entity state' can also be found in this issue, in his article 'The Future of Irish Literature', 55–63.

F. S. L. Lyons's famous comment about Plato's cave appears on pages 557–558 of *Ireland Since the Famine* (London, 1973). The *Irish Times* editorial, entitled 'Out of the Shadows', appeared on 12 May 1945. The similarity was pointed out by Geoffrey Roberts in his article 'Three narratives of neutrality: historians and Ireland's war', in Girvin and Roberts, eds., op. cit. I am grateful to Eibhear Walshe for a copy of Kate O'Brien's unpublished typescript for her radio talk, 'Anglo-Irish Writing since 1945', which is held in the O'Brien Papers at Northwestern University, as well as access to the O'Brien letters quoted in chapter 1. See also Walshe, *Kate O'Brien: A Writing Life* (Dublin, 2006).

I THIS EMERGENT IRELAND

On Irish culture and society during the 1930s, in addition to the standard histories such as Lee (op. cit.) and R. F. Foster, *Modern Ireland 1600–1972* (London, 1988), see Francis MacManus, ed., *The Years of the Great Test 1926–1939* (Cork, 1967); David Fitzpatrick, *The Two Irelands, 1922–1939* (Oxford, 1998); F. S. L. Lyons, *Culture and Anarchy in Ireland, 1890–1939* (Oxford, 1982); Gabriel Doherty and Dermot Keogh, eds., *De Valera's Irelands* (Cork, 2003); Joost Augusteijn, ed., *Ireland in the 1930s: New Perspectives* (Dublin, 1999); John P. O'Carroll and John A. Murphy, eds., *De Valera and his Times* (Cork, 1983); J. H. Whyte, *The Church and State in Modern Ireland 1923–1970* (Dublin, 1971); Dermot Keogh, *The Vatican, the Bishops and Irish Politics, 1919–1939* (Cambridge, 1986) and *Ireland and Europe, 1919–1949* (Dublin, 1988); Patrick Murray, *Oracles of God: The Roman Catholic Church and Irish Politics 1922–1937* (Dublin, 2000); John M. Regan, *The Irish Counter-Revolution, 1921–1936* (Dublin, 1999); Diarmaid Ferriter, *The Transformation of Ireland 1900–2000* (London, 2004).

On the New York World's Fair see the coverage in the *New York Times* in the first half of 1939; *'Building the World of Tomorrow': Official Guidebook of the New York World's Fair, 1939* (New York, 1939); *Michael Scott, Architect*, in conversation with Dorothy Walker (Kinsale, 1995); 'The International Style Comes to Ireland', in Sean Rothery, *Ireland and the New Architecture, 1900–1940* (Dublin, 1991). The script of de Valera's January

1939 radio broadcast and correspondence about the Fair are held at NA DFA 233/24. For an analysis of New York's Irish-American culture during the 1930s see Francis Hackett, 'The Greater Ireland', *Ireland Today* 1.1 (June 1936), 31–40.

On the need for Ireland to 'grow up' politically see Sean O'Faolain, 'Editorial', *The Bell* 2.6 (September 1941); Sean O'Casey, 'There Go the Irish', in *They Go, The Irish,* ed. Leslie Daiken (London, 1944). On the modernisation of the Irish countryside see Sean O'Faolain, *An Irish Journey* (London, 1940); John Gibbons, *Ireland, the New Ally* (London, 1938). For information on electrification I have relied on Michael Shiel, *The Quiet Revolution: The Electrification of Rural Ireland 1946–1976* (Dublin, 1984). I quote from Dáil Debates, Vol. 29, 8 March 1945 on the impact of rural electrification. Michael Tierney's critique of Irish 'suburbanity'and 'the fever of dancing' appeared in 'The Problem of Partition', *Studies: An Irish Quarterly Review of Letters, Philosophy and Science* 27 (Dec. 1938), 637–646; James Hogan's article, 'The Pre-Conditions of a Rural Revival', appeared in *Irish Monthly* 67 (July 1939), 457–473. On dancing and joy-riding I also quote here from the *Donegal Democrat* of 14 January and 8 April 1939, and the *Clare Champion* of 13 March 1937 and 13 February 1938 (where Most Rev. Dr Fogarty's Lenten Pastoral, 'The Growth of Secularism', is reproduced in full). On sociability and sexuality during this period see Sandra L. McAvoy, 'The Regulation of Sexuality in the Irish Free State 1929–1936', in Greta Jones and Elizabeth Malcolm, eds., *Medicine, Disease and the State in Ireland 1650–1940* (Cork, 1999), 253–266; Maria Luddy, 'Sex and the Single Girl in 1920s and 1930s Ireland', *Irish Review* (2007); Mark Finnane, 'The Carrigan Committee of 1930–31 and the "moral" condition of the Saorstát', *Irish Historical Studies*, 32, 128 (November 2001), 519–536; James M. Smith, 'The Politics of Sexual Knowledge: The Origins of Ireland's Containment Culture and the Carrigan Report (1931)', *Journal of the History of Sexuality* 13.2 (2004), 208–233. The literary perspectives quoted are from Frank O'Connor, *Dutch Interior* (London, 1940) and Myles na gCopaleen, *The Poor Mouth – An Béal Bocht: a bad story about the hard life*, trans. Patrick C. Power (London, 1975), originally published 1941. See also Flann O'Brien, 'The Dance Halls', *The Bell* 1.5 (February 1941).

For de Valera on the 'suicide' of entering the war see Dáil Debates, Vol. 91, 16 November 1943. Aiken's statement on 'civil war' is from his Memorandum on 'Neutrality, Censorship and Democracy', 23 January 1940 (NA DT S 11586A). Bowen's comment on the contracted peace in Ireland appears in the epilogue to *Bowen's Court* (Cork, 1998), first published in 1942. On the IRA during the 1930s and the English campaign see: J. Bowyer Bell, *The Secret Army* (Dublin, 1979); Donal Ó Drisceoil, *Peadar O'Donnell* (Cork, 2001); Conor Foley, *Legion of the Rearguard: The IRA and the*

Modern Irish State (London, 1992); Brian Hanley, *The IRA, 1926–1936* (Dublin, 2002); Henry Patterson, *The Politics of Illusion: Republicanism and Socialism in Modern Ireland* (London, 1989). See also Eugene Coyle's articles on the 'Dictatorship' in Northern Ireland, reprinted as a series in the *Donegal Democrat*, Feb–March 1939; *Ireland and the War* (Ballyshannon, 1939). On the question of German support for IRA military attacks on Britain, and the visit of the German agent Oskar Pfaus to Dublin in February 1939, see Mark M. Hull, *Irish Secrets: German Espionage in Wartime Ireland 1939–1945* (Dublin, 2003); Fearghal McGarry, *Eoin O'Duffy: A Self-Made Hero* (Oxford, 2005).

On the fear that neutrality would prove ineffectual, see Col. J. J. O'Connell, 'The Vulnerability of Ireland in War', *Studies* 27 (March 1938), 125–135 and 'Can Ireland Remain Neutral?', *Studies* 27 (December 1938), 647–655. On defences see Dáil Debates, Vol. 74, 8 February 1939, 'Protection Against Air Attack' and Vol. 73, 15/16 February 1939, 'Finance: Army'. See also John P. Duggan, *A History of the Irish Army* (Dublin, 1991); Eunan O'Halpin, 'The Army in Independent Ireland', in Thomas Bartlett and Keith Jeffrey, *A Military History of Ireland* (Cambridge, 1996); Donal MacCarron, *Step Together!: The History of Ireland's Emergency Army as Told by its Veterans* (Dublin, 1996). For de Valera at the League of Nations see Maurice Moynihan, ed., *Speeches and Statements by Eamon de Valera, 1917–1973* (Dublin and New York, 1980), 282–285; see also in the same volume his speech to the Dáil on 18 June 1936 on the failure of the League of Nations and the policy of neutrality (273–276), and his broadcast from Geneva to the United States during the Munich crisis (355–357). See also Kennedy, *Ireland and the League of Nations*, op. cit.; M. J. MacManus, *Eamon de Valera: A Biography* (Dublin and Cork, 1944).

2 TALK OF ESCAPISM

For descriptions of the events in Ireland on the outbreak of war, including the blackout, see Dáil Debates, Vol. 77, 2 September 1939; Seanad Debates, Vol. 23, 2 September 1939; Dáil Debates, Vol. 77, 17 September 1939, 'Blackout Regulations'; Vol. 77, 19 October 1939, 'Lighting Restrictions'; I have also consulted local and national newspapers and quote from 'Neutral Ireland', *Round Table* 117 (December 1939), 138–139. For J. J. Walshe's memo on 'positive' censorship see Aiken Papers UCD P104/3433 (2). On Emergency legislation see O'Halpin, *Defending Ireland*, op. cit., 201–203; Seosamh Ó Longaigh, 'Preparing Law for an Emergency, 1938–1939' and 'Emergency Law in Action, 1939–1945' in Keogh and O'Driscoll, eds., op. cit., 36–47 and 63–80. The anecdote about Basil Brooke appears on p. 105 of Fisk and the comment of the British foreign office official on de Valera's difficulties over Danzig on p. 100.

On unemployment as a consequence of the war see *Dáil Debates* Vol. 77, 18, 19 October 1939, 'Statement of Government Policy'; on milk riots See *Dáil Debates* Vol. 78, 22 November 1939 'Milk Situation'. On volunteers travelling to Britain see Richard Doherty, op. cit.; the summaries of the Volunteers Project Oral Histories (VP); Aidan McElwaine, 'The Oral History of the Volunteers', in Girvin and Roberts, op. cit., 107–120; Myles Dungan, *Distant Drums: Irish Soldiers in Foreign Armies* (Belfast, 1993). The debate about conscription at Queen's University, Belfast can be found in *The Queensman*, 21 November 1939 and 30 January 1940. On voluntering I also quote here from a Mass Observation Diary for autumn 1939, Belfast (MO, 5102). See also Patrick Maybin's letters to John Hewitt (PRONI D/3838/3/10); NA DFA 241/100 contains pleas for help in gaining discharge from the British army for minors and those who think they should not be liable for conscription. On Irish volunteers see also, A. J. Liebling, 'Paddy of the RAF', *The New Yorker War Pieces* (6 December 1941); Devlin Papers, IWM 89/13/1; Dunlop Papers, IWM 76/271/1; Brian Inglis, *West Briton* (London, 1962).

Hubert Butler's letter to Dulanty is held at NA, DFA 241/15, along with other 'Applications to serve in Eire' during the war. See 'The Kagran Gruppe', and 'The Children of Drancy' in Butler, *The Children of Drancy* (Mullingar, 1988). Dermot Keogh's *Jews in Twentieth-Century Ireland* (Cork, 1998) and Katrina Goldstone's article, '"Benevolent Helpfulness"?: Ireland and the International Reaction to Jewish Refugees, 1933–9', in Kennedy and Skelly, eds., op. cit., offer interesting background on the Irish Co-ordinating Committee for Refugees, which was set up in 1938 and in which Butler was very active. See also R. F. Foster, 'The Salamander and the Slap: Hubert Butler and his Century', in *The Irish Story: Telling Tales and Making it Up in Ireland* (Penguin, 2001). On Kate O'Brien see *The Last of Summer* (London, 1990); Vivian Mercier, 'Kate O'Brien', *Irish Writing* 1 (1946), 86–100; Adele Dalsimer, *Kate O'Brien: A Critical Study* (Dublin, 1990); Lorna Reynolds, *Kate O'Brien: A Literary Portrait* (Gerrards Cross, 1987); Eibhear Walshe, ed., *Ordinary People Dancing: Essays on Kate O'Brien* (Cork, 1993); Walshe, *Kate O'Brien*, op. cit.

On the Irish Left see in particular chapter 9, 'Communism in the Second World War', in Mike Milotte, *Communism in Modern Ireland: The Pursuit of the Workers' Republic since 1916* (Dublin, 1984). See also Michael O'Riordan, *Connolly Column* (Dublin, 1979). I quote here also from *Irish Front,* 11 May 1935; *Irish Workers' Weekly* (published by Communist Party of Ireland), 1 January 1940; J. Higgins, 'England's Enemies, Ireland's Friends?', *Workers' Republic* (June 1938); William Clare, 'Goering in the Bay?', *Workers' Republic* (July 1938); 'German Nazis at Work in Ireland', *Workers' Republic* (August 1938).

On Behan see: *Borstal Boy* (London, 1958); E. H. Mikail, ed., *The Letters of Brendan Behan* (London, 1992); Ulick O'Connor, *Brendan Behan* (London, 1979); Michael O'Sullivan, *Brendan Behan, A Life* (Dublin, 1997); John Brannigan, *Brendan Behan: Cultural Nationalism and the Revisionist Writer* (Dublin, 2002); Seamus de Burca, *Brendan Behan: A Memoir* (Dublin, 1985); Colbert Kearney, *The Writings of Brendan Behan* (Dublin, 1977).

On Irish attitudes to the war in Spain, and the differences between the Irish and English intellectual left (associated with *New Signatures* and *New Writing*), see *Ireland Today*, particularly the Foreign Commentaries by Owen Sheehy Skeffington, poetry by Charles Donnelly, short stories by Charles Ewart Milne, and the 1936 Symposium on the war; Máirín Mitchell, *Storm over Spain* (London, 1937); Kate O'Brien, *Farewell Spain* (London, 1937). Peadar O'Donnell, *Salud! An Irishman in Spain* (London, 1937) is particularly useful in outlining how the Spanish war caused 'uproar' in Ireland 'where it rekindled the antagonisms of the Civil War'. See Ewart Milne, *Letter from Ireland* (Dublin, 1940) and *Listen Mangan* (Dublin, 1941), for an anti-fascist perspective which is also pro-neutrality (Milne was a member of the Spanish Medical Aid Committee and co-edited *Irish Front* with Donnelly). For Irish sympathy with the nationalist cause see Eoin O'Duffy, *Crusade in Spain* (Dublin, 1938); Aodh de Blácam, 'Can Ireland Help Spain?', *Irish Monthly* 64 (October 1936), 645–665 and *For God and Spain* (Dublin, 1936) where de Blácam argues that the fascist and the Catholic cause are one; for a royalist perspective see Walter Starkie, *Grand Inquisitor* (London, 1940). See also William Tierney, 'Irish Writers and the Spanish Civil War', *Éire–Ireland* 7.3 (1972), 36–55; Fearghal McGarry, *Irish Politics and the Spanish Civil War* (Cork, 1999) and *Eoin O'Duffy*, op. cit.; R. A. Stradling, *The Irish and the Spanish Civil War, 1936–1939* (Manchester, 1999).

Louis MacNeice's *Autumn Journal* was first published by Faber in 1939. The fullest version of MacNeice's 'The Coming of War' appeared in *The Last Ditch*, published by the Yeats sisters' Cuala Press in 1940; a shorter version appeared in *Plant and Phantom* (London, 1941), and another in *Collected Poems 1925–1948* (London, 1949). See also *The Poetry of W. B. Yeats* (London, 1941) and *Modern Poetry* (London, 1938) for MacNeice's developing sense of his relationship with the modernism of both Yeats and Eliot. MacNeice's prose recollections of the period are from *The Strings Are False, An Unfinished Autobiography*, ed. E. R. Dodds (London, 1965), which he wrote during 1940 and 1941. For MacNeice's movements in auturm 1939, and his debate with Eleanor Clark, see Jon Stallworthy, *Louis MacNeice* (London, 1995), 258–67; See also Edna Longley, *Louis MacNeice: A Critical Study* (London, 1988); Peter McDonald, *Louis MacNeice: the Poet in his Contexts* (Oxford, 1991); Richard Danson Brown, 'Neutrality and Commitment: MacNeice, Yeats, Ireland and the Second World War', *Journal of Modern Literature* 28.3 (2003), 109–129; Miranda Carter, *Anthony Blunt, His Lives* (London, 2001).

On Dublin's literary drinking culture see Tony Gray, op. cit. and *Mr Smyllie, Sir* (Dublin, 1991); For the description of the Palace Bar as 'very far away' from the war see Anthony Cronin, *No Laughing Matter: The Life and Times of Flann O'Brien* (London, 1989), 158. See also Lionel Fleming, *Head or Harp?* (London, 1965); John Ryan, *Remembering How We Stood* (Mullingar, 1987); Antoinette Quinn, *Patrick Kavanagh: A Biography* (Dublin, 2001).

A copy of Bowen's letter to Humphry House was kindly given to me by Dierdre Toomey. Bowen's story 'Summer Night' was first published in *Look at All Those Roses* (London, 1941). See also 'Meet Elizabeth Bowen', *The Bell* 4.6 (September 1942); Hermione Lee, ed., *The Mulberry Tree: Writings of Elizabeth Bowen* (London, 1999); Hermione Lee, *Elizabeth Bowen* (London, 1999); R. F. Foster, 'The Irishness of Elizabeth Bowen', *Paddy and Mr Punch* (London, 1993); Victoria Glendinning, *Elizabeth Bowen: Portrait of a Writer* (London, 1977); Patricia Craig, *Elizabeth Bowen* (London, 1986); Phyllis Lassner, *Elizabeth Bowen* (London, 1990); W. J. McCormack, *Dissolute Characters: Irish Literary History through Balzac, Sheridan le Fanu, Yeats and Bowen* (Manchester, 1993); Heather Bryant Jordan, *How Will the Heart Endure: Elizabeth Bowen and the Landscape of War* (Ann Arbor, 1992); Maud Ellmann, *Elizabeth Bowen: The Shadow Across the Page* (Edinburgh, 2003); Neil Corcoran, *Elizabeth Bowen: The Enforced Return* (Oxford, 2004).

The best guide to O'Faolain's wartime development is his contemporary journalism and editorials. 'Irish Blackout' was published in the *Manchester Guardian*, October 1939 and reprinted in *Irish Digest* 5.1 (November 1939), 1–3; *An Irish Journey*, which he was completing at the time of his visit to Bowen, was published by Longmans in 1940. See also *The Story of Ireland* (London, 1943); *The Great O'Neill: A Biography of Hugh O'Neill, Earl of Tyrone 1550–1616* (London, 1942); *Vive Moi! An Autobiography* (London, 1965); Maurice Harmon, *Sean O'Faolain, a Life* (London, 1984). For Séamus Ó Néill's comment on Poland see *Tonn Tuile* (Baile Átha Cliath, 1947), 8.

3 MOBILISATION

Butler's letters to his wife from Kilkenny are held at Trinity College Archives (TCD MS 10304/625/158/1). On the possibility of German invasion see: *Militär-geographische Angaben über Irland* (Berlin, 1940); O'Halpin, *Defending Ireland*, op. cit., 172–6; Charles Burdick, '"Gruen", German Military Plans and Ireland, 1940', *An Cosantóir* (March 1974); Comdt Colm Cox, 'Militargeographische Angaben über Irland', *An Cosantóir* (March 1975); Cox, 'Wir Fahren Gegen Irland?', *An Cosantóir* (March 1976); John P. Duggan, 'The German Threat – Myth or Reality?', *An Cosantóir* (September 1989). For debates on expansion of the army and Volunteer Forces see *Dáil Debates*, Vol. 79, 17, 18, 24, 25 April 1940; *Seanad Debates*, Vol. 24, 7 June 1940.

On discreet help to Britain see O'Halpin, *Defending Ireland*, op. cit., 225–231 and *MI5 and Ireland,* op. cit., 55–59, 85–89. On Malcolm MacDonald and the offer of unity see Fisk, 190–206. On northern mobilisation see Brian Barton, *Northern Ireland in the Second World War* (Belfast, 1995); John W. Blake, *Northern Ireland in the Second World War* (Belfast, 1956). The description of defence emplacements comes from Moya Woodside's Mass Observation Diary (MO 5462). Several local publications fill in the picture of specific bases in Northern Ireland, e.g. Breege McCusker, *Castle Archdale and Fermanagh in World War Two* (Irvinestown, 2000); John Quinn, *Covering the Approaches: the War Against the U-boats* (Coleraine, 1996); Quinn, *Wings Over the Foyle: A History of Limavady Airfield* (Belfast, 1995). On cross-border intelligence and fortifications south of the border see: NA DJ 8/ 832 (the Garda report of June 1940) and DFA 241/187; the Boyne–Blackwater line of defence is described in 'The Modern Landscape' in Geraldine Stout, *Newgrange and the Bend of the Boyne* (Cork, 2002), 116–173. See also Lt. Col. M. T. Duggan, 'Autumn Exercises, 1940', *An Cosantóir* (June 1980); Comdt Padraic O'Farrell, 'Remembering the War', *An Cosantóir* (November 1979); Special Issue of *The Irish Sword,* 19/75–76 (1993–94).

On internal 'subversive activity' during the war see: NA DT S 11564A, 'IRA Wartime Publications' and DJ 8 752; O'Halpin, *Defending Ireland*, op. cit., 245–253; Uinseann MacEoin, *The IRA in the Twilight Years, 1923–1948* (Dublin, 1997). Brian Hanley offers a concise assessment of IRA involvement in German plans against Britain through Sean Russell, and analyses the increasingly pro-Nazi and often anti-semitic stance of *War News* in the context of declining support for the IRA during late 1930s. He argues convincingly that German success in 1940 gave impetus to this faction in the IRA, which by late 1940 was supporting the idea of a German invasion of Ireland. '"O Here's To Adolf Hitler"? The IRA and the Nazis', *History Ireland* 13.3 (May/June 2003). See also the final chapter of McGarry's biography of Eoin O'Duffy, op. cit. For the story of the IRA message to the Luftwaffe see Eunan O'Halpin, 'British Intelligence, the Republican movement and the IRA's German Links 1935–45', in Fearghal McGarry, ed., *Republicanism in Modern Ireland* (Dublin, 2003), 108–131. See Aiken Papers, UCD P104/3377 on the need for parents, teachers and clergy to rein in anarchical young men.

On morale-building and the recruitment drive see Aiken papers, UCD, P104/3374; Duggan, *Irish Army*, op. cit. and MacCarron, op. cit.; *Step Together!* pamphlets produced for regional fairs held at the National Library, Ireland. For General McKenna on recruitment for the LSF see the first issue of *An Cosantóir* (December 1940); Aiken's Memo on Censorship, NA DT S 11596A. On tableau and pageant in an earlier period see Mike Cronin, 'Projecting the Nation through Sport and Culture: Ireland, Aonach Tailteann and the Irish Free State, 1924–32', *Journal of Contemporary History* 38.3,

395–411; T. H. Nally, *The Aonac Tailteann and the Tailteann Games. Their Origin, History and Development* (Dublin, 1924); Comdt P. Young, 'Pageantry and the Defence Forces', *An Cosantóir* (September 1985). On regional drama see Michael Farrell's series on Country Theatre during the first two years of *The Bell*. On Easter 1916 as 'National Morality Play' see Denis Johnston, 'Public Opinion', *The Bell* 1.6 (March 1941). See also Christopher Morash, *A History of Irish Theatre, 1601–2000* (Cambridge, 2002), 193–198. The script of RTÉ's series on Irish film-making, *Memories in Focus*, (dir. Peter Canning, 1995) including an interview with Jack Millar on filming army manoeuvres, is available at IFC, along with a large archive of newsreels of the army and Step Together activities and the 1940 recruitment film. The Dutch journalist was Kees Van Hoek; see *An Irish Panorama* (London, 1946) and *Country of My Choice* (Dublin, 1945). For 'Applications to Serve in Eire' see NA DFA 241/15; for fear of 'pressganging' of Northern Catholics see NA DFA 241/103.

4 WAR AT SEA

For information on the sinking of the *Mohammed Ali El Kebir*, including newspaper reports, see mohamed.ali.el-kebir.freewebspace.com. I am greatly indebted to Michael Kennedy and Simon Nolan for access to their meticulous and moving database of bodies washed ashore and logged by gardaí, and for alerting me to the file on bodies washed ashore at the National Archives, on which I have drawn heavily.

For Richard Mulcahy's comment on the sinkings near Malin Head see Fisk, 301. Both Frank Forde, *The Long Watch: The History of the Irish Mercantile Marine in World War Two* (Dublin, 1981) and Trevor J. Allen, *The Storm Passed By: Ireland and the Battle of the Atlantic, 1940–41* (Dublin, 1996) provide details of the sinking of both Irish and Allied ships near the Irish coast. The principal public discussion on the ports in Ireland occurred during a debate on External Affairs, Dáil Debates, Vol. 84, 17 July 1941.

On the Admiralty and British attitudes towards the ports early in the war see O'Halpin, *Defending Ireland, 172–173* (cited p. 115). For the memo by Rear Admiral Phillips see Fisk, 117–118; for general discussion of the ports see Fisk, 104–127, and 279–332. For British, Irish and US propaganda for and against neutrality and the use of the ports see: Nicholas Montsarrat, *The Cruel Sea* (London, 1951); Tom Ireland, *Ireland Past and Present* (New York, 1942), which includes the text of the American Irish Defense Association's call for Ireland to lease the ports; Henry Harrison, *The Neutrality of Ireland* (London, 1940); Máirín Mitchell, *Atlantic Battle* (London, 1941); Jim Phelan, *Churchill Can Unite Ireland* (London, 1940); *Ireland: Atlantic Gateway* (London 1941). Phelan provides a novelistic treatment of the situation in ... *And Blackthorns* (London, 1944) complete with 'Nezzies' in league with the big farmers. Reports on Éire by Elizabeth Bowen, J. H. MacDonnell,

A. A. Mowat and W. K. Hancock are held in the PRO DO 130/28. These frequently comment on a posture of 'isolationist virtue' in Ireland and the tendency to condemn both sides as equally malign. I quote from p. 36 of Robert Brennan, *Ireland Standing Firm: My Wartime Mission to Washington* (Dublin, 2002), on American special correspondents in Ireland. I am grateful to Eunan O'Halpin for a copy of Robert Brennan's poem; Dorothy L. Sayers's poem appears in Colville, *The Fringes of Power: Downing Street Diaries, I: The Gathering Storm* (London, 1949).

MacNeice's plea for understanding of de Valera's difficulties was first published as 'London Letter', *Common Sense* 10.5 (May 1941), reprinted in *The Selected Prose of Louis MacNeice*, ed. Alan Heuser (Oxford, 1990). Elizabeth Bowen's 'A Love Story' was first published in *Horizon* 1.7 (1940), 481–498; her letter to Virginia Woolf is reprinted in *The Mulberry Tree*, op. cit., 214–216. Hubert Butler's critique of the Irish 'ocean of indifference' appeared in 'The Barriers', *The Bell* 2.4; see also *Escape from the Anthill* (Mullingar, 1985), and *Grandmother and Wolfe Tone* (Mullingar, 1990), particularly the essays 'The Invader wore Slippers' and 'The Two Languages'. On Dillon see Maurice Manning, *James Dillon: A Biography* (Dublin, 2000).

On the Marine and Coast-Watching Service see: Dáil Debates, Vol. 77, 6 December 1939, Vol. 79, 18 April 1940, Vol. 90, 19 May 1943; *Irish Sword* 19/75–76 (1993–94); Patrick Campbell, *Come Here Till I Tell You* (London, 1960); Campbell, *An Irishman's Diary* (Dublin, 1951). On the problem of bodies washed ashore see NA DFA 241/184 A (Bodies Washed Ashore); DFA 241/194 (Articles Washed Ashore); DFA 241/230 (Coroners); reports of recovery of bodies, coroners reports, and local Board of Health meetings in local papers; Hewitt's letter to Patrick Maybin, 9/8/43, PRONI D/3838/3/12; Peadar O'Donnell, 'Why Blame the Seagulls?', *The Bell* 1.3 (December 1940); Margaret Barrington, 'Village Without Men', Daiken, ed., *They Go, The Irish*, op. cit. For Gillespie's testimony see mohamed. ali-el-kabir. freewebspace.com. See also the *Belfast Newsletter* and *Belfast Telegraph* for November 1940.

5 INVISIBLE ENEMIES

On German activity in Ireland and fears of IRA collaboration see: Duggan, *Herr Hempel*, op. cit.; Mark M. Hull, *Irish Secrets*, op. cit.; Sean O'Callaghan, *The Jackboot in Ireland* (London, 1958); Enno Stephan, *Spies in Ireland* (London, 1963); Carolle J. Carter *The Shamrock and the Swastika: German Espionage in Ireland in World War II* (Palo Alto, 1977); O'Halpin, *MI5 and Ireland*, op. cit. Richard Mulcahy's letter to Boland is quoted in Fisk, 149. For de Valera's speech on 8 May 1940, G2 reports on subversives, and copies of *War News* see NA DT S 11564 A; further copies of *War News* are at NA DJ 8752. For the description of Dublin 'reverberating' with rumours see O'Halpin, *Defending Ireland*, 244.

THAT NEUTRAL ISLAND

On border crossings see: NA DFA 241/187 on southern residents as members of B specials; NA DJ 8/868 on cross-border shopping and smuggling; NA DFA 231/84 on British food-rationing cards. Tom Harrisson's report on the atmosphere and security difficulties in Northern Ireland in 1942 is held at the University of Sussex Mass Observation Archive, MO 12/6/42 (F 1309). On British security services' attitude towards the border see *MI5 and Ireland*, 26–27 and 54. I am grateful to Peter Rigney for the story of Belfast women smuggler passengers (Irish Railway Record Society Archive, Great Northern Railway: General Manager's file 70/5). I have also consulted local newspapers, in particular the *Dundalk Examiner* and the *Donegal Democrat*, trade journals, and Great Northern Railway excursion leaflets held at the Ulster Museum. Rayner Heppenstall's description of travel to the North appears in 'People Who Live in Glass Houses', in Stefan Schimanski and Henry Treece, eds., *Wartime Harvest* (London, 1943).

On British and Irish intelligence organisations, including SIS, see Eunan O'Halpin, '"Toys" and "Whispers" in "16-land": SOE and Ireland, 1940–42', *Intelligence and National Security* 15.4 (Winter 2000), 1–18, and *Defending Ireland*, op. cit., 166. On communications censorship and domestic surveillance see O'Halpin, *Defending Ireland*, 213–220. On the use of postal censorship to collect as much information as possible see Aiken Papers UCD P104/3456. For the main public debate on postal censorship see Seanad Debates, Vol. 25, 30 January 1941 (Censorship and Constitutional Rights); On the battle between an 'ascendancy clique' and supporters of neutrality see Aiken Papers, UCD P104/3433 (2); Duggan, *Herr Hempel*, 107.

On 'informing' and the attempt to encourage the civic sense see: Sean Dorman, 'Irishmen Should be Informers', *Commentary* (August 1942); Lionel Pilkington, *Theatre and State in Twentieth-century Ireland: Cultivating the People* (London, 2001); George Shiels, *The Rugged Path and the Summit* (London, 1942). T. P. Murray credits Shiels with rooting out a 'social cancer' in a review in the *Irish Press*, 10 February 1942. T. H. White's letter to Garnett appears on p. 73 of David Garnett, ed., *The White/Garnett Letters* (London, 1968). *The Godstone and the Blackymore* (London, 1959) describes the visits to Inishkea as part of rather unlikely folklore investigations. White's views on Irish neutrality became increasingly caustic as the war progressed. He was later to produce a viciously satirical – and pathetically self-aggrandising – attack on neutrality in his novel *The Elephant and the Kangaroo* (London, 1948), where he presented himself as a latter-day Noah, building an ark against the flood tide. The Irish gawp and mock until the rains come, when their derision turns to envy and White's ark floats out to meet and be saved by the lucky arrival of the English mailboat in Dublin Bay.

Much of the information on 'comforts', dances and functions to provide funds for British forces, including 'informing' letters and garda reports, can be found at NA DFA 241/125. For Bowen's essay, 'The Big House', first published in *The Bell*, 1.1 (October 1940), see *The Mulberry Tree*, op. cit., 25–29. I also quote here from Hubert Butler, '*The Bell*: An Anglo-Irish View', *Irish University Review* 6.1 (1976), 66–72; Henry Green, *Loving* (London, 1949). For Green's attitude to Ireland see *Surviving: The Uncollected Writings of Henry Green*, ed. Matthew Yorke (London, 1992), 264–265; see also Green, *Pack My Bag: A Self Portrait* (Oxford, 1989); Jeremy Treglown, *Romancing: The Life and Work of Henry Green* (London, 2000).

6 WAR IN THE AIR

For Bowen's description of an island of quietness see *Bowen's Court*, op. cit., 456–7. On British wartime radio propaganda see: Siân Nicholas, *The Echo of War: Homefront Propaganda and the Wartime BBC, 1939–1945* (Manchester, 1996); Asa Briggs, *The War of Words* (London, 1970); Briggs, *The BBC: The First Fifty Years* (Oxford, 1985). Correspondence over *Irish Half Hour* and written scripts for the programme are held at the BBC Written Archives Centre. See R19/568 for policy on *Irish Half Hour*, including objections from the Northern Irish government and Nicholas Mansergh's and Betjeman's letters on radio propaganda. Chapter 14 of Bernard Adams, *Denis Johnston: A Life* (Dublin, 2002) provides interesting background on *Irish Half Hour*, as well as on Johnston's own broadcasts, quoted on p. 195. See Rex Cathcart, *The Most Contrary Region: The BBC in Northern Ireland 1924–1984* (Belfast, 1984) for J. M. Andrews on *Irish Half Hour*. See the Aiken Papers UCD P104/3436 (2) for J.J. Walshe's less than complimentary views of Johnston's broadcasts, and criticism of Betjeman. For MacNeice's radio work see Stallworthy, op. cit., 291–333; Barbara Coulton, *Louis MacNeice in the BBC* (London, 1980); Terence Brown and Alec Reid, eds., *Time Was Away: The World of Louis MacNeice* (Dublin, 1974); Brown, *Louis MacNeice: Sceptical Vision* (Dublin and London, 1975); John Drakakis, ed., *British Radio Drama* (Cambridge, 1981). Scripts of MacNeice's plays and features are held at BBCW.

On Betjeman see: Candida Lycett Green, ed., *John Betjeman, Letters*, Vol. 1: 1926 to 1951 (I quote here from letters to Oliver Stonor, 19 April 1941, p. 285, and to Douglas Goldring, 14 July 1941, pp. 292–293). See also Patrick Taylor-Martin, *John Betjeman: His Life and Work* (London, 1983). For wartime letters held at the Betjeman archive at the University of Victoria, Canada, I have relied on Robert Cole, '"Good Relations": Irish Neutrality and the Propaganda of John Betjeman, 1941–43', *Eire/Ireland: A Journal of Irish Studies* 30.4 (1996), 33–46; Antoinette Quinn, op. cit., 165–8.

On Irish radio see: Patrick Kavanagh, 'Europe is at War', *Irish Times*, 25 October 1939, reprinted in Peter Kavanagh, ed., *Patrick Kavanagh: Man and Poet* (Newbridge, 1986). This volume includes a useful annotated bibliography of Kavanagh's uncollected works. Martin McLoone quotes Bryan Cooper's 1924 comment about Irish radio in *Broadcasting in a Divided Community: Seventy Years of the BBC in Northern Ireland* (Belfast, 1996), 31. See also Maurice Gorham, *Forty Years of Irish Broadcasting* (Dublin, 1967). I quote from Dáil Debates on wireless broadcasting, Vol. 83, 4 June 1941, Vol. 87, 17 June 1942, Vol. 88, 26 November 1942, Vol. 91, 9–10 November 1943. I have drawn on Alacoque Kelly, *Irish Radio Data 1926–1980* (Dublin, 1981) for much of the information here on scheduling, numbers of radios, and programme details; see also Desmond Fisher, *Broadcasting in Ireland* (London, 1978); Eileen Morgan, 'Question Time: Radio and the Liberalisation of Irish Public Discourse after World War II', *History Ireland* (Winter 2001); E. Arnot Robinson, *The Signpost* (London, 1943).

For German radio propaganda to Ireland and the text of Mahr's report, I have primarily drawn on David O'Donoghue, *Hitler's Irish Voices: the Story of German Radio's Wartime Irish Service* (Belfast, 1998); for Tomás de Bháldraithe's story of listening to Irland Redaktion in Cois Fharraige in Galway see O'Donoghue, 46–7. O'Donoghue's study includes the complete text of Mahr's report on radio propaganda to Ireland as an appendix, 183–193. See also J. A. Cole, *Lord Haw-Haw: The Full Story of William Joyce* (London, 1964). See chapter 2 of Séamus Ó Néill, *Tonn Tuile,* op. cit. for the visit to the storyteller in Donegal; Máirtín O Direáin offers a comparably pessimistic view of the fortunes of the Irish language and traditional culture in his poem 'Blianta an Chogaidh' ('The War Years'). Like Ó Néill, O Direáin was a civil servant. Originally from Aran, he moved to Dublin in 1937 and worked in the postal censorship during the war. In 'Blianta an Chogaidh' he compares the arid life in the city, trading cheques for filing documents, with memories of a fulfilled life in the Gaeltacht. Both writers were to an extent attempting to create a new form of Irish-language community through their works. For two versions of 'Blianta an Chogaidh' see Eoghan Ó hAnluain, 'Nóta Faoi "Blianta an Chogaidh" le Máirtín O Direáin', *Scríobh* 2 (1975), 21–29. For the Czech diplomat's report see McGarry, *Eoin O'Duffy,* op. cit., 327.

On the response to the Dublin bombing see local and national newspapers. I quote here from Editorial, *Kilkenny People,* 4 January 1941; Seanad Debates, Vol. 25, 29–30 January 1941. J. L. Hodson, *Towards the Morning* (London, 1941), 48–78 includes Ed Murrow's assessment of the effect of the bombs. See also T. H. White to David Garnett, 22 September 1940, *The White/Garnett Letters,* op. cit., 73; Sylvia Townsend Warner, *T .H. White, A Biography* (London, 1967).

For the Belfast blitz I have drawn on Brian Barton, *The Blitz: Belfast in the War Years* (Belfast, 1989) and Fisk, op. cit. (who quotes Lindsay Keir on p. 474 and John MacDermott on p. 510). See also *Bombs on Belfast, The Blitz*

1941 (Belfast, 1984, first pub. *Belfast Telegraph* 1941); Benedict Kiely, *Land Without Stars* (Dublin, 1945); Brian Moore, *The Emperor of Ice-Cream* (Belfast, 1965); Woodside Diary (MO 5642). For de Valera's speech at Castlebar see *Irish Press,* 21 April 1941; see Dublin newspapers for April/May 1941 on the refugee crisis in Dublin and in the Northern Irish countryside; Maurice Craig, 'Ireland Rides the Storm', *Irish Digest* 9.2 (December 1941), 1–3. *The Strings Are False* was first published in Paul Vincent Carroll, *Three Plays* (London, 1944). See also Shelagh Richards, 'Producing *The Strings Are False*', *Commentary* (June 1942).

7 IMMOBILISATION

Ritchie's diary entry is from Charles Ritchie, *The Siren Years: Undiplomatic Diaries, 1937–1945* (London, 1974). Information about Görtz is from Hull, op. cit., 145, 171. See also Stephen Hayes (former Chief-of-Staff of the IRA), 'My Strange Story', Part I, *The Bell* 17.4 (July 1951), Part II, *The Bell* 17.5 (August 1951); W. J. McCormack, *Blood Kindred: W. B. Yeats, the Life, the Death, the Politics* (London, 2005). For O'Casey's response to the attack on Russia see David Krause, ed., *Letters of Sean O'Casey,* Vol. 1 1910–1941 (London, 1975), 891. See also Vol. 2 1942–1954 (London, 1980); O'Casey, 'There Go the Irish' in Daiken, op. cit.; O'Casey, *Oak Leaves and Lavender* (London, 1946).

On shortage of equipment and morale in the Irish army see MacCarron, op. cit., xi; *Irish Sword* 19.75/76 (1993–94); Charles J. F. McCarthy, *Regional Defence* (Cork, 1944); *Step Together!* (Cavan, 1943). The statement by General McKenna on army recruitment is quoted in O'Halpin, *Defending Ireland,* 168; see also Romie Lambkin, *My Time in the War: An Irishwoman's Diary* (Dublin, 1992), 5; VP Summaries of interviews.

On Ireland and the USA see: T. Ryle Dwyer, *Irish Neutrality and the USA, 1939–1947* (Dublin, 1977) and *Strained Relations: Ireland at Peace and the USA at War, 1941–45* (Dublin, 1988); Troy Davis, *Dublin's American Policy: Irish–American Diplomatic Relations* (Washington, 1996); Robert Brennan, *Ireland Standing Firm,* op. cit.; de Valera, 'America's Entry Into the War' and 'Statement on the American Landings', in *Ireland's Stand: A Selection of the Speeches of Eamon de Valera during the War* (Dublin, 1946); for de Valera's speech in Navan, and some responses, see *Dundalk Examiner,* 17 January 1942; 'Plot to Embroil Country in War', *Irish Press,* 30 January 1942. See also *Speeches and Statements by Eamon de Valera 1917–1973,* ed. Maurice Moynihan (Dublin, 1980). On Irish-American newspapers see Matthew O'Brien '"Hibernians on the March": Irish American and Ethnic Patriotism in the Mid-Twentieth Century', *Éire–Ireland* 40.1 and 2 (2005), 170–182; Raymond James Raymond, 'American Public Opinion and Irish Neutrality 1939–1945', *Éire–Ireland* 18.1 (1983), 20–45; Brian Hanley, 'The Irish World,

FDR and the Great Depression', *New York Irish History Review* 17 (2003). David Reynolds, *Rich Relations: The American Occupation of Britain 1942–5* (London, 1995), quotes the US consul in Belfast, and the GIs' *Pocket Guide to Northern Ireland*, 117–121; For propaganda issued to the AEF see *Booktab* Vol. 1.2, 'Is Ireland Next?' (June/July 1942). See also Jim Phelan, 'Mild and Bitter', in Daiken, op. cit. I am grateful to Geoffrey Roberts for copies of OSS Reports; I quote from OSS 'Report on the Present State of Éire', 27 Jan 1943, RG22b, entry 106, box 0039, file 347, on pages 233 and 235. See also Louis MacNeice, *Meet the US Army* (London, 1943). *March of Time* Irish newsreels are available at IFC; Sean O'Faolain's 1942 radio script is held at BBCW. Denis Ireland's speech to Craobh na h-Aiséirí, 'An Ulster Protestant's Attitude Towards Partition', is quoted in *Irish Press*, 9 February 1942.

On the stagnating economy and shortages of food and fuel, in addition to editorials in local and national newspapers and advertisements issued by the Department of Agriculture and Department of Supplies on the wheat drive, coupons and rationing, see James Meenan, 'The Irish Economy During the War', in *Ireland in the War Years and After*, op. cit.; Barney Heron, 'Winning the Turf', *The Bell* 2.6 (1941); on coal and electricity see Michael Shiel, op. cit.; Tony Gray, *The Lost Years*, op. cit.; on tea see Batstone Letters, IWM (86/61/1); Dáil Debates, Vol. 85, 4 March 1942, 'Supply and Distribution of Bread'; Vol. 86, 16 April,1942, 'Agriculture'; Vol. 95, 2 February 1945, 'Poverty Amongst Unemployed'; Elizabeth Bowen, 'Eire', *New Statesman* 21 (12 April 1941), reprinted in *The Mulberry Tree*, op. cit., 30–35; C. S. Andrews, *Man of No Property* (Dublin, 2001); Lambkin (op. cit.). For pictures of wartime plenty see: Moya Woodside (MO 5642); Ben Robertson, 'So You're Neutral, Too', *Irish Digest* 8.4 (February 1941), 1–3; John Cudahy, 'You're Neutral – Why Not?', *Irish Digest* 8.6 (April 1941), 4–5; Beverley Nichols, 'Ireland's Wartime Problems', *Irish Digest* 9.4 (February 1942), 1–3; Michael Burke, 'Eating in Dublin', *The Bell* 2.3 (June 1943); Cyril Connolly, 'Comment', *Horizon*, op. cit. page 6; Hodson, op. cit. page 50. For Flann O'Brien's *Irish Times* column see Myles, *Cruiskeen Lawn* (Dublin, 1943); Kevin O'Nolan, ed., *The Best of Myles: A Selection from Cruiskeen Lawn* (Dublin, 1968), where the Research Bureau's plans for trains fuelled by bogland appears on page 114; John Wyse Jackson, ed., *Flann O'Brien at War: Myles na gCopaleeen 1940–1945* (London, 1999). I quote here too from *Irish Half Hour* scripts and Johnston's BBC broadcasts from Dublin, 'Irish commentary'. For the glimmer man story see Chapter 16 of Dunlop Papers, IWM 76/271/1.

For Kavanagh's occasional poems see Peter Kavanagh, ed., The *Complete Poems of Patrick Kavanagh* (New York, 1972). I quote here from 'White Bread' and 'The 6.40 pm from Amiens Street'; 'The Great Hunger' is most easily available in Antoinette Quinn, ed., *Patrick Kavanagh, Selected Poems* (London, 2000); Robert Greacen's review was published in

Horizon 5.25 (January 1942), 217–219. See also Greacen, 'Irish Letters and the War', *Modern Reading 6*, ed. Reginald Moore (London, 1943); Antoinette Quinn, *Patrick Kavanagh: A Critical Study* (Dublin, 1991); Eamonn Wall, '"It is midnight in Dublin and Europe is at war": Patrick Kavanagh's Poems of "The Emergency"', *Colby Library Quarterly* 31.4 (1995), 233–241.

On Irish radio's fare for housewives see Alacoque Kelly, op. cit.; on wartime cooking see Maura Laverty, *Flour Economy* (Dublin, 1941); *A Simple Guide to a Wholesome Diet* (Dublin, 1942); Josephine Marnell et al., *All in the Cooking* (Dublin, 1946). On the development of women's organisations see Pat Bolger, ed., *And See Her Beauty Shining There: The Story of the Irish Countrywomen* (Dublin, 1986); Hilda Tweedy, *A Link in the Chain: The Story of the Irish Housewives Association 1942–1992* (Dublin, 1992); Geraldine Mitchell, *Deeds Not Words: The Life and Work of Muriel Gahan* (Dublin, 1997). Caitriona Clear, *Women of the House: Women's Household Work in Ireland 1922–1961* (Dublin, 2000), is an excellent study of women's work, and public attitudes to women and domesticity, throughout the period, and is particularly good on the Commission on Vocational Organization.

Poverty and disease, particularly tuberculosis, were frequently discussed in the Dáil from 1942 onwards. See in particular Dáil Debates, Vol. 86, 13 May 1942 (on petrol for nurses), Vol. 87, 16 June 1942 (on TB and public health). On page 259 I cite Mary Daly, *Social and Economic History of Ireland since 1800* (Dublin, 1981), 156 and 190–191. On typhus see Laurence Geary, 'What People Died of During the Famine', *Famine 150 Commemorative Lecture Series*, ed Cormac Ó Gráda (Dublin, 1997); Ó Gráda, *Black '47 and Beyond* (Princeton, 1999). Contemporary discussions of TB can be found in J.E. Counihan and T.W.T. Dillon, 'Irish Tuberculosis Death Rates', *Journal of the Statistical and Social Inquiry Society of Ireland* XVII (October, 1943), 169–188; T.W.T. Dillon, 'The Statistics of Tuberculosis', *Irish Journal of Medical Science* 199 (July 1942) 221–43. W.R.F. Collis 'Some Facts and Figures in Relation to Health', in *Dublin Irish Journal of Medical Science* 173 (May 1940), 192–200; Eithne MacDermott, *Clann na Poblachta* (Cork, 1998); Kevin Rafter, *The Clann: The Story of Clann na Poblachta* (Cork, 1996). See also Greta Jones, *Captain of All These Men of Death: The History of Tuberculosis in Nineteenth and Twentieth Century Ireland* (Amsterdam, 2001); For the report by D. P. O'Brien for the Rockefeller Foundation, *Report on Conditions of Ireland*, see Jones,192–194. Robert Collis, *Marrowbone Lane* (Dublin, 1943); the play is discussed by Christopher FitzSimon, *The Boys: A Double Biography* (London, 1994), 126–7; James Deeny, *The End of an Epidemic: Essays in Irish Public Health 1935–65* (Dublin, 1995) and *To Cure and to Care* (Glendale, 1989).

8 THE STATIC GENERATION

For descriptions of cultural stagnation see Frank O'Connor, *The Backward Look: A Survey of Irish Literature* (London, 1967), 224–5; Hubert Butler, 'The Barriers', op. cit.; Margot Moffett, 'Young Irish Painters', *Horizon* 11.64 (April 1945), 261–267; Betty Chancellor's letter to Denis Johnston is quoted in FitzSimon (op. cit.), 138; The quotation on page 277 from Sean O'Faolain is from his unpublished radio broadcast held at BBCW; Bowen's description of a 'ban on feeling' and 'claustrophobia' appears in 'Éire', op. cit., 30. Cyril Connolly's description of cut-off Ireland, 'In Éire Today', appeared in *Picture Post* 15.2 (11 April 1942). For Daniel Corkery's criticism of the denationalised Irish see *What's This About the Gaelic League?* (Dublin, 1942). For Irish-language writers in 'limbo' in Dublin and a discussion of the Cumann na Scríbhneoirí (Society of Writers), see Eoghan Ó hAnluain, 'Nóta Faoi "Blianta an Chogaidh" le Máirtín O Direáin', *Scríobh* 2 (1975), 21–29.

The principal wartime debate on literary censorship can be found at Seanad Debates, Vol. 27, 18 November, 2, 3, and 9 December 1942. See also Sean Dorman's Interview with Sir John Keane, *Commentary* (December 1942). On wartime political censorship, particularly with reference to the press, I have drawn on Donal Ó Drisceoil's detailed analysis of the files held at the National and Military Archives in *Censorship*, op. cit. See also Aiken papers (UCD P104), which were closed during Ó Drisceoil's research, for Aiken/Walshe correspondence and the Chief Press Censor's monthly reports on activities of the censorship. The debate on Sir John Keane's motion can be found at Seanad Debates, Vol. 28, 27 January, 24 February 1944. See Aiken papers UCD P104 3436 (2) for Aiken's attempt to head off the debate. See also Michael Adams, *Censorship: The Irish Experience* (Alabama, 1968). For James Dillon's criticism of the use of censorship see Dáil Debates, Vol. 82, 3 April 1941.

On British film propaganda and Irish responses see, in addition to Ó Drisceoil, Luisa Burns-Bisogno, *Censoring Irish Nationalism* (London, 1997); 'Meet Dr. Hayes', *The Bell* 3.2 (November 1941). See Rockett, *Irish Film Censorship*, op. cit., 318–325 on Republican objections to royalist films and cinema riots. *Yesterday's News: British Cinema Newsreels Reader*, ed. Luke McKernan (London, 2002), describes audience response to newsreels in Britain; Martin Quigley, *A US Spy in Ireland* (Dublin, 1999) contains the text of Quigley's letter to Betjeman. For Aiken's views on Quigley see Aiken Papers, p104/3445. On Irish film see the series of articles by Rev. R. S. Devane SJ in the *Standard* from 1937 onwards. *The Irish Cinema Handbook* (Dublin, 1943), edited by Rev. R. S. Devane, collects more than thirty articles by film enthusiasts debating the future of Irish film and the film trade, including Devane, 'The Film in National Life', Liam O'Laoghaire, 'Documentary Film', Edward Toner, 'The Irish Film Society', and a Symposium, 'What Kind of Films should we Make?' *Memories in Focus* op. cit. outlines the beginnings of the Irish Film Society and developments in wartime film. See also Kevin Rockett, 'Documentaries' in Rockett, Luke Gibbons and John Hill, *Cinema and Ireland* (London, 1985); Liam O'Laoghaire, *Invitation to the Film* (Tralee, 1945); John Martin Hayes, ed., *The Mind of Canon Hayes: Writings and Speeches of the Founder of Muintir na Tíre* (Tipperary, 1961); Stephen Rynne, *Father John Hayes* (Dublin, 1960).

On émigrés and the Irish art scene see the wartime journal *Commentary* which published reviews of art exhibitions, and also interviews and articles by practitioners on drama, painting and set design. On the Irish Exhibition of Living Art see Mainie Jellett, 'The R.H.A. and Youth', *Commentary* (May 1942) and Brigid Ganly's reply, *Commentary* (June 1942); Con Leventhal's response to the Irish Exhibition of Living Art was published, along with a series of articles on wartime movements, in *Irish Art: A Volume of Articles and Illustrations* (Dublin, 1944); Herbert Read's introduction to the Subjective Art Exhibition catalogue was reprinted in *The Bell* 7.5 (February 1944), 424–449 and his lecture which was to have opened the exhibition, 'Art and Crisis', in *Horizon* 9.53 (May 1944), 336–350; see also Rex MacGall, 'Basil Rakoczi Interviewed', *Commentary* (March 1946); Thomas Bodkin, *Twelve Irish Artists* (Dublin, 1940); Bodkin, *Report on the Arts in Ireland* (Dublin, 1949). Herbrand Ingouville-Williams, *Three Irish Painters: Basil Rakoczi, Kenneth Hall, Patrick Scott* (Dublin, n.d.), includes the painters' statements on their approach to their art. S. B. Kennedy, *Irish Art and Modernism 1880–1950* (Belfast and Dublin, 1991), provides a detailed analysis of the various art movements in Ireland during this period. Stephen Rynne's comment on art and neutrality, first published in *The Leader*, 1 September 1945, is quoted by Kennedy on page 127; Máirín Allen's judgement of the Exhibition of Living Art appears on page 122. See also Róisín Kennedy, 'The Emergency: A Turning Point for Irish Art?', *From the Edge: Art and Design in Twentieth Century Ireland, Circa* 92 (Summer 2000); Radharc ar gCúl: *A Backward Glance: 'Twelve Irish Artists', New Hibernia Review/Iris Éireannach Nua* 6.2 (Summer/Samradh 2002).

For the National Planning Exhibition of 1944 see Harry Allberry, ed., *Reconstruction Pamphlets 1–7* (Dublin, 1944), which includes pamphlets on 'Planning for Leisure', 'Afforestation', 'Transport', 'The Economic Farm Unit'. See also Durdin Manning Robertson, *Town Planning* (Dublin, 1944). For O'Brien's views on 'internationalism', in addition to the edited collections of Myles na gCopaleen columns (especially *Flann, O'Brien at War* op. cit.), see the excellent article by Steven Curran: '"Could Paddy Leave Off from Copying Just for Five Minutes?": Brian O'Nolan and Eire's Beveridge Plan', *Irish University Review* 31.2 (2001), 353–375.

Christopher FitzSimon offers by far the most wide-ranging and atmospheric description of Dublin's wartime theatre in *The Boys*, op. cit., which includes a comprehensive list of plays produced at the Gate and the Gaiety during the war. I quote him on Dublin's 'rakish international life' on page 282. See also Earl of Longford, 'New Season at the Gate Theatre', *Commentary* (October 1942); Shelagh Richards and Michael Walsh, 'Our Autumn Season at the Olympia Theatre', *Commentary* (August 1942); Mícheál Mac Liammóir, *Theatre in Ireland* (Dublin, 1950); Brinsley MacNamara, *Abbey Plays 1899–1948* (Dublin, 1949). A full list of Abbey plays, including casts, in the period is included in Lennox Robinson, *Ireland's Abbey Theatre: A History, 1899–1951* (London, 1951). See also Christopher Murray, *Twentieth-Century Irish Drama: Mirror Up to the Nation* (Manchester, 1997); Nicholas Grene, *The Politics of Irish Drama* (Cambridge, 1999); D. E. S. Maxwell, *A Critical History of Modern Irish Drama* (Cambridge, 1984); Robert Welch, *The Abbey Theatre: Form and Pressure, 1988–1999* (Oxford, 1999); Robert Hogan, *After the Irish Renaissance, A Critical History of the Irish Drama since* 'The Plough and the Stars' (London, 1968); Peter Kavanagh, *The Story of the Abbey Theatre, from its Origins in 1899 to the Present* (New York, 1950).

On *The Bell*, I quote from O'Faolain's editorials during the war years. Frank Shovlin, op. cit., offers the best overall assessment of the journal. For examples of *The Bell*'s documentary mode see, for example, 'I Live in a Slum' (Recorded), *The Bell* 1.2 (November 1940); 'The Life of a Country Doctor' (Anonymous), *The Bell* 3.1 (October 1941); Peadar O'Donnell, 'People and Pawnshops', *The Bell* 5.3 (December 1942). For contemporary responses to *The Bell* see the following: Frank O'Connor's criticism of *The Bell* was included in 'The Future of Irish Literature', *Horizon*, op. cit.; Vivian Mercier, 'The Fourth Estate, VI – Verdict on *The Bell*', Donat O'Donnell [Conor Cruise O'Brien], 'A Rider to the Verdict', and O'Faolain, 'Speech from the Dock', all in *The Bell* 10.2 (May 1945); Hubert Butler, '*The Bell*: An Anglo-Irish View', and Dermot Foley, 'Monotonously Rings the Little Bell', *Irish University Review* 6.1 (Spring 1976), 54–62. A copy of A. J. Leventhal's article 'Credo 5: What it means to be a Jew', showing the censor's cuts, is printed in full in 'What the Censor did in 1944', *The Emergency: A Supplement to the Irish Times*, 8 May 1985, 4–5. The uncensored article was published after the war in *The Bell* 10.3 (June 1945). See also John V. Kelleher, 'Irish Literature Today', *The Atlantic Monthly* (April 1945), 70–76, reprinted in *The Bell* 10.4 (July 1945); Conor Cruise O'Brien, *Maria Cross: Imaginative Patterns in a Group of Catholic Writers* (London, 1954).

The Runa Press published a series of wartime collections and anthologies of poetry in Ireland: *Bannered Spears* (Dublin, 1943), *Apocalypse* (Dublin, 1944), *Earth Fire* (Dublin, 1943), *Outriders* (Dublin, 1943), *Tidings* (Dublin, 1943), *Winter-Sheaf* (Dublin, 1944). See also Robert Greacen, Bruce Williamson, Valentine Iremonger, *On the Barricades* (Dublin, 1944) and

Greacen ed., *Irish Harvest: An Anthology of Prose and Poetry* (Dublin, 1946); Greacen, ed., *Northern Harvest: An Anthology of Ulster Writing* (Belfast, 1944); Geoffrey Taylor, ed., *Irish Poems of Today* (Dublin, 1944); Donagh McDonagh, ed., *Poems from Ireland* (Dublin, 1944). See also Greacen and Iremonger, ed., *Contemporary Irish Poetry* (Dublin, 1949); D. A Garrity, ed., *New Irish Poets* (New York, 1948).

For versions of provincial nostalgia see Maura Laverty, *Never No More: The Story of a Lost Village* (London, 1942); Kevin Neil, *I Remember Karrigeen: An Account of Life in a Small Town in Ireland* (Dublin, 1944); Michael McLaverty, *Lost Fields* (New York, 1941). On Laverty see Caitriona Clear, '"I Can Talk About It, Can't I?": The Ireland Maura Laverty Desired, 1942–46', *Women's Studies* 30.6 (2001), 819–835. See also Seán Ó Súilleabháin, *A Handbook of Irish Folklore* (Dublin, 1942); D. L. Kelleher, *Ireland of the Welcomes* (Dublin, 1943).

9 THE VANISHED GENERATION

The most comprehensive study of Irish migration to Britain in the mid-twentieth century is Enda Delaney, *Demography, State and Society: Irish Migration to Britain 1921–1971* (Liverpool, 2000). I draw heavily on this work for figures and the background to wartime migration. Delaney gives the figure of 1,500 migrants per month in February 1941 (p. 118); the memo from the Department of Industry on 'involuntary idleness' is cited on p. 121. See also Delaney, *Irish Immigration since 1921* (Dublin, 2002). I also draw on Jackson, *The Irish in Britain* (London, 1963) who cites the figure of 6,500 migrants a month in spring 1942 (p. 100); Ultan Cowley, *The Men Who Built Britain: A History of the Irish Navvy,* (Dublin, 2001); and *MI5 and Ireland,* op. cit., on the UK permit office and British need for Irish labour, 54–55 and 59–60. See also Peadar O'Donnell, 'Emigration is a Way of Keeping a Grip', *The Bell* 3.2 (November 1941) quoted on pages 310 and 312; O'Donnell, 'Call the Exiles Home', *The Bell* 9.5 (February 1945); Anne O'Dowd, *Spalpeens and Tattie-hokers: History and Folklore of the Irish Migratory Agricultural Worker in Ireland and Britain* (Dublin, 1991); Gerard Quinn, 'The Changing Pattern of Irish Society', in *Ireland in the War Years and After,* op. cit.; James Meenan, 'Irish Industry and Post-War Problems', *Studies* 32 (September 1943), 362–363; John Healy, *The Death of an Irish Town* (Cork, 1968); Anne O'Grady, 'Irish Migration in the 1940s and 1950s', *Irish in Britain Research Forum Papers* (London, 1988); Sean Glynn, 'Irish Emigration to Britain, 1911–1951: Patterns and Policy', *Irish Economic and Social History* 8 (1981), 50–69; P. Inman, *Labour in the Munitions Industries* (London, 1957). On the frequent migration of Irish doctors during the period see Earl McCarthy, 'Éire's Surplus Doctors', *The Bell* 9.2 (November 1944).

The County Clare librarian was Dermot Foley; see 'Monotonously Rings the Little Bell', *Irish University Review* 6.1, op. cit. NA DFA 41/228 and DFA 241/248 contain documents on women land-workers and conscription of women; NA 241/99, on Agents for work in Britain and advertisements in Irish newspapers. For wartime literary treatments of migration see Michael J. Molloy, *The Old Road* (Dublin, 1961); Frank Carney, *The Righteous Are Bold* (Dublin, 1951). On emigration from rural Ireland I have referred to Dáil Debates, Vol. 86, 16 April 1942 (Agriculture); Vol. 87, 1 July 1942; Vol. 91, 1 July 1943. See also George A. O'Brien, ed., *The Vanishing Irish: The Enigma of the Modern World* (London, 1953); Hugh Brody, *Inishkillane: Change and Decline in the West of Ireland* (London, 1973); Damien Hannan, *Displacement and Development: Class, Kinship and Social Change in Irish Rural Communities* (Dublin, 1979).

For Peadar O'Donnell on Burghfield, see Ó Drisceoil, *Peadar O'Donnell*, op. cit. N. O'Connor, 'Irish Versus Irish', IWM 87/14/1 provides an account of riots, strikes and absenteeism amongst Irish women workers at Burghfield Hostel in 1943. Out of a thousand women living in the hostel, and working in a private munitions factory owned by the tobacco firm Wills, eight hundred were Irish. Pat Dooley, *The Irish in Britain* (London, 1943), published by the Connolly Association, provides details of wages in factories and sites, and includes the article by Flann Campbell on working and living conditions. On the journey to Britain see H. L. Morrow, 'Journey into Fear', in *They Go, The Irish*, op. cit. James Deeny discusses the disinfecting process at the Iveagh Baths in *To Cure and to Care*, op. cit., 79. See also Dáil Debates, Vol. 92, 14 and 16 December 1943 (on the Health Embarkation Certificate, and the criticisms made by Flann Campbell). Unemployment, wage levels and remittances received from England were frequently discussed in the Dáil throughout the war period. Seán MacEntee gives the figures for 1942 in Dáil Debates, Vol. 91, 19 November 1943.

Statistics on sexuality and reliable information on sexual behaviour are notoriously difficult to determine. In addition to the studies already referenced by McAvoy and Luddy, I have drawn here on Sandra Larmour (McAvoy), 'Aspects of the State and Female Sexuality in the Irish Free State', (Dissertation, UCC, 1998). Larmour quotes the Department of Health memo on VD (NA DT S13444A); Moira Maguire generously provided me with information on numbers of illegitimate births and the details of wartime cases of infanticide from her dissertation, 'The Myth of Catholic Ireland: Unmarried Motherhood, Infanticide and Illegitimacy in the Twentieth Century' (American University, 2000); see in addition Maguire, 'Foreign Adoptions and the Evolution of Irish Adoption Policy, 1945–52', *Journal of Social History* 36.2 (2002), 387–404. See also the government report, 'The Suppression of Prostitution', 1947 (NA DJ 72/94/A), quoted on pp. 323 and

324; Pauline Jackson, 'Outside the Jurisdiction: Irishwomen seeking Abortion', in Chris Curtin et al., eds, *Gender in Irish Society* (Galway, 1987); Greta Jones, 'Marie Stopes in Ireland: The Mother's Clinic in Belfast', *Social History of Medicine* 5.2 (1992), 255–278; J.C. Cherry, 'The Control of Venereal Disease in Ireland', *The Irish Journal of Medical Science* 210 (June 1943), 161–170. I am grateful to Leanne McCormick for the quotation from the Bishop of Derry's sermon, which was published in the *Londonderry Sentinel*, 29 April 1944. Mary Lavin's story 'Sunday Brings Sunday' was published in her 1944 collection *The Long Ago and Other Stories* (London, 1944). This was not Lavin's only story about illegitimacy in this period. Her story 'Sarah' in *Tales from Bective Bridge* (London, 1943) focuses on a young domestic servant in a rural community who bears children by different men and is eventually forced out of her home by her brothers to die in a ditch. Hewitt's letter to Maybin is dated 1/4/44. See PRONI, Hewitt Papers, D/3838/3/12.

On migrant work in Ireland see Barney Heron, 'Winning the Turf', op. cit.; Michael O'Beirne, 'A Month on the Bog', *The Bell* 3.6 (March 1943); Peter Rigney, 'Report on the Coalfields in the Arigna District in 1942', *Breifne* 10 (2002), 509–516 and Rigney, 'Arigna Coal Mines and the Emergency', *Breifne* 12 (2004), 290–293. For de Valera's St Patrick's Day Speech, 1943, see Moynihan, op. cit., 466–468. On the 1943 election see Lee, op. cit., 236–242; Michael Gallagher, *Electoral Support for Irish Political parties 1927–1973* (London, 1976). For prisoners on hunger strike, see Dáil Debates, Vol. 91, 7 and 9 July 1943.

I am extremely grateful to Geraldine Parsons for her thoughtful translations of passages of *Cré na Cille* and related work, and to Máirín Nic Eoin for additional material. On Ó Cadhain see *Cré na Cille: Aithris i nDeich nEadarluid* (Baile Átha Cliath, 1949); see also his letters from prison, *As an nGéibheann: Litreacha chuig Tomás Bairéad* (Baile Átha Cliath, 1973); the letters are reviewed by Tomás de Bhaldraithe, 'Litreacha Géibheannaigh', *Comhar* (Feabhra, 1974), 22–3; see also Ó Cadhain, 'Mo Chairde', *Irish Times*, 29 September 1954. For biographical information on Ó Cadhain see An tSr Bosco Costigan, with Seán Ó Curraoin, *De Ghlaschloich an Oileáin: Beatha agus Saothar Mháirtín Uí Chadhain* (Béal an Daingin, Conamara, 1987). This includes the description of Ó Cadhain's burial of an old neighbour in Connemara in winter 1944 (p. 72); see also Éamon Ó Ciosáin, *An t-Éireannach 1934–1937: Nuachtán Sóisialach Gaeltachta* (Baile Átha Cliath, 1993). The idea of 'concentration camps' to learn Irish is discussed on pp. 87–88 of this book.

On internment at the Curragh see the fascinating series of accounts collected by Uinseann MacEoin, op. cit. The information about radio and newspapers in Arbour Hill and the Curragh comes from Sean O'Neill's testimony

(p. 741). For a parallel vision of rural Ireland as a living death see Paul Vincent Carroll's 1941 play *The Wise Have Not Spoken*, published in *Two Plays* (London, 1948), which offers a tragic version of the situation treated in Molloy's *The Old Road*, centred on the family of a young farmer who has returned from fighting for the republicans in Spain.

10 SACRED EGOISM

For the US perspective on Catholic social theory and sympathy for fascism I quote from the Records of the Office of Strategic Services, Reports on the Present State of Éire A–2071–216A; A–3711 (Report of April 1943). For contemporary Irish views on corporatist thought see, for example, E. J. Coyne, 'Corporative Organisation of Society', *Studies* 13 (March 1934), 185–202; Coyne, 'Oliviera Salazar and the Portuguese Corporative Constitution', *Studies* 64 (February 1936), 81–94; Michael Tierney, 'Vocationalism and Parliamentary Democracy: Are they Reconcilable?', *Irish Monthly* 66 (June 1938), 369–377. (This issue of *Irish Monthly* is devoted to vocationalism, with other essays by Hugh O'Neill, M. P. Linehan, and E. J. Coyne, SJ.) James Meenan, *The Italian Corporative System* (Cork, 1944); *Report of the Commission on Vocational Organisation* (Dublin, 1943); Bishop Browne, *Bulwark of Freedom* (Dublin, 1945); *Muintir na Tíre: Parish Guilds, Parish Councils: The Official Handbook* (Dublin, 1945). See also J. J. Lee, 'Aspects of Corporatist Thought in Ireland: The Commission on Vocational Organisation 1939–1943', in Cosgrave and McCartney, eds., *Studies in Irish History* (Dublin, 1979); Kieren Mullarkey, 'Ireland, the Pope and Vocationalism: the Impact of the Encyclical *Quadragesimo Anno*', in *Ireland in the 1930s*, op.cit.; Susannah Riordan, 'The Unpopular Front', op. cit.; Maurice Manning, *The Blueshirts* (Dublin, 1970); Mike Cronin, *The Blueshirts and Irish Politics* (Dublin, 1997); Peter J. Williamson, *Varieties of Corporatism* (Cambridge, 1985); Donnchadh Ó Corráin, ed., *James Hogan, Revolutionary, Historian and Political Scientist* (Dublin, 2001).

For Irish intellectual perspectives on fascism during the 1920s and 1930s see, for example, Walter Starkie, *The Waveless Plain: An Italian Autobiography* (London, 1938); 'Whither is Ireland Heading – Is it Fascism?', *A Survey of Fascism: The Year Book of the International Centre of Fascist Studies* (London, 1928); Odon Por, *Fascism* (London, 1923); James Hogan, *Could Ireland Become Communist? The Facts of the Case* (Dublin, 1935) and *Election and Representation* (Dublin, 1945); Louis MacNeice, *Station Bell* (Berg Library Manuscripts). For Yeats's dalliance with fascist and eugenicist ideas, and brief involvement with the Blueshirts, see R. F. Foster, *W. B. Yeats: A Life, II: The Arch-Poet* (Oxford, 2004), 466–495; W. B. Yeats, *On the Boiler* (Dublin, 1938); Conor Cruise O'Brien, *Passion and Cunning* (London, 1990); Elizabeth Cullingford, *Yeats, Ireland and Fascism* (London, 1981);

Joseph Hone, *W. B. Yeats, 1865–1939* (London, 1942); Michael North, *The Political Aesthetic of Yeats, Eliot and Pound* (Cambridge, 1991); W. J. McCormack, *Blood Kindred*, op. cit.; Grattan Freyer, *W. B. Yeats and the Anti-Democratic Tradition* (Dublin, 1981). See also Nicholas Allen, *George Russell (AE) and the New Ireland 1905–1930* (Dublin, 2002).

On Ireland's distinctive destiny I quote from an editorial in the *Donegal Democrat*, October 1939. See also the series by Father Devane, 'Our House', *Irish Rosary*, 1942; Donat O'Donnell [Conor Cruise O'Brien], 'The Catholic Press', *The Bell* 10.1 (April 1943). For Joseph Walshe's letter to the Irish envoy in Vichy see Dermot Keogh, *Ireland and Europe*, op. cit., 140. On the Capuchin Annual group see Máirín Nic Eoin, *Eoghan Ó Tuairisc: Beatha agus Saothar* (Baile Átha Cliath, 1988).

For Denis Devlin's poem 'Lough Derg', see J. C. C. Mays, ed., *Collected Poems of Denis Devlin* (Dublin, 1989); for Patrick Kavanagh's 'Lough Derg' see *Selected Poems*, op. cit. For the assumption that peace and neutrality are linked see Professor Agnes O'Farrelly, 'Let's Work for Peace', *Irish Digest* 8.6 (April 1941), 9–11. T. H. White's perspective on the Peace Pilgrimage to Knock is quoted by Townsend Warner, op. cit., 171. For Connolly's view see 'Comment', *Horizon* 5.25, op. cit., and T. L. Murray, 'Another View', in the same issue of the journal, 22–26.

On fascist groups and anti-semitism in Ireland see: Dermot Keogh, *Jews*, op. cit., for background and G2 reports; Josephus Anelius, *National Action* (Dublin, 1942); *Aiséirghe Says!* (Dublin, 1943). The Blythe Papers contain Blythe's correspondence with Ó Cuinneagain and his editorial suggestions on drafts of Aiséirí manifestos: UCD P24/969 and P24/974; the 1943 film of Ailtirí na h-Aiséirí is held at IFC. See also Proinsias Mac Aonghusa, 'Aiséirí Faisisteach na Gaeilge', *Aimsir Óg* (2000), 280–288; 'Ailtirí na h-Aiséirí', *Saoirse* (Mean Fomhair, 1997); TG4 documentary on Ó Cuinneagain, "Mo Sheanathair, An Fuhrer Gaelach" (My Grandfather, the Gaelic Fuhrer), Kairos Productions, first broadcast 1/1/2004. For Hewitt's description of Ó Cuinneagain see Hewitt Papers, PRONI D/3838/3/12, letter of 9/10/43. NA DJ 233/24 'Alleged Campaign Against Jews in Ireland' contains documents relating to the anti-semitic manifesto of the 'Irish Ireland Research Society' distributed in Jan/Feb 1939. See also Peadar O'Donnell, 'Cry Jew!', *The Bell* 5.5 (February 1943).

On German–Irish relations see: Andreas Roth, *Mr Bewley in Berlin: Aspects of the Career of an Irish Diplomat, 1933–1939* (Dublin, 2002); W. J. McCormack, ed., *Charles Bewley, Memoirs of a Wild Goose* (Dublin, 1989); Sean Cronin, *Frank Ryan: the Search for the Republic* (Dublin, 1980); Joachim Fischer, *Das Deutschlandbild der Iren 1890–1939* (Heidelberg, 2000); Joachim Gerstenberg, *Eire: Ein Irlandbuch* (Hamburg, 1940); Thilo Schulz, *Das Deutschlandbild der Irish Times 1933–45* (Frankfurt, 1999);

Horst Dickel, *Die Deutsche Aussenpolitik und Die Irische Frage* (Wiesbaden, 1983); Cathy Molahan, *Germany and Ireland 1945–55: Two Nations' Friendship* (Dublin, 1999).

On Francis Stuart see *Things to Live For: Notes for an Autobiography* (London, 1934); *Blacklist, Section H* (Dublin, 1995); *Pigeon Irish* (Dublin, 1932). Brendan Barrington, ed., *The Wartime Broadcasts of Francis Stuart, 1942–44* (Dublin, 2000), offers, along with the texts of the broadcasts and a detailed bibliography including Stuart's occasional writings, by far the best analysis of Stuart's broadcasts and his stance towards Nazism. See Hull, op. cit., p. 68, and Róisín Ní Mheara-Vinard [Róisín], *Cé hí seo amuigh?* (Baile Átha Cliath, 1992), p. 151, on Stuart as IRA courier; see also Francis Stuart, *Der Fall Casement: Das Leben Sir Roger Casements und der Verleumdungsfeldzug des Secret Service*, trans. Ruth Weiland (Hamburg, 1940); Stuart, *Redemption* (Dublin, 1994); *The Pillar of Cloud* (Dublin, 1994); Ruth Weiland, ed., *Irische Freiheitskämpfer* (Berlin, 1940), contains essays by Ní Mheara (on Patrick Pearse, and under the name Nora O'Mara) and Stuart, who contributed the introduction and a piece on de Valera. See also Madeleine Stuart, *Manna in the Morning: A Memoir, 1940–1958* (Dublin, 1984); J. H. Natterstad, *Francis Stuart* (Lewisburg, Penn., 1974); Geoffrey Elborn, *Francis Stuart: A Life* (Dublin, 1990); W. J. McCormack, ed., *A Festschrift for Francis Stuart on His Seventieth Birthday* (Dublin, 1972); Clair Wills, 'The Aesthetics of Neutrality', *boundary* 2 31.1 (2004), 119–146; Simon Caterson, 'Francis Stuart, Hitler and the Lure of Fascism', *Irish Studies Review* 16 (Autumn 1996), 18–22; Anne McCartney, *Francis Stuart: Face to Face, A Critical Study* (Belfast, 2000).

On Social Credit see Alfred O'Rahilly, *Money* (Dublin, 1942); Denis Ireland, *Eamon de Valera Doesn't See it Through* (Dublin, 1941). I am grateful to Brian Hanley for much of the background here on interest in Social Credit and corporatism within the IRA. I also quote here from Maud Gonne MacBride, 'Letter of the Month: Fascism, Communism and Ireland', *Ireland Today* 3.3 (March 1938), 241–244. For Frankie Hannafey's critique of the 'money system' see O'Faolain, *Come Back to Erin* (London, 1940), 162.

11 PAYING FOR NEUTRALITY

For the fictional Irish collaborator Patrick Rosse, see Douglas Brown and Christopher Serpell, *Loss of Eden* (London, 1940). For Churchill's statement on the travel ban see Fisk, 531–532. For a British perspective on travel and security arrangements see O'Halpin, ed., *MI5 and Ireland*, op. cit., 87. On the Axis legation radio see Duggan, *Herr Hempel*, 185–190. On the 'American Note' and Gray's attempts to discredit the Irish government see Ryle-Dwyer, *Irish Neutrality and the USA*, op. cit., 179–200. On the Irish-American response to these events see Matthew O'Brien, '"Hibernians on the March"',

Éire–Ireland, op. cit. de Valera's letter to Robert Brennan is quoted in Keogh, *Ireland and Europe*, op. cit., 191–192; Sir John Maffey's assessment of the legation visit is quoted in Ryle-Dwyer, *Strained Relations*, op. cit., 164. For Churchill's attack on Irish neutrality and de Valera's defence see Fisk, 537–541, and 'Reply to Mr Churchill (17 May 1945)', in *Ireland's Stand*, op. cit., 89–94.

Much of the information here on de Valera's knowledge of the persecution of the Jews, and on the diplomatic moves behind the scenes, is from Dermot Keogh, *Jews*, op. cit., Ó Drisceoil, *Censorship*, op. cit., and Katrina Goldstone, op. cit. For British policy towards the Jews in Europe see, for example, Bernard Wasserstein, *Britain and the Jews of Europe, 1939–1945* (Oxford, 1979); Louise London, 'Jewish Refugees, Anglo-Jewry and British Government Policy, 1930–1940', in David Cesarani, ed., *The Making of Anglo-Jewry* (Oxford, 1989).

For Denis Johnston see *Nine Rivers from Jordan* (London, 1953); *Dionysia* (British Library, n.d.); Johnston papers, TCD MS 10066/287–290 (Correspondence), MS 10066/168 (Diary 1940–1942), MS 10066/27–32 (War Field Books); MS 10066/362/191–204 (Translations of the 'Sichermann Papers, 1941–2'). The War Field Books make no mention of an encounter with an SS officer, although Johnston does record the attempted suicide of an officer on 19 April 1945. He also mentions possessing a Luger. I quote from Bernard Adams, op. cit., 216, on Johnston's idea of himself as a neutral reporter. See also Vivian Mercier, 'Perfection of the Life, or of the Work?', in Joseph Ronsley, ed., *Denis Johnston: A Retrospective* (Gerrards Cross, 1981); Terry Boyle, 'Denis Johnston: Neutrality and Buchenwald', in Kathleen Devine, ed., *Modern Irish Writers and the Wars* (Gerrards Cross, 1999).

On the Irish response to the camps I quote here from Liam MacGabhann, 'Buchenwald Becomes Box Office', *Irish Press* 11 June 1945, 5; Benedict Kiely, 'To Tell of Horrors', *Standard*, 15 June 1945, 5; Lucy Glazebrook, 'Ireland sees the War', *The Bell* 10.5 (August 1945); Sean O'Faolain, 'The Price of Peace', *The Bell* 10.4 (July 1945). For MacGreevy's analysis of Ireland's relationship to the world of war see Thomas MacGreevy, 'Postscript', *Jack B. Yeats* (Dublin, 1945). Beckett's review of the book is published in *Disjecta: Miscellaneous Writings and a Dramatic Fragment* (London, 1983). For Beckett at Saint-Lô, see Lois Gordon, *The World of Samuel Beckett 1906–46* (New Haven and London, 1996); S. E. Gontarski, ed., *Samuel Beckett: The Complete Short Prose 1929–89* (New York, 1995). See also Robert Collis, 'Journey to Czecho-Slovakia', *The Bell* 11.5 (February 1946), an account of his work at a children's hospital at Belsen. For Beckett's letter to Freda Young see Cronin, *Samuel Beckett: The Last Modernist* (London, 1996), 343.

For Dáil debates on humanitarian aid see for example Vol. 30, 9 May 1945, 'Distress in Europe'. For a disturbing contrast see Senator O'Duffy's comment in Seanad Debates (Vol. 30, 25 July 1945): 'I have yet to learn who are the victors', and because of the imprisonment of Irish republicans the concentration camps were 'not unfamiliar . . . A big number of the people in the country are well aware of the nature of concentration camps.'

For most of the text of 'Aifreann na Marbh' and a parallel translation see Éamon Ó Ciosáin, ed., *Une île et d'autres îles: Poèmes gaéliques du XXième siècle* (Paris, 1984), 66–89. See Mícheál MacCraith, 'Aifreann na Marbh: Oidhe Chlainne Hiroshima', in Pádraig Ó Fiannachta, *An Nuafhilíocht: Leachtai Cholm Cille XVII* (Maigh Nuad, 1986), 61–94; Máirín Nic Eoin, '"Our hearts go out to you": The Representation of War in Twentieth-Century Poetry in Irish', 'Scéal an Tuirimh Nua-aoisigh: Téama na Cogaíochta i Nuafhilíocht na Gaeilge', in Breandán Ó Conaire, ed., *Aistí ag iompar Scéil* (Baile Átha Cliath, 2004). For Flann O'Brien on Hiroshima see *Flann O'Brien at War*, op. cit., 171–174.

ACKNOWLEDGEMENTS

A great many people have helped in the research and writing of this book, sharing information, discussing ideas, and reading drafts. In addition to specific debts noted in the bibliography, I should particularly like to thank Adrian Beamish, Richard Bourke, Mike Cronin, Seamus Deane, Luke Gibbons, Lisa Godson, Warwick Gould, Brian Hanley, Marjorie Howes, Anne Janowitz, Michael Kennedy, Siobhán Kilfeather, Maria Luddy, Ian McBride, Margaret MacCurtain, Mícheál Mac Graith, Moira Maguire, Sandra McAvoy, W.J. McCormack, Ronan McDonald, Patrick Murray, Bruce Nelson, Máirín Nic Eoin, Simon Nolan, Matthew O'Brien, Dáithí O'Ceallaigh, Bernard O'Donoghue, Eunan O'Halpin, William O'Reilly, Peter Rigney, Geoffrey Roberts, Robert Savage, Caitríona Scanlan, Robert Tobin, Deirdre Toomey, Eibhear Walshe. I am deeply grateful to Geraldine Parsons for her translations and invaluable advice on the Irish language texts. Roy Foster and Joe Lee kindly read the penultimate draft and I have benefited greatly from their comments. In Victoria Hobbs I have had the good fortune of a wonderfully supportive agent, while my editor Neil Belton guided my book through to press with far more knowledge and insight into my topic than any author could reasonably hope for. I could not have seen this project through without the encouragement, critical insight and practical help offered by family and friends – Toby Buxton, Claudia FitzHerbert, Helen Miles, Ian Patterson, Niall and Oona Roycroft, Karen Van Dyck, Frances Wilson, Philomena and Bernard Wills, Siobhan Wills, Bridget Wills, and above all Peter Dews, and Jacob, Luan and Philomena Wills.

I had long and illuminating conversations about the war years with a number of people who lived through them. I contacted some by placing advertisements in Irish local newspapers. All were wonderfully generous with their time. I am grateful to Alan and Betty Haughton, Hugh Gibbons, Gladys Leach, John Joe McCarthy, Peggy McCarthy, Nealie McCarthy, Sheelagh Martin, Michael Martin and members of Cobh Historical Society, Jimmy Moxley, Michael O'Connor, Philomena and Bernard Wills.

457

I am grateful to librarians and archivists at the British Library, including the Newspaper Library at Colindale, the National Library of Ireland, the National Archives of Ireland, the BBC Written Archives Centre, University College Dublin Archives, Trinity College Library Manuscript Department, the Public Records Office, the Northern Ireland Public Records Office, the Berg Collection at New York Public Library, the Imperial War Museum, and Sussex University Library. I should particularly like to thank Sunniva Flynn at the Irish Film Archive, Jane Leonard at the Ulster Museum, Tim Cadogan at Cork County Library, Michael Smallman at Queen's University Belfast Special Collections Archive and Bob Bruns at the John J. Burns Library, Boston College. I am grateful to the following institutions for supporting my research: the Leverhulme Trust awarded me a Research Fellowship in 2002; the Arts and Humanities Research Council granted me a Research Leave Scheme Award in the same year; Queen Mary, University of London granted me a period of study leave in 2001.

My thanks to the following for permission to reproduce the extracts herein:

Nicholas Monsarrat, *The Cruel Sea* © The Estate of Nicholas Monsarrat 1951 with kind permission of Mrs Ann Monsarrat. Nicholas Monsarrat, *The Cruel Sea*, published by Cassell/Penguin Books.

Louis MacNeice, 'Autumn Journal', *Collected Poems* (London: Faber and Faber, 1979). Reproduced with kind permission of David Higham Associates.

Louis MacNeice, 'The Closing Album', *Collected Poems* (London: Faber and Faber, 1979). Reproduced with kind permission of David Higham Associates.

Louis MacNiece, 'Neutrality', *Collected Poems* (London: Faber and Faber, 1979). Reproduced with kind permission of David Higham Associates.

Extracts from *Jack B. Yeats: An Appreciation and an Interpretation* by Thomas MacGreevy (Dublin: Victor Waddington, 1945). Reprinted with the kind permission of Margaret Farrington and Robert Ryan.

Extracts from *Surviving: The Uncollected Writings of Henry Green* edited by Matthew Yorke, published by Chatto and Windus. Reprinted by permission of The Random House Group Ltd.

ACKNOWLEDGEMENTS

Extracts from *Borstal Boy* by Brendan Behan, published by Hutchinson. Reprinted by permission of The Random House Group Ltd.

The lines from Patrick Kavanagh's 'The Great Hunger' and 'Lough Derg, are reprinted from *Collected Poems*, edited by Antoinette Quinn (Allen Lane, 2004), by kind permission of the Trustees of the Estate of the late Katherine B. Kavanagh, through the Jonathan Williams Literary Agency.

The extract from the letter from Elizabeth Bowen to Humphry House is reproduced with kind permission of Curtis Brown Group Ltd, London on behalf of the Estate of Elizabeth Bowen, and of Professor John House. Copyright © Elizabeth Bowen

The Woodside Diary, the Harrisson Report on Northern Ireland and extracts from the diary of diarist number 5102 (September 1939) reproduced with permission of Curtis Brown Group Ltd, London on behalf of the Trustees of the Mass-Observation Archive © Trustees of the Mass-Observation Archive.

My thanks also to the Estate of Hubert Butler for permission to quote from the Hubert Butler papers held at Trinity College, Dublin and to the Department of Documents of the Imperial War Museum, London for permission to quote from the Batstone letters and the Dunlop papers.

Extracts from the John Hewitt papers (PRONI D/3838/312) are reproduced with kind permission of the Deputy Keeper of the Records, Public Record Office of Northern Ireland.

Extracts from 'Irish Half-Hour' (R19/568) Reproduced with kind permission of BBC Written Archives.

Extracts from Denis Johnston, 'The Six Countries at War', 17th August 1940. Reproduced with kind permission of BBC Written Archives.

Extracts from Denis Johnston, Irish Commentary of 1st September 1941 and 31st May 1941. Reproduced with kind permission of BBC Written Archives.

Every effort has been made to obtain permission for quotations and the Faber Editorial Department would be delighted to hear from you with any information concerning works used.

I am grateful to the Irish Electricity Supply Board Archives for permission to reproduce the illustration that appears on page 16; to

459

Gandon Editions for the image of the Irish Pavilion at the World's Fair that appears on page 19. The recruitment advertisement which appears on page 91 and the photograph reproduced on page 157 are printed courtesy of the *Irish Examiner*. The cartoon by David Low, which appears on page 120, and by Neb [Ronald Niebour], which appears on page 232, are printed courtesy of the Centre for the Study of Cartoons and Caricature, University of Kent © Solo Syndication / Associated Newspapers. I am grateful to Todd Hirn at poseal.com for permission to reproduce the illustration on page 142, and to www.world-covers.com for the illustration on page 165. The cartoons from *Dublin Opinion* on pages 205, 240, 247, 248, 392, 393 are reproduced courtesy of the British Library. The illustrations on pages 55, 56, 155, 202, 241, 255, 266, and 328 are from *The Bell*; those on pages 300 and 303 are from the *Irish Cinema Handbook* (Dublin, 1943); those on pages 97, 225, and 226 from Charles J. F. McCarthy, *Regional Defence* (Cork, 1944); those on pages 365 and 368 from *Aiséirí Says!* (Dublin, 1943); the illustration by Charles Lamb R.H.A. on page 339 is from Máirtín Ó Cadhain, *Cré na Cille: Aithris i nDeich nEadarluid* (Baile Átha Cliath, Sáirséal agus Dill, 1949).

INDEX

Figures in italics indicate illustrations.